AF658526

V.S. Naipaul and Postcolonialism

Writing History, Politics, Culture, Self

Prakash Chandra Pradhan

Published by

PUBLISHERS & DISTRIBUTORS (P) LTD
7/22, Ansari Road, Darya Ganj, New Delhi-110002
Phones : +91-11-40775252, 23273880, 23275880, 23280451
Fax : +91-11-23285873
Web : www.atlanticbooks.com
E-mail : orders@atlanticbooks.com

Branch Office
5, Nallathambi Street, Wallajah Road, Chennai-600002
Phones : +91-44-64611085, 32413319
E-mail : chennai@atlanticbooks.com

Printed in India at Nice Printing Press, A-33/3A, Site-IV, Industrial Area, Sahibabad, Ghaziabad, U.P.

DEDICATION

For my mother, father, brother, parents-in-law, and my teachers whose memories constantly haunt me, and shape coherence and direction(s) of my life.

Preface

V.S. Naipaul has been critical of the postcolonial societies—their history, politics and culture. He has combined fiction, history, autobiography and facts to present his ideas and vision, relevant to the contemporary conditions. As a valued author, he has generated enormous interest/debate among the readers and scholars across the globe. The present book explores Naipaul's concerns for suppressed histories of various civilizations and the related complex issues concerning the intriguing confusions regarding rootlessness, identity crisis and cultural predicament of the marginalized individuals, communities and nations, their directions/misdirections of different movements after the end of colonialism as well as the prevailing political, cultural and psychological contradictions faced by the postmodern societies, more specifically the third world countries. Postcolonialism signifies a contemporary condition, and embodies various intellectual approaches, influenced by poststructuralism, deconstruction and cultural criticism. Postcolonial cultural interpretation of texts brings out new areas of meaning by destabilizing the existing fixed notions and assumptions. As a diasporic writer, Naipaul subverts the existing social order and history emphasizing the aspects of his immigrant experience related to the burning postcolonial issues such as search for identity, marginality, ethnicity, political disorders and neocolonial ills.

This book discusses Naipaul's fictional and travel worlds which are sad, enigmatic and baffling as they raise the core issues of identity crisis, immigration, metaphysical alienation and search for roots. In his early fiction, Naipaul presents the complex fate of individuals delineating their spiritual crises in their struggle to find meaning to their marginalization in an enigmatic world of alienation and disillusionment. In his shorter fiction, Naipaul explores the existing confusions regarding identity of communities and nations, politics and conflicts in national and international levels, and racial discriminations in the postmodern and postcolonial context. The societies portrayed in these fictions reveal that political liberation has not enabled these societies to have cultural, economic, intellectual and psychological decolonization. Focusing on the suppressed histories, racial conflicts, ethnicity, political violence, sexual promiscuity and neocolonial ills in the half-made, newly-liberated postcolonial societies in his later fiction, Naipaul also examines his own moods, doubts and confusions as well as his development as a writer in an alien exotic world surrounded by enigmatic foreigners. In these novels, the protagonists move away from one place to another in search of meaning, thereby falsifying their own selves, being uprooted from their societies incurring a loss of culture. Naipaul, therefore, explores how man's metaphysical alienation situates him in his vulgarity, sordidness, brutality and irrationality. His travelogues explore a painful experience of the author in connection with the postcolonial paradoxes and neocolonial imperialism, marginality, cultural contradictions, racism, ethnicity, suppressed histories and political chaos. His extensive travelling has immensely benefitted him as it has equipped him with objective perception and sensibility about multicultural societies to which his fictional and nonfictional discourses have some bearings. Writing has, therefore, become an integral part of self-definition for Naipaul. His travelogues on India explore Naipaul's critical and objective examination of India's socio-cultural, political and economic conditions, which have become rotten due to neocolonial ills, social malaise, economic disorder and political corruption. Naipaul observes that both India and West Indies, though decolonized, still hold on to imitate their former colonizer by perpetuating the British establishment in the functioning of education, law and administrative machinery, thereby creating ripples of mental colonization of elitists. He portrays the Islamic civilization in the four converted Islamic nations, namely Iran, Pakistan, Indonesia and Malaysia. Analyzing the intricacies of Islamic culture, he has interpreted the split personalities of the intellectuals and the miserable conditions of the marginalized people in these Muslim nations. He also examines the culture of the Black societies of American South and primitive African society in his travelogues on South America and Africa, respectively. His travelogues are serious explorations of civilizations that have developed his deeper insight about man, society and culture. The present book is, therefore, a useful analysis and interpretation of Naipaul's perception of civilizations and cultures across the globe.

Prakash Chandra Pradhan

Acknowledgements

It is my pleasure to acknowledge the financial support by The University Grants Commission, New Delhi, India for sanctioning a major research project on V.S. Naipaul during 2009-2012 that extended a helping hand to me to study V.S. Naipaul's writings from a postcolonial perspective. That was the genesis of preparation of the manuscript of this book. I thank Banaras Hindu University, Varanasi, India, (my employer) for sanctioning me sabbatical leave for a year during 2015-2016 for finalizing the manuscript for its publication. I appreciate the gestures of the publishing house, Atlantic Publishers & Distributors [P] Ltd., New Delhi, India for signing the contract. I also appreciate the sincere efforts of Shweta Kumari, my research scholar, a Senior Research Fellow in the Department of English, Banaras Hindu University for resolving some of the key formatting issues before submitting the manuscript to the publisher. I acknowledge the help of Jyoti, Manjeet, Vinamrata and Ram Prakash, my research scholars, during the processing of the manuscript.

I owe special thanks to my wife, Bini, and my children, Papul and Gudul, for their love and emotional support to me for writing this book. The book is dedicated to my parents, elder brother, parents-in-law and teachers who are no more, but their memories constantly haunt me, and shape the course of my life.

Prakash Chandra Pradhan

Contents

PART III
Travelogues: Writing History, Culture, Civilization

PART IV
Conclusion

List of Abbreviations

The Mystic Masseur	:	Mystic
The Suffrage of Elvira	:	Suffrage
Miguel Street	:	MS
A House for Mr Biswas	:	House
The Middle Passage	:	MP
Mr. Stone and the Knights Companion	:	Mr. Stone
India: An Area of Darkness	:	AD
The Mimic Men	:	MM
A Flag on the Island	:	Flag
The Night Watchman's Occurrence Book and Other Comic Inventions	:	Night [Suffrage, Mr. Stone, Flag]
The Loss of El Dorado: A History	:	El Dorado
In a Free State	:	FS
The Overcrowded Baracoon and Other Articles	:	Barracoon
India: A Wounded Civilization	:	IWC
Guerrillas	:	GS
A Bend in the River	:	BR
The Return of Eva Peron with Killings in Trinidad	:	Eva Peron

Among the Believers	:	AB
Finding the Centre: Two Narratives	:	FC
The Enigma of Arrival	:	EOA
A Turn in the South	:	TS
India: A Million Mutinies Now	:	MMN
A Way in the World	:	WW
Beyond Belief	:	Beyond
Half a Life	:	HL
Magic Seeds	:	MAS
Literary Occasions	:	LO
A Writer's People	:	WP
The Writer and the World	:	TWW
The Authorized Biography of V.S. Naipaul The World is What It is	:	Biography
The Adventures of Gurudeva	:	Gurudeva
The Wretched of the Earth	:	WE
Black Skin, While Masks	:	BW
The Sacred Wood	:	SW
Illustrated Weekly of India	:	IWI
Modern Fiction Studies	:	MFS
The Atlantic Critical Review	:	ACR
The Discovery of India	:	DI

PART I
Introduction

1

Situating Postcolonialism

The relevance of a theoretical approach to literary discourses often baffles the scholars and readers. In recent times so many theoretical approaches have emerged thereby questioning the validity of the traditional approaches for study of literature. The recent approaches have destabilized the existing fixed notions and assumptions. They have tried to demonstrate how meaning of a discourse is not fixed/stable. Postcolonial studies have posed challenges to the dominant western epistemology which has all along been totalitarian leaving little space for other knowledge systems and assumptions to interpret literary texts. Although the other knowledge, other experience is important for understanding the universe, it has been kept under domination for a long time. Postcolonial studies are emphasizing and employing alternative hypotheses to understand the other experiences and knowledge systems which have remained unexplored. Now a section of critics however thinks that postcolonial studies have no relevance in a postcolonial world. But the questions arise: Are we really in a "postcolonial world"? Does the term "postcolonial" refer to a situation after "colonialism"? Has "colonialism" really ended? Or does "postcolonialism" refer to a condition, a state, and a situation which are more relevant today? Many such questions disturb us when we encounter "postcolonialism" in its transformed perspective. A pertinent situation in this context is the U.S. attack on Iraq in 2003. Such attacks were also conducted on Iraq and Afghanistan earlier in 2001. Ania Loomba et al. point out appropriately:

> The shadow the 2003 U.S. invasion of Iraq casts on the twenty-first century makes it more absurd than ever to speak of ours as a postcolonial world. On the other hand, the signs of galloping US imperialism make the agenda of postcolonial studies more necessary than ever. In a context of rapidly proliferating defenses of empire (not simply *de facto* but *de jure*) by policy-makers and intellectuals alike, the projects of making visible the long history of empire, of learning from those who have opposed it, and of identifying the contemporary sites of resistance and oppression that have defined postcolonial studies have, arguably, never been more urgent. In many ways, the new global reality has made the analysis of imperialism, in all its historical variants, more pressing, but also more difficult, than ever before. (2008:1)

The relevance of postcolonial studies has been discussed vividly in the conference, namely "Postcolonial Studies and Beyond" held at the University of Illinois, Urbana-Champaign, April 25-28, 2002, organized by Ania Loomba et al. The discussions and assumptions by the contemporary postcolonial critics upheld "all the material and ideological tensions and inequities" (Loomba et al. 2008:1) that led to the subsequent events in the neo-imperial situation created by the administration of George Bush. Before the organization of the conference, Loomba and others had scrutinized whether postcolonial studies had proved important to the task of analyzing, with intellectual power and political clarity, both the colonial past and the new empire of the contemporary times. They did so because all ideas, methods and movements "tend to have a distinct and bounded lifespan" (Loomba et al. 2) after which they lose the contemporary relevance.

Postcolonial studies from their inception have been carrying on with many controversies. For example, the appropriateness of the term "post" in postcolonial and the continuance of the term "colonial" for making us understand the term "post", relationship of postcolonial studies to anticolonial nationalism and to post-structuralist theories are some of the debates that have questioned the validity and future of postcolonial studies. The increasing roles of information technology, globalization, transnational capitalism and alternative modernities have often motivated some scholars to examine the viability of postcolonial methods.

1.1. Postcolonialism and V.S. Naipaul

Since the early 1980s, postcolonial cultural analysis has been concerned with theoretical frameworks that contest the previous dominant Western ways of seeing things. Claiming the right of all people on the earth to the same material as well as cultural well-being through their emancipation and empowerment, postcolonialism shifts its emphasis on the marginal sections in the society. It aims at subversion of the existing social/world order and reconstruction of history and culture. Postcolonialism is concerned with removing the conditions of exploitation and poverty in which the larger sections of the marginalized live every day. Through its alternative ways of perception, it "seeks to change the way people think, the way they behave to produce a more just and equitable relation between different peoples of the world" (Young 2006: 6-7). Young argues that postcolonialism is about a changing world "that has been changed by struggle and which its practitioners intend to change further" (2006: 7). In its attempt to subvert the existing world-order, postcolonialism threatens privilege and power. Its radical agenda is for the well-being of the marginalized, "the wretched of the Earth" (Frantz Fanon 1961) and aims at destabilization of the margin-center equation (Said 1978; Spivak 1990) emphasizing cultural identity (Hall 1990; Bhabha 1994). V.S. Naipaul deconstructs the "margin-center equation" repositioning the "margins" and "the center"—pushing the margins into the center and the center being pushed to the other side of the margin. The collision of cultures and ideologies in the social structure with reference to the "Center-Margin" paradox is central to the world of V.S. Naipaul. In his texts, Naipaul portrays cultural predicament of the displaced and the marginalized individuals, communities and nations; and he revisits the history of these people to explore culture-conflicts and ideological clashes. This immigrant writer in his works subverts the existing social order and history emphasizing the aspects of immigrant experience of a diaspora in relation to such burning postcolonial issues as search for roots, cultural identity and suppressed histories. An analysis and interpretation of Naipaul's texts drawing on the insights and precision of multiple approaches of postcolonial theories will enable us to have a deeper understanding of such issues as marginality, cultural identity and deconstruction of history in relation to current global, socio-political, economic and cultural concerns.

Postcolonialism, as a politics and philosophy of activism, contests the social disparity and economic inequality between the West and the non-West and continues the anticolonial struggle in a new way for the rights of the deprived and marginalized sections to access the material resources equally and assert their cultural identity. The postcolonial writers deconstruct the societies of the West through intervention of dynamic power of their cultures. In many ways, the Bandung Conference of third world countries in 1955 marks the origin of postcolonialism as a self-conscious political philosophy. The more militant version of third-world politics as a global alliance, resisting the continuing imperialism of the West, however, cropped up at the Tricontinental Conference held in Havana in 1966 when the writings of postcolonial theorists and activists such as Amilcar Cabral, Frantz Fanon, Che Guevara, Ho Chi Minh and Jean Paul Sartre were brought together in the journal titled *Tricontinental*. The terms "tricontinental" (Asia, Africa and Latin America) and "third world" retain their power because they suggest an alternative culture, an alternative "epistemology" or system of knowledge. Until now, the "institutionalized knowledge corporation" of the West has been produced by the Westerners during the past three or more centuries. Postcolonialism however rejects the Western epistemology and begins from its own knowledge systems with the premise that the Westerners should take such other knowledge systems, other perspectives as seriously as those of the West. To Robert Young, postcolonialism or tricontinentalism refers to these insurgent knowledge systems that come from "the subaltern, the dispossessed and seek to change the terms and values under which we all live. For acquiring such knowledge one is to look at the world not from above, but from below" (2006: 20).

After decolonization, the West started neocolonial strategies to rule the Third World nations indirectly by interfering in their internal affairs. Such strategies have been exposed by Frantz Fanon who argues that the West uses "organized violence" for domination and legalization of its colonial/neo-colonial rule for which the Third World people must use violence in their anti-colonial struggles. His book *The Wretched of the Earth* (1961) was a landmark in the history of postcolonial aesthetics that inspired many kinds of struggles against domination and oppression across the world. Edward Said has defined "Orientalism" as a "Western style for dominating, restructuring, and having authority over the Orient" (*Orientalism* [1978] 2001: 3) and pleads for the study of the postcolonial texts in the context of European imperialism. Gayatri Chakravorty Spivak corroborates this view when she writes that "the political claims that are most urgent in decolonized space are tacitly recognized as coded within the legacy of imperialism, nationhood, constitutionality, citizenship, democracy, socialism, even culturalism" (*Outside in the Teaching Machine* 1993: 60). Homi K. Bhabha, one of the diasporic intellectuals like these two, has discussed such concepts as "cultural hybridity", "ambivalence" and "contingency" which have further developed the theory of postcolonialism and which have been useful in the interpretation of postcolonial texts (*The Location of Culture*, 1994). While Said and Spivak argue that culture and imperialism are the distinguished factors that shape postcolonial literature, Fredric Jameson (1986: 69) stresses on the allegorical nature of such literature and history of the colonies as its shaping force. Jameson also speaks in terms of the binary opposition of the First and Third Worlds. Aijaz Ahmad, however, questions Jameson's views by alleging that the latter's concept of national allegory is "positivist reductionism" (1994: 97). Frantz Fanon talks of the psychological aspects of colonialism and myths of racism (*Black Skin, White Masks* 1967; *The Wretched of the Earth* 1961). Ahmad also elaborates how the term "postcoloniality" conjoined the two terms "postcolonial" and "postcolonialism" in literary and cultural theories and in deconstructive forms of history writing (Mongia 1997: 281) during the 1980s. Stuart Hall made useful discussions on the concepts of marginality, cultural identity and reconstruction of history (Mongia 1997: 110-21). The critique of Fanon, Said, Spivak, Bhabha, Ahmad, Jameson, Hall and many others helped to evolve the postcolonial theories for analysis of literary texts. Ashcroft, Griffiths and Tiffin argued that postcolonial literature included literatures of all former colonies including the USA because "they emerged in their present form out of the experience of colonization and asserted themselves by foregrounding the tension with the imperial power, and by emphasizing their differences from the assumptions of the imperial centre" (*The Empire Writes Back* 1989: 2). Ella Shohat writes that "postcolonialism...evokes the contemporary theoretical writings, placed in both the First and Third Worlds generally on the left, and which attempt to transcend the (presumed) binarisms of the Third Wordlist Militancy" ("Notes on the Postcolonial" in Mongia 1977: 324-25).

Postcolonialism is a state of consciousness in the continuum of our cultural process which can only be understood with reference to colonialism. Postcolonial theories claim that the major theme of literature for postcolonial countries is resistance to the former colonizer, and the postcolonial writers represent the people of their society authentically. These theories use such terms as "the oppressed", "the colonized other" and "the indigenous" to describe postcolonial societies. They therefore destroy internal hierarchies and divisions in these societies and confer "subaltern status" on the entire postcolonial world. At present, the term "postcolonial" does not however refer to "periodisation". In recent years, it refers to both literary writings and literary criticism. Discourse of postcolonialism is not about the colonizer, but about the colonized other (the non-West). In this framework, "the colonized other" has been placed at the center of the dominant discourse of the Western Academy. Critics often argue that postcolonial theory makes use of structuralism and post-structuralism which are the theories of the West. Although postcolonialism is about the non-West, the postcolonial intellectuals still look to the West for intellectual guidance. It is now time for these intellectuals to make use of their indigenous convictions and ideas for interpretation of postcolonial texts.

In the perspective of such theoretical and methodological developments on postcolonialism, there is a need for analysis and interpretation of V.S. Naipaul's novels, shorter fictions and travelogues. A comprehensive analysis of Naipaul's discourses in the light of insights and precision of recent postcolonial theories rather than drawing on critical writings on Naipaul will be more useful and a worthwhile pursuit in exploring new areas of meaning. We cannot, however, ignore some important critics on Naipaul. Many of them like Bruce King (1993), Selwyn Cudjoe (1988), Simon Gikandi (1992), Andrew Gurr (1981), Landeg White (1975), Fawzia Mustafa (1995), B. Chandra Joshi (1994), Shashi Kamra (1990), Rob Nixon (1992), William Walsh (1973), M.I. Singh (1998), Bhat (2000), Chandra Chatterjee (2000), Robert Hamner (1977) and many others are perceptive, and have contributed much to understand V.S. Naipaul's vision. In spite of that, the focus shall however be on his primary materials in the light of our insights of recent postcolonial critical assumptions to make the study first-hand, authentic and authoritative. This book therefore aims at exploring Naipaul's holistic vision on contemporary issues embedded in his texts.

Postcolonialism as a critical discourse aims at subversion of existing colonial mindset and imperial values. It also encourages an alternative way of seeing things from the perspective of the Other Knowledge systems, rather than being guided by the Western Metaphysics. Its objective is to focus on the contemporary social problems and contradictions. Postcolonialism as a political philosophy means the right to autonomous self-government of those who still find themselves in a situation of being controlled politically and administratively by the dominant power. It also aims at empowering the poor, the dispossessed and the disadvantaged; tolerance of difference, diversity and multiculturalism; and establishment of women's rights, minorities' rights and cultural rights. It resists all forms of exploitation, both human and environmental; and all oppressive conditions to suit the interests of corporate capitalism. In short, postcolonialism stands for the rights to all basic amenities such as security, sanitation, health care, food and education for all people on the earth—the young, the adult and the aged. It champions the cause of the marginalized and aims at demolishing the hierarchies of power. In its objective to sympathize the subaltern, the peasantry, the poor and the exploited class, postcolonialism undermines the importance of high culture of the elite and espouses subaltern cultures which are the rich repositories of culture and counter-knowledge. It thus focuses its emphasis on those at the margin of the society whose cultural identity has been dislocated by the forces of global capitalism. These margins are the refugees, the migrants who have moved from the countryside to the edges of the city, the migrants who struggle in the first world for a better life while working at the lowest levels of those societies. Postcolonialism aims at removal of inequality in all levels of the world systems of social hierarchies that operate in all social and cultural relations. The Westerners therefore consider that postcolonialism turns the world upside-down as it perceives the world from below rather than from above. Although postcolonialism draws on elements from radical socialism, feminism and environmentalism and combines them, it is fundamentally different from all of them as it begins from a tricontinental, third world, subaltern perspective and its priorities always remain there. V.S. Naipaul as a novelist or as a writer of shorter fiction and travelogues delineates the human situations from such a subaltern perspective. The implicit agenda of the writer is to bring the marginalized to the centre by changing different socio-cultural, political and economic systems and ideas. Since postcolonialism is concerned with analysis of the nervous conditions of the deprived of being marginalized in a postcolonial environment in respect of social oppression in the postcolony or the metropolis, a postcolonial reading of V.S. Naipaul's texts will result in greater emphasis on social and political campaigns for material, cultural, educational and legal rights of the marginalized in the globe. A study of this kind will yield in such dividends by which it can influence the policy-makers, politicians and the people in power to shift their focus of attention on the subaltern, the deprived and the marginalized for their respectful human existence on the earth. An understanding of V.S. Naipaul's ideas and visions in his texts by following the postcolonial critical methods will therefore enable us to understand this world better and deeper. This study has global relevance as it is useful for the larger sections in the globe.

This book constitutes the following chapters:

Part I: INTRODUCTION

Chapter 1: Situating Postcolonialism

Chapter 2: Contextualising V.S. Naipaul as a Postcolonial Writer

Part II: INTERPRETING FICTIONAL DISCOURSE

Chapter 3: Society, Politics and Culture in Early Novels

Chapter 4: Neocolonialism, Expatriacy and Cultural Identity in Shorter Fiction

Chapter 5: Hegemony, Ethnicity, Political Disorder and Diasporic Identity in Later Novels

Part III: TRAVELOGUES: WRITING HISTORY, CULTURE, CIVILIZATION

Chapter 6: The Caribbean Journey: Exploring West Indian History, Society, Culture

Chapter 7: The Image of the Indian Nation: A Diasporic Perspective

Chapter 8: The Islamic Journeys: Deconstructing History, Religion, Civilization

Chapter 9: The South American Expedition: Exploring Racism, Culture, Civilization

Part IV: CONCLUSION

Chapter 10: Self, Culture and Universal Civilization

In chapter 1, a perspective of postcolonial theories has been discussed for interpretation of literary texts. The focus has been on "marginality", "cultural identity" and "deconstruction of history" with reference to socio-political and cultural issues of global concern. In chapter 2, V.S. Naipaul as a postcolonial writer with reference to his portrayal of human situations has been discussed. The substantial part of the book has been presented in chapters 3-9. The fictional world of Naipaul is sad, enigmatic and baffling. The core issues of identity crisis, immigration, search for roots and metaphysical alienation have been discussed. Then, the focus has been on his non-fictional discourses, more specifically the travelogues which explore a painful experience of the author in connection with postcolonial paradoxes and neocolonial imperialism, marginality, political and cultural conflicts, cultural/racial identities and so on. The focus has been on the postcolonial experience of the writer with the colonial past, social history, politics, culture and conflicts of nations/communities.

In chapters 3, 4 and 5, Naipaul's fictional texts have been interpreted. The fictional texts deal with complex fate of individuals, societies and cultures. Naipaul delineates the individual's predicament in his search for roots and identity; and tries to find a meaning to his marginalization and alienation. This is a reflection of the general disillusionment that seriously affected the two post-War generations and deep spiritual isolation felt by man in an enigmatic universe. As in the case of Conrad, the other immigrant modern British novelist, his mentor, Naipaul's alienation too springs from a spiritual crisis resulted from his strong disliking for the two worlds to which he has significant connections—his strong repulsion for the Trinidadian milieu with a multi-racial composition competing for pseudo-Westernization through mimicry of the colonial masters and disliking for cultural-spatial milieu of London as a Diaspora. In *A House for Mr. Biswas* (1961), the protagonist Mr. Biswas has been marginalized against the conventional, customary and conservative Hindu ideas and ideology. He is the lone fighter against the degraded system filled with rotten myths, customs and rituals of a Brahmin cultural system. In *The Mystic Masseur*, the marginalization of Ganesh and that of Ralph Singh in *The Mimic Men* shows that these novels are more about displacement, isolation and identity crisis rather than about politics or about a particular race or society. *The Suffrage of Elvira* explores the possibility of a democracy and political awakening among the natives in a multi-racial, multi-religious and multi-ethnic society. *Mr. Stone and the Knights Companion* focuses on post-War English middle class who feel frustrated under a new post-imperial order because of their continuous displacement although they are rooted in their own culture and society. In *The Enigma of Arrival*, the Caribbean expatriate in England examines his own moods, doubts and confusions as well as his developments as a writer in the perspective of an alien or exotic world surrounded by enigmatic foreigners. Both Willie Chandran in *Half a Life* and Ralph Singh in *The Mimic Men* move from one place to the other in search of meaning thereby falsifying their own selves and uprooting themselves from their societies, and incurring a loss of culture. This cultural loss is a threat to identity. His exploration of man's metaphysical alienation situates him in his vulgarity, brutality and irrationality. *Guerrillas* and *A Bend in the River* deal with the gloominess of a postcolonial disorder rotten by violence, sexual promiscuity and racial bias in the newly independent societies of West Indies and Africa. In *A Way in the World* he has illustrated how there are no definite ways by which the world is governed. He thinks that the world should be understood in the perspective of history, politics and culture in relation to both the place and the individual. That is why he emphasizes that the identity of an individual is not merely associated with inheritance or history but by both. Naipaul's concern for the complex issue of Identity of an individual has been a dominant perspective in *Magic Seeds*. That is because Willie Chandran's identity has been continuously evolved in a postcolonial perspective.

In chapter 4, shorter fictional texts have been discussed from the perspective of neocolonial ills in the postcolonial nations. These shorter fictional texts explore the existing confusion regarding identities of communities and nations, politics and conflicts in national and international levels, and racial discrimination in the post-modern, postcolonial context.

Miguel Street (*Miguel Street*, 1959) symbolically represents Trinidad, a multi-racial and multi-cultural society comprising the Negroes, Asians, Chinese, English and Spanish all of whom are expatriates. Political liberation has not yet been able to decolonize them intellectually and culturally. Such a society is portrayed by Naipaul in *The Middle Passage,* and he considers these people to be "unimportant, uncreative, and cynical" (*MP* 43). Despite having achieved their independence, they have no dignity and "every person of eminence was held to be crooked and contemptible" (43). *A Flag on the Island* deals with different places and times for which the characters do not form a "society-street". On the other hand, they are full of vices such as selfishness, superstition, intolerance, corruption, hypocrisy and exploitation. They are complex individuals fighting for their rights and identities. *In a Free State* (1975) deals with the predicament of free individual expatriates, staying away from their roots in an alien world. These alienated figures belong to different nations—India, Africa, Sweden, Germany, China and America. Though free from political colonialism, they are living in an atmosphere surcharged with hostility; and they have not yet attained psychological and cultural freedom. Naipaul's penetrating analysis of futility of freedom in an alien land reveals the enigmatic situation of the postcolonial societies which achieved political freedom without attaining psychological and cultural independence. These three collections of stories, therefore, deconstruct the impact of colonialism on the displaced migrants.

Chapter 6 discusses the painful situation of West Indies, and chapter 7 explores India in a postcolonial environment. Naipaul's extensive travelling to different parts of the world has immensely benefited him as a writer. As a product of three different cultures such as the native West Indian culture where he was born, the English culture that shaped his adulthood and the Indian culture that formed his psyche Naipaul has been equipped with the objective perception and sensibility of a multi-cultural society to which his fictional/non-fictional writings have some bearings. Writing is an integral part of self-definition for Naipaul. His three travelogues on India explore an objective examination of her socio-cultural, political and economic conditions. Just like other post-Independent nations, India has also been rotten by neocolonial ills, economic disorders, social malaise and political corruption. India, though decolonized, is still imitating the former colonizer and their power hierarchy and perpetuates the presence of British Establishment in the functioning of education, law and administrative machinery thereby creating vibrations of mental colonization of the elitists. That is why postcolonial theory undermines the significance of political liberation without economic liberation. In *The Middle Passage,* Naipaul has presented difficult situations of racial tension, violence and disorder of his native land vividly. He delineates that India is progressively ravaged by moral and historical degeneration in *An Area of Darkness*. He, therefore, painfully utters that India is "the featureless area of darkness" (35). In *India: A Wounded Civilization*, Naipaul very sadly points out that India's crisis is the crisis of "a wounded old civilization that has at last become aware of its inadequacies and is without the intellectual means to move ahead" (18). However, in *India: A Million Mutinies Now*, Naipaul becomes optimistic as he thinks that liberation of spirit "had to come as rage and revolt. India was now a country of a million little mutinies" (517). Chapter 8 has examined Naipaul's portrayal of the Islamic civilization and culture in the four Islamic countries, namely Iran, Pakistan, Indonesia and Malaysia, and chapter 9 has examined the culture of Black societies of American South.

This book therefore examines the extent of reversal of normal perspectives in history, politics and culture "in allowing peripheral figures their place in the momentousness of great literature" (Ray xi) as Dr. Horace Engdahl has rightly pointed out in his presentation speech for 2001 Nobel Prize award ceremony. Naipaul explores "suppressed histories" of nations and communities to bring truth to surface, and reconstructs history ethically and accurately. This book has focused on prominent issues faced by contemporary world in general and the third world countries in particular. The book discovers some of the complex issues regarding rootlessness, identity crisis and cultural predicament of marginalized individuals, communities and nations, different movements of these nations after the end of colonialism and the prevailing political, cultural and psychological conflicts faced by the post-modern societies.

1.2. Postcolonial Studies: A Historical Perspective

Before interpretation of Naipaul's works in the perspective of postcolonial theories, it is imperative to discuss postcolonialism in its historical context and subsequent developments. In the human history, colonialism has always persisted in all situations and all times. Colonialism exists whenever we find a situation of domination of the more powerful over the less powerful, exploitation of the economically disadvantaged labourers and marginalized sections, appropriation of material resources of other's territory, cultural and political domination. If power is the basis of such domination over the less advantaged, then the question arises: where from this power comes? Referring to Foucault, Ania Loomba says that "power does not emanate from some central or hierarchical structure but flows through society in a sort of capillary action" (2007: 40). Foucault's idea of power is therefore important even if it is sometime problematic: "Power is everywhere; not because it embraces everything, but because it comes from everywhere" (1990: 93). Such a concept of power is relevant to the context of all-pervasive repression that exists in all social structures across the globe. Foucault's conception of power does not however explain the complexity of social formation which is not a unitary whole. Stuart Hall's concept of power explains the relations of power between different social structures:

> The question of the relative power and distribution of different regimes of truth in the social formation at any one time—which have certain effects for the maintenance of power in the social order—that's what I call the 'ideological effect'. So I go on using the term 'ideology' because it forces me to continue thinking about that problem. By abandoning the term I think that Foucault has let himself off the hook of having to retheorize it in a more radical way i.e. he saves for himself "the political" with his insistence on power,

> but he denies a politics because he has no idea of the "relations of force". (1996: 136)

Hall's concept elucidates how resistance can be organized in a social structure, rather than being confined to the resistance of an individual. In colonial imperialism, these ideas of power are important because they focus on the systematic exploitation of the marginalized sections in a colonial society.

As we know, colonialism is related to conquest and domination of other people's land and materials. In this sense it has a long tradition, travelling from ancient times to the present era. However, there is a marked distinction between ancient colonialism and modern European colonialism in Asia, Africa and America from the sixteenth century onwards. The European colonialism is more ruthless and organized in exploiting both the human as well as the material resources in their colonies unlike the ancient Empires. The modern Empire is capitalist and inhuman. Loomba therefore comments:

> Modern colonialism did more than extract tribute, goods and wealth from the countries that it conquered—it restructured the economies of the latter, drawing them into a complex relationship with their own, so that there was a flow of human and natural resources between colonial and colonized countries. (2007: 9)

The economies of the colonial countries were ruined because the profits always flowed back to the so-called "mother country". The European colonialism, being a capitalist outfit, applied a number of techniques to produce economic imbalance for growth of European industry. It is appropriately said that "colonialism was the mid-wife that assisted at the birth of European capitalism" (Loomba 10).

The cheap but immense human labour of the colonies was exploited for abundant industrial growth by the imperialistic rulers as they invested capital for their own profit. Through colonial domination, European industry and finance-capital was achieved to a considerable measure. Imperialism can be explained in two ways, namely "political imperialism" and "economic imperialism". Granting political independence results in the end of political imperialism whereas economic imperialism continues in an independent country through control of market and economic interference by the imperialist superpower. Direct political rule is not required in this case. Loomba therefore posits:

> Thus the imperial country is the metropole from which power flows, and the colony or neo-colony is the place which it penetrates and controls. Imperialism can function without formal colonies (as in United States imperialism today) but colonialism cannot. (12)

Since colonialism does not perish in spirit, it always continues in the postcolonial nations. Hence, the term "postcolonial" poses many problems. We cannot say exactly when "postcolonial" begins (Shohat 1993: 103). Moreover, the prefix "post" complicates the issue further because the colonial conditions still persist in the independent nations because the new global order allows the " economic, cultural and political penetration of some countries by others" (McClintock 1992). The European values still exist in many so-called postcolonial countries. Even the marginalized sections in an independent nation are still being exploited thereby challenging the appropriateness of the term "postcolonial" to such societies and nations. The issues of postcolonialism seem to be baffling:

> These internal fractures and divisions are important if "postcolonialism" is to be anything more than a term signifying a technical transfer of 'governance'. But at the same time, we cannot simply construct a global 'white' culture either. There are important differences of power and history between New Zealand or Canada and the European (or later United States) metropolis. Internal fractures also exist in the countries where postcolonial status is not usually contested, such as India. Here the ruptures have to do with class and ethnicity in a different sense. (Loomba 2007: 14)

Postcolonialism is thus full of contradictions because the newly independent nation-states selectively facilitate the benefits of liberation to the selected few. The end of colonialism has therefore not improved the conditions of the marginalized sections. Loomba pleads:

> The newly independent nation-state makes available the fruits of liberation only selectively and unevenly: the dismantling brings about changes for the better in the status of women, the working class or the peasantry in most colonial countries. "Colonialism" is not just something that happens from outside a country or a people, not just a thing that operates with the collusion of forces inside, but a version of it can be duplicated from within. (2007: 16)

de Alva (1995) argued in this direction earlier: the term "postcolonialism" should be understood through post-structuralist approaches to history which have suggested that the lives of various oppressed people can only be explored by emphasizing that there is no single history but multiple histories. Even the feminists and anticolonial intellectuals have argued in this light. It is difficult to brand who belongs to a minority group. Who is marginalized? Who shares a history of colonial exploitation? Who shares the cultural roots? In postcolonial study, it is necessary to reconstruct the cultural identity of the marginalized. There should be authentic representation of their social history and culture. This implies that their existing history is to be dismantled and deconstructed.

It is noteworthy that the term "postcolonial" refers to the specific groups of oppressed people or individuals within them rather than to a location or a social order. In this sense postcolonial theory shifts its focus from location and institutions to individuals and their subjectivities. That has been so because it depends on literary and cultural criticism and post-structuralism as well. Another important thing is that colonialism should not be the measuring rod for defining the third-world countries. Their histories, cultures and indigenous ideologies should have to be understood authentically rather than judging them in relation to colonialism as a standard. That is why Vaughan thinks colonialism "as a minor interruption" in a long, complex history (1993: 47). To Hulme, postcolonial should be a "descriptive not an evaluative term which refers to a process of disengagement from the whole colonial syndrome" (1995: 120). The postcolonial studies have marked that the process of decolonization has restructured both the "metropolis" and the "colonies" although both are not postcolonial in the same sense. Postcoloniality is to be understood alongside other economic, social, cultural and historical factors and therefore, in practice, it works differently in various parts of the world. Postcolonial situations therefore vary in various contexts and locales. For example, the situations in Latin America, India, Africa and West Indies are not the same. For understanding postcoloniality meaningfully, it should have to be entangled to specific locations notwithstanding the term postcolonial as useful in indicating a general process with some shared experiences across the globe.

The ideas of Frantz Fanon in *Black Skin, White Masks* and *The Wretched of the Earth* on colonial racism are relevant. His concern for the marginalized is noteworthy because he believes in the dignity of man. He pleaded that "the third world must start over a new history of man" (*WE* 238) by resisting the condition of coloniality. He writes that "the thing colonized becomes a man through the very process of liberation" (*WE* 2). The divisive colonized world's border is represented by the "barracks and the police stations" (*WE* 3). Thus the "police officer" or the "soldier", the agent of the colonizer, carries on with the oppressive measures enforcing "violence into the homes and minds of the colonized subject" (*WE* 4). Fanon vividly describes that the colonist's sector is a sector of all good things—"lights and paved roads, without garbage, clean and smooth—meant for white folks and foreigners". Contrarily the native colonized black people are to live anywhere, die anywhere. They are a kind of people who are deprived of good food and all civilized amenities. They are to live in barbaric conditions. Although the colonists appropriate the land of the natives, they remain foreigners, the outsiders, and the so-called civilized people who have settled in the colony to civilize the colonized, the native barbaric. Due to this bipolarity in the attitudes of the two sections, the colony is a world divided into two, always in conflict in temperament and behavior. Fanon says that the colony is a "compartmentalized" world divided into two territories where two different species live:

> The singularity of the colonial context lies in the fact that economic reality, inequality and enormous disparities in lifestyles never manage to mask the human reality. Looking at the immediacies of the colonial context, it is clear that what divides this world is first and foremost what species, what race one belongs to. In the colonies the economic infrastructure is also a superstructure. The cause is effect: you are rich because you are white; you are white because you are rich. This is why a Marxist analysis should always be slightly stretched when it comes to addressing the colonial issue. (*WE* 5)

What Fanon views in the above oft-quoted passage is that Marx's analysis of class struggle of pre-capitalist society for social change is to be modified in the perspective of anti-colonial struggle where racial discrimination is more important than domination of the higher class over the working class. To Marx, colonialism is a brutal precondition for liberation of the colonized societies:

> England, it is true, in causing a social revolution in Hindustan was actuated only by the vilest interests, and was stupid in her manner of enforcing them. But that is not the question. The question is can mankind fulfill its destiny without a fundamental revolution in the social state of Asia? If not, whatever may have been the crimes of England she was the conscious tool of history in bringing about that revolution. (1973: 306)

The views of Marx need to be revised because the division between the poor and the rich is based on race rather than class. Aime Cesaire's (1972: 9) emphasis on the negative aspects of European colonialism is worth mentioning because it is nearer to the ideas of Fanon. His indictment of European colonialism, imperialism and capitalism is due to its dehumanizing aspects. Fanon in his *Black Skin, White Masks* points out that the colonist tries to inculcate the inferiority complex to the mind of the colonized thereby traumatizing them psychologically.

In addition to appropriating their land and labor the colonist brings out the death of the culture of the local people in "whose soul an inferiority complex has been created by the death and burial of its local cultural originality" (*BW* 18). Loomba argues that Marxist analysis has not theorized exploitation of labor of women, pointed out by the feminists. She demands for a reexamination of the colonial context:

> The question of race and colonialism demanded rethinking for similar reasons. The impact of colonialism on culture is intimately tied up with its economic processes but the relationship between them cannot be understood unless cultural processes are theorized as fully and deeply as the economic ones. In recent years some of the fiercest disagreements among scholars are about this interrelation. Colonial intellectuals consistently raised the question of their cultures, both as the sites of colonial oppression, and as vital tools for their own resistance. Thus the analysis of colonialism demanded that the categories developed for understanding capitalism (such as class) be revised but also that the relation between the realms of 'culture' or 'ideology' and the sphere of 'economics' or 'material reality' be reexamined. (2007: 26)

Marx and Engels, and subsequently Lukacs view that human consciousness is constituted by an ideology which consists of beliefs, values and ways of thinking and feeling through which human beings perceive reality. Since ideology is the production of a particular dominant class, the "dominant ideology embodies, and serves to legitimize and perpetuate, the interests of the dominant economic and social class" (Abrams 1993: 241). Loomba however rightly argues that there is no correspondence between ideologies and classes: "Classes are heterogeneous groups, fissured by gender, race and other divides. Different people within the same class do not hold the same relationship to the production process, or other aspects of reality" (2007: 28-29). Gramsci (1971: 324, 371) posits that ideologies are conceptions of life, manifested in individuals and collective existence. He holds the view that hegemony is achieved through a combination of coercion and consent. He thus conceptualizes that the ruling class domination is achieved by the consent of the oppressed by creating appropriate ideologies by which the ruled willingly surrender to the ruling class. Loomba comments on Gramscian concepts of hegemony regarding the centrality of colonial rule:

> Gramscian notions of hegemony stress the incorporation and transformation of ideas and practices belonging to those who are dominated rather than simple imposition from above. Such transformations are being increasingly seen as central to colonial rule. The dimension of Gramsci's work that has most inspired revisionary analysis of colonial societies is his understanding that subjectivity and ideology are absolutely central to the process of domination. (2007: 32)

In his essay "Ideological State Apparatus", Althusser pleads that ideology is more autonomous, and suggests that "ideology" has a material existence: "...an ideology always exists in an apparatus, and its practice, or practices" (1971: 166). Althusser's formulations have strongly influenced postcolonial studies through Michel Foucault, his student, who held the view that, the "human subject is not an autonomous entity" (1970: ix). He argued that all human ideas and all fields of knowledge are "structured and determined" by the "law of a certain code of knowledge. All utterances are to be contextualized since no single source is sufficient for the full meaning of a text." Foucault's innovative ideas have advanced the theory of postcolonial studies via postmodernist and post-structuralist ideas. Loomba postulates:

> At the same time, following upon Althusser's interest in language and psyche, subject formation is often taken to be an effect of language and ideas, and a matter of individual psyche developments alone. These innovative as well as reductive effects are both visible in postcolonial studies, often refracted through the writings of Althusser's student Michel Foucault. Foucault's work stands at the intersection of innovations in theories of

> ideology, subjectivity and language, and has exerted an important (some would say even definitive) influence on the shaping of post-modernist and post-structuralist ideas and, via Edward Said's *Orientalism* (1978), on postcolonial studies. (2007: 34)

Ferdinand de Saussure pleads that language is a system of signs whose meaning is relational. Through the signs or words a community shares their assumptions and identity as a community. Language is ideological rather than objective. Macherey (1978) considers that a text is produced under determinate conditions, rather than being created by an intention (78). To Derrida, no utterance or text is capable of conveying its meaning fully. Close analysis or deconstruction of texts reveals their own instability and contradictions (1994: 347-58). He, therefore, argues that meaning is to be understood in the gap between words or signs in the text i.e. in "differance" (difference and deferral). Words and images become fundamental for an analysis of historical processes such as colonialism. Quite rightly, intellectual developments clearly point out that ideological and social practices are interconnected. These intellectual debates have established linkages of the economic realities of colonialism with "all that was excluded from hard social analysis—sexuality, subjectivity, psychology and Language" (Loomba 2007: 37). It is, therefore, established that the real relations of society do not exist in isolation from its cultural or ideological categories. In other words, it is imperative on our part to bring out linkage between event and representation, history and text, rather than segregating them. History is not merely a background to the study of texts; it is an essential part of textual meaning. Texts or representations are thus regarded as fundamental to the creation of history and culture. Such a perspective destabilizes the fixed meaning of texts thereby questioning the dominant canonicity of literary texts. So also the anticolonial movements questioned the dominant ideas of "history, culture and representation". Loomba cogently sums up how postcolonialism is making use of the poststructuralist notion of destabilizing the canonical texts, ideas, and cultures and epistemologies:

> Post-structuralist's suspicion of established truths was shared by various new social movements which also challenged the 'meta-narratives' that excluded them. Anti-colonial or feminist struggles emphasized culture as a site of conflict between the oppressors and the oppressed. The decentring of the human subject was important to them because such a subject had been dominantly theorized by European imperialist discourses as male and white. They also paid attention to language as tool of domination and as a means of constructing identity. (2007: 39-40)

Anticolonial and feminist struggles therefore strived hard for the much needed social change. Such struggles are great challenges against colonialism, patriarchy, canonicity, phallocentrism and logocentrism.

In his "Foreword: Framing Fanon" (2004), Homi K. Bhabha discusses the contemporary relevance of Fanon's ideas in the present era of globalization. He argues that even if there is scope for wider opportunity and choice, "the colonial shadow falls across the successes of globalization" (*WE* 2004: xii). The globalization, a "dual economy" is not a developed economy because it creates inequality in the economic conditions. Bhabha illustrates this idea:

> Dual economies create divided worlds in which uneven and unequal conditions of development can often mask the ubiquitous, underlying factors of persistent poverty and malnutrition, caste and racial injustice, the hidden injuries of class, the exploitation of woman's labor, and the victimization of minorities and refugees. (*WE* xii)

These views are noteworthy because the decolonized man, who has been free from the shackles of colonialism very recently, is still under the civilizing mission of new global empires which are also guilty of "psychological terror, cultural arrogance and even physical torture" (*WE* xi). Fanon was actually angry because of such a situation in the fresh conditions of neocolonialism in the decolonized scenario. These new western saviors want to civilize the third world in the name of democracy and free markets. That is why Fanon feels that "the colonized, underdeveloped man is today a political creature in the most global sense of the term" (*WE* 40). Reflecting on this view of Fanon, Bhabha correlates the condition of the "colonized man" to the "globalized man" rather than to the "decolonized man". The intersection and association between decolonization and globalization is complex:

> The global aspiration of "Third World" national thinking belonged to the internationalist traditions of socialism, Marxism and humanism, whereas the dominant forces of contemporary globalization tend to subscribe to free market ideas that enshrine ideologies of neo-liberal technocratic elitism. And finally, while it was the primary purpose of decolonization to repossess land and territoriality in order to ensure the security of national polity and global equity, globalization propagates a world made up of virtual transnational domain and wired communities that live vividly through webs and connectivities "on line". (*WE* xi)

Global duality can be understood when we correlate it to the compartmentalized structure of colonial society which is described by Fanon as the "geographical configuration of colonial governance" (*WE* 3). Such a society is divided into two as discussed in the previous section. Fanon was interested in creating a world-system of Third-World nations that cultivated a postcolonial consciousness founded on a "dual emergence" of national sovereignty and international solidarity. He, therefore, writes: "...it is at the heart of national consciousness that international consciousness establishes itself and thrives" (WE 180). Fanon wanted a world-system which should be founded on the political and ethical principles of independence and security rather than based on a "metaphysical principle" of cultural authenticity or geopolitical exceptionalism like the African tradition, the Asian temperament and the Latin American spirit. The regional solidarity should have been given to the nation because it is to face challenges for internal squabbles and threat from the external, hegemonic "quasi-colonial powers". But there is some trouble in implementation of Fanon's ideas wherever there is some natural calamity in a decolonized nation in extending economic and technological support for underdeveloped regions. Bhabha is hopeful that Fanon's ideas have eternal value for the wretched of the earth in all situations and times:

> However, Fanon's proleptic proposal that the postcolonial narrative of independent nation building could enter its international phase only after the end of the Cold War telescopes that long history of neglect into our times, whence it reveals the poignant proximity of the incomplete project of decolonization to the dispossessed subject of globalization. Caught up in this spirit of history, the wretched of the earth, in our time and Fanon's, enter the zone of psycho-affectivity and echo the horrifying call to violence Fanon for our times. And Fanon for other times and places. (*WE* xxvii-xxviii)

In his preface to Fanon's book *The Wretched of the Earth*, Jean-Paul Sartre denounces the attitude of Europeans and North Americans for their inhuman exploitations on the marginalized people, "the wretched of the Earth". He argues that the colonists have taken the "gold and minerals and then oil from the new continents and shipped them back to the old metropolis" (WE lviii). With that wealth the colonists built "palaces, cathedrals and centers of industry". From colonial exploitation with so much wealth, Europe granted humanity to its inhabitants who have all been profited. Referring to Fanon, Sartre is pungent on his attack on the exploiters, namely Europe and North America. He therefore utters in anger:

> This pale, bloated continent ended up by lapsing into what Fanon rightly calls "narcissism". Cocteau was irritated by Paris, "this city that never stops talking about herself". And Europe, what else is it doing? And that super-European monster, North America? What empty chatter: liberty equality, fraternity, love, honor country, and what else? This did not prevent us from making racist remarks at the same time: dirty nigger, filthy Jew, dirty Arab. Noble minds, liberal and sympathetic neocolonialists, in other words—claimed to be shocked by this inconsistency, since the only way the European

> could make himself man was by fabricating slaves and monsters. (*WE* lviii)

Sartre believes that the colonists are exposed, and therefore now turned into a race of subhuman. The marginalized majority are up against these inhuman colonizers:

> There is worse news: since the others are turning into men against us, apparently we are the enemy of the human race; the elite is revealing true nature—a gang. Our beloved values are losing their feathers if you take a closer look there is not one that isn't tainted with blood. (*WE* lix)

Sartre believes that everybody has a right to all privileges on the earth. The colonist should not exercise power to prevent the marginalized other from enjoying rights and privileges. He therefore thinks that a mature human race will define itself as the "infinite unity of their reciprocities" rather than the sum of the inhabitants of globe" (*WE* lix). Postcolonialism is a mode of alternative way of thinking to "produce a more just and equitable relation between the different people of the world" (Young [2003] 2006: 7). It is neither a single set of ideas nor a single practice. It rather involves multiple ideas and practices which are not static. They are relational, and might be in conflict or harmony with each other thereby generating and creating new set of relations between them. Postcolonialism is revolutionary because it has the objective of demolishing the existing thinking based on irrationality of western epistemology. In other words, postcolonialism is interested in challenging the existing power structures of imperialism. Young justifiably writes:

> Postcolonial theory, so called, is not in fact a theory in the scientific sense that is a coherently elaborated set of principles that can predict the outcome of a given set of phenomena. It comprises instead a related set of perspectives, which are juxtaposed against one another, on occasion contradictorily. It involves issues that are often the preoccupation of other disciplines and activities, particularly to do with the position of women, of development, of ecology, of social justice, of

socialism in broadest sense. Above all, postcolonialism seeks to intervene, to force its alterative knowledge into the power structures of the west as well as the non-west. (2006: 6-7)

The main purpose of postcolonialism is to develop a thinking which emphasizes the equal rights and privileges of the marginalized sections on the earth. It aims at liberating them. Beginning with Edward Said's monumental book *Orientalism* (1978), postcolonialism has destabilized the dominant culture of the West. Said has been categorical to point out how the West has created the concept of "Orientalism" through its knowledge systems. Young pleads that the racial attitude of the European domination has created anthropological theories to denigrate the oriental cultures and knowledge systems:

> Colonial and imperial rule was legitimized by anthropological theories which increasingly portrayed the peoples of the colonized world as inferior, childlike, or feminine, incapable of looking after themselves (despite having done so perfectly well for millennia) and requiring the paternal rule of the west for their own best interests (today they are deemed to require development). The basis of such anthropological theories was the concept of race. In simple terms, the west-non-west relation was thought of in terms of whites versus non-white races. White culture was regarded (and remains) the basis for ideas of legitimate government, law, economics, science, language, music, art, literature—in a word, civilization. (2006: 2-3)

These notions about the dominant West were also written long back by Edward Said when he defined Orientalism as "a western style of dominating, restructuring, and having authority over the Orient" ([1978] 2001: 3). To Said, "the Orient is not only adjacent to Europe ; it is also the place of Europe's greatest and richest and oldest colonies, the source of its civilizations and languages, its cultural contestant, and one of its deepest and most recurrent images of the Other" (2001 [1978]: 1). Said argues that "Orientalism" produced by the West was to be understood as a discourse because through this discourse

'European' culture was able to manage—and even produce—the Orient politically, sociologically, militarily, ideologically, scientifically, imaginatively during the post-Enlightenment period" ([1978] 2001: 3). Said considers that Orientalism is "a sign of European-Atlantic power over the Orient than it is a verdict discourse about the Orient" ([1978] 2001: 06). The dominion of the West over the Orient therefore thrived on the "Western cultural hegemony" ([1978] 2001: 7). The colonial administration in most of the colonies tried to peep through the discourse of Orientalism that Western cultural standards were upheld and "all other notions of culture, of art or literature or philosophy, were denounced as inferior and subordinated to western standards" (Klages 2008: 149). Klages argues that postcolonial theory is a deconstruction of the Western hegemonic ideas. She therefore believes that postcolonial theorists examine how the colonizers created the colonial subject, the subaltern, through various discursive practices, and also scrutinize how "subaltern cultures both participated in and worked to resist colonization through various overt or covert, direct or subversive, means" (153). Hence postcolonial reading is concerned with examining the mechanisms through which the colonizing powers persuaded the colonized people to accept a foreign culture as better than their own indigenous methods of government and social organization. The colonizers thus brought one of the most important kinds of "power knowledge by constricting the concept of 'race', more specifically the racial binary opposition of white and the other be that other 'black' 'yellow', 'brown', 'red' or whatever other color became the signifier for the 'otherness' of the colonized people" (153).

Within the system of race, a dark skin color becomes a signifier to represent some "signified". In this case a dark skin color may signify "athletic ability". Theorists interested in race and postcolonialism study how distinctions are made on the basis of race. They have observed that some physiological features have been irrationally connected to specific ideological signifieds. Actually race as a genetic or biological construct does not exist. It is a signifying system wherein physical signifiers become connected with concepts of ability to create meaning of one's "race" appearance. As in other signifying systems, these connections are arbitrary. Hence there is no essential connection between the physical signifiers of race and the cultural conceptions which those physical signifiers are supposed to point to. Now the question disturbs us how these connections between signifiers and signifieds are made arbitrarily or modified. Referring to Foucault's idea of discourse, it is understood that writings about race from the disciplines of anthropology, sociology, psychology, criminology, biology, medicine and literary studies connect a certain kind of eye shape with a certain kind of intelligence, or a hair texture with a social behavior. In this way, "racial traits" are created, and elaborated. When these associations are made by connecting certain signifieds with corresponding signifiers, then those signs of race are considered true and factual. Said, following Foucault, thinks that discourse works to create knowledge about a supposed racial group. Said illustrates how signifiers get connected to signifieds through discursive means "to create the ordering system we call race". He argues that "Orientalism" is a discipline to create "knowledge", from the perspective of dominant, more specifically western culture, about the subordinated/colonized culture. In this context Mary Klages pleads that "this knowledge wielded power, as it defined and described a culture of racial group, and thus produced the social attitudes, the ideological practices which surrounded and delimited the group or culture being written about" (154).

Said therefore elaborates how the cultural knowledge about, and representations of "the Orient" and "the Oriental" constructed by the West produce "the Orient" as a place of otherness. Said shows how the West projects the Orient as negative with values related to body, evil and feminine. These negative values, the West considers, are to be repressed for building up a society with positive values associated with mind, goodness and masculinity. Said points out that creation of discourse about a colonized culture, about 'the other', works also to silence that colonized culture which cannot retaliate or write about it. Such discourse renders the colonized people powerless and helpless subjects of Western power/knowledge. If at all anything is written by the colonized, it is considered illegitimate, non-knowledge and irrational. A postcolonial approach to literary texts examines what happens when the formerly colonized culture starts producing its own knowledge about itself. It also focuses on what happens when "the empire writes back" to the dominant culture, when the silenced subjects of knowledge insist on becoming the producers of knowledge. When the subaltern writes back all the binary oppositions are deconstructed. These binary oppositions start collapsing when a colonized subject insists on taking up the position of "self".

Homi Bhabha's idea of "hybridity" is in conformity with the poststructuralist political critique of the binary oppositions that structure racial, ethnic and national identities. In between race and ethnicity, the latter is a less definite category than race because the signifiers of ethnicity are less prominent than those of race. Ethnicity is sometimes a more important category in the contemporary world. In most of the cases the question of ethnicity has much to do with national identity. However, it is difficult to find out the interrelationship between race, ethnicity and national identity. In a multicultural situation in most of the countries in the globe, it seems extremely difficult to define any "national identity" or "racial identity" or "ethnic identity". These identifications pose serious challenges in a nation where the individuals have multiple identities simultaneously. This is problematic in postcolonial theory/postcolonial studies. From a postcolonial perspective, an individual is delimited as a subject within the framework of ideology of his/her race / gender / age / education / profession / socio-familial relations and obligations. The individual's identity therefore comes from his/her position within the ideologies and discourses he/she inhabits. But the point is, the individual is generally constructed by multiple discourses and ideologies simultaneously and the various subject positions are quite dissimilar. Because of his/her position, beliefs and assumptions, the individual might have multiple subjectivities and identities which may even be opposite and contradictory to one another. In other words, the individual's identity is not determined by just one discourse or ideology. The individual is not a single position as per the humanist tradition. Klages therefore rightly pleads that one might have innumerable identities because his subjecthood is constructed multiply and infinitely. For example, a child who has an Indian mother and an African-American father, then he or she does neither belong to one race nor to the other. He is rather a mixture of both. Such people occupy a hybrid position in poststructuralist theories of race and ethnicity. Since such hybridity breaks down any possibility of a stable binary opposition, it is therefore deconstructive. If race is divided into white/black or white/non-white, then someone born to white and non-white parentage destabilizes and deconstructs these categories.

The idea of hybridity is crucial in Bhabha's idea of culture. This notion of hybridity is functional for all kinds of subject positions when one crosses categories, inhabits two subject positions simultaneously or finds the space between defined subject positions. Bhabha wants us to look into the issues of transsexuals, multiracial and multi-religious people to think about national identities and national boundaries. In the beginning of his "The Location of Culture" he talks about ethnocentric ideas that focus on particular definitions of self-hood by referring to a unified and unitary set of beliefs, practices, and configurations. He then challenges these ethnocentric ideas with the idea of dissonant, dissident and dislocated voices whose identities are excluded from these fixed categories and presumed to be stable ones. He segregates these marginalized voices as women, the colonized, minority groups, and bearers of political sexualities. He also focuses on another category of hybridity such as the migrant, the homeless, the refugees, the displaced indigenous peoples.

Citing Serbian "ethnic cleansing" Bhabha argues that "the idea of a homogenous, stable concept of belonging to a nation" is under profound redefinition because a nation goes too far in killing its inhabitants in order to produce a unified national identity. Bhabha says that "a defined and unified" nation is countered by recognizing the idea of hybridity. He then talks that our identity is shaped by the "imagined communities" we consider our own. A "nationality" is also such an imagined community and "hybridity" or transnationalism is a challenge to that idea of a unified "imagined community". Hybridity brings up the idea that one might belong to many communities or cultures simultaneously, and transnationalism brings up the idea that identity may not be determined by national boundaries, either political or geographic. The idea of a nation is a fiction, an "imagined community", an entity created to forge a new sense of identity, to unite peoples who may have had in common only the fact that they inhabited the same general geographical region. Bhabha reflects on the questions what holds a nation together, when nations are imagined communities of widely disparate and different peoples? And who is taking decisions in global geopolitics? He thinks that capitalism is the connective narrative, an economic practice that holds the idea of nation together. Nations are therefore defined by their economic positions in a global economy, as well as by their political positions in global organizations.

Bhabha is interested in the disruptive forces and identities that destabilize the idea of a unified nation, a homogenous "imagined community". He pleads that the concept of nation is built upon the exclusion or extermination of those who are described as not belonging to that nation. Bhabha is categorical about those marginalized people when the world, after World War II, was carved up into nations. He talks about the refugees, the displaced stateless persons, the nomads, as something that is not contained within the concept of nation, and, specifically which is not contained within a nation's conception of its history. The idea of a 'nation', the idea of an entity has its own history, its own narrative of progress and success. Bhabha argues that the hybrids, the displaced, the non-nationals, must invent their own "history" through art which renews the past, refigures the past as an in-between space that innovates and interrupts the performance of the present. Bhabha therefore locates the project for those not included in unified definitions of nationhood: "The performance of identity as iteration, as recreation of the self in the world of travel, the resettlement of the borderline community of migration" (Rivkin and Ryan 1998: 939-40). This is more than just relocating the lost past or re-invoking the indigenous cultural traditions, creating an identity for an imagined community, not based on geopolitical or economic ideal of nationhood. Bhabha traces one important field where this happens is in literature where literatures are defined by nationalities such as English Literature, American Literature, French Literature, Indian Literature, Chinese Literature and so on. Now literature needs to incorporate the transnational, postcolonial, hybrid experience. Actually, this hybridity, this refugee experience, this non-national identity must transform how we think about literature and its relation to nationality. Klages therefore argues: "postcolonial literature, literature by people who can't be identified as belonging to one specific nation, challenges us to think about how we might organize our universities and our systems of knowledge so that we don't reproduce the narratives of nationhood and thus silence or lose the voices which are excluded from the narratives" (2008: 161). Anzaldua thinks that the border is that where "two or more cultures, classes, races, ideologies, edge or confront each other. The border is both the space between cultures, classes, races, sexual orientations—the slash—and the place where they melt and mix, where they are both sides of the slash and neither side of it" (Rivkin and Ryan 895). Klages writes that this marginalized, liminal space is a space of, contradictions, a space between and "disruptive of defined categories of race, class, nationality, sexuality and other identity formations" (162).

Anzaldua's Chicana lesbian feminist analysis of "the border" in her essay "Borderlands/La Frontera" (Rivkin and Ryan 1998) is concerned with naming rather than "mapping—the 'multiplicity of identity formations she inhabits simultaneously and contradictorily" (Klages 162). Writing both in English and Spanish she wants to highlight how the politics of language operates within and around the politics of racial, ethnic, nationals, gender, and sexual identity. She supports the poststructuralist view that language speaks us, and agrees with Bakhtin on the notion that the languages we speak define our identity, our cultural make-up, our ideologies, and our definition of self. Anzaldua therefore writes: "Language is a homeland, *Un leguaje que corresponde a un mode de vivir*" (Rivkin and Ryan 1998: 89). She emphasizes that ethnic identity is "twin skin to linguistic identity—I am my language" (Rivkin and Ryan 898). But those who occupy "the border", those who have multiple and conflicting subject positions or identity categories—such as Chicana lesbian—are "*deslanguadas*" (without language) according to Anzaldua:

> *Somas las del español deficience.* We are your linguistic aberration, your linguistic *mestizaje*, the subject of your *burla*. Because we speak with tongues of fire we are culturally crucified. Racially, culturally and linguistically *somas huerfanas*—we speak an orphan language. (897)

Homi Bhabha argues for a hybridity imagined and articulated through transnational literatures, but Anzaldua asks in what language such texts can or should be written: "what happens when your language is illegitimate, an unacceptable language?" Anzaldua's own essay, both in English and Spanish (sometimes translated, sometimes not) embodies her answer to the problem of dominant and subordinated languages and identities. Her concept of *la frontera* is a deconstructive place where everything is '*mita y mita*'—half half. Anzaldua sees her linguistic mixture, her *lenguaje mestiza* as a mode of empowerment, rejecting both sides of a choice structured as a binary opposition in favor of a more multiple version of 'double voiced discourse'. In her text, as in her multiple identity positions, Anzaldua is constantly shipping in and out of two or more worlds and world-views, and she claims this slippage as a form of power: "Maimed, mad, and sexually different people were believed to possess supernatural powers by primal cultures' magico-religious thinking. For them abnormality was the price a person had to pay for her or his inborn extraordinary gift" (890).

With the insights and precision from various theoretical formulations elucidated above, postcolonial Reading has been acclaimed as a recognized interdisciplinary method of interpretation of literary texts. It draws on insights of radical socialism, historical knowledge of colonialism, political philosophy, culture, economics, and cultural-anthropology, poststructuralism, post-deconstruction and postmodernism. It rejects the analysis of literary texts from the standpoint of Western Metaphysics. It also draws on "the indigenous experience of the colonized other". Like postmodernism, postcoloniality signifies a contemporary condition and embodies different intellectual approaches which are influenced by post-structuralism, post-deconstruction and cultural criticism. Postcolonialism is a state of consciousness, a crucial stage in the continuum of our cultural process and self-awareness. Since colonialism involves two types of imperialism, namely political and cultural, the important elements in postcolonialism are "Myth and History", "Self and the other", "Language and Landscape". Applying the insights and precision of postcolonialism, the study of V.S. Naipaul's texts will be a worthwhile pursuit for understanding his vision and ideas deeper and better because we will be in a position to explore cultural contradictions, ambiguities and ambivalences that underlie in a social structure. In spite of its certain limitations, postcolonialism is useful because it goes beyond anticolonial, nationalist theory and signifies a movement beyond specific point in history. Postcolonialism is transnational in dimension and multicultural in approach. It is a movement beyond the binary opposition of the power relations between the colonizer and the colonized, and center and periphery as well.

2

Contextualising V.S. Naipaul as a Postcolonial Writer

Although New Critics have rejected the relevance of knowledge of a biographical perspective of a writer for interpretation of his texts, it is however essential to know the writer well before interpretation of his texts. The arguments of the "New Historicists" to rehistoricise texts support this standpoint because they hold the view that "text" and "historical context" influence each other rather than being static. A writer is therefore to be placed in the perspectives of his contemporary situations, personal life and ideas. It is true that his books are more important than the writer; but it is equally true to know how the writer formulates his ideas, what circumstances determine his style of writing. That does not mean a writer's biography is an exemplary one. The writer as a man has all the lapses like other human beings. However, it is always important to know the writer through his books, his ideas and visions. That is therefore Patrick French postulates:

> Vidia Naipaul, born in rural poverty in colonial Trinidad in 1932, would rise from this unpromising setting to become one of the great writers of the twentieth century. This achievement does not mean that all his writing was good or that his behavior was exemplary, but rather that his cumulative accomplishment outstripped his contemporaries, altered the way in which writers and readers perceived the world. Using simple sentences, he

> would look at complex modern subjects: extremism, global migration, political and religious identities, ethnic difference, the implosion of Africa, the resurgence of Asia and the re-making of the old European dispensation in the aftermath of the empire. His achievement was an act of will, in which every situation and relationship would be subordinated to his ambition. His public position as a novelist and chronicler was inflexible at a time of intellectual relativism; he stood for high civilization, individual rights and the rule of law. (2008: xi-xii)

Stylistically Naipaul does not find any difference between fiction and nonfiction. He wrote about the world; and his distinction in narration lay in his memory of history of the empire, "the history of the vanquished" (Engdahl in Ray: xi). The Nobel Committee's remarks reflected in the prize citation of the Swedish Academy are therefore a testimony to Naipaul's genius. In the Nobel Prize Award Ceremony at the Stockholm Concert Hall in 2001, the permanent secretary acknowledged his genius:

> The Nobel Prize in literature for 2001 is awarded to the British writer, born in Trinidad, V.S. Naipaul "for having united perceptive narrative and incorruptible scrutiny in works that compel us to see the presence of suppressed histories". (Ray xi)

Dr. Horace Engdahl concludes the presentation speech for the 2001 Nobel Prize in literature by acknowledging Naipaul's distinctive way of "a presentation of his experience with nonattachment":

> Sir Vidia! Your life as a writer calls to mind what Alfred Nobel said to himself: "my homeland is where I work, and I work everywhere". In every place, you have remained yourself, faithful to your instinct. Your books trace the outline of an individual quest of unusual dimensions. Like a Nemo piloting a craft of your design, without representing anyone or anything, you have manifested the independence of literature. (Ray xvi)

In reply to the award, Naipaul in his "Nobel Lecture" titled "Two Worlds" said that everything of value about him was in his books (*Literary Occasions* 181). Elaborating on this idea he says that each book intuitively sensed and in the case of fiction, intuitively worked out, stands on what has gone before and grows out of it: "I feel that at any stage of my literary career it could have been said that the last book contained all the others. It's been like this because of my background. My background is at once exceedingly simple and exceedingly confused (*LO*: Mishra 183). He continues his speech clarifying further: "In Trinidad, bright boy though I was, I was surrounded by areas of darkness. School elucidated nothing for me. I was crammed with facts and formulas. Everything had to be learnt by heart; everything was abstract for me" (190). After he became a writer, "those areas of darkness as a child" always haunted him. He therefore becomes nostalgic:

> The land; the aborigines; the New World; the colony; the history; India; the Muslim World, to which I also felt myself related; Africa; and then England where I was doing my writing. That was what I meant when I said that my books stand one on the other, and that I am the sum of my books. That was what I meant when I said that my background, the source and prompting of my work, was at once exceedingly simple and exceedingly complicated. You will have seen how simple it was in the country town of Chaguanas. And I think you will understand how complicated it was for me as a writer. (190)

Naipaul does not follow any plan, he has no system. His sole interest is to do a book which would be unique and interesting to read. He could only work within his "knowledge and sensibility and talent and world-view" (191). He wrote the books on the specific subjects because there were no books written on those. He had to clear up his world, and elucidate it for himself. Naipaul says that his books have a focus though he seems to be diverse: "So just as there is a development in narrative skills and knowledge and sensibility, so there is a kind of unity, a focus, though I might appear to be going in many directions" (192). He has no political or literary bias. He invents his own methods and means for exploring the materials of his books, one after the other. He thinks that his ancestors such as R.K. Narayan and his father had neither any literary or political idea as a guiding principle for their writing. It is the case because his ancestry is far from authority for many centuries. He however, considers it positive because it gives them a special point of view as they are "more inclined to see the humour and pity of things" (194). Concluding his Nobel Lecture, Naipaul says that every book has amazed him because he has been able to handle the "baffling" nature of his material through his "intuition". Referring to Proust's book *Against Sainte-Beuve,* Naipaul believes that a little luck and labour could enable a writer to create beautiful things by capturing "the blurred memories" (195) and transforming them into his world of creation.

For understanding a writer's vision and world of his art, his biography is as important as his contemporary situations and thoughts. However, the writer as a "social man" is quite different from the writer as an "artist" who is doing his work in "seclusion". The deepest conviction comes to the artist when he is engaged in his works with full concentration, completely free from the world outside it. The background and his experiences on different occasions come to him indirectly whenever he is deeply engrossed in his work. Referring to Proust, Naipaul thinks that it is "a beguiling method using the man to illuminate the work" (181). Proust believes that the biography of a writer is not much helpful to know the work which is the product of a different self from the self we manifest in our habits and social life. If we try to understand that particular self, we are to locate it in our heart and try to reconstruct there. Naipaul quotes Proust to elucidate the idea:

> ...it is the secretions of one's innermost self, written in solitude and for oneself alone, that one gives to the public. What one bestows on private life—in conversation...or in those drawing-room essays that are scarcely more than conversation in print—is the product of a quite superficial self, not of the innermost self which

> one can only recover by putting aside the world and the self frequents the world. (Quoted in *LO*: Mishra 2004: 182)

Supporting Proust Naipaul believes that the details about the life of a writer may give us some impressions, but the mystery of the writing will remain: "No amount of documentation however fascinating, can take us there. The biography of a writer—or even the autobiography—will always have this incompleteness" (182). The "new historical approach" however believes in interpreting literary texts from the perspective of their historical and cultural conditions of productions. In his "new historical approach" to Lawrence's novels Prakash Chandra Pradhan argues:

> Lawrence's 'letters' hitherto regarded as 'marginal' can be studied as 'central' to his ideas and visions in the context of his major cultural products, the novels. By that way, there will be constant and continuous interactions between the events of his life, his contemporary history and culture as well as his concepts and visions. Such an approach in the context of ideologies of our era will reveal many areas of meaning in Lawrence hitherto escaped our notice. This will also enable us to bring out the current relevance of Lawrence's ideas and vision in the context of our own culture and social set-up. (2009: 3-4)

New historical approach to literary study therefore argues for a dialectical relationship between past and present and rejects the concept of history as a record of the past event. Such an approach deconstructs the notion of "history as context" because the text should be understood as "a privileged moment within a network of discursive and material practices". Greenblatt argues that the "historical situation" along with "intentions and genre" are important for understanding a text because all are social and ideological. He therefore pleads: "...in response to the art of the past we inevitably register, whether we wish to or not, the shifts in value and interest that are produced in the struggles of social and political life" (1990:

112). The creator of the text cannot be disconnected from his life, past and present altogether. He is simultaneously historical, political and cultural. Greenblatt therefore pleads that "a work of art is the product of a negotiation between a creator or class of creators, equipped with a complex communally shared repertoire of connections and the institutions and practices of societies" (1990: 158). Though Naipaul thinks that biography and autobiography can never fully reveal the source of the books of the writer, Patrick French, his biographer however thinks that "the best writing can be examined only in its effect. Sometimes, a critic or biographer can see the things the author cannot." An individual is so complicated that it is difficult to bring out a parallel between the incidents of a writer's life and the key ideas in his literary texts: "the best thing a biographer can hope is to illuminate aspects of a life and seek to give glimpses of the subject, and that way tell a story" (2008: xviii).

In the essay "Conrad's Darkness and Mine" Naipaul says: "to understand Conrad, then, it was necessary to match his experience" (*LO* 171). He also pleads that every great writer is produced by a series of special circumstances. All the circumstances of the writer are to be considered deeply. The most imaginative writers, Naipaul believes, discover themselves through their works: "To take an interest in a writer's work is, for me, to take an interest in his life. One interest follows automatically on the other" (174). Experience of a writer is important to mould his visions and ideas. It is the foundation of his basic assumptions and thoughts. To Naipaul, the myths of the great writers usually have to do with their works rather than their lives. The work is more important than the writer. The novel must contain convictions rather than experimentation. Naipaul's ideas of the world in writing more specifically in a novel should be related to the world which is renewed every moment. The novelist should involve himself in his interpretive function of the "new world" which is changing every moment. To Naipaul, the Nobel was "a great tribute to both England, my home, and India, the home of my ancestors" (French 2008: xii). French points out Naipaul's misdemeanor: "Creating tension, insulting his friends, family, or whole communities left him in excellent spirits" (xiii). He comments on Naipaul's attitude for rejecting his homeland altogether:

> Naipaul's dismissal of his own homeland became part of his persona, a persona he invented in order to realise his early ambition to escape the periphery for the centre, to leave the powerless for the powerful and to make himself a great writer. I sometimes thought of him as a man running up a beach with the advancing tide behind him managing to stay a bare step ahead of the water. In order to become what he wanted to be, he had to make himself someone else. He could not remain regional. His ambition was linked to fear, as it often is in an author or creative artist: fear of failure, fear of not being able to write, fear of disappearance, fear of mental or physical breakdown, fear that people were trying to do him down, fear of being faced down, fear of losing face, fear of being found out. (xv)

A perspective of Naipaul's life—his frustrations and anxieties, his notions and assumptions, his formulations and constructions about the world at different stages of life—is necessary to understand his visions and ideas in his works.

2.1. Indenture and Indian Diaspora in Trinidad

Nothing prevented Naipaul from executing his work: neither the prospect of "death" of his ailing wife nor the prospect of marriage to Nadira in November 1995: "Vidia traveled swiftly to Malaysia anxious that neither the prospect of 'looming death nor marriage' should interfere with his work, and returned to Wiltshire for Christmas" (French 2008: 487). This refers to the context of dying Patricia, Naipaul's wife who was suffering from cancer and his future prospect of marriage with Nadira, the Pakistani journalist who would marry him on April 15, 1996 after the death of Patricia on 3rd February 1996. V.S. Naipaul, the grandson of Indian migrant and indentured labourer, Capildeo Maharaj, was deeply engaged in his works to understand the people of the world, to unravel their "suppressed histories" for his fictions and travelogues. In other words, he was busy in representing their history authentically.

As a serious writer he worked hard for understanding cultures, beliefs, nations, ideologies and religions. He travelled different countries—Trinidad, India, Pakistan, Iran, Indonesia, Malaysia, Africa and South America—to understand the ideologies of marginalized sections, their religions and cultures. It is necessary to focus on the various incidents of his life that had influenced him in formulating his perceptions, ideas and visions.

Naipaul was born in Trinidad in 1932 to poor parents, namely, Seepersad Naipaul and Dropatie, the daughter to the "formidable" Soogee and the migrant Pundit Capildeo Maharaj in a peasant world of Trinidad. He spent his childhood and completed his formal education there in 1950, and then left for Oxford where he studied till 1954. Before he could complete his education, his father died in 1953. However, he could not go back to Trinidad without being a writer although his family needed his support the most. It has been an enigma to understand Naipaul. He was always more occupied with his work rather than with the crisis in the family. Naipaul writes about his apprehensions in "Prologue to an Autobiography" in 1982:

> And it was that fear, a panic about failing to be what I should be, rather than simple ambition, that was with me when I came down from Oxford in 1954 and began trying to write in London. My father had died the previous year. Our family was in distress. I should have done something for them, gone back to them. But, without having become a writer, I couldn't go back. In my eleventh moth in London I wrote about Bogart. I wrote my book; I wrote another. I began to go back. (*LO* 111)

Naipaul's fear made him adventurous for which he was a great success. It is interesting to know about the formative years of a writer's life which shaped his ideas and visions. It is therefore necessary to interpret the colonial set-up of Trinidad from 1932 to 1950 with reference to the destitute life of the indentured labourers from North India wherefrom his grandfather migrated to Trinidad along with other helpless bonded labourers during the maladministration of the British colonial rule in India. After the abolition of slavery in 1834, the cheap labour needed for the sugar cane plantations of the white masters, was filled by the "malnourished" Indians, shipped from Calcutta and Madras. In Northern India, the "destitute peasantry" under British dominion took "a voyage across the oceans and a stint as a bonded or indentured labourer" (French 2008: 5) as an alternative to destitution. However, after reaching Trinidad the North Indian indentured labourers had strange experience with the Black, Negro agricultural labourers who regarded the East Indians as heathens, with peculiar customs, who took strange food and worked long hours in the field like slaves. To these destitute Indians, the Negroes seemed to be ruffians with the dark skins, and identified with the lower caste Hindus. In such an alien society the North Indians tried to establish a Hindu society of their own. *The Handbook of Trinidad and Tobago* (1924) recorded that Kopil, a Brahmin from a village near Gorakhpur in the Nepalese border with India, was brought to Trinidad in the ship "Hereford" from Calcutta in 1894. Leaving the large country and ancient civilization far behind Kopil was indentured to Woodford lodge in Chaguanas, an estate in central Trinidad. Under the strict work atmosphere, Kopil aged 21, a Sanskrit knowing Brahmin was to do different jobs like weeding the field and sweeping the dung from animal pens for which he fell ill. He was however rescued by an Indian Sirdar, an Overseer who cut his name from indenture by paying a sum to the government, gave his fifteen years old daughter Soogee in marriage, and established a house in Chaguanas where he would manage a general store for his father-in-law, Govinda. Kopil changed his name as Capildeo Maharaj, and became famous as a pundit "explaining sacred text and duties at impromptu services, and conducting pujas or ceremonies" (7). Having a sharp business attitude, he could make a lot of money, purchased land and built a mansion in North Indian style. He had also "nine surviving daughters and two sons". On his trip to his village along with Yosodhara, he fell ill at Calcutta and died in 1926. Soogee however managed the show of the empire her husband had established in Trinidad. Seepersad Naipaul, 22 years old was employed in her establishment to paint a sign at the general store. He fell in love with Dropatie, one of the daughters of Capildeo, and got married to her in 1929. Vidyadhar Naipaul was born to them in 1932 as their second child, Kamala being their first daughter born in 1930.

Naipaul's grandfather Capildeo's ancestry traces back to a Hindu village near Gorakhpur where caste had given a structure to Indian society for thousands of years. It was based on Hindu idea of Karma, where past action in previous life determined a person's status in the present. Pundits, learned Brahmin men with knowledge of the Sanskrit teaching traditions, performed ritual duties in order to safeguard social order: "At its best caste gave a sense of identity and community; at its worst, it condemned people to a degraded life based on an inherited social position, and provided an excuse for inhuman cruelty" (9). Not only Hindus did practice the caste system, the Indian Muslims, Sikhs and Christians too used it as a form of social stratification. Most of the indentured Indians came from North India, ravaged by famine, drought and social upheaval in the beginning of the second half of the nineteenth century. By the time Capildeo was recruited, around 15 percent of immigrants were from the higher castes (Brahmins, Thakurs, Rajputs and Khatris); 34 percent were from farming or artisan castes; 37 percent were from lower or backward castes and 14 percent were Muslims. Though caste played a dominant role in their native places for establishing their identities, the immigrants had a very hard choice by emigrating overseas as it might end their community life and identities. The destitute had no option but to migrate. Even single women from urban areas chose to migrate with a hope of changing their misfortunes:

> Most single women who chose to emigrate were recruited from urban areas rather than villages, and in many cases they had already run away from home or a bad husband, or been expelled for a social transgression, and were seeking to avoid prostitution. (10)

Life of this first wave of Indian diaspora was very hard in the plantation field of Trinidad. In the name of discipline the planters were very cruel and brutal to these destitute, indentured labourers. Even though the protectors of immigrants were to look into the interest of these marginalized people, they always supported the planters:

> On the plantation, coolies would start work at six in the morning, stop for breakfast at ten-thirty and continue work until four in the afternoon; they were paid a token wage of two to four schillings a week. At Woodford lodge estate they would cut sugarcane, a rough, sharp, brutal crop, haul into the refinery on ox-carts and move casks of sugar by barge to the road. (11)

The Indian communities however did not split: they lived together under an ordinance from the Indian government. As a result, they developed a sense of "community identity" which was not the case with Trinidadians or African descent Negroes. The emphasis on Indian culture founded on strong family and caste ties enabled them to retain and build a sense of community abroad. After the tenure of their indenture, some Indians preferred to live in Trinidad rather than return to their homes in India. The Indian community lived in rural Trinidad where diseases like hookworm, Malaria, dysentery and skin infections were rampant. There were not many latrines because of which people were forced to defecate in the open nearby fields. By the time World War I ended, the indenture-system was almost abolished because of the protest by Mahatma Gandhi and other Indian National Congress leaders like G.K. Gokhale. Ethnic tension grew in Trinidad when the Black soldiers returned there after World War I. By the time Vidyadhar was born, the population of Trinidad was almost four lacs, one-third of which were Indians, employed as agricultural labourers, merchants, spirit-vendors, clerks and shopkeepers. Very few Indians were teachers or lawyers or government officials. By the 1930s, the Indians were "depicted as poor, mean, rural, heathen, aggressive, ethnically exclusive and illiterate" (13). Vidyadhar Naipaul was born to such a rotten Hindu world.

2.2. Marginality and Identity: Reclaiming Self

A writer's ideas and visions, perceptions and thoughts are often shaped by his situations, experiences, aspirations and frustrations. V.S. Naipaul's childhood and youth in Trinidad, Oxford education, his parents' conditions, their Indian and Hindu background, the socio-political cultural milieu of Trinidad together have immensely contributed to his writings.

Since Seepersad Naipaul was not mentally well during the early 1930s, V.S. Naipaul was to spend the first six of his formative years with women in the Lion House: his grandmother, his mother, his aunts, his teacher and his sister, Kamla. Dropatie, always conscious of her role as a traditional Hindu woman, was very tough and powerful in a way that could have been matched by few Indian women in Trinidad. She was a strong woman with a strong personality. She was too reluctant to forgive the Muslims for their numerous invasions of India and for forcing the partition of the subcontinent. Dropatie Naipaul was always a confident, self-assured and straight-forward woman: "Ma's bright, certain, robust, slightly mocking tone of voice would be inherited by Vido; without the impetus of Ma and her family, his later achievement would have been impossible" (28). Seepersad, though intelligent and ambitious, hailed from poor parents. His siblings were yet to recover from indenture. His ambitions to become a journalist were therefore in disarray in the 1930s under the pressure of poverty and family obligations. During the period of breakdown Seepersad had long-standing conflicts with his wife although he loved the children. Seepersad was however not violent to Dropatie. He was a man of progressive outlook. He could neither find a solution to his mental breakdown from the old-fashioned Hinduism based on superstitions, rituals, animal-sacrifice and caste-system nor from traditional Christianity. He was however influenced by a modern rational Hindu philosophy based on Dharma or duty. He also studied the texts of the late 19th century reform movements like the Arya Samaj, J.S. Mill, Gustavo Flaubert, Mulk Raj Anand, Mary Wollstonecraft and J.S. Van Teslaar or Psychoanalysis. Being a young nationalist Indian, he held the view that mixed marriages were responsible for race-dissolution; and if they continued, the Indian community in Trinidad would lose their distinctive identity. He complained against the adoption of Western dress, a trend known then in Trinidad as Bobism. Although Seepersad started as a freelance reporter on the *Trinidad Guardian* in 1929, the year of his marriage, he was paid a meager salary of $4 a week. He was to adopt Bobism in this new role, dressing in a tie, short and cotton blazer. As a reporter of the *Trinidad Guardian*, Seepersad Naipaul was given a weekly column on Indian affairs by the editor, Gault McGowan. He earned the wrath of the Indian community by writing against the superstitions of Hinduism. Though his writings against Kali, the Indian goddesses, were sensational, subsequently under the pressure of the Indian community and in-laws he was to offer goat sacrifice to goddess Kali to avoid her wrath. Both the editor and Seepersad were removed, and thereafter by 1935 he had a serious mental breakdown. Afterwards he was to leave the Lion House for his destination where he would live with his wife and children.

But before that Vidyadhar (young Naipaul) was to be a part of the situation of the Lion House where 40 odd children of Capildeo family were to live under the strict discipline of Nanie, the "formidable Soogee" who was the supreme commander in the extended joint family with her daughters, sons, sons-in-law and grandchildren. The children were to do whatever they were told to do. They were not encouraged to think. It was a sort of emotionally restricted way of bringing up children. Though Nanie believed in Hindu way of life, she wanted her children to speak English. They should also remain aloof from the non-Indian Negro community. She was very much "ethnic" in this sense. Nanie was an imperialist in her attitudes and actions. She kept the sons-in-law under her control. Taking advantage of their poverty, she used them as coolies in her land and trade, and expanded her empire. Whenever the sons-in-law needed money, they were to come to Nanie because she controlled the finance of the family. She also implemented the policy of "divide and rule" in the household to keep everybody under her dominion. Under such empirical domination, the relationship was not warm. The children were forced to behave in the most disciplined manner. V.S. Naipaul in an interview on 12 July 2002 disapproves of such treatment to children:

> Children were beaten with a strap or with a stick. Outside, we were surrounded by language that came from the days of slavery. Parents would say: 'I will peel your backside. I will beat till you pee. I will make you fart fire.' You can hear the language of the plantation. I think there is a lot of violence in Indian peasant families. But my father and mother did not punish people too often, though we were surrounded by the people being punished...what happens in that kind of awful set-up is that lots of quarrels break out between people, and those quarrels were my training for life, my training in life and society—propaganda, alliances, betrayals—all these things. So, in a way, nothing that happened later ever really shocked me. (Quoted in French 27)

Vidyadhar joined Kamla at the school established in the country town of Chaguanas where strict discipline was imposed. As a boy of five, Naipaul enjoyed his school days much although the focus was on rote learning. In colonial societies like Trinidad opportunities for personal development were rare. Rudranath Capildeo, the younger son, was intelligent, and hence to facilitate his studies through Island Scholarship in the overseas, the great Nanie purchased a house at 17 Luis Street in 1938. After the recovery of Seepersad from mental breakdown in 1938, his family was asked to shift to that house in the Port of Spain along with Rudranath and Nanie so that they could help Nanie in looking after the new properties that were purchased. As Seepersad had rejoined his job as a *Guardian* journalist, it was a great coincidence for the Naipaul family to live in Port of Spain. It was rather unusual on the part of an Indian by origin to work as a journalist since the Indian community in Trinidad were the marginalized people who were doing low status work such as street vending, carrying head loads, and collecting garbage. All higher status activities such as work in the bank, newspapers, civil services and higher police services were actually performed by the white people who generally constituted the British expatriates, Portuguese, French Creole, Spanish or Red Africans. The gradation was strict and instinctive, part of a way of thinking that was instilled early in this ethnically diverse colonial setting. The experience of such social gradation and racial discrimination had a great impact on the perception and thinking of V.S. Naipaul as a writer at a later stage. In his Tranquility School, Vidyadhar was however enjoying with friends and teachers who hailed from diverse cultures and community. At Tranquility he was given a solid grounding in grammar, spelling, vocabulary, arithmetic and geography. On Empire Day, the children were to sing "'God Save the King', and 'Land of Hope and Glory' including the immortal line 'Britain never, never, never, shall be slaves'." Vidyadhar's schooling at Tranquility was suddenly affected when Seepersad and Dropatie were asked to move to a new family commune Petit Valley in 1940. In his 12 July, 2002 interview Naipaul remarked how the house at Petit Valley was frightening with incompleteness: "It was all so improvised, all so dreadful. We were given a very low idea of human needs. I think without anybody knowing, this was coming from Mother India from a beaten down broken down people" (French 34).

Seepersad hated to be a part of the extended family. In such an atmosphere one loses one's identity. The children were also subjected to too many unusual things like molestation and homosexuality for which Vidyadhar had strong repulsion. Vidyadhar was however spending much of his time with his father who acquainted him with different writings of European literature. As a result, they lived "in an ordered fantasy world derived from European literature, far from the noise, squalor and their own powerlessness in Petit Valley" (37). Later Naipaul described that the Petit Valley was like a hell for him. In the July 19, 2002 interview he held the view that Petit Valley provided him everything for his writing, his "understanding with which civilization can be destroyed" (37). Simbhoo and Rudra, the maternal uncles to the children were tyrants who always terrorized them. One of the cousins, Brahmananda, complained that they were harsh and brutal towards the children because they had the financial power to control the entire family under the patronage of the formidable Nanie. Due to World War II, which was still continuing, the children were to suffer without food occasionally. Despite this, both Kamla and Vidyadhar were doing excellent at Tranquillity. Vidyadhar always remained an exemplary to his cousins as a bright boy at Petit Valley; he developed the ambition of becoming the writer. The Naipaul family shifted to Luis Street again in 1943 so that Vidyadhar and Kamla would be able to study in Queens Royal College. Vidyadhar understood quite well the two different worlds: one at home and the other at school. The social world at the college was an elite and metropolitan world whereas the world at home was ravaged by poverty. In 1943, Seepersad got financial help from Simbhoo and published *Gurudeva and Other Indian Tales* which described "the picaresque progress of its title character, a rogue who starts out as a juvenile husband, becomes a boastful but a cowardly village stick-fighter, gets sent to jail, and ends up as a phoney pundit before sacking his wife, Ratni in favour of Daisy, who bobs her hair and dumps him" (43). The book was set in the 1930s and the 1940s, and depicted how Indian community in Trinidad was cut off from their origins and were in terms with a confusing, changing world. Although the book had no high literary value, still it was an exceptional book, "an early text in the tradition of Indian diasporic fiction that was to develop vigorously later in the century" (44). *Gurudeva* was written in lucid style based on intimate experience, quite illustrative and economical. It has precision, clarity and simplicity. This book was the guiding principle for V.S. Naipaul who believed that his father's book had helped him a lot when he wrote the books in the first phase, namely *The Mystic Masseur, Miguel Street, A House for Mr. Biswas* and *The Mimic Men.* Naipaul appreciates his father's book as a landmark piece and comparable to Leo Tolstoy's *Master and Man,* Homer's *The Odyssey.* It cannot be dismissed as a peasant writing about peasant's details. His father's book had taught him a lot how to write well. He therefore thinks that *Gurudeva* is his own epic: "The more I look at it, the more I (can) see the actual way I write—very pictorial, very fast, the details. I knew that I had been given a feeling for language and it was very beautiful, and it was my own epic" (Naipaul's interview on 26 September 2002, quoted in French 46).

Search for identity is an important aspect in postcolonial literature because identity gives one a mark for establishing himself in any society. V.S. Naipaul wanted to establish his identity in course of time. While he was studying in Queens Royal College, he was always haunted by the poverty of his father and his struggle for his own identity to be a writer and a journalist. He was seriously disturbed by his father's marginalization at the extended family of Capildeo's. After the end of World War II, the British Empire became bankrupt and decolonization was being discussed freely. Elections to the Legislative Council were planned for the following year, the first to be based on a universal franchise. The senior Capildeo's son, Simbhoo was unsuccessful in the elections. *Gurudeva* gave Seepersad some identity as a result of which, he was given a job to make a survey of the rural Indian community, and therefore he was to get training in Jamaica. By that time, Capildeo landholdings and properties were divided on the basis of patrilineal stand taken by Nanie so that the sons inherited the properties. The daughters were given one each a plot. Seepersad dismissed the gift because he considered the agricultural plot "Swamp lands, lagoon lands, rice lands". In the meanwhile Vidyadhar did worse in his examination. Seepersad, distressed, took a loan from his rich relation, Sookdeo Misir to build a house at Nepaul Street at Port of Spain. This helped the Naipaul family to be a nuclear one with father, mother and children. Seepersad, being a man of independent nature, taught his children to question the way things were done. He hated the Capildeo family for their high-handedness and attitude of cheating.

Identity is problematic in Trinidad. With so little common heritage between communities, attributes could be borrowed. It was necessary to have a public face since whatever one's ethnicity is aspects of home life would be culturally alien to those one met outside. The Trinidadian people had no sense of history since they did not know it. Ancestry is clear in the case of only a few individuals whether they have come from West Africa or Venezuela, or Madeira or South India. In all the communities, there were divisions and sub-divisions on the basis of caste, religion or faith. Each Trinidadian had a void in him because dispossession and extermination haunted him. That was so because it was not his land, and he thought he possessed the land of the native Amerindians who had been killed or chased away. Trinidad was therefore a borrowed island. After independence an attempt was made for a shared "Trini identity". Seepersad as an individual rejected orthodox Hinduism though he was identified by "Indianness". He believed in the cultural and religious reformation in Hinduism. To him, Hinduism should be such a philosophical system in which all the old rituals should be rejected altogether. As a true son to his father, rationalist Vidia rejected all group activities linked to the caste. It was also difficult to know his critical attitude to caste status when he rejected to shave his head like his cousins for the sacred thread ceremony in one case, and on the other as a Brahmin boy he refused to touch the pipe in his mouth in the Science class. He was however a talented boy, and was very serious for his high school certificate examination. As he wanted to escape the Trinidadian world, he was to establish his identity as the best boy for an overseas scholarship. But he failed to win scholarship in 1949 examination because of the wrong combination of papers although he was able to achieve double distinction in both French and Spanish. The government however granted a special scholarship to V.S. Naipaul when the QRC authorities sent a proposal for his outstanding performance even if there were protests and criticisms in the press. Naipaul later admitted that he would have been doomed and collapsed without a scholarship. In a primitive society like Trinidad, the Negroes had talent in intrigue. His victory to win the scholarship was a grand moment in his survival and establishment of his identity. The education board of Trinidad decided to send Vidyadhar to Oxford in 1950. Vidyadhar was therefore to escape from the "hole" to seek freedom in the mother country, England. In a letter to Kamla who had already gone to India to study in Banaras Hindu University, Vidyadhar wrote about his ambition to become a writer "to see something of life". By the time he left for England he was educated, intelligent, emotionally immature but ambitious. By the time he left for England, "the epicenter of civilization", he had been influenced by three strong women—Nanie, Ma and Kamla. He had however great reverence for his father because of his desire to serve the cause of literature. On first August Vidyadhar was driven in a car by his father to the airport to fly to New York from where he flew to live in an alien world. In his later life Naipaul fictionalized his departure from Trinidad in *Miguel Street,* and in *The Enigma of Arrival.* He depicted an account taken from life, presenting himself as an epic figure destined to what lay ahead.

By this time cities like London were no more national cities; they had become international cities where refugees from Europe, and students of Asia and Africa settled down. Naipaul's early experiences in Oxford had been frustrating. His struggles to establish his identity as a writer were also the struggles and frustrations of his father who had felt himself discriminated due to racial bias as a reporter in the *Guardian.* The ethnic bias against him was so much that he was getting half of the salary given to the white people who were less talented than him:

> Like Vidia, Pa felt the racial prejudice underlay his own lack of advancement. He had been on the *Guardian* for 'sixteen months now, but they have not given me a raise. A thing that is making me bitter—I suppose that's how a Communist comes into being—is that a third rate English boy...is getting a far bigger salary than I am getting'. (French 83)

Both men felt that their talent was being stifled. While in Oxford Vidia would write to his father: "I have always admired you as a writer. And I am convinced that, were you born in England you would have been famous and rich and pounced upon by the intellectuals" (80). While working as a feature reporter in *Isis* in 1951, he wrote to his parents how people rose to high positions not only by intelligence, but by arranging parties: "To get on you must throw sherry parties; take the editors out to dinner" (80). In response to this letter, "Pa sent Vido $ 10 to hold a sherry party. 'I know full well what this thing means and how necessary it is'" (80). Seepersad stood strongly by his son and wrote him: "You don't have to worry about us—so long as I keep going. Give yourself all the chance" (81). Understanding the difficult situation at home and his father's predicament to run the family at Trinidad, he wrote to Kamla from Oxford:

> A feeling of emptiness is nearly always on me. I see myself struggling in a sort of a tunnel blocked up at both ends. My past—Trinidad and the necessity of our parents—lies behind me and I am powerless to help anyone. My future—such as it is—is a full four years away. (76)

The situation of V.S. Naipaul at Oxford was quite frustrating: "Oxford had been presented to him as the pinnacle of achievement, but now it was failing to give him what he wanted. The past, meanwhile, was receding as Trinidad was rendered absurd" (79). The first success as a writer came to Naipaul when the poem, "Two Thirty A.M.", an adolescent cry of anguish was broadcast on "Caribbean Voices", an influential half-hour weekly radio program on the B.B.C. His first story "This is Home", was grounded in the memory of his father's building a house at Petit Valley. This story, which is symbolic, contains some key themes such as dislocation, homelessness, anxiety about man-woman relationship. These aspects of the story recur in many of his writings. Struggling himself in his Oxford days, he would encourage his father to write because the essential thing about writing is writing. His father, Naipaul considers, is the best writer in the West Indies. He believed: "there are many would-be great writers, but the only ones who became great writers are those who sit down and write" (87). After completion of his father's manuscript, Naipaul showed it to his tutor Peter Bayle who later thought that it contained the seeds of Vidia's first four novels: "I found there *The Mystic Masseur, The Suffrage of Elvira* and of course quite a lot of *Miguel Street* and indeed anticipations of *Mr Biswas*" (87). Impressed with Vidyadhar's literary ambition Peter Bayle asked the dean to sanction a grant of 30 Shillings from college to repair his type-writer.

In 1951 September, he had a very enjoyable experience in France. In 1952 he gave up his work at *Isis* and started designing the Oxford Tory and enjoyed the work there. When he wrote to his parents that he had been under severe mental upset, Mira wrote to him: "I hardly know what to say except...to assure you, if assurance is necessary, that we are all looking forward to the day when V.S. Naipaul will have become a famous name in the world of letters" (89). His mother wrote to him in late January 1952 to choose an Indian girl for his marriage rather than a white girl to which his father also agreed because "most intermarriages end in failures". He however advises him to choose his own wife with much consideration. V.S. Naipaul would start loving Patricia Hale, a white girl whom he met at his college play on 9 February 1952, a few days after receiving his mother's letter. Patricia came from a poor background. Her entry to Oxford University was through her intellectual merit by virtue of getting a state scholarship. Her parents and only sister lived in a "decrepit two bedroom flat above the Buckingham Municipal Bank in Kingstanding" (91). In 1952, Naipaul was undergoing tremendous mental upheaval. The two psychological consultations did not help much. He was also desperate due to financial crisis. His talks over the phone with Patricia could not help him much. A great sense of loneliness and insecurity brought so much mental anguish. When Seepersad learnt about his traumatic agony, he wrote to Kamla: "I am really very, very sorry for him. He is so impulsive, so unpredictable" (95). The emotional shock of Naipaul lasted for eighteen months during which period the only consolation to him was Patricia. In his 14 November 2002 interview Naipaul recalls his period of depression: "it was a great depression verging on madness... Pat was a great solace to me at that period; probably I clung to her because of that depression" (quoted in French 96). This depression was caused due to lack of money, solitude and sexual deprivation. Despite that, Naipaul stood by his own convictions:

> Rationalist, culturally Hindu with a dose of Trinidad's practical Christianity, having grown up in an island society where each religion and race had to exist in parallel, private and public sphere, the son of a questioning father and morally upright mother, Vidia had formed his own ethical notions and applied them

stringently; he did not want to reform, convert or emancipate; he was a watcher, a writer. (103)

As a beloved and friend, Patricia was rather critical of literary merit of Naipaul. Pointing out that Naipaul had tremendous literary potential she added that he should go beyond his imaginative penetration of futility, and misery. She also suggested him to write his story which should contain humanity with full sense.

Since the relationship between Patricia and V.S. Naipaul was not approved by her father, it could not be turned into a marriage. By mistake a love letter to V.S. Naipaul was redirected to Trinidad. The whole family read it and therefore Naipaul explained to his father that their relationship was virtuous and pure. Seepersad was a little unhappy because the relationship between them was objected by Patricia's father and all family members of Vidia wanted him to marry an Indian girl. Naipaul however clarified to his father that he would settle with Patricia in England although he wished to meet all his family members as many times as possible. Soon after these correspondences, Naipaul however had consummation of love with Patricia and therefore proposed her to come forward for marriage.

A couple of incidents at Trinidad relating to Naipaul's family were quite disturbing. First, the formidable Nanie, Soogee, Capildeo Maharaj, Queen Victoria died at the age of 65 in September 1952. In January 1953, Seepersad Naipaul had cardiac problems for which *The Guardian* dismissed him from his service. Kamla therefore wrote to a depressed Naipaul to do something for the publication of his father's book failing which their father might not survive. Kamla's appeal to her brother was touching: "now something immediate regarding the publishing of his story means life or death for him and consequently life or death for us, especially those poor children at home..." (113). Naipaul replied that their father should not be worried since he was making efforts for publishing their father's manuscript by a reputed publisher. However, he did not proceed further since he knew that the manuscript was not in a good state for publication. So far as his private emotional life was concerned, Patricia suggested that they should not formally engage in 1953. After getting a damn second class in graduation, he wanted a job; but he could not get one. His frustration had therefore multiplied, and his writing career was seriously affected. He thought, "My stories remain merely ideas for stories. What would he do if inherited dream of becoming a writer could not be fulfilled? He wanted to be an Indian diplomat, he wanted to be wealthy, he wanted to succeed" (122). Patricia also reprimanded him for being a hurdle on her way to do acting. In the meanwhile he decided to work half-heartedly for a postgraduate research degree, a B.Litt. in English literature with a specialization in Spanish literature.

During such frustration of Naipaul, on 3 October 1953 Seepersad had a heart attack when the family had been to *puja* in Luis Street to commemorate Nanie's death. Though Dr. Navis Rampersad attended to him, he cried out in pain as the evening approached. His heart was in agony and his life went out like a candle: "At the age of 47, Seepersad Naipaul, the writer who had lifted himself out of nowhere and tried to make his way in the world, was dead" (125). The following day, his body was cremated in Trinidad as per the Hindu custom. After his death the whole family was in despair. Ma and six children solely depended on Kamla's earning. The loan from Sookdeo Misir was yet to be paid back. Savi remembered that they were left to wind: "Vidia could not come back; he had his own life, his own problems.... I know that for Mira and I to get shoes and clothing, I sewed clothing for my friend and they would pay me, that's how we outfitted ourselves..." (126). Naipaul wrote a touching letter to his mother after getting the news of his father's death: "Please don't worry about me...everything that I am is directly due to him...he worked for all of us; what we are he has made us. And when you think from what he started, you ought to feel proud" (126). As a tribute to his father he wrote his father's book in 1961, eight years after his father's death. *A House for Mr Biswas* was a great fictional tribute to his father; and the last gift of his father, "brass base" was his constant companion to any place he moved throughout his life. After a fortnight of his father's death Naipaul wrote to his mother that his life would be a continuation and a fulfillment of Pa's. His father's death made him lonely and unprotected.

Although Naipaul was a man of strong conviction and sensitivity, he was to sacrifice a lot for establishing his identity as a writer. In the context of the proposal of marriage to Patricia, Seepersad wrote to his son: "...it is felt by everybody at home (not excluding myself) that if you get married at all you will be lost to us. We cannot afford losing you; I am not good any longer for hard work" (124). This is not a small appeal of a broken father to his ambitious son who would harden his heart to be a writer. Naipaul lost his father, his great protection in life so far. The world in which he struggled was also not congenial towards the non-white. England was rather "racial" towards him in relation to his B.Litt. Though he did excellent in the written paper, he was intentionally harassed by F.P. Wilson, a retired professor of English. As a result he could not get his B.Litt. Degree. It was a serious example of racial discrimination. He wrote to Patricia: "I wish you to know that I was failed deliberately...I was viva'd—not on the paper—but on the Spanish theological temper" (131).

Naipaul had the notion that his future lay at the centre rather than on the periphery. He was the man of the world; he was not to be confined to a particular nation/notion. From Madrid, he wrote to Patricia that she was an embodiment of purity and cleanliness with all the prized qualities of his future wife. Since "identity" always haunted him, he therefore wrote to her: "from a purely selfish point of view you are the ideal wife for a future G(rand) O(ld) M(an) of letters" (129). His views on English people as a race are worth mentioning. From Madrid he wrote to his family in Trinidad: "England is by comparison dead and the English are made of wax. They are the most immoral people I have yet known; yet they set about the matter with grimness and a sense of determination that is frightening" (129). Thinking the attitude of F.P. Wilson, the English Professor who was a "just one big sneer" (131), he felt insulted : "he did ask me once more where I came from...it is just another one of hundred and one insults that make my life in England hell—that also gave me my breakdown" (131). Naipaul, however, got a testimonial from his tutor Peter Bayley who was an inspiring figure for him. In the testimonial he wrote that V.S. Naipaul "is a sympathetic and a delightful person with a most attractive sense of humour (and) outstanding literary gifts who deserved a job. More than most I think he could be said to be a citizen of the world. He is a British subject of Indian descent domiciled in the West Indies" (131). This remark will remain a permanent identity for Naipaul who would concentrate on this theme of identity in his writings. Being broken hearted after Wilson rebuff, V.S. Naipaul would write to his mother to understand his state of mind. He believed that his life in Trinidad would be a dead one without any worthy work for him because Trinidad is a small place with "wrong values" and "petty people". Even his life in England was also miserable because of "racial prejudices". In spite of his traumatic experiences in his Oxford life he does not become hopeless: "The world is a pretty awful place, but our star will shine bright yet" (132).

In spite of his best efforts Naipaul, an Oxford student, would not be able to get any job. He tried for jobs in Britain, India, and America. To his misfortune he could not get a single job out of 26 he applied for. He could not get a job in India because he was British, and he could not get a job in England because he was an Indian. His "name, face and colour" were responsible for not getting a job in America. Out of frustration he told Patricia that the letter he received from home "tore his heart": "their trust, their faith, their love—never mentioned, but underlying every word. My little brother needs me now. I can feel it" (134). By November 1954, his predicament was so intense that he was undone. He could not go back to his country to serve. He questioned himself how he could serve his country by going back. He reflected too much to know his identity. He thought of his predicament as the product of complex historical circumstances. He was an East Indian West Indian who escaped his own society by getting a superior British education, leaving him a double exile. Naipaul had been so perturbed that he was not happy with the freedom he was enjoying in England because such freedom was meaningless for an individual without "freedom of opportunity". He told Patricia that his "freedom of speech and religion" would in no way help him from starvation. He therefore wanted to know his place in the free world. He wrote to Patricia:

> You tell me I talk a lot of rot about history. But I wonder whether you ever consider that my position has been caused by several complex historical factors: the slave trade, its abolition; British imperialism, and the subjection of Indian peoples; the need for cheap labour on the Caribbean sugar plantation; Indian indentured immigration...so today, you have me—disowned by India. Well, I belong to the Commonwealth. (138)

This outburst of Naipaul was not skin deep. This came from the core of his heart because he was not only subjected to "physical oppressions", but he was also subjected to "spiritual oppression". At this moment, he had been disturbed due to the recurring "racial humiliation" that he faced in London and his "epic uncertainty over his future" (139). He also wrote to Patricia how people in authority felt his qualifications fitted him only for "jobs as porters in kitchens, and with the road gangs" (139). His predicament was rather devastating, suicidal and outrageous. Such anxiety and predicament would occupy Naipaul's mind throughout the second half of the 20th century when he would establish himself as one of the best writers of the century. It is significant to know how Naipaul was too much critical of the free world and its policy which could not provide opportunities to the needy people who were starving. In a free world very often people do not suffer due to "political persecution"; but they suffer from "insidious spiritual persecution". Naipaul's "insidious spiritual persecution" has been aimed at breaking his spirit: "They want me to forget my dignity as a human being. They want me to know my place.... No fire in my room for two days and only tea and toasts in my stomach" (140). That is what the whole policy of the free world amounts to Naipaul. At this moment of crisis and mental anguish he remembered his "poor father" who had died a broken, frustrated man without any achievement: "He was ghettoed—in a sense more cruel than that in which Hitler ghettoed the Jews. But there was an element of rude honesty in the Nazi approach; they at any rate killed swiftly. The approach of the free world is infinitely subtler and more refined" (140). The dilemma of the young Naipaul was the dilemma of a lot of migrants in the free world of the second half of the twentieth century who had to migrate to different countries in search of opportunities. In explaining his breakdown to Patricia Naipaul remembers:

> What happens in this: One's life is so unsatisfactory, so terribly insecure, so haunted by fear & doubt & sense of failure—that the mind in a clever beastly way removes attention from these truths so hard to swallow, and fixes it on an alien dread. It seems to be a different spirit within that says: Little boy finds these things so frightening, here, little boy, exercise your mind on this. Oh God, I wish, I do deeply wish that I don't lose my balance again. (142)

In such a mental condition, V.S. Naipaul was supported by Patricia for his food and basic needs of life. However, in December 1953, he got an offer from Swanzy, "a renewable three-month contract presenting *Caribbean Voices*" (142) in B.B.C. This offer actually saved him from his doom and he therefore wrote to his mother that he would save 20 to 25 Shillings every week to send home to mitigate their difficulties.

The B.B.C assignment was a great opportunity for V.S. Naipaul to widen his intellectual circle and extend his talent to establish himself as a writer. Leaving the White world of Oxford University, he would now work with *Caribbean Voices* boys. He got a chance to review the novels, interviewed writers and chaired discussions on West Indian literature. French comments: "Like Willie in *Half a Life*, involvement with the B.B.C. gave Vidia a sense of power and wealth of London that he did not find elsewhere; like Willie he went to interview a rising African Carver, a man named Felix Idubar, a sculptor and seducer from Nigeria..." (147). Despite Naipaul's denial, his colleagues at *Caribbean Voices* played a crucial role in shaping the structure and vision of his writings. In the beginning of 1955, Naipaul walked over the streets of Post-War London, "a world of Lyons Corner Houses, down-at-heel bars, lodgings, poverty, friendship, alcohol, prostitute, racial mingling and the sexual fascinations and dissatisfaction that he would later depict in fiction" (148). Through such intimate experiences, he gained larger knowledge than what he had. He was always haunted by two central ideas, namely "race and sex": his relationship with friends and colleagues at the B.B.C. such as Jan Carew, John Stockbridge, Gordon Woolford and Willie Edmet was central to his life at this time. He explored London and the world through their stories, romances and the experiences which he himself did not dare to have.

In the beginning of his tenure at B.B.C. his marriage took place with Patricia in January 1955. However, it was kept a secret from the family members of both of them. After some weeks, he started writing *Miguel Street*. This book portrays a part of Spain Street in the 1940s in a series of linked stories, the narrator of which is a fatherless boy. Written in a simple language with humorous tone the book implicitly deals with ethnic issues. This book was really ambitious, and through his writings Naipaul wanted to establish his identity in the Free World. Soon after this book, Vidia wrote the next novel *The Mystic Masseur,* which dealt with the rural Indians in Trinidad. In December 1955, he wrote to his mother about his success as a writer. However, the mother was unhappy to learn from Kamla that he had already been married: "Well I am very disappointed that you really don't know your mother.... In future always remember that I am a very good mother to all my children. I have given all of you freedom to marry who they like, but choose wisely. No secret from now" (161). Even Patricia's parents were also not happy when they knew about her marriage. It is however significant that Patricia would sacrifice her life after marriage to serve the cause of her husband who would become one of the great writers of the world. French's sympathetic comments for Patricia's sacrifice to this noble cause is worth-mentioning: "Like many people, Pat could see the mistakes her parents had made with their lives, but was unable to avoid making different, though related, mistakes in her own. She too would, finally, sacrifice life to self-sacrifice" (French 164).

Naipaul reached Trinidad to meet his distressed mother and his family in September 1956. Initially he was highly pleased to see the improvement of his family under Kamla's care. After a few days he could understand that Trinidad had been under a severe ethnic conflict. The Indians, especially the Hindus, were the target of the racial discrimination: "It was an irreversible shift; like Trinidad itself, V.S. Naipaul went through a hardening of racial attitudes in 1956. Old relationships died as old certainties unraveled" (170). Naipaul found that the official policy in Trinidad was racial, more dangerous than the colonial rule. The ruling government under Eric Williams was offensive against Hindus, Muslims, and Chinese: "But with the present government of noble Niggers, all sorts of racialist laws might be passed; and life for minority communities could become tricky. Indians are talking of leaving; so are the Chinese" (172). He felt that it was hundred times better to have a colonial rule rather than self-rule by these Negroes who were racial, offensive, damned and nasty. He therefore believed that "his future as a Trinidadian was now fatally circumscribed, and that he would need to look to a new, wider identity" (173). He was really disheartened to see the marginalized position of the Indian communities who were "too much of a majority to assimilate, too much of a minority to dominate" (173). After visiting his home in Trinidad he felt very sad. Staying here for two months, he only got some new materials for his writings. In November 1956, he returned to England with a very, very sad heart while leaving his family at Port of Spain and hoping that he would come there soon. Coming back to England, Naipaul hurriedly wrote his third book, *The Suffrage of Elvira*, about an election with a "crazy twist to the whole story" (178). In June 1957, he was excited to see the good reviews of his first novel *The Mystic Masseur*. He therefore wrote to his mother: "They are really rather good reviews for a first novel by a completely unknown writer.... And I believe I will be able to send some sums of money home" (179). The identity of Naipaul was being established through *The Mystic Masseur*:

> *The Sunday Express* critic called *The Mystic Masseur* 'The deftest and gayest satire I have read in years.' *The Sunday Times* decided he was 'a sophisticated and witty young Trinidad novelist who immediately takes

> a front-line place in the growing West Indian school'. Vidia wrote out the entire *Daily Telegraph* review for his mother, including the lines: 'V.S. Naipaul is a young writer who contrives to blend Oxford wit with home-grown rumbustiousness and not do harm to either. He is a West Indian Gwyn Thomas [a Welsh novelist and radio personality of the moment]—pungent, charitable, Rabelaisian, who deals with a small change of human experiences as though it were minted gold.' (French 179)

When Naipaul sent all these reviews to his mother, she was intensely happy, and offered *Puja* for his success. In 1958 his third book *The Suffrage of Elvira* was published. It was also highly praised by the reviewers: "a beautifully contained and balanced book...extremely funny and accurately cruel" (Penelope Mortimer in *The Sunday Times*); "unusual elegance and sense of style" (Anthony Powel). Kingsley Amis, Arthur Calder Marshall and many others also praised the merit of the book. In 1959, Andre Deutsch Limited published *Miguel Street. The Times Literary Supplement* remarked that Naipaul had a "fresh and original talent and an ability to show the humanity of the very poor" (181). *The News Chronicle* remarked that "the time has come for Naipaul to move on to something bigger" (181).

These successes however did not resolve his hard realities of life. Naipaul's humiliations were immense. His efforts to get work on the General Overseas Service were rejected by Mary Trade Gold because he was not a European as per the official policy of B.B.C.: "*Caribbean Voices* was a place of opportunity, but it was also a racial ghetto" (183). P.H. Newby, the 1969 Booker Prize winner novelist and the head of the third programs of B.B.C. noted that V.S. Naipaul's stories in *Miguel Street* were disappointing because they lacked precision and proper perspectives. However, the third program took him seriously in 1960 when he planned to visit the country of his ancestry, India. Naipaul was a determined person to establish himself as a writer. Andre Deutsch, despite being a professional publisher to survive in publishing business, still helped him a lot for his recognition:

> For all this, Vidia's early books enjoyed a good critical reception with the help of his publisher and won important Prizes aimed at encouraging younger writers. He received the John Llewellyn Rhys Prize for *The Mystic Masseur* and the Somerset Maugham Award for *Miguel Street*. (190)

However, the most important book during his first phase of writing career *A House for Mr Biswas* (1961) is regarded as a seminal postcolonial text, "later set against novels such as *Things Fall Apart* by Chinua Achebe or *Midnight's Children* by Salman Rushdie" (200). The publication of the book raised strong reactions from Capildeo family, persuading the publisher to suppress the book. However, the British press acclaimed the book as a landmark text. The Capildeo family regarded the book as an act of betrayal and misrepresentation. In *The Observer* Colin, MacInnes remarked: "*A House for Mr Biswas* has the unforced pace of a master work: it is relaxed, yet on every page alert" (201). In *The London Magazine* Francis Wyndham wrote that the book is "one of the clearest and subtlest illustrations ever shown of the effects of colonialism...he has succeeded in filling an unusually large frame without sacrificing the finesse of the miniaturist's technique" (201). *A House for Mr Biswas* was "the most interesting novel to have been published in England in 1961" (Dan Jacobson: *The New Statesman*), and to Angus Wilson, the novelist, "V.S. Naipaul has now joined the small group of unquestionably first class novelists" (201). Writing a full page report in the *Trinidad Guardian,* Derek Walcott commented on the gap between Naipaul as a man and the author: "Naipaul seems on first acquaintance to have alienated himself from all the problems of our society and particularly those of his race. But the books are almost of our society and particularly those of his race. But the books are almost contradictions of the man" (201). Later on Edward Brathwaite remarked: "the novels of Vidia Naipaul...have come almost overnight to topple the whole hierarchy of our literary values and set up new critical standards of form and order in the West Indian novels" (201). A kind letter came from Seepersad's editor Gault MacGowan (the former editor of *The Trinidad Guardian*) who mistakenly thought Seepersad Naipaul succeeded to such peak. As Trinidad was on the way to independence in 1954, the Chief Minister, Dr. Eric Williams invited V.S. Naipaul on a government scholarship. Being exhausted due to enormous work that *A House for Mr. Biswas* had demanded, both Naipaul and his wife decided to go to Trinidad for a change in 1960. When he was there, Dr. Williams asked him to write a book which turned out to be *The Middle Passage.* Naipaul was very critical of the way West Indies moved; he was very much concerned with the dangers of decolonization and rising racialism in the West Indies. His observations on colonialism are perceptive and authentic: "He presented the West Indies now as barely redeemable, a region colonized only for the cruelties of slavery" (208). In *The Middle Passage* he wrote: "The History of the islands can never be satisfactorily told. Brutality is not the only difficulty. History is built around achievement and creation; and nothing was created in the West Indies" (*MP* 20).

The West Indians had been infected with the disease of "racial hostility" because their "identity" was not singular. Naipaul sees dangers in this "corruption of identity": "Like monkeys pleading for evolution, each claiming to be whiter than the other, Indians and Negroes appeal to the unacknowledged white audience to see how much they despise one another" (78). At a time when the country was preparing for freedom, Naipaul's strong resentments against false nationalism in West Indies seemed to be insulting though afterwards his convictions were certainly proved exact: "Nationalism was impossible in Trinidad.... There were no parties, only individuals. Corruption, not unexpected, aroused only amusement and even mild approval" (69). He was disgusted to observe the predicament of the people in Surinam where slavery ended late and the people were still slaves in their choice of food, and savagely beat their children. In Jamaica, he was not happy with the local culture as people were not punctual. He however reached Stratham Hill in May, 1961 and planned to complete the book by the end of the year so that he could go back to India to search for his further identity in the land of his ancestors. By 1962, when he was preparing to go to India, he felt that the mother-country,

England, had betrayed the cause of immigrants by bringing the new Commonwealth Immigrants Act which did not give the Commonwealth citizens, automatic rights to move to U.K.:

> At the start of 1962, as Vidia prepared to travel to India for the first time, he was aware that his identity had been compromised by external events. Trinidad faced black majority rule, with the unstable Capo R. claiming to represent the interests of the island's many Indians. Britain was closing the doors to immigrants. (French 213)

In a changing scenario, Naipaul therefore tried to change his focus from West Indies to other issues. At 29, he established his identity as the author of *A House for Mr Biswas,* an epic text of postcolonial literature. He therefore decided to move forward to see the land of his ancestors:

> Ambitious, protean, made of smart material, deracinated by the accelerated politics of the end of empire, Vidia made a conscious choice to refashion himself. The vogue of West Indian writing was over and, uniquely among his contemporaries, he saw the implications of this early enough to do something about it. (214)

2.3. Deconstructing History: Writing Self and Civilization

From 1962 to 1972, the writings were *Mr Stone and the Knights Companion* (1963), *An Area of Darkness* (1964), *The Mimic Men* (1967), *A Flag on the Island* (1967) *and In a Free State* (1971). Along with his wife Naipaul reached India, the land of his ancestors, in 1962 when Jawaharlal Nehru was the Prime Minister. Despite five-year plans and efforts of the leaders, India was still very poor and the suffering of the people was immense. Because the leaders had no proper vision for development, and were unable to tackle the burning issues, India still remained a backward country, rotten by poverty and uncleanliness. By traveling different parts of the country, Naipaul was too much moved by the people who were on the margin—the poor people, the coolies and the peasantry:

> Vidia was struck above all by Indian indifference to suffering. 'Porters are called coolies; they have no

> barrows, which would simplify their labour; they carry incredible loads on their heads and people who are no doubt friendly and hospitable and charitable walk behind them, concerned only that their luggage should not be stolen. (French 223)

After his observation of the Indian way of life for a month he settled in a Kashmiri hotel to record his experiences. He observed that Indians did not see the happenings around them though they "saw" them physically. He condemned the Indians for dirtiness and defecation everywhere, their irrationality, superstitions, caste divisions, religious hypocrisy and above all inhuman approach to suffering of the deprived. During his trip he had met many dignitaries like Khuswant Singh, I.A.S. officer Moni Malhotra, Ravi Dayal who worked for Oxford University Press, Karan Singh, the Maharaja of Kashmir, the novelist R.P. Jhavwala and many others. Ravi Dayal explained how the Indians by that time were guided by the national ethos to take the responsibility to lift the miseries of the people; and they never felt "marginalized" in the world. Pat persuaded Naipaul to soften his stand on India in his book *An Area of Darkness*, but he would not relent. He wrote what he saw, what was truthful to him. Though he was frustrated as to how to go ahead with the book, he would finish it with his experiences that he encountered in different places including Bombay, Delhi, Agra, Vijaynagram, Lucknow, Moradabad, Gorakhpur, and Madras. He was bound to write the book failing which he would pay back Deutsch, his publisher a sum of £500. He was much puzzled to start the book because he was unable to understand the Indians fully. While staying in Kashmir, he was able to write a short novel, titled *Mr Stone and the Knights Companion* about an old man with regular habits leading a mechanical life. French writes that this short fiction was "a feat, but it did not offer a way forward as a writer. He could not write further novels about dull life in London. Nor could he return to the world of *Miguel Street*" (226).

Back in England, Naipaul was to face the consequences of the publication of the book, *An Area of Darkness* (1964). For decades, the book could continue to provoke readers both in

India and outside. In his analysis of India, he has pointed out the lapses of the Hinduism and its failure to improve the quality of human life in absolute terms. Though Naipaul attributed "India as an area of darkness", it was not true because he nurtured a "love-hate relationship" towards India. After the publication of the book, Francis Wyndham, to whom it was dedicated, wrote: "Your book is really an important book I suppose it will make some people angry" (236). French notes:

> John Wain in *The Observer* judged it 'tender, lyrical, explosive and cruel'. *The Times Literary Supplement* praised it as 'beautiful, sensitive and sad'. *The Daily Telegraph* thought it "sore recital". V.S. Pritchett called it the most compelling and vivid book about India to appear for long time. (236)

The remark of Rudranath Capildeo in a speech in Parliament in the Port of Spain is worth mentioning: "...Pope Paul VI went to India and he left his heart in India, but one of our countrymen went there but left his excrement" (236). Actually Naipaul's concern for the ancestral land was that India as a nation was doomed as a civilization; it had no future.

By 1964, there was serious ethnic prejudice against the migrants of Indian subcontinent in England because they did not integrate with the culture of England as they had less interest in marrying the white women unlike the Negroes who integrated to the white culture. Naipaul's writing to *Illustrated Weekly of India* from England upholds that a scientist or an industrialist is more important than the politicians because they produce a country's wealth which is the power. After finishing his two writings as per the agreement with *Illustrated Weekly of India* at the end of 1964, he was much depressed. Around this time C.L.R. James came to his rescue. After World War II and the end of Empire, London was a disturbing city due to ethnic violence and tension. Many writers who have migrated to London from within the Commonwealth "have become refugees, victims of the idea of London and England, of self-delusion and sentimentality, which are always dangerous" (*IWI*, 27 December 1964). By that time there was correspondence between James and Naipaul. Being a Marxist critic, James suggested that a country's problems were based on economic, social and political foundations. It was therefore not wise on the part of a writer, a former colonial subject, to write so harshly, when the countries were struggling for development after independence. V.S. Naipaul however believed that he did not belong to any country—India, West Indies or any other: "Contrary to the depredations that would be launched against Vidia with increasing force overcoming decades, his moral axis was not white European or pre-Islamic Hindu Culture, or any other passing culture: it was internal, it was himself" (245). V.S. Naipaul wanted to confront the convictions in fiction that he had already done in travel writings such as *The Middle Passage* and *An Area of Darkness*.

At this juncture of his own crisis in creativity, Naipaul was preoccupied with a very important question; what should be the function of the novel? He felt that the novel had become a worn out form unsuitable for capturing the complexity of modern societies. In 1999 he therefore wrote in the *New York Review of Books*:

> Literature is a sum of its discoveries...what is good is always what is now in both form and content...the new novel gave 19th century Europe a certain kind of news. The late 20th century, surfeited with news, culturally far more confused, threatening again to be as full as tribal or folk movement as during the centuries of the Roman Empire, needs another kind of interpretation...it is a vanity of the age (and of commercial promotion) that the novel continues to be literature's final and highest expression. (Quoted in French 245-46)

During this time, he kept himself aloof from his West Indian colleagues from *Caribbean Voices* and entered a new circle of Antonia Frazer, Hugh Frazer, Francis Wyndham, Anthony Powell, Powel's wife Violet and Antonia's aunt who were educated and well connected in social status and political circles. Naipaul admired Lady Antonia's ability to bring together discrete social, political and literary spheres. Naipaul and Antonia continued good relationship as friends, and through

Antonia, he could come in contact with political leaders, writers and socialites. Taking some loan later on he purchased a two bedroom flat which needed to be renovated. In the meanwhile Shiva came to Oxford for studies after getting a scholarship. By this time, Naipaul had severe monetary crisis. From 1960 to 1969 Naipaul's gross income after expenses averaged £1963 a year. Due to high rate of personal taxation in the 1960s much of his money never reached him. In 1969 he was saved by an Arts Council bursary of £3500 secured by Francis Wyndham and Angus Wilson. In 1970 his income was reduced to £773, and he was forced to sell the Stockwell house.

Before such financial crisis, he went to Trinidad and wrote a script for a film. The material was later transformed into *A Flag on the Island.* The film-maker gave him £5000. Back in London from Trinidad he wrote *The Mimic Men* (1967). Naipaul had a strong desire to see Africa, the ancestors of his fellow Trinidadians though he had already encountered the land of his own ancestors. He therefore readily accepted an invitation to be the writer in residence offered by Farfield foundation at Makerere University in Uganda. Naipaul now got a chance to move on as a writer because he was able to produce *In a Free State* and *A Bend in the River* as a result of his African journey. It was a very fruitful journey because it helped Naipaul move on.

Both Naipaul and Patricia reached Kampala in early 1966. After reaching Uganda in Africa, Naipaul engaged himself in writing after two years of false start. Uganda was a newly independent nation with King Freddie and Milton Obote as the Prime Minister. Naipaul was always concerned with the marginalized sections. Even in Africa he met the Indians whom he told that his book *An Area of Darkness* was about the marginalized people, their pains and sufferings rather than about India. Naipaul's encounter with the places and people during his nine months stay in Africa was quite productive because it provided immense materials for his writing later on. The displaced international characters and restricted campus setting of Makery provided substantial material for *In a Free State* and *A Bend in The River.* The publication of *The*

Mimic Men raised Naipaul's critical reputation to a significant height. Angus Wilson compared the ironies in the book with Conrad's. The noteworthy remark was made by V.S. Pritchett in *New York Review of Books* on 11 April 1998: "Among the younger English novelists Mr. V.S. Naipaul is a virtuoso. A brilliant chameleon from the Caribbean the descendant of Hindu immigrants, he has grown into the English novel with more lasting assurance than almost all contemporaries in the West Indies or Africa who are in the same case" (quoted in French 263). In 1970 Eric Williams remarked: "V.S. Naipaul's description of West Indians as 'mimic men' is harsh, but true... psychological dependence leads to an ever-growing economic and cultural dependence on the outside world. Fragmentation is intensified in the process" (French 263). Naipaul always played the role of a "displaced, unaffiliated, unCaribbean writer" for which he was to keep distance from all political movements in West Indies. He returned to London from Africa in October 1966. Then he went to Trinidad and wrote the book *The Loss of El Dorado*, neither a travel nor a history book, a reconstruction of the history of Trinidad. From 1966 to 1970 after his African travel it was a period of frustration without any significant literary output. French assesses Naipaul's mood:

> He was profoundly frustrated by his lack of sexual fulfillment, despairing himself for brothel sex; he did not know how to convert his singular background and recent experience into new fiction; he mistrusted the social and political movements of the time: the creative *avant garde* seemed to him an irrelevant indulgence, and he detested Hippies, Yippies, beatniks, free schools, flower power, Black Power, flag burning, hair growing, sit-ins, be-ins, teach-ins, and love-ins. The sharp Naipauline vision that had arisen from his family background and sound colonial education now appear to be at odds with current thinking, particularly about what was coming to be called the Third World. (266)

In 1967, Naipaul visited India and wrote an article for *Telegraph Magazine,* and then he proceeded to Japan and interviewed a businessman. Naipaul's relationship with Paul

Theroux, the novelist was critical—sometimes warm and sometimes detached. By 1968, the Naipauls were financially miserable and new restrictions on immigration made them think to move to Canada. They therefore sold their house Stockwell Park Crescent. Since Naipaul was to complete the book *The Loss of El Dorado*, Antonia and Hugh Frazer lent them their country house in the north of Scotland, namely Eileen Airgas. While staying here, Patricia unhappily confided with Antonia about their childlessness and consulted a gynecologist who suggested that she was normal. However without taking further tests, she left it to her luck and concentrated on the care of Naipaul. By November 1968, the Naipauls were ready to leave first for the Caribbean then for Central America, the U.S.A. and Canada. Before departing, Naipaul in a farewell interview condemned the British politicians as "shabby sharp dealers". Before that he spoke on *The World At One* on the B.B.C. about the "plight of immigrants and ethnic minorities" and how cruelly they were treated in Britain. Naipaul's statelessness was a condition imposed on him when he left Trinidad in 1950:

> Now it was something he sought, from a position of experience. Creatively and personally, he needed something fresh...displacement gave Vidia a distant view of the world. At this time, there was no other writer of stature who was analyzing society in this detached global way. V.S. Naipaul was of everywhere and nowhere, rooted in English literary tradition, but outside it. His attitudes and outlook had been formed by his family background, his colonial education and his experiences in Britain and beyond in the 1950s and 1960s: his instincts and prejudices were intact, but his eyes were wide open, missing nothing. (279)

From Jamaica in 1969 Naipaul couple went to British Honduras or Belize, London's last colony on the American mainland. In New York their social and intellectual work was facilitated by Robert B. Silvers through Francis who had given an introduction to Silvers about Naipauls. The Naipauls traveled many important places in America; they met writers and journalists. They went to Canada where they encountered many

Indians and West Indian East Indians. However by September 1969, Naipaul changed his mind by being "anguished, angry and feeling lost" (283) and returned to England. Later on, he blamed his wife for the decision to go to Canada. The Naipauls had therefore been homeless at the start of 1970s. While staying in Gloucester with aunt Lu, Naipaul was able to complete the fiction *In a Free State* which was published in Autumn 1971. Francis remarked that it was magnificent, amazingly original, most extraordinary and ambiguous. To Maomi, the style is unique so far. Critics like Nadine Gordimer, Anthony Powell and many others praised the book for its extraordinary form and excellent rich content. In October 1971, *Times* reported about the book:

> *In a Free State* is a book of such lucid complexity and such genuine insight so deft and deep, that it somehow manages to agitate, charm, amuse and excuse all at the same pitch of experience. Do not miss the exhilaration of catching one of the most accomplished writers reaching towards the full stage of his talent - our? Well, yes, no. (209)

At the end of 1971, the Naipauls would shift from Gloucester to Teasel Cottage in Wiltshire, "beautifully situated close to the river but on a bank above it" (290). After *In a Free State,* Naipaul traveled India to write about an election in Ajmer for the *Sunday Times Magazine*. In 1971 March, he went to Jamaica to see Kamla, and to Trinidad to see his mother and sisters. When he was reading his paper in a meeting at the Jamaican Campus of the University of the West Indies, a black Jamaican librarian, Cliff Lashley, shouted that Naipaul should be killed with a gun. The organizers neither apologized Naipaul nor reprimanded Lashley. Then he traveled to Mauritius to write "The Overcrowded Barracoon". Mauritius was a country ravaged by colonial imperialism where people suffered severely. Naipaul was deeply hurt to note the plight of the helpless and the malnourished boys who came to a political meeting in oversized jackets that belong to fathers or elder brothers to listen to empty slogans: "The rain, the bush, the cheap houses, the poor clothes, the mixture of races, the umbrellaed groups who have come out to watch the hysterical scene is yet to intimate: adults fighting in fronts of the children, the squalor of the overcrowded barracoon, the politics of the powerless" (298). Though Mauritius prospered significantly after a few years, Naipaul's analysis of the situation of the moment was correct. Returning to Britain, he was laid low due to bronchial pneumonia. Naipaul's depression continued due to illness. However, soon he would be informed that he won the Booker Prize for his book *In a Free State*. The prize lifted his spirit too high as he received it at a time full of depression, frustration and financial crunch. After the Booker prize, he was praised highly by friends and critics. Peter Bayley, his former tutor remarked quite truly:

> I thought *A House for Mr. Biswas* was wonderful—in a wild marvelous Dickensy imaginative way; *In a Free State* seems astonishingly far beyond that. But as a result I found it profoundly disturbing...perhaps I was wrong to see personal unhappiness, alienation, loneliness, humiliation so clearly behind it all. (300)

His tutor was proved true because soon after the Booker dinner, after Christmas 1971 the Naipaul couple flew to West Indies wherefrom they would go to some other destination—Argentina, Nigeria or Bangladesh. By 1972, there was a turning point in the life of V.S. Naipaul. Before he left for Argentina, Patricia was losing her weight due to the developing cancer that would finish her life in 1995. There was diminishing sexual relationship between the couple. Funded by Bob (the editor), when Naipaul went to Argentina to observe the situation there and write articles for *New York Review*, he had already completed *In a Free State*. After this great work, he was exhausted and had nothing substantial to write about. He therefore confided to Norman Mailer, the great novelist, there in Argentina that his marriage was in trouble and therefore after each book he was hung with whores. In addition to this he might have to leave England due to racial tension. Mailer therefore introduced him to the "slim, tanned healthy young woman", Margaret Gooding, wife of Roy Gooding. Naipaul's relationship with Margaret had brought freshness into his life because it was a terrific sensual fulfillment, full of passion and wonder. Naipaul felt a sense of completeness after his experience with Margaret. This experience had a great impact on his books that were written afterwards. He would therefore confess: "the books stop being dry after Margaret, and it was a great liberation…nothing was missing. The world was complete for me. I have often thought how strange it is that I lived for so long in England and I really had no English affair" (French 314). Coming back to Trinidad while Naipaul was going through the emotional turmoil he wrote an article about the political situation of Argentina, which was well appreciated. After that he was invited to go to New Zealand by UNESCO. He went there with an intention of meeting Margaret who revolutionized his life and thinking during the next 25 years of his life. However after reaching New Zealand, he admitted guilt of his adultery in a letter to his wife. He also wrote that the state of their homelessness had brought a lot of strains in their life and damaged more to Patricia's physical and psychological life: "A woman needs a house, a fortress of her own, which she creates and governs; I wonder how that we never thought of that. I think that we must…find some kind of house which will be yours and, because it will be yours, will also be mine" (318). However, Naipaul did not materialize this fine intention of giving his wife a fortress so that he would lead a life of comfort and peace. He rather embraced the other life with his mistress Margaret that enabled him to produce such great works as *Guerrillas*, "the Congo", *India: A Wounded Civilization* and *A Bend in the River.* It is interesting to mention the remarks of French:

> Margaret was Vidia's ideal woman, a woman of a kind who has existed previously only in his fantasy life: he could string her along and mistreat her, with her abject consent. Margaret was unlike Pat in almost all respects: tempestuous, cynical and sexy. Their relationship, battered and disturbed would endure for almost a quarter of a century; a kink in his personality met a kink in hers, and snagged. The affair was to be intense, and intensely sexual, and sexually aggressive to their mutual pleasure.… She was in thrall and addicted to

> him, sexually and emotionally. She liked to be his slave and his victim, and he was snared by her: although he appeared to be in control of how things unfolded, he was mentally hooked. Margaret gave him the power much of which was generated out of a new self-belief and physical confidence, to push ahead with his literary ambition. (320-21)

Naipaul finished the first draft of the novel, *Guerrillas,* in May 1974 and immediately left for Argentina. Patricia was unhappy because people in London knew that he was going to Margaret, his mistress. Spending two months with Margaret in Buenos Aires, he returned to England. Before this event, Margaret left her husband and children. She was employed by Massey-Ferguson, manufacturer of tractors. Naipaul and Margaret were violently engaged to each other either in Argentina or in England. Naipaul arranged a London flat for Patricia to live there alone. The distressed wife was to spare her kitchen and home at Wiltshire to Naipaul and Margaret to live together. From 1975 to 1995, the next 20 years, "the triangle between Vidia, Pat and Margaret persisted shifting from an equilateral to scalene depending on his work, mood and location and the emotional pull exerted by each woman" (367).

In 1975, Naipaul along with his mistress Margaret went to Mobutu's Zaire to write for *The Sunday Times* and *The New York Review of Books.* Naipaul was disturbed after reaching the Congo due to the chaotic condition of the country. The Congo, formerly a Belgium colony, is an African kingdom, known as Zaire. He returned some of the important ideas that would be incorporated in the novel *A Bend in the River* which sounded the prophetic future of Zaire under its dynamic leader Mobutu Sese Seko KuKu Ngbendu Wa Za Bonga. Back in Europe he spent five weeks with Margaret in Spain working hard on the article while his wife was spending a distressed lonely life in Wilfred Cottage and London flat. His relationship with Margaret made him stable partially and therefore he focused on his work when Bob Silvers asked him to visit India and write a series of articles about India's economic and constitutional crises under the Emergency rule of Indira Gandhi, the then Prime Minister.

V.S. Naipaul, along with Margaret reached Bombay during the monsoon time. During his visit Naipaul observed that people were not interested in talking to him because there was curtailment of freedom of speech during the Emergency rule: “Indira Gandhi had suspended elections, censored newspapers, imprisoned political opponents and banned strikes. Middle class society in the capital was split between those who were delighted that the buses were running on time, and others who were frightened believing democracy in India was finished (371). Naipaul was trying to interpret India in a new way. He was making an effort to deconstruct the Indian history—to reconstruct the history of Indian civilization. He understood that the Indians should have a sense of History rather than simply accepting the invasions as some normal events. He also focused on the analysis of India, writing about its poverty, Chawls of Bombay, the rise of Shiv Sena, bonded labor, caste, rural stagnation and the Naxalite movements. Referring to R.K. Narayan, Mahatma Gandhi and Vinoba Bhave, he analyzed the Indian psyche, which never tried to understand history. Working through 1976 in Wilsford, Naipaul was able to publish his book *India: A Wounded Civilization* in 1977. Although Naipaul focused on some important issues in this book, his analysis of India was far from accuracy because he could not comprehend the vast India fully. The book, *The Return of Eva Peron*, was written during 1970-1973 when no novel was produced by him. The publication of the book resulted in mixed responses from the *New York Review, The Observer* and *The New Statesman*. The essays on South America were considered brutal, obsessive and brilliant. While in Argentina with Margaret in March 1977, Naipaul was arrested, “an experience he would use in *A Bend in the River*” (377). He was released afterwards as he was not on the list of suspected guerrillas.

After this South American trip, Naipaul along with Margaret visited Trinidad, a new republic under a new constitution. Except Kamla, no other family members went to the airport to receive them. All the family members were not happy with Naipaul because of his relationship with Margaret. His mother refused to see Margaret when he went to Nepaul Street to meet her. None of his sisters and their children liked Margaret. Despite Naipaul's stand on importance of Margaret in those days of his life, nobody approved it for which he broke with all of them. From Trinidad, Margaret went to London to stay with her sister, Diana. The love-hate relationship between them had started to be disintegrated. Margaret felt that Naipaul's family members including his wife wanted her to get out of Naipaul's life. She also felt insecure, but there was no "alternative" in her life. Naipaul's action at this point was really not praiseworthy. He neglected Patricia who sacrificed her life for her husband. Her care and affection for the husband as if her own child was not considered by Naipaul for his self-interest of "sensual fulfillment" to have stability in his own life. He did not bother the sentiment of his childless wife, Patricia and his distressed mother, a widow who depended on her son. V.S. Naipaul did all this to serve the cause of becoming a great writer. But then, such notions and actions are far from being human, compassionate and considerate. He sacrificed one thing for the sake of the other.

Naipaul was however preoccupied with writing a new book on the paradox of civilization in the early autumn of 1977 for which he needed the help of his devoted wife Patricia. She therefore returned to Wilsford to give him company because "it was her sacrifice, her destiny, the life of her choice" (382). Naipaul worked hard, reading and thinking during late night. Due to cooperation of his wife Naipaul was able to write *A Bend in the River* which "brought together all his experience and uniqueness of his perspective, a late 20th century global narrative that could have been written by no one else" (383). This book is

> a mature work of the imagination rather than disguise autobiography: it was the product of assimilated experience. Although it contained much that was observed or personal—Africa, Margaret—his travels and memories were a starting point for invention. The book was a work of a middle aged novelist marked by experience but in full command of his creative powers.

It lacked the anger of *Guerillas* or *India: A Wounded Civilization.* (384)

After completing this great work in 1978, with the company of Patricia, Naipaul would however go to U.S.A. to live with Margaret.

Naipaul became famous as a great writer. His *Guerrillas* was a tremendous success in America. His reputation reached to great heights. He was nominated for Neustadt International Prize for Literature by Derek Walcott. He was invited to speak by the Cambridge Union. He was invited to become a Regent's Professor at Berkeley. He was invited to open a conference at the University of the West Indies. He was requested to become a Knight of Mark Twain. He was also invited to be a writer-in-residence at the University of Western Australia. Naipaul accepted an invitation from Phyllis Rose of Wesleyan University's English department to spend an academic year teaching courses in creative writing and literature and "alien cultures" at the small, private liberal arts college in Middletown, Connecticut, in exchange for $30000. He planned to spend the year along with Margaret in a rented house taken by the University. The anonymous evaluation at the end of the year showed that students either loved or hated him too much. After the publication of *A Bend in the River* (1979), the author still remained "an elusive man". Now he was reckoned as a world class novelist rather than as a Calypso writer. During this time he received a telegram from Deutschs that he might receive the Booker Prize but he could not win because it was awarded by compromise to Penelope Fitzgerald's *Offshore*. He however turned down both the James Tate Black Memorial Prize and The Royal Society Literature's Winifred Holtby Award that were offered to him.

Naipaul, who was seen as the voice of truth, could see it by virtue of his ethnicity and intellect. He opens *A Bend in the River* with a philosophical stance: "The world is what it is; men who were nothing, who allow themselves to become nothing, have no place in it" (1979: 3). Though this book brought him high reputation from the book-reviewers, Edward Said did not agree with Naipaul on his dismissal of all national liberation movements against colonialism. In 1980, *Newsweek* reported that Naipaul was the strong contender of the Nobel Prize of that year though he was not awarded. In his opinion:

> The great Arab civilization of the seventh to twelfth centuries was the world's most eclectic civilization. It was not closed to outside influences. It was endlessly incorporating the art of Persia, the mathematics of India, what remained of the philosophy of the Greece. The mistake of Western vanity is to think that the universal civilization that exists now is a purer racial one. It's not the perspective of one rule, one country but has been fed by many. (Quoted in French 396)

Such a view deconstructs the Western dominance of knowledge and epistemology. While in Wesleyan, Naipaul was fascinated by the Iranian revolution. He believed that the development of the Islamic radicalism might become a serious threat to the world. He therefore decided to write a book by traveling to four non-Arab Muslim countries such as Iran, Pakistan, Malaysia and Indonesia. He assumed that "Islam, with its emphasis on a text written in Arabic and on Pilgrimage to holy places in Saudi Arabia, was innately imperialist, requiring its followers to diminish their native culture" (396). His traveling to these Muslim countries would result in the book *Among the Believers*. In this book he has focused on the "Islamic revivalism" or "fundamentalism" in the postcolonial era. In the context of postcolonial situation in this book, he opens up his heart to the *New York Times* on 13th May, 1979:

> Each country has a quarrel with the modern world; and my own feeling is that Islam, in these countries, is as much a looking away as a looking back. Is it despair, recognition of intellectual and scientific incapacity? Is it nihilism? Doesn't this kind of anti-intellectual movement...commit these countries to a counting dependence on the technologies and the science of the West? Independence, then leads back to dependence... in tone and form I will be aiming at something like my *Middle Passage* of 1960-62. (French 396-97)

Naipaul, aggrieved due to less publicity in financial terms, decided to change his publishers in 1977. He settled all his accounts with Graham Watson, and New Gillon Aitkin took his place. It resulted in his financial gains to a considerable amount. He would therefore buy a dilapidated house in Salterton, up the valley from Wilsford Manor and renovated it in his own way. Fed up with Margaret, he spent the summer with Patricia in England in 1979. Despite the troubled relationship with Margaret, he however took her with him to visit Iran and Pakistan. The relationship was on the verge of collapsing in Kuala Lumpur for which Naipaul asked her to leave him alone. In his usual dominant style, he asked his wife to come to Indonesia after the departure of Margaret. After the traveling in Indonesia, both of them went to India. Patricia did not accompany Naipaul to Pakistan from India. She came to London. Finishing his work in Pakistan, Naipaul came back to England by spring trying to lead a regular, smooth married life. They entertained Lady Antonia and her new husband, Harold Pinter. Naipaul, though a little depressed, was rigorously busy in writing his new book *Among the Believers* (1981), and Patricia engaged in helping him for completion of the work. After its publication, there were positive and negative responses from critics across the world. Naipaul has been much critical of the lies, mediocrity, cruelty, violence, self-indulgence of the postcolonial world. In February 1982, the Naipauls finally shifted to the converted Diary Cottage, a four bedroom house. However after the completion of the book, Naipaul went to Brazil and Venezuela leaving Patricia alone in their new house. His reputation jumped to new peaks in the 1980s. He was to travel to different countries to receive so many prizes and Honorary D. Litt. He turned down some including the D. Litt. offered by the University of Leicester. He traveled Holland, Israel and Jerusalem in this connection. Naipaul was a fully committed writer. He never wanted to keep the work pending. He always remembered the instructions given to him by William Demos at the Cricket nets of QRC: "never put things off until tomorrow" (414). In the summer of 1982, he completed his project, "A Prologue to An Autobiography". In November 1982 he was in West Africa researching the life and situation there. In 1983 he was in Grenada. Wherever Naipaul went, his sole concern was to know the truth, to explore the unknown and undiscovered. In 1984 he published the book *Finding the Centre* that included "Prologue to An Autobiography" and "The Crocodile of Yamoussoukro". In the mid 1980s, Naipaul had a feeling that his years of writings were to be over very soon. The impulsive mood was declining. It was being replaced by a "technical brilliance". Though he would now be preparing to write such great books as *The Enigma of Arrival* (1987) and *India: A Million Mutinies Now* (1990), they would lack the lyricism of *Miguel Street,* the extraordinary originality of *A House For Mr Biswas* or the robust vigor of *A Bend in the River.* He would therefore rely more on thought rather than on intuition.

Though Naipaul had a sense of belonging to his family, he had less contact with his mother and sisters except Kamla since his "ill fated visit to Trinidad in 1977" (421). However, in November 1984, the family members met in Trinidad, after the death of Sati, where he met all of them. Nine months later in 1985, the death of Shiva was another disaster in the family. He was deeply in grief due to sudden death of his brother for which his mother advised him to be brave enough to fight any kind of "break down" like his brother or father. By this time Patricia was undergoing sudden weight loss. Though not diagnosed early, her weight loss was due to breast cancer. At this critical moment of his life, Naipaul was writing *The Enigma of Arrival* (1987), "a work of intermittent brilliance, a cross between a partially fictional autobiography and an essay and a slowly revealed study of the life of the mind but billed as a novel. It was an unusual masterpiece" (427). Naipaul has depicted the rural England in the end of the 20th century in a unique discourse which combines "the sense of innocence and wonder with an eye and understanding that are quietly and totally penetrating" (427). Salman Rushdie, though praised the book very highly in *The Guardian*, observed the lapses of the writer for making the book sad, and avoiding the use of the word 'love'. This book's worth was also acknowledged by the Nobel Committee in 2001:

> In his masterpiece *The Enigma of Arrival*, Naipaul visits the reality of England like an anthropologist studying some hitherto unexplored native tribe deep in the jungle with apparently short-sighted and random observations he creates an unrelenting image of the placid collapse of the old colonial ruling culture. (430)

In 1987, Naipaul and Margaret travelled through South Africa. For helping him, Margaret was paid $ 40000 with which she bought a flat. Observing the plights of the poor black and the poor white, he wrote the book *A Turn in the South* (1987). After this work Naipaul travelled India for his book, *India: A Million Mutinies Now*. When Naipaul was busy in formulating and shaping his work on India soon after his travels in India in 1989, Patricia learnt that she had breast cancer. She was to lose her right breast after the operation. After its publication in the late 1990, *India: A Million Mutinies Now*, "he journeyed through United States, being paid to lecture; he won the Premio Nonino and the British Book Awards Prize for the best travel book of the year" (453). His publisher, Helen Frazer at Heinemann informed that he was at number 10 in *The Sunday Times* best seller list. The book was quite different in tone from his earlier books on India. The reviewers noted that Naipaul had become more tolerant, kind and gentle; and presentations in the book were superb. Naipaul received the Knighthood from the Queen in 1990. He was also offered Trinidad and Tobago's highest award 'The Trinity Cross'. He received the award from Noor Hassanali, the country's first Indian President. His mother, who attended the award ceremony, was overjoyed at her son's achievement. Savi arranged a party in honor of her brother. Next year in 1991, Naipaul's mother died in her sleep. He could not however attend the funeral though he went to Trinidad in 1992 to give a lecture organized by Selby Wooding. Back in England Naipaul received a number of awards and honorary degrees from Oxford, New York and London. Besides, he was awarded the first ever David Cohen British Literature Prize for a life's achievement. His global stature as a great writer was established. In an address to Manhattan Institute in New York, he analyzed his own philosophy on the title "Our Universal

Civilization". He was quite optimistic as he suggested that a "Universal civilization or modernity" existed in the world. He was quite happy to note that the civilization had at last transcended the racial boundaries. To him the pursuit of an idea of happiness is at the heart of this universal Civilization. He thinks that this idea is elastic without any rigidity and fixity. Such an immensely human idea cannot generate fanaticism, and hence it is able to blow away any rigid narrow system.

In 1992, V.S. Naipaul started *A Way in the World*, not in the standard novel form. Because of his pain in spine, he was to undergo operation that year. When Babri Masque was demolished in India in an interview to *The Times of India*, he approved of the passion that took the youth to dome to destroy it. Patricia was seriously suffering from cancer in 1992. In January 1993, she had to undergo surgery and received radio therapy and chemo-therapy in April. After her mother's death Patricia and her sister, Eleanor shared £ 70000 from their mother's will. Thinking of her approaching death and Patricia's illness Naipaul made arrangements for the archives to be sold. Losing the Nobel Prize for literature in 1992 to Derek Walcott, Naipaul concentrated on completing *A Way in the World*. Two months before the publication of *A Way in the World* (1994), he flew to America to present his archives to the University of Tulsa. In 1994, Naipaul visited the British Council as a guest to write a book. In 1995, he went to Buckingham Palace to watch the head of Teachers' Union, the Governor of Brixton. Without much progress in his work in Brazil, he would return to Iran, Indonesia, Malaysia and Pakistan to look at the future of Islamic ideology in a new global political scenario. In his new book on Islam *Beyond Belief* (1998), he would once again reject the usual academic convention that all cultures, peoples and belief systems are different but equal. He would publish another book *Letters between Father and Son* (1999). After traveling five months in 1995 to four non-Arab countries, he finished the book during the course of 1996 and early 1997. In Naipaul's view *Beyond Belief* is about people, not a book of opinion. It is the book about Islam: "ritual purification, sacrifice, Islamic martyrs, mujahidin, talebeh or students Chance Taliban" (478). In 1996, Naipaul wrote to a Tulsa Oilman:

> ...totalitarianism has been the great curse of the century, and you know in your heart of hearts that every form of totalitarianism has pretended to have a core of virtuousness: this illusion of serving virtue makes us look away.... A writer who does this looking away...is betraying his essence and cannot be a good writer. The good writers have always looked for truth. Nothing else is worthwhile if you are a writer. (478)

After a number revisions *Beyond Belief* has been a thought-provoking book.

When Naipaul was doing research on *Beyond Belief* in 1995, he was aware of Patricia's serious illness. As Margaret refused to accompany him to Pakistan, he went there alone and there he met Nadira, a divorced journalist, 21 years younger to Naipaul. Before he left for Malaysia both Nadira and Naipaul had developed close relationship. After finishing his research on the book, Naipaul returned to England but early in January 1996 Patricia was swiftly proceeding towards her death. Before her death, when she came to learn about Naipaul's relationship with Nadira, she remarked that her death would make easier for him to lead his life with the new woman. Patricia, in fact, died in February 1996. After the death ritual was over, Nadira would come to England and later on both of them would marry at Salisbury in April 1996. On 18 October 1996, V.S. Naipaul, the writer and Nadira, his new wife scattered the ashes of Patricia, which event touched to the core of his heart resulting in tears rolling down his cheeks. French has made positive remarks about Naipaul in the context of his achievements as a writer:

> V.S. Naipaul has been writing now for nearly half a century. He has twenty-three books to his name—brilliant combinations of travel, fiction, history, politics, literary criticism and autobiography. It is a body of work of astonishing scope and subtlety, giving him a fair claim to be Britain's greatest living writer.... Although he often brings the reader to a moment of

> realization elliptically, there is candour to his writing, a constant precision at its heart. It is this quality of integrity—the closer analysis of human conduct...that enables Naipaul's work to transcend the peculiarity of his general theories as he narrates the extraordinary lives of ordinary people from his singular perspective. (480-81)

After Patricia's death Naipaul's marriage to Nadira has not prevented him from writing some more books. Patricia did not survive to see that her husband would be awarded Nobel Prize in literature in 2001. She did not survive to see his other publications such as *Beyond Belief* (1998), *Half a Life* (2001) and *Magic Seeds* (2004). His other important books published by Picador, were *The Writer and the World* (2002), *Literary Occasions* (2004), *A Writer's People: Ways of Looking and Feeling* (2007) and *The Masque of Africa* (2010). Even then Naipaul, the perceptive writer understands very clearly the great contributions of Patricia, the devoted wife who sacrificed her life to the cause of her husband to establish his identity as a world writer of repute.

PART II

Interpreting Fictional Discourse

3

Society, Politics and Culture in Early Novels

Naipaul's life and works are intimately connected. He is concerned with the condition of the human world, their wretchedness, isolation and rootlessness. Naipaul declares that he does not belong to any country, society or religion or culture; he is a man of the world. He perceives a clear vision of human situations that are disturbing. Moreover, as a writer of fiction and travelogues he does not follow the traditional forms as he thinks that they are inadequate to uphold the complexities of the contemporary human world. He is therefore iconoclastic in his approaches to both fictions and travelogues. Joshi posits:

> Naipaul has himself insisted that a novelist's function goes beyond documentary realism, that he must impose his vision on the world, not merely record what he sees. He describes the novel as "a form of social inquiry" and sees the writer as one who owes a responsibility to society. Although for a writer with such a positive prescription his is a singularly negative vision, Naipaul's work is of the utmost relevance in a world in which we are all in a sense exiles. (1994: xiii)

Naipaul has tried to explore the predicament of all of us who are more or less exiles in our own surroundings. Joshi therefore postulates: "His ruthless adherences to his own dark vision, his refusal to pretend to an optimism he cannot feel, give a compellingly persuasive power to his depressing fictional world" (1994 xiii-xiv). What is important for the author is that he is not pretentious in his descriptions and analyses even though there is an element of brutality in it. He is not optimistic for the sake of it. So his character Salim utters in *A Bend in the River:* "The world is what it is: men who are nothing, who allow themselves to become nothing, have no place in it" (3). His early novels underlie such a dark vision of the later works through their comic exuberance.

Naipaul writes in *The Return of Eva Peron*: "The great societies that produced the great novels of the past have cracked. Writing has become more private and more privately glamorous. The novel as a form no longer carries conviction" (218). Such a view was also expressed in the 1960s when many believed that the novel was dead because the novel as a traditional form lost its vigor and appeal to the people in the New world. In a changing scenario of the postcolonial people, the new materials for the novel could not be incorporated in the old form. Naipaul experimented with new materials in his novels. Bradbury (1977), Steiner (1969), Massey (1990), and Parrinder (1987) argued how the traditional form of novel lost its relevance to be suitable for the new materials of the postcolonial people. The notion of history plays a prominent role in the postcolonial world. The contemporary novelists of his time therefore emphasized the concept of history and reinterpreted it. The novelists deconstructed history of the people to know the truthfulness of their culture, society as well as political and economic conditions. V.S. Naipaul, Salman Rushdie, Gunter Grass, Albert Camus, Dorris Lessing, Samuel Beckett and many others adapted the form of novel according to their needs in a fast changing global situation. Yashoda Bhat therefore argues:

> A new way of looking at the novel with the abundant experimentation going on within it under the influence of post-modern theories, is its close association with history. The novel today, especially in the growing Third world countries is a reflection of the history in the making at every minute there. History in action and the concept of history are alive as subject and theme in recent fiction. (2000: 5)

During the 1980s and 1990s, history has a potential meaning for the novelists:

> The novel receives and absorbs history, transforms it into a creative stream and pours itself out into a form which may coincide with the previous novel forms or under the impact of the new experiments, emerge as a completely transformed unit. The novel exists today, as much truthfully as the sun blazes or the moon shines. (Bhat 2000: 5-6)

The novel has therefore been recharging through new materials of the new world. The New Literatures in English emerged in Australia, West Indies, India, Africa, New Zealand and many Third World countries. The diasporic writers regenerated this art form from its decay. Naipaul, being a diasporic writer in England, contributed immensely to the new novel of today with his own experiments about the Third-world countries and societies. First, he made use of the West Indian life and societies as materials for his fiction. However, he used the British European structural models and his inherent Hindu perspectives also interacted. As a result, his novels gave a new dimension to English fiction, widening and extending its frontiers. Naipaul dealt with the contemporary problems of postcolonial societies. He had great concerns for the marginalized, who were dominated and suffered. That is why Bhat says: "In these experiments, he emerged as a true post-modernist, using the form of the novel for analyzing the postcolonial predicament, neo-colonialism and the global phenomenon of Diaspora" (68).

This chapter will focus on Naipaul's concerns in the early novels, especially the novels written till 1967. His shorter fictions will however be discussed in the chapter 4. Both *The Mystic Masseur* and *The Suffrage of Elvira* deal with the exposition of Trinidadian world of immigrant Hindu community with a focus on postcolonial Third-world politics. *The Mystic Masseur* narrates the situations about Trinidad during the first General Election in 1946 whereas *The Suffrage of Elvira* focuses on the second General Election in 1950. *A House for Mr Biswas* (1961) deconstructs the social history of Trinidad. It is a prose epic that brings out how a protagonist on the margin with a progressive outlook is set in contrast with the conservative people in the centre trying to colonize him at every stage of his life. However, Mr Biswas tries to liberate himself from the imperialistic Tulsidom. *The Mimic Men* (1967) deals with politics, and illustrates the predicament of a decolonized country that strives hard for its independent existence. Though *Mr Stone and the Knights Companion* is about English life, the protagonist Mr Stone has almost the same predicament like Mr Biswas, and struggles to overcome the tyrannical forces.

3.1. Politics, Mimicry and Corruption

The Mystic Masseur presents typical characters of the Caribbean world. The novel highlights the personality of Ganesh who yearns for power and prestige for which he finds "politics" as an easy means. He is vigilant to every situation. Whatever he finds suitable for his interest, he avails himself of the opportunity as he is well aware of the limited resources of his nation. Politics becomes a means for personal gains and achievement rather than for any social or national cause. The themes presented in the novel are displacement, dislocation, mimicry of democracy, chaos and corruption in the postcolonial Trinidad. The novel opens with the description of the struggle of Ganesh, as a masseur. The narrator reports: "...but when I first met him, he was still a struggling masseur, at a time when masseurs were ten penny in Trinidad" (*Mystic* 1). Though the profession of a masseur is not much promising in Trinidad, Ganesh plunges into this field because the natives still prefer these unqualified doctors to the qualified ones. The narrator says: "My mother distrusted doctors and never took me to one. I am not blaming her for this because in those days people went by preference to the unqualified masseur or the quack dentist" (1).

This illustrates that the colony is exploited of all its resources, and is rotten with ignorance, illiteracy and superstition. The natives are not sensitive to their situations; they are rather involved in playing on the innocence and weakness of other native fellows. Ganesh has a number of books with him in his shelves but he has nothing to do with these books. He never reads them but he has kept them to befool the illiterate natives easily: "Four hundred Everyman, two hundred Penguin—six hundred. Six hundred, and one hundred Reader's Library, make seven-hundred. I think with all the other books, it have about fifteen hundred good books here" (5).

Though he aspires to be a writer and a reader, he is not much proficient in this quality. He just practices this habit as a fashion. It is the result of his Christian education. He does not have the knack of being a good writer/reader at all. Simultaneously he has an adherence to the Hindu culture and religion only to exploit the religious sentiments of the innocent Trinidadians. In fact he is caught up in between the East and the West for his identity:

> I tried to forget Ganesh thumping my leg about and concentrated on the walls. They were covered with religious quotations, in Hindi and English, and with Hindu religious pictures. My gaze settled on a beautiful four-armed god standing in an open lotus. (6)

At the age of 15 Ganesh is sent to Queens Royal College. His father feels proud of sending his son to this college. Before sending the son to the college, he shows off to the people that his son is going to attend an English school. The people are also fascinated to see that Ganesh is going to Royal College. It shows their colonial mentality. Trinidadians have not developed a sense of their own identity, and still they are happy to imitate English men in their life:

> Mr. Ramsumair made a lot of noise about sending his son to the "town college", and the week before the term began he took Ganesh all over the district, showing him off to friends and acquaintances. He had Ganesh dressed in a khaki suit and a khaki toupee and many people said the boy looked like a little sahib. (9)

In fact he was looking ridiculous in his dress. When they reached St. Joseph, Ganesh began to feel shy. Their dress and manner no longer commanded any respect. People were smiling, and when they got down at the railway terminus in Port of Spain, a woman laughed. Harveen Sachdeva Mann rightly comments:

> Queens Royal College in Port of Spain is a mere secondary school that imparts a Victorian education system ill-suited to the need of an emergent nation and that succeeds only in fostering in the students a need to mimic the English. (472-73)

In addition to this, his father is humiliated in the principal's office due to his cultural difference from others: "Then there was the scene in the principal's office: his father gesticulating with his white cap and umbrella; the English principal patient, then firm and finally exasperated; the old man enraged, muttering, '*Gaddaha! Gaddaha*!'" (*Mystic* 10). Though Ganesh is sent to school to behave like an Englishman, he never stops being a country boy. He just proves to be a mimic man of the English. He also changes his name. His indigenous culture and beliefs are in his instinct though he tries his best to shed them off:

> Ganesh never lost his awkwardness. He was so ashamed of his Indian name that for a while he spread a story that he was really called Gareth. This did him little good. He continued to dress badly. He didn't play games, and his accent remained too clearly that of the Indian from the country. He never stopped being a country boy.... He went to sleep with the hens and woke before the cocks. (10-11)

Ganesh goes back home to become a complete Brahmin following one of the rituals and when he returns from home he is again insulted by the principal: "Ramsumair, you are creating a disturbance on the school. Wear something on your head?" (11). It is important to note that the religious and cultural differences bring in deplorable plight for the marginalized group through their humiliations and insults inflicted on them by the dominant colonizers.

Though Ganesh is not able to adjust himself to the circumstances in the Christian school, the modern city life and education have a great influence on him. His rejection of the marriage proposal of his father's choice is the result of his modernity. He goes to the extent of accepting himself as an orphan: "...when his father replied that if Ganesh didn't want to get married he must consider himself an orphan, Ganesh decided to consider himself an orphan" (13). For his survival Ganesh becomes a teacher, but he is once again insulted due to his cultural differences: "This teaching is an art, but it have all sort of people who thinks they could come up from the cane field and start teaching in Port of Spain" (15). Chandra B. Joshi rightly comments:

> In Ganesh's instinct to hide behind the name Gareth, the author is sympathetically aware of the pains of adjustment to an unfamiliar environment. This is an important theme in Naipaul's work, a way in which he has explored the challenges to the preservation of identity in an alien environment. That many Indians felt the compulsion to take on Anglicized names does suggest that they found it difficult to preserve their cultural identity in the Creole world. However, even when they surrendered their names in a move to identify with their environment they met with a measure of contempt and hostility. (115-16)

After the death of his father when he returns to Fourways, he feels quite relieved:

> For it was indeed a singular conspiracy of events that pulled me away from the emptiness of urban life back into the stimulating peace and quiet of the country.
>
> Ganesh was happy to get away from Port of Spain. He had spent five years there but he had never become used to it or felt part of it. It was too big, too noisy, too alien. (*Mystic* 21)

Though he returns to the place where he is known and honoured, he is still under the influence of the English education and city life which create a sense of alienation in him. He knows the people of Fourways, and they also like him but he sometimes feels that he has been alienated from them. Joshi comments on the existential condition of Ganesh:

> Ganesh's sense of displacement and his groping towards a solution are presented with full understanding of his predicament, caught as he is between an Indian past and

> Creole present. To see Ganesh merely as a character in a farce does not quite do justice to the author's treatment. (116-17)

Ram Logan, an illiterate fellow, has western attitudes. His longing for Ganesh as his son-in-law is due to Ganesh's Christian education. Ganesh, for him, is a modern man in the European sense. His flattering to Ganesh is just to placate him for his daughter's engagement with him:

> Look Ram Logan marrying off his second and best daughter to a boy with a college education, and this is all the man giving." Is that what eating me up, sahib? I know that for you, educated and reading books night and day, it wouldn't mean much, but for me, sahib, what about my ch'acter and sensa values? (*Mystic* 40)

To Ram Logan's amazement, Ganesh plays greater trick on him. Ganesh grabs a lot of dowry from his father-in-law. "In the end Ganesh got from Ram Logan a cow and a heifer, fifteen hundred dollars in cash, and a house in Fuente Grove. Ramlogan also cancelled the bill for the food he had sent to Ganesh's house" (45). In fact everyone is an opportunist here. All human relations are based on vested interest only. In a decolonized country, it unfolds colonial traits. Ganesh's treatment to his wife, Leila, emphasizes the subordinate condition of women in the society. It seems that Ganesh's treatment to his wife is the result of his sense of insecurity. He perhaps feels insecure of his wife's modernity and education. As the Great Belcher tells Ganesh: "these modern Girls is hell self", she said. "And from what I see and hear this Leela is a modern girl. Anyway, you got to make the best of what is yours" (46).

For writing books also, Ganesh is encouraged by the great Belcher. Ganesh doesn't have the instinct of writing or massaging. He has the only motive that behind every profession the intention is to accumulate money. After robbing Ram Logan, Ganesh robs most of the Trinidadians and thus continues to be a mimic man, mimicking the colonial masters who have exploited the country for a long time. Trinidadians are crazy for anything that makes them important in the European sense. All the admirers, friends and acquaintances of Ganesh wish him to be like a great European writer. Beharry who has anglicized his name as Behary encourages Ganesh. He says: "The Americans is nice people. You must write this book for them" (64). The use of colonial language and style may have some other implications as well. Manjit Inder Singh makes a remarkable point in this context:

> The notable point is the realization of the necessity to exploit language to enter a class which will ensure recognition and importance. However, Ganesh doesn't exemplify a subversive strategy or design to undermine the power of the colonizer. On the other hand the acquisition of literary through the colonizer's language becomes a technique to conquer the empty spots, the vacuum in the colony that only waits to be filled by the intelligent mimic like the hero of *The Mystic Masseur*. (1998b: 102)

In Trinidad, a newly independent country, a few people have access to education and Ganesh who has got a little Christian education is, for the uneducated natives, equal to the Governor. His apparent habit of reading brings an unexpected reputation for him. It helps him when his profession as a masseur has disappointed him:

> But Ganesh's reputation, lowered by his incompetence as masseur, rose in the village; and presently peasants, crumpling their grimy felt hats in their hands, came to ask him to write letters for them to the Governor or to read letters which the Government curiously had sent them. (*Mystic* 69)

Then there is Soomintra, the other daughter of Ram Logan, who hangs between the two cultures: on the one hand the modern European style and on the other hand her fascinations for India:

> She had a son whom she had called Jawaharlal, after the Indian leader; and her daughter was called Sarojini, after the Indian poetess.

> 'The third one, the one coming, if he is a boy, I go call him Motilal: if she is a girl I go call she Kamala.'
>
> Admiration for the Nehru family couldn't go much farther. (74)

Her hypocrisy reveals in her showing off her wealth and concealing the poor educational background of her husband to show herself as a modern. She is the representative of the Trinidadians who deceive their culture and social ethos by following the western way of life:

> Soomintra jangled her gold bracelets and at the same time coughed, howled, but didn't spit—another mannerism of wealth, Leela recognized. Jawaharlal father start reading the other day too. He always say that if he had the time he would do some writing, but with all the coming and going in the shop he ain't really have the time, poor man. I don't suppose Ganesh so busy, eh? (75)

Beharry has also fascination for western modernity even more than Ganesh. Their appreciation for Basdeo's printing machine reveals their indifference to anything Trinidadian:

> You think they have that—sort of type in Trinidad. All they have here is one sort of mash-up type, ugly as hell.
>
> 'But this boy, this man I was telling you about, Basdeo, he have a new printing machine. It like a big typewriter: ...'It does just show you how backward this Trinidad is. When you look at those American magazines; you don't wish people in Trinidad could print like that?' (77-78)

When the little book of Ganesh, *101 Questions on Hinduism*, was published, it brought a lot of reputation and love for him from his wife and relatives but the book did not have wide circulation in the market. Ganesh blamed the Trinidadians for their inability to appreciate a quality work. Harveen Sachdeva Mann posits:

> Occasionally the narrator shows Ganesh to damn himself. When he becomes an author, Ganesh, who had brought books for their size, complains that people 'want a book

> that looks big. Once it looks big they think it good'. In exposing the publics' illiteracy, he unwillingly reveals his own hypocrisy and pretentiousness of his status as scholar. (*MFS* 1984: 475)

Ganesh seems to hang between two cultures—Indian and Western. But in fact Indian culture is a kind of recourse to him to cover his failures. When he fails as a writer, at the suggestion of the Great Belcher, he again plunges in mystic business of masseur. To have the real looking of mystic masseur he wears dhoti-kurta but it doesn't have any religious implication because he doesn't like Indian dress. Beharry comments on his dress: "Nobody would believe now that you did go to the Christian college in Port of Spain. Man, you look like a pukka Brahmin" (*Mystic* 13). The Negro family, his clients come on the appointed time. The following passage reveals how Ganesh cheats innocent people:

> Shortly after twelve the boy, his mother and father arrived, in the same taxi as before. Ganesh, dressed once more in his Hindu garments welcomed them in Hindi and Leela interpreted as arranged. They took off their shoes in the verandah and Ganesh led them all to the darkened bedroom, aromatic with camphor and incense, and lit only by the candle below the picture of Lakshmi on her lotus. Other pictures were barely visible in the semi-darkness: a stabbed and bleeding heart, a putative likeness of Christ, two or three crosses, and other designs of dubious significance. (122)

By curing the boy successfully, he becomes the most successful masseur in Trinidad superseding all other masseurs. With the prosperity of his business Leela like Soomintra, starts displaying her wealth. Even the change also comes in the behavior of Ganesh. Such changed behavior creates a distance between him and Beharry's family. Beharry's wife says: "Suraj Poopa, you ain't listening to me. Every Sunday morning bright and early you jump out of your bed and running over to kiss the man foot as though he is some Lord Lallo" (131). Ram Logan, the father-in-law of Ganesh, who had grudge against Ganesh, now starts taking the advantage of the reputation of Ganesh.

He hires taxis at high rates for the patients, though later he is checked by Ganesh. Ganesh also gets a temple built for himself by an Indian architect from British Guiana but it does not have any religious or cultural implications. In fact, it is meant to enhance his mystic profession and reputation. This indicates the opportunistic attitude of Trinidadians. After having riches and prosperity, Leela behaves like a colonial master: she starts imitating western manners and style. She tells Suraj Momma: "This house I are building, I doesn't want it to come like any erther Indian house. I wants it to have good furnitures and I wants everything to remain prutty prutty. I are thinking about getting a refrigerator and a few other things like that" (143). The following passage reveals the two aspects of Ganesh's character:

> He didn't forget the smaller things. From an Indian dealer in San Fernando he bought two sepia reproductions of Indian drawings. One represented an amorous scene: in the other God had come down to earth to talk to a sage. Leela didn't like the first drawing. 'It are not going to hang in my drawing-room.'
>
> 'You have a bad mind, girl.' Under the amorous drawing he wrote, will you come to me like this? And under the other, or like this? (145)

Bruce King remarks:

> But there are the resulting incongruities as an unsuccessful Hindu masseur becomes, through the study of modern psychology, a rich successful medicine man for the black Trinidadian and then a leading national politician who is eventually knighted by the British. (1993: 29)

Ganesh cheats the innocent and uneducated natives very easily. The numbers of books are his weapons. He plays with the emotion of the people by impressing them with the numbers of books in his shelf. Though his preaching is supposed to be spiritual, it seems that his behavior is self-contradictory. He himself is ambitious; but he instructs people to shun desires:

> He spoke about the good life, about happiness and how to get it. He borrowed from Buddhism and other religions and didn't hesitate to say so.... He spoke

> in Hindi but the books he showed in this way were in English, and people were awed by this display of learning. His main point was that desire was source of misery and therefore desire ought to be suppressed.... At other times he said that happiness was only possible if you cleared your mind of desire.... (*Mystic* 149-50)

In Trinidad, politics is a vehicle of the natives to be a part of a larger society. But it is not used in a proper way. It becomes the means of personal gain and advancement. Social justice, cultural identity and independence are kept aside. Democracy becomes a plaything in the hands of a few selfish leaders like Ganesh and Narayan. Bruce King therefore comments:

> British political culture is seen as absurd in Trinidad when at the time, 1946, there was no strong sense of nationhood and a common past, little education, little political discussion, no political ideals or politics. Ganesh is an Indian version of Man-man, the unemployed, apparently untalented, marginal man who finds a career and employment first in religion and then as a leader of the people. (1993: 30)

Ganesh's clash with Narayan for getting thirty thousand rupees granted by Indian government is not for any religious cause. He has his motive of misappropriating the fund granted for the spread of Hindu religion in Trinidad. Bruce King posits: "...religion, ethnic organizations and politics offer for personal advancement. This is a marooned, impoverished, disorganized, neglected colonial society which has been given a gift of elections" (1993: 30). However the conflict between the two proves to be destructive for Hinduism in Trinidad. The Hindus are divided into political parties—Hindu Association led by Narayan and Hindu League led by Ganesh. Though Ganesh wins, their conflict results in some kind of indifference towards Hinduism by others who had earlier strong faith in it:

> The bearded Negro stood up and made a long speech. He said that he had been attracted to Hinduism because he liked Indians; but the corruption he had seen that day was entirely repugnant to him. It had, as a matter of

> fact, decided him to join the Muslims, and the Hindus had better look out when he was a Muslims. (*Mystic* 183)

The ultimate ambition of Ganesh is to enjoy the privileges like colonial masters. In this context Manjit Inder Singh comments:

> The political fraud and metropolitan mimicry is a simpler theme, compared with the life and times of the master-trickster Ganesh Ramsumair in *The Mystic Masseur*. Yet, Naipaul traces another facet of the destitution and derivativeness of Trinidad society to survive, for Ganesh, the successful mystic turned politician is an illustration of the scandalous ways to ascend the ladder in the colonized outpost. (1998b: 98)

A week before the polling of M.L.C. Ganesh organized a recitation of *Bhagwat,* a seven-day prayer meeting. Leela's comment regarding the nature of natives towards religion is noteworthy: "Is easy for you, just sitting down and reciting prayers and thing to the people. But they don't come to *Bhagwat* just for prayers; I can tell you they come for the free food" (*Mystic* 191). It exposes that the Trinidadians do not have a deep sense of involvement and sincerity in religious matters. On the last day of *Bhagwat* while introducing Indarsingh to the audience, Ganesh highlights his European education and praises his English though for the last seven days he had been organizing a prayer meeting related to his own culture:

> I got to talk English to introduce this man to you, because I don't think he could talk any Hindi. But I think all of all you go agree with me that he does talk English like a pukka Englishman. That is because he have a foreign education and he only *just* come back to try and help out the poor Trinidad people. Ladies and gentlemen—Mr. Indarsing, Bachelor of Arts of Oxford University London, England. (192)

Both Leela and Ganesh are living a very unreal life. Their aspirations and ambitions have put them in a situation of uncertainty and instability. They are torn between two cultures.

On the one hand, they want to be modern in European sense and on the other hand they also wish to retain their own cultural identity. When the members of the new Legislative Council and their wives are invited to dinner at Government House, Leela does not go though she has always an inclination towards European manners: "Leela was shy but she made out that she couldn't bear the thought of eating off other people's plates. "It are like going to a restaurant. You don't know what the foods are and you don't know who cook it" (194). Though Ganesh attends the dinner party, his awkwardness shows the cultural confusion: "The meal was torture to Ganesh. He felt alien and uncomfortable. He grew sulkier and sulkier and refused all the courses. He felt as if he were a boy again, going to the Queen's Royal College for the first time" (197). The humiliation at Governor's dinner forces him to leave rural Fuente Grove for urban, Port of Spain. Chandra B. Joshi comments:

> The move from Fuentes Grove to Port of Spain is a wrench too and Ganesh cries out: "I wish the whole thing did never happen".... It is not only leaving Fuente Grove that is distressing Ganesh. He knows that he is leaving behind something of his past forever. (1994: 118)

Though he becomes an M.L.C., very soon he becomes a puppet in the hands of the government led by whites. Second time, even after losing the election he is made M.B.E. because of his loyalties to the ruling government. He is sent to England when the narrator meets him. The narrator is amazed at the new "look" of Ganesh:

> 'Pundit Ganesh!' I cried, running towards him, 'Pundit Ganesh Ramsumair!'
> 'G. Ramsay Muir,' he said coldly. (*Mystic* 208)

This word "coldly" suggests a sense of loss in Ganesh as he has no passion or involvement. Chandra B. Joshi rightly argues:

> In that "coldly" is conveyed all the loss involved in that transformation. Through all the stages of his career Ganesh had never really lost the reader's sympathy—because he was shown as retraining always a certain

> warm humanity. Now, with that one word "coldly" that sympathy seems to be withdrawn. (1994: 119)

Bruce King's critique on the novel *The Mystic Masseur* and its protagonist is noteworthy:

> The life of Pt. Ganesh in *The Mystic Masseur* can be seen as a humorous success story during a time of social & political change, but it also illustrates a rapid deterioration of Hindu culture which, historically, parallels the movements towards self-Govt. in the colony. If Pt. Ganesh is a colorful figure he is without culture or moral standards. He unashamedly surrounds himself with symbols from many religions when he seeks business as a faith healer, he appeals to Hindu Nationalism, however, to win an election. After a period as a radical fire-brand he becomes a supporter of the colonial government and receives a knighthood. (1980: 102-03)

3.2. Failure of Democracy: Racism and Ethnicity

The Suffrage of Elvira presents the theme of election in Trinidad. It deals with the second general election in the village of Elvira which is remote to the outside world. It explores the possibility of democracy and political awakening among the natives in a world which is multiracial, multi-religious, and multiethnic. Like all other third-world nations, the political forms and social institutions of Trinidad "...were imitated rather than created, borrowed rather than relevant, reflecting the forms existing in the particular metropolitan country from which they were derived" (Williams 1970: 501). The very beginning of the novel, in the prologue, anticipates the mimicry of democracy in a newly decolonized nation. Harbans, who is contesting for M.L.C., has to bargain for votes of the people. Such a step is undemocratic to bring in a fair democracy in the country:

> He (Harbans) had done all his bargaining for the election; the political correspondents said he had as good as won already. This afternoon he was going to offer himself formally to Baksh and Chittaranjan, the

> powers of Elvira. The bargains had only to be formally sealed. (*Suffrage* 10-11)

Baksh and Chittaranjan are dominant in the society. They are the agents of power thereby suggesting still a colonial situation in a newly independent country. In such a situation Harbans purchases votes from different communities. Since Baksh and Chittaranjan are the leaders of Muslim and Hindu communities respectively, Harbans has some secret deals with them. When Harbans meets Baksh, he is puzzled to understand as to how a man like Baksh could be the leader of Muslims:

> It was a puzzle: how Baksh came to be the Muslim leader. He wasn't a good Muslim. He didn't know all the injunctions of the Prophet and those he did know he broke. For instance he was a great drinker; ...He had none of the dignity of the leader. He was a big talker; in Elvira they called him "the mouther". (12)

According to Harbans another Muslim, Haq, should have been the leader of Muslims but he could not become because he was poor. As Harbans puts it: "...though the position should have gone in all fairness to Haq.... Haq was orthodox, or so he led people to believe, but Haq was poor" (12-13). Baksh is mentally colonized and lacks the spirit of nationalism as his statement makes it clear:

> 'Only', he used to say, 'they just ain't have the sort of materials I want for my house. This Trinidad backwards to hell, you hear.' He kept the designs of California-style houses from American magazines to show the sort of house he wanted. (13)

Baksh is the representative of Muslim vote bank, and he might support anyone, either Harbans or Preacher, depending on the money he gets. As the elections are nearer, Baksh is well aware of his position and importance. When Harbans comes to him, he does not pay any attention to him: "Foam kept on tacking. Baksh made more marks on his cloth. Two months, one month ago, they would have jumped up as soon as they saw him (Harbans) coming" (15). At last the bargain is settled. Foam would campaign for Harbans for seventy-five dollars a month:

> Baksh said, "I promise you the boy going to work night and day for you. And the Muslim leader kissed his crossed index fingers.
>
> 'Seventy dollars a month.'
>
> 'All right, boss.'
>
> Foam said, 'Eh, I could talk for myself, you hear. Seventy-five.' (20)

Baksh has not only aspirations for a house of California-style, but his whole family has a liking for western fashions. Mrs Baksh doesn't wear her Muslim dress but western knee length skirt: "Harbans thought there was a little of her husband's recklessness about her as well. Perhaps this was because of her modern skirt, the hem of which fell only just below the knee" (20). Even Baksh has chosen alternate Christian and Muslim names for his children: "Baksh boys: Eqbal, Herbert, Rafiq and Charles. (It was a concession the Bakshes made to their environment: they chose alternate Christian and Muslim names for their children)" (21). After the negotiation with Baksh, Harbans along with Foam moves to Chittaranjan to have a bargain for Hindu votes. The bargain with Chittaranjan is settled on the condition that Harbans would marry his son with Chittaranjan's daughter Nelly:

> 'Daughter?' Harbans asked. As though he didn't know about Nalini, little Nelly; as though all Elvira didn't know that Chittaranjan wanted Nelly married to Harbans's son, that this was the bargain to be settled that afternoon. (30)

In most of the Trinidadian novels, the protagonists do not plunge into politics with an interest to serve people. It is just by means of money power and opportunity that they try their hands in politics. Harbans is not at all aware of Elvira, the people and their problems: "'Foam,' Harbans said, 'is a good thing I have a campaign manager like you. I only know about Elvira roads. I ain't know about the people'" (28). But as his political journey proceeds further, he realizes that society is more hostile to him rather than supportive. Foam is well aware of the political reality, and his awareness also exposes that the upcoming generation is in the process of being mature in politics. Foam summarizes well the political situation of Trinidad:

> 'You shy, Mr. Harbans,' Foam said. 'I know how it is. But you going to get use to this waving. Ten to one, before this election over, we going to see you waving and shouting to everybody, even to people who ain't going to vote for you.'

Harbans shook his head sadly.

Foam settled into the angle of the seat and the door. 'Way I see it is this. In Trinidad this democracy is a brand new thing. We is still creeping. We is a creeping nation.' He dropped his voice solemnly: 'I respect people like you, you know, Mr. Harbans, doing this thing for the first time'. (25-26)

Shashi Kamra comments on this mimicry:

> The younger generation is as entrapped as their elders but they are aware of it and wish to get away from it. As individuals they might escape their physical and economic deprivation. But the lack of educational opportunities or the mimic nature of those available has entrapped them in repetitive patterns of behavior though the elections have brought the promises of a wider world. (69-70)

Though the novel is about political awakening and rise of democracy, the excitement and enthusiasm of the people of the country is not for democracy but for imitation of European systems and institutions. The fascination for western superficialities is seen in the use of instruments during the campaign. Since the people are mostly orthodox and superstitious, the use of western instrument turns out to be mere western mimicry. And this mimicry proves to be a mockery of Democracy as Mr Baksh puts it: "I been telling him, Teach, a hundred times if I tell him one time, that this election begin sweet sweet for everybody, but the same sweetness going to turn sour in the end" (*Suffrage*, 125). This is also anticipated by other characters. Teacher Francis thinks: "This new constitution is a trick, Miss Chittaranjan. Just another British trick to demoralize the people... 'No point in voting. People in Elvira don't know the value of their vote'....

Elvira was a good friendly place before this universal suffrage nonsense" (89-90). Dhaniram says, "This democracy is a damn tinny thing." Even Harbans accepts "This democracy is a strange thing. It does make the great poor and the poor great" (164). At last the novel concludes with the illustration of democracy only as a loss:

> So, Harbans won the election and the insurance company lost a Jaguar. Chittaranjan lost a son-in-law and Dhaniram lost a daughter-in-law. Elvira lost Lorkhoor and Lorkhoor won a reputation. Elvira lost Mr. Cuffy. And Preacher lost his deposit. (220)

However, mimicking the west is not only restricted to political arena; it is also reflected in social life. Harveen Sachdeva Mann observes:

> Nalini Chittaranjan becomes 'Nelly' and Surajpat Harbans becomes 'pat' Harbans. The Indians own allegiance not to one but to three countries—Trinidad, England and India—as do those immigrants from Africa Portugal, Spain, and China, their names emphasizing ethnic confusion yet the same time indicating assimilation in to a national identity. The Baksh children have alternate Muslim & Christian names—Iqbal and Herbert, Rafiq and Charles, Zilla and Carol—as 'a concession...to their environment'. (*MFS* 1984: 480)

There are persons who are living a hybrid cultural life. Although Dhaniram is a Hindu pundit, he is proud of his Christian education:

> Pundit Dhaniram had been educated at one of the Presbyterian schools of the Canadian Mission where he had been taught hymns and other Christian things. He cherished the training. 'It make me see both sides,' he used to say; and even now, although he was a Hindu priest, he often found himself humming hymns like 'Jesus loves me, yes I know'. He slapped his thigh and exclaimed, 'Armageddon!' (*Suffrage* 50)

The social welfare activities, which should be the core of democracy, are used in Elvira only as tools for securing votes. As Pundit Dhaniram says:

> It go take some money. But not much. Here in Elvira the campaign committee must be a sort of social welfare committee. Supposing one of those Negroes fall sick. *We* go to them. *We* go take them to doctor in a taxi. *We* go pay for their medicine. (53)

The politicians even think of the poor Negroes to be dead so that they may help in their burial ceremony and win their sympathy and votes. The novel presents people who are selfish, having no definite ideals. They are rather playing with democracy for self-interest. Baksh tells Harbans that if he does not purchase a van and a loudspeaker, he may not get the Muslim votes: "you ain't got no Muslim vote" (17). Harichand says: "...if you want my vote, you want my printery" (77). A large population of Elvira does not know how to make an "X" on their ballot papers as they are uneducated and ignorant. Superstition prevails not only among simple ignorant villagers but it also affects people like Harbans who are well educated:

> He was nearly seized with another fit of pessimism.... Then he thought of the sign he had had; the white women and the stalled engine, the black bitch and stalled engine. He had seen what the first meant. The women had stalled him in Cordoba.
>
> But the dog. What about the dog? Where was that going to stall him? (55)

Though the population of Elvira is divided in the name of religion during the electioneering for bargain of votes, the people of different cultures and races live a culturally mix-up life in Elvira:

> Things were crazily mixed up in Elvira. Everybody, Hindus, Muslims and Christians, owned Bible; the Hindus and Muslims looking on it, if anything, with greater awe. Hindus and Muslims celebrated Christmas and Easter. The Spaniards and some of the Negroes celebrated the Hindu festival of lights.... Everybody

> celebrated the Muslim festival of Hosein. In fact, when Elvira was done with religious festivals, there were few straight days left. (69)

Like other Trinidadian novels, *The Suffrage of Elvira* reinforces lack of moral codes in the society. "The only character who has a complete ethical system, who lives by traditional values, is Chittaranjan, and he is one of the few losers connected with the election" (King 1993: 34). Although Nelly is already engaged, she still spends nights with Foam:

> Nelly Chittaranjan hadn't been thinking when she agreed to meet Foam that evening and take the dog.... She didn't believe the dog existed at all. But the thought of meeting a boy at night in a lonely lane had kept her excited all afternoon. She had never walked out with any boy: it was wrong; now that she was practically engaged, it was more than wrong. (88)

Lorkhoor doesn't care for women and disapproves of the marriage as an institution, but during nights he visits a woman in his van: "He said he didn't care for women that marriage was unnatural, and here he was driving out Elvira at night with a woman who wasn't anxious to be seen" (91). Ultimately the daughter-in-law of pundit Dhaniram runs away with Lorkhoor, taking away all clothes and jewellery, "The *doolahin* gone, Goldsmith. She run away with Lorkhoor" (187). But the elopement of *doolahin* (The daughter-in-law of Dhaniram) may be considered as a step of liberating herself from the ruthless patriarchal domain of pundit Dhaniram. In fact she symbolizes the marginalized condition of women in the society. Her husband is living away from her in England, and here in Elvira, she is just like a servant of Dhaniram; she doesn't have any identity of her own.

Elvira is a place which is full of differences of religion, race or culture but in some context we find cohesion among its inhabitants. As Shashi Kamra puts it rightly:

> Elvira, like Miguel Street, has a public personality. Its striking feature is the cohesiveness of its inhabitants in spite of the conflict of race, religion and personal

> interests. They live very much in the present propelled by immediate needs. They can put aside their differences to unite in the demand for cases of whiskey for the whole community or for a religious thanksgiving ceremony for the victory of Harbans: they can recognize justice when they see it and can speak as one voice in their claim for fair play. (65)

There are different kinds of representatives, representing Elvira. The first category of people like Lorkhoor, Doolahin, Teacher Francis and Nelly has the feeling of alienation and deprivation by staying in Elvira. They wish to go away from Elvira. Secondly people like Harbans and Chittaranjan, who are entrapped in Elvira, can't get away from there even if they wish. For example, Harbans has spent so much money to win the election that he can't leave it though he wishes to get away:

> When Harbans had left Elvira and was in Country Caroni, he stopped the lorry and shook his fist at the dark countryside behind him.
>
> 'Elvira!' he shouted. 'You is a bitch! A bitch! A bitch.' (*Suffrage* 154)

Although Chittaranjan knows that there is less chance of his daughter getting married to Harbans's son, yet he tries for it. He is not much worried at the loss of his money because his failure in a way is one of the tools to establish democracy in Elvira. There are also people who are instrumental in the success of democracy in Elvira. Nelly, Chittaranjan, Foam and Doolahin may be mentioned in this context. In fact these characters facilitate the hope for democracy in Elvira. Chittaranjan is fully democratized during the electioneering on behalf of Harbans. Nelly is granted the permission to go to England for her further studies. The long-standing enmity between Chittaranjan and Ram Logan diminishes with mutual understanding. Though Harbans is hopeless after the election, we find in Foam, an upcoming leader of Elvira. Bhat makes perceptive remarks:

> The novel is superb in its exposition of the mechanism of the functioning of the democratic process and its initial filtering down to the common people. The machinery of

> election is educative and brings out not only the dormant differences but also a temporarily forged unity created by a common involvement in the election. (2000: 71-72)

The coming of democracy has also unveiled so many realities and the inhabitants are disillusioned. When Harbans is asked about the next election he says, "Next election? This is the first and last election I fighting in Elvira" (*Suffrage* 177). When Harbans returns to Elvira first time (and perhaps last time after winning the election, the people of Elvira are hurt to find an entirely new Harbans:

> He wasn't the candidate they knew. Gone was the informality of dress, the loose trousers.... Harbans didn't wave. He looked preoccupied, kept his eyes on the ground....
>
> The people of Elvira were hurt.
>
> He didn't look at anybody, didn't look at anybody. He made his way silently through the silent crowd....
>
> They didn't like it at all. (*Suffrage* 207-08)

Chittaranjan's expectations are totally shattered when he goes to see Harbans in Port of Spain.

> And Chittaranjan. But he had lost. He sent many messages to Harbans but got no reply. At last he went to see Harbans in Port of Spain; but Harbans kept him waiting so long in the veranda and greeted him so coldly, he couldn't bring himself to ask about the marriage.... Harbans said... 'But we can't let our children marry people who do run about late at night with Muslim boys.' Chittaranjan accepted the justice of the argument. And that was that. (219)

The failure of political career of the protagonists and unsuccessful democracy in the novels of Naipaul emphasize the fact that colonial institutions could not be utilized by the newly decolonized countries as people are not well-equipped with intellectuality to handle them. This fact has been well elaborated by Shashi Kamra:

> The protagonists of these novels realize the self only through political failure. Such failure for island politicians becomes not only the 'point of return' but is also a dead end. The trap manufactured out of the colonial condition is strengthened by the colonizer's inability to perceive its structure as it inheres in his personality and environment....
>
> The political despair of the protagonist as experienced absurdity provides the narrator with an entry into the very particular Trinidadian sensibility. Through it alone can he hope to make the reader aware of the essential simplicity and literalness of a colonized mind without a concrete past or a promising future, product of a system which recognizes only its market value living out an isolated fantasy of fulfillment which rivals the amorphous subjective trapped existence of Beckett's protagonists—unable to live or die. (55-56)

3.3. Imperial/Post-imperial Disorder and Human Predicament

A House for Mr. Biswas is Naipaul's first phenomenal novel, a great classic of New English Literature. It foregrounds the previously devalued colonized culture and its complexities. It has been set in Trinidad around the time of World War II. It reveals the colonial situation of Trinidad quite comprehensively. Mohun Biswas, the protagonist of the novel, revolts against the imperial paradigm of Tulsis, their conservative Hindu ideas and ideology. He alone fights against the oppressions of the Tulsis. He wants to liberate himself from the narrow circle of ideologies of rotten, obsolete Hindu cultural system and wishes to assert his own identity. Bruce King posits:

> Biswas' story is both representative of the history of the Trinidadian East Indian and a special case. The history of the Trinidadian Asian Indian could be put together from aspects of his life and the lives of those to whom he was related by birth and marriage. Yet no one single character in the novel can be said to be typical of the Trinidadian Indian. (1993: 41)

Naipaul presents in Biswas, a rebel. In the first part of the novel, there is focus on the futility of his rebellion. Such rebellion is of no use for those who are almost slaves, and without any means of self-support. Under such circumstances, Biswas can only show his resentment for them upon whom he is dependent. On the other hand, Shama, his wife, is closely attached to the Tulsi family. She moulds herself in conformity with the limitations of the Tulsis. Hanuman House represents a feudal/colonial set-up where those who conform to its rules and regulations are given some kind of privilege. For example, Hari, one of the Tulsi sons-in-law becomes a family priest. However except the mother and the two sons, everyone is treated as colonized, dependent and slave. Biswas is a marginalized man, detached from society at an early age. Fate makes him orphan in the very childhood. His actions are motivated by the confrontation between his sense of freedom and sense of insecurity. Society plays the role of a malignant fate against his life. He doesn't have any grudge against social ideologies. He abides by every rule and regulation of the society; his initial freedom makes him unfit to live in harmony with society which demands compromise. He demands a certain sense of security from the society which the society fails to provide.

Alienation foregrounds itself even in the narrative technique. There is a distance between the relationship of the hero and the narrator. The narrator's addressing to Mohun Biswas as Mr Biswas brings out his distance from the protagonist. Though the narrator shows a kind of sympathy for Mr Biswas, both the narrator and the protagonist are the outsiders to the society in which Mr Biswas lives and the society the narrator portrays. Mr Biswas is destined to be an outsider. During a religious ceremony at Tara's house he even felt this pinch:

> In Tara's house he was respected as a Brahmin and pampered: yet as soon as the ceremony was over and he had taken his gift of money and cloth and left, he became once more only a laborer's child-father's occupation: laborer was the entry in the birth certificate F.Z. Ghany had sent-living with a penniless mother in one room of a mud hut. And throughout life his position

> was like that. As one of the Tulsi sons-in-law and as a journalist he found himself among people with money and sometimes with graces; with them his manner was unforcedly easy and he could summon up luxurious instincts: but always, at the end, he returned to his crowded, shabby room. (House 47-48)

Lack of enough opportunities in his society makes him move towards sign-painting which is his hobby as well as casual occupation. Here again fate determines his future sending him to Hanuman House where he goes with a sense of security but becomes a slave: "The world was too small, the Tulsi family too large. He felt trapped" (92). As a matter of fact, his struggle starts from this very stage. When he attempts to set up his own home with Shama, he realizes his poverty and economic dependence on the Tulsis. Under the domineering nature of Mrs Tulsi, his dream of having an independent home remains only a day-dream. But his initial sense of security and freedom enable him to stand and rebel against such a colonial situation of Hanuman House:

> The organization of the Tulsi house was simple. The daughters and their children swept and washed and cooked and served in the store. The husbands, under Seth's supervision, worked on the Tulsi land, looked after the Tulsi animals, and served in the store. In the return they were given food, shelter and a little money; their children were looked after; and they were treated with respect by people outside because they were connected with the Tulsi family. Their names were forgotten; they became Tulsi. There were daughters who had, in the Tulsi marriage Lottery, drawn husbands with money and position: ...formed no part of the Tulsi organization.... Mr Biswas had no money or position. He was expected to become a Tulsi. At once he rebelled. (98-99)

Very soon Mr Biswas realizes that this place doesn't suit his taste and temperament. His love-marriage also does not prove to be a happy one. He always receives taunts that seriously destabilize his state of mind. He finds himself trapped in the grip of the Tulsi family. He therefore wants to liberate himself. His dream of a home is not just to own a house; it is an aspiration for stability and permanence in his life, an escape from the confinement of the Tulsi set-up. It is an attempt of Biswas to assert his identity. Maureen Warner Lewis observes:

> Into this apparent monolith of conversions, prejudices and conservatism, then Mr Biswas barges. He openly disapproved of many of the Tulsi practices and policies. He even challenges their religious belief and associates with Hindus of another set with whom the Tulsis disagree...the religious ambiguity and syncretism and in some case, even neglect of traditional religion, is one of the earliest aspects of cultural confrontation with which Naipaul deals in his novel. And he progressively shows sometimes subtle, sometimes obvious, in which the western oriented Creole culture of Trinidad corrodes Hindu traditional customs and beliefs, and the shifting of attitudes and psychological bewilderment this produces. (1977: 87)

Though Mr Biswas enjoys freedom, it is just like those newly independent colonies which are deprived of all economic and intellectual resources. His freedom also lacks the material, emotional and intellectual resources for which he is compelled to depend on the Tulsis. Hanuman House is just like a slave house. Gordon Rohlehr rightly remarks:

> Hanuman House reveals itself not as a coherent reconstruction of the clan, but as a slave society, erected by Mrs Tulsi and Seth who need workers to help rebuild their tottering empire. They therefore exploit the homelessness and poverty of their fellow Hindus and reconstruct a mockery of the clan which functions only because they have so completely grasped the psychology of a slave system. (Quoted in Hamner 87)

In this house men serve two functions: husbands for Tulsi daughters as well as labourers for the Tulsi's estates. The sons-in-law of the Tulsi house are meant for working on the Tulsi land, and looking after the animals. But Mr Biswas does not fall in the line, and hence suffers. The novel reveals a colonial situation in which the colonizer (Mrs Tulsi) demands service in exchange for food and security; and "Mr Biswas's personal battle with the stronghold of the Tulsi household, a symbol of the colonial Manichean world, is a quest for existential freedom and the struggle for personality. (Singh 1998a: 126)

The condition of women in the Hanuman House is also not a happy one. They lead a miserable and marginalized life. They are just used like machines to maintain the house. They are subjected to the monotonous life of the house. It is only on the occasion of funeral or marriages that they get relieved from the tedious life of the house. The novel describes a world of loneliness and homelessness in a dry, sterile landscape. With such a background, the character of Mr Biswas is seen struggling for stability in his life. Mr Biswas's desire for a house symbolizes his desire for permanence, stability and self-identity in life. But as long as the Tulsis support him in his struggle for his stability, all his efforts end in fiasco because the freedom they offer him is in consonance with his being a shopkeeper at the Chase and a sub-overseer of the Greenvale sugar estate but his aspiration for literary activities is not the part of the liberty they provide. He realizes the futility of this freedom:

> In all Mr Biswas lived for six years at the Chase, years so squashed by their own boredom and futility that at the end they could be comprehended in one glance. But he had aged....

Though he never ceased to feel that some nobler purpose awaited him, even in this limiting society, he gave up reading Samuel Smiles.... But now, though his philosophical books gave him solace he could never lose the feeling that they were irrelevant to his situation. The books had to be put down....

> And at least once a week he thought of leaving the shop, leaving Shama, leaving the children, and taking that road. (188-89)

Mr Biswas's marriage into the Tulsi family with Shama derails his progress as an individual. The Tulsis have created such a powerful and dominating structure that there is no scope for the progress of a freedom loving individual. Santosh Chakrabarti observes:

> The Tulsi house is the microcosm of an authoritarian Hindu world with an efficient hierarchy of control. The Tulsi society is actually founded on a system of classic slavery: food and security are bartered with independence. ...Any demonstration of individualism is treated with exemplary ruthlessness. (Ray 47-48)

Mr Biswas doesn't simply accept the oppressive systems imposed on the colonized periphery of the Tulsi world but rebels against them who torture him: "Biswas may be colonized in the physical, economic and political sense, but his emotional urge for freedom, his sensibility to humiliation and slavery are signs of a temperament that bristles with rebellious subversion" (Singh 1998b: 114). Mr Biswas is trapped in the Tulsi family, a "totalitarian organization". But he is the first to revolt against this feudal-capitalist hierarchy and asserts his individual identity. Mr Biswas's desire to own a house is a pre-requisite for asserting his identity. That is why "the 'House' in this novel is a symbol not for 'rootedness' but for freedom—freedom from slavery and oppression" (Das 1995: 103). The Tulsi House presents the neo-colonial situation in the newly independent colonies. After the political independence of Trinidad, the local masters adopt the skills of the colonial rulers to satisfy their own petty ends. Even after the independence, Trinidad is an impoverished, disorganized country where African and Indian descents have been brought to improve the conditions of their lives but without being provided with opportunities and resources. Naipaul criticizes colonialism and reveals the effect of colonization after decolonization of the colonies. He declares that assertion of local culture and complaining against victimization cannot alone provide any redemption from the problems left by history. Bruce King makes perceptive comments in this context:

> Trinidad in *A House for Mr Biswas* lacks the resources required for authentic independence. As Biswas discovers when he attempts to find employment or build

> his house, freedom can be dangerous, humiliating and self defeating. Biswas's situation is that of the colony, his own attempts at independence are limited by the condition of the society into which he is born; frustrated self-assertion turns into self-destructive rage, the tempest that temporarily disorders Biswas's mind. (1993: 46)

A House for Mr Biswas highlights the way man is pressurized by complex forces that make his escape from the past impossible. According to Eric Erikson society and history are the important factors in the development of an individual. Such psycho-analysis can account for Mr Biswas's mental and spiritual colonization and the cause of his rebellion. Such study can give a proper focus on the theme of slavery in the novel. Though Mr Biswas is free from actual slavery unlike his ancestors, he still carries the burden of their attitude and sensibilities. Mr Biswas's personal battle with the stronghold of the Tulsi-household symbolizes the quest for a place in the hostile universe.

The autobiographical elements of the novel synthesize Naipaul's quest as a writer, his displaced position and the fragmented history of West-Indies. When Mr Biswas dreams about his own house in the prologue of the novel, it reveals the historical wound which his ancestors had suffered:

> How terrible it would have been, at this time to be without it, to have died among the Tulsis, amid the squalor of that large disintegrating and indifferent family; to have left Shama and the children among them in one room; worst, to have lived without even attempting to lay claim to one's portion of the earth; to have lived and died as one had been born, unnecessary and unaccommodated. (*House* 8)

Mr Biswas's house is not simply a four-walled shelter with a roof but it works as a metaphor which compensates all that he lacks in his life. It erodes his placelessness; it is a place of peace and freedom, a fortress against the evils of the outer world. It is a kind of declaration of freedom from the sense of slavery and oppression which he had inherited from his ancestors. It is a symbol of an identity, a place and respect to a slave.

A House for Mr Biswas can also be studied as the socio-cultural change of Trinidad around the Second World War and its social history. M.I. Singh thus remarks:

> "...the rebellion of Mr Biswas can be understood in cultural, psychological and economic sense. His symbolic position as a historical and cultural orphan is evident. He is an uprooted man; his assertions of the self, day dreaming, evasion of responsibility are the results of the plurality of his nowhereness. (1998a: 127)

The Hanuman House with its colonial fortress suggests the psychology of slavery. Mrs Tulsi, like the traditional white colonizers, presents herself as the protector of her subjects (her daughters and sons-in-law). Seth, the second-in-command represents the ruthless colonial power, the agent of exploitation. Thus they maintain the colonial ideology through both consent and coercion, a hegemonic tool according to Gramsci. In colonial period in Trinidad, the uneducated and unskilled labourers were exploited under the impression of egalitarianism to the underprivileged and if anyone tries to break this accepted ideological system, it was considered punishable. Mr Biswas's rebellion could be seen as the continuation of that struggle for a more balanced and feasible society in Trinidad. Though the Tulsi family provides Mr Biswas's protection and job, he rebels against them. But his rebellion is not unreasonable. In fact, the Tulsi family is a mimic world of colonialism. On the surface, the Tulsis have founded a very admirable reconstruction of the clan in the hostile conditions. It has its own schemes, law, order and rituals, and it also helps the men of their own community on the basis of merit. On the other hand, they take advantage of the poverty and homelessness of men like Biswas and others. It is not the consent but the economic deprivation which has brought different elements under one roof of Hanuman House. To survive under the rules and order of Hanuman House is just like accepting their slavery. In the beginning Mr Biswas is made to believe that he is a part of the Tulsi household. But later on he is insulted and told that he has intruded the clan at his own. This is the way of assertion in the colonial system in which the ideology is created so that the colonized must be obliged to benevolence and legitimacy of the colonizers. In this context Albert Memmi has made a remarkable comment:

> In order for the colonizer to be the complete master, it is not enough for him to be so in actual fact, but he must believe in its legitimacy. In order for that legitimacy to be complete it is not enough for the colonized to be a slave; he must also accept this role. (Quoted by Gordon Rohlehr in Hamner 1977: 88)

Another instance of oppression in the Tulsi house is the attempt to erode the individualism. Even the children and wives don't escape; they are beaten whenever they try to raise their voice. This was the way to neutralize any alteration in the given system: "Mr. Biswas's greatest sin and crime is to have tried to act as an individual. His malice, rebellion or the rhetoric of protest eventually becomes paralyzed and he retreats into his insulted weariness and shame like the physically lacerated slave" (Singh 1998a: 130). Biswas's dream of his own house is frustrated every time whether at Greenvale or Port of Spain (where he is partly owner of the house as he pays the rent for the house) or Shorthills. But Biswas's constant faith in him provides him the taste of success. He buys a tall square house in Sikkim Street on loan and moves into it. Though in the beginning the children and Shama start finding defects in it, gradually they accommodate in it. For the first time Mr Biswas finds self-fulfillment with his house. Not only Mr Biswas but also his family shares his happiness and satisfaction. The whole family for the first time, not only gathers under the same roof but this gathering also brings the fragmented loyalties of the each member of the family:

> Soon it seemed to the children that they had never lived anywhere but in the tall square house in Sikkim Street. From now their lives would be ordered, their memories coherent. The mind while it is sound is merciful. And rapidly the memories of Hanuman House, the Chase, Green Vale, Shorthills, the Tulsi House in Port of Spain would become jumbled, blurred; events would be telescoped, many forgotten. (*House* 614)

With the possession of his own house, Mr Biswas gets stability in his life and this stability also brings the favour of Shama who had been dependent on her mother till then. Now she starts sharing the economic burden of the house, and helps Mr Biswas instead of depending on the Hanuman House. This house has not been the day-dream of Mr Biswas; it is true to his expectations. We find the growth of the career of his children. He is able to send his children, Anand and Savi, to England for further studies. Though this house is not without any unusual occurrence, it brings the family members closer to one another. Mr Biswas gets the heart stroke, and is hospitalized in this very house; but this incident reveals the intensity of the love and care among family members. Kamala, Myna and Shama all face this situation and Mr Biswas recovers and resumes his work. His possession of the house not only brings peace and his family together but it also erases his sense of incapacity and dependency on the Tulsis. In this context Shashi Kamra remarks:

> His powers of imagination and observation now become the source of a full and whole life. His personality subsumes the house, the garden, the car and the furniture. But his pleasure in them is intensified by a sense of sharing them with his family. Each item has a personality which expresses itself in its history, recalled with pleasure. They are no longer mere possessions over which he gloats in miserly loneliness erecting them as barriers against his existential insecurity. This is the house in which he dies in peace and triumph. For he has provided adequate shelter for Shama and the children. (97)

Though in itself Biswas's victory is not of much importance, it is justified in relation to the gradual fragmentation of the Tulsi power. The Tulsi family starts disintegrating into smaller, independent units. A quarrel arises between Shekhar, the elder son of Tulsi and Seth who feels himself now marginalized as an outsider. He moves to a new house next to Hanuman House and opens a new bigger store. Some other sons-in-law also start dispossessing themselves from the loyalties of the Tulsi power. Even Shekhar moves to his in-law's family after his marriage to Dorothy, a daughter of a rich Christian. In fact all these changes stand as a precursor to a new order. And the root cause behind all these changes is Biswas's rebellion. M.I. Singh rightly observes:

> Finally the Tulsi autocracy crumbles in the face of larger social complexities which pave the way for a general rebellion. His struggle against the apparently indestructible system of brutality and humiliation affirms the universal nature of values he fights for by remaining within the system. This problem of losing identity and cultural moorings has been faced by all racial groups in Trinidad, while later, education assumed greater importance for personal success in a highly materialistic and competitive world. (Singh 1998a: 130)

Mr. Stone and the Knights Companion succeeds *The Middle Passage* and precedes *An Area of Darkness*. This novel is the outcome of the shock, disillusionment and alienation which Naipaul experienced during his first visit to India in 1962. It is not strange that the first and only book Naipaul wrote about English characters in an English setting was written in distant Srinagar in India. Naipaul posits: "You've got to get some sort of distance between yourself and your experience in order to use it well. I can only write about a place when I am away from it. The experience must be complete and I must be able to look back" (Mel Gussow, "Writer Without Roots", *The New York Times* Magazine, 26 Dec. 1976: 9). *Mr Stone* deals with the story of an old bachelor, Mr Stone, a librarian in a firm, called Excal. He is sixty-two, living alone in a quiet suburban London Street with an old maid, Miss Millington. Mr Stone is just three years away from his retirement, and he is disturbed to see a poster assuring people of the coming of spring. The return of the spring symbolizes his retirement and a sense of nearing death. It is due to this state of fear that he marries a widow, Mrs Springer. Even the marriage does not bring any solace to him. After a year when he goes on a honeymoon trip, he comes across a wretched, retired old man. The pathetic condition of the man moves him, and therefore he plans to start a scheme that could help the retired men of his firm to be in touch with each other after their retirement. The purpose is to help the needy physically as well as financially. The firm approves his scheme, and he is made the officer in-charge of a unit formed to implement the scheme. He also gets an assistant named Whymper, who suggests the name "Knights Companion" for the scheme. In the beginning, the scheme tastes much success but very soon, Mr. Stone is deeply disillusioned. He therefore finds himself in the same state of alienation and fear in which he has been in the beginning of the story.

The book is entirely different from his preceding Trinidadian novels as till now he was writing about the things he knew such as his roots and native land. He writes this book about English life as an outsider. In defense of its authenticity in the presentation of English life, V.S. Pritchett says: "The best novels come out of native ground. But where now-a-days is it? Outside of pockets which no longer have any interest, aren't we all uprooted? What is the ground? Is it a country, a race, a class, a culture? Is it now and for all of us anything more than the homeless English language" (105). *Mr Stone and the Knights Companion* can be studied in comparison with *A House for Mr Biswas* as Naipaul himself says: "...after *Mr. Biswas* I felt the need to react against this luxuriance and expansiveness, so instead I set out in *Mr Stone and the Knights Companion* to write a compressionist novel pared to the bone.... I determined to put in nothing inessential, however alluring..." (V.S. Naipaul, "Speaking of Writing", *The Times*, 2 January 1964: 11). Mr Stone has certain zeal, energy, restless curiosity but he does not possess a favourable society where he could use them. Like Biswas, he is an outsider in his society but it is he himself rejects his society because he has never felt the need of a society. He spends his spare time in gardening, and also with his fantasies:

> It was in the empty house, on these occasions of Miss Millington's absence, that he found himself prey to fancies which he knew to be grotesque but which he ceaselessly indulged. He thought of moving pavements: he saw himself, over-coated and with his briefcase, standing on his private moving strip and gliding along, while walkers on either side looked in amazement. He

> thought of canopied streets for winter, the pavements perhaps heated by that Roman system he had seen at Bath. He was able to fly. (226)

Mr Biswas's rootlessness is considerable as he is a displaced Indian in an alien and chaotic society, without having any place of his own. His search for a house is symbolic of exploration of his roots. But Mr Stone, in his ordered and established life, having a house for last twenty-four years, feels as restless as Mr Biswas. Mr Stone does not find solace anywhere. He feels a sense of futility and waste in his life. He doesn't feel at ease even with familiar sights. Miss Millington, who has served him for last twenty years, is not able to arouse any feeling in his heart for her. She strikes him as a woman "slowed down by age and by flesh which was bulky but not robust, was soon to die" (*Mr Stone* 236). In a way, the predicament of Mr Stone dismantles the notion of West as an ideal place among colonized countries or third-world countries. Chandra B. Joshi argues:

> The displaced colonials of the first four books had cherished a notion of England as the refuge from all the ills that beset their own deprived and barren lives. Mr. Stone exposes this as a hollow myth. Man in metropolitan London is as vulnerable, as susceptible to all the pains of living, as the residents of Miguel Street. (1994: 151)

The irony is that Mr Stone is unable to trace out the cause of his restlessness and fear which disturbs his life. Though he has created a reserved world for him, he apprehends that his world is being intruded:

> But this morning the familiarity of the scene did not soothe him. He felt only a faint unease, whose origin he couldn't place and which, persisting, gave him a twinge of alarm, for it seemed that all the ordered world was threatened. (*Mr Stone* 236)

Mr Stone's mood of despair heightens with his focus and categorization of his present restlessness. He observes his surroundings and the people around him from different point of view, different from what he earlier thought about them.

But all his thoughts move him to feel a sense of loss and death. The posters in "London underground train advertising spring tourism" seem to him of emphasizing the cold and dark winter. Even the jokes at the Tomlinson's Christmas party turn the atmosphere into a serious silence. He visits Olive but even his visit to Olive does not mitigate his uneasiness. It only suppresses his uneasiness for the time being. In such a state of depression and despair, he accepts any kind of diversion which may make him feel his former carefree life. That's why he accepts Mrs Springer's invitation to tea though he does not like the places like Earls court which is "a disreputable, overcrowded area" (243). While returning he also invites Mrs Springer home for tea. He is trying in many ways to break away from his habits which are obstructions in his happiness. Subsequently he gets married to Margaret Springer. But the marriage disillusions him afterwards. After marriage, he meets with new kind of fear and anxieties which intensify his old uneasiness. His marriage creates a distance from his colleagues in the office. The young girls no more tease him. The jokes of his colleagues remind him of his growing age and coming retirement. Even he thinks that the tree in the yard symbolizes his approaching old age:

> But beneath the apparent calm which marriage had once more brought to him, there grew a new appreciation of time. It was flying by. It was eating up his life.... Every ordered week reminded him of failure, of the uncreative years once so comfortingly stocked away in his mind. Every officeless Sunday sharpened his anxiety, making him long for Monday and the transient balm of the weekdays, false though he knew their fullness to be, in spite of the office diary he had begun to keep, tabulating appointments, things to be done, to flatter himself that he was busily and importantly occupied.
>
> The tree, changing, developing with the year, made its point every day. (263-64)

Mr Stone therefore represents the monotony and insecurity of English life especially of lower-middle class. It also deals with the Indian notion of fate and action. Bruce King therefore comments:

> ...it is infused with Indian fatalism and notions of activity as futile illusion, a view which it struggles against, and instead offers an existential alternative of life as intensity and a struggle against annihilation (1993: 56)

Mr Stone can be seen as another portrait of Biswas in England. But unlike Biswas, in spite of owning a house and pension, he is still very unhappy. Bruce King comments: "This is another portrait of the rebel, this time the insider who suddenly sees the void, experiences a sense of nothingness, turns a corner and feels a wind which changes his life" (1993: 56).

The novel portrays life in England after World War II. It presents the agonies of English men by presenting the miseries of a librarian who works for a firm; lives alone except for a housemaid; has a dingy house and a garden which he doesn't like. He has neighbors but he doesn't have any interaction with them; he is only obsessed with the neighbor's cat. Naipaul presents the dreary life of London. When Naipaul wrote this novel, it was the time, English writing turned inward from serious issues. It presented dull manners, morals and lives rather than the sophisticated ones. Mr Stone also reveals the existential drama in which one searches for self-definition. Bruce King comments:

> ...it comes to someone so old, near retirement—the prospect of retirement sets off the drama—is why we might not realize that Mr. Stone is a brother to Camus' rebel, although in the many references to Stone's solitude and loneliness, and in his lack of close relationships, we can see the alienation, the significant toneless voice, of Camus' Outsider. (1993: 59)

While writing *Mr Stone*, V.S. Naipaul might have had Biswas in his mind. Mr Stone is also a portrayal of Biswas in England. He reflects the life of V.S. Naipaul as a writer in England. Mr Stone's tensions, aspirations, achievements and expectations are identical to Biswas and Naipaul himself. Here Bruce King's comments are worth mentioning:

> Security, a homogeneous society, pension, cultural roots, a home is an attractive ideal, but the energies of life,

> the desire for stimulus, the need for change, the need to conquer, to active, for what hobbies termed glorification, even the need for new companionship, create the uprooted rebel, the artist, the modern individual, and put us in the existential situation of self-creation, a self-creation limited however by our circumstances and society. (1993: 61)

Stone gets married to Margaret to get a kind of solace; but when Margaret makes him realize his responsibility of a husband, he escapes. After marriage he has become a man of the world, the master and husband; but he is unable to discharge his roles, and therefore escapes from home, as well as from his office. But there is no chance of his escape:

> Now there was no escape. From his role as their brave bull, going froth day after day to "business" (Miss Menzies's word, which was Margaret's as well), he hoped to find rest in the office. But rest there was none, for increasingly his manner, to his disquiet, reflected his role. (*Mr Stone* 252)

In the office Whymper creates problems for him, and therefore he wishes to escape from him by retirement from service. But unfortunately Whymper intrudes on his personal life as well. He elopes with Stone's niece Gwen. The disgust and hatred against Whymper further intensifies when he comes to know about the appointment of Whymper as publicity director at Gow's. He is also declared as the real architect behind the success of Knights Companion scheme for its retired pensioners. Thus Stone feels that his identity was snatched away. In this context, Shashi Kamra makes noteworthy comments:

> Stone's isolation from his milieu is a usual feature of contemporary cosmopolitan ethos. This superimposed... human alienation which is at the same time cultural and a personal bias, privacy being highly valued by the English, makes a direct unfiltered response to raw experience impossible. The narrator's exposition of Stone's situation enables Naipaul to give fictional shape to his concern with those conditions in contemporary

> society, which hinder a man from attaining 'a fix on reality'. (112)

The novel therefore focuses on post-war English middle class who feel frustrated under a new post-imperial order. It is not that the people of the colonized nations are the marginalized lot who have been continuously displaced and uprooted; it is also the case with the people of the imperialistic nations. Mr Stone feels that through his initiation of the scheme of Knights Companion for the firm employees has brought him some identity for which he would be remembered. But actually he has been displaced of this identity by Whymper who has taken the credit for Mr Stone's work. It has caused some new frustrations for him. This is quite natural in all societies. Every individual is constantly displaced from his identity. It is not that a diasporic individual is uprooted of his roots. Even a rooted man to his own soil, his own country, is also displaced and uprooted constantly. In the context of the theme of alienation in the novel Mustafa postulates:

> The novel has been productively read as another of Naipaul's explorations into states of alienation. Mr. Stone's Prufrockian disaffection does suggest that life in the metropole, so fantasized about by distant colonials, houses its own varieties of rootlessness and inner frustrations. Comparisons with both Mr. Biswas of *House* and Ralph Singh of *The Mimic Men*, furthermore also suggest that Naipaul's preoccupation with existentialist questions breaks down the center/ periphery dichotomy so prevalent in colonial and postcolonial representations. (1995: 91)

Alienation is the condition of every individual. Mr Stone's ordered life has been broken down in a middle-class sub-urban English set-up. Disorder has been a dominant postimperial social structure in England.

3.4. Identity Crisis: Impact of Imperialism on Decolonised Society

The novel, *The Mimic Men* in the first person narrative, reveals the condition of the hero, Ralph Singh, shipwrecked first on his native island, and then in England. The image of shipwreck has a deep symbolic meaning, referring to the sense of abandonment and dereliction. This sense of abandonment comes into focus as a sharp contrast with ambition to achieve success and identity. Naipaul once again reinforces the theme of psychic damage to the colonial subjects. Naipaul examines the social, historical and political reality of the third world countries and reveals how hollowness of colonial set-up compels people to pose as the mimic men: "These men live in the memory of the past or in the fantasies of the future, and cultivate an ambivalent personality" (Veena Singh in Ray 2005: 156). Naipaul reveals the static condition of the newly decolonized country where there is no hope for change because of the deep impact of the colonial master on its inhabitants' psyche. Manjit Inder Singh postulates:

> ...Ralph Ranjit Kripalsingh, the exiled ex-politician hero of *The Mimic Men* is an 'insider', one who has practiced the most dubious forms of colonial mimicry as a politician and dandy, as husband and businessman and sees through the charade of politics, the deep humiliation and self-contempt that results from defeat and failure. Ralph Singh is the example of a thoroughly, psychologically colonized man, one who knows both the hurts and the excitements of the short-lived euphoria of inconsequential 'empires of our times'. (1998b: 105)

The protagonist of the novel, a Caribbean Indian (Hindu) politician, is living an exiled life in London because of racial discrimination. The protagonist is writing his memoirs of island in a hotel in London. He examines the ideas of decolonization and identity, and how they are accepted by the society without an awareness of history. He observes the causes of instability of the newly liberated colonies, his own past and identity. He realizes that writing the book itself becomes his identity and success. He presents himself as a completely psychologically wounded person who faces only failures in love, marriage and long-lasting relationships. It is his passion for order and coherence for which he examines history in order to find a meaning and order in his life:

> I know that return to my island and to my political life is impossible. The pace of colonial events is quick, the turnover of leaders rapid. I have already been forgotten, and I know that the people who supplanted me are themselves about to be supplanted. My career of the colonial politician is short, and ends brutally. We lack order. Above all, we lack power and we don't understand that we lack power. (*MM* 6)

Ralph Singh is able to dismantle the old order but he does not succeed in creating a new order. Throughout his life he tries to find order, and therefore fights against corruption and other social ills. In the process, he experiences a lot of challenges in a bewildering world. Veena Singh makes noteworthy comments on mimicry and metaphysical alienation of man:

> In an individual the mimicry is caused by loss of sense of belonging, and in the society it is caused by loss of culture. Naipaul like other commonwealth writers considers this cultural loss a threat to identity. The constantly shifting character of life is the cause of rootlessness. There are no place associations; as a result the individual becomes impotent rendering all values meaningless. Naipaul depicts the metaphysical alienation of man which is a significant aspect of the modern sensibility in literature. (Ray 157)

In fact *The Mimic Men* presents the hurdles which the colonized face in getting independence in real sense. Isabella is a small colony which lacks economic resources, skills and knowledge for which it tends to be dominated by neo-imperialistic order. The inhabitants belong to various cultures, traditions, and races. Isabella therefore lacks the unity which is the foremost requirement of a nation:

> Because the nationalist movement has been driven by racial hurt, nation and race have become confused, and those who do not share in the dominant vision are treated as enemies. While the whites move to safety elsewhere; the Asians, especially the Indians, are left as victims of the new black rulers. (King 1993: 67)

Such kind of racial fear existed in Trinidad just after the independence when there was the rule of Eric Williams. Ralph Singh mentions how violence is inflicted on the Indians. He is accused of racial exclusiveness in developing Cripple Ville because he does not feel comfortable around blacks. Even his mother does not give consent to his marriage with an English woman. The colonial rule had influenced the inhabitants so much that even after decolonization; they are still in the grip of psychological and mental slavery. They have lost their sense of liberation. They are unable to cope with the new system and order, and therefore they have lost coherence and direction in the process of achieving cultural, political and social identity. This influence forces them to be victims of mimicry. Ultimately they are found culturally displaced as John Thieme comments:

> Escape has become a way of life and displacement a perennial condition. For the dispossessed colonial, political independence solves no problem. A kind of cycle determinism makes it possible for them to find home. Neither colony nor mother country provides matrix. Dependence and displacement are his ultimate. (1975: 11)

The memoirs of R.R.K. Singh includes a wide range of themes as he is not writing continuously but he recalls and contemplates his past and, then he writes. He writes on the influence of colonial educational system, slavery of the past, loneliness, and racial discrimination, disillusionment of the world of fantasies, homelessness, power and politics. We do not find any ordered sequence in different episodes of his life. The only fact which holds them together is that he examines each episode in the context of his present situation.

The Mimic Men reflects the similar situations of the first four novels of Naipaul. However, the first four novels are set in Trinidad while *The Mimic Men* is set in an imaginary island, namely Isabella. In fact, he presents this novel as a representative of all the other colonies of the world. As Kripalsingh says: "It has happened in twenty places, twenty countries, islands, colonies, territories...I cannot see our predicament as unique" (*MM* 209). In the four preceding novels set in the Caribbean islands, the chief characters escape to England as they find their land incomplete and unreal, and not providing any opportunity. *The Mimic Men* depicts their conditions after escape. Chandra B. Joshi rightly comments:

> Kripalsingh comes from his Caribbean island to England with the usual expectations of the people from his. Refusing to consider the island of his birth as his home, looking on himself as marooned on this island, soon to be rescued he comes to England seeking fulfillment, completion, a sense of belonging to a well-established order. He finds only a greater isolation, a more acute sense of being adrift, of being shipwrecked. Sexual promiscuity, role playing—these are his ways of fighting the overwhelming sense of loss, the shock of disillusionment. On the verge of a breakdown he marries a London girl in a desperate bid for reassurance. She seems to him strong and secure, full of certainties. (1994: 166-67)

Another concern of *The Mimic Men* is the influence of colonization and slavery on the third-world politics and how it affects the individuals psychologically. Though they are liberated from slavery, and have enjoyed freedom and democracy, they are devoid of any social, political, economic and cultural past of their own. In such a situation they look towards their colonial masters as their model and thus they are unable to release themselves from mental slavery. Peter Nazreth posits:

> Slavery did the greatest damage to them by destroying their value, and setting before them the ideals of their civilization. Unfortunately this white civilization is not really the civilization as it is in Europe, it is a form of behaviors represented by the third rate people who have had a chance to become rich in the West Indies in a way they wouldn't be in England.... Such a society has no inner values. It merely copies its way of life from the Western Consumer society. (Nazreth in Hamner: 146)

Singh belongs to a poor family in Isabella. His father is a school teacher but his mother is from a prosperous family.

His mother's family owns the Bella Bella Bottling Works which business makes them rich by unfair means. They practice white master's trickery of "exploit and plunder". When Singh reads "The Missionary Martyr of Isabella", he comes to know how his father had come to this slave Caribbean Island:

> When I read this book I used to get the feeling that my father was a man who had been cut off from his real country, which in my imagination was as glorious as the Isabella described in the diary of the missionary's lady: nowhere else would people see magic in a white turban, hibiscus hedge, a bicycle and the Sunday-morning sun. I used to get the feeling that my father had in some story book way been shipwrecked on the island and that over the years the hope of rescue had altogether faded. (*MM* 94)

He feels a kind of inferiority complex due to his ancestral origin of India, and shows inclination towards western manners/ fashions. Such a condition throws him into a clash of the inherited culture and modern culture. To achieve success, he goes to the extent of changing his name from Ranjit Kripalsingh to Ralph Singh. Through such a step, he becomes an evil in the eyes of his father who is a staunch Hindu:

> He was not pleased at having to sign an affidavit that the son he had sent out into the world as Ranjit Kripalsingh had been transformed into Ralph Singh. He saw it as an affront, a further example of the corrupting influence of Cecil and my mother's family. (*MM* 101)

His fascination towards western world is strengthened by the description given to him by the English expatriate teacher at school. The description of England given to Ralph Singh reinforces his restlessness in Isabella. He feels himself alienated and experiences a sense of loss in Isabella, his homeland because it is an obscure, colonial and barbarous transplantation. Whenever he thinks of the preservation of his identity and culture, he feels insecure and his fear is heightened. He therefore contemplates:

> I have read that it was a saying of an ancient Greek that the first requisite for happiness was to be born in a famous city.... To be born on an island like Isabella, an obscure New World transplantation, second-hand and barbarous, was to be born to disorder. From an early age, almost from my first lesson at school about the weight of the King's crown, I had sensed this. (*MM* 127)

But at the same time he becomes nostalgic when he thinks of escaping from Isabella: "Even as I was formulating my resolve to escape, there began those series of events which, while sharpening my desire to get away, yet rooted me more firmly to the locality where accident had placed me" (*MM* 127).

One important aspect of the novel which, according to Molly Mahood, many critics don't observe is how Naipaul focuses on the consequences which affect the colonized nations. And these effects have been caused by the capitalist production of the imperial centre. Molly argues that most of the critics do not observe distinctive wrongness of the Caribbean colonialism in its different phases that has been portrayed in *The Mimic Men*:

> ...the primal wrongness of Caribbean colonialism in all its phases—the creation of a slave society and economy, the prolongation through indentured labor of a form of serfdom long after black slavery ended, and the relegation of the islands for many decades to the status of slums of empire, a relegation culminating in an ill-prepared "granting of independence". This was the violation the novel never lets us forget, as it traces out the pattern of rejection, impairment, alienation, in individual lives as well as in the groups that compose this heterogeneous society. (1977: 161)

MM reveals that the colonial subjects feel alienated and exiled because of their separation from their original home, their past and culture which are not possible to be recompensated in this situation. Mixing up of cultures, hybridity cannot substitute their alienation. As Ralph observes:

> The restlessness, the deep disorder, which the great explorations, the overthrow in three continents of

> established, social organizations, the unnatural bringing together of peoples who could achieve fulfillment only within the security of their own societies and the landscapes hymned by their ancestors.... The empires of our times were short-lived, but they have altered the world forever; their passing away is their least significant feature. (*MM* 32)

Isabella is a new democratic world and the dilemma of this new political society is exposed in the mimicry of its inhabitants. The Mimicry authenticates the west and makes them real while the Caribbean world becomes the symbol of mimicry, absence and unreality. The following passage from the text reveals this fact. This passage also signifies that the island is not a "unified and unitary identity" but "a fragment, a part of some greater whole from which it is in exile and to which it must be related in an act of (never completed) completion that is always also, as it were, an exile, a loss of the particular" (Bongie 1998). In this context, let us consider this passage from the novel:

> There, in Liege in traffic jam, on the snow slopes of the Laurentians, was the true, pure world. We, here, on our islands, handling books printed in this world and using its goods, had been abandoned and forgotten. We pretended to be real, to be learning, to be preparing ourselves for life, we mimic men of the New World, one unknown corner of it, with all its reminders of the corruption that came so quickly to the new. (*MM* 157)

Though Ralph is a colonial man who reflects the dominant power, there is something of the subversive ambivalence of mimicry in *The Mimic Men.* According to Bhabha: "colonial mimicry is the desire for a reformed, recognizable other, *as a subject of a difference that is almost the same but not quite the same.* This is to say that the discourse of mimicry is constructed around ambivalence; in order to be effective, mimicry must continually produce its slippage, its excess, its difference" (1994: 96). Ralph and his wife belong to a group on the island of Isabella which represents the colonial state of Indian men and their expatriate wives. The consequence of the colonization is that they mimic the memories, stories, myths, lives and landscapes that don't belong to them. This distance and separation from their own culture, home, life and self is the result of the colonial past and this situation leads them into a state of fragmentation. Ralph belongs to the generation which sees the Caribbean world from the point of view the English and recreates "home" through English mythologies. Ralph also changes his name Ranjit Kripalsingh to the anglicized Ralph Singh. But colonialism turns out to be a rupture, an absence, a displacement for this generation because they don't have their own authentic experiences and identities.

Though on the one hand Ralph's generation finds recourse to English mythology, his mother's generation on the other hand looks back to the Indian culture and landscape as shelter. But the performance of the following ritual of Indian culture by his mother's generation also serves to be a kind of mimicry. When Ralph and his wife return, his mother performs a specific Hindu religious ritual for them. Such a ritual is rather a form of mimicry. Though Ralph knows the incongruity of the rituals, he realizes that the maintenance of such rituals is an attempt to acquire a sense of continuity and wholeness: "My mother's sanctions were pretence, no doubt; but they were also an act of piety towards the past towards ancient unknown wanderings in another continent. It was a piety I shared" (*MM* 59). As Ralph belongs to the third generation of expatriates, he desires for an ordered society. It is his irresistible desire for a well-regulated society that he leaves for England. Ralph is so much concerned with his personal dilemma that he does not realize the fact that being "lost" is "the universal condition of man in the twentieth century" (Bruce 1975: 45). He goes to England in search of order but his dilemma intensifies when he experiences a crisis of identity. He is disillusioned. When he attends the Christening Party of Lieni's baby in the church, he feels suffocated because there is a big gap between his imagination and the reality which he faces:

> The priest hallowed the baby with his saliva, his thumb and his fingers. With his nose he made the sign of the cross over the baby. I believe—my memories of the ceremony are now a little vague—that at a certain stage

> he put a pinch of salt into the baby's mouth. John Cedric made a sour face and worked his tongue. (*MM* 12)

Ralph's marriage to Sandra also seems to be a means to secure his identity and certainty which he had in Isabella; but even in this he is unsuccessful. And here he realizes the futility of coming to an alien culture: "It was my hope to give partial expression to the restlessness which this great upheaval has brought about" (32). When Sandra leaves him, he joins politics, but here also he is humiliated. When he goes to England regarding bauxite contract, the minister refuses to talk about colonial problems. When he goes to another minister, he also treats him in the same way. His disillusionment with these representatives of power and democracy touches the soul of Ralph. He therefore finds a release from his frustration in his writing. Ultimately he is able to free himself from his dilemma. Though he does not get success in creating an ordered world, he at least recreates himself as an independent man. Singh himself expresses: "Yet I feel that in this time I have cleared the decks, as it were, and prepared myself for fresh action. It will be the action of a free man" (*MM* 274). Ralph's self-discovery is crucial to liberate the man. The novel is therefore not depressing as has been criticized by some critics. Ralph's exploration of his "self" and Naipaul's authentic portrayal of social reality heighten its aesthetic effect. Veena Singh's comments subscribe to this point:

> Naipaul like the modern writers of the age mirrors the tortured and twisted psyche of man, and also his ambiguous and irrational self. Like Ellison's *The Invisible Man, The Mimic Men* is not about politics or about a particular race or society but about the dissociation of sensibility about the displacement, isolation and identity crisis. (Ray 165)

4

Neocolonialism, Expatriacy and Cultural Identity in Shorter Fiction

Naipaul's shorter fictional texts explore the post-colonial situations in the third-world countries. He portrays the evil impact of colonialism in greater details in these texts, namely *Miguel Street* (1959), *A Flag on the Island* (1967) and *In a Free State* (1973). Kamal Mehta postulates:

> The issues that he picks up for fictional exploration and construction pertain to the prevailing confusion regarding the identity of the communities and nations, the mis/direction of different movements for various purposes in these countries, the politics together with all its anarchical intrigues and incompetence, the human life in general, the complex national and international conflicts and maneuverings, the problems faced by the post-modern society like rootlessness, disillusionment and prevalent racial discrimination. (Ray 279)

Naipaul, grounded in three cultures—the Trinidadian, the English and the Indian, and then disowning all the three, has objectively portrayed the post-colonial situations. Naipaul's distinction lies in not only what he writes about Trinidad but he also universalizes the issues of freedom, culture, history and postcoloniality referring to the life outside the island. *Miguel Street* deals with the problems of the newly independent rural Trinidad; *A Flag on the Island* is concerned with different periods of various places, referring to the apprehensions of losing cultural identity; and *In a Free State* refers to the condition of expatriates, outsiders and aliens in a world without stability and order. Naipaul has explored the predicament of exile, loss of roots and culture, and pain of homelessness. One remarkable fact about Naipaul is that he does not pretend to be an optimist. He presents the dark reality and vision with authenticity. Salim's utterance in the opening lines of *A Bend in the River* is noteworthy: "The world is what it is; men who are nothing, who allow themselves to become nothing, have no place in it" (3).

Naipaul describes the difference between the newly independent countries and their former colonizers (Europeans). The difference is not only geographical and cultural but also financial. This creates obstruction in the development of the decolonized nations. First, these countries were colonized by Europeans for exploitation of their resources and later on when they were freed; they still remained as the former colonies of Europe being economically dependent on them. Psychologically, they were in the grip of their colonizers, and politically they just became the mimic men of Europe. Bill Ashcroft et al. postulate, "Post-colonial culture is inevitably a hybrid phenomenon involving a dialectical relationship between the grafted European culture systems and an indigenous ontology, with its impulse to create or recreate an independent local identity, such construction or reconstruction occurs as a dynamic 'peripheral' subversion of them" (1989: 195). The problem with the inhabitants of these countries is that they don't live with their indigenous culture or history of their own. They know about their cultures through their parents, but they live as mimic men of European manners by attending English schools. They don't have a sense of importance of their own history and culture for which they suffer from identity crisis and rootlessness. They are cut off from their mother country, and the politics of racialism does not allow their acceptability.

In a Free State reveals how 'freedom' turns out to be mimicry in a disordered world. Kamal Mehta remarks:

> Naipaul reveals the fate of newly independent nations who do not know the significance of a 'Free state'. The

> forest Africans is having integrity and identity but they are illiterate, ignorant and poor. They, thus, cannot take up the responsibility of providing a direction to their state. The city Africans are rootless and sorts of parasites, concerned with their material prosperity and least dedicated to the cause of their state.... The state passes into chaos as the President and the King, belonging to separate tribes, pull it into opposite directions, making the situation worse. (Ray 293)

Naipaul has the experience of a cross-section of a society, and therefore he has been successful in representing the problems of rootlessness, dislocation, quest for identity and cultural dilemma. He has often been severely criticized for castigating his own people. George Lamming therefore considers his books satirical:

> His books can't move beyond a castrated satire, and satire may be useful element in fiction, no important work, comparable to Selvon's can rest safely on satire alone. When such a writer is colonial, ashamed of his cultural background and striving like mad to prove himself through promotion to the peaks of a 'superior' culture whose values are gravely in doubt, then satire, like the charge of philistinism, is for me nothing more than a refuge. But it is too small a refuge for a writer who wishes to be taken seriously. (1960: 37)

Naipaul however denies the charge of being a satirist. Gordon Rohlehr defends him:

> Irony enables Naipaul to get down to the bare humanity beneath his history. Because he is dealing with his own personal past, his irony doesn't preclude sympathy but reinforces it. He is also to answer in terms of creative sensibility, a question to which he could find no satisfactory academic answer. (James 1968: 122)

All the three shorter fictions reveal the impact of colonialism on the inhabitants and their land as well. *Miguel Street* explores the physical, intellectual, emotional and social lives of the people of the Street. In *A Flag on the Island*, Naipaul expands his stories from the Trinidadians, and then tries to convey the same phenomenon symbolically with different characters, different times and different places. *In a Free State* portrays the predicament of the citizens in a country which is not their ancestral land though they have complete freedom. It explores the conditions of the people who are displaced, irrespective of their nationality.

4.1. Postcolonial Disorders: Multiculturalism and Ethnicity

Miguel Street consists of the earliest short stories though they were published later. "Miguel Street" stands for Trinidad which is a newly independent country. The different stories in the collection together represent the crises—changes, unrest, confusion, dilemma—in the newly independent colony. Naipaul presents the impoverished area of the Miguel Street with its cultural diversity, fantasies, chaos and changeable standards. The society in this street is composed of different ethnic, racial and colour groups like Negroes, Asians, Chinese, English and Spanish. All of them are expatriates. The noticeable fact about the street is that its inhabitants are not permanent settlers. They are rather "flitting in and out": "new tenants come and go, old ones move away suddenly and come back as suddenly, making little difference to the life on the street" (Joshi 1994: 105). Homogeneity prevails so far as their aspirations, disappointments, failures and struggles are concerned. Colonial past has influenced their beliefs, habits and attitudes. Though they are politically free, intellectually and culturally they still bank on the past colonizers. They don't have any history or past to be proud of. It is also because they are all expatriates. It doesn't mean that they don't have potential or they are not capable of innovation. In fact in the absence of proper opportunities, they only meet failures. In such a situation all their efforts to assert their identity become synonymous to absurdity. One chief reason of the backwardness of Miguel Street is that all the natives belong to different roots; there is nothing common among them except their present residence. They don't have holistic approach to the development and achievements; they are rather individualistic and isolated. Naipaul is critical of such a society in *The Middle Passage:*

> Though we know that something was wrong with our society, we made no attempt to assess it. Trinidad was too unimportant.... There was no nationalist feeling: there could be none...it was only our Britishness, our belonging to the British Empire, which gave us any identity. So protest could only be individual, isolated, unheeded. (MP 36)

Miguel Street consists of seventeen stories related to seventeen persons of different ethnicity, race, color and culture; but all of them have similar problems. Social and psychological issues have been inculcated into their thoughts by the colonizers. They still consider themselves inferior to foreigners and their lifestyles. They demean their own virtues and manners. Their indigenous culture is not of any significance to them. They speak about their shortcomings frankly. The society has many talented people; but they do not get any scope for development of their potentialities. They wish to take revenge on the society because they feel that they are the victims of this society and its conventions. They don't develop a sense of belonging to their land. The society does not facilitate the inhabitants for fulfillment of their aspirations. As a matter of fact, people have tension between ambition and opportunity because "talent is squandered in eccentricity, romance lies only in escape" (White 1975: 49).

The first story is about a character named Bogart. The title of the story is also after his name. The very beginning of the story creates an atmosphere of doubt, mystery, confusion and indecisiveness. Though he doesn't do any creative work, he has so much concern for it. His involvement in absurd activities leads to assertion of his identity and existence: "Before they called him Bogart they called him Patience, because he played that game from morn till night. Yet he never liked cards" (*MS* 1). Though he is not a man of action, he has so many friends because he is very popular in Miguel Street. In this Street, there is no resource to meet his talent and taste. His pretence of making a living by tailoring reinforces his identity crisis: "I never could imagine him competing with anyone; and I can't remember him making a suit" (2). Time and again he leaves the street and goes somewhere and returns after a long time. There is a kind of sense of loss in him. In the beginning, he is a silent figure but after returning he seems to be boasting. After his return from British Guinea, the natives are scared of him. Consequently, he becomes the most feared person of the street: "They had never seen Bogart drink so much; they had never heard him talk so much; and they were alarmed. No one dared to ask Bogart where he had been" (4). It exposes that the natives are still mentally and psychologically colonized. We find that Bogart is a mimic man: "His mouth was twisted a little, and his accent was getting slightly American" (5). On the disappearance of Bogart, Hat's guess about his whereabouts shows the aspiration of almost all the inhabitants and it seems to be the cause of their predicaments: "Everyone accepts these unaccountable disappearances as a natural part of the treacherous instability of events, and perhaps as a condition of surviving their implacable advance" (Walsh 1973: 13). It is surprising why Bogart doesn't marry the girl who gave birth to a child through their sexual relationship. It shows how this society is morally rotten. All the men in the street assert their superiority by suppressing women:

> "You see", Hat said on the pavement that evening, "the man leave his first wife in Tunapuna and come to Port of Spain. They couldn't have children. He remains here feeling sad and small. He go away, find a girl in Caroni and he give she a baby...."
>
> "But why he leaves she?" Eddoes asked.
>
> "To be a man, among we men." (*MS* 7)

"The Thing without a Name" is about Popo, an idle fellow without doing any work. Though he seems to be "always busy hammering and sawing and planning", his activities are fruitless. It signifies that his involvement in the work is only for assertion of his superiority. The occupation which he has chosen does not suit his taste and talent. He has hanged a signboard of a carpenter, but whenever someone comes asking about him, he says that he doesn't live there. His signboard is, actually, the symbol of his identity crisis. He lives in the world of fantasy.

He talks about serious things such as life and death, and work. His wife works outside. Though Popo is financially dependent on her, she has no importance in the family. Popo's relation with his wife explains that women are just a kind of machine for the family, for housekeeping, for money making:

> Popo never made money. His wife used to go out and work, and this was easy because they had no children. Popo said, "Women and them like work. Man not make for work." (10)

Popo's wife elopes with the gardener. It emphasizes lack of moral codes in the society. It also exposes the looseness of the bond in human relationship. It is puzzling if women are materialistic or having any deeper relationship with their husbands. When Popo facilitates all the amenities, his wife returns to him. Hat's comment is relevant when he says: "You see the sort of thing woman is. You see the sort of thing they like. Not the man. But the new house paint up, and all the new furniture inside it" (13). Moreover till now Popo's every way to assert his identity is unrecognized but as soon as his wife flees away, he becomes popular in the street:

> Popo found himself then a popular man. The news got around very quickly.... And then all the men began to gather in Popo's workshop, and they would talk about cricket and football and pictures—everything except women—just to try to cheer Popo up. (11)

After returning from the jail, when Popo becomes a changed man, and starts his workshop fruitfully, his gang of friends becomes sad because they don't want any change in him. It seems that they do not want any change in Popo; they rather want him to remain the same.

The story "George and the Pink House" concentrates on the absurdities of George. It is strange that George doesn't have any kind of responsibility for his family. However his wife, son and daughter have no complaints against him, and they bear with his absurdities, beatings and abuse readily. In Miguel Street child-beating and woman-battering are acceptable. George doesn't need any company because he gets all the recreations he wants from beating his wife, daughter and son. Such an attitude of George has been presented with a tone of disapproval: "George never became one of the gangs in Miguel Street. He didn't seem to mind. He had his wife and his daughter and his son. He beat them all" (17). It is a matter of great concern that even after decolonization, patriarchal ideologies in the Street dominate as we see in the case of Popo. This society is rather destroying the perspective of decolonization. In this society people do not bother to do something meaningful applying their own minds because they lack such intellectual vision. Even these people do not find any leader for guidance. It seems that this society is ill prepared for a future responsibility to move forward for effecting the much needed socio-economic transformation to lead it in the path of progress. They enjoy freedom physically, but mentally they are still rooted in their colonial past. One form of colonization is over, and a new form of colonization has taken place. The ill-treatment to children and wives is so conspicuous that it proves to be a barbaric society without sophistication of any civilized standard. A woman, for example, George's wife has no distinctive identity of her own in such a patriarchal society: "George's wife was never a proper person. I always thought of her just as George's wife, and that was all.... And while George sat on the front concrete step outside the open door of his house, his wife was busy" (17). Such male-hegemony in Miguel Street is rather a psychological issue. Going back to the colonial exploitation, we understand that the past colonial masters had terrorized the natives, especially the males, so much that these natives now feel the best use of power and freedom is to rule over the other weaker people in the society. They therefore now enjoy their authority over children and women by terrorizing them at home. They are yet to understand the real meaning of freedom: a set of rules; systems; a democracy, equal rights and opportunities for everyone. The condition of George's wife and his daughter Dolly thus reinforces the subordinate condition of women in the society of Miguel Street. The story concludes with the marriage of Dolly, but the marriage is not going to do any good to her. She seems to be the living victim of this mechanical relationship as the narrator observes: "I never knew what happened to Dolly. Edward said one day that she was living in Sangre Grande. Hat said he saw her selling in the George Street Market. But she had left the street, left it for good" (23).

The story "His Chosen Calling" is about Elias's struggle for education and aspirations. It presents the educational backwardness of Miguel Street. There is no proper arrangement for education in the country. Education is a "prestige issue" in the society. Although George always bullies his son, Elias, "he was very proud that his son was getting an education: 'The boy learning a hell of a lot. You know. He reading Spanish, French and Latin'" (27). But we find that Miguel Street is unable to fulfill the aspirations of the boy. Corruption is growing as Elias began saying, "But what the hell you expect in Trinidad? You got to bribe everybody if you want to get your toenail cut" (31). "Man-man" is about the cynical activities of a character, Man-man, who has been declared a mad man in the society. This story, in fact, reveals the hollowness of the Street. As the narrator himself says, "I can think of many people much madder than Man-man ever was.... He never stared at you the way I expected a mad man to do; and when you spoke to him you were sure of getting a very reasonable reply" (33). The way people judge him shows that they don't have any capacity to have an insightful look in his activities. His participation in every election and getting only two votes exposes the political hollowness, instability or mimicry of democracy in the newly independent colony. His witty remarks on the school going of the narrator are a satire on the standard of education:

> "Boy, where you going?" Man-man asked.
>
> "I going to school", I said.
>
> And Man-man, looking at me solemnly, said in a mocking way, "So you go to school, eh?" (34)

After the death of his dog, when Man-man becomes a preacher and people start gathering to listen to him, he shows the intellectual dearth among the natives. It is strange that the man, who is declared a mad man, suddenly becomes God's apostle to the public. Swinden Patrick's view is worth quoting:

> Clearly a society that responds to Man-man's non-sensical self-crucifixion by hurling stones at him has next to no moral sense, the crude aesthetic spectacle, not the inner psychological anguish, is what appeals to them. Man-man is taken away to an asylum. Outside authority removes what might otherwise have been a problem to be dealt by the street itself. The framework of social convention which allows people to amuse them by stoning a lunatic is obviously very weak. (1984: 215)

The story "B. Wordsworth" reveals so many aspects of Trinidadian life. The leisure of B. Wordsworth's life explains lack of action in the country. He is a worthless, idle fellow who spends his time in staring at odd things and justifies his activities as the work of a great poet. When the narrator asks his full name, he says "Black. Black Wordsworth. White Wordsworth was my brother. We share one heart. I can watch a small flower like the morning glory and cry" (*MS* 42). It seems that in this society people don't have awareness of their past, history and culture. Even they don't try to dig out their past; but at the same time they want to have an identity and individuality. The views of William Walsh are remarkable:

> Because the myths are so thin, so social code, so derivative, the people pour their individuality. These people are no derivations of some rich history of which they are part, the inheritance and part the function. They are wholly here and now and there is in each of them an extraordinary concentration of life. (1970: 66)

He is well aware of his deficiency and absurdity of his work, yet he does all these things to assert his individuality:

> He said, "Good. Well, listen. That story I told you about the boy poet and the girl poet, do you remember that? That wasn't true. It was something I just made up. All this talk about poetry and the greatest poem in the world, that wasn't true, either. Isn't that the funniest thing you have heard?" (*MS* 48)

"The Coward" is a story about Big Foot who is a terror in the street. Hat compares Big Foot's act of bullying with the policeman's son and the priest's son. Hat said, "You does only get policeman son behaving in that way. Policeman son and priest so" (52). It signifies that law and order is not equal for everybody in the society. After the defeat of Big-foot in the boxing match, the laughing of the crowd exposes that the people are accustomed to failures, though Big-foot leaves Miguel Street feeling humiliated:

> But the crowd was laughing, laughing.
>
> I looked at the ring.
>
> Big foot was in tears. He was like a boy, and the more he cried, the louder he cried, and the more painful it sounded. (59)

Success can't be expected in this place as stated by Hat, "Well, what you expect in a place like this?" (60). The inhabitants of the Street don't feel the sense of belonging to their land. That's why we find them always, talking about European countries:

> "Boyee said, 'you people just don't know the Germans. The Germans strong like hell, you know....' Errol said, 'But we have Americans on we side now'". (56)

"The Pyrotechnicist" is about a typical character of Trinidad who tries to overcome his story of failure. Although he gets success, the victory turns out to be pathetic. It reveals the personal and social consequences of failure and distress. Morgan, the Pyrotechnicist is the illustration of the weakness of a West Indian male who is unable to carry out the responsibility of his family. He tries to show his manliness in bullying and beating his children and wife. Morgan has his own written constitution—"Crime and Punishment" in his family, which prescribes certain codes of conduct and punishment for his children in case they violate the codes. The narrator portrays the proceedings:

> We all stood up, and Morgan appeared smiling all round.
>
> I asked Hat, "Why he smiling so?"
>
> Hat said, "That is how the magistrates and them does smile when they come in court." (66)

Kamal Mehta aptly remarks:

> Naipaul humorously narrates the things and raises the question of the state of constitutions in such countries. Secondly, he seems to be examining the fact whether the constitutions are effective at all, particularly, when the citizens are like these children, either adamant or insincere? He perhaps wants to convey that in the absence of true regards such a constitution solves no problem. (Ray 2005: 287)

Like all other inhabitants of the continent, Morgan also lives in the world of fantasy. He always wants to be the best fire-maker in the street but he never becomes; and when out of frustration he burns his own home, it turns out to be the best fire. Thus ultimately he achieves his identity, but at the cost of losing everything.

The hero of the story, "Titus Hoyt, I.A." is one of the most versatile persons in the Street. He is a man of vision, but there is lack of opportunity for him to materialize his vision. As the narrator himself says: "This man was born to be an active and important member of a local road board in the country. An unkind fate had placed him in the city. He was a natural guide, philosopher and friend to anyone who stopped to listen" (*MS* 72). Titus Hoyt exposes the reason of the backwardness of the society appropriately. People are superstitious, they don't have the sense of belonging to the nation; they are not interested in the history and past of their culture and country. Titus Hoyt would therefore say:

> The thing that really matter is faith. Look, I believe that if I pull out this bicycle-lamp from my pocket here, and set it up somewhere, and really really believe in it and pray to it, what I pray for go come. That is what I believe. (77)

> You see you people don't care about your country. How many of you know about Fort George? Not one of you here know about the place. But is history, man, your history, and you must learn about things like that. (80)

Hoyt is interested in educating the youth, but they are not interested and cooperative. It seems that the boys are puzzled.

> Hoyt used to say, "Is a science man. The trouble with Trinidad is that the teachers don't have this science of teaching".
>
> And "Is the biggest thing in the world, man. Having the minds of the young to train. Think of that. Think." (*MS* 78)
>
> Further when Hoyt said to Boyee, "Remember that you have just attended a meeting of the youth Association as our delegate. Remember these things." Boyee said, "Go to hell, Hoyt." (81)

The story "The Maternal Instinct" centers on the character, Laura, who has eight children by eight men. But she doesn't feel ashamed; she is cheerful; she doesn't think that her children are burden to her. Sometimes she becomes furious only due to her financial crisis. Though she is a concubine, she is actually challenging the patriarchal supremacy and order of the society. She never lets her any husband to live with her for a longer period. She doesn't want to be dominated by any male as in the case of Nathaniel, her last husband. She rather becomes violent towards him:

> Nathaniel said, "But who go mind your children?"
>
> Laura said, "That is my worry, I don't want you here. You is only another mouth to feed. And if you don't leave me right right now I go go and call Sergeant Charles for you." (90)

She doesn't need any male to support her family. However, she can't be blamed alone for the disorder in the society as the men are equally responsible for it: "The men, who cycled slowly past Laura's house in the evening, whistling for Laura, were not going to give any of their money to Laura's children. They just wanted Laura" (85-86). But her maternal instinct arouses when her own daughter, Lorna, becomes pregnant. She breaks all the moral and patriarchal ideologies. She feels relieved with the death of her daughter. When the police came to tell Laura about it, she expressed: "It good. It good. It better that way" (92).

"The Blue Cart" is about Eddoes, a scavenging-cart driver. People's appreciation for his profession and his habit of keeping tooth-brush in the mouth, show that they have not developed their own standard manners.

> He was one of the aristocrats of the street. He drove a scavenging-cart and so worked only in the mornings. ...Eddoes was a real "saga boy"...he was a "sweet-man", a man of leisure, well-dressed, and keen on women. (93)

In this story Laura was not the only one but there are so many other women who give birth to babies without being married. Hat's comment is rather a general opinion about the women of the street: "Well, boy, woman these days funny like hell. They go run after a dwarf if he got money" (94). Girls giving birth to babies before marriage reinforce lack of moral and social standards in the society. When Eddoes said to Hat, "A girl making baby for me", Hat's reply was: "But don't be stupid, man. Is the sort of thing that does happen to anybody?" (99). It also reveals the mimicry of democracy in the newly independent colony. One's approach to higher authorities matters a lot rather than one's hard work. The narrator's mother rightly says:

> You see what sort of thing life is. Here, I is, working my finger to the bone. Nobody flinging me a pair of shoes just like that, you know. And there you got that thin—arise little man, doing next—to nothing, and look at all the things he does get. (96)

"Love, Love, Love, Alone" is about the strange love story of Mrs. Hereira and Mr. Toni. They are White, and have come from somewhere else to live in Miguel Street. They buy a house. They are not welcomed warmly. The narrator describes, "We were prepared to dislike the new people even before they came" (104). The narrator also thinks that the lady is not fit for Miguel Street:

> This lady didn't fit in with the rest of us in Miguel Street. She was too well dressed. She was a little too pretty and a little too refined, and it was funny to see how she tried to jostle with the other women at Mary's shop trying to get scarce things like flour and rice. (*MS* 105)

We find the cultural difference in the interaction between the narrator's mother and Mrs. Hereira:

> "My mother remained calm. She said 'All right, then. Go back to the great man. Is my own fault, you hear.' Meddling in white people business." (108)
>
> My mother said, "You know, Mr. Hereira, I really wish you was like me. If somebody did marry you off when you was fifteen, we wouldn't been hearing all this nonsense, you hear. Making all this damn fuss about your heart and love and all that rubbish." (114-15)

Hereira is always ill-treated by Mr. Toni. Even then she is not ready to leave him. This treatment to Mrs. Hereira generalizes the subjugated condition of women. It is reinforced in the statement of Hat, "Is a good thing for a man to beat his woman every now and then, but this man does do it like exercise, man" (108).

William Walsh's comments on the man-woman relationship are noteworthy:

> Life in Miguel Street is lived, at least by the men, outside, on the pavement. The women, the power centre of the family, live in less external existence out of a caustic sense of disillusioned reality.... Love in this sense, as distinct from sex, doesn't occupy too much of the consciousness of those beating out living in Miguel Street. They are too much aware of the helplessness of the subject, too obviously witness to the brutality of events, what they look for in conduct is not conformity to blunder value, but that it be stamped with the seal of authentic self. (1970: 12)

The story "The Mechanical Genius" is about the eccentric activities of Bhakcu with his motor vehicles. We find him dismantling and repairing his car in which he never gets success. His obsession with the mechanism of his car is just the mimicry of Western technology. When the mechanic of the company comes to see his car, he says: "When you have all sorts of ignorant people messing about with an engine the white people build with their own hands, what the hell else you expect?" (*MS* 125). Whenever he is in stress, we find him reading the *Ramayana*. Perhaps in the recitation of the *Ramayana* he tries to avoid his failures and frustrations. The annoyance of the other inhabitants with his recitation shows the cultural clash of the Street. Hat said, "Hear the two of them now. She with that voice she got, and he singing that damn sing-song Hindu song" (130). After the failure of his car and lorry business, his wife starts rearing hens and selling them but she does not succeed in it. Ultimately at the suggestion of the narrator's mother, Bhakcu chooses the profession of a *pundit*, a profession related to his own culture: "My mother said, 'Well, it easy easy. He is a Brahmin, he know the *Ramayana*, and he have a car. Is easy for him to become a pundit, a real proper pundit.'" (132). It expounds that one's last recourse is one's own culture and any type of cultural transgression leads only to failure.

The story "Caution" is concerned with the dreams and expectations of Bolo from Trinidad and his disillusionment for being unsuccessful. He has been so much disappointed due to his failures in his profession that he even does not rely on his own ability. When the narrator asks him: "But why you stop cutting hair regular, Mr. Bolo?" he replies, "Ha, boy that is asking a big big question. The fact is, I just can't trust myself" (135). When he doesn't get success through his actions, he tries his luck in the missing Ball competition run by *The Trinidad Guardian*. But in this case he becomes a victim to racial discrimination. As he says: "Is just a big bacchanal, you hear. The proper people done make up their mind long-long time now who going to win the week prize. They only want to get all the black people money" (136).

Once again he tries his hand in a project for house advertised in the newspaper but the company proves to be a bunch of crooks. Bolo doesn't stop here. He starts buying "sweep-stake ticket" but here again he faces failure. For the next three years he doesn't get any draw. He is so much disappointed that when at the Christmas meeting of 1948, the narrator informs him about his draw; he doesn't believe and becomes infuriated. Bruce King makes pertinent remarks in this context:

> Bolo, in "Caution", fails so often at everything he does that when he wins some money on the sweep stake he refuses to believe it, as it would destroy his sense of being a victim, and tears up the ticket and withdraws into himself. It is easier to blame the imperial powers or racial discrimination of Trinidadian corruption than to accept his own past foolishness and failures of character. (1993: 28)

"Until the Soldiers Came" is about Edward, the brother of Hat. This story reveals that there is no opportunity for work in the country as with the coming of the war: "For the first time in Trinidad there was work for everybody, and the Americans paid well" (*MS* 148). Till now Edward was living a very peaceful life without any ambition; but with the coming of Americans, he joins a job provided by them. He not only joins the job but becomes a mimic man imitating the Americans and despising the Trinidadians:

> Edward surrendered completely to the Americans. He began wearing clothes in the American style, he began chewing gum, and he tried to talk with an American accent. We didn't see much of him except on Sundays, and then he made us feel small and inferior. (149)

Before the coming of Americans, he didn't have any interest in women, but now he criticizes the Trinidadians for the cases of women having babies before marriage. However, it is rather hypocritical when he himself impregnates an American girl and after that plans to marry her. But after the marriage, his wife doesn't feel comfortable with him and tries to commit suicide because there is so much cultural difference between them. One day she therefore elopes with an American soldier and his Americanism becomes a matter of derision in the society: "Edward said sadly, 'Yes, she run away. With a American soldier; And I give the man so much of my rum to drink'" (158). He turns towards the Americans because of he fails in fulfilling his aspirations in Miguel Street. When he participates in the poster competition and doesn't even get a consolation prize, he gets angry with Trinidad:

> "I was stupid to send in anything I paint with my own two hands for Trinidad people to judge. What they know about anything. Now, if I was in America, it would be different." (149)
>
> And when "somebody had the idea of organizing a Local Talent on Parade show and Edward said, 'Don't make me laugh. What sort of talent they think Trinidad have?'" (151)

The story "Hat" reveals some strange facts about Hat and his society. From the very beginning, it becomes clear that the society is not restricted to any moral, social or traditional code. He openly declares that Boyee and Errol are his illegitimate children:

> Hat loved to make a mystery of the smallest things. His relationship to Boyee and Errol, for instance. He told strangers they were illegitimate children of his. Sometimes he said he wasn't sure whether they were his at all, and he would spin a fantastic story about some woman both he and Edward lived with at the same time. (160)

Even the boys are ready to accept any kind of identity attributed to them by Hat as they don't know anything about their past. Hat is accused of adulterating milk even though he is not involved in it. In his conversation with Edward, we find how corrupt the judiciary system is, and bribery is prevalent in police department:

> Hat said, "Edward, you talking as if Trinidad is England. You ever hear that people tell the truth in Trinidad and get away? In Trinidad the more you innocent, the more they throw you in jail, and the more bribes you got to hand out. You got to bribe the magistrate...you got to bribe the inspectors. By the time you finish bribing it would be better if you did take your jail quiet quiet." (164-65)

He is so much disappointed with the systems of Trinidad that he wishes to follow the Americans. "I think I was a damn fool not to go and work with the Americans, like Edward and so much other people" (167). After returning from jail, he gets married. His wife seems to be very docile but once she flees away with all the jewelry Hat has bought for her. This reinforces that women of this society are materialistic rather than standing for values of family life.

The last story "How I Left Miguel Street" is about the narrator. The story reveals how the youths of Trinidad are wayward due to lack of opportunity for work in Trinidad. The narrator himself says: "We made wild parties and took rum and women to Maracas Bay for all-night sessions" (174). Further he said to his mother, "Is not my fault really. Is just Trinidad. What else anybody can do here except drink?" (174). In the absence of proper employment, they become aimless, and it happens so that even if they are given chance to make their future, they are in dilemma as in the case of the narrator. Pt. Ganesh arranges a scholarship for his studies for him after taking a suitable bribe from his mother. While leaving for America, the narrator becomes nostalgic in the Airport for Trinidad. He therefore expresses:

> The airport lounge frightened me. Fat Americans were drinking strange drinks at the bar. American women, wearing haughty sun-glasses, raised their voices whenever they spoke. They all looked too rich, too comfortable. (178)

But when he returns home for a few hours as his flight was late, he finds the people as usual not feeling his absence though they had given a warm farewell to him some hours before. He is thus disillusioned:

> I was disappointed. Not only by Hat's cool reception. Disappointed because although I had been away, destined to be gone for good, everything was going on just as before, with nothing to indicate my absence. (178-79)
>
> And his disillusionment perhaps made his journey for exile easier.

It is obvious, through interpretation of these stories, that the colonial society portrayed in *Miguel Street* was a society without any deep-rooted values and cultural ethos. Moreover, it was a society without any coherence and direction. People had neither aims nor dreams to materialize. They were rather swayed by superficialities of modern life. Since the colonial administration before decolonization was not much concerned with the improvement of the intellectual horizon of these people, they therefore remained ignorant. They did not bother to take any interest in the higher aspects of life. They simply lived without any meaningful activities. These marginalized people needed to move to the centre only through proper education and sustaining economic development that were not possible without a welfare government. They needed to be rooted in a certain cultural tradition that might inculcate a sense of identity and pride in them. By deconstructing the social history of these people Naipaul brings out the painful truths about that society.

4.2. Own Flag, Colonial Mindset

In *A Flag on the Island*, Naipaul brings together several short fictions written at different times. Unlike in *Miguel Street*, the narrator is not the same throughout the book. The narrator is different from story to story. All these stories talk of different communities, different times and different places. *A Flag on the Island* was written during the time Naipaul was writing *The Mimic Men:*

> The two stories and the novel are in part about communal antagonism, and the cultural confusions and mimicry of cultural behavior that occur when different groups are brought together and society is in a period of change. (King 1993: 65)

The stories describe the condition of expatriates from different regions—India, China, Africa—, and also they describe the Whites who have emigrated. They are all victims of the social changes on the Island. The first story "My Aunt Gold Teeth" revolves round the character, Gold Teeth, her dilemma, her culture-crisis and religious uncertainty. The story reveals the effect of cross-cultural confrontation on the island. Gold Teeth belonged to an orthodox Hindu family. She had a great adherence to the rituals, ceremonies and taboos of the religion, though she knew little about their relevance:

> She ate little and prayed much. Her family being Hindu, and her husband being a pundit, she, too, was an orthodox Hindu, of Hinduism she knew little apart from the ceremonies and the taboos, and this was enough for her. (*Flag* [Night] 351)

She had firm belief that the practice of religious rituals kept her family away from every kind of curse. But as she couldn't be relieved of the curse of childlessness, she turned to Christian practices which as a matter of fact, brought all the commotions in her life.

She was such a stern Hindu that she did not yield before the Presbyterian for conversion. When she was inclined towards the Christian rituals, she had some doubts regarding the alien culture. She did not allow Christianity to dominate her own religion and rituals: "...Hinduism was a superior religion. She was willing to select, modify and incorporate alien eccentricities into her worship; but to abjure her own faith—never." (352). This is the real cause of her suffering—neither she abjures Hinduism nor does she rely totally on the efficacy of Christianity. Her cultural dilemma does not let her rely on the advice of the doctor and she gives in before the mystic masseur, Ganesh Pundit who tells her that she has been bewitched by some evil spirits though the fact was that her husband had diabetes:

> The District Medical Officer at Chaguanas said it was diabetes, but Gold Teeth knew better. To be on the safe side, though, she used the insulin he prescribed and, to be even safer, she consulted Ganesh Pundit, the masseur with mystic leanings, celebrated as a faith-healer. (353)

It is her ignorance of the religious connotations that makes her feel guilty and she thinks that her husband's illness is due to her religious transgression. Ultimately her husband dies and then she realizes the futility of religious transgression and destroys all the idols of Christianity:

> "It is my entire fault", she cried, "My own fault, Ma. I fell in a moment of weakness. Then I just couldn't stop...."

> That evening Gold Teeth ritually destroyed every reminder of Christianity in the house. (359)

The story focuses on one's happiness by being rooted in one's own culture, religion and a set of rules. Any kind of mix-up, transgression leads nowhere but to destruction. Kamal Mehta rightly argues:

> The author exposes the society for which religion remains confined to rituals only and the values upheld by it remain neglected. People are after convenience. If things run smoothly, there is no problem but if they go wrong, people blame the habit, person or institution. (Ray 289)

The story "The Raffle" is about the influence of borrowed institution of education system on a totally different culture. The brutality of the teacher, Mr. Hind, symbolizes a colonial situation. In the school, he is more like a dictator than a teacher. The story also exposes the poverty of the teachers but such poverty has a dignity in the society and perhaps this dignity is bestowed upon them because they belong to a system of a foreign institution: "They don't pay primary school teachers a lot in Trinidad, but they allow them to beat their pupils as much as they want" (*Flag* 360). The school boy, Vidiadhar, the favorite of the school teacher, Mr. Hind, very soon realizes the misery of being the favorite student. Sudha Rai thus comments:

> The exploitation of the child by adults especially within the colonial school system, where two-way communication is absent, generates the more serious implications of the story. Whipped for the first time by the school master because Vidiadhar (and his mother) have taken the liberty to dispose of the goat, the boy decides to stay away from the school altogether. (Panwar 119)

The story "A Christmas Story" is about the conversion of the protagonist, the narrator. Gold Teeth had association with root culture and religion, but the narrator in this story is detached from his root culture and religion. He has even changed his name to a Christian name Randolph. He has so much hatred for his roots that he shows his scorn for every ritual of Hindu culture:

> "I had up to that time eaten with my fingers, a manner of eating which is now so repulsive to me, so ugly so unhygienic, that I wonder how I managed to do it until my eighteenth year." (*Flag* [Night] 368)
>
> "I cannot understand why these people persist in this admiration for the cow, which has always seemed to me a filthy animal far filthier than the pig, which they abhor." (369)

But very soon it becomes clear that it was his vested interest that drew him towards conversion:

> I was interested in teaching—there was no other thing a man of my limited means and limited education could do—and my Presbyterianism was a distinct advantage. (366)

It seems that he has been confined to certain sets of ideologies in which progress and development mean that Christianity and other cultures are uncivilized and backward. But at the same time even after the conversion he feels alienated from and nostalgic to his old religion. He therefore says: "My life thereafter was a lonely one. I had cut myself off from my family...in the event of real trouble there would be people to whom I could turn. Now I was deprived of this solace" (370). Sudha Rai makes remarkable comments:

> Naipaul grapples with the treatment of the perils of hybridity in the colonial situation. Through the use of flashback the story traces the events in the life of Randolph (Chunilal) who despite his commitment to the teaching profession is unable to attain worldly success. In contrast, his friend Hari who is in the truck business is far better off. Alienated from Traditional Hindu family ties, rejection is his lot. Failure stares him in the face; not even the religious theme of the destruction of vanity can console him for the nonentity he is. (Panwar 123)

Randolph says that "progress is not a matter of outward show, but an attitude of mind; and it was this that my religion gave me" (*Flag* [Night] 367). Such type of hypocrisy in him, according to Kamal Mehta, has very well been exposed by Naipaul:

> Randolph considers Hinduism unfit for the modern world as it means "animistic rites", "idolatry" and "cow dung". He hates rituals but himself goes to Church on all Sundays. He despises dhotis of Hindus as they reveal the legs.... At the same time, he praises the Christian girls who wear short-frocks, leaving their legs totally bare. He praises missionaries who work among the backward people but he himself does not sympathies with the backwards.... While commenting on the Hindu wives, he despises them saying that he would marry an intelligent, educated and all cultured lady. However the readers know that his wife is neither intelligent nor cultured.... Moreover, when an inspection committee arrives to investigate into the matter, she sets the very building on fire to hide the poor construction and thus destroys the evidence of financial corruption. (Ray 291)

"The Mourners" is about the superficiality of relations and emotions. Romesh, the narrator visits Miss Sheila, who is mourning the death of her son Ravi. When she talks to Romesh, her hypocritical nature is exposed. It seems as if she wants to show off her modern fashions, higher status and relationships with Whites. "The Night Watchman's Occurrence Book" is in the form of a diary. It exposes the relationship between the night watchman, Hillyard and the Hotel Manager and the White guests. Hillyard does his duty honestly; yet he is always abused and scolded by the Manager and the guests because of his illiteracy and belonging to a different religion. Hillyard says: "I am a poor man and you could abuse me, but you must not abuse my religion sir, because the good Lord sees all and will have His revenge sir" (*Flag* [Night] 398). The story also presents drinking and merrymaking of the hotel guests throughout the night which indicates, "the pointless frenzied self-indulgence of the rootless people as also of the tourists in the Island" (Walsh 1973: 47).

"The Enemy" is about the author's childhood when he feels himself torn between his mother and father. The very opening of the story gives us a shock: "I had always considered this woman, my mother as the enemy" (*Flag* [Night] 401). Sudha Rai comments: "The story develops the marital conflicts of Naipaul's own parents stemming from the culturally sanctioned divide between "the mother's side" and "the father's side" of Naipaul's family" (Panwar 119). The daily quarrels of the parents have left the child unattended by them. "Greenie and Yellow" is a story about three birds owned by a landlady, Mrs. Cooksey. At the surface level it seems to be a fable but it has metaphorical connotations, presenting the clash among the three cultures, their survival, cultural predicament, relation between the Aborigines and the settlers. The three birds are Bluey, Greenie and Yellow. Bluey symbolizes the native of the island, who is having a happy life in the cage but after some days a new bird Greenie is brought in to the cage, which symbolizes a foreign settlement. Greenie starts dominating Bluey and after a period of time Bluey becomes marginalized on her own island. But this domination of Greenie doesn't last for long because after some days the land (cage) is invaded by Yellow, who represents a new culture. There begins a cultural clash between Greenie and Yellow, in which Greenie loses, and now the land is colonized by Yellow. But the reign of Yellow also does not last for long. She is calm and alone in the cage. Her isolation symbolizes cultural alienation—she is able to set up herself in an entirely different cultural milieu. And one day Yellow also passes away and now again the cage is owned by its true owner, Bluey, the Aborigine. But the wound given to the legs of Bluey never recovers though she has recovered her health again. The wound of her leg symbolizes that the colonized land can never shed off the colonial effect entirety.

"The Baker's Story" is about the struggle of a Grenadian baker in Trinidad. Though he is a very proficient baker, he is the victim of the ideology that blacks are only to serve others. They can't own their own bakery: "They get so used to working for other people that they get to believe that because they black they can't do nothing else but work for other people" (*Flag* [Night] 453). The story also presents the antagonism among blacks from different races, culture and nations. Ultimately the narrator sheds off his cultural and social identity and becomes an anonymous Chinese and becomes one of the successful bakers of the island. Sudha Rai has rightly observed: "In the early phase of colonial history, economic survival takes precedence over more dignified needs such as self-expression, anger and protest. The narrator conveys only his dogged determination to become a rich man, despite the price he pays for it" (Panwar 123).

The title story "A Flag on the Island" reveals the condition of Trinidad through the comparison between the past of Trinidad and that of present. The narrator is an American soldier, named, Frankie who comes to revisit the land as a tourist and finds that the past cannot be reclaimed. Yashoda Bhat rightly argues: "Naipaul, the novelist is steeped in historicism, like other Third world Writers. The writer of the post-colonial world shows past history as receding and new History, which the writer of the New World projects. Naipaul's novels of Trinidad are an illustration of this principle" (86). The narrator had been an American soldier on the island during the war and now again some years later, he revisits the island as an American tourist. He halts on the island due to a threatened hurricane. Just to pass the time, he moves to different places of the island. The island has won the political independence as its flag symbolizes this: "But just as it could be said that there is no real difference between an island depending on soldiers and one depending on tourists, so a new mimicry has replaced the old" (King 1993: 66). The second part of the story goes into flash-back when he has been posted on the island as a soldier. This was the time when the land was not free: it was colonized; it had not its own flag. The characters present the typical Trinidadian traits—sense of loss, inferiority-complex, living in fantasy and remote from reality. Blackwhite says: "this island doesn't exist". Embarrassed by English civilization, he decides to prove that black people can also write; and therefore he imitates English fiction of lady Theresa Phillips: "Lady Theresa Phillips was the most sought-after girl in all the country of Shorpshire. Beautiful, an heiress to boot, intelligent, well-versed in the classics..." (*Flag* [Night] 495). When this foreign fantasy is frustrated by his own native reality, he turns towards the West Indian art and culture. Now he follows the model of African decolonization. Further he mimics black Americans by writing "I hate you", subtitled "One Man's Search for Identity". This book turns out to be a good seller among the tourists and makes him popular West Indian writer of American foundations and he makes a lot of money out of it. Though Blackwhite calls himself the representative of the Black, in the book he presents the version of the life, the Americans require. As Landeg White comments: "Mr. Blackwhite becomes H.J.B. White, writing stories called "I Hate You" with the help of money from American foundations, producing versions not of the life he lives but of the myths the Americans require" (146).

It seems that financial backwardness and unawareness of the past make its inhabitants "mimic men" of the Americans. Though they are hosting the Americans for their own livelihood, they feel it a noble work to work for the Americans. It therefore shows their colonial mentality. The narrator ironically comments: "We brought the topics to the island.... Everyone worked for us. You asked a man what he did; he didn't say that he drove a truck or was a carpenter: he simply said he worked for the American" (*Flag* [Night] 480). In part III, we find that the island is free; it has its own flag. Yet there remains a complexity. Chandra B. Joshi therefore rightly thinks that people have not yet achieved their real independence despite their own flag: "It has an identity now—as the flag declares—but the lives of the people have become more unreal because now they are all living up to a tourist image of themselves" (160).

4.3. Trajectory of Displacement: Expatriacy and Dangers of Freedom

Naipaul's art of writing short stories reaches its height in *In a Free State*. He universalizes the theme of freedom and exile. The danger of freedom of an individual without a sense of belonging to a community has been focused in this collection of stories:

> The main characters in the fiction of this period are mostly outsiders, expatriates or alien minorities—those who have become uprooted from their origins, travelers without a home to which they can return, minorities at the mercy of others, those stranded by the withdrawal of protecting governments, former enemies brought together by the artificial boundaries of the new nations, and those who have come to the capitals of the world without the necessary skills and resources to survive. (King 1993: 83)

The first story, "Prologue, from a Journal, The Tramp at Piraeus", deals with the theme of competition, struggle, lack of resources, group-consciousness of communities and alienation. The passengers on the ship belong to different groups and cultures, and they are in the competition of self-comfort. "The tramp", an Englishman who looks like a romantic wanderer, is actually a poor, lonely old man, afraid of other groups. He is marginalized because he is without his group community. Though he brands himself as cosmopolitan, in reality he needs company for his own survival, "But what's nationality these days? I think of myself as a citizen of the world" (*FS* 3). Though all the passengers on the ship are expatriates, they are segregated on the ground of social, cultural and national differences. The ship also symbolizes the commotion and disorder after the decolonization of the various colonies:

> The old roles have become dangerous as power has changed and order is unstable. The ship in the prologue is an example of this new disorder in which relationships, identity, dignity, depend on what one achieves by one's own means or by the group to which one belongs. No one really governs; the law is the law of the jungle. (King 1993: 96)

The story "**One out of Many**" centers around Santosh, who goes to America with his employer but he has to go through so many trials and tribulations in adjusting himself there. In Bombay, he is a servant, but is quite happy. Immigration to America has been his dream but when it turns into reality, he is disillusioned. King explains this episode explicitly:

> Santosh's transfer to Washington and expectation of a green card through marrying an African-American may seem like paradise to some in the "third world", and his memories of life in Bombay may seem the immigrant's usual idealized nostalgia for a lost home, but his life in America is impoverished, lonely and filled with anxieties. (1993: 92)

Santosh becomes conscious of his freedom and responsibilities, but he does not know how to use it. In America, he thinks of enjoying freedom, but he is only confused and humiliated. He is always under the fear of being deported. To get the citizenship he has to marry a black woman. He thus ponders over his situation: "All that freedom has brought me is the knowledge that I have a face and have a body, that I must feed this body and clothe this body for a certain number of years. Then it would be over" (*FS* 3). A sense of loss affects him in New York when he sees people of different cultural groups dancing together. He feels that in such cultural mix-up the minority culture would be marginalized by majority culture: "I thought that these people were now strangers, but that perhaps once upon a time they had been like me. Perhaps...they had been brought here among the *hubshi* as captives a long time ago and had become a lost people...turns to be degraded, like a deformed man, or like a leper, who from a distance looks whole" (25). Though physically Santosh has migrated to America, he always nostalgically remembers India. William Walsh therefore comments:

> The various terrors his extradition from his own world submits him to are constructed with a brilliant, unpushing certainty: the horrors of the aeroplane flight, the incomprehensible lavatories, the weird food and the contemptuous company, the continuous enclosure in hissing, air-conditioned buildings, the corridors, the doors, the illuminated ceiling, and then the alien inhabitants themselves the wild and terrifying *hubshi* and the strange Americans. (66)

Santosh's inclination towards American lifestyle exposes his sense of protection in an alien community and culture.

"Tell Me Who to Kill" is about Dayo's brother, the protagonist who also goes through the same sense of despair and loss as in the preceding story. The story reveals the pathetic life of a simple rural man from Trinidad, who sends his brother to England for higher studies so that he will have a better career. However, all his aspirations are shattered. While Santosh has a community life and rich culture that makes him nostalgic, Dayo's brother is devoid of such culture and community. Even he has not been given any proper name. He remains only Dayo's brother. This story repeats the themes of Naipaul's earlier works—the effect of the dissociation between land and people, education and life, reality and borrowed ideals of the individual. Dayo's brother also lives in the world of fantasy. Realizing that there is something wrong in his country that does not facilitate him to fulfill his aspirations, he focuses on Dayo, his younger brother, for achieving his goals.

Dayo's brother sends his brother to England because he does not want Dayo to lead the ugly, brutal life he himself has lived. Dayo's brother also leaves for England to see the progress of his brother. But he is disappointed to see his brother smoking and talking very high of himself. He finds a job in a factory and pays for the studies of his younger brother who has stopped his studies long before. He also saves some money to open a small roti-shop; but due to racial prejudice, he has to lose his shop. Now he feels alienated as his younger brother whom he trusted so much has betrayed him. Thus the lives of the two brothers are in a state of disorder and uncertainty. Though Dayo seeks shelter in marriage with a English girl, his brother is left alone. Thieme therefore thinks that Dayo's brother has to suffer considerably in his aspiration for self-liberation:

> "In Tell Me Who to Kill" the Trinidadian narrator, nourished on Hollywood myths, devotes himself to furthering the education of his good looking brother, Dayo, in England, only to discover that metropolitan achievement is as far beyond Dayo as himself. He loses his carefully accumulated savings in the ill-conceived enterprise of running a roti-shop in England, and later salt is jabbed in the wound when he returns and finds

> the shop has been converted in to a joke-shop. For him the human condition has become horror comedy. The immediate occasion of the story is Dayo's escape through marriage to an English girl. The narrator is left with only a vision of his own deadness and a desire to kill the 'enemy' who is the author of his sufferings. But no enemy is to be found. The English among whom he now moves are as guiltless as his brother and himself. The only enemy (but it is something he doesn't realize) is the human condition which leads the dice against the colonial in his quest for self liberation. (1975: 19)

"In a Free State", the title story also deals with the disorder and uncertainty of a new independent colony. The focus is on the advantages and dangers of those who travel, become expatriates or who have no home. Naipaul points out that the state of freedom is universal but at the same time, it is also true that dangers of freedom exist for all human beings. Freedom is especially dangerous when individuals are cut off from their own communities, and fall into a society where order has disappeared, where there are no accepted social and cultural traditions. Naipaul demonstrates that the interference of the first world with the lives of the third world may lead to a dangerous position. Bruce King observes:

> The white liberal thinks he or she is being helpful but is shown to be exploitative and harmful. It is impossible to transcend the self through larger causes; the appearance of doing so is a luxury of the economically and racially secure who use others to feel a purposefulness they themselves lack or to overcome their failures in their own society. (1993: 85)

The story reveals the condition of a newly independent colony. Just after getting freedom, the people of the territory are divided between two groups—King's and President's. The army is under the control of the President, and they have started an operation against the King. The White men, who once were in favour of the King, now support the President for their political motives. The White men "had liked the king personally. But the president was stronger; the new army was wholly his, of his tribe, and the White men decided that the president was to be supported" (*FS* 99).

Naipaul has presented in this work a wide gap between rural and urban Africans. The rural Africans still do not know anything about their freedom; they are engrossed in their own culture and tradition, while the urban Africans, cut off from their roots, are following European lifestyles. Naipaul presents a situation of disorder of a newly "Free State". Bobby's discussion with Zulu in the bar of New Shropshire, and the breaking of the screen of his taxi on the way to southern collectorate, exposes the racial feeling among the Africans. Bobby realizes that master-slave relationship has changed. Further when he is beaten up, stripped naked by the President's soldiers, he realizes that the natives do not need his help and encouragement: "His arms were twisted harder and he was thrown forward.... Feeling the boots thump him on the back...intended to kill. He thought: I must protect myself, I must play dead" (233). Kamal Mehta comments on Naipaul's vision:

> *In a Free State* reveals the sad fate of the postcolonial societies which attained political freedom without being socially, psychologically and culturally free. Freedom has no meaning when the individual is cut off from his communities. The writer states that it is dangerous to be free in an alien land, as it is likely to lead to perversion in the absence of any check on oneself. (Ray 2005: 293)

Naipaul has explored the various aspects of postcolonial context by creating characters and situations with utmost integrity and sincerity. His own experience of postcolonial conditions and cross-cultural situations has enabled him to present the facts authentically.

4.4. Conclusion

Naipaul writes in *The Middle Passage* that Trinidad was a place where the stories were not stories of success but of failures: "History is built around achievement and creation; and nothing was created in the West Indies" (20). Failure is very much vivid in *Miguel Street*. Nearly every story of *Miguel Street* ends with the failures of the characters. Black Wordsworth passes away without writing a line of poetry though his aspiration was to be a great poet. Elias aspires for becoming a doctor; but all his efforts end in fiasco, and therefore becomes a driver of the scavenging carts. Man-man, who aspires to be a Jesus, is confined to a mental asylum. Bolo ends up with the feeling of hatred and distrust for everybody. Mrs. Hereira, having failed in finding true love, returns to her husband whom she does not like. Hat is disillusioned when his wife runs away with somebody else taking all his jewellery. With Hat being imprisoned, the narrator is disillusioned: "When Hat went to jail a part of me had died." Now it is impressive for him to admire Eddoes or Titus Hoyt. At eighteen he was "drinking like a fish and doing a lot besides". Like all others, the narrator also feels that Trinidad is not a proper place for him. Bruce King therefore writes:

> The stories allude to a time when Trinidad was important for its plantations, a former economy which is recalled by the remains of decaying buildings. There is a history here, a possible 'usable past,' when Trinidad was a significant place in the Empire and part of world trade and worth fighting over in contrast to the impoverished, neglected Trinidad of the 1930s and 40s in which the outside world seems distant and incomprehensible to Bolo and others. (1993: 27)

Seeing the miserable condition of every inhabitant the narrator decides to leave Trinidad soon, otherwise he will also become another failure like those he mistakenly admired. *A Flag on the Island* addresses the variety of themes and the formal experimentation. The stories raise issues regarding the predicament of the protagonists in the post-colony whose traditional structures are eroding. Flag depicts the dilemmas and confusions of colonial/postcolonial situations. Sudha Rai makes noteworthy comments:

> The stories take an ironical view of the lives of the colonials, young and old, men and women trapped in family situations which permit them no rebellion. The stories also relate to life in the colonial school, a life of meagre opportunities, making an ample contribution to the wrapping of identity. Poverty thwarts the ambition

> of most of the characters in this selection of stories and it is only in the title story "A Flag on the Island" that Trinidad is projected in its economic development, benefiting from its growth as a tourist paradise." (Panwar 2007: 117)

The themes which Naipaul deals with in this collection are related to poverty, insecurity, the void of expatriation, lack of opportunities on the island, the peril of accepting an alien culture/religion. It puts forward to the confused pulls of the colonial experience, and the predicament of the inhabitants molded in such situations. We find the characters fighting their battles for their rights and identity. In the first book, the narrator is the same throughout, and his attitude to the street remains the same, whereas in this book, there is no common narrator. The narrator changes from story to story.

In *In a Free State*, Naipaul's art and vision reaches its maturity. Looking beyond the Caribbean world, Naipaul universalizes the concept of freedom and exile. The book consists of five different pieces which are about the people who are away from their home. Chandra B. Joshi postulates:

> While the Prologue sounds the themes to be explored in the three stories, the Epilogue sums up the conclusions to be drawn from them. Homelessness is seen as a universal feature of the modern world, afflicting all races. The book ends on the sober thought that perhaps, like El Dorado, the unviolated, 'Home' never did exist but as a cherished ideal, a dream, a vision of the artist. (178)

It reveals the conditions of the individuals who are expatriates, staying away in an alien world. The book is about the displacement and hostile atmosphere. In the newly independent colonies, though the colonial period is over and the states are free, they are psychologically and culturally still colonized. Shashi Kamra therefore posits:

> Sontosh's loss of an ideal self, Dayo's brother's loss of a complete love and Bobby's sense of the loss of a supporting environment, all as a consequence of a

> growth in knowledge through disillusioning interaction with reality, reflect analogously the lonely tramp at odds with his environment deeply conscious of vulnerability. (148)

In a Free State reveals the predicament of the postcolonial countries which achieved political freedom although they were socially, psychologically and culturally not free. Freedom turns out to be a danger when the individuals are cut off from their communities. Naipaul suggests that freedom is dangerous in an alien land as it may lead to perversion in the absence of any check on oneself.

5

Hegemony, Ethnicity, Political Disorder, and Diasporic Identity in Later Novels

In the shorter fictional texts, Naipaul has been vivid in his portrayal of postcolonial societies where marginalized people's sufferings perpetuate. However, the protagonists try to overcome the difficulties and establish their identities. This chapter focuses on interpretation of Naipaul's later novels, namely *Guerrillas* (1975), *A Bend in the River* (1979), *The Enigma of Arrival* (1987), *A Way in the World* (1994), *Half a Life* (2001) and *Magic Seeds* (2004). The predominant issues in these novels are representations of the suppressed histories of the peoples and nations, and racial conflicts as well. In *Guerrillas* and *A Bend in the River*, the external world is "chaotic, disordered, violent and almost deranged" (Kamra 116) just like the mental state of the characters. In these two novels, the political and social realities of the earlier novels have been retained. The concept of power is central to these novels because the survival of an individual in a democratic set-up is possible only when he is associated with power-groups. These two novels portray racially and culturally complex societies where the cultures are in conflict with each other although these have already been distorted in the course of history. So the white people's claim of superiority has been altogether rejected. The cultural conflicts between the whites and the non-whites are of paramount importance to understand the intricacies of power politics and the concept of "liberation". Naipaul brings out the dichotomy between the past and the present. Kamra expresses her disapproval of hegemonic exploitation:

> He (Naipaul) shows it in its most ugly form in situations where the third and first world meet deliberately or accidentally to exploit each other, the one culturally and the other economically. This coming together for mutual gain does not constitute a society. (142)

Such a society is rather self-centered to take advantage of each other at the time of crises.

The Enigma of Arrival (1987) is an autobiographical novel which opens with the reflective thinking of the narrator-protagonist after his arrival to his workplace. The protagonist, a marginalized third world expatriate, struggles to create an order out of the disorder in the outside world. Naipaul sees a great change in the fortunes of the less privileged people, the barbarians, the people of the forests and deserts, Africans, Arabs, Malays and all other marginalized sections of the globe in the new situations of change. He understands that all the centralized Western knowledge that he has acquired through his colonial education is not the absolute truth about the world. He therefore tries to understand the world by acquiring knowledge through a process of continuous change and evolution. Naipaul as an expatriate has always been disillusioned because even in England he has been treated differently because of his color, and background of coming from a third world colonized country. Bruce King therefore comments:

> Besides feeling a foreigner in Wiltshire, there is his feeling that he is an accident of imperial history—an Indian earning a living as a writer in English in England—and his view that his own life is part of a larger historical process which began with the sending of indentured Indian laborers to Trinidad. (140)

This sense of history and imperialism, domination-dominated dichotomy has always been in Naipaul's psyche as an individual or as a writer. King rightly comments:

> It is the figurative representation of the decay of the imperial order and the rise of the postcolonial that makes

> it unlikely that the people and world observed by the narrator are always factually real. The disruption of the fictional and distanced with the factual and undisguised personal is what makes *Enigma* post-modern, post-colonial. (146)

In *A Way in the World* Naipaul critiques the situations of the postcolonial world in relation to the colonial history drawing examples from Spanish and British Imperialism. In a paper titled "The Politics and Poetics of Diaspora in V.S. Naipaul's *A Way in the World*" Stephanie Jones rightly points out how Naipaul is critical of the nationalist governments who often became racialists:

> Again, Naipaul comprehends historical continuities in perceived discontinuities, routes beyond roots, hybridity beyond "whole" communities in order to debunk the mythological epochal sense of—or betrayal of—history justifying an exclusionist racial politics. From a critique of Lebrun's diasporic metaphysics of a "pure" homeland, the text becomes a critique of the very brute implications of a "pure" racialist government in national power. *A Way in the World* becomes an indictment of the falsely clarifying narratives of "authenticity" and racial power which he understands as characterizing many of the recent governments of the Caribbean, South Americas, South Asia and Africa. (2000: 93)

In his next novel *Half a Life*, Naipaul portrays the character, Willie, who is put to live in alien places, and searches for his identity. Indian born Willie Somerset Chandran, moves to London, lives a bohemian life, publishes a book, and marries Ana, a woman of mixed African descent and then moves with her to Africa to her family estate. Willie is split in himself because he is unable to reconcile with his father's marriage to an untouchable, though he is a Brahmin. Even in Africa, he has a sense of "homelessness", and therefore leaves it for search of his true identity because he thinks he has only lived a half life, a shadow life. The novel is open-ending because Willie's search for his existence continues endlessly, and we do not know what happens to him as a rebellious man. The last novel by V.S. Naipaul is *Magic Seeds* which deconstructs the Indian belief-system inherited from the British Empire. The Indians have been made to believe throughout history that "in India there were servile races, people born to be slaves, and there were martial races" (*MAS* 10). This notion of British Empire has been outright rejected by Sarojini, Willie's sister, who believes that such false belief system has been an imperialistic idea of the British. She understands that the so-called martial classes have been abused by the British for their ulterior motives whereas "some servants" have often exhibited courage to fight for justice against the oppressors. This is central to the thematic structure of this novel. This postcolonial notion deconstructs the idea of "servile" class and "martial race" with reference to history. It is therefore important to study Naipaul's later novels in the context of racial issues, suppression of histories, and oppression of the marginalized people. The interpretation of these later novels elucidates Naipaul's concerns for liberation of the oppressed classes by the oppressor.

5.1. Neoimperial Tools: Racism, Sexual Promiscuity and Political Violence

In *Guerrillas*, Naipaul portrays the multiple problems a postcolonial nation faces on its way for progress. More specifically, Naipaul traces the racial conflicts and black-white politics in rebuilding West Indies in his novel *Guerrillas*. Bruce King is fairly perceptive when he argues:

> *Guerrillas* (1975) brings together many of Naipaul's recurring themes—the inability of small, underdeveloped nations to be truly independent; mimicry; the relationship between whites and blacks in which assertions of black authenticity so often are part dependency; the ways in which Christianity blending with Black Messianism. (1993: 99)

In *The Return of Eva Peron*, Naipaul views that Black power outside the United States perpetuates the negative, colonial politics of protest. It is "deep corruption: a wish to be granted a dispensation from the pains of development, an almost religious conviction that oppression can be turned into an asset, race into money" (1980: 73). In *Guerrillas*, Naipaul shows the tension that exists between the Whites and Blacks through their mutual deceptions and pseudo-colonial concerns to lift the fortunes of the postcolonial people who are on the margin. However, it is only a showdown. In the Caribbean, there were two types of people: the so-called liberal Whites posed to be revolutionaries to uplift the people from their miseries so that they would be their leaders and enjoy power; the other categories were the black people who wanted to be the leaders of the blacks and enjoy power and control the economy of the country. With such interests, there was always racial tension among the revolutionaries and common people as well. In the process, there were a series of violence, rapes and murders. In his paper "Writers and Readers, the Written and the Read in V.S. Naipaul and *Guerrillas*", Neil ten Kortenaar makes a commendable remark: "V.S. Naipaul's novel *Guerrillas* is about the mutual deception practiced by Black power enthusiasts in the West Indies and white liberals in the West and their sometimes fatal self-deception" (1990: 324). In the very beginning of the novel when Jane and Roche drive on the city roads, they notice a slogan surcharged with racism: "Basic Black, Don't vote; Birth Control is a Plot Against the Negro Race" (*GS* 1). On their way to Thrush cross Grange from their house on the Ridge, they were to cover a long distance of ride across the hilly, barren areas. Some of the foreign investors, getting the affair of tax-holidays, had started projects for their industry and later on moved elsewhere. Jimmy Ahmad was the people's commune leader who had established a commune hut in that of Grange. Sablich's were thinking of buying all the land for investments. However, after Jimmy stepped in, "they disgorged this bit. A twenty-five years lease. Gifted just like that" (5). The racial issue, that is predominant in this part of the land, is obvious from the reactions of Roche when Jane moves towards the commune hut in Grange:

> When he saw Jane waking up the slight slope to the hut door he felt, as he had feared, that her presence

> there was wrong, and looked like an intrusion. The flowered blouse, through which her brassier could be seen, the right trousers that modeled stomach groin and cleft in a single, sudden curve: that could pass in the city and in the shopping plaza of the Ridge would be hardly noticeable but here it seemed provocative, over-casual enough to be dressy: London, foreign, wrong. And again it occurred to Roche that she was very white, with a colour that wasn't at all like the colour of White people. She was white enough to be unreadable; even her age might not be guessed. (6)

Roche rushed to her protectively near the hut when Jimmy Ahmad came. Jane saw that he gave an increasing physical neatness with a slender waist, trimmed moustache, closely-shaved cheeks and all other physical gestures and clothes. Jane however had expected this Ahmad to be more Negroid and awkward in appearance. Jane saw a poster of Ahmad which was looking more Negroid with roughly lettered words below: "I'm Nobody's slave or Stallion. I'm a warrior and Torch Bearer—Haj James Ahmed" (10). To her amazement, Jane thought that this Grange was another complete world: "...in that hut, with the junked office equipment on the table, the posters and the black pin-ups from newspapers on the walls with the boys on the metal beds, with the light and the emptiness outside, and the encircling forest. She felt she had entered another, complete world" (10). Jimmy had been deported from England on charges of rape and assault. As he himself told he was a *bakwai* Chinese (a nigger Chinese). In his outburst at his home, Jimmy showed off his strength as a leader and claimed that he was a friend to everybody, the investors, the government and the people. He was a worker, who fought for the cause of the Negroes. He was not a street-corner politician to change the government. On the other hand, he was a friend to every capitalist, even to Sablichs and he was not a Guerrilla: "I have no gun. I'm no guerrilla" (21). On their return, Jane saw how people were still living like derelicts in the postcolonial scenario: "And Jane thought that was something else she had stopped seeing. People like the runner, people like the wild men who lived in the hills, among the new developments, or down in the city, in the backyards of certain thoroughfares: derelicts, a whole parallel society" (23). It is startling to note the chaos and disorder in the postcolonial society. The Government is unable to take care of the suffering of people who have no minimum basic needs of life. They still live like the aborigines in rags:

> Wild men in rags, with long matted hair; wild men with unseeing red eyes. And bandits. Police cars patrolled these hillsides suburbs. Sometimes at night and in the early morning there was the sound of gunfire. The newspapers, the radio and the television spoke of guerrillas. (25)

Jane coming from England had a startling experience of the derelicts: people in rags, chaotic law and order situation and self-styled commune revolutionaries. People's suffering perpetuates. Only there is high publicity of development and fight for the people's cause. But Jane observes: "So bogus...so hidden away. The High Command. All the publicity. All that found. Of course, it's a perfect cover for the guerillas, isn't it?" (25). Jimmy Ahmed, the black revolutionary contemplates and urges to Roy, his friend that he is frustrated to see the dispossessed people's continuous suffering. It is very difficult to change their fortunes. He reflects on how he has been deported from England during the time of crisis. The people who win are the people who have won already. Jimmy mentions this in his letter to Roy:

> Perhaps after all Roy the world is only made for the people who possess it now, and there are some people who will never possess anything. The people who will win are the people who have won already and they're not taking chances now, like the liberals. (36)

Jimmy Ahmad has been aggressive towards those white liberals who have deported him from England after using him and making him his playboy. They are not sparing him even after deporting him from England: "Even here they are coming after me.... These liberals who come flashing their milk white thighs and think they're contributing to the cause" (36). Then he is also attacking Peter Roche, the Public Relations officer of the imperialistic firm of Sablich's great slave traders in the old days. Mr. Roche the great White revolutionary and torture hero of South Africa has written a book, the bestseller in Caribbean island is working on behalf of in the Sablich's who now pretend that black is beautiful and they think Mr. Roche can prove it. To Jimmy the situation on the Ridge is quite desperate because betrayal has been frequent there: "it's always a case of black faces white masks, you don't know who your enemy is, the enemy infiltrates your ranks all the time" (82). He is frustrated and hopeless because in the night he loses courage and considers that he is fighting a losing battle. When Stephen is vanished, they are sending other agents and he has no means to cope with. His despair makes him a pessimist very often. He therefore expresses his state of mind to Roy:

> Things are desperate Roy, when the leader himself begins to yield to despair, things are bad. The whole place is going to blow up; I cannot see how I can control the resolution now. When everybody wants to fight there's nothing to fight for. Everybody wants to fight his own little war, everybody is a guerrilla. (83)

Roche's frustrations, although internal, disturb him often. He thinks about his futile life: "I've built my whole life on sand" (87). Though people think that he is working for a cause, he understands that he has neither any political ideology nor vision to go forward: "If he had a system, a set of political beliefs, it might have been easier for him to have set it aside, to have admitted error, as some of his associates had done, to have blamed the system to have blamed the world for not living up to the system, and without any sense of reneging to have made a fresh start" (87). He has been disillusioned with his job of public relations officer with Sablich's. He has also been waiting for Jane to leave for England: one failure after the other. Analyzing his life and actions of the past, he feels that he is responsible for his actions by ignoring certain truths about his life in South Africa and Ridge and his relationship with Jane. He therefore considers his life futile.

The chaotic situation in a municipal area of the city is rather deplorable. Once upon a time the area had been a "respectable lower-class area" (99). The municipalities have not bothered to maintain the civility in this area:

> It was a community now without rules; and the area was new apparently without municipal regulation. Empty house-lots had been turned into street-band yards or open-air motor-repair shops; cars and lorries without wheels choked the narrow lanes where garbage dammed the open gutters wrinkled white films of scum formed on the black water. The walls were scrawled, and sometimes carefully marked, with old election slogans, racial slogans, and made-up African names *Kwame Mandingo* (*Slave Name—Butler*). There was something competitive and whimsical and it seemed at variance with the words of threat and anger. (100)

The novel therefore demonstrates that a society without the established inbuilt structures cannot give stability during transition from colonial to postcolonial stage. Since the society is independent, and without a visionary political system, it has been dragged to chaos. The revolutionaries have no definite plans and ideas to take the country in the path of progress. They have only fantasies rather than any redeeming movement that can remove the chaotic situation. Jimmy's claims of "back to the land" by black people and the racial attitude of black consciousness have the strength of moving forward. Nor even the white liberals' notion of personal power and involvement can redeem these third world situations so effectively. In *Guerrillas*, there is no treatment of political events directly. The Caribbean island has a history of racial humiliations. After independence, there is no viable alternative plan to provide a better life to its people. The political events are thought of being a kind of communal frenzy. The people therefore turn to "quasi-religious notions of racial deliverance" (King 1993: 101). Naipaul is not supportive of the outsiders' interference in the distress of the Third world countries after they enjoyed their freedom. He scrutinizes their motivations in the affairs of these postcolonial nations that normally do not welcome the whites who apparently involve themselves to improve their conditions. Naipaul portrays them as the heirs of the Empire, who carry their emotional needs to the former colonies for dramatization of their sexual excitement and access to power after the shrunken condition of their societies during postcolonial period. After the end of Empire, the imperial centre has lost its glamour and the Europeans have therefore turned to these third world nations for their excitement. But these expatriates, the outsiders have no connections and roots in the local context and hence they are not acceptable. These white liberals however cling to local ethos and activities.

In *Guerrillas* Naipaul portrays Jimmy Ahmed, who is a half-Chinese Negro, as Black Power. Jimmy is treated as a play-boy in England by the liberal whites. He was made a black-power leader in England, and he is also used sexually for excitement of the Whites. Then he is deported to the Caribbean island on the charges of rape and assault. Even in the Caribbean he is not spared. He is used by Roche in order to provoke that he has a cause for the Negroes for their upliftment. Jane, an outsider white woman, tempts him sexually for fulfillment of her excitement. Jimmy Ahmed has always the potential for violence, and Jane has rightly marked that Ahmed has the thrill of playing with fire.

Though Jimmy is a Chinese Negro, he is also an outsider in the Caribbean. Despite his rise as a black-power leader, he is neither black nor a leader and hence he is not protected by any group. Despite his London reputation, he is rather unsuccessful to fulfill the cause of the blacks. His revolution has no vision to inspire, and he had not worked out a political system to expedite the cause of the dispossessed blacks. In England Jimmy was admired initially for his potential concern for the blacks by the progressive politicians but at the time of crisis because of the rape charge he was not supported by any group as he was an alien, a non-White. Roche, the liberal White, faces a similar situation in South Africa. For a time, he was highly admired by the left and considered to be the hero of South African resistance, but he was to flee to England when he was threatened by a South African agent. That was because he was an alien there. Both these heroes are not the true and serious revolutionaries. They have not worked any definite political system to rescue the distressed blacks. Both of them are activists without any ideology or plan. They are associated with the commune in the Caribbean in which they have no trust. They are themselves confused and often reflect upon the credibility of the commune. Both of them as activists attract women because of their reputation as leaders. It is rather difficult to "read" Jimmy who finally indulges in the brutal murder of Jane, the white woman who has tempted him to violent sex. The novel therefore highlights the "black-power rising, killing of a black leader, eruption of violence and the crumbling of the government" (Bhat 94-95). Naipaul thus explores the predicament of the newly decolonized countries. Kamra's remarks on the postcolonial set-up of the Ridge society are worth-mentioning:

> The various subjective realities of the expatriate society of the Ridge, through whose eyes we see the town and Grange, provide the outsider's view of third world chaos, disorder and subhuman existence. Theirs is the despair of having come as messengers of good will to uplift and present a new hope on behalf of the Western World only to find that they are at the mercy of "beasts" and their own similar hungers. Jimmy and indirectly Bryant's consciousness pervade the novel from beginning to end. (132-33)

Jimmy, the so-called half Chinese Negro, murders Jane after his violent sex with her; then he plans to murder Roche, but fails. If this is the vision of the leader, then naturally he is a lost case. Jimmy is such a black-power leader who is a scheming villain without morality and ethics. He is a guerrilla no doubt; but the question is, for what he is fighting, for whom? A leader who fled from England on the charges of rape and assault is indulging here at Grange in rape, murder and conspiracy to murder. He is a leader with no humanity and, having no concern for values. He is not a leader in the true sense of the term. He is both perverse and subversive. Despite his tall claims of being a friend to everybody, in his lifestyle, there is no such quality and behavior. It is simply impossible on his part to contribute substantially to bring about development and order to that kind of Ridge society. After the end of colonialism what is required at this juncture of a leader is that he should be a man of vision with positive values, design and real concern for the people of the land who are under-living, starving, without clothes and, also uncivilized. A barbaric and racialist as Jimmy is, no change could be possible through his revolution. In other words, he is a secret terrorist who can murder people who have some trust on him. Naipaul, portraying such a character as a black-power leader, is emphasizing that postcolonial societies under the hands of these villains are not safe. The governments are unable to tackle the chaotic situation created by them. Even the white liberals, who claim to have been working for the cause of the blacks, are also unable to counter them because they are also working on without any concrete plan based on ideologies to uplift the miserable people and discarded society economically, socially and culturally. Naipaul is scrutinizing the activities of the different groups as well as governments if these have the potentiality to improve the postcolonial situation in these countries. What is conspicuous in this context is that both these people and the governments are great failures to discharge their responsibilities with clarity, precision and effectiveness. *Guerrilla* supersedes the harsh and black realism that *The Mimic Men* and *In a Free State* establish in Naipaul's fiction. Mustafa's interpretation of the novel is convincing:

> Its (Guerrilla's) unpleasant tale of a doomed quasi-cooperative enterprise on a Caribbean island between the skewed Black Power initiatives of Jimmy Ahmad and his corporate sponsors, Sablichs, is played out amongst a cost of characters confused by their missions and arrogant in their ignorance. The resulting posturing between the expatriates Roche and Jane and the returned "revolutionary", Jimmy, is from the start fated to abort at the level of a grass theatricality because of their failure to grasp anything but their own misplaced vanities. Against a political climate that remains controlled by

> outside forces, Jimmy's Black Power commune is like the thwarted and stunted vegetables that they profess to cultivate, while the importations of both Roche's anti-apartheid South African resume and Jane's London-chic third-world slumming are similarly misallied. All three characters have in different degrees been molded by a metropolitan liberalism that has utterly failed to discern that its attitude to and understanding of decolonization are necessarily blinded by its own glint-ridden complicity in the prior colonial enterprises. (1995: 125)

The characters in this novel, who consider themselves self-righteous, are deluded and confused and hence are careless "expounders of rhetoric mouthed by the generation of decolonization" (Mustafa 126). Their actions cause more harm to the natives because these are of villainous nature. In the context of inappropriate sexuality and violence Mustafa's comments are worth-noting in relation to such characters as hypocritical Jimmy, his male-lover Bryant and sexually-licentious Jane:

> While she is neither mysterious nor compelling, she nevertheless represents a sexual license that within the island setting is both threatening and inappropriate. Thus, towards the end of the narrative Jimmy's act of sodomy upon her is the novel's twinning of her with Bryant, the foundling of the commune and Jimmy's male lover, and serves as the narrative's impelled sexual mirroring, making sex and sexual promiscuity the novel's frame for political misadventure and misalliance. (127)

The discussion of Roche with Stephens's mother just before Police gun down Stephens is very important to understand the complexity of the island's political option within a framework of a confined, urban, neo-colonial setting. Mrs. Stephens is acutely critical of the lie that Jimmy represents to the community. Stephens endorses "the frugal but functional rhetoric of redemption and liberation that still exists among the island's population" (Mustafa 128). Roche's encounter with Mrs. Stephens makes him reflective on excessive role of England on the island to control it although it is no more under the colonial rule: "England, Roche thought: it was so hard to get away from England here. And there were so many Englands: his, Jane's, Jimmy's, Lloyd's, and the England—hard to imagine—in that old woman's head" (*GS* 104). Mrs. Stephens's hatred for Jimmy is obvious: "That Chinese man I never like that Chinese man. But I am a supporter of this government, Mr. Roche. This government will never fall" (*GS* 106). Mrs. Stephens has therefore no illusions of the commune's objectives guided by London ideas. Britain has not promises for the people of island either. She therefore represents that "silent constituency that helps maintain the status quo through its balance between the revivalist faith of the redemption-minded servant-class and a distinct communal identification, despite the harsh realities of poverty and abandonment" (Mustafa 128).

Guerrillas reveals that the borrowed ideas from England cannot be applied to the complex situations of the island people, recently liberated politically. Their economic woes still continue. The neo-colonials like Sablichs and Black power commune leader Jimmy do not fit into the set-up of island's design either politically or economically. They are rather inadequate to deal with the complexities of the multiple problems the myriad people in the Island face with.

5.2. Ethnicity and Political Chaos in Postcolonial Africa

Naipaul discusses the chaos and disorder in the postcolonial African Society in the novel *A Bend in the River* as he presents the West Indian chaotic situation after the end of colonialism in the novel *Guerrillas*. The African society referred to here is rotten by violence and a mimic civil war because of group clashes. The African attitude towards the whites was based on hatred because of their memory of the past when they were slaves to the whites. They therefore went back to the remote past when their society had no whites and other outsiders. Naipaul is concerned with the disorder of the postcolonial world in Africa. Both the white forces and the extremist militarism of the nationalistic outfits create havoc and disorder in the country dragging it to the brink of disaster. Naipaul gives us a fearful picture of different historical forces clashing with each other. It has therefore been rightly argued:

> A vision of the enactment of historical forces clashing with one another gives a fearful picture. It is as dreadful a picture as that of postwar England in T.S. Eliot's *The Waste Land*. Postcolonial Africa torn by the rival and clashing forces of varied types is a new version of "Wasteland", where there seems to be no redemption. (Bhat 94)

The group clashes are thus based on narrow racism and conflicts of culture. Naipaul perhaps inquires into a democratic world which explains how an individual's existence is possible only by power groups; otherwise there is always a threat to his existence. Only the man in power enjoys dignity through his power of exercising choice and freedom. In this context, Kamra's comments on the positions of individuals in such societies represented in *Guerrillas* and *A Bend in the River:*

> In the racially and culturally complex societies of these two novels the narrator enables Naipaul to present a cross-section of a placeless world without intrinsic value in which the self is prostituted into a commodity to purchase "a fix on reality" sex, violence, money, speech—the coins of exchange and communication—are all encompassed by the shopkeeper's jargon of buying and selling the sense of misuse and waste and assessment of this world as a junkyard. (124)

The confrontation of cultures takes place in a third-world society which is an unreal society because of the continuous presence of the dominated whites who try to control such a society economically, though political independence has already been achieved. However, the whites who pose that they have come to do good to such a society impose their "secured" superiority upon them and consider the native culture inferior. This sort of attitude of the whites is altogether rejected by the natives resulting in group clashes and cultural conflicts. Kamra thinks that the associations between "colonial West" and the "colonized third-world" have damaged the psyche of the natives to an irreparable loss:

> The significance of *A Bend in the River* can be better understood if the two social situations are contrasted. In these two novels the narrator comes to groups with the psychological reality of the association between the colonial West and the colonized third world. Evoked subjectivity with an ample expression of moods, passions, sentiments and emotions, they leave a deep impression of the far-reaching and almost lasting damage done to the third world psyche. (133)

Although in Africa the sons of the soil like Ferdinand and the boys at the lycee question the white man's religion, culture and education regarding their domination and seriously think about the future of Africa, they do not have the vigor and intellectuality that can counter them. Their ideas and thoughts are rather borrowed, and have no viability and strength to take the country forward in the path of progress. In the absence of an alternative, viable system of beliefs, the society therefore sinks into disasters and disorders. Chaos prevails, and hence violence, sexual promiscuity, civil war and bloodshed do occur frequently. These young people have only despair to react to the immediate present rather than having any sense of "nationhood" of the American Negro. *A Bend in the River* is set in an unnamed African country after independence. Salim, an ethnic Indian Muslim shopkeeper, the narrator, though born in another part on the east coast, observes the rapid changes in his homeland with an outsider's distance. The very first sentence in the book is significant to Naipaul's world-view and his sense of history: "The world is what it is: men who are nothing, who allow themselves to become nothing, have no place in it" (*BR* 3). Salim, who bought the shop cheap from Nazruddin, noted that "the town in the interior, at the bend in the great river, had almost ceased to exist" (3) because of which Salim was advised to start everything afresh. His sense of history helped Salim know about the place: "The place had had its troubles: the town at the bend in the river was more than half destroyed. What had been the European suburb near the rapids had been burnt down, and bush had grown over the ruins; it was hard to distinguish what had been gardens from what had been streets"

(4). However, from the ruins the activities of the day-to-day life bloomed again. Though Salim was an Indian Muslim, Africa was his country and a home for his family for many centuries:

> Africa was my home, had been the home of my family for centuries. But we came from the east coast, and that made the difference. The coast was not truly African. It was an Arab-Indian-Persian-Portuguese place, and we who lived there were really people of the Indian Ocean. True Africa was at our back. Many miles of scrub or desert separated us from the up-country people; we looked east to the lands with which we traded—Arabia, India, Persia. Those were also the lands of our ancestors. But we could no longer say that we were Arabians or Indians or Persians; when we compared ourselves with these people, we felt like people of Africa. (12)

Salim understands the sort of history he has learnt only from history books written by the Europeans: "Without Europeans I feel, our past would have been washed away, like the scuff marks of fishermen on the beach outside our own" (13).

In contrast to the Europeans, the Arab and the Indian Muslims were more moral. They did not tell lies or manipulate things to their own advantages:

> We didn't lie because we never assessed ourselves and didn't think there was anything for us to lie about; we were people who simply did what we did. But the Europeans could do one thing and say something quite different and they could act in this way because they had an idea of what they owed to their civilization. It was their great advantage over us [...]. Being an intelligent and energetic people; and at the peak of their powers, they could express both sides of their civilization; and they got both the slaves and the statues. (19)

In course of time, the Arab energy that had pushed them into Africa was vanished. At the bend in the river a European town had grown. Salim going back to history tells us that "one tide of history [...] had brought us here [...] another tide of history was coming to wash us away" (22). Salim therefore smells change in the African set-up and in their lives as well. In the changed scenario when Salim reaches the interior at the bend of the river, the town where Nazruddin lived, had been destroyed: "Ruins had been left as ruins; no attempt had been made to tidy up [...]. The wish had only been to get rid of the old, to wipe out the memory of the intruder. It was unnerving, the depth of that African rage, the wish to destroy, regardless of the consequences" (30). This African attitude towards destruction is rather chaotic. Nazruddin's town looked ghastly with the ruins and its deprivations. In such a deadly, ruinous destruction, the past, present and future mingled and seemed to be one, confused and disturbing:

> Sun and rain and bush had made the site look old, like the site of a dead civilization. The ruins, spreading over so many acres, seemed to speak of a final catastrophe. But the civilization wasn't dead. It was the civilization I existed in and in fact was still working towards. And that could make for an odd feeling: to be among the ruins was to have your time-sense unsettled. You felt like a ghost, not from the past, but from the future. You felt that your life and ambition had already been lived out for you and you were looking at the relics of that life. You were in a place where the future had come and gone. (30)

Actually, there was a publicity that feudalism was going to be over. It was a positive move for a great change: "Some papers spoke of the end of feudalism and the dawn of a new age. But what had happened was not new. People that had grown feeble had been physically destroyed. That, in Africa, it was not new; it was the oldest law of the land" (33). Nobody could prevent changes when they would come. The world was in a flux, it is not constant. However in Africa, the change was not to the better. The colonial administration had been harmful to the psyche of the natives. However in its absence, the country needed an alternative modern government which could rule on democratic norms to make the country economically viable. But that did not happen because the country was dragged into disastrous chaotic situations because of lack of an alternative vision on democratic as well as economic developments. Even Salim wanted to break away from his own family: "I had accepted his offer because I wanted to break away. To break away from my family and community also meant breaking away from my unspoken commitment to Nazruddin and his daughter" (27). Reaching there in the town of Nazruddin, Salim was shocked to note that the town had been destroyed. In such a town Salim had to start his life afresh in a hostile atmosphere without any substantial social life: "My life was unconstricted, but narrower than it had ever been; the solitude of my evenings was like an ache. I didn't think that I had the resources to last" (32). Such a barren life was a great burden for Salim. In the post-independence Africa there was racial tension, and hence the white people were driven away from some towns. However, the tall warrior African class loved the whites, hated the Africans: "The white people had been driven out from our town, and their monuments destroyed. But there were a lot of white people up there, in another town, and warriors and slaves. And that was glamour for the warrior boys, glamour for Metty, and glamour for Ferdinand" (61).

Salim notes that people like him, who are less educated, are at peace. However people like Ferdinand at lycee are not simple because their minds are not empty: "It was a jumble, full of all kinds of junk" (61). The local Africans were *malins* who chased men as their prey. Mahesh explained that the English expression "wicked", "mischievous", and "bad-minded" are wrong substitutes for *malins,* the French word: "The people were *malins* the way a dog chasing a lizard was a *malin*, or a cat chasing a bird. The people were *malins* because they lived with the knowledge of men as prey" (63). In that town there were no laws and regulations. The town had been ruined because there was no order. Even if there was order, there was also dishonesty: "There had been order once, but that order had had its own dishonesties and cruelties—that was why the town had been wrecked. We lived in that wreckage. Instead of regulations, there were now only officials who could always prove you wrong, until you paid up" (65). Father Huismans, a European, had a greater understanding of Africa, its history and civilizations.

To him the relics and carvings were words that helped him to see himself and Africa as part of an immense flow of history. He could see the destruction of the European town in a new way because he thought such destructions always yielded to some new beginnings "when the course of history was being altered" (72). Father Huismans considered all colonial relics to be as precious as African things because he saw that true Africa was going to die. While that Africa still lived, it was necessary to understand and preserve its things. Naipaul reflects on Huismans's idea of his civilization: "So old, so new. And out of his stupendous idea of his civilization, his stupendous idea of the future, Father Huismans saw himself at the end of it all, the last, lucky witness" (73).

While still the town was under recovery from the semi-tribal war that had broken out during the independence struggle, and shattered and emptied the town, there was again the declaration of a war between the army and the rebels. Soon after the independence, the people of the town at the bend went mad with anger and fear with the memory of the colonial period when they had been suffering so much under the Europeans and the Arabs. They refused to be ruled now by the new government. The people were so much raged unreasonably that they did not consider the town at the bend to be theirs: "But they had hated the town for the intruders who had ruled in it and from it; and they had preferred to destroy the town rather than take it over" (76). However after the destruction, they had a great grief and wished to see the town again as a living place: "And seeing it come to a kind of life again, they had grown afraid once more" (76). However, the war started again inculcating fear and horror among the people. Salim wished that neither the army nor the rebels should win the war. He wished that the old balance should continue. But war is war. Destructive as it is, it took lives from both sides. Many people and soldiers were killed. However, peace could be established for some time. And during this period of peace that father Huismans was gunned down. Salim was shocked at his death:

> It was terrible. His death made his life seem such a waste. So much of his knowledge was buried with him, and

> what to me was more than knowledge—his attitudes, his relish for Africa, his feeling for the beliefs of the forest. A little bit of the world was lost with him. (92)

Such kind of waste was frequent in such a society of chaos and disorder. Violence had no limits in destroying people and property: "It had sent him looking, inquiring; it had made him find human richness where the rest of us saw bush or had stopped seeing anything at all. But his idea of civilization was also like his vanity. It had made him read too much in that mingling of peoples by our river; and he had paid for it" (93). In spite of his death, it is significant to remember father Huismans's comments on the historical process of civilization: "After each setback, the civilization of Europe would become a little more secure at the bend in the river; the town would always start up again, and would grow a little more each time" (99). During the peace time, the town could be reestablished again and the rebellion as well as the death of father Huismans receded fast. The Big man in the capital started many developmental projects to provide different modern amenities to the people—order and money, telephone system, bus service and taxis, the steamer service and so on. New cities were built up to accommodate the movement of villagers to the cities. However, the growth of population was reflected in the heap of rubbish in the streets. It was a great reflection of civil disorder with which the new government could not cope:

> The growth of the population could be gauged by the growth of the rubbish heaps, in the *cites*. They didn't burn their rubbish in oil drums as we did; they just threw it out on the broken streets—that sifted, ashy African rubbish. Those mounds of rubbish, though constantly flattened by rain, grew month by month into increasingly solid little hills, and hills literally became as high as the box-like concrete houses of the *cites*. (101)

Naipaul mocks at the inefficiency of the health department and other administrative functionaries. Though there were officials in all the departments, the system did not function properly. The streets in the cities remained dirt, the roads were neglected, and the disinfectant system was merely an eye-wash.

Every system was just a hollow although the number of the officials was very high:

> All the people—like the health officials—who performed services for ready money were energetic, or could be made so—the customs people, the police, and even the army. The administration, however hollow, was fuller; there were people you could appeal to. You could get things done, if you knew how to go about it. (101)

With such pompous and secured atmosphere provided by the government, people became enthusiastic to work with new confidence although the occasional thought, that they might be replaced any time in the historical process, caused some kind of pain in them. With the new vigor, people maintained their tempo of work. The government officials in all the departments became corrupt to accumulate wealth. Even the army people were no exception to this kind of temptation. In spite of their roughness, the warrior tribes were preferable to the army people who had no "warrior code". They were rather aggressive, crooked and graceless. They thought that they had the license to do anything they liked:

> With their guns and jeeps, these men were poachers of ivory and thieves of gold. Ivory, gold—add slaves, and it would have been like being in oldest Africa. And these men would have dealt in slaves, if there was still a market. It was to the traders in the town that the army turned when they wished to clear their gold or, more especially, the ivory they had poached. Officials and governments right across the continent were engaged in this ivory trade which they themselves had declared illegal. It made smuggling easy; but I was nervous of getting involved, because a government that breaks its own laws can also easily break you. Your business associate today can be your jailer or worse tomorrow. (106)

But Mahesh was associated with the army people in this kind of business knowing full well that it was dangerous to deal with them in this illegal work. He therefore argued:

> But if they let you down, you pay up. That is all. In your costing, you make allowances for that. You just pay. I don't think you understand, Salim. And it isn't an easy thing to understand. It isn't that there's no right and wrong there. There's no right. (107)

In this way, Mahesh could accumulate a lot of wealth and gold. Many people could turn into rich millionaires through this corrupt business practices in postcolonial Africa when the government machinery was corrupt and inefficient. By the orders of the "Big" man, the President, modern Africa was being built with new buildings and structures.... In reference to the subsequent turn of events in Africa, the appreciation of the President seemed to be satirical:

> The president had wished to show us a new Africa. And I saw Africa in a way I had never seen it before, saw the defeats and humiliations which until then I had regarded as just a fact of life. And I felt like that—full of tenderness for the Big man, for the ragged villagers walking around the Domain, and the soldiers showing them the shabby sights—until some soldiers played the fool with me or some official at the customs was difficult, and then I fell into the old way of feeling, the easier attitudes of the foreigners in the bars. Old Africa, which seemed to absorb everything, was simple; this place kept you tense. What a strain it was picking your way through stupidity and aggressiveness and pride and hurt! (117)

Though the buildings at the Domain were grand, they had consumed millions of dollars. The objective was not materialized because neither the Chinese nor the Taiwanese turned up to the land of the new model African farm. However in an ironical turn, the Domain became a University City and research centre. Though in the new turn of the events Ferdinand, Metty's friend, got a chance of going for higher studies with govt. scholarship, Metty lost his friend. Such changes however made Salim see "a disordered future" for the country where nobody was going to be secure. Salim also thought the Domain, with its shoddy grandeur, as a hoax: "Neither the President who had called it into being nor the foreigners who had made a fortune building it had faith in what they were creating" (119). Actually the Domain was the creation of the President. In the presence of the foreigners in the Domain, Ferdinand and the other young Africans had a high, romantic idea of Africa: "So foreigners and Africans acted and reacted on one another, and everyone became locked on an idea of glory and newness" (139). Despite the Domain being a "hoax", Salim moved between the Domain and the town because he thought whatever man made, it was real. However to him the town was reassuring and secured because in the Domain, Africa was more in words and ideas of excitement. Raymond, the European historian, is concerned with the record of the historical events. He therefore questioned Indar and Salim about the past wars and rebellions in Africa: "Do you think we will ever get to know the truth about what has happened in Africa in the last hundred or even fifty years. All the wars, all the rebellions, all the leaders, all the defeats?" (151). It is important to understand the concern of Raymond to write about the history of Africa. But what is interesting is that he had to work on the behest of the Big man. It would therefore be difficult on his part to represent an authentic history, without distortion and modification. Salim was also concerned with the history, the record of the Past. To him, history should be free from suppression of facts. It should be fairly authentic:

> History was something dead and gone, part of the world of our grandfathers, and we didn't pay too much attention to it; even though, among trading families like ours, there were still vague stories—so vague that they didn't feel real—of European Priests buying slaves cheap from the caravans before they got to the depot on the coast. The Africans (and this was the point of the stories) had been scared out of their skins—they thought the missionaries were buying them in order to eat them. (210)

Referring to the article about the missionaries and the ransomed slaves by Raymond, Salim sees that the writer heavily depended on the quotations from the Archives. His knowledge was not based on interaction with people. Despite his vast researched knowledge about Africa, "he had less true knowledge of Africa, less feel for it, than Indar or Nazruddin or even Mahesh; he had nothing like father Huismans's instinct for the strangeness and wonder of the place" (210-11).

Noimon, the Greek businessman sold his property secretly and left Africa smelling the boom was going to an end. However this man's departure marked the end of boom of property in Africa. All the businessmen lost confidence thereafter. By this time, when there was sluggish economy without acknowledging it, the President declared that the youth guard in the region of the bend would be disbanded because they were unfaithful, and also forgot their duty to the people. It was the hidden agenda of the President to take the bend into disorder and chaos again for his own selfish purposes: "The officers would lose their stipend; there would be no government jobs for any of them; they would be banished from the town and sent back to the bush to do constructive work there. In the bush they would learn the wisdom of the monkey" (243). Behind this declaration, the Big man had just the opposite motive. People were happy initially to see the disbanding of the youth Guard, but after the disbanding things were changed from bad to worse. After this, the police and other officials tormented people for money. Salim notes:

> It was harassment, and the purpose was money, and money fast, before everything changed. These men had sniffed some change coming; in disbanding of the youth Guard they had seen signs of the President's weakness rather them strength. And in this situation there was no one I could appeal to. Every official was willing for a consideration, to give assurance about his own conduct. But no official was high enough or secure enough to guarantee the conduct of any other official. (245-46)

That is so because the country has been dragged into disaster and disorder once again. Salim observes: "But men had lost or rejected the idea of an overseeing authority, and everything was again as fluid as it had been at the beginning. Only this time, after all the years of peace and goods in all the shops, everyone was greedier" (246).

Every businessman was facing the same situation. To Mahesh, there was no question of stable relationship at the bend. In a crisis, peace was to be bought afresh every day. Salim could not read the fluid political situation properly for which like Raymond, he believed in the power and wisdom of the President who could do something to reassert his authority. The officials like hawks would disturb Salim for money. However, it was a great relief for him when violence came to the town: "Not the evening drama of start brawls and murders but a steady, nightly assault in different areas on policemen and police stations and officials and official buildings" (247). One night the statue of the African Madonna and child in the Domain was smashed. There had been riots about water, riots due to death by car accident and so on. The violence was organized, widespread and sudden. In a circulated leaflet, it was written:

> ....since war is an extension of politics; we have decided to face the ENEMY with armed confrontation. Otherwise we all die for ever. The ancestors are shrieking. If we are not deaf we can hear them. By ENEMY we mean the powers of imperialism, the multinationals and the puppet powers that be, the false gods, the capitalists, the priests and teachers who give false interpretations. The law encourages crime. The schools teach ignorance and people practice ignorance in preference to their true culture.... Our people must understand the struggle. They must learn to die with us. (248)

The leaflet was a call to the people to participate in the general disorder of the region such as violence, bloodshed, chaos, murder and looting: "There was a lot more blood as a result; and the violence, which at first seemed directed against the authorities alone, became more general. African stalls and shops in the outer areas were attacked and looted. People began to be killed in horrible ways, by rioters and police and shanty town criminals" (249). Raymond was stunned to note the insurrection. He became nervous when the structure of

Madonna was demolished: "And Raymond now lived in fear of dismissal. This was what it had come down to for him—a job, a house, his livelihood, simple security. He was a defeated man; and the house in the Domain was like a house of death" (251-52). When such a disorder was prevailing in the town, the villages were not also spared. Zabeth noted that her business was sluggish in the village since the days of insurrection: "Young men were being kidnapped here and there by the police and the army: it was the new government tactic" (261).

After his engagement with Nazruddin's daughter in London, Salim returned to Africa with the idea of home where he would live with Kareisha the rest of his life. But Salim did not know whether he could wind up his business establishment there, after reaching Africa. He was to live in a world that was given to him. He could not create his own world according to his whims and desires: "There could be no going back; there was nothing to go back to. We had become what the world outside had made us; we had to live in the world as it existed" (286). Reaching there he learnt that his business had been nationalized by the President and he was to work as a manager to Citizen Theotime, who was appointed state trustee by the President. With nationalization or radicalization, he had to lose all his money deposited in the banks. He was no more the owner, but a mere employee of his own business establishment. It was a rude shock to Salim when he arrived in his flat to note the coldness of Metty in the changed circumstances: "You don't have anything. They take away your shop. They give it to Citizen Theotime. The President made a speech a fortnight back. He said he was radicalizing and taking away everything from everybody: "All foreigners. The next day they put a padlock on the door. And a few other doors as well" (299). Even before this news Salim was astonished to learn the destruction created by the insurrection, the Liberation Army: "We passed a burnt out building, a new ruin. It had been a primary school, never much of a place, more like a low shed.... It didn't lessen my relief of being in the town, seeing the night-time pavement groups, and finding myself, so quickly after arrival. Something of the forest gloom still on me, in my own street—all there, and as real and loss ordinary as ever" (298). After losing all his money in the banks, Salim explored opportunities to make money through gold and ivory business quite secretly so that he could get his commission in the European banks which would enable him to go to Europe afterwards. It was however quite a Dangerous business: "It was a slow, taut-like, humiliating business" (304). Although money could be made through such business quite slowly during this time of political disorder, it was however difficult to get away from the country. Salim understood human behavior during this crisis in a rather curious way:

> But then I proved Indar's point about trampling on the past: the Domain quickly ceased to be what it had been for me. It became a place where honorable people—many of them first-time law-breakers, who were later to use their respect for the law to cheat me with a clear mind, tried to get better rates than the ones we had agreed. What was common to these people was their nervousness and contempt, contempt for me, contempt for the country. I was half on their side; I revived them the contempt that it was so easy for them to feel. (304-05)

In the Domain, Salim notes the changes of this structure gradually to on African hailing settlement. The easily grown maize in the African soil created "make-believe" of garden shrubs. Salim therefore wonders about the mysterious changes at the bend of the river:

> This place of earth—how many changes had come to it! Forest at a bend in the river, a meeting place, an Arab settlement, a European outpost, a European suburb, a ruin like the ruin of a dead civilization, the glittering Domain of new Africa, and now this. (306)

The behavior and attitude of Theo in the shop gradually became unbearable to both Salim and Metty. Metty wanted some money from Salim to go away but Salim comforted him by saying that sooner the situation would change. But it did not change however. Being enraged Metty betrayed Salim for which the police under the leadership of Prosper could search the ivory in Salim's flat. He was however asked to give the police officer three/four thousand dollars. Since Salim had no such amount to give them as bribes, he was arrested, and jailed. The interference of Ferdinand, the commissioner, could however help him in his release from the jail. Salim's experience in the jail was startling. He was raged to see so many young men picked up and their lives destroyed. The state had specific plan or law for restoring order. Jailing people was rather a futile, meaningless exercise:

> If there was a plan, these events had meaning, if there was law, these events had meaning. But there was no plan; there was no law; this was only make-believe, play, a waste of men's time in the world. And how often here even in the days of bush, it must have happened before, this game of warders and prisoners in which men could be destroyed for nothing. I remember what Raymond used to say—about events being forgotten, lost, swallowed up. (313-14)

Salim observes that the press was not reporting these awful events of jailing—kidnapping the young people and jailing them and the operations of the torture of the Liberation Army. In the morning, these young people, picked up from villages, were compelled to sing the hymns of praise to the President and African Madonna. In this exercise, the young people from the villages had been "trussed up and dumped in the courtyard and were being maltreated in ways I don't want to describe" (315). Looking at them Salim was really shocked to think about the collapse of African state machinery and vision:

> Those faces of Africa! Those masks of childlike calm that had brought down the blows of the world, and of Africans as well, as now in the jail: I felt I had never seen them so clearly before. Indifferent to notice, indifferent to compassion or contempt, those faces were yet not vacant or passive or resigned. There was, with the prisoners as well as with their active tormenters, frenzy. But the frenzy of the prisoners was internal; it had taken them for beyond their cause or even knowledge of their cause, for beyond thought. They had prepared

> themselves for death not because they were martyrs; but because what they were and what they knew they were all they had. They were people crazed with the idea of who they were. I never felt closer to them, or more far away. (316)

Before his last encounter with Ferdinand, the commissioner, Salim reflected on his rising to the top position from a village boy, starting from nothing. He did not see Ferdinand to create an impression on him. He was rather looking shrunken and characterless in the regulation uniform that made him look like all those officials. It was really a strange thing to think about the pomp and infinite power of these officials: "These men, who depended on the President's favor for everything, were bundles of nerves. The great power they exercised went with a constant fear of being destroyed. And they were unstable, half dead" (318). Ferdinand, the commissioner, whose guardian was Salim himself during Ferdinand's Lycee days, was quite warm to him in their final meeting. He advised Salim to stop business and escape in the only steamer that would be starting the next day. There were no plane seats because all the officials were coming for the President's visit. The commissioner assured Salim to keep Prosper busy in the airport to facilitate Salim's escape. Salim quietly agreed and asked Ferdinand how he was feeling in the present situation. It was really frightening to note the reactions of Ferdinand, the commissioner:

> You don't have to ask. You mustn't think it's bad just for you. It's bad for everybody. That's the terrible thing. It's bad for Prosper, bad for the man they gave your shop to, bad for everybody. Nobody's going anywhere. We're all going to hell, and everyman knows this in his bones. We're being killed. Nothing has any meaning. That is why everyone is so frantic. Everyone wants to take his money and run away. But where? That is what driving people mad. They feel they're leaving the place they can run back to. I began to feel the same thing when I was a cadet in the capital. I felt I had been used. I felt I had given myself an education for nothing. I felt I had been fooled. Everything that was given to me was given

> to destroy me. I began to think I wanted to be a child again, to forget books and everything connected with books. The book runs itself. But there is no place to go to. I've been on tour in the villages. It's a nightmare. All these airfields the man has built, the foreign companies have built—nowhere is safe now. (319-20)

This reflective philosophical gesture of Ferdinand on the state of affairs of Africa is quite revealing of the collapse of the state machinery. It indicates the bankruptcy of the vision of the state administration. It is a great political disorder. The people in the administration lack the intellectuality to run the state. They have become nothing to take the state to nothing. This nihilism is rather startling. The execution is going on every day, but the person who is to be executed does not know about it. He is one of the witnesses of the execution place. Thereafter on his way to the steamer, Salim meets Metty who is quite depressed because he learns about the mass killing. He learns that nobody will be spared. The Liberation Army will kill everybody—the Govt. officials and all people—the masters and servants:

> They say they have to do what they did the last time, but they have to do it better this time. At first they were going to have people's courts and shoot people in the squares. Now they say they have to do a lot more killing and everybody will have to dip their hands in the blood. They're going to kill everybody who can read and write, everybody whoever put on a jacket and tie, everybody who put on a *jacket de boy.* They are going to kill all the masters and the servants. When they're finished nobody will know there was a place like this here. They're going to kill and kill. They say, it is the only way, to go back to the beginning before it's too late. The killing will last for days than to die forever. It is going to be terrible when the President comes. (322)

The collapse of the state machinery was really gloomy and depressing for everybody. These Africans got their independence to rule themselves for the cause of the people—for their progress and development. But they had no intellectual strength, and a constructive vision to go forward. Now they therefore indulge in such kind of mass killing and violence. It seems that the postcolonial situation is rather more brutal and destructive than the earlier colonial administration. That has become so because the leader has no proper vision for his country. Salim tried to calm down Metty's rage which was rather impossible. He told him to take the car and be careful. He could also own his flat after his departure. However it was not convincing: "He wasn't comforted. But it was all I could do now. He recognized that and didn't press me any further. Then he left to go to his family" (323).

Salim quickly proceeded to get his ticket for the steamer. Some young people with guns tried to take the steamer under their custody, but the captain could manage to outwit them. Darkness was approaching among the gunshots for which the searchlight of the steamer was turned off for the barge to be unseen: "The steamer started up again and moved without lights down the river, away from the area of battle. The air would have been full of moths and flying insects. The searchlight, while it was on, had shown thousands, white in the white light" (326). Salim's life was therefore subject to flux. It was not stable. He did not know where he was going next, how long or how far. Joshi comments:

> Salim maintains a camp-life existence always nursing the idea that he was only passing through. Not only Salim, but all the others who pass through his life illustrate the book's related themes of exile as a universal condition of a changing world, of their being no more safe places left to run to and of the ache of homelessness. (214)

Commenting on the life of Salim, Michael Neil refers to the false apocalyptic endings of some books that are negative in contrast to the positive qualities of the book *A Bend in the River:*

> The book chronicles a whole series of new beginnings and false apocalyptic endings: it envisages a disintegrating world in which there are neither new starts to be made, nor old homes to return to. In this the life of the

> hero, Salim, mirrors that of the town to which he has come. (45-46)

Bruce King makes appropriate comments when he argues that the diasporic Indians were made homeless soon after the "withdrawal of the imperial order and the resulting chaos; the need for ruthlessness to survive; the dangers of the involvement—especially through romantic love and interbreeding: the universality of suffering; the effect of modern transportation in bringing into close contact such former enemies as various African tribes and the British and Arabs; the threat of the modern African state to the traditional ways of Africa" (119). He further thinks that *A Bend in the River* even though brings out a depressing vision by representing the futility and vanity of life; it also represents how Africa is a "metaphor for the modern way of living in a free state":

> It is perhaps Naipaul's most pessimistic novel, filled with a sense of apocalypse, of the futility and vanity of life, of an impending world-wide disaster and coming of a new dark age—it is suggested there is a parallel between the decline of the West and the invasion and fall of the Roman Empire. Yet it is also a strong statement about the need to struggle to survive and to be lucid and rational. Sentiments, whether of the past, race, religion, place, home, family or others, are dangerous. It is a book in which the small lives of individuals in an obscure part of Africa become a metaphor for the modern condition of living in a free state. (119)

Naipaul expresses his views in his interview by Adrian Rowe-Evans published in *Transition*, 40 (1971) on the postcolonial situation of Africa. He is critical of the collapse of a disorder which is not necessarily the cause of colonialism:

> I do have a great distrust of causes, simply because they are causes and they have to simplify, to ignore so much...for example in Africa you can get a profound refusal to acknowledge the realities of the situation; people just push aside the real problems as if they had been settled. As though the whole history of human

> deficiencies was entirely explained by the interlude of oppression and prejudice, which have now been revived; any remaining criticism being merely recurrence of prejudice to be dismissed. (57)

In the same interview, he dismisses that Africa was advancing technically, educationally, culturally and politically. It is rather baffling. He therefore views differently in the interview. This sums up the breakdown of Africa:

> I was appalled to find that people who possessed a few tiny skills were so convinced that they, simple people, were carrying the seeds of all civilization, all culture, all literature, all technology. That was rubbish.... The idea that all the things which have been presented to Africa have somehow been already assimilated and appropriated by Africa in the most hideous type of conning. It may be a willing conning, voluntary on both sides but remains conning. (58)

5.3. Post-imperial (Dis)Order: Collapse of Old Colonial Culture in England

Naipaul has often been in a state of homelessness. The novel, *The Enigma of Arrival,* concentrates on the state of mind of the narrator. It is related to the situation of England after the end of imperialism. His "enigma" after his arrival to an alien country like England has been vividly brought out. He belonged to the Trinidad-Asian community in the West Indies, which was a Third world country. Immediately after his arrival at the centre of the Empire, he had his puzzles and dilemmas. He therefore recorded his experiences lucidly in his beautiful descriptions in the autobiographical novel *The Enigma of Arrival.* The protagonist, a third-world fellow, a stranger, arrives at a strange society where he feels himself alienated and therefore seriously disturbed. In England writing was considered aristocratic pastime. However, the protagonist-narrator, who arrives in England, is a Third-world fellow who writes and subverts the chronology of the existing novel of manners. His journey to the centre from the margin is a metaphorical journey of subversion: "The metaphor of entrapment and the journey undertaken to escape the constricting influence of such situations encapsulates Naipaul's fiction so that the third world protagonist's anguish of homelessness is pressed upon the consciousness of the audience" (Kamra 170). Through his long restlessness the writer, the narrator-protagonist, imagines to move to an ideal setting. His journey to the countryside of Wiltshire is quite different from all his previous journeys because this arrival is qualified with a difference: "It is a changed man who though excited about his own surroundings, yet exercises *restraint* and *caution* in interpreting them as they are in themselves and how they matter to him" (170). Kamra elaborates on the enigma of the writer-narrator: "The 'island innocent' is, however, disillusioned on arrival at the land of his imagination. The sameness and ordinariness of life everywhere leaves him annulled. The only recovery is to travel once more to continue searching for a 'resting place for the imagination'" (171). The state of mind of Naipaul was affected by the rejection of his book *The Loss of El Dorado* because of the great financial loss. He was disillusioned with the Caribbean islands at this juncture. He therefore returned to England this time to Walden to set up a new home. The idea of home under the changed circumstances posed a new enigma after his arrival in England out of which he created *The Enigma of Arrival.*

By the time Naipaul was writing this book, his sister Sati died. This event influenced his theme of decay and regeneration that he has expressed through a number of images and metaphors. Naipaul's concern with the end of imperialism and imperialistic literature is obvious. The colonial situation in the most of the Third-world countries ended. Not that the third-world countries were regenerated through the end of colonialism; England was also regenerated because of the presence of the Third-world writers and intellectuals. Such a situation provided also some enigma to the people in general. Bhat therefore comments:

> He (Naipaul) is aware of the decay and ruin of the imperial order in all the colonies—Africa, Caribbean islands, India and other South American countries, which he has visited. However, there is also a regeneration of another sort—English society and literature are being

> regenerated through the strength of the people of the colonies reflected in the changing face of England and English literature, which is being revived by new writers from the colonies like Naipaul himself. The new writers from the Third World have arrived and are establishing themselves on the scene and the transformed situation is also an enigma to the reading public. (97)

Jack's death and his wife's remarriage are symbolic of decay and regeneration. Naipaul's landlord of the manor firm is also symbolic of the fading imperialism and the writer himself stands for the newly emerging Third world writer merging with the main tradition of English literature. The protagonist, like Mr Biswas, makes an effort to establish an order but he finds complete disorder outside himself: "Empires fall; metropolitan cities grow and become mega cities. The forces of history are furiously at work and Naipaul the writer has a touching vision of it" (Bhat 99). These ideas have been delineated in the book:

> It was to become an Australian and South African a white-colonial, enclave in London, presaging a greater mingling of peoples. Cities like London were to change. They were to cease being more or less national cities; they were to become cities of the world, modern-day Romes, establishing the pattern of what great cities should be in the eyes of islanders like myself and people even more remote in language and culture. They were to be cities visited for learning and elegant goods and manners and freedom by all the barbarian peoples of the globe, people of forest and desert, Arabs, Africans, Malays. (*EOA* 154)

Naipaul's such vision of cosmopolitanism and internationalism is significant. His focus on the death of colonial dominance is reflected in the above passage. Naipaul's expatriate sensibility that makes him restless due to his condition of homelessness brings a lot of disillusionment to him. He feels that he is treated differently due to his skin and color. This racialism was even present in England by that time. He hopes that there would be an international order soon after the demise of imperialism: "Besides feeling a foreigner in Wiltshire, there is his feeling that he is an accident of imperial history—an Indian earning a living as a writer in English in England—and his view that his own life is part of a larger historical process which began with the sending of indentured Indian laborers to Trinidad" (King 1993: 140). Naipaul effectively brings out two parallel themes of decay and regeneration of English society and Literature. He also hints at the postcolonial situation after imperialism. In *EOA*, Naipaul delineates the collapse of the colonial order, and establishment of a new order of the English society symbolically represented by the new people in the manor Estate and new Third World writers who symbolize the collapse of old colonial culture of English writers: "From a British or American perspective that much overused word postcolonial means the collapse of a tradition and cultural fragmentation as a result of internationalism, cultural relativism and cultural pluralism" (King 1993: 148-59). In the opinion of Mustafa, "The new social order which he has learned to see himself a part of...has come about through a curious transfer of power, a rewriting of the imperial configuration" (173).

In this novel, which consists of five sections, the most important theme is the theme of decay and regeneration. This idea can also be related to the demise of empire and its subsequent revival of new life. In the first section of the novel, "Jack's Garden" the protagonist understands this decay:

> ...and the taut lines of barbed wire made me feel, although the life of the valley was just beginning for me, that I was also in a way at the end of this thing I had come upon.... But already I had grown to live with the idea that things changed; already I lived with the idea of decay. (I had always lived with this idea. It was like my curse: the idea, which I had even as a child in Trinidad that I had come into a world past its peak.) Already I lived with the idea of death, the idea, impossible for a young person to possess, to hold in his heart, that one's time on earth, one's life, was a short thing. These ideas, of a world in decay, a world subject

> to constant change and the shortness of human life, made many things bearable. (*EOA* 22-23)

This idea of death and regeneration is predominant throughout the novel. Even Naipaul's personal loss of his sister Sati because of her untimely death is always there in his psyche during the period of writing of this enigmatic novel. This is obvious when the narrator utters:

> My theme, the narrative to carry it my characters—for some years I felt they were sitting on my shoulder, waiting to declare themselves and to possess me. But it was only out of this new awareness of death that I began at last to write. Death was the motif; it had perhaps been the motif all along. Death and the way of handling it—that was the motif of the story of Jack. (376)

In the context of his personal loss, Naipaul correlates his psychological obsession with the idea of death to Sati's death which was a very disturbing incident to him by that time. Towards the end of the novel he explores the theme of regeneration through Sati's death:

> Sati's husband said, "I would like to see her again." His voice sounded whole; but there were tears in his eyes.
>
> The pundit didn't give a straight reply. The Hindu idea of reincarnation, the idea of men being released from the cycle of rebirth after a series of good lives—if that was in pundit's mind, it would have been too hard to pass on to people who were so grief-stricken.
>
> Sati's son asked "Will she come back?" Sati's husband asked, "Will we be together again?"
>
> The pundit said, "But you wouldn't know it is her."
>
> It was the Pundit's interpretation of the idea of reincarnation. (381)

With such a state of mind of death the narrator reflects upon the life of Jack who lives among the ruins. The ruins in Jack's surroundings have also some bearing on the life of the narrator:

> That idea of ruin and dereliction of out-of-placeless, was something I felt about myself, attached to myself: a man

> from another hemisphere, another background, coming to rest in middle life in the cottage of a half-neglected estate, an estate full of reminders of its Edwardian Past, with few connections with the present. An oddity among the estates and big houses of the valley, and I a further oddity in its grounds. I felt unanchored and strange. Everything I saw in those early days, as I took my surroundings in, everything I saw on my daily walk, beside the windbreak or along the wide grassy way, made that feeling more acute. I felt that my presence in that old valley was part of something like an upheaval, a change in the course of the history of the century. (13-14)

Though Jack lived among the ruins and the narrator-protagonist was a new person to the Estate, still Jack's life was deep-rooted to the landscape unlike the diasporic state of the narrator. He was a "remnant of the past". However, Jack might have been a stranger to the place at a particular time of the past. In course of time he became rooted, fixed to the place. It is not right to think that life is constant and things are not changing. Death and regeneration are natural in the scheme of things. Changes are going in a place on different levels and planes:

> But that idea of an unchanging life was wrong. Change was constant. People died; people grew old; people changed houses; houses came up for sale. That was one kind of change. My own presence in the valley, in the cottage of the manor, was an aspect of another kind of change. The barbed-wire fence down the straight stretch of the droveway—that also was change. Everyone was ageing; everything was being renewed or discarded. (32)

The idea of change takes away disappointment because even "decay" will pass away in the cyclic process of change. Therefore the idea of decay gives him some knowledge about the idea of regeneration:

> On this walk, as on the longer walk on the downs past Jack's cottage, I lived not with the idea of decay—that idea I quickly shed—so much as with the idea of change.

> I lived with the idea of change, of flux, and I learned, profoundly, not to grieve for it. I learned to dismiss this easy cause of so much human grief. Decay implied an ideal, perfection in the past. (228)

In the context of imperial link between the narrator and his landlord, he elaborates on the concept of change. Empire continued for a long time ruling many countries. So also, the landlord was empirical as many people were governed as his tenants. As a landlord, the owner of the manor farm had certain privileges of owning the houses, his staff, and income. The narrator-protagonist had no such privileges because he was a tenant, who depended on him for his accommodation:

> I was his opposite in every way, social, artistic. And considering that his family's fortune had grown, but enormously, with the spread of the empire in the nineteenth century, it might be said that an empire lay between us. This empire at the same time linked us. This empire explained my birth in the New World, the language I used, the vocation and ambition I had; this empire in the end explained my presence there in the valley, in that cottage, in the grounds of the manor. But we were—or started—at opposite ends of wealth, privilege, and in the hearts of different cultures. (208)

The end of imperialism has facilitated Naipaul to explore his own facilities as a writer because "the world had changed; time had moved on". He has been able to find his own "talent and subject" in the postcolonial situation. Had it not been so, the imperial link would have been burdensome. It would have tormented him as a man (or boy) to be racial oddity in the valley. He would have been able as a writer to deal with the material only by suppressing certain aspects of himself. Due to change the role-reversal takes place. The narrator-protagonist, though a stranger to the manor farm, culturally and racially different from the people of the place, had great sympathy for the landlord whose fortunes were going to change:

> My career had changed; my ideas had changed. And coming to the manor at a time of disappointment and

> wounding, I felt an immense sympathy for my landlord, who, starting at the other end of the world, now wished to hide, like me. I felt a kinship with him; was deeply grateful for the protection of the manor, for the style of things there. I never thought his seclusion strange. It was what I wanted for myself at that time. (208)

The existing conditions of manor farm were fairly congenial for the narrator-protagonist to pursue his writing career with a sort of easiness and peace. That is why he had a great good will towards his landlord, though he was living with a great seclusion: "So though we had started at opposite ends of empire, and privilege, and indifferent cultures, it was easy for me, as his tenant now, to feel goodwill in my heart for him" (209). Change is very often refreshing and progressive. Dismantling of the empire has helped the world move on the path of progress and liberation from oppression. It has helped people enjoy freedom and think about their own culture and politics of governance. In the valley, the narrator-protagonist initially thought of Jack as a socialist, having a long beard and leading a self-conscious, imposing life. Even though he sensed ruins around him, he was not perturbed. He was assertive in his death because he never thought beyond life:

> All around him was ruin; and all around, in a deeper way, was change, and a reminder of the brevity of the cycles of growth and creation. But he had sensed that life and man were the true mysteries; and he had asserted the privacy of these with something like religion. The bravest and most religious thing about his life was his way of dying. The way he had asserted, at the very end, the primacy not of what was beyond life, but life itself. (100)

His attitude of imposition in his establishment is being challenged by the passage of time. Change has been all around him. The ruins are symbolic of this although he does not smell it till his death that is symbolic of the collapse of his imperial order. It had been reflected in his wife's remarriage in the town, and her living quite happily enjoying her freedom. In his own

way he had been a tyrant, imposing, in addition to the long hair and the bun, a style and way of life that had been irksome to his wife. Now living in another valley, she thinks her life as a small success story:

> For her, Jack's wife, the move away from the cottage had been good. She saw her life as a small success story. Father a forester, a gamekeeper of sorts: Jack the farm worker, the gardener; and now she half a townswoman. One cycle for me, in the cottage, in the grounds of the manor; another cycle in the life of Jack's wife. (101)

Naipaul understands that Jack and other townsmen, who had worked on the land and lived there, were not the remnants of the past. Jack had created his own world and never regarded the tenuousness of his hold on the land. The narrator wanted to record his observation of the land from time to time because everything might be dissolved in course of time. He had thought like that because of so many changes in his life:

> I had thought because of my insecure past—peasant India, colonial Trinidad, my own family circumstances, the colonial smallness that didn't consort with the grandeur of my ambition, my uprooting of myself for a writing career, my coming to England with so little, and the very little I still had to fall back on—I had thought that because of this I had been given an especially tender or raw sense of an accommodating world. (99)

The narrator reflected on how there were changes on the land. He gave a historical perspective of true changes that ha undergone on the land through different stages:

> The history had repeated, had radiated outwards as were: much of the wealth for the Victorian-Edward manor, its gardens and ancillary buildings, had c from the empire, ventures abroad. Once the m estate had covered many of the acres of my after walks. But its glory had lasted one generation family had moved elsewhere; the estate had b the manor and grows alone; it had shed its far land. Others had taken over these acres, built

> houses in villages or on the sites of hamlets once full of working people. And now on the last of the peasant or farm cottages along the droveway had been taken over. What had once been judged a situation suitable only for agricultural cottages—next to a farm, far from roads and services—had become desirable. The farm had gone; the very distance from the public road was a blessing. And so, the quality or attributes of the site changing, the past had been abolished. (98-99)

There were transformations: destructions, renovations and new constructions, new buildings, pre-fabricated shed, and new fences. After reaching the valley, the narrator felt a kind of perfection about the place. Soon, the narrator found that the things were changing. He had therefore a sense of longing for the perfection. He had fallen back on old ideas of flux and the constancy of change to fight the distress he felt at everything—a death, a fence, departure—that altered or threatened the perfection he had found. This overwhelming sense of ruin and destruction was very much with the narrator due to his background, which was subject to so many moves and changes: "To see the possibility. The certainty, of ruin, even at the moment of creation: it was my temperament" (55). Those nerves had been given to him from his family circumstances due to the living condition of the family in half-ruined buildings they lived in. To this mode of feeling went deeper an ancestral inheritance that came with the history of his making. It was not only India, with its ideas of a world outside men's control, but also the colonial plantations or estates of Trinidad, to which his impoverished Indian ancestors had been transported in the last century.

Fifty years ago, the narrator would not have a chance to live there on the estate. There was historical perspective to his existence in the manor cottage. His migration within the British Empire, from India to Trinidad had given him the English language as his own and also a particular kind of education he acquired. That helped him pursue his literary career for the last twenty years. His sense of history, acquisition of education and his personal ambition had sent him to "the world with a

sense of glory dead" (55). In the changeable world everything changes. The glory of the manor farm too changed. Through its decay, there would be movements again:

> The narrator goes back to his earlier life through his reflections after coming to the manor farm. His later life at manor farm had been necessary to write about Jack, his cottage and his garden. It was necessary for him to have lived a second life in the valley, and to have had a second awakening to the natural world there. But a version of that story—a vision—came to him just days after he came to the valley, to the cottage in the manor grounds. The narrator's first life is related to his attaining consciousness through his concerns in his writings such as novels, travelogues, and his history. This has been reproduced through his references to the background information of producing these writings. He also explains how Giorgio de Chirico's one painting titled "The Enigma of Arrival" has influenced him to work on his present project which would uphold his own enigma, the second life at Wiltshire of Jack's Garden. Mustafa postulates: "Where the second life, in the Wiltshire of Jack's Garden, is documented as a developing perception of setting that grows to match the intimacy and familiarity of place already achieved in the first life, the dialectic of these two lives prepares the ground for the novel's other major theme: the end of empire" (171). Close to his stay for about twelve years in the cottage, the narrator's insights were transformed to understand the newly constituted social order, through movements and migrations, changing patterns of life through new ideas and ideologies. His own movement to England, as an expatriate, is also the signal of the end of empire. Even his subsequent journey through his writings takes him back to the knowledge he had already acquired. This duality of the narrator's life allows him to see his settlement in Wiltshire as a second life, "one that has come about through his recognition that settlement

itself is as subject to change and as self-willed a state of being as was his first life as a colonial" (171).

Toward the end of the section "The Journey", the narrator is reminded of his early life in England when he receives a letter from the hotel waitress Angela. Already ten years have passed since he moved to the valley: "More than ten years after I had moved to the valley, when I was almost at the end of my time there, my time in the manor cottage, my second life, I was strongly reminded of my first week in England. I had a letter from Angela" (*EOA* 191). It was a letter which took the narrator to the past when he was engaged in writing an important book about a generation of young people becoming restless and finding consolation in a revealed religion. This was the time Naipaul was engaged in writing his book *Among the Believers*:

> I was also deep in a book. My thoughts were of a whole new generation of young people in remote countries, made restless and uncertain in the late twentieth century not by travel but by the undoing of their old certainties, and looking for consolation in the mind-quelling practices of a simple revealed religion. Angela took me back to the past. I wasn't living there, intellectually and imaginatively, any longer. My world and my themes had come to me long after I had ceased to write of Angela. (196)

The narrator had no time to either telephone Angela or see her though the letter was a disturbing element for him. It made him reflective to understand his surroundings deeply. Change is constant in life and all other things are variables. Looking at the different sides he could see the changes all around in the meadows, hedges, aspens, beeches, yews and so on: "Though I had never noted it down, I had had an intimation of a world in flux, a disturbed world, when I had first seen Angela and her friends in Earls Court. We had both, it seemed, continued to travel versions of our old route; we had both made circular journeys returning from time to time to something like our starting-point" (195). The narrator kept her letter in the piles of accumulated papers in various places in his cottage on the plea that he had no time to share her concerns: "After some months it would not have been possible for me to get at it easily. She never wrote again" (196). Mustafa argues that the anecdote of Angela is crucial to establish a link between the two sections of the novel, "The Journey" and "IVY", in relation to the crucial theme of imperialism that Naipaul has been concerned with:

> ...Just as Angela's memory must remain in the narrator's tidy archeology of his past; her letter now must become submerged under a pile of papers. What is more interesting about this anecdote; however is that it is a class as well as a racial anxiety that is revealed. This becomes evident in the positioning of the anecdote rather than in its actual account. By serving as a transition between "The Journey" and the novel's following section, "IVY", the class stratification among his neighbors that the narrator gradually discerns as part of his newly acquired familiarity with a late twentieth-century settler's England lacks firmly into place. It allows "IVY" to be an examination of post-imperial Britain through a pitching of the narrator's arrival—at middle age, at a late stage in his journey—against his landlord's decaying health and fortunes. (172)

"IVY", the parasitic plant symbolically expresses the dependence of the landed gentry and also the Empire on the tenants and colony for their economic resources and exploitations. In the novel the plant "ivy" is responsible for the death of the trees. Even the landlord of the narrator is quite happy for the wild growth of "ivy" and orders his staff not to disturb the plant. This elucidates his attitude of the landed gentry to dominate his workers. The colonized-colonial relationship finds a symbolic relationship here. It also illustrates how the landed gentry are the parasites depending on the workers of the estate for their economic survival. a chance to walk over the private estate of his landlord the narrator finds that his landlord was rooted in his own "security, wealth, empire, the idea of glory, material satiety, a very great security" (231). The narrator observes how the landlord considers the ivy plants mysterious:

> What did he see? Sitting there in his canvas-backed chair. Did he see tall weeds in the solid greenhouse, the tops of some of the weeds flattened against the glass? Was he agitated by the wish to put things right or by the idea of decay and lack of care? Did he see the ivy that was killing so many of trees that had been planted in the garden? He must have seen the ivy. Mrs. Phillips told me one day that he liked ivy and had given instruction that the ivy was never to be cut. (233)

The narrator is critical of the attitude of the landlord towards the ruins of his garden, collapse of the tree, the wild growth of the reeds. The ivy is responsible for the collapse of the cherry tree. Its wildness is responsible for the ruins of his garden. The narrator doubts if the landlord sees it or he is happy to see the ruins of his garden because of the dominant growth of the ivy on other trees: "Did he in fact see decay? Or did he—since vegetable growth never stopped—simply see lushness? Or did he cherish the decay, seeing in it a comforting reflection of his own accident" (234). The narrator wonders what type of this ivy is which "covered and smothered some trees". It killed many trees including a cherry tree during the previous year. It was rather surprising to note the attitude of the landlord who did not realize the importance of his property:

> A man with a simpler idea of himself, a simple idea of his name, would have seen the great value of his property, might have realized its value, and lived elegantly elsewhere on the proceeds. But my landlord preferred to be with what he knew. Other people might contemplate a move for him. He himself could not think of a life away from his house and garden, which perhaps he continued to see his own way, perhaps even saw as whole and perfect, the way we fail to see the tarnishing that has gradually come to flats or houses where we have lived a long time. (238)

The narrator saw that ruins were pervasive in the garden—in the frames just outside his cottage. His knowledge about Phillipses pained him because though they belonged to the locality "they were in fact rootless people; less rooted than Jack, over the hill" (241). They were less aware of the dereliction around them. They had neither nausea nor had planned to have one. They even seemed to bother less about the time when they would be old. Like their employee the landlords Mr. and Mrs. Phillips appeared to think that there would always be shelter for them. These Phillipses were not country people; they were townish and events and festivities outside their home gave rhythm, pattern and savour to their life. Pitton, the gardener, did never realize that he was also living around the ruins. Bray, the car driver, who was fond of his father's service as a head-gardener, was too living in illusion and never bothered about the ruins in the estate. Pitton had been able to keep only part of the garden going. His successors were creating only an allotment:

> A cycle in the life of the manor had come to an end. There might one day be the beginning of a new cycle. But for the moment or for some years ahead the great walled garden, calling for the labor of many hands, had returned to a modest human scale, had become the setting for a small allotment. (303)

The narrator's grief had been immense for the departure of Pitton with whom he had worked in the garden. Though he himself was getting consolation by replacing the idea of decay by the idea of flux; his association with manor, caused a lot of anguish. But change would go on in a cyclic process. Pitton left the estate for his new work as a laundry man and worked with new vigor and enthusiasm. His style had now been changed in all aspects. The landlord had always a life free from "restlessness and creative abrasion" when he thought about the world from his back window being "a complete, untouched, untroubled world" (309). Now this idea of world turned his life into "morbidity, acidia, a death of the soul" (309): "That morbidity had been like a long sleep. Then he had miraculously awakened, and he had still found his world about him. He knew that the spaciousness of earlier days had gone. But he was prepared, as he had always been prepared, to live with what he found—that was how, projecting myself on to him, I read him" (309). The landlord did not bother about his empire diminishing, declining and ruining. With much curiosity, the narrator read the book of his landlord given to him by Bray. The book contained a story about a young English woman, who was eaten on her mission in Africa. The narrator regards the idea in the book as the "joke knowledge" of his landlord:

> This was the joke knowledge of the world the young boy of eighteen had arrived at; this was the knowledge (which would have appeared like sophistication) that had been fed by the manor and the grounds. And perhaps later knowledge had not gone beyond the joke; outside England and Europe, a fantasy Africa, a fantasy Peru, or India or Malaya. And perhaps passion too had never gone beyond the titillation of the Beardsley-like drawings of this book. And that was the most amazing thing about the book Bray had preserved and cherished: the drawings. (308)

Forgetting the past has become a way of life. The narrator refers to the encounter between him and Pitton: "One day in Salisbury, in that pedestrian shopping street where he had tried to fill me with his own panic, one day he saw me. And then—the new man—he didn't see me" (310). This indicates the willful distancing of Pitton from the narrator as the narrator himself distances from Angela. This is the end of relationship. Pitton's similar gesture of resistance denies any communion he had had with the narrator. The gesture acts as yet another kind of release for the narrator so that 'Rooks', the penultimate section and 'The Ceremony of Farewell', the novel's *envoi*, are each able to bring to a close the combination of the inverted imperial theme. In the manor, there were so many changes. People came and went. Trees collapsed. People suffered from illness and died. Alan, the writer friend died. Mr. Phillips who was protective to the landlord and the manor also died before the ambulance reached. In the life of manor changes continued like chains. The narrator was always having consolation with the idea of change rather than decay to avoid grief. In spite of the existence of the manor, the series of changes that persisted had shaken the narrator because philosophy failed him when he could not face the ravages of the land:

> I had lived with the idea of change, had seen it as a constant, had seen a world in flux, had seen human life as a series of cycles that sometimes ran together. But philosophy failed me now. Land is not land alone, something that simply is itself. Land partakes of what we breathe into it, is touched by our moods and memories. And this end of a cycle, in my life, and in the life of the manor, mixed up with the feeling of age which my illness was forcing on me, caused me grief. (366-67)

All preparations were made for the move of the narrator. He was to move to a place of ruins where a woman had lived. The narrator fully understood that he would be moving one day to another place from the very first spring when he came to the manor. But now the moment of departure was causing a lot of anguish in him: "now that it had come, it was shocking. And as at a death, everything here that had been a source of pleasure and surprise, everything that had welcomed me and healed me, became a cause for pain" (367). After the death of Mr. Phillips, the strong man of manor Mrs. Phillips deserted the landlord because she thought he was unmanageable for her. She would leave the manor and the landlord because she would marry some other. Mr. Bray referring to the landlord said: "old age is a brutal thing. I suppose they'll just sell up. In the end there will be nothing left" (371). The narrator responded to it: "It's lasted all his life. Now many people can say that. That's happiness" (371). But Bray was emotional when he thought of the old age of the landlord who was deserted by his staff because of his old age. In spite of his talk he had some emotional attachment to the dignity of the house in the manor: "The dignity of the house had given value to his independence, it was what he measured his own dignity against" (371).

Decay and Death, the end of the things brought a state of melancholy to the narrator. After his illness, he left the manor cottage; he put an end to the kind of life there, and awakened by the thoughts of death. This state of melancholy prompted him to write the book *The Enigma of Arrival*. He was preoccupied with the fantasy as he observed that there was a great change in the ancient social order through modifications over the years. The story of the book became autobiographical because the writer's journey and the journey of the manor were mixed together, and in this context "Death" was the motif. Naipaul therefore suggests that the ancient social order in England was collapsing after the end of empire. However, many new social transformations have emerged in England after the demise of colonialism. The English life, language, culture and literature have been regenerated shedding their smugness and the dead quality of life. Reflecting upon his personal loss in the death of his sister Sati, Naipaul understands that "death" leads to regeneration. Attending his sister's death ritual, he understands that every generation takes us from the sanctities of our childhood. He therefore concludes *The Enigma of Arrival* with his vision:

> But we remade the world for ourselves; every generation does that, as we found when we came together for the death of this sister and felt the need to honor and remember. It forced me to face the death I had been contemplating at night, in my sleep; it fitted a real grief where melancholy had created a vacancy, as if to prepare me for the moment. It showed me life and man as the mystery, the true religion of men, the grief and the glory. And that was when faced with a real death, and with this new wonders about men, I laid aside my drafts and hesitations and began to write fast about Jack and his garden. (387)

Jack and his garden were subject to death and destruction leading to new emerging energy and regeneration. The "death" motif is a recurring motif of regeneration in the novel.

5.4. Hybridity as Identity: Racialism in Colonial West Indies

For Naipaul the documentation, the sequence of history along with its strange ironies is of significant interest. This is quite obvious when we read *A Way in the World*. *A Bend in the River* emphasizes the importance of history in the same manner. M.I. Singh postulates: "His own sense of rootlessness, derived from the experience of growing up in an immigrant community and then living as a fitful, rather restless exile in England provides a sharp edge to his emphasis on the social necessity and a practical knowledge of history" (1998a: 141). In his later works, integration of myth, history and fiction has been an inseparable part of Naipaul's works. In most of these novels, he emphasizes that the individual and the whole community should understand their history to make sense of the present. In *A Bend in the River*, Naipaul points out that African history is easily forgotten or else too much simplified without going into the intricacies in relation to the modern complexities of reality. Naipaul considers "history" from a different perspective. A historian represents human events in an abstract manner whereas Naipaul reconstructs the human story, and his representation of human story is supported by his own story: Colonial events, revolutions, chaos and disorder after revolution, plantation colony, and slavery, demolition of the social order and construction of new social order. Colonialism, its history, and the revolutionary as well as other human activities are well interwoven in most of Naipaul's works. M.I. Singh posits:

> What happens quite often is somewhat like this: the writer starts with a set or a burden of a real material of life, resolves to turn it into a creative one, but along the line somewhat that material gets assimilated into other, parallel and personal recollections to alter its appeal radically. One "narrative" of Naipaul—non-fictional and fictional—as it were answers and echoes other stories, other narratives of travel and reflection to complicate and illuminate a given knowledge of the World. (1998b: 205)

The diversified elements of knowledge and experience are further dislocated for working out the meaning of one's location in a culture or historical framework. A number of human encounters with historical elements are connected to a dominant metaphor to precipitate a cultural crisis that brings the ideologies to the surface, and these ideologies explicate the human conditions. Naipaul critically examines the various fractured socio-cultural issues of which he himself is a product, and creates his work by binding the various historical forces with his artistic thread. Peter Hughes remarks: "If Naipaul's West Indian world and its history comes to seem a makeshift fantasy, writing about it forces him to recognize other worlds that make new claims on his consciousness" (1988: 76). In most of the works after *In a Free State,* Naipaul deals with politics, history, ideology and class that structured the imperial history itself. Analyzing the post-imperial situations in different parts of the world, he brings out the corrupting and dehumanizing forms of neo-colonialism, which are destructive. Because of his traveling life he has been able to give interpretation of the contemporary situations by way of dramatizing his own ancestry and background as a significance of similar manifestations. Some of these aspects have been illustrated in *A Way in the World.* In a comparative framework, *In a Free State* explores the post-imperial human encounters in the Arab World, Africa, the United States, the Caribbean and England which are presented in the context of power-relations. *A Way in the World* confines its focus on the Caribbean scene by fusing the autobiographical, historical, socio-cultural, political and literary materials into a kind of "sequenced unity". It is the complex journey of time about which Naipaul contemplates.

The chronology of history in *A Way in the World* is diffused. The novel has nine narratives which have "a loose geo-historical connection" (Mustafa 202). In the first few narratives Naipaul focuses on his ancestral memories and childhood; in some middle narratives he tells us real life stories of an author and a black "revolutionary"; in the other two middle sections he draws upon sequences of history of European colonialism. In the last section "Home Again", Naipaul recalls his stay in Uganda in the 1960s. In the novel the term "way" most probably refers to a pattern of life, shaped by a number of circumstances and acts of history. The way becomes "synonymous with one's mental reflexes, a pattern of absorbing things, the quest for meaning, one's place or location in the world" (Singh 1998b:

207). More importantly, Naipaul has brought out the unusual relation between the "colonizer" and the "colonized" by way of bringing the apparently unrelated figures such as the author himself, Lebrun, Foster Morris, Manuel Sorzano, Walter Raleigh, Francisco Miranda.

The book begins with Naipaul's cyclic pattern of visits to Trinidad. The writer narrates his impressions and experiences each time. Referring to Leonard Side, a mortician of Port of Spain, with devilish looking having hairy fingers, he questions the "mystery" of one's roots in Trinidad. Leonard Side, a Muslim, decorates the dead bodies. The idea of making the dead bodies beautiful upsets the narrator. He becomes also curious about the way things are mixed: a Muslim decorating the dead bodies of Christians and a dead, wasted thing being made beautiful. Such aesthetic sense of Side baffles the narrator. In the context of this peculiar, mysterious character his mystery of inheritance or ancestry puzzles Naipaul. He therefore writes:

> I can give you that historical bird's eye-view. But I cannot really explain the mystery of Leonard Side's inheritance. Most of us know the parents and grandparents we come from. But we go back and back, forever; we go back all of us to the very beginning; in our blood and bone and brain we carry the memories of thousands of beings. I might say that an ancestor of Leonard Side's came from the dancing groups of Lucknow, the lewd men who painted their faces and tried to live like women. But that would only be a fragment of his inheritance, a fragment of the truth. We cannot understand all the traits we have inherited. Sometimes we can be strangers to ourselves. (*WW* 9)

The idea of hybridity is core to the issue of ancestry and inheritance for which very often this is contentious and mysterious. Few people want to know about their origins and ancestry; and even if they try, they may not be able to reach any finality. The first narrative of the book concludes with the thesis that all of us are strangers to ourselves. This issue of hybridity be it biological or cultural is of paramount significance in the subsequent narratives. Mustafa believes that all the key characters in the novel operate within the framework of hybridity in the postcolonial context: "Side, it transpires, is emblematic of all the principal figures of the subsequent narratives who at different times and in different situations also emerge from the hyrbidity of their cultural compositions—be the historically constituted or the result of developments during their lifetimes—as ultimately deluded by their philosophical subscriptions" (202). For an individual's identity, inheritance and history are both important because "history and inheritance serve as propositions which Naipaul can imaginatively locate and play off against each other" (203).

In the chapter "History: A Smell of Fish" Naipaul focuses on the awakening of racial politics in Trinidad in the historical perspective. During the conversation with the lawyer, he uttered: "The race! The race, man!" (*WW* 15). Naipaul understood that the lawyer referred to various races: "The black race, the African race, the colored races" (15). Evander, the lawyer was obsessed with the white racial bias. Naipaul considers it to be mimicry: "What was stranger was the public idea of Evander; my friend's father was not like this at all. In the gossip Evander was the self-made Blackman who wanted only to be white, wanted to have nothing to do with black people, and in everything he did was fighting only for himself" (16). Though Naipaul's friend and his father, Evander, had a feeling of belonging to a group, he considered his "idea of a great racial movement forward too sentimental" (16). Before coming to England, Naipaul worked in the Registrar General's office to maintain the birth and death records. Through his inheritance and linkage to history, he carried in his "blood and brain very old Indian ideas about the indifference of the arbitrariness of rulers and governments. They were simply there; you looked to them for nothing" (18). He remembers his ancestors' suffering due to the cruelty of circumstances:

> There was an ancient, or not-so-ancient, cruelty in the language of the streets: casual threats, man to man and parents to children, of punishments and degradation that took you back to plantation times. There was the

> cruelty of the extended family life; the cruelty of the elementary school, the bad beatings by teachers, the bloody end-of-term fights between boys; the cruelty of the Indian countryside and the African town. The simplest things around us held memories of cruelty. (18)

Naipaul thus analyses the anarchy and cruelty of the colonial rule where the marginalized people suffered considerably. Referring to the ill administration and torment of colonials towards the migrant Indians, he interprets their miseries and sufferings in life. These marginalized, homeless Indians were the people "without money, job, without anything like a family, without the English language; without any kind of representation. They were utterly destitute" (19). These people had been lifted from the peasantry of India and were set in Trinidad. Therefore, in the colonial setting of Trinidad, they could be tormented by the people of town in Trinidad. However, the people with such background died by the 1940s. In course of time, when Trinidad got independence, it was in a state of racial tension, a state of black exaltation—"almost a state of insurrection—and with its new well-defined racial division: the Indian countryside, the African town" (33). The transformations from colonial to postcolonial situations had brought in some disorder and negative things including racial politics, pre-industrial disorders in the landscape, violence and disorder in the society:

> It was though, with the colonial past, all the colonial landscape was being trampled over and undone; as though, with the past the very idea of regulation had been rejected; as though, after the sacrament of the square the energy of revolt had become a thing on its own, eating away at the land. (35)

Naipaul understands the much promised "redemption" by the leaders after colonialism came to many, but some people felt betrayed because of the inflated black causes: "so disaffection grew, feeding on an idea of an impossible racial righteousness; and there was always the threat of an insurrection within the insurrection" (36). In the postcolonial new politics, the new leaders refer to slavery and local history. This politics traces back to the overtaking of Trinidad and many other islands following the 1937 Oil-Workers strikes: "This climacteric, radical shift in the mind of the average man is Naipaul's recall of these distressing years in the 1950s. While this demonstration in public of the suppressed cruelty and turmoil leads to the celebration of the local and the ethnic, the limitations of an uneducated politically uninitiated mass of populace are mockingly stressed" (M.I. Singh 1998: 215). However, there was some release from the racial tension when the narrator visited Trinidad. Recalling the racial conflicts, bloody confrontations and general looting, the narrator puts them against his vision of the calm, ordered state of the city, St. Vincent Street the Red House and the Woodford Square. The narrator focuses on the chain of events which match the terrible moments of a history of uncertain developments:

> But all scenes of human habitation are touched by violence of this kind. Nearly every town has been besieged and fought over and has known this kind of blood. And as soon as I thought back even to my own nerves at the time of my first return from England, I saw that there was an immense chain of events. You could start with the sacrament of the square and work back to the black mad men on the benches, the Indian destitute, the plantations, the wilderness, the aboriginal settlements, and the discovery. And you could move forward from the exaltation and that mood of rejection to the nihilism of the moment". (*WW* 39-40)

M.I. Singh rightly explains:

> Always having existed with the idea of the 'other' in someone else's perception of power, the Trinidadian man has lived with a set of unsure ideas of himself. The memory of worst and oppressions, of holocausts and revolts are etched in the memory of the narrator and he draws up the intertwined history marked in edifices, geography and the faces of the people. But the narrator, as the writer behind him, looks at the whole "chain of

> events" from a distance, meditated by the English visits. (1998b: 217)

In the middle part of the book, especially in the chapters 3, 4, 5, the focus is on three figures, Blair, Lebrun and Morris. Blair and Lebrun represent the corrupt power of politics and racism. Morris, the mediocre writer of England visits Trinidad in the 1930s to write on the real issues. He writes about the Oil Strike of 1937. Lebrun was associated with the oil strike of 1937. *A Way in the World* is a prelude to the modern political awakening. In the chapter 4, "Passenger", Lebrun as a leader of the oil field workers' strike is fully discussed. Lebrun's life history is discussed in the chapter 5 "On the Run". The other emerging politician of the decolonizing period, Blair, was one of senior clerks in the Red House, where the narrator was working during his apprenticeship. The deceptive politics in the half-modern societies after colonialism helps Blair rise to the top as a politician in Uganda. However, his fatal death indicates how dangerous these half-made societies are and how they disillusion the young people who aspire to rise as politicians during the postcolonial period: "After his introduction as the one person who appears to transcend the limitations built into the island existence, Blair's political career recedes from the narrative's immediate attention and is only alluded to as an unemployable domain that his death, years later in Uganda, may explain" (Mustafa 206).

In the chapter "New Clothes" the narrators views how tribes once displaced lose their wholeness, their true identity. Migration of people not only makes them homeless, they also become displaced, fragmented.

> Everywhere else, in Asia, Europe north and south, Africa, tribes and peoples have been in collision since the beginning of time. These people, after the migration of their ancestors from Asia, have become people entirely of themselves, without resilience or the talent to adapt. Once their world was broken into, they lost their wholeness. (*WW* 56)

Naipaul, by going back into antiquity and history reflects upon the various processes and stages in the colonial setting of Trinidad:

> Going back into antiquity and history the writer's vision of the original aboriginal island, the sudden cerebral reversion to the colonial setting. He had known as a child; conjure up the many versions of history in a superb literary reflection. Beyond this, what is looked at through the complex mental process is the void before anything else existed the colonizers, the colony, the races, the plantations. (Singh 1998b: 217-18)

After the First World War, the Caribbean islands attracted the tourists. These tourists not only came for the sights and the sun to escape the European Depression of winter, they also came for history:

> The tourists came for the sun, to get away from winter and the depression; they came to be in places that were unspoilt places that time had passed by, places it might be said, that had never been discovered. So history was set on its head; the islands were refashioned. (*WW* 73)

In the absence of Empire and the 19th century nationalistic rhetoric, the modern travel writer refashioned their travel writing by digging into the past to make them attractive for a good selling of their writing. These travel writers never brought out a totality of the West Indian society and history in their writings. It is difficult to uphold the multi-racial setting of Trinidad in the totality of the historical perspective:

> Centuries on, we needed our visitors to give us some idea of where and what we were. We couldn't have done it ourselves. We needed foreign witness. But disregard came with this witness. And that was like a second setting of history on its head. Because in this traveler's view—this distant view of people eating bananas and wearing squeaky shoes, this view of the smallness that a cruise passenger could take in a morning or a day—we, who had come in a variety of ways from many continents, were made to stand in for the aborigines

> and were held responsible for the nullity which had been created long before we had been transported to it. (77)

A Young English writer in 1937, Foster Morris, came to Trinidad and wrote his book *The Shadowed Livery* which was based on the big oilfield workers' strike in Trinidad that year. Naipaul was not sure if Morris knew fully about the local conditions of Trinidad when he wrote about the strike. Most of the workers in Trinidad were Africans from the small island of Grenada to the north. The leader was a man with small beard and a long name, Tubal Uriah Buzz Butler. As a preacher he was able to take the strikers to a pitch of frenzy. He was able to attract the radicals who described themselves as socialists or communists. The strike turned into an insurrection resulting in the burning a policeman alive. This is what Foster Morris wrote about in his book. However, Naipaul argues that Morris's depiction of the local conditions is inappropriate:

> What was missing from Foster Morris's view was what we all lived with the sense of the absurd, the idea of comedy, which hid from us our true position. The social depths he gave to ordinary people didn't make sense. That idea of a background—and what it contained: order and values and the possibility of striving: Perfectibility—made sense only when people were more truly responsible themselves. We weren't responsible in that way. Much had been taken out of our hands. We didn't have a past for most of us the past stopped with our grandparents; beyond that was a blank. If you could look down at us from the sky you would see us living in our little houses between the sea and the bush; and that was a kind of truth about us, who had been transported to that place. We were just there, flouting. (79)

What Naipaul focuses on the above passage is the diasporic identity of the Trinidadian people. They have no roots, no history. Morris's portrayal of the characters with family, history and tradition is unrealistic, and does not conform to the people's reality though Morris's portrayal was well-intentioned. Morris was unable to understand the nature of deprivation of these people. He considered these people as a simplified version of English men. Though people supported Butler as a leader, however educated people like lawyers "felt at the same time, in their bones, that he was a crazed and uneducated African preacher, a Grenadian, a small-islander, an eater of ground provisions boiled in a pitch-oil tin" (80). This man, after the strike, was imprisoned and when released was "a clown, a preacher with grey beard, a fly whisk, a fondness for suits" (80): "He was an embarrassment to the lawyers and others who had drawn strength from him in the great days of 1937. He had brought on a new kind of politics; but he had himself become an anachronism" (80).

Lebrun is the other figure narrated in the Chapter 5 "On the Run". Actually Naipaul came to learn about him in 1959 from Foster Morris at a lunch. Lebrun, the Trinidadian-Panamanian communist of the 1930s was spoken by Morris as one of the most dangerous men around Butler the oil strike leader. This black writer was hated by Morris, the white writer.

M.I. Singh remarks that "Lebrun is certainly more complex and protein figure compared with Foster Morris, for Naipaul brings into, prominence some really contentious issues in the West Indian racial politics and its queer practices" (1998b: 221-22). He further comments:

> The disappearance of Morris from the narrative brings in Lebrun, to start the next sequence of colonial 'histories' what is interesting about Lebrun and Foster Morris is that they serve as foils to Naipaul's explorations of the colonial subjects. He involves his own person with their professions and views to often mischievously make use of them, just as he often made malign uses of his exile as a writer. (1998b: 222)

Naipaul actually demeans both Morris and Lebrun as writers of inadequate perception to represent the complex West Indian societies. In 1956, Lebrun had talked about "history and the production of sugar" (*WW* 125). He theorized the idea of slavery in the perspective of production of sugar during the last two hundred years. He argued that the black people were the earliest industrial workers in the world. The black people of the islands were therefore not to be categorized racially because they were not like the peasantry of Africa and Asia and large areas of Europe: "They were a very old. Industrial proletariat and the history of slavery had shown them to be always a revolutionary people. Now they were destined to be in the forefront of the revolution in the New World" (121). Initially, the narrator was puzzled, but his emphasis is on the industrial nature of slavery in the Caribbean. Later on he thought it was an ideology for the sake of an ideology. At a dinner at Maida Vale Lebrun explained that political resolution had "enabled him to lay aside the shame he had grown to feel because of his mother's uncle, the old coachman, who looked back to a time nearer slavery as the good time, when white people and black people were one" (122). The narrator was impressed with such a confession: "every black man...had some tormenting secret like that". Despite that the political resolution was concealing something the narrator identified himself:

> Yet the words, political resolution, had appeared to conceal something. And now I felt—with shame, grief, sympathy, admiration, recognizing something of myself in his struggle—that, as much as the uneducated old coachman of ninety years before and the middle-aged black man in bowler and pin-stripe suit stepping out of the queue in Regent Street in 1950 to show the photographs of his house and English wife, Lebrun had always needed to find some way of dealing with the past. (122)

His ideology enabled Lebrun to do more than the most with its fixed structures, its clear enemy, and its clear morality. It was possible to move forward with the revolutionary writing. During the time of slavery, such writing was like a guerrilla war. However after abolition of slavery, such writing was "flat, directionless, without moral issues" (122-23). Naipaul illustrates the political resolution of Lebrun: "Lebrun's political resolution was very far from this sensationalism. It enabled him, not to embrace the period of slavery, but to acknowledge it without pain and presenting in his own way to make a claim for its universality and even its precedence" (123). In course of time, Lebrun fades out except in his articles and his last book, *The Second Struggle: Speech and Writing 1962-1972.* Nobody read Lebrun's book. However, the narrator reading his book comments on the changed world: "Thinking about the ironies of Lebrun's life that at the end he should have been like the people he had written about in his first book, and feeling almost superstitiously that there was a circularity in human lives" (129). In his old age Lebrun is an oddity to those who are interested in colonial and postcolonial history: "Ironically, no one stood any risk of eulogizing Lebrun in an age in which issues for which he and his likes had fought for, had long ago been won.... Lebrun's intellectual cast and his fantasies have meanings elsewhere but in the Caribbean context it is only a form of words to witness a more primeval struggle to power, as his later deportation from the island substantiates" (Singh 1998b: 226). Singh explains how Lebrun was removed from the scene of central revolutionary politics:

> The role of the black intellectual in ex-colonies or elsewhere yields self-satisfaction which inhibits growth. This self-satisfaction results in either dogmatic submission to and upward mobility in sectarian formations, or marginal placement in the bourgeoisies enclosures in the West, utterly divorced from the integral dynamics, concrete realities and progressive possibilities of the black community. Lebrun, a self-styled black Marxist intellectual slowly alienates himself from the centre of practical life to camouflage his role in the western metropolitan culture. He represents another variety of the exited West Indian Writer/intellectual, unnecessary and unwanted in the last changing politico-historical scenario. (*WW* 226-27)

Naipaul's delineation of the stories of Raleigh and Miranda in the novel is related to the colonial adventures of these two men and the disastrous results emerged therefrom. These adventures were also described in *The Loss of El Dorado*: "To make the structure of the book emblematic, the narratives are culled out of the larger historical detail which forms the content of *The Loss of El Dorado*. The theme of imperial adventure, the fierce novel battles between European powers in the Caribbean and South America underscore the greed, politics and corruption at the heart of a search of El Dorado, or the plan for a revolution with Trinidad as a base" (Singh 1998b: 227). The protagonists of these episodes, both Raleigh and Miranda, were to meet with their death at the end. Naipaul chooses the final parts of their career and relates them to the human experiences in the perspectives of colonial history.

Walter Raleigh conquered Indies on his first expedition in 1595 after which he went back to London as a hero. During the expedition, he captured Berrio, the governor of Trinidad and plundered the islands, and was accepted as hero by the local Indians. Then he claimed to have brought the samples of gold, turned out to be nothing more than sand. He was therefore imprisoned in The Tower of London. He was released on the condition that he would be given a second chance to find gold at El Dorado failing which he would be executed. After twenty-two years of his first expedition, Raleigh, an old man along with his son and soldiers went to find gold, but failed also miserably. Running short of food, he was losing his men everyday to the ghost of death. Raleigh, obsessed with power and wealth, faced defeat because the Indians were now siding with the Spaniards, the ruling people of the islands. His disaster and hopelessness was conspicuous when we read the dialogue between him and the Surgeon. Losing everybody including his son and his lieutenant Keymis, he was frustrated. The Surgeon was therefore critical of the whole expedition of the General Raleigh:

> We do things for all kinds of reasons.... And it may be that one of these reasons—just one, perhaps—at the bottom of this venture—so chivalric now, at the limit of the world, so heroic so doomed to failure, an old man's nobility—bringing us all here, at the cost of so many lives—it may be that one of the original reasons for this might have been your wish, all these years ago to prove

> that you were not a fool, that you had not brought home a cargo of sand as a cargo of gold. (*WW* 167)

The Surgeon therefore condemns Raleigh for his greed and corruption. Raleigh, the man of self-aggrandizement, was responsible for the death of so many soldiers and others. He was a plunderer and murderer. This plunderer, a man of self-glorification, vainglorious was to be executed on his return to England without gold. Naipaul's presentation of Raleigh's story exposes the European colonizer's mindset of cruelty of looting, plundering and murdering and bringing miseries, subjection and death to the helpless marginalized people of the colonies.

Naipaul's delineation of the storm of Francisco Miranda is a story of exploitation and corruption to attain political power. He was also a man obsessed with the desire to possess power and wealth. These were their visions of the new world for exploitation. That is why Naipaul comments: "Separate stories, different people changing style of clothes, but the episodes would have developed one out of the other, as in a serial (237). Naipaul's presentation of the degraded Miranda has been examined by M.I. Singh:

> The madness and self-deception, followed by surrender that marks the later career of Miranda, is however, not marked by any "historical myth"—it is just fabulous and attractive. His rank opportunism, seeming character and shifting loyalties—from Spain to England to France to Russia—conjure up fast changing roles of a play-actor in the European colonial power games. Living thus, purely on his wife, Miranda is runaway from his Venezuelan ancestral past, ranked by his ordinary background, being a shopkeeper's son. (1998b: 231-32)

After his Venezuela life, Miranda had an eventful life by making endless journeys between Europe and South America during which he acquired a deep sense of history because of his exposure to the politics of power. However, his acquired knowledge was utilized for personal gratification. Miranda served as a lieutenant-colonel in the American war of Independence. Then he had a scandal about money and smuggling in Cuba for which he was arrested and thereafter released. He had to have a break with Spain and then flew to the United States. Finally he was an exile in Europe. Miranda was the first South American Europe had known. He went to Russia and impressed the Empress Catherine. In Caracas, he lad longed for Europe, for a civilization and society, more demanding than the plantation Kingdom of Venezuela. He was able to convince the English to launch a British-American Revolution to liberate Venezuela, making Trinidad as base after his two decades of talk. However, the people who had invited him to lead the revolution betrayed him and handed him over to the Spaniard. Like Raleigh he was to lead an identical career in the prison towards the end of his life. Naipaul posits:

> He is sixty-two now. He has four more years to live. All these years will be spent in jail; some of the time he will be chained. He will never see London and his family again.... As though he is content at the end to lay aside the fantasies of thirty years-fantasies of immense Spanish-American republic-fantasies of Incas worthy of Plato's republic, fantasies which (Like Columbus's ideas about the New World and Raleigh's) also contained a dream of a fabulous personal authority. (242-43)

Naipaul here sums up the futility of Miranda's life, dreams, his career and imperial ambitions. Heaslop, the colonial Governor was however disillusioned of colonial squabbles of fortune-making, and conspiracies. He hates the slave-trade in the land. It is thought-provoking when we read the fatal end of Miranda:

> He was buried unceremoniously, lifted from the hospital of the jail in the mattress and sheets of his death bed, and in the clothes in which he had died, and set down with it all in his grave. The men who took him away then came back and gathered up his clothes and possessions and burnt them. Knowledge of the spot where he was buried was soon lost. (339-40)

The stories of Raleigh and Miranda illustrate the grand mad illusions of two ambitious colonizers who aspired for power, wealth and fame. The absurdity of their political exploits and expeditions, is their plunder and killing, false vanity and ego. The very attitude of killing the aboriginal people is based on their self-aggrandizement and aggressive attitude. Their vision of the new world is also absurd because they never thought that the original inhabitants had a right to their own land and wealth. Singh observes:

> The core idea around which Naipaul constructs *A Way in the World*—European privilege and non-European disorder—is extended to a reworking of the 'dichotomy' from pre-colonial times to the present day. But Naipaul, despite the keen note he takes of the enormous gap between histories, cultures and epistemologies of the two painfully connected sets of experiences, his malice towards the non-Europeans is strikingly consistent. None of the figures is allowed authenticity or a place in the landscape he inhabits. Indeed Naipaul sees a necessarily fleeting and absurd wish in them to cross barriers, erected by the limitation of colonized culture that in the end can only lead to a falsity of purpose, supplemented and aggravated by a consciousness of unimportance. Like the 'slave' he refers to at the end of *The Loss of El Dorado* who "has no story" the ways in the world seem to be ineluctably inscribed and allotted in one's actions and responses. (1998b: 235-36)

Naipaul illustrates the ways in which the world is governed. There is no definite way which can be considered exemplary and ideal. The patterns of life cannot be controlled. Life should be understood in the perspective of history, politics and culture of a place. As such, the identity of an individual is not merely governed by the inheritance or history, but by both. That is why the issue of identity is a complex one. It is also related to homelessness, displacement and multiple associations of diasporic aspects.

5.5. Diasporic Identity in a Postcolonial World

The theme of exile and longing for roots is central to *Half a Life*. The central idea of the novel revolves around the protagonist Willie Somerset Chandran, born in India in the 1930s, moves to London with a scholarship to study in Nottingham, remains in a state of tension, publishes a book, marries Ana, a woman of mixed African parents, and then goes along with her to Africa, her family estate. Willie is not mentally stable, and questions his own background. His father is a Brahmin who has married an "untouchable", and lives in a monastery. Willie does not like such a haphazard life of his father although he also leads a life of that sort, more or less. Even if he lives there in Africa with his wife, he does not feel Africa as his home, and therefore he is an outsider. That is why after eighteen years of his stay in Africa he divorces her and tries to explore his existential identity. In Africa he has led a half-life, an unreal "shadow life". The ending of the novel is exploratory. Willie realizes that he has led a meaningless, futile life in his wife's native country, Africa: "But now the best part of my life has gone, and I've done nothing.... And even if we go to Portugal, even if they let me in there, it would still be your life. I have been hiding for too long" (*HL* 227). Ana reacts to Willie's realization of living a Half Life: "Perhaps it wasn't really my life either" (227). Actually, nobody leads a full life. At the beginning of the novel, Willie questions his father, "Why is my middle name Somerset?" (1). This existential question is related to the identity of Willie. From the very beginning Willie is curious to know about his identity. While giving Somerset's name to his son Willie's father is a split personality by mixing illusions and reality. Willie's father is not only leading a half life himself, he rather creates a background to the dilemma of his son who is leading a half life throughout. Choubey comments that this question forms the very essence of a person's existence: "The answer to this question brings into light the irony of Willie's existence and at the same time prepares the background of his half-life in half-made societies with people who are themselves leading a life which is half-discovered, half-realized and half-lived" (2002: 1).

Naipaul presents the anguish and predicament of "unanchored Souls" (Nandan 2000: 56). Willie tries to explore his self to know his identity. In India or London or Africa he is always a half-man, and therefore leads a half-life only. The book is therefore about the half lives of various people: "In a larger sense the novel points to various predicaments of various half-and-half people uprooted from a way of life on account of factors often out of their own control. A war, an uprising, a change of government, ethnic hostilities that make people feel threatened.... The book also suggests that most of us get only 'half a life'...to live choices of various kinds that we make do shut out other ways of life to us" (Sharma 176-77 in Panwar 2007). Krishna Barua comments on the narrative strategy: "If there is a narrative strategy, it is a patterning of plurality, in voice, in distance, in focalization. Therefore in this paper, my aim shall be to analyze the rhetoric of 'hiding', of the use of psychological substratum as an essence of identity, of different narrative strategies shifting between reversible consciousness of unscrupulous truth and the structuring of the discourse of lying and hiding which had not always be verbal" (*ACR* 3.2, 2004: 116). The protagonist, uprooted from his home and ancestry, is facing a crisis of identity. Other characters are also swayed by this social chaos: "*Half a Life* continues the existential search of Willie in particular and other characters in general. Percy, Marcus, Rozer, Ricardo, Carla, Grace, Correias, Alvaro, and Noronha are searching for a meaning in their lives. The social chaos in the form of wars is the hostile condition, which invigorates them. The search for their identity paves the way to their self-discovery" (Mishra *ACR* 3.2, 2004: 134-35).

The postcolonial linkage to *Half a Life* can also be considered from the point of view of Willie being portrayed as a postcolonial intellectual. Willie being a postcolonial migrant has a deeper understanding of the cultural life of London as well as of Africa than the natives of these places:

> The experiences he (Willie) received in London remained within him as latent properties which are compared with his experiences in Africa and then the 'codes' received in London are 'translated' in Africa. The existential suffering of the exile that Willie had to undergo in the multiracial society of the Portuguese Africa prepared him to assert his individuality. (Haldar in Ray 246)

Willie's father had a crisis of his own identity which he thought he could achieve through his children. That is why to the query by Willie he says: "You were named after a great English writer. I am sure you have seen his books about the house" (*HL* 1). Somerset Maugham, the renowned novelist met children, Willie's father, and after his return to England, eighteen months later, he writes two to three pages about him. That writing brought a lot of fame to Chandran, who was leading the life of a priest after he was charged of being corrupt in the court of the Maharaja. Chandran recalls: "That was how I became famous. Not in India, where there is a lot of jealousy, but abroad. And the jealousy turned to rage when the writer's famous novel came out during the war, and foreign critics began to see in me the spiritual source of *The Razor's Edge*" (3). Because of the writer, the Maharaja and his officials changed their mind-set towards Chandran and pretended to treat him as a man of sacrifice and great personality like the writer "They pretended to see me as the writer had seen me: the man of high caste, high in the Maharaja's revenue service, from a line of people who had performed sacred rituals for the ruler, turning his back on a glittering career, and living as a mendicant on the alms of the poorest of the poor" (3). Chandran could not drift away from such "a strange life that fate had bestowed" on him because the maharaja along with his courtier came bare-backed to him for some religious performance and offered him gifts and clothes. In course of time Chandran accepted the life that was thrust upon him as his destiny:

> In some such way, contemplating the strange life that had been forced on me by that meeting with the great English writer, I began to see that it was a way of life that for some years I had been dreaming of: the wish to renounce, hide, run away from the mess I had made of my life. (5)

Chandran's grandfather, who was to lead a life of starvation through his life of temple inheritance, shunned such a way and became a letter writer of the maharaja. His son however wanted to go back to the security of temple life. During his old age Chandran's grandfather reacted against the falsity of the secured temple life. Chandran went a step forward and thought of the insecurity of the life around the maharaja that they led: "I began to have some idea that this life we were all living in the big town around the maharaja and his palace couldn't last, that this security was also false. When I thought like that I could panic, because I couldn't see what I could do to protect myself against that breakdown" (8). Chandran was an ambitious boy. During his studies in the college, there was the freedom movement led by the Mahatma. Around 1931-32, Chandran, a student of B.A., burnt all his books and wanted to break away and join politics to become a great man in his life. He would be able to explore a proper identity for his self. Through his own crisis, Chandran wanted to sacrifice everything to achieve "greatness" in his life like the Mahatma so that he can have the freedom to be away "from the servile life around the palace of the Maharaja" (10).

Being influenced by the Mahatma he wanted to sacrifice his life for the cause of the lowest caste. He wanted to marry the lowest person he could find. He therefore wanted to trample on the wishes of his father who wanted Chandran to be in the service of the Maharaja and marry the Principal's daughter. Chandran however decided to marry a girl of backward caste, his classmate in the college, the daughter of a firebrand leader. But after such a decision, he was again in a state of another crisis. Thinking of remaining away from the Maharaja's service and leading a life of sacrifice by marrying the girl of a lower caste, his mind was in a state of raging flood:

> Now in almost every particular my life had altered. It was as though, like a child seeing the sky reflected in a puddle after rain, I had, wishing to feel fear while knowing I was safe, let my foot touch the puddle, which at that touch had turned into a raging flood which was now sweeping me away. That was now in a few minutes I had begun to feel. And that in a few minutes became my view of the world about me: no longer a dull and ordinary place where ordinary people walked and worked, but a place where secret torrents flowed which might at any minute sweep away the unwary. It was what came to my mind now when I looked at the

girl. All her attributes changed: the thin black feet, the big teeth, the very dark skin. (16-17)

Chandran hid the backward caste girl in a sculptor's room, and also boycotted the examination as he had not studied properly. He had to borrow money to support the girl though she did never believe that the idea of working in the office of the Maharaja frightened Chandran: "But I went to school yesterday. That was the way I felt about going to work in the Land Tax Department, and the thought of going to work in a place like that every day every year until I died frightened me" (22). There was rampant corruption in the office of the Maharaja: the tax-collectors and surveyors would collect tax from people and then they would destroy all records. They would compel the illiterate peasants to give tax again: "It was endless, the petty cheating that went on among the poor" (22). Chandran, when transferred to the audit section, scrutinized this type of corruption and he himself indulged in destroying the receipts, which was a kind of civil disobedience. Despite his inefficiency, he was promoted as an Assistant Inspector which surprised him. His father thought that the principal had a hand in it because he had a great ambition for his son-in-law. However Chandran revealed his father that he was married to another girl of lower caste which shocked his father who told him: "You've blackened all our faces. And now we'll have to face the anger of the school principal. You've dishonored his daughter, since in everybody's eyes you are as good as married to her" (24). Chandran thought that it was a strange thing to be trapped like that: "So, though I hadn't touched either of them, and though I had gone through no form of ceremony with either of them, there were two women whom I dishonored" (24). The father was worried about the revenge the principal could take on the family. That actually happened when the Chief Inspector told him: "I think, I should tell you right away. You are being investigated for corruption. There have been complaints by senior officials. It's a serious matter, corruption. You can go to jail. RI, rigorous imprisonment. There is enough in these files to convict you" (25-26).

After this threat of imprisonment, Chandran began to think of running away and taking sanctuary in the famous old temple in the town like his grandfather: "At this moment of supreme sacrifice I fell, as if by instinct into old ways" (26). One day early in the morning, after shaving his head he left his father's house like the "Lord Buddha leaving the revels of his father's palace" (27). Dressed like a Brahmin, Chandran walked to the temple barefooted and barebacked and declared himself as a mendicant and claimed sanctuary there. Later on the scandal came out after three days. When the firebrand took a procession, nobody—the Principal or the officials of the Land Tax department—touched him: "And that was how to my mortification and sorrow, and with every kind of grief for my father and our past, I became part of the cause of backwards" (27). Like him another lawyer of a backward caste walked past the temple. There was civil disobedience for the actions of the lawyer and Chandran. Because of the one day strike and civil disobedience Chandran was able to be safe from the school Principal and the courts. In Maharaja's state there was the petty politics of caste when people elsewhere in the country were talking about Gandhi, Nehru and the British. Though Chandran wished to follow only the Mahatma, fate had made him a hero of the people, who fighting their own petty caste war, wished to pull them down. Chandran took a vow of silence for an indefinite period and people came to him and offered gifts. Once Haxton with the Principal, the director of the state's tourist publications, came to the temple. On Haxton's [the writer's] insistence he explained about Chandran, who had high background of ancestry and good prospects of life, but gave up them all for the life of an ascetic, though he continued to hate him. However, the writer took his interview which enhanced his reputation. Chandran chose the life of a mendicant under the circumstances. He thought he was trapped though he had wished to be free from the life of servility. It was rather his destiny controlled by some unseen power:

> ...I understand one day that, through a series of accidents, tossed as in dream from one unlikely situation to another acting always on the spur of the moment

> wishing only to reject the servility of our life, with no clear view of what was to follow, I had fallen into ancestral ways. I was astonished and awed. I felt that some higher power had taken a hand and I had been shown the true path. (32)

However, his father and the Principal had thought that Chandran was irredeemably a fallen man of caste, and his path was a mockery of the sacred ways. Chandran was to regularize his life by establishing himself with the girl though he was ashamed of his act. Through shame, he contemplated to live on melancholy:

> This shame was always with me, the little unhappiness always at the back of my mind, like an incurable illness, corrupting all my moments, all my little triumphs (another reference in a book, another magazine article, and another titled visitor. I began...to take refuge in my melancholy. (33)

Though he took "a vow of sexual abstinence" (33), in course of time Willie and Sarojini were born to Chandran. After the birth of Willie when he was growing up, Chandran would repent and would think "Little Willie, little Willie, what have I done to you? Why have I forced this taint on you?" (33-34). After Sarojini was born, Chandran, looking at the ugliness of the girl, would think that it was a kind of divine punishment. However, he named her Sarojini in the hope that some similar blessing of the poet of independence movement, might fall on her.

Listening to the story of "wretchedness" and "self-disgust" of his father, Willie expressed his hatred towards him: "I despise you...what is there for me in what you have said? You offer me nothing" (35). However, Chandran would argue: "It has been a life of sacrifice. I have no riches to offer you. All I have are my friendships. That is my treasure" (36). About Sarojini, Chandran said to his son: "her prospects in this country are not bright. But foreigners have their own ideas of beauty and certain other things, and all I can hope for Sarojini is an international marriage" (36).

In the first chapter, the novel focuses on the life of Chandran, who actually goes through a series of upheavals in search of his identity. In an effort to break with the ancestry through his insistence on marrying a dalit woman by following the ideals set by the Mahatma during the pre-independence period, Chandran had an obsession with becoming a great man like him. His "compelled life of spirituality" gave him an identity, which his son now challenges. His grandfather's lineage to the temple life elucidates that the man was to undergo starvation till he broke with it to become a letter-writer outside the Maharaja's palace. Chandran's father, who continued as a courtier of the Maharaja, was however obsessed with the temple cult. Chandran, who understood his grandfather's rage against the poverty of the Brahmins by sticking to their ancestral profession, wanted to do something by which he could be a free man and live with dignity. Though he studied in the Maharaja's college, he was however disillusioned to learn the stereotype mechanical way of learning. He found no interest in learning the romantic poets and other renowned writers who told only lies. He therefore wanted to do something greater for which he burnt his books as a protest against the English education in India. Later on when he joined the service in the Maharaja's Tax Department, he was also frightened to think of leading such a life of servility to work in the office throughout his life. He did not even agree to marry the Principal's daughter for which he was framed under the charges of corruption. Finally, he kept away from power, and led a life of sacrifice under confusion, compulsion and disillusion.

Though he could establish his identity as a spiritual man, later on Chandran was rather disillusioned to see that Willie, his son was drifting away from his ideals. In the beginning of the second chapter, there is also a reference to both the identities of Chandran and Willie in the question of the Canadian teacher in the mission school: "What does your father do?" (37). The strange reply of Willie with irritation is also interesting to note: "You all know what my father does" (37). In the mission school where their mother had been a student, Willie and Sarojini studied. But it was a branded school where backward caste children also read. It was noteworthy that Willie was doing excellent in the composition class by composing stories of inventive nature. However, the father noted that Willie invented stories of lies like Shelley, Wordsworth and others. He thought about his son:

> But I have done him nothing. He is not me. He is his mother's son. All this mom-and-pop business comes from her. She can't help it. It's her background. She has these mission school ambitions. Perhaps after a few hundred rebirths she will be more evolved. But she can't wait like other decent folk. Like so many backwards nowadays, she wants to jump the gun. (41)

A week later when Chandran again went through the exercise book of his son, he found another offensive composition against mom and pop. He therefore thought that the boy, "true son of his mother, was challenging him, with all the slyness of a backward, and he wasn't sure what he should do" (41). Remembering the Mahatma's "Civil disobedience", he did nothing to the exercise book. Willie, back from school, thought about his father: "Not only is he a fraud but he is also a coward" (41). Though Chandran did not discuss anything regarding the composition with his son, he was rather disturbed. He thought there was something treacherous in the exercise book. He read the next composition in the exercise book titled *King Cophetua and the Beggar-Maid*. This time he was more disappointed about the attitude of his son: "We've created a monster. He really hates his mother and his mother's people, and she doesn't know. But his mother's uncle was the firebrand of the backwards. I mustn't forget that. The boy will poison what remains of my life. I must get him for away from here" (43). Thinking so he told him to pursue his higher education in Benares, Bombay or Calcutta, but Willie insisted that he would go to Canada with the help of the fathers of the Missionary school. He further persuaded his son that he himself led "a life of sacrifice" and did not get his degree, but Willie must have to get his degree. He did not approve of the missionary idea of his son: "They will turn you into little monkey and send you right back here to work with your mother's family and other backwards. You are a fool." A few days later Willie would write a longer composition titled

"A Life of Sacrifice". By reading this composition, Chandran was greatly disturbed and thought about Willie:

> His mind is diseased. He hates me and he hates his mother, and how he's turned against himself. This is what the missionaries have done to him with mom and pop and Dick Tracy and the Justice Society of America comic magazine, and Christ on the cross movies in Passion Week, and Bogart and Cagney and George Raft the rest of the time. I cannot deal rationality with this kind of hatred. I will deal with it in the ways of the mahatma. I will ignore it. I will keep a vow of silence so far as he is concerned. (47)

During his crisis Chandran was practicing this "vow of silence". However, two or three weeks later he was to break the silence due to a breakdown of Willie after seeing a picture of a priest with glasses and a wristwatch standing with one foot on a statue of the Buddha. Willie had decided not to go to school, nor even to go to Canada to become a missionary. The boy therefore stopped going to school. Chandran was moved to see his son one day sleeping with his face down with the closed copy of the school edition of *The Vicar of Wakefield*:

> There was such unhappiness and such energy there that he was overwhelmed with pity. He thought, 'I used to think that you were me and I was worried at what I had done to you. But now I know that you are not me. What is in my head is not yours. You are somebody else, somebody I don't know, and I worry for you because you are launched on a journey I know nothing of. (49)

This realization of his father was a great compliment to his son. To his father Willie was meant for a special purpose. He therefore wrote to the contact persons abroad whom he helped in India to help him to get a place for his son in some institute. But it was not that easy. Many letters came with no concrete help. Finally, there was a positive response: "But he was spared the humiliation of an all-round refusal. There came a letter in a blue envelope from London, from the House of Lords, from a famous man who had paid a brief visit to the ashram just after independence. His fame and his title had made him memorable to Willie Chandran's father" (50). This man wanted to display his power to Willie's father. It was a letter containing some gold for Willie: "The letter contained a little of the gold the little man had spun: a place and a scholarship had been found for Willie Chandran in a college of education for mature students in London" (51). This letter created an opportunity for Willie to go to London. Willie's father could not know the concrete journey of his son. He could not know what his son's destiny would be. Even Willie did not know what his London life would bring for him in future:

> And that was now, when he was twenty, Willie Chandran, the mission-school student who had not completed his education, with no idea of what he wanted to do, except to get away from what he knew, and yet with very little idea of what lay outside what he knew, only with the fantasies of the Hollywood films of the thirties and forties that he had seen at the mission school, went to London. (51)

In his early London days, he would realize his ignorance, and therefore he read a number of books on world history and politics. He could not understand many of them. Meeting many people he would realize the hardships of a real life. He would therefore admire his father's ability: "I misjudged my father. I used to think that the world was easy for him as a Brahmin and that he became a fraud out of idleness. Now I began to understand how hard the world must have been for him" (58). Willie knew a lot of rules to cope with the college as well as London life. At the end of his second term, he saw clearly that the old rules no longer bound him. He therefore wanted to write his own revolution: "The possibilities were dizzying. He could within reason, re-make himself and his past and his ancestry" (60). He reconstructed his identity through his father's connection to the greater writer and the journalist, his mother's uncle as a kind of "trade union leader, a pioneer of worker's rights"; his mother as "belonging to an ancient Christian community of the subcontinent, or a community almost as old as Christianity itself", and his father a Brahmin, his grandfather as "a courtier" and so on (60-61). In this way, Willie remade himself which gave him a feeling of power. This seemed that Willie was settling down in London. With some confidence Willie moved on in London first making friendship with Percy Cato, a Jamaican of mixed parentage.

Willie realized that it was necessary for everybody to establish his identity in the world. Through Percy, Willie was being introduced to the "special, passing bohemian-immigrant life of London of the late 1950s" (72). A number of immigrants from the Caribbean the white colonies of Africa and Asia along with some English people were also exotic to have a taste of social adventure. Willie led a bohemian life of the writers in London along with such friends as Percy, Roger, Richard and Perdita. Rogers, a Lawyer suggested Willie to write stories not necessarily having a neat beginning and a neat ending because life in reality is not like that: "Life doesn't have a neat beginning and a tidy end. Life is always going on. You should begin in the middle and end in the middle and it should all be there (83).

Willie, accepting Roger's suggestion, revised his early stories of missionary school days, and then wrote more stories. He was anxious for the publication of the book. Finally Richard agreed to publish the book that had India as a background setting. Through it, he wanted to have an identity. However, his book could not be reviewed much favorably. Willie was gradually being fed up with those bohemian parties with Percy and June and others. In the meanwhile he was informed about the international marriage of Sarojini with a German in Berlin. Willie could learn in London that everything goes on a bias: "The world should stop, but it goes on" (113). Without getting so much favorable reviews of the book, Willie was a little frustrated:

> Let the book die. Let it fade away. Let me not be reminded of it. I will write no more. This book was not something I should have done, anyway. It was artificial and false. Let me be grateful that none of the reviews spotted the way it was done. (123)

Richard's catalogue contained a half page somewhere in the middle. It was rather depressing because it presented Willie as "a subversive new voice from the subcontinent and the stories having an universal Indian Provincial setting: "The catalogue entry, modes, even bleak commercially self-denying, seemed less a tribute to the book than a tribute to Richard and the well-known politics of his firm" (122). Willie felt that his book was now "tainted" and "dead". However Willie got two letters of compliments for the book from Roger, his friend and Ana, a young woman from an African country. To Willie, the letter from Roger seemed to be "cool and distant". The other letter from the Portuguese-sounding name, doing a course in London, contained some positive remarks about the book:

> I feel I had to write to you because in your story for the first time I find moments that are like moments in my own life, though the background and material are so different. It does my heart a lot of good to think that out there all these years there was someone thinking and feeling like me. (124)

When Ana came to meet him in the college, Willie could understand that for the first time in his life he met someone who accepted him completely. At home in India, his life was governed by mixed inheritance, rules and regulations. In England, he lived with the idea of difference to be liberated from the cruelties and rules of home. At this point of time Willie received a letter from Sarojini, his sister from Cuba enquiring about his plans for future and the publication of his book: "Was your book published? You kept it to yourself. You didn't send us a copy; and I suppose it's come and gone. Well, now that you've got it out of your system, it's time for you to put that kind of vanity aside, and think more constructively about the future" (130).

But Willie had not planned anything for his future. He had been living in a fool's paradise. His time was going to be over in the college. It was time for him to get a job and a place to live in with Ana. After much contemplation he realized that he would have to go to Ana to Africa where they could live together. After such a proposal Ana, though agreed, told him:

"Let's see how you like the bush. We need a man on the estate. But you have to learn the language" (131). It was significant to understand the views of Sarojini to her brother in her last letter before Willie left for Africa:

> Outsiders who go to India have no idea of the country even when they are there, and I am sure the same is true of Africa. Please be careful. You are putting yourself in the hands of strangers. You think you know what you are going to but you don't know all of it. (131)

These words of his sister that represented mimicking adulthood had no much impact on him. He rather took it differently: "She likes her own international marriage, but she is worried about mine" (131). Thereafter he undid the centre of his London life, he started himself with Ana to African city, he did not know.

Africa was a strange country with its strange people and strange language. Initially, he thought of staying in Africa for a few nights only and then he would leave the place: "I am not staying here. I am leaving, I will spend a few nights here and then and I will find some way of going away" (133). After reaching Ana's estate house Willie was disturbed seriously: "I don't know where I am. I don't think I can pick my way back. I don't ever want this view to become familiar. I must not unpack. I must never behave as though I am staying" (135). However, Willie spent eighteen years in Africa with Ana. After he shipped one day, he was injured for which he was to be treated in the military hospital among the wounded black soldiers. Willie expressed his desire to leave Ana in the hospital itself. However, Ana consoled him and told him: "People exaggerate the fighting in the bush. You know that. There's not going to be a new war" (135). Such a hopeful consolations did not have any effect because Willie did not think about the war, he rather thought about the world, which is full of slippery substances. It is important to understand the mindset of Willie after his shadow life in Africa for long eighteen years. It was a life he desired without knowing its consequences. Now after experiencing it, he thought that his life had become meaningless. Then he decided to go away to some unknown destination again without knowledge of its consequences. The dialogues between Willie and Ana elucidate his half-life:

> When she came back, he said, "Do you think it would be possible for someone to look at all my bruises and cuts and work out what had happened to me? Work out what I have done to myself?"
>
> "You're recovering your spirits."
>
> You've had eighteen years of me."
>
> "You really mean that you are tired of me."
>
> "I mean I've given you eighteen years. I can't give you any more. I can't live your life any more. I want to live my own."
>
> "It was your idea, Willie. And if you leave, where will you go?"
>
> "I don't know. But I must stop living your life here." (136)

Willie's unknown destination was Berlin. Reaching there he told his sister about his life in Africa in the manner his father had told him about his story in India. Willie was a rootless man throughout his life. When he was in India, he was too much restless, and when he came to London, he still felt that he was unsettled although his tutors felt that he seemed to settle. In Africa he led a very adventurous life of a diaspora without being settled though once Ana commented that he was settling there. Coming Berlin he saw that Tamil boys, displaced and uprooted, were raising funds for a war. His friend, Percy went back to Jamaica, his native land. He himself returned to his sister in Berlin after spending eighteen years, the best part of his life. He didn't know how to move on and where to go in future. This postcolonial dilemma of Willie is reflected in his thoughts when he saw the Tamil boys in Berlin:

> They were unsmiling, boys with a mission, raising funds for the great Tamil war far away, and they hardly looked at Willie or his sister. They were of another generation but Willie saw himself in them. He thought, "That was

> how I appeared in London. That is how I appear now. I am not as alone as thought." Then he thought, "But I am wrong. I am not like them. I am forty-one, in middle life. They are fifteen or twenty years younger, and the world has changed. They have proclaimed who they are and they are risking everything for it. I have been hiding from myself. I have risked nothing. And now the best part of my life is over. (138)

Willie's experience of postcolonial Africa is illuminating. Without knowing anything about this colonial country—its people, its racial tension, strange manners and situations—he went there because he loved Ana and lived there with a belief on her luck. Willie needed Ana for his idea of himself being a man. He depended on her strength and authority to be secured, to lead a comfortable life: "She was a woman who had given herself to me. I believed that she was in some essential way guided and protected, and as long as I was with her no harm could come to me. It may be because of something in our culture that, in spite of appearance, men are really looking for women to lean on" (141). His life was complete and quite different. Ana liberated him, he had no fears now:

> These were the days of my intense love-making with Ana. I loved her—in that room that had been her grandfather's and her mother's with a view of the nervous branching and the fine leaves of the rain tree—for the luck and liberation she had brought me, the undoing of fear, the granting to me of full manhood. (145)

The loss of passport of Willie was symbolic. Willie, by losing his passport, perhaps lost his identity, the pastness of his past, his ancestral inheritance. In Africa, he was completely a new man: "the loss of passport worried me more than everything else. Without my passport I didn't see how I could prove to any official in Africa or England or India who I was" (157). Willie knew that without the passport he would be lost. He would not have claims over anyone: "I wouldn't be able to move. The more I thought about it, the more unprotected I felt. For some days, I could think of nothing else. It began to be like my torment, on the way out, all down the coast of Africa, about losing the gift of language" (158). However, he felt safe after getting the passport back. For one year Willie was quite exciting about his new rich life in Africa. He enjoyed substantially by meeting new people and the excitement of the Africans in a postcolonial world. Ana's authority on the estate helped a lot in removing people's doubts about Willie: "But then after a year or so I began to understand—and I was helped in this understanding by my own background—that the world I had entered was only a half-and-half world, that many of the people who were our friends considered themselves, deep down, people of the second rank. They were not fully Portuguese, and that was where their own ambition lay" (160-61).

Africa is a strange country with strange attitude of the people about their security there. The Correias, proud of their aristocratic name, lived with the idea of great disaster about to happen when they would lose their security both in Portugal and Africa for which they had bank accounts in New York, London and Switzerland so that when that disaster came, they could move easily to these places with a good sum of money. This was their idea of security in Africa. The way of life changes in seconds. There was certain uprising in a region in Africa in the third year of Willie's stay there for which people must learn shooting with a gun as the government would increase the strength of garrison. Willie was to undertake this shooting work on Ana's Estate:

> In a second the scale of things could alter and I could be lost in something like a private universe. It was strange being on the shooting range in Africa and thinking in a new way of my father and his Brahmin ancestors, starveling servants of the great temple. I bought a gun. I set up targets in the grounds of Ana's grandfather's house and practiced whenever I could. Our neighbors began to look at me with a new regard. (168)

With the passage of each year in Africa Willie was acquiring new identities with new experiences. However, each time with a new experience he goes back to his ancestral roots even though he has already denounced such a life of Indian ancestry with rule codes and regulations. The postcolonial government in Africa was authoritarian though people thought that they were far away from the capital. The function of the postcolonial government was questionable in its approach to administration for giving people welfare governance because the authoritarian government heavily depended on some local people who exploited the resources of the country and practiced corrupt means for becoming richer and richer:

> There was no challenge to our authoritarian but easy-going government for many years, and it had grown strangely lazy. In his security the ruler had grown to feel that the details of governing were a burden, or so it appeared; and he had farmed out or leased out important governmental activities to eager, energetic and loyal people. These people became very rich; and the richer they became the more loyal they were and the better they did the jobs that had been farmed out to them. So there was a kind of rough logic and effectiveness in this principle of government. (169)

The authoritarian government often dumped the half-and-half man of Africa. Curia was a rich man of the colony, who transacted Govt. business for commission, was a Portuguese having bank accounts abroad. But when, there was a crisis in relation to the Govt. deal, such people were destroyed. Willie understood how a half man like him in a half-made African society could be destroyed any time. Naipaul's observations of this African life are rather convincingly illustrated here: "There was no trouble at all in throwing a man of the second rank into the darkness, someone from the half-and-half world, educated and respectable and striving unusually knowledgeable about money, and ready for many reasons to do whatever he might be required to do" (174).

Willie's experiences along with the Alvaro, the estate manager of the Correias in the warehouse were startling initially. It was a reflection of the great disorder in the African country in a postcolonial period when the army was pampered for the eventuality of an uprising or a war. The warehouse business was meant for the pleasures of the army soldiers. It was a shock for Willie to note that the tiny aged girls in the prime of their life are forced to such brutality of institutionalized prostitution for the pleasures of the soldiers and the other town people. It was an experience of horror, brutality and shock to Willie. He was surprised how the African waiters and the owner conducting the sex business could be so indifferent:

> I wish I had his detachment. But I was not trained for this kind of life, and I was full of shame. The girls were all African. It had to be like that, I suppose; but I wondered whether the two African waiters didn't suffer a little. And the girls were so young, so foolish, with so little idea, as I thought, of the way they were abusing their own bodies and darkening their likes. I thought with old unhappiness of things at home. I thought of my mother and I thought of my poor father who had hardly known what sex was. I thought of you, too, Sarojini. I imagined that the girls might be you, and my heart shrank. (185)

Even Alvoro, who enjoyed the excitement of village sex every month with a fresh crop of innocent girls, was subdued in that warehouse. After that spur moment in that warehouse, Willie was disturbed a lot for his betrayal to Ana. However, there was a self-discovery in Willie in his experiences with the girl in that "split-second" when he was commanded by the tension of the body of the girl. However, it was a void, without any satisfaction, but this experience led him to a new idea of himself as a human being that he did not know during his life with Ana in the last ten years in Africa. That was so because both Ana and Willie were not guided by true sensuality or true desire. Willie had his own nervousness and fear at being in Africa. Even Ana had been half-timorous at that time of passion because of her family history. However, they led their half-life together: "We each found comfort in the other; and we had become very close, not looking beyond the other for satisfaction, not knowing, in fact, that another kind of satisfaction was possible" (189). With such knowledge, Willie was moving in the wilderness for some years, but gradually that also became a mechanical experience with Willie in course of time. He therefore needed to revive with some new experience that was provided to him with Graca, Carla's convent-school friend, the wife of the new manager at-the-German-castle, an abandoned estate house:

> The long drive had been a strain. Graca's need matched my own. That was new to me. Everything I had known before—the furtiveness of London, the awful Provincial prostitute, the paid black girls of the places of pleasure here, who had yet satisfied me for so long, and for whom for almost a year I had felt such gratitude, and poor Ana, still in my mind the trusting girl who had sat on the settee in my college room in London and allowed herself to be kissed, Ana still so gentle and generous—over the next half-hour everything fell away and I thought how terrible it would have been if, as could so easily have happened, I had died without knowing this depth of satisfaction, this other person that I had just discovered within myself. It was worth any price, any consequence. (204-05)

When his life with Graca was known, Ana suggested him after two years of his drive with Graca that as a man of self-respect and order, he should refrain from all these ungentle ways.

The situations in postcolonial Africa were fluid, constantly changing the life of the common men in the colonies. The colonial government in the capital eased down and the Guerrillas took over. The Portuguese began to leave and the army withdrew from the town: "The barracks were empty; it seemed unnatural after the activity and the daily military rituals, like Church rituals, of the past twelve years" (223). However, the army did not fight the African war in the town. The war was a distant game. It was rather tactical move to keep the town in peace. Graca's house, which she got through her friend Carla, was taken for sharing. Her children were taken to Portugal. It was strange that the children were to prepare papers to say who they were. This was the problem of displacement and rootlessness. However, Ana was firm in not giving anything: "But I'm not running away. Half of what my grandfather gave me was stolen by my father. I will stay here and protect the other half. I do not want people squatting in my house or sleeping in my bed" (226). After the normalcy, there was again rumor of a tribal war:

> The guerrillas had had the support of the black governments over the border. The new insurgents had the support of the white government to the West, and they were far more deadly. It was their policy to "blood" new recruits, to get a recruit to kill someone. They raided the outskirts of towns and killed people and burnt houses and spread terror. (226)

Willie thought of leaving Africa because he would not be able to live through another war. When he was treated for his injuries, the physical pain of his "damaged body" was like the other pain that had been with him for years. Now that Willie was forty-one and had spent the part of his life with Ana during the last eighteen years, he expressed his gratitude to her for obliging him. However, he had done nothing because he had led a half-life by hiding there for a long time. To Willie, his life was a shadow life, the life of Ana rather than his own. Even to Ana, this was not her life either. The anguish of Willie is the result of the shattering of all his illusions in the postcolonial scenario of Africa. After his dreams were shattered he prepared to go to Berlin, his sister, but then it was not his home. Willie had not yet arrived at his final identity. He was yet to explore something more about his identity. Mishra has interpreted the anguish of Willie appropriately: "Willie's anguish is not only his own but in a way; it also describes the agony of all individuals who have been separated by time and place. It is the anguish of people whose fondest dreams are ravaged and yet have something to fall back upon (136, ACR 3.2: 2004). *Half a Life* therefore explores the predicament of an individual in a postcolonial society. The individual's high hopes and dreams of keeping away from his roots were frustrated finally, and the individual perhaps reconciles with his roots. His journey is spiritual because through it he acquires new experiences and new knowledge that evolve his identity which is therefore not complete because experience does not end when he reaches

Berlin. The novel ends with Willie's realization of the whole perspective of his journey from India to Africa via England. His identity is exploratory because it is continuously evolved, adding new experiences and new knowledge. Naipaul however takes up Willie's further crisis in the novel *Magic Seeds* after his return to his sister Sarojini in Berlin.

5.6. Journeying through Homelessness, Longing for Home

Magic Seeds is a novel of philosophical significance. It explores how life has its own ways and moves without being subjected to any kind of structured pattern. This novel deals with the aftermath of Africa life of Willie who comes to Berlin to his sister, Sarojini after spending a "half-life" with Ana. Sarojini does not approve of Willie's actions because she believes that her brother has run away from life without facing the guerrilla war. Such cowardly action is denounced by her. She therefore persuades him to join the guerrilla war perpetuated by the Tamils in the Indian forests. He therefore spends his life for seven years among the revolutionaries, and is imprisoned. After the release, he goes to London once again after a gap of thirty years; he however has different kind of experiences in London in the late 1980s / early 1990s. It is important to note Willie's evolutionary significance as an individual. Through his journey, he goes to London from India, and then moves to Africa, from Africa to Berlin, then to the Indian forests and jail, and therefrom to London. His homelessness makes him a romantic to have a house of his own like Mr. Biswas in *A House for Mr Biswas*. It is interesting to note his psychological set-up and mature reactions to the world which is not governed by any scheme of an individual:

> All night Willie heard the music. It invaded his sleep and mingled with other memories. Africa, with the conical grey stone hills and Africans walking on the red paths beside the asphalt road. The burnt-out concrete houses, smoke-stained around the windows. The forest and the men in olive uniform with caps with the red stain star, and the endless marching. The strange jail where, as

> on a slave ship, the prisoners lay side by side on the floor in two rows separated by a central aisle. All night it seemed to him as well that he had found something good to write to Sarojini about. This thing eluded him. He looked for it, through all the slave music, and in the morning all he was left with was, "It is wrong to have an ideal view of the world. That's where the mischief starts. That's where everything starts unraveling. But I can't write to Sarojini about that. (*MAS* 280)

The novel ends with such a state of mind of Willie who has attempts to write a letter, but fails because he changes his mind three or four times every week. As a result, he writes the letters, but neither completes them nor sends any one of them to his sister.

Going back to Willie's life of ten years back, it is interesting to understand his frame of mind. When he divorces his wife Ana after living with her for eighteen years, he thinks that he may lead a full life in future if he leaves Africa. But then, in Berlin his sister challenges his "running away" and "hiding" life without facing the hard realities. Sarojini reminds him of his short existence in Berlin because his visa cannot be renewed:

> It had begun many years before in Berlin. Another World. He was living there in a temporary, half- and—half way with his sister Sarojini. After Africa it had been a great refreshment, this new kind of protected life, being almost a tourist, without demands, without anxiety. It had to end, of course; it had begun to end the day Sarojini said to him "You've been here for six months. I may not be able to get your visa renewed again. You know what that means.... You've got to start thinking of moving on. Do you have any idea of where you can go? Is there anything you feel you want to do? (5)

As usual, life is not subject to well-structured design to Willie. He therefore says: "I don't see what I can do. I don't know where I can go" (5). When Sarojini reprimands him for his callous attitude towards action in life he questions: "What could I have done in India? What could I have done in England in 1957 or 1958? Or in Africa?" (6). But Sarojini is aggressive towards her brother: "You've always preferred to hide. It's the colonial psychosis, the caste psychosis. You inherited it from your father. You were in Africa for eighteen years. There was a great guerrilla war there. Didn't you know?" (6). She further elaborates the significance of the guerrilla war:

> It was a glorious war. At least in the beginning when you think about it, it can bring tears to the eyes. A poor and helpless people, slaves in their own land, starting from scratch in every way. What did you do? Did you seek them out? Did you join them? Did you help them? That was a big enough cause to anyone looking for a cause. But no. You stayed in your estate house with your lovely little half-white wife and pulled the pillow over your ears and hoped that no bad black freedom fighter was going to come in the night with a gun and heavy boots and frighten you. (6)

She suggests her brother that he should have joined the war, the African revolution for the cause of liberating the people of Africa. When Sarojini is reprimanding him, a Tamil rose-seller, a revolutionary is seen selling roses. Citing the activities of this Tamil revolutionary who is working for the cause of the liberation of the Tamils, Sarojini tells her brother that the rose-seller has more worth than Willie because he has found his war. He is brave enough to face the reality whereas Willie has not that courage. Sarojini argues that it is necessary to know the authenticity of history to understand a revolution in its proper perspective: "He had the look of a man with a cause, the look of a man apart. It's something you might have noticed in Africa, if you had learned to look. This man's selling roses here, but those roses are being turned to guns. Somewhere else far away. It's how revolutions are made. There is no more disciplined guerrilla army in the world. They are quite ferocious, quite ugly. And if you know more about your own history you would understand what a miracle that is" (9-10).

Sarojini's interpretation of history of India from the point of view of imperialism is significant. She believes that the first history book about India written by a British school Inspector is biased and, not authentic representation of facts because Roper Lethbridge, the historian was motivated by the imperialistic bias. Even then, his British way of presenting facts, though commercial, still gave us some learning:

> One of the most important of those ideas was that in India there were servile races, people born to be slaves and there were martial races. The martial rules were fine; the servile races were not. You and I half belong to the servile races. I am sure you know that. I am sure you half accept that. That is why you have lived as you have lived. The Tamils selling roses in Berlin belong wholly to the servile races. That idea would have even been impressed on them in all kinds of ways. And that British idea about the servile and the martial races of India is utterly wrong. (10)

Such deconstruction of history deserves special mention because it leads us how the British administration is denigrating the Indian people in their own land. That is the functioning of imperialism: "It is what happens to captive people" (11). Sarojini further explains: "Since in India we have no idea of history we quickly forget our past and always believe what we are told" (11). In the new British dispensation, the Tamils in the South were considered dirt, fit only for labor for which they were sent off as serfs to the plantations of Malay and Ceylon and other places. Sarojini pleads that these Tamils who are selling roses to buy guns are the truly martial races who have thrown off a great weight of history and propaganda: "They have made themselves a truly martial people and they have done so against the odds. You must respect them, Willie" (11).

Sarojini's assertive talk on injustice and cruelty, and the need for revolution has the force of serenity to have a great influence on Willie. Sarojini's understanding of the politics of revolution has given her a complete intellectual system: "Her world-view was able to absorb everything political murders in Guatemala, Islamic revolution in Iran, Caste riots in India and even the petty theft practiced as a matter of shopkeeping habit or principle by the wine-shop men in Berlin..." (12). Willie now sees a Sarojini of a different brand. She has evolved to understand everything with so much calmness and poise. By staying with his sister for six months in Berlin, "the world began to change for him. Just as he felt she could enter all his emotions...so he began to enter her way of looking. There was a logic and order in everything he said" (13). Sarojini has shown Willie the two worlds: one is ordered and settled where people live quite happy; and the other world is desperate to enter the simpler, ordered world. In this sound world, "a hundred loyalties, the residue of old history tied them down; a hundred little wars filled them with hate and dissipated their energies" (13). In Berlin, Willie understood that the two worlds co-existed. Going back to his life twenty years back, he felt ashamed: "His half-life in London; and then all his life in Africa, that life when he was permanently in semi-hiding, gauging his success by the fact that in his second class, semi-Portuguese group he didn't particularly stand out, and was "passing"; all that life seemed shameful" (14). He therefore decided that he would no more lead a life of hiding and would join some revolution.

Referring to history, one day while both of them were walking below the trees in the shopping avenue, Sarojini told Willie that Kandapalli would be comparable to Lenin or Mao when the history of the twentieth century revolution would be written in future. He is an important person because he has the capacity to bend the course of history: "When, in a hundred years, the definitive history of twentieth century revolution comes to be written, and various ethnocentric prejudices have disappeared Kandapalli will be up there with Lenin and Mao of that I have no doubt. And you haven't even heard of him now" (15). To Kandapalli, "Revolution was to come, from below from the village, from the people. There was to be no place in this movement for middle class masqueraders" (18). Kandapalli has been able to spearhead a true revolution. He is a simple man from Warangal, a school teacher without qualifications, is always moved with tears, when he talks about the poor, the marginalized sections of the society.

During his five months stay in Berlin with his sister, Willie was given the mental exercise of thinking about the desperate places of the world he had known: "he found himself reconsidering Africa and his marriage, acknowledging everything in a new way, hiding nothing, submerging all the pathos of his nondescript past in an ennobling new ideal" (14). The knowledge of his own "self" and other things and situations as well brought a new kind of joy in Willie: "...at the same time he felt the excitement of the new movements of his heart and mind; and he felt above everything around him" (25). Willie's condition of homelessness as a refugee from Africa with no place to go to, had not dumped him like many others who were to lead a life of a tramp like another Indian he met in Berlin, who was having "no place to sleep, his mind no longer whole, his breath very bad, a broken arm in a sling black with grime, complaining of his torments at the hands of young thugs" (25). He understood that he had spent a shameless life in Africa, but then his varied experience and false longings of the past were only a preparation for what was to come to him in the near future. After receiving the letter from Joseph to her husband Wood, Sarojini would tell her brother that he would meet that University teacher in India to join the revolution of Kandapalli which was being regulated by him in his forest Headquarters. It was therefore a great chance for Willie to go to India after a gap of twenty years: "After more than twenty years Willie saw India again. He had left India with very little money, the gift of his father; and he was going back with very little money, the gift of his sister" (28).

Willie in India understands now that he has a different identity. Twenty years ago he had gone to England with the identity of his father's son to have a degree / diploma in England. In the meanwhile, through different phases of his life in London, Africa and Berlin he has become a different man. He therefore sees India from a different perspective when he reaches the airport from Berlin:

> Twenty years ago I wouldn't have seen what I am seeing now. I am seeing what I see because I have made myself another person. I cannot make myself that old person

> again. But I must go back to that old way of seeing. Otherwise my cause is lost before I have begun. I have come from a world of waste and appearances. I saw quite clearly some time ago that it was a simple world, where people had been simplified. I must not go back on that vision. I must understand that now I am among people of more complicated beliefs and social ideas, and at the same time in a world stripped of all style and artifice. This is an airport. It works. It is full of technically accomplished people. That is what I must see. (30)

From the airport Willie went to the distant town of Joseph by a train. When they had their initiation to each other Joseph told Willie about his impressions of Africa:

> Like you, my attitude to Africa was the colonial one. But that's where we all have to begin. It was the colonialists who opened up Africa and told us about it.... We are in one of the saddest places in the world here. Twenty times sadder than what you saw in Africa. In Africa the colonial past would have been there for you to see. Here you can't begin to understand the past, and when you get to know it you wish you didn't. (38-39)

Joseph goes to the Indian history of four hundred years back to illustrate the catastrophe that fell on this sacred last Indian kingdom which was invaded by the Muslims to destroy the kingdom completely. After ruining the capital city, they killed the entire human resources and talent: "they killed the priests, the philosophers, the artisans, the architects, the scholars" (39). The only people spared were the serfs, the low class people during this military defeat. It was a "war of annihilation, a war without limits and restraints" (40). There was no resistance against this destructive war. The serfs were the people who were completely divided. "They were of various low castes, and there is no caste hatred greater than that of the low, one up-caste for another" (39). They all belonged to serving class, slaves in some sense. After the great demolition and destruction they ruled people by force and imposed forty types of taxes.

As a result, people were to live with much poverty. Through such rules of exploitation people have now thought that this is their eternal condition of poverty and slavery. Joseph further interprets how the people did not have sense of dignity and rage against such destructions and exploitations. They are rather callous and indifferent to their self-dignity:

> But this was the origin of our sacred Indian poverty, the poverty that India could offer the world. And there was something else. Thirty years after the destruction of the last Indian Kingdom the conquerors built a big gate of victory. The gate of victory is now an Indian heritage site. The destroyed city has been forgotten. (40)

Joseph has been enraged to its climax when he utters that there should have been a great revenge by the rulers after independence. But that did not happen:

> Defeat can be terrible. You would have thought that at independence all the lords of the conquered people would have been hanged with their families and their bodies left to turn to bones. That would have been a kind of redemption, the beginning of something new. But nothing like that happened. It was left to some very simple people to raise the standard of revolution. (40-41)

The extremist revolutionary outrage of Joseph is quite conspicuous in his anger of expression: "Yes, I would leave nothing better than to see a revolution sweeping everything away" (42). He also suggested Willie to move to Neo Anand Bhavan from the hotel Riviera because none of the revolutionaries would come to see him in such a high class hotel. In Neo Anand Bhavan Willie would have the "tormenting" and "emptiest" days? With the new way of life in the forest that he has come to terms with initially Willie is a bit disturbed: "I have to understand now that, in this venture, books are a cheat. I have to depend on my own resources" (46). Being now trapped he reflects: "I no longer know where I am. I don't think I will be able to pick up my way back. I am in their hands now" (48). Willie was in having serious mental imbalance in the early days of the forest life. He questioned himself why he jumped into the revolution of Kandapalli:

> Kandapalli preached the Mass Line. Kandapalli wished the villagers and the poor to fight their own battles. I am not among the poor and villagers in this camp. There has been some mistake. I have fallen among the wrong people. I have come to the wrong revolution. I don't like these faces. And yet I have to be with them. I have to get a message out to Sarojini or to Joseph. But I don't know how. I am completely in the hands of these people. (50)

Willie's predicament in the forest is well understood because he has come to the forest to join the revolution after his life of high luxury in Africa and Berlin. One night when he is asked to do sentry duty Willie becomes emotional and cries: "That night Willie cried, tears of rage, tears of fear, and in the dawn the cry of the peacock, after it had drunk from its forest pool, filled him with grief for the whole world" (50). In the training camp of the organization, Willie was not feeling comfortable. Even then he was to hide his feelings. He could not be explicit to make his disgust known to these people: "I have never known such boredom. Ever since I have come to India I have known these terrible nights of boredom. I suppose it is a kind of training, a kind of asceticism, but for what I am not sure. I must look upon it as another chamber of experience. I must give no sign to these people that I am not absolutely with them" (52). During the camp life, Willie thought of going to the poor people to understand their "unreserved sorrows over the centuries". From the training camp, Willie was sent to the village Dulhipur along with Bhoj Narayan who guided Willie in all critical situations.

With the meager amount of ₹ 150, both of them were to ration money for daily expenses to survive in the forest. Willie's patience was now lost without money. He thought of running away, but Bhoj Narayan guided him to keep patience, and if possible they might return to the forest wherefrom they came. Keeping his conscience he did not run away. By this time of crisis in his life his sister writes to him about his father's serious illness.

However a "peasant-disguise" man brings some money for both of them to survive. The idea of home is much important for Willie: "Willie looks for home everywhere. Even in the bagasse yard he looked at home" (74). He is always disturbed by the idea of home: "It's the one thing I have worked at all my life: not being at home anywhere, but looking at home" (74). Being on the move always, Willie along with Bhoj Narayan enjoyed the duty of a courier. To him as a courier, the guerrilla territory was no more a series of unconnected landscapes. Bhoj Narayan, the revolutionary and companion to Willie suspected Raja, the weaver, whose last deliveries of supplies were captured by the police. Thinking that both Raja and his elder brother would be great threat by passing information to police, Bhoj shot Raja dead. After so many weeks, Willie reflected upon his own state of mind:

> I could say various things about justice and people on the other side. But it couldn't be true. The fact is I have arrived at a new way of feeling. And it is amazing that it should have happened just after fourteen or fifteen months of this strange life. (89)

Near the post office, when Bhoj Narayan was captured by the police, Willie was on his own way to a village by a passenger train. However, he became too much reflective on the two lives—Bhoj's and Raja's which were wasted after the success stories of their family lineage of two or three generations. There were possibilities of prosperity. But these two lives came to nothing. He reached Shivdas's house before eight in the night, and he was given their main bed room for that night's rest. Such generosity of Shivdas, a peasant revolutionary, made him quite reflective on the course of revolution:

> We think, or they think, that Shivdas does what he does because he is a peasant revolutionary, someone, created by the movement, someone new, and very precious. But Shivdas does what he does because he is instinctively following old ideas, old ways, old courtesies. One day he will not give up his bed to me.... That will be the end of the old world and the end of the revolution. (97)

After elimination of Bhoj Narayan, Willie felt alone in his "room in a commandeered long hut" (99):

> The hut for some months had become a kind of home. It was where he returned after his expeditions; and it was an important addition to the list he carried in his head of places he had slept in, and was able to count, (as was his habit) when he felt he needed to get hold of the thread of his life. But now the hut he had also become a place where, without Bhoj Narayan, he was horribly alone. He was glad to have got there but then, almost immediately, he had become restless. (99)

At this juncture of his life Willie was in crisis because he had been trapped in such a revolutionary organization from which he could not escape. Sometimes a sort of emptiness and frustration had shaken him; therefore he was thinking of death as an escape from this state of psychological crisis: "The most comforting thing about life is the certainty of death. There is no way now for me to pick my way back to the upper air. Where was the upper air? Berlin? Africa? Perhaps there is no upper air. Perhaps that idea has always been a mirage" (100-01). Willie's role in the revolutionary organization was suddenly changed from a courier to a member under the commander Ramchandra, a bony handsome man with a gun, AK-47. Under the chairmanship of the leader, the section meeting took place in the hut of Ramchandra for about three hours. Many issues were discussed including the loss of the squad which was inevitable in any kind of revolution or war: "All the weapons that had been assembled piece by piece over a year had been lost. That was a loss of many hundreds of thousands of rupees, and there had been nothing to show for it" (103). The leader further argued that it was not a ripe time to expand the revolutionary base in the small towns. It was rather important to expand the bases in the villages in the deep forest areas. Einstein, a critic of Kandapalli, pleaded for a shift in change to the approach of the revolution because the peasants, from which background he himself came, were to be roughed up a bit to be disciplined in the organization. Even he pleaded that people like Shivdas, needed the help of the revolutionaries to enhance his wealth:

"But (Shivdas) is a crook and a thing. The big landowners and the old feudal officials have run away. There is no policeman or surveyor in his village, and every year shades reap many acres of the other people's crops and plough many acres of other people's land.... The day Shivdas thinks it will serve him better he will betray us to the police" (104). Such type of neo-colonial situation exists in many villages. A revolutionary, according to Einstein should have clarity of vision and precision of thought. He therefore now blames Willie for the misfortune befell on their commander Bhoj Narayan because of such lack of vision and clear thoughts. Though generously Willie accepted his mistake, he was highly appreciated by the leader. Finally it was resolved that the revolutionary base should be expanded in the deep forest among the villages.

This new idea of liberating more areas in the villages of forest was a strange thing for Willie: "It was a step down into yet another kind of life; patternless labor without reward or goal, without solitude or companionship; without news of the outside world, with no prospect of letters from Sarojini, with nothing to anchor himself to" (105-06). In the deep forest, Willie developed some sort of relationship for which he gave an outline of England, Africa and Berlin. Ramachandra explains his idea of revolution is different from Kandapalli. As a revolutionary, Kandapalli believes in dialogue whereas Ramachandra and many others believe that revolution can be achieved through blood and violence. The young people who join the revolution believe in action and change. However, the villagers, who are landless and poor, are not accepting the suggestion to take over the land. To them the land does not belong to them, so they cannot plough. To bring them to sense, you need violence so that there will be radical changes in the society and the landless poor will be free from their slavery mentality. Having faith in revolution, they will think that their poverty is not permanent and the idea that the poor will remain poor and the rich will remain rich will go away. Ramachandra's idea of revolution to transform the villages through social equality has a flaw. Willie therefore thinks: "They all want the old ways to go. But the old ways are part of people's being. If the old ways go, people will not know who they are, and these villages, which have their own beauty, will become a jungle" (117). The background of Ramachandra being a revolutionary lies in his poverty and shame. "Shame" is eternal. It can only die with the person who has been ashamed: "Little things drive people more than we sometimes imagine. I have so many causes of shame. In India, London and Africa. They are fresh after twenty tears. I don't think they will ever die. They will die only with me" (120). Ramachandra, the commander with a gun, has to grow strength and skill to face the police. He was therefore killed in the police encounter and after which Willie and others were to go back on their tracks for their survival. Willie is now puzzled what to do: "Now I'm truly lost. In every way, I don't know what lies ahead or behind. My only cause now is to survive, to get out of this" (122).

Though Willie had been with the movement, he had always the pastoral vision of the area: its beauty, its sanctity and its serenity:

> He had persuaded himself that outside the noise and rush and awfulness of cities was this quite different world where things followed an antique course, which it was the business of the revolution to destroy. This pastoral vision contained the idea that the peasant labored and was oppressed. What this pastoral vision didn't contain was the idea that the village—like those they had liberated on the march (and then let go of) and might one day with luck liberate again—was full of criminals, as limited and vicious and brutal as the setting, whose existence had nothing to do with the idea of labor and oppression. (124-25)

So Willie and others came back to their old places after the wish of the high command to extend the liberated areas had failed. Different section meetings were conducted to chalk out the plan for further action when police arrested their leader of the forest and also Kandapalli, the leader with humanity and tears for the poor. However, all their plans failed even to kidnap a minister to protest the arrest of Kandapalli. It was therefore presumed that the movement could not be run any further. There was more brutal action by the police. Finally Einstein and Willie also decided to surrender to the police in a planned manner. That was done with meticulous care and caution: "Einstein telephoned the police, and the day came when they went to the police headquarters of the town where they were" (145). The police superintendent received these political prisoners with full civility. The gesture of civility moved Willie and therefore he reflected on his revolutionary life:

> Bhoj Narayan was my friend. My heart went out to Ramachandra. Without Einstein I wouldn't have known how to get here. But the man in front of me in this office is much more my kind person. My heart and mind reach out at once to him. His face radiates intelligence. I have to make no allowances for him. I feel we are meeting as equals. After my years in the bush—years when in order to survive I made myself believe things I wasn't sure of—I feel this as a blessing. (146)

Willie had the idea that soon after his surrender; he might be arrested and released afterwards. But then, his case was seriously viewed because of the killing of three police men by Ramachandra and he was close to him. Though he himself was idle and not involved in any murder during his revolutionary days, he was charged as an accessory which was quite unfair: "But the superintendent has quite another idea of my life as a guerrilla.... He would not believe that things merely happened around me. He just counts the dead bodies" (150).

After his worried London life and African life of purposelessness, and Berlin plan Willie's revolutionary life was rather a life of a floater: "But he had been undone by the India of his return. He could see no pattern, no thread. He had returned with an idea of action, of truly placing himself in the world. But he had become a floater, and the world had become more phantasmagoric than it had ever been. That unsetting feeling, of phantasmagoria had come to him the day when poor Raja, with boyish excitement, had taken him for a ride in his three-wheel scooter, to show him the "enemy" (150-51). After the hearing in the court, Willie was sentenced to ten years' imprisonment. However after some days, his sister came to visit him in his jail and therefore planned his release. As a result of which Willie was released from the prison under terms of special amnesty, and went to London: "Willie understood that just as his father, thirty years ago, had by his begging letters to great men in England set certain wheels in motion that had eventually taken him to London, so now Sarojini, out of her great political experience, had begun to act on his behalf" (168).

At every stage of his life, Willie is disturbed by the question of his identity. So in London, he felt his old stirrings and the beginning of old grief. He then made up his mind:

> I have been there. I have given part of my life and I have nothing to show for it. I cannot go there again. I must let that part of me die. I must lose that vanity. I must understand that big countries grow or shrink according to the play of international forces that are beyond the control of any one man. I must try now to be only myself. If such a tuning is possible. (169-70)

Reflecting upon his changing situations and adaptation of his delicate brain to all these including his life of tormenting in the jail he tells his friend Roger in London: "The whole thing was so strange, such a string of unreal episodes, I feel in time I would have gone mad like the others. The brain is so delicate, and man can adapt to so many situations. That's how it's been for me" (172). Roger tells him that in some ways life has been the same for everybody. However, unlike Willie, Roger has always lived in the real world. Contrarily Willie's life has been full of surprises without having any control over things. That night Willie had a heavy sleep in Roger's house after taking a large amount of whisky. Awakening, he was disturbed a lot when he thought of his homelessness:

> I have never slept in a room of my own. Never at home in India, when I was a boy. Never here in London. Never in Africa. I lived in somebody else's house always, and slept in somebody else's bed. In the forest of course there were no rooms, and then the jail was the jail. Will I ever sleep in a room of my own? (177-78)

Such a thought had never occurred to him. This idea of homelessness is an important diasporic consciousness. Even Naipaul himself has often been disturbed by such an idea though willingly he led such a life of homelessness. Perdita met him in the room and showed him his paperback ball and also told him how Roger made the plan of his release from the jail through this book arguing that he is not a political writer, but a real one. Willie read that "his book was a pioneer of Indian postcolonial writing" (180). Walking in the streets of London, Willie thought that he was a free man. He was not bound by any organization to join for a revolution as when came to India from Berlin. He is now a completely free man: "Now I can only celebrate what I am or what I have become" (188).

After two weeks Willie's mood of exaltation vanished because of the repetitive, mechanical life he had fallen into. Since he had already seen enough of London life, he therefore did not get any pleasure. Even his past life in London was not exciting: "To see it too often was to strip it of memories and in this way to lose precious pieces of himself" (159). Willie wanted to join a job because he was feeling bored day by day. Roger suggested that work might make him a slave. A man might get some self-fulfillment in work, but then seeing people at work in the office made him awful. Willie however got a job in the magazine office at Bloomsbury, London for which he was to go in the morning. After six weeks in the Bloomsbury office Willie went to Barnet, to be trained in architecture in the company's training centre. When Roger drove Willie to the training centre, Willie saw on the way the immigrant Indians, Pakistanis and Bangladeshis from the subcontinent that repeopled London during the last thirty years assuming that London is still the centre, not a periphery. When Roger dropped in Willie in the hostel, he talked about his crises and problems in personal life. Willie however found the course at the training centre richer and profounder sidelining the problems of his friend in his mind. The course on architecture interested Willie significantly because whatever he learnt was quite relevant to correlate to what he saw around him. At this late age he began to learn things and saw life in a new way:

> It is terrible and heartbreaking that this way of seeing and understanding has come to me so late. I can't do anything with it now. A man of fifty cannot remake his life. I have heard it said that the only difference between the rich and the poor in a certain kind to economy is that the rich have money ten or fifteen or twenty years before the poor. (220)

In the same manner people who come to see things in a way quite late, they are fools. He therefore mocks at all those attending the courses because all of them are in the forties or fifties who have already crossed the prime of their life: "I was so condemning of other people on the course. How vain and foolish. I am no different from them" (220). People from various countries like South Africa, Australia, Egypt, India, Pakistan, Malaysia, and China were sent by their companies to undergo the training in this course to get at knowledge that was simply there seemingly divinely provided knowledge that had for a long time been unfairly denied them for racial or political reasons but was now, in a miraculously changed world, theirs to claim as their own. And this claimed knowledge confirmed each man in the rightness of his own racial or tribal or religious ways. Up the greasy pole and then letting go. The simplified rich world, of success and achievement, always itself; the world outside always in disturbance (225).

Though Willie enjoyed the course, in the weekends he felt desolated and nostalgic when other trainees moved to different places. He went back to his roots, his past life in Africa and India. He became emotional when he thought of the misfortunes of his "caste" father and "low" caste mother: "...understanding as a result with the deepest kind of ache that there was no true place in the world for him—back to that childhood when on some especially unhappy evenings there came, with the utmost clarity, a child's vision of the earth spinning in darkness, with everyone on it lost" (228).

It was not that Willie was undergoing tremendous psychological pressure by being uprooted from his roots. Even Roger in his country England had his own predicament. As a friend of Willie, Roger opened his heart to him and when he talked about his crisis, both personal and that of his country, tears rolled down his cheeks:

> He talked of socialism and high taxes, and the inflation that inevitably followed high taxes, destroying families and the idea of families. This idea of families (rather than the family) passed on values from one generation to the next. These shared values held a country together; the loss of these values broke a country up, hastened a general decline. (233)

Roger, like Willie himself, believed in liberal ideas. He was a man of "inherited liberal ideas, a man rooted in this liberalism, concerned with human rights all over the world, and at the same time at ease with his country's recent history going with flow" (233). However, Roger had his own personal tragedy with Marian though she had long back inspired him to work with optimism.

Willie writes a letter of optimism to his sister, Sarojini, regarding his plan for future. He would study architecture for the next eight years; then he would work about fifteen years till seventy-five. By that way, he could at least lead an active life of ten to fifteen years in the profession: "The difficulty there is that to any logical mind it is absurd for a man of fifty to start learning a profession. The main difficulty is that to carry it out I would need an injection of optimism" (271). He further writes to his sister:

> If I was born new, in the same place, the world would have a different look. Too late for me unfortunately. And with that pathetic little self that now exists inside me somewhere, the self that I recognize so easily, I put aside the architecture dream and think that I should get some understanding little job somewhere and live in some little flat somewhere and hope that the neighbours are not too noisy. But I know enough now to understand that life can never be simplified like that and that there would be some little trap or flow in that dream of

> simplicity, of just letting one's life pass, of treating one's life only as a way of passing the time. (272)

That is how most of the dreams in life remain unfulfilled. These dreams are the "magic seeds" which never fertilize and never grow. However these "seeds" facilitate optimism in life to make it dynamic. Willie writes to his sister that a successful man is a happy man who has "precise goals, limited and attainable" (272) like their friend Marcus whose only goal was to have sex with white women and have a white grandchild. He has succeeded in achieving both:

> His half-English son, Lyndhurst, now a man of about thirty, has had two children by a pure-white aristocratic lady. One of these children is as white as white can be. The whole thing is being sealed this Saturday by the wedding up the half-English boy and his lady, mother of his white child. It is the fashion here, babies before wedding bells. (272-73)

Referring to the wedding of Marcus's son's two children before marriage, Naipaul perhaps suggests that these two children—white and black—are the magic seeds who would grow in future. He has brought out the racial memory and the slave music in the wedding. Further, the imprecise dreams of the individuals are the magic seeds, which are not often easily achieved in life. They seem to be things in a magic, in a dream. However, the "magic seeds", which symbolize optimism in life, help it move on to an unknown destination. This is the blurred identity of an individual who is moving towards "the unknown" submerged in the dreams to achieve the magic seeds in his life.

PART III

Travelogues: Writing History, Culture, Civilization

6

The Caribbean Journey: Exploring West Indian History, Society, Culture

Naipaul's obsession with Trinidad is intensely personal. Though he left Trinidad after getting an overseas scholarship for pursuit of his higher studies, he had a sense of attachment to this place despite his repeated denials. He therefore writes in "Author's Foreword" to *Finding the Centre*: "A writer after a time carries his world with him, his own burden of experience, human experience and literary experience (One deepening the other) and I do believe...that I would have found equivalent connections with my past and myself wherever I had gone" (1985: 10). A writer's imagination is therefore sharpened by the complexity of his experiences in an alien land by being displaced from the land of his roots. Naipaul, after moving to the centre from the margin, went to different places of margin to "broaden his worldview" (*FC* 11):

> It broadened my worldview; it showed me a changing world and took me out of my own colonial shell; it became the substitute for the mature social experience—the deepening knowledge of a society—which my background and the nature of my life denied me. My uncertainty about my role withered; a role was not necessary. I recognized my own instincts as a traveler, and was content to be myself, to be what I had always been, a looker. And I looked in my own way. (11)

Naipaul was travelling to explore his experience. "Exile" is important for diasporic writers like Naipaul. Terry Eagleton argues that the past of an exiled writer creates tension in his mental set-up lending his writing new associations and creating freshness: "...great art is produced, not from the simple availability of an alternative, but from the subtle and the involuted tensions between the remembered and the real, the potential and the actual, integration and dispossession" (1970: 8).

Naipaul's contemporary, George Lamming, the Caribbean exile writer, is sympathetic to his native people in his work *The Pleasures of Exile* (1960). Naipaul is however critical of the West Indian society in his travelogue *The Middle Passage*. It is difficult to respond to the mixed, half-formed West Indian culture and way of life. Naipaul is satirical and humorous in his portrayal of the societies and peoples in his travelogues. In memory of the colonial rule in the Third World countries, M.I. Singh puts a right argument:

> While most Third world countries have memories of colonial rule and cultural displacement as a result of forced migrations or white political strategies, the general decline in almost all areas of development is common. Naturally enough, these nations have had to depend on external sources and the economic infrastructure to overcome poverty and their underdeveloped state. (1998a: 37)

It is therefore natural that large-scale migration takes place from the Third World Nations to the European metropolitan cities in search of better career prospects. Coming back to the Third World Nations from the metropolis in search of order and pattern of life, Naipaul is rather unhappy because of the imitative nature of these Third World societies. His disapproval of the Third World societies has been well reflected in his travelogues on West Indies, India, Africa, Islamic countries and South American provinces. Initially Naipaul encountered the Caribbean multi-racial society and then he undertook his journey to India in search of his roots. He was however disillusioned. This is obvious in *The Middle Passage, India: An*

Area of Darkness and *India: A Wounded Civilization*. India traumatized Naipaul. He was surprised by its strangeness and vastness—its poverty, mediocrity and loss of its cultural and mythical identity. However, in *India: A Million Mutinies Now,* Naipaul is emotionally involved to comprehend India as a country of immense possibilities. Naipaul's traveling to non-Arab Muslim countries has enabled him to comment on the rootlessness and identity crisis of Muslims in Pakistan, Indonesia, Malaysia and Iran. The suffering of the marginalized slaves in the Latin American countries has made him understand the crisis of values in these South American countries.

In his travelogues, Naipaul is concerned with a sense of history, and loss of identity and culture. M.I. Singh pleads that "the overwhelming sense of defeat, exploitation or passive obedience inherited from the historical feeling of shock and amnesia turns the Third World writer's hero proverbially shipwrecked, without any mental resting-place or moorings in the historico-cultural terms" (1998a: 104-05). It is seen that the loss of indigenous cultures and traditions in Asia, Africa and the Caribbean is linked directly to the colonial history and its legacies. Colonialism did a lot of harm to the indigenous people and their cultural traditions and identities. The colonized were tortured psychologically. Though apparently it seemed to be economic reason of the shame of the colonized, it was actually a moral and spiritual chaos. It is therefore rightly argued:

> Colonialism, with its own norms and detested traditions, threw up all kinds of divisions; the native vs. the settlers, the rich vs. the poor, the illiterate vs. the literate, Black vs. White, or the oppressors vs. the oppressed. These modes and oppositions formed the system of relationships which developed out of the Black vs. White or the oppressor vs. oppressed. These modes and oppositions formed the system of relationships which developed out of the Black-White contact which in turn led to the Black economic and cultural subordination. Whether it is the forced transfer as laborers or indentured servants into an alien environment, or the voluntary migration into metropolitan cities in search of a better economic

> future, the end-product has been a native inferiority and the sense of feeling at the margin of success and creation. (Singh 1998a: 105-06)

What is conspicuous therefore in colonialism is immense inequality. The colonial period was thus a period of inhumanity because there was large-scale exploitation, marginalization and psychic-subordination. Despite their claim of civilizing the natives, the European colonialism had been a system of systematic robbing of the native resources, lands and cultures. Sometimes it was seen that the inhabitants in colonial system, did not have any coherent, central way of life or a common cultural identity as in the case of the Caribbean community. Naipaul has explored all these in his Caribbean writings and has tried to give a sense of viable identity and nationalism to its people. Through long suffering due to marginalization, the native communities become introspective and try to know their identity. Fanon posits: "Because it is systematic negation of the other person and a furious determination to deny the other person all attributes of humanity, colonialism forces the people it dominates to ask themselves the question constantly. In reality, who am I?" (1963: 250).

This question of "identity" leads the natives to try for psychic-liberation by revolting against the White, colonial supremacy. In his travelogues, Naipaul is concerned with the psychological "slavery-mentality" of the natives during colonialism. He is trying to penetrate into the psychic state of natives to explore their socio-cultural history. In *The Middle Passage* he observes that the Caribbean people have remained the mimic men, though they are on the verge of getting their freedom. In *An Area of Darkness*, Naipaul believes that the Indo-British encounter during the colonial rule has not any positive results for India as a nation. In *India: A Wounded Civilization*, he has engaged in analyzing the very foundation of Indian culture and civilization. In the third book on India, *A Million Mutinies Now*, he describes India stirring into new life. By traveling to the Islamic countries he understands that Islamic fundamentalism has been a serious threat to the First and Third World Nations. *Among the Believers* and *Beyond Belief* are therefore serious explorations that make us think about the global policies that are reshaped due to threat of Islamic fundamentalism. In *A Turn in the South*, he has pursued the truth of racial question of interrelationships between the white and black communities living together. Naipaul's travelogues have therefore been written for finding truth about people's history, politics and culture. In *The Masque of Africa*, his latest and last travelogue, Naipaul portrays history, culture, and civilization of the continent of Africa. Among many other evil aspects of African life, he has been moved by the "kitchen cruelty" of the continent. The people are obsessed with eating their domestic pets—cats and dogs. Referring to a report published in *The Sunday Times* in London, *The Times of India* reports:

> The Trinidadian-born author, who has previously been in hot water for alleged racism, misogyny and a disregard for Islam, now writes about witch doctors, buildings allowed to fall into ruin and streets strewn with rubbish. Naipaul is perhaps disheartened in the barbaric act of the Africans who kill their kitten for their food. (2010: 9)

Traveling is a kind of exploration for Naipaul. It is a kind of discovery about human history—their cultures, political systems, fundamental values and moral behaviors. Traveling for Naipaul has been an obsession, a kind of restlessness. That has been so because of his search for his own identity as well as the location of human values and cultures. Moreover, his voluntary homelessness has encouraged him to know the global situations. This global vision has made him not merely a writer of Trinidad or a writer who valued his Indian ancestry only. Such an approach to literature has enabled him to remain above all cultures, communities and nations. It is therefore necessary to analyze his travel writings indepth so that we will be in a position to know to what extent he valued the fundamental aspects of human life. Naipaul as a travel writer is truthful. He is above partisan ideas, comments and observations. In the next three chapters i.e. in chapters 7, 8 and 9, his travelogues will be discussed under four groups: his Caribbean Journey, India vision, Islamic excursions and South American explorations. The focus is on the truth that has shaped his vision and imagination. This chapter will however discuss Naipaul's concerns about his native place in the travelogue *The Middle Passage*.

The Middle Passage (1962) is a representation of colonial society in the West Indies and South America. This book was the result of Naipaul's three-month stay at Trinidad on a scholarship grant in 1960 by the Government of Trinidad and Tobago. Though it was risk to venture upon a non-fiction work like this, he however undertook it at the suggestion of the then premier, Dr Eric Williams. In the "Foreword" to this book Naipaul writes: "While I was in Trinidad the premier, Dr Eric Williams, suggested that I should write a non-fiction book about the Caribbean. I hesitated. The novelist works towards conclusions of which he is often unaware; and it is better that he should. However, I decided to take the risk. The Trinidad Government paid for the travel" [(1962): 2001: x]. On his way to the West Indies from England, Naipaul was pained to note group identity in the level of "color groups, race groups, territory groups, money groups" (*MP* 19). There was no fixed West Indian Identity among the people. They were a divided lot: "As England receded, people prepared more actively for the West Indies. They formed color groups, race groups, territory groups, money groups. The West Indies being what they are, no group was fixed; one man could belong to all (19). Naipaul did not feel any substantial gain by the West Indian adventure of the British because neither any civilization nor revolution grew out of it: "For nothing was created in the British West Indies, no civilization as in Spanish America, no great revolution as in Haiti or the American colonies. There were only plantations, prosperity, and decline: neglect: the size of the islands called for nothing else" (19). Naipaul is much critical of the West Indian society which is "without standards, without noble aspirations, nourished by greed and cruelty: a society of whose illiteracy metropolitan administrators continued to complain right until the middle of the last century" (19-20). He even contrasts the grossness of West Indian slavery with the "gracious culture of the slave society" in Southern states of America. He therefore questions himself how to write the history of such a society in which men ate "like cormorants" and drank "like porpoises" (19):

> How can the history of this West Indian futility be written? What tone shall the historian adopt? Shall he be as academic as Sir Alan Burns, protesting from time to time at some brutality, and setting West Indian brutality in the context of European brutality? Shall he, like Salvador de Madariaga, weigh one set of brutalities against another, and conclude that one has not been described in all its foulness and that this is unfair to Spain? Shall he, like the West Indian historians, who can only now begin to face their history, be icily detached and tell the story of the slave trade as if it were just another aspect of mercantilism? The history of the islands can never be satisfactorily told. History is built around achievement and creation; and nothing was created in the West Indies. (20)

The above passage reveals Naipaul's dilemma how to handle the history of his native land which he left in 1950. Soon after reaching Trinidad by the ship, *The Francisco Barbadilla*, he felt again the old fear of Trinidad: "I did not want to stay. I had left the security of the ship and had no assurance that I would ever leave the island again" (33). But he would have the place of his birth once again. However before leaving for England he would reflect upon the colonial societies of Trinidad, British Guiana, Surinam, Martinique and Jamaica. He would scrutinize the "crude philistinism of the British settlers and the culture of other peoples" (King 1993: 52). The British colonizers were unscrupulous due to their interest in exploitation. They did not work in the direction of any substantial economic development. Consequently, the worst sufferers were the people, their cultures and regions. King rightly argues that "the basic situation in the region has not changed since the last century; the Europeans created no worthwhile society or culture, established no lasting economic foundations, had no vision, but imported as slaves and laborers large numbers of people from different cultures when they discriminated against and then abandoned to their mental antagonism without providing means of improving their situation" (1993: 52). Naipaul observes that the existing ethnic differences in the region might result in political fantasy and violence. The West Indian Society is a mimic society and a positive nationalism can only be inculcated among the people through some cultural pride. Naipaul is not blind to the loopholes of his native people. Critics often charge him as a colonial. Bhat however views that *The Middle Passage* is "an account of the return journey of an immigrant to England, settled there as an expatriate, officially visiting his native country, as an outsider. He was an insider but now he visits Trinidad as an outsider" (2000: 110).

Naipaul's portrayal of Trinidad's social history is impartial and authentic, without any prejudices. His impressions and descriptions are not merely factual. They are based on keen observations of life-styles, manners, racial and ethnic conflicts. The Trinidadian society is a colonial society with no progressive mindset, without visionary dimensions. Naipaul considers Trinidad to be "unimportant, uncreative, cynical" (*MP* 34). The contempt for such a society is obvious when he views: "Power was recognized, but dignity was allowed to no one. Every person of eminence was to be crooked and contemptible" (35). A Society without directions and coherence will not be able to guide its people to definite goals. Hence, the stories of Trinidad were the stories of failures: "scholarship winners, who had died young, gone mad, or taken to drink; cricketers of promise whose careers had been ruined by disagreements with the authorities" (35).

Unusual skills were not appreciated in the Trinidadian society which did not require such talent. People with exceptional qualities were made to "boil down". As such a society could not produce "scientists, engineers, soldiers or poets" (35), a cricketer is the only heroic-figure. Despite the fact that such a society had wrongs; no attempt was made to assess it:

> Trinidad was too unimportant and we could never be convinced of the value of reading the history of a place which was, as everyone said, a dot on the map of the world. Our interest was all in the world outside, the remoter the better; Australia was more important than

> Venezuela, which we could see on a clear day. Our own past was buried and no one cared to dig it up. This gave us a strange sense of time-sense. The England of 1914 was the England of yesterday; the Trinidad of 1914 belonged to the dark ages. (36)

Such an attitude of emulating the white people indicates that those Trinidadians had no sense of their own values and culture. There was no sense of national feeling. People remained individuals to establish their own identities. So Naipaul comments sarcastically:

> Everyone was an individual, fighting for his place in the community. Yet there was no community. We were of various races, religions, sets and cliques; and we had somehow ourselves on the same small island. Nothing bound us together except this common residence. There was no nationalist feeling; there could be none. There was no profound anti-imperialist feeling; indeed it was only our Britishness, our belonging to the British Empire, which gave us any identity. So protests could only be individual, isolated, unheeded. (36)

Naipaul's critical scrutiny of the crude Trinidadian society needs to be reflected upon because such a society could not offer any opportunity for the people to establish themselves. Hence exceptional people tried to escape from such a society and around the end of World War II; some of them became distinguished outside Trinidad. Naipaul therefore comments: "The threat of failure, the need to escape: this was the prompting of the society I know" (37).

Naipaul critiques the so-called "modern" attitudes in Trinidadian society. Though the Trinidadian society was accepting changes in their lifestyles and manners, they were not based on some deeper values of life. They were rather superficial, and went against indigenous cultural aspects. Naipaul observes that modernity in Trinidad means "a constant alertness, a willingness to change, a readiness to accept anything which films, magazines and comic strips appear to indicate as American. To be modern is to ignore local products and to use those advertised in American magazines" (40). Naipaul disapproves of such attitude of the people. In their choice of food, dress and furnishing, they wanted to be modern. They had no modern vision because they were swayed by so-called glamorous, superficialities of modernity:

> The excellent coffee, which is grown in Trinidad, is used only by the very poor and a few middle-class English expatriates. Everyone else drinks Nescafe or Maxwell house or Chase and Sanborn, which is more expensive but is advertised in the magazines and therefore acceptable. The elegant and comfortable morris chairs, made from local wood by local craftsmen, are not modern and have disappeared except from the houses of the poor. Imported tubular steel furniture, plastic- straw chairs from Hong Kong and spindly cast-iron chairs have taken their place. (40)

People were however not sure of being guided by a particular type of modernity, "having no taste or style of their own" (41). They depended much on the advertising agencies which emphasized the American commodities as modern. The indigenous things were thus considered old-fashioned. The changing scenario in Trinidad was reflected in the specific events:

> No dying horses surrounded by helpless jabbering men will be found on a Trinidad race-ground today. Pigtails, no calypso folk costume; and turbans are rare. Dress is uniform, national tastes emerging only in colors. The three groups in the Kingsley engraving stand in three isolated cultures. Today, these cultures are modified. One, the Chinese, has almost disappeared; and the standards of all approximate to the standards of those who are absent in the engraving: the Europeans. (46)

After the abolition of slavery in 1834, the Spanish law, which used a little torture, was replaced by the English Law in Trinidad. This resulted in the refusal by the Negroes to work on the estates and large-scale migration of indentured laborers from Madeira, China and India. The Indian migrant community, which proved to be the most suitable, increased to 1,34,000 in Trinidad by 1917, when the migration from India stopped. Trinidad, therefore, remains a materialist immigrant society, continually growing and changing never settling into any pattern, always retaining the atmosphere of the camp; unique in the West Indies in the absence of a history of enduing brutality, in the absence of a history; yet not an expanding society but a colonial society, ruled autocratically if benevolently, with the further limitations of its small size and remoteness. All this has combined to give it its special character, its ebullience and irresponsibility. And more: a tolerance which is more than tolerance: an indifference to virtue as well as to vice (49).

Trinidad was thus a land of failures, without any roots and deep-rooted culture and tradition. There was no guiding spirit for the people. The taste of the old Trinidad was individualistic, and anarchic. In architecture, behavior and education there were no set patterns or standards and Naipaul's resentment is conspicuous: "There was no guiding taste because there was no taste" (52). Local talent was undermined in the field of journalism. The dominance of colonials was too much intense in this field. The newspapers relied too much on "space-filling syndicated American and English columns, comic strips, the film gossip…" (53). The colonial society in Trinidad did not require the efficiency of Trinidadians; "it never required quality, and these things, because unrequired, became undesired" (53). Such aspects of inefficiency and fraudulence were marked in every aspect of life. Naipaul therefore observes:

> If curiosity is a characteristic of the cosmopolitan, the cosmopolitanism on which Trinidad prides itself is fraudulent. In the immigrant colonial Society, with no standards of its own, subjected for years to the second-rate in newspapers, radio and cinema, minds are rigidly clashed; and Trinidadians of all races and classes are remaking themselves in the image of the Hollywood B-man. This is the full meaning of modernity in Trinidad. (56)

Discussing the origin of the Negroes in Trinidad, Naipaul felt that the deprivation from their native soil of African home damaged the Negro-psyche. Being rootless, they supposed the white civilization to be their own and hated other civilizations: "Deprived as a slave of Christianity, education and family he set himself after emancipation to acquire these things; and every step on the root to whiteness deepened the anomaly of his position and increased his vulnerability" (62). The Negro had to expose himself to the "cruelty of the civilization which had overpowered him and which he was mastering" (63). Naipaul refers to the writings of Anthony Trollope:

> They (Creole Negroes born of Africa) have no idea of a country and no pride of race. They have no religion of their own, and can hardly as bet be said to have, as a people, a religion by adoption. The West Indian Negro knows nothing of Africa except that it is a term of reproach. If African immigrants are put to work on the same estate with him, he will not eat with them, or drink with them, or walk with them. He will hardly work beside them, and regards himself as a creature immeasurably the superior of the newcomer. (Quoted in *MP* 62)

Such attitude of self-contempt was due to their rootlessness and identity crisis. But the West Indian took pride considering himself to be the part of the Western civilization. Naipaul quotes the views of Dr Hugh Springer published in an issue of *Caribbean Quarterly:*

> ...ours is not a separate civilization, but a part that great branch of civilization that is called Western civilization. At any rate this is where we begin our national life. Our culture is rooted in Western culture and our values, in the main, are the values of the Christian Hellenic tradition. What are the characteristics of that tradition? They can be summed up in three words—virtue, knowledge and faith—the Greek ideals of virtue and knowledge and the Christian faith. (Quoted in *MP* 63)

Because of the prejudices and jaundiced vision of the Negro writers, they were unable to provide literature of high order with universal appeal. To Naipaul, "a literature can grow only out of a strong framework of social convention. And the only convention the West Indian knows is his involvement with the White World. This deprives his work of universal appeal" (*MP* 66). Though it is not a sin on the part of the writer to reflect upon his society, the West Indian writer is blamed because "by accepting and promoting the unimpressive race-and-color values of his group, he has not only failed to diagnose the sickness of his society but has aggravated it" (66).

In Trinidad the fundamental aspects of life, related to culture and nationalism, were lacking. Calypso, a local form, dealt with local incidents and local attitudes in a local language. However, the situation by 1960 was such that the form of Calypso was no more pure because of the interference from outside culture: "The promotion of a local culture was the only form of nationalism that could arise in a population divided into mutually exclusive cliques based on race, color, shade, religion, money" (68). The divided people in Trinidad had no sense of nationalism. They were rather self-centered and corrupt. So Naipaul remarks: "Nationalism was impossible in Trinidad. In the colonial society every man had to be for himself; every man had to grasp whatever dignity and power he was allowed, he owed no loyalty to the island and scarcely any of his group" (69). Such a society encouraged violence and corruption considerably. It was rather difficult to bring a sense of responsibility among the people:

> To bring political organization to the picaroon society, with its taste for corruption and violence, and its lack of respect for the person, has its dangers. Such a society cannot immediately become responsible, but it can be re-educated only through responsibility. Change must come from the top. Capital punishment and corporal punishment, incitements to brutality, must be abolished. (71)

To bring a change in the society, the civil service must be free from corruption. The civil servants must realize that they were not to exercise their authority over the poor and marginalized sections. The police should understand that they were more than "a licensed bull" (71).

The rich-poor polarization in Trinidad was quite obvious. People were divided by class and racial divisions. The community spirit was killed and "The shutting up of people in their separate prisons of similar ambitions and tastes and selfishness: the class struggle, the political struggle, the race struggle" (74-75). The racial problem in Trinidad was not related to the Negro-White polarization. It was rather Negro-Indian rivalry. Naipaul was puzzled to note this rivalry because there was no clash of interests between these two communities: "Their interests don't clash. The Negro is a town-dweller; the Indian is an agriculturist. The Negro with a good handwriting and a head for intrigue goes into the civil service; the Indian similarly equipped goes into business" (76). Naipaul felt that Trinidad was proceeding towards a racial war. The liberals were unable to handle the situations with proper interest. The Negro's obsession with white culture and his hatred towards everything other than white was more responsible for it: "The Negro has a deep contempt...for all that is not white; his values are the values of white imperialism at its most bigoted. The Indian despises the Negro for not being an Indian; he has, in addition, taken over all the white prejudices against the Negro and with the convert's zeal regards as Negro everyone who has any tincture of Negro blood" (77-78).

The Indians had a sense of their own identity by connecting themselves to India whereas the Negroes had no pride in their origins. The Indians were alienated from the rest of the white society because they stood in contrast to the white values nurtured by the rest of Trinidadians. This alienation however gave them strength and insulated them from the black-white conflict. The religion of an Indian gave him values "which were not the white values of the rest of the community, and preserved him from self-contempt, he never lost pride in his origins" (79). His family organization, which was an enclosing self-sufficient world rotten by quarrels and jealousies, protected and imprisoned his static world awaiting decay. Though Hinduism, the religion of Indians, was constantly renewed, the Trinidadian Indian was not aware of it. Despite that the Trinidadian Indian world was "a world of its own, a community within the colonial society, without responsibility, with authority doubly or triply removed" (79-80). Naipaul is rather harsh towards the Indian community:

> A peasant-minded, money-minded community, spiritually static because cut off from its roots, its religion reduced to rites without philosophy, set in a materialist colonial society: a combination of historical accidents and national temperament has turned the Trinidad Indian into the complete colonial, ever more philistine than the white. (80)

This racialism created by the Trinidadian politicians is crucial to destroy Trinidad:

> Indian politicians have created Indian racialism out of a harmless egoism. Negro racialism is more complex. It is overdue assertion of dignity, it has elements of bitterness; it has something of the urban mob requiring to be satisfied with bread and circuses. It has profound intellectual promptings as well in the realization that the Negro problem lies not simply in the attitude of others to the Negro but in the Negro's altitude to himself. (81)

This Negro-Indian rivalry was destructive. The white man was more responsible for it. The Negro was not able to shake off the prejudice that he inherited from the white man, a duality which was responsible for what the Jamaican novelist John Hearne, on a visit to British Guiana in 1957, described as the "pathetic nostalgia". That this Negro-Indian rivalry would bring disaster to the whole country was not understood by the two communities. They considered that their sides would win. Whoever might win the battle, but the suffering would go to the country, its people. Naipaul's analysis of Trinidadian socio-cultural history therefore exposes the basic defects of this society. He scrutinizes their manners, styles, attitudes and conflicts from human angle. Naipaul critiques other societies in British Guiana, Martinique and so on reflecting on their culture and Nationalism.

British Guiana was a vast country with a more population of six hundred thousand people. Though in size, it was like

England, it provided fewer opportunities to its inhabitants. The people in British Guiana were colonized by the outsiders. Naipaul writes: "Booker's are one largest firm of merchants and planters in British Guiana and at one time virtually controlled the country; according to the people's progressive party, they were and perhaps still are the villains of the piece" (86). Chedi Jagan, the Prime Minister was blamed for the disastrous condition of B.G.: "The Jagans and their party were accused of fomenting strikes, undermining the public service and the public force, spreading racial hatred, and generally advancing the cause of international communism" (92). In B.G. "questions of nationality seemed unimportant.... Here the Negro Policeman could speak of himself as English, and it seemed right. Everything on the other side of the border was Brazilian; everything on this side was English; and the English had no doubt which was superior" (96). Racialism was a dominant issue in B.G.: "Some of this resentment is undoubtedly racial. Government officials, the police in particular, are Negroes; and in the Rupununi the Negro, the Blackman from the coast, is still a symbol of threat and terror: the runaway slave, once the enemy of Amerindian and now his corrupter" (98). Though the Trinidadian Society had no memory of slavery, in B.G. such memory continues: "The very word 'Negro' because of its associations with slavery is resented by many black Guianeses; the preferred word is "African", which will cause deep offence in Trinidad" (98). In this futile Guianese society there is a sense of futility and purposelessness among the people: "Among more complex peoples there are certain individuals who have the power to transmit to you their sense of defeat and purposelessness: emotional parasites who flourish by drawing you of the vitality you preserve with difficulty" (101). In this respect the Amerindians surpass everybody in B.G.

Naipaul's perceptive resentment against the uncleanliness of the Amerindians is noteworthy. When he entered the hut of the village chief, Felix, he was too much disgusted: "Later in his trance-like way he took us to his hut. It was dark and dirty and dusty and disordered, like most Amerindians' huts. The sight of exposed food in the midst of dust and mud has the same effect on me as the screech of chalk on a board..." (101). Naipaul writes about the hopelessness of the Guianese society frankly:

> It is my view that it would be hypocritical to wish a bright and prosperous New Year to Guianese generally at this period of their country's history when there is so much hardship and distress in the land through unemployment and underdevelopment and the consequent absence of the means of securing the essentials which make for brightness and prosperity. (113)

Naipaul has quoted this message of Mr. D'Aguiar published on the front page of the *Sun*—Vol. 1, No. 8. Mr. D'Aguiar, the managing Director further pleaded that their country was rich and prosperous. It was the duty of the Guianese people to make endeavors "to put an end to the depressing conditions" which surround their homeland. He believed that the country would be prosperous if only their county was "wide open to and its wealth brought within easy reach of its people by the expenditures of large sums of money" (113).

In British Guiana, the exploitation of the labor force was also remarkable: "The indenture system, which replaced slavery and brought over hundreds of thousands of Indians to the West Indies, operated most harshly in British Guiana for the efficient running of the latifundia, the workers must be regarded as a caste apart and must continually be reminded of their condition" (119). Though malaria had a great adverse impact on the Guianese society, Naipaul believed that the history was more responsible: "Slavery lasted for three hundred years and was of exceptional brutality: in this matter of slavery the Dutch record is even blacker than the French!" (118). Naipaul has exposed the ruthless attitude of the Bookers although they have done some good to B.G.: "And though bookers must be given credit for their radical reforms of recent years, they must bear responsibility for what they have been and what, with the best will, they could not help being. Nor harsh and unimaginative employers which was unavoidable even on the latifundia; but for being, for creating, a colonial society within a colonial society: a double confinement for the Guianese" (119). The sufferings of the people in B.G. have been intensified due to multiple factors like slavery, the land, the latifundia, Bookers, indenture, the colonial system and malaria. When people in a society are marginalized they grudge against the privileged and exploiters. It is quite natural that the Guianese had become also "revolutionary and intensely reactionary". All these adversaries had made the Guianese "slew, sullen, independent though deceptively yielding; proud of his particular corner of Guiana, and sensitive to any criticism" (120). Naipaul observed that there was some political consciousness among the people who tried to pressurize the elected Government to undertake developmental programs in their areas:

> This is the level of political judgment in British Guiana. Wherever ministers go they are met with trivial complaints; whenever, in a country area, Dr Jagan stands still he is at once surrounded by people who have favored to ask. That the government is elected does not matter; the people require it to be as paternalistic as before, if a little more benevolently; and a popular government must respond. The people have learned their power and the sensation is still so new that every new voter regards himself as a pressure group; in this way the people, not the politician's abstraction, but the people who wish to beg, bribe and bully because this is the way they got things in the past—in this way the people are a threat to responsible government and a threat finally, to their own leaders. It is part of the colonial legacy. (121)

The West Indians did not have any sense of history. They were least concerned with the past. To them "history" was irrelevant and dead. That is because, "past is unimaginable; perhaps it is the light; perhaps it is because so much is makeshift and new and the squalor so wholly contemporary. To feel the past you need the emptiness of these Guianese rivers" (122). Despite the fact that there was some understanding between the races in British Guiana, there were however rifts among the races: the racial conflict was a dominant problem in British Guiana:

> However the rift exists, and it has divided the country racially, created a situation which reflects, as in a mirror, the Trinidadian situation: in Trinidad the Negroes are the majority group, in British Guiana the Indians. With almost one half of the population contracting out of the self-government experiment, the country is dangerously weakened. Racial antagonism, endlessly acting and reacting upon one another, and, encouraged by the cynical buffoons who form so large a part of the politically ambitious in every population, are building up pressures which might easily overwhelm the leaders of both sides and overwhelm the country; though British Guiana, because of its physical size and the isolation of its communities, can better withstand disturbance than Trinidad. (134-35)

Racialism in B.G. was against the peaceful co-existence. It did not help in development. The British Empire was responsible for so much suffering of the people due to landlessness and poverty. There was also large-scale political corruption. Power and privilege of a few helped them to amass wealth. There was no sign of a progressive society even after the end of colonialism. Although the Christian values sometimes helped in preventing corruption in the West Indian colonial society, it "has not lost its racial associations, its association with power and privilege and progress" (161). Naipaul therefore comments:

> The West Indian colonial situation is unique because the West Indies, in all their racial and social complexity, are so completely a creation of Empire that the withdrawal of Empire is almost without meaning. In such a situation nationalism is the only revitalizing force. I believe that, below the ebullience and bravado, a positive nationalism existed in British Guiana in 1953. (142)

To Naipaul, a true perspective of nationalism could rescue B.G. from the evil of racial conflicts.

V.S Naipaul's representation of Surinam society is perceptive. Surinam, a former Dutch Guiana, is situated next door to British Guiana, on the north-eastern coast of South

America. Since 1955 it has been virtually an independent kingdom. Some people of Surinam call it England's twelfth province. In comparison to Trinidad and British Guiana, Surinam have a diverse population of Negroes, East Indians, Dutch, Chinese and Javanese. However, "it does not have the racial problems of these territories, though there is inevitably a growing rivalry between the Negros and the East Indians, the two largest groups" (168). Although the political parties are racial, the government is however a coalition of these parties. There are neither any "inflammatory political issues" on any "acute racial problem". Despite the two-third contributions of financial needs by the Dutch government for the development of Surinam, a kind of nationalism is arising. Such an aspect is "unsettling the established order, proving that the objection to colonialism in the West Indies is not any economic or political or...racial" (*MP* 169). Colonialism is distorting the distinctive identities, cultures and basic characteristics. That is why it has some negative impact on the social lives of peoples and nations:

> Colonialism distorts the identity of the subject people, and the Negro in particular is bewildered and irritable. Racial equality and assimilation are attractive but only underline the loss, since to accept assimilation is in a way to accept a permanent inferiority. Nationalism in Surinam, feeding on no racial or economic resentments, is the profoundest anti-colonial movement in the West Indies. It is an idealist movement and a rather sad one, for it shows how imprisoning for the West Indian his colonial culture is. (169)

The Surinam Nationalists argue that Europe is not the only source of enlightenment. They plead that the alternative continents such as Asia and Africa are also to be considered. The Nationalists have assimilated the ideas of Europe in their bones. They therefore sometimes think that Africa and Asia are "contemptible and ridiculous" (169).

There were language problems in Surinam, and also the general cultural struggle which were not known to the outside world. The Surinam nationalists were not happy with the poet Lorly who loved Holland, Dutch literature and the Dutch people. That was because he preferred to write in Dutch rather than in the local dialect on themes not related to Surinam. Naipaul disapproves of mother country fixation in so many things in the West Indian territories of British dominion when he looks at the architectural design of Paramaribo. Naipaul writes: "In Georgetown I had longed for the liveliness of Port of Spain. Now I longed for Georgetown, and the people of Paramaribo told me I didn't know what dullness was: I should go across the border to French Guiana" (172). Naipaul refers to Dr. Voorhoeve's radio talk on the analysis of colonial society which was rejected by the Nationalists: His "Intelligent, temperate talk" was interesting:

> A colony is a strange sort of society without elite.... The leaders come from the motherland, from another culture.... The colonial cultural ideal has pronounced bad consequences for the individual. It is in fact an unattainable ideal.... A few exceptional people...come to great achievement, but thereby lose their nationality.... And what goes for them does not go for ten thousand others who must remain stuck in a soulless imitation, never achieving anything of their own. They learn to despise their own, but get nothing in its place. So, after the war there were many in Surinam who thought themselves far above the ordinary people because they had been able to assimilate the Dutch Language and the Dutch Culture. Sometimes they wrote a pretty little poem in a la Kloos, or painted a pretty little picture, or played a Mozart sonata not without skill; but they were not capable of any true cultural achievement. When this new generation was able after the war to go to Holland in great numbers...they dissolved their cultural emptiness with a shock. They came into contact with the great world, the community of nations, and stood there with empty hands. They did not have their own songs; they hardly had Mozart. They did not have their own literature; they had only Kloos. They had nothing and were worthless elements in the life of nations. What once was reasons for pride—'Surinam is

> the twelfth province of Holland'—was reason for shame and disgrace. (173-74)

It is remarkable to note that there were no elites in a colonial society. The colonial attitude in Surinam was that everything was reflected as "barbarous" if it was not coming from the "mother country". Naipaul remarks: "One reason for this British West Indian passivity is that the British have never attempted to turn that colonials into Englishmen" (174). In their Empire, the British behaved like Europeans. These British were even irritated when the French or Dutch West Indians assumed that "equal opportunities existed in the mother country" (174). Naipaul notes the paradoxical situation in Surinam: "The paradox is that Dutch idealism is leading to rejection, while out of British cynicism has grown a reasonably easy relationship between colonials and metropolitans" (174). The Dutch administration was interested in assimilation of cultures, but there was no enforcement. The Dutch were supportive of tolerance and understanding of their cultures unlike the French arrogance and denigration of other's cultures. Even the British had no such understanding and tolerance like the Dutch. Surinam had been able to cultivate the cosmopolitan outlook. Naipaul therefore comments:

> The cosmopolitism of Trinidad is now fundamentally no more than a matter of race; in Surinam diverse cultures, modified but still distinct, exist side by side. The Indians speak. Hindi still; the Javanese live, a little bemused, in their own world, longing in this flat unlovely sad for the mountains of Java; the Dutch exist in their self-sufficient Dutchness; the Creoles in their urban Surinam Dutchness; in the forest, along the rivers, the bush-Negroes have recreated Africa. (175)

The Surinamers had no much idea of the diversity and richness of their own country though very often the concept "culture" was much discussed. The Creoles were rather Eurocentric. Some Nationalists thought the existence of Javanese and Indian culture in Surinam was "a barrier to the development of a national culture" (175). Naipaul therefore argues: "This pointed to the confusion and the unexpected racial emotions that lie at the back of the Nationalist agitation. The cultural problem in Surinam is mainly a problem for the Negro; it is only he who has rejected his past, all that attaches him to Africa" (175).

Though the Nationalist agitation in Surinam led by Eduard Bruma, a Negro Lawyer, was carried on, it had no official status. The movement had "a touch of the underground". Despite the tall claims by Bruma that his organization had no "racial bias", it was not true. It was difficult to avoid the racial feelings because the organization was more inclined towards the Negro problems in the New World. Naipaul postulates:

> In Trinidad and British Guiana there is no widespread realization that such a problem exists, and it is to the credit of the Nationalists in Surinam that they have made it a public issue without going to the extremes of the back-to-Africa Ras Tafariana in Jamaica or the Black Muslims of the United States. There is much in their thought, however, to frighten the respectable and excite the cry for *Jehad*. Their view of Christianity is historical: they see it as much a part of European culture as the Dutch language. (184)

Since "Christianity" for the West Indies was more than a faith, it would be difficult to replace it by any rule. Since there was a large gap between the bush-Negroes, the forest dwellers and the continental Surinamers, there was little sympathy and understanding between them. The solution if at all attempted, there might be large-scale violence and racial tension. So, a solution to this problem was less important than developing some sort of "profound awareness" to understand that countries and cultures exist beyond the White mother country, beyond Europe and America. To create this awareness is not easy. It would be difficult for the Nationalists to create such awareness in Surinam without recourse to "a futile black racism". The language issue was also a great problem in the National Movement. Paradoxically, the Dutch inheritance of the Surinamers was responsible for that. Naipaul observes:

> Speaking a language little understood by the outside world, the Dutch have become great linguists. So have the

> Surinamers. English, Dutch, French, *negerengels*: these are the languages spoken by the educated Surinamer; and to this the Indian adds Hindi, the Javanese. Having access to so many worlds, the Surinamer is not as colonial-provincial as the British West Indian and is able to have a more objective view of his own situation. (185)

Though slavery was abolished in Surinam in 1863, still its impact was felt when Naipaul visited the island. Slavery was felt in all aspects of life such as vegetation, food, and salt fish, racial abuse, physical brutality of strong to weak, child-beating and so on. Slaves had been tortured to an unimaginable level in Surinam. Referring to Stedman's analysis of the Surinam society of the past, Naipaul understands that Surinam was like a vast concentration camp:

> The slave-owner had less on his conscience than the concentration camp commandant: the world was divided into black and white, Christian and heathen. White might conceivably be expected to show some scruples in his relations with black; but the Christian had no such inhibitions in his relations with the heathen. (191)

Naipaul went to Coronie to see the situation of the dullest Surinamers. In that part of Surinam, the miseries of those poor Negroes were indescribable:

> The land was flat, always flat. The forest lay immediately behind the huts that were strong along the road. Surinam is an under populated country. Here it felt neglected and abandoned and, oddly, related to nothing else, with the inhabitants, mainly Javanese, lost in an unfamiliar landscape, whose monotony invited no exploration. (194)

Naipaul along with the companions walked to the coconut fields full of the thick grass and the ditches were choked. The mosquitoes were large in number and they stung Naipaul through his whole body. Naipaul was so much pained to note the untold miseries of the Surinamers in this part of dumpy land, full of mosquitoes. He therefore writes:

> A derelict man in a derelict land; a man discovering himself, with surprise and resignation, lost in a landscape which had never ceased to be unreal because the scene of an enforced and always temporary residence; the slaves kidnapped from one continent and abandoned on the unprofitable plantations of another, from which there could never more be escape: I was glad to have Coronie, for, more than lazy Negroes, it had the full desolation that came to those who made the middle passage. (197)

After observing the miseries of the poor Surinam society Naipaul describes the miseries of the marginalized in Martinique. After reaching Martinique, a French colony, Naipaul observes: "Martinique is France.... The policemen are French; the street name-places in blue-and-white enamel are French; the Cafes are French; the menus are French and are written in a French hand" (199). This country was full of little French villages, "each with its church, *Mairie* and war memorial (*Aus Enfants de-Morts pour la Franca*), each with its history and its illustrious, for whose descendants pews are reserved in the Church" (199). Naipaul further observes:

> The radio station announces itself as 'Radioffusion Franchise'. The political posters—*voler ovi a de Gaulle* (the referendum had taken place not long before) and *Meeting de Protestation: Les Colonialistes ont Assasine Lumumba*—are metropolitan France and unlike anything else in the Caribbean. The tobacco Kiosks stock *Gauloises;* and the advertisements are for cinzano and St. Raphael and *Paris-soir*. Only most of the people are black. (199-200)

Even though people in Martinique were black in color, they were French in all respects. They imitated every aspect of French civilization. The Martinique French felt privileged because they were allowed to enjoy all sorts of facilities like French people. That was not the case in England where the non-English people were discriminated in housing and employment because of the color prejudices: "More than England to the British West Indian or even Holland to the Surinamer, France is the mother country to the Martinique. The highest positions are open to him in France; it is a cause for pride, and not surprise, that a French West Indian represents an important French town in the National Assembly and was for some time the constitutional successor to president de Gaulle" (201). The Martiniquans were French in their speech, manner and gestures. In appearance it seemed that the French Empire had been successful in implementing her "*mission civilization*" (203-04) in Martinique. Leigh Fermor wrote in 1959 that the distance French territories should consider the success of Martinique project in civilizing the people. However in 1967, there were "race riots in Martinique in which three people were killed" (203-04). Though all Martiniquans were simple French men outside Martinique, they were still a divided society in Martinique. In Martinique they are black French men or brown Frenchmen or white Frenchmen. Racial discrimination is a dominant issue in Martinique although it was said that the French were not bothered about color. In the days of slavery, the free colored were forbidden by law to wear clothes similar to those worn by the whites, and "Pedigrees are so carefully watched that there is no possibility whatsoever of anyone with the least tincture of Negro blood, however unapparent, passing as white" (204). Naipaul compares the Trinidad situation with Martinique where things were rather different. In Martinique a white-skinned, light-eyed, straight-haired person was "colored" whereas in Trinidad a reasonable white-looking person was passed as white. The color discrimination in Martinique was more oppressive than in Trinidad. Naipaul says that this is well marked when Lloyd Braithwaite's *Social Stratification in Trinidad* is compared with Michel Leiri's *Contacts de Civilization en Martinique.*

Along with the exportation of their civilization to Martinique, the French had also exported their social structure. The social prejudices of metropole for bourgeois and racial distinction derived from slavery coalesced to produce the most organized society in the West Indies. In this society, Negro-blood was a mark of slave ancestry. Education, money and cultured Frenchness really mattered. With its single standard of bourgeois Frenchness, social or racial prejudices are rather struck with amazement to note such marked significance in Martinique:

> No social prejudice, no social sanction really matters in Trinidad: standards are too diverse and society is split into too many cliques. Living in Trinidad and then as an outsider in England, I had never before experienced, the organized, single-standard society where sanctions could cripple; and in Martinique I felt choked. Prejudices have been imported wholesale from metropole. (205)

The Martinique society was divided into three concrete sections: white (of certified purity), mulatto and black. In such a society, the white man called his woman *Cherie*; the mulatto would call his woman *dou-dou*; and the Negro called his woman "a stinking bitch". The white man would eat in ware-plate, the mulatto in earthen ware, and the Negro in 'calabash'. Naipaul therefore comments: "At all levels in Martinique 'race' is important and inescapable. This is one reason perhaps why Martiniquans are all Frenchmen. All cannot be white, but all can aspire to Frenchness, and in Frenchness all are equal" (206). In the metropolitan France, the prejudices of Martinique had no validity. In Martinique too, the metropolitan Frenchmen were free from the racial regulations of the society. Despite this, the Martiniques were not enjoying the same status, privilege and representations in all fields of life:

> The social benefits at metropolitan France have not been extended to Martinique: the island's economy would have been disrupted, it is said, and the expanse would have been too great anyway. Investments have not come to Martinique. With the fierce jealousy characteristic of petty, tight, self-important communities, every Martinique capitalist ridicules and does his best to block every project in which he does not have a hand. (207)

The Martiniquan Capital was therefore not included in Martinique for its overall development. The money was invested in France or elsewhere. Moreover, no industry of Martinique could compete with French industry. Martinique therefore depended on France for everything and it had no existence without French economic patronage. This was a colonial situation because the raw materials were exported to France and the products were imported from France. Since Martinique was part of France, her unique rum could not be exported direct to North or South America, but must first cross the Atlantic to Paris and be redirected from there, enriching middlemen, all the way: "Assimilation has not made Martinique an integral part of prosperous France, but has reduced the island to a helpless colony. Where now more than ever the commission agent is King" (207).

Martinique was a pettily feudal country where a white or colored gentry and a respectful mass of straw-hated black people could only be described as "peasants" (209-10). In this society people were mostly poor. The apparently civilizing mission of the French Govt. was merely a mask rather than doing any good things that might help the nation to become progressive. Naipaul's remarks on the Caribbean situations are worthwhile because they focus on the evil attitudes of the colonizers in exploiting people. The colonizers needed the cheap labor for their benefits. They therefore exploited the marginalized black Negroes, indentured Indians and other working class people. Because of their ulterior motives they did not emphasize the economic development of the people or else the overall development of the country through industry or modern methods of agriculture. The Caribbean situations are rather Satanic:

> The Caribbean has been described as Europe's other sea, the Mediterranean of the New world. It was a Mediterranean which summoned up every dark human instinct without the complementary impulses towards nobility and beauty of older lands, a Mediterranean where civilization turned satanic perverting those it attacked. (212)

Though Naipaul was glad to leave Martinique, he was "inexpressibly saddened to land in Antigua" (219). Since there was no direct flight to Jamaica, he was to land in Antigua, a costly town, unaffordable by Naipaul. Naipaul quotes the following extract written by M.G. Smith, Rog Augier and Rex Nettle Ford in 1960 in "The Creed of a Ran Tafari Man":

> Jamaica was a nice island, but the land has been polluted by centuries of crime. For 304 years, beginning in 1655, the white man and his brown ally have held the black man in slavery. During this period, countless horrible crimes have been committed daily. Jamaica is literally Hell for the Black man, just as Ethiopia is literally Heaven. (Quoted in *MP* 223)

For outsiders, Jamaica was, on the one hand, an expensive winter resort for the tourists with its "turquoise sea white sands, reverential bowtied black servants, and sun-glassed figures below striped umbrellas" (224). On the other hand, one can see immigrants living in miseries and poverty in their slums after reaching Jamaica:

> The tourists are on the North coast, which is separate from the rest of the island and almost like another country. And the Jamaica middle-class world, in which the visitor moves, with its spaciousness and graciousness, its tradition of hospitality, its PEN meeting and art exhibitions, its bars expensive or bohemian, its clubs and hotels, its cocktail parties and dinner parties, is physically so disposed...that one can move from suburb to suburb and never cease to be sheltered from offending sights. On drives to the country peasants can of course be seen; but these people have little in common with the desperate and rebarbative immigrant stereotype; their manners are gentle, they have a welsh feeling for rhetoric, and they speak the purest English of all West Indians. (224)

The slum-dwellers in Kingston of Jamaica were living a very wretched life. The houses were "so close in street so narrow that there is no feeling of openness. Filth and rubbish are disgorged everywhere; everywhere there are puddles; and on the rubbish dumps latrines are forbidden by law. Pigs and goats wander as freely as the people and seem as individual and important" (224-25). There was no distinction between the animals and the slum-dwellers. Among these slum-dwellers the sects known as the "Ras Tafarians" or "Rastas" developed their own "psychology of survival" (224):

> They reply to rejection with rejection. They will not cut their hair or wash; and for this neglect of the body, this expression of profound self-contempt, they find biblical sanction. Many will not work, turning necessity into principle; and many console themselves with marijuana, which God himself smokes. They will vote for no party. Because Jamaica is not their country and Jamaican Government not one they recognize. (225)

They considered their country to be Ethiopia and they worshipped Ras Tafari, The Emperor Haile Selassie. They did not consider Babylon, the world of the white, Brien and yellow men and ruled by Pope, to be repatriated to Africa and Ethiopia. They were not interested in the improvements in Jamaica because such a case would perpetuate their condition of being slaves in Babylon. Ras Tafarianism in Jamaica was a proletarian movement which aimed at the "death of whites":

> Nationalism in Surinam, a movement of intellectuals, rejects the culture of Europe as Tafarianism in Jamaica is nothing more than a proletarian extension of this attitude, which it carries to its crazy and logical limit. It resembles African nationalism, which asserts the importance of African personality, and is the opposite of middle-class West Indian Negro Nationalism, which is concerned only to deny the existence of a specially Negro Personality. It is regarded by the largely brown Jamaican middle class as a black lower-class contagion, a sort of backyard mau-mau. (227)

The Ras Tafarians in Jamaica expressed the basic racial attitudes of the majority black people who constituted the eighty percent of the population in the land. Racial conflict between black and white (even against Yellow and Brown) was the most burning issue in Jamaica: "Hypocrisy which permitted the middle-class brown Jamaican to speak of racial harmony while carefully maintaining the shade distinctions that preserved his privilege is at last provoking anger and creating a thoroughly black racism which could conceivably turn the island into another Haiti" (328). Naipaul felt that in Jamaica one always lived in two unrelated worlds, "the world of the middle class—the businessman's Jamaican—grand, pseudo-American talk, the women's chatter about the wages of servants and the treachery of servants—and the vaster, frightening world beyond it" (233). Naipaul had been traveling for seven months and therefore he was being exhausted for seven months for which his diary entries grew shorter and shorter. Moreover, he was to record only the same things—unemployment, ugliness, overpopulation and race. Naipaul understood the futility in the same circular arguments of the young people whose rage was self-destructive and wild with anger against something which was not in existence. He therefore concluded his assessment of the Jamaican society of the late 1950s and the early 1960s:

> The young intellectuals, whose gifts had been developed to enrich a developing, stable society, talked and talked and became frenzied in their frustration. They were looking for an enemy, and there was none. The pressures in Jamaica were not simply the pressures of race or those of poverty. They were the accumulated pressures of the slave society, the colonial society, the underdeveloped, overpopulated agricultural country; and they were beyond the control of any one "leader". The situation required not a leader but a society which understood itself and had purpose and direction. It was only generating selfishness, cynicism and self-destructive rage. (234)

The Middle Passage is the record of V.S. Naipaul's keen, perceptive observations during his travels to Trinidad, British Guiana, Surinam, Martinique and Jamaica. The Caribbean Journey undertaken by Naipaul for about seven months with the Govt. scholarship offered by the Trinidadian Govt. under Eric Williams was a serious one because he tried to understand the serious problems of the people in relation to their socio-economic conditions, political outlook, racial conflicts, identity crises and conflicts of cultures. His delineation of human concerns in *The*

Middle Passage is based on truth, the perceptive observations made by the writer as an impartial recorder. Whatever he saw, he recorded with a judgment of his own. He has been very harsh on the colonial masters of Europe who did not have a proper vision for establishing any permanent economic strategy for these imported slaves and indentured laborers. They did not bother to design the development of these regions for improvement of this helpless, unfortunate labor class. They exploited their labor only for their self-interest. They used their power to subjugate them for their permanent use. They did not take any care for their education, health and nourishment. The marginalized people that they imported from different cultures and regions—African Negroes, indentured laborers from India, China and other Asian Countries—were treated with discrimination and were abandoned to engage amongst themselves in racial and cultural conflicts. These people in the periphery did not bother to have any cultural or National pride. Naipaul believed that the people must have to overcome the racial differences to develop any cultural or National pride so that these societies might develop some stability to engage in clear-cut developmental programmes to upgrade their living standards by eradicating their miseries. In the above perspective King (1993) postulates:

> Many of the problems raised by Naipaul are still relevant; but as they were expressed without the usual of black-white conflict, victimization and cultural assertion, they became uncomfortable.... The increasing racial conflict between blacks and Indians in British Guiana, and the example of the Martinique Indians who had lost knowledge of their culture, heightened his feelings about the insecure place of the Asian Indians in the West Indies. (53)

Naipaul thought that Nationalism was the only revitalizing force in these islands; but these societies were rotten by racial conflicts. As a result, they were divided societies without any common agenda, culture and vision for overall development. However, such a judgment is not accepted without critical examination:

> The nationalism of *The Middle Passage* seems the usual fare of the independence era of the early 1960s and should have been unexceptional. But Naipaul hurt feelings in bringing attention to racial conflicts and prejudices, offering dismissive summaries of the region's history, and criticizing the existing culture. Some found offensive such remarks as, "for nothing was created in the British West Indies, no civilization as in Spanish America, no great revolution as in Haiti or the American colonies" (27). (King 1993: 53)

Naipaul believed that the woes of these regions owed to the mimicry of the colonizer, racial resentment, political fantasy, envy, violence and corruption. He therefore commented: "Colonialism distorts the identity of the subject people, and the Negro in particular..., since to accept assimilation is in a way to accept permanent inferiority" (*MP* 181). Though people talked of nationalism, they were not interested in surrendering any of their privileges. There was cultural and political vacuum. Despite many changes in the Caribbean islands, there were no strong economic foundations on which the people could build their nation. These societies continued to be slave societies because people still remained the mimic men imitating the imperialistic colonizers. The total picture was therefore full of disillusionments, and Naipaul was very harsh on his judgments. Bhat considers Naipaul's comments stereotype:

> This judgment of the author on the Caribbean islands may have arisen out of authentic observation of the Islands but they also sound stereotypes and appear like platitudes. This was the view held by many an imperialistic traveler to the Caribbean islands. Naipaul accuses the islanders of mimicry. Critics have asked the question, "Is he also not a mimic man, mimicking the imperial travel writer? Naipaul is both an outsider and insider in Trinidad". (2000: 112)

Though *The Middle Passage* brought a lot of tirade from the native Caribbean community for Naipaul, it would be far from truth if his authentic observations, though painful, are not taken seriously. *The Middle Passage* is a landmark book in his career.

It looks back to the first four novels and forward to the writing that followed it. It signals the beginning of a new reflective trend in his writing. This book is a culmination of a phase of Naipaul's career which is marked by a reconstruction of his West Indian background on the basis of his memory of childhood and early youth. It is an attempt to explain the reasons for his self-exile. The examination of West Indian society is also an examination of his relation to that society and of the reasons why he reflected it.

Naipaul is against the colonial mindset of the West Indian people. He disapproves of their mimicry. These people should have to establish their own identity which can only be achieved through their cultural identity and National pride. They have to create their own world rather than being the mimic men. They are to prove their own worth rather than imitating the Europeans in all walks of life. Kanika Batra posits:

> It is in his analysis of Martinique, a tiny island which is an overseas department of France that Naipaul makes his most strident attack on colonial mimicry. He begins with the statement that 'Martinique is France.... Only most of the people are black.... They are black, but they are Frenchmen (*MP* 192). He concludes on an exasperated note by saying that "I was getting tired of the French colonial Monkey Game" (*MP* 210). (Panwar 181)

Batra's further remarks on the mimic West Indian societies are also appropriate: "The implicit essentialist assumption of an 'original' rigorous and untainted culture, be it European, African or Indian, is discordant with the history of intercultural contact in the Caribbean" (Panwar 185).

7

The Image of the Indian Nation: A Diasporic Perspective

Travelogue as a mode of literary discourse has a rich tradition. The distant lands have often enchanted the creative writers for exploration of "the unknown and the undiscovered". In recent times, travel writings have interpreted the political scenario, socio-economic conditions and cultural specifications of a nation. Diaspora has become an important feature of the New World during the 1950s/1960s, when most of the colonies achieved their independence after World War II. A Third World diaspora, soon after his journey to the imperial metropolis in search of a prosperous life of his dream, suddenly experiences a sort of culture-shock and alienation that make him restless to quest for his roots. Such an urge motivates him to undertake reverse journeys from the metropolis to the indigenous cultures associated with his roots resulting in historical, socio-anthropological and ethnological enquiries. V.S. Naipaul's travels to India from the metropolis of London have stirred his expatriate sensibility prompting him to record the experiences in his "discourses on India" that interpret the complex situations of the Nation. This chapter will focus on Naipaul's inquiries into the complex pluralistic ideologies of the Indian Nation, imagined in *An Area of Darkness* (1964), *A Wounded Civilization* (1977) and *A Million Mutinies Now* (1990) after the three successive visits to his imaginary homeland. In the Trilogy, Naipaul negotiates the gap between the indigenous cultural specifications of India, and his own perceptions and representations about it. A close reading of the Trilogy reveals that a strong ambivalence is marked because of Naipaul's threshold positions both as an outsider and as an insider. Naipaul therefore strikes a balance between his world-view and the actual experiences in the country. National identity is not a unitary concept. It is therefore difficult to define it in absolute terms. In *An Area of Darkness,* Naipaul has constructed India only as a world of "myth and darkness", "chaos and confusions". In *A Wounded Civilization*, he is rather shocked by noticing the strangeness of India, "a whole vanished world", a seriously wounded civilization. In his third travelogue, he has however been able to comprehend the pluralistic ideologies of the Indian Nation as a view of the everyday life for which he accepts multiple Indian Identities and rejects the so-called nationalist discourse built up by a totalizing image. He therefore accepts that old caste or clan boundaries can't disappear. He thinks that they are the people's support systems and within those boundaries people are beginning to have a greater sense of themselves.

7.1. Idea of Nation in a Postcolonial Situation

Postcolonialism seeks to disrupt the workings of colonialism, and it acknowledges that the historical fact of colonial oppression still exists under different forms in contemporary society. It was influenced by the ideologies of colonialism itself. The negative effects of colonial oppression gave postcolonialism its anti-colonial perspective. Its obvious manifestation reached a climax during the Independence struggle and the achievement of political freedom. In such a cultural space as well as resistance against the power of colonization, an articulation of all that was perceived to be indigenous, took place. This coincided with the political idea of nation building and nationalist discourse formulated by totalizing image of the Indian identity. In this sense nationalism, a western cultural formation played the role in uniting the diverse ethnic and racial groups under the idea of nation. To R.N. Tagore, "this narrowness of freedom is an evil which is more radical, not because of its quantity but because of its nature. And we cannot but acknowledge this paradox, that while the spirit of the West marches under its banner of freedom, the Nation of the West forges its iron chains of organization which are the most relentless and unbreakable that have ever been manufactured in the whole history of man" [(1971) 1976: 14]. Chandra Chatterjee observes that in India the evils of caste system and poverty perpetuate the process of recolonization: "Within the gamut of postcoloniality then is the realization of a recolonising process. This continues even after the historical and political process of colonization, especially in the perpetuation of the caste system and poverty in India..." (2000: 3). Carole Boyce Davies understands that "...countries and people have become effectively recolonised to various political, commercial and military operations and interests" (1994: 83). She therefore argues that it is not right to define postcolonialism within a temporal framework. Thus Chatterjee rightly believes that "...Postcolonial studies should not be periodised but postcolonialism should be recovered as a process of hegemonization by various power-structures all over the world today" (4). Tagore has however disapproved of such an organized, mechanical power of a nation with its emphasis on strength and efficiency undermining the idea of human creativity (Nationalism 1917: 14). In his novel, *Countdown,* Ghosh points out the issue of a nation-state's appropriation of its people within the folds of its organized ideologies:

> ...at about noon a squad of soldiers had driven up and asked the villagers to move out of their houses to open ground. They guessed what was going to happen. Some of them possessed refrigerators and television sets. They carried these out of doors and set them down in the sand, under the noon day sun, then they sat under the trees and waited. It was very hot. The temperature touched 48 degrees centigrade. (1999: 9)

The origin of the "nation" has to be traced back to the idea of freedom. It is hard to deny that the same nation which came into existence as an effect to liberate the country will have the same stand in allowing freedom to the people. B.R. Ambedkar holds the view that nationalism is "at once a fellowship for one's own...and an anti-fellowship for those who are not" (1947: 32-33). Liberation Movements are therefore influenced by the concept of a nation which means "self-assertion is a vital tool for survival amongst nations of the world" (Chatterjee 2000: 5).

In *Countdown,* Ghosh dramatizes the thought of his character Chandran who considers 'Bomb' an icon of self-assertion and national pride:

> Now fifty years down the line we know that the moral force isn't enough to survive in this world: it doesn't count for very much. When you look at India today and ask how best you can instill a sense of national pride or overcome those feelings of inferiority which have been ingrained in your mind for two hundred years, the bomb seems to be as good as an answer as any. (16-17)

The paradox of India's liberation struggle was unique because it was non-violent. This has led to the building up of a nation that feels weapons of mass destruction will sustain its prestige in the world. Albert Memmi understands the process of marginalization of the colonized by the design of the colonizer: "An urge to dominate has been a toll in the hands of the colonizer which he used indefatigably to sustain the process of scaling down the colonized economically, socially and culturally. The political system of oppression depends on this spectacle of power (1990: 205). The various communal uprisings based on religion are forcing the Hindus to uphold their identity and lean towards it with self-consciousness unknown in the last two centuries. Ashish Nandy's view is relevant to understand this aspect better: "In the 19th century Hindu religious reformers like Sri Aurobindo, Swami Dayanand and Swami Vivekananda tried to instill in the Hindu 'a sense of community as Hindu and a sense of History as a community'" (1983: 103). This Hinduism became a challenge to the invasion by western values in Indian culture. It also helped in decentring of the position of "postcoloniality". The most dominant image of Indian Culture is its ability to absorb the culture and ways of its invaders, and incorporate them as part of its own religion and way of life. Before independence anti-colonialism in the form of rebellion against an imperialistic nation was a form of protest. All the strands of this rebellion were gathered up into an ideological unity which formed the basis of national construction. However, democracy in India was protest-ridden. The ethnic and religious minorities protest against any singular definition of nation—the politically marginalized groups protest against inadequate representation in government policies. Numerous insurgencies all over the country relate their revolts to wars for independence at the sub-national level which the dominant national ideology has been unable to either outwit or neutralize.

In both Tamil Nadu and Kashmir anti-national issues spilled over the geographical boundaries of the nation, questioning the very basis of its formation and bringing back the issues of liberation where regional separatism has to counter internal colonialism. It is therefore partly true that independence opened the doors to liberation. The political structure of the nation-state that replaced the colonial government has continually been forced to keep up with world politics by being true to its name of an emergent third world nation. The nation follows the colonial structure of administration, a structure that was designed to oppress, exploit and suppress people. There are innumerable defects in administration by giving less emphasis on the safe drinking-water and making provisions for huge defense budget. Chatterjee views that "...it is the task of the nation to constantly adjudicate between competing nationalisms at the world level and the numerous cultural nationalisms that seek legitimacies of their own within its geographical boundaries" (2000: 10). The third world nations do follow the same form of nation-state like the colonial structure. Though the nation-state aims at providing the opportunities of equality and liberty, it seems difficult to keep itself aloof from the colonial system. Benedict Anderson views that postcolonial nation-states have been modeled on colonial patterns because the native intelligentsia of the colonies were trained into European values and adept in western culture and the "models of nationalism nation-ness, and nation-state produced elsewhere in the course of the nineteenth century" (1991: 116) although formation of nation-states is based on anti-colonial struggles. This problematic has also been discussed by Foucault in "The Ethic of Care for the Self as a Practice of Freedom":

> When a colonized people tries to free itself of its colonizer, that is truly a practice of liberation in the strict sense of the word. But as we also know this practice of liberation does not define the practices of liberty which will then be necessary for this people, this society and those individuals to define themselves receivable and acceptable forms of their existence or of a political society. (Bernauer and Ramussen 1988: 13-14)

Partha Chatterjee's arguments are however more appropriate with regards to the formation of Indian Nation. He argues that nationalism in the non-European context was "historically fused with the colonial question" (1986: 18). The anti-colonial struggles of these nations assert the national identities at the time of colonial exploitation. The intellectuals in the non-European World were fully aware of the Enlightenment idea of rationality and progress as well as autonomous identity of a national culture. It is however difficult to revitalize the shaky economic structure of a colonized nation such as India where intellectual tradition is deeply rooted in religions and moral ideologies. Chatterjee therefore questions the function of ideologies of a nation set in contradictions:

> What significance do these elements of modernity acquire when looked in the context of the evolving colonial economy of massive deindustrialization and destitution...of the crushing of peasant resistance, of the growing gulf...between a modernized, western educated, urban elite and the rest of the nation. (1986: 23)

Chatterjee thinks that the nation may depend partially on the Western ideas in the matters related to politics, science and economics to lead itself in the path of modernization. He however regards nationalism as a cultural sentiment fused with emotional attachment to a politically organized entity. He therefore pleads for a judicious combination of the material and spiritual worlds:

> Nationalism launches its most powerful, creative, and historically significant project: to fashion a "modern" national culture that is nevertheless not western. If the

nation is an imagined community, then this is where it is brought into being. In this, its true and essential domain, the nation is already sovereign, even when the state is in the hands of the colonial power. (1993: 6-7)

Studies on the freedom struggle show that the native resistances on the basis of groups and regions were vital in India and other colonized nations. These subaltern struggles are quite different from the national movements in the Western culture. They were based on regional needs and interests. Ranajit Guha therefore argues that it is necessary to understand the difference between the anti-colonialist imaginations of the 'nation' by the bourgeoisie nationalist and peasant nationalist. Chandra Chatterjee thus argues: "Questions of identity and selfhood are central to any discursive formation of a nation. The individual in the postcolonial situation is consciously looking for a bounded, linear and ideological concept wherein he can safely place his idea of nationhood" (2000: 12).

An Indian identity is pluralistic. The multiple images of the nation and the national self are sometimes complex as well as contradictory. Due to multiple languages, races, ideologies, cultures, castes and religions, the concept of the nation-state of Western model does not fit into India. A compromise among the various group identities is therefore necessary for national integration. Stuart Murray posits: "The desire for a bounded, linear and empirical version of selfhood that is so strong in many postcolonial societies finds in nationalism a set of useful ideological tools, yet the consequences of these ideological moves may actually produce multiple and often contradictory images of the national self" (1997: 8). Anti-colonial nationalism poses a duality because it has to decide whether it should encourage the richness of cultural diversity in the geographical boundary of a nation or it has to create a political discourse with an authoritarian stand to be imposed by the nation-state. It is perhaps correct for the nation-state to "use historically inherited cultural religious tradition to legitimize its version of nationalism and mark its difference from colonial rule" (Chatterjee 2000: 14). During the anti-colonial struggles in the colonial countries, people should have to form organizations based on their national cultures with certain agenda of socio-cultural progress. Fanon writes in *The Wretched of the Earth*:

> National culture is the collective thought process of a people to describe, justify, and extol the actions whereby they have joined forces and remained strong. National culture in the underdeveloped countries, therefore, must lie at the very heart of the liberation struggle these countries are waging. (2004: 168)

To Aurobindo, "nation-building" is a deep-rooted conviction. It should not be done in a mechanical way: "But a nation cannot be made,—it is an organism which grows under the stress of a principle of life within. We speak indeed of nation-building and of the makers of a nation, but these are very convenient metaphors" [(1907) 1972: 309]. The common bond of a people is evident when there is some serious threat to the nation. A nation is therefore an expression of its people which may be marked well. Aurobindo therefore argues that a nation involves the collective interest of its people:

> A nation is indeed the outward expression of a community of sentiment, whether it be the sentiment of a common blood or the sentiment of a common religion or the sentiment of a common interest or any or all of these sentiments combined. Once this sentiment grows strong enough to develop into a will towards unity and to conquer obstacles and make full use of favoring circumstances, the development of the nation becomes inevitable. [(1907) 1972: 309]

He emphasized "the organized strength of the nation, gathering to a powerful central authority and guided by the principle of self-development" ("The Doctrine of Passive Resistance," Introduction, 1907: 95). He also viewed that the power of the people should have to be invested in a strong political ideology. Aurobindo's concepts of organized strength of nationalism and the self-development of the individual were idealistic. These were based on a united moral basis which could not be questioned in those days. He viewed that political freedom was an essential component of spiritual strength. This idea of Swaraj or 'self-rule' was based on uniting all disparate political arguments under one i.e. "nationhood". He however believed in the democratic principles of fraternity by which there would not be any tendency among the individuals to dominate or subjugate others. He also advocated for A League of Nations—an association of friends and allies which would be a world-state. As a result, the marginalized people of Asia and Africa could be protected through such a world-state. Like Aurobindo, Gandhi's idea of Nationalism is also rooted in moral and ethical principles. To liberate India, Gandhi believed that the people of India must reject violence and should be organized as true Indians. They must be "swadeshi" to have the swaraj i.e. self-rule by the method of Satyagraha, sticking to the principles of truth and non-violence: Gandhi expresses his political manifesto in *Hind Swaraj* where he writes that every Indian must impose self-rule on himself before Home-rule is achieved. Gandhi's conclusions in *Hind Swaraj* reveal that Gandhi emphasizes moral rigidity which does not give any scope for democratic pluralism. Morality, according to Gandhi, should be cultivated within the framework of "idea of Dharma" which is violated because of the modern civilization. He therefore asks the individuals for spiritual orientation:

> There is yet time to escape it, but everyday makes it more and more difficult.... My first complaint is that India is becoming irreligious. Here I am not thinking for the Hindu, the Mohammedan, or the Zoroastrian religion, but of that religion which underlies all religions. We are turning away from God.... We should remain passive about worldly pursuits. ....[and] set a limit to our worldly ambition, our religious ambitions should be illimitable. (*Hind Swaraj*: 42-43)

Gandhian thinking was not flexible on maintenance of moral codes. Sometimes it seemed impossible on the part of the common people to practice it. The leaders, who continued the struggle, preferred the use of power and domination in practice rather than Gandhian theories of ethics and morality. Nehru went to the past to understand the idea of nation. He also traveled to most of the places to understand the people so as to find out a means of organizing them. Chandra Chatterjee comments on Nehru's perception of the Indian Nation:

> The political flavor of this anti-colonial rhetoric sought to bind on enormous social and religious diversity under a pre-conceived state umbrella. Nationalism had to seek the sanction of antiquity to be accepted by the enslaved masses. Nehru's critique of ancient Indo-Aryan society not only brought history into contemporary focus, it also began to establish the principles which the modern Indian Nation would set itself. (2000: 39)

In visualizing the societies described in Upanishads, Nehru aspires for a political objective of social unity:

> It is obvious that the ideas of the authors of the Upanishads were confined to a small body of the elect who were capable of understanding them. They were entirely beyond the comprehension of the vast mass of the people. A creative minority is always small in numbers but, if it is in tune with the majority, a stable and progressive culture results. Without that creative minority a civilization must inevitably decay. But it may also decay if the bond between a creative minority and the majority is broken and there is a loss of social unity in society as a whole. (The *Discovery of India* 70)

However Nehru does not approve of "the intense individualism of the Indo-Aryans" (*DI* 71) fully because "individualism" led men away from society. To him caste-system was also responsible for that. Moreover, the tolerant inclusion of every belief and superstition harmed the society considerably. He therefore pleaded for heroic "self-sacrifice" of the individuals for the sake of building the nation. Nehru wanted to awaken this "amazing spirit of man" (*DI* 16) among the enslaved people to "recharge the battery of India's spirit and awaken her for her long slumber" (*DI* 37). Chatterjee thinks that "this national spirit also included making people politically aware of their subjection. It was supposed to help them to see their position as timid and subservient and this burden of subjection was to unite them in their fight for freedom" (2000: 41). To Nehru, nationalism is thus "a group memory of past achievements, traditions and experience" which has relevance in the present in the form of national memories. He wanted the foundation of a nation—a state that could be linked to national tradition:

> Nehru's ideas have a strong political structure. The constructive role of history is restricted to its ability to identify its commonness with the present and to emphasize the adaptability of its ideas to changing situations. Both past and present are then to be seen as dominated by the idea of national progress. (Chatterjee 2000: 43)

Gandhi and Nehru made efforts to force a unity among people. They aimed at social equality on the basis of ethical values. They desired that the national strength can be achieved by bringing all the cultural diversities together by the force of morality and religion. The ideology of unity later on was transformed to a totalitarian and monopolising effect. Aurobindo had however been very careful not to emphasize a pluralistic society in his world-view. To him a nation could be evolved when the smaller living units developed closer links, and he did not want an erasure of cultural differences. He therefore wanted a unification through a spiritual religion of humanity rather than mechanical unification imposed by the state. For Aurobindo the ideal of unity should be combined with the fact of liberty. Nehru viewed that the individual should give up his ego by self-sacrifice and this sacrifice is 'nationalistic'. He is more practical than Gandhi because of his less emphasis on moral stringencies. He tried to arouse popular sentiments of truth, faith and honor within the framework of a political movement. In their own ways, these illustrious personalities have searched for alternative, relevant ideological and realistic structures to build up the nation from the ruins of the colonial empire: "The anti-imperialism of Aurobindo, Gandhi and Nehru was the site where a strong affirmation of morality was the hallmark of political ideology. They emphasized this to be a particular characteristic of Indian patriotism which was inspired by more than geographical barriers" (Chatterjee 2000: 46).

In *Illegitimacy of Nationalism*, Ashis Nandy writes about the ideas of Nationalism of Aurobindo, Gandhi and Tagore: "They saw themselves belonging to a civilization that refused to view politics only as a secularized arena of human initiative. While associating the country with maternity and sacredness, they...imposed a responsibility on the individual to maintain that sacredness" (85). Frantz Fanon believes that such a force is capable of cutting the barrier of class distinctions and uniting the peasants and landowners, the workers and capitalists, and revitalizing a decadent, colonial society. He argues: "This dispossessed population, used to living in a narrow cycle of conflict and rivalry, solemnly sets about cleansing and purifying the local face of the nation. In a state of genuine collective ecstasy rival families decide to wipe the slate clean and forget the past. Reconciliations abound...Faith in the nation furthers political consciousness. National unity begins..." (*WE* 2004: 83). The chief goal of nationalism is not merely to achieve the political freedom; it should also focus on the moral well-being of the common people and their self-discipline. The fight for freedom should go along with validation of a national culture which was developing simultaneously. The problem lies here because neither "the masses" nor "national culture" are monolithic, static units. The efficiency of the nation-state depends on its strong political, social and religious mechanism. That does not mean it will be ruthless and crush the liberty of the people for the sake of an ideal unity for the existence of a nation. Within the framework of the nation, the pluralistic existence of people's cultures must be understood in the proper perspective. In the Indian context, the pluralistic existence of people needs to be understood properly. That is because it is a country of diverse cultures and peoples. In order to grant dignity and liberty to the individuals, the nation-state may have to be liberal and shun its totalitarian standing. Chatterjee's arguments are befitting:

> Populations live between the constructed official "nation" and the very opposition they had tried to contest against. Liberation is still a fight for political Justice and the affirmation of individual dignity.... Before the doors of liberty, then, nation and nationalism fall apart. The

nation-state has to overcome its totalitarian outlook and nationalism has to find a way to re-imagine its diversities within the sentiment of unity. (2000: 47-48)

Before interpretation of Naipaul's travelogues on India, it is necessary to understand that the 'idea of India' is baffling, and complex. The concept of the "Indian Nation" should be considered in the perspective of polyphony of its indigenous people spread over the country and abroad. The emigrant population of different parts of the world has their own nations and ideas of our nation. The various diasporic writers like Bharati Mukherjee, Salman Rushdie, Amit Chaudhuri, V.S. Naipaul and many others have their own formulations and ideas about India as a nation. Even the writers like Arundhati Roy, Amitav Ghosh, Shashi Tharoor and many others have begun to question the validity of popular, self-complacent notions about India as a nation and a culture. V.S. Naipaul, a third generation Indian born in Trinidad, has also his own formation of India as a nation and a civilization. His Trilogy on India, namely *An Area of Darkness*, *A Wounded Civilization* and *A Million Mutinies Now* interpret India according to the understanding and perception of the writer. Naipaul is sometimes baffled and traumatized to comprehend the complexity of its situations. He has tried to understand a visible India, but then India is not visible. The "invisibility" of India is deeply rooted in its tradition and culture. In the first two travelogues, Naipaul could not comprehend the "total India" though his interpretation is quite perceptive, authentic and deeper. In the third travelogue, he acknowledges the potentiality of India as a nation, people, culture and an ideology. Before interpretation of these travelogues, it is necessary to discuss the experiences of a diasporic writer that constantly haunt him while he reconstructs his own homeland in his first-hand experience about the systems of the nation physically. A migrant's experience is important after the end of colonialism. In the context of one's identity "home" plays a prominent role. A journey to the land of his ancestors arouses a number of questions in the migrant writer. These questions lead him to make some formulations and reconstructions about himself and also about the nation of his ancestors. As everything is in a flux, the traditions of a nation are also subject to changes by the passage of time. Reconstruction of one's homeland is also subjective, and hence it cannot be generalized. After colonialism, the experiences of a migrant have some specific relationship with the ideas of home, tradition, identity and past history. The perception of the nation by the emigrant is therefore multi-dimensional based on his myriad experiences. As discussed earlier, Fanon and Said view that "anticolonial nationalism" should emphasize the concept of an "open-minded global community". To Fanon, "National consciousness" not nationalism can only give the people of a nation, an "international dimension". To Said, this is "postnationalism" that can give us a "pluralistic vision" of the world (1993: 277). Chatterjee rightly adds to this idea when she argues that "the perspective offered by a diasporic reading of the nation may possibly avoid the pitfalls of the fixities and the fetishes that form part of the single minded notion of nation-building after the achievement of political independence from the colonial ruler" (2000: 145). Spivak believes that the culturally displaced diasporic people form their own ethnic island which retains the archaic rarities of a distant land. It can therefore be emphasized that "diasporic thought can have independent validity when the plurality of its cross-cultural perspective can be used to provide constructive ideas of socio-political progress" (Chatterjee 2000: 145). Naipaul's interpretation of India in his Trilogy explores his ideas about India, the land of his ancestors, a postcolonial India in the diasporic perspective. In these travelogues, he has been very critical, perceptive and sometimes subjective rather than objective. Moreover, his obsession with rootlessness has made him more anxious and hence his perceptions have occasionally not been properly judicious. Further, since he has not been an Indian citizen, he has no such emotion to be blind to the defects of Indian society. Being a Westerner, he is unable to understand the mysteries that are inherent in Indian culture, society and life. For understanding everything, he makes a physical scrutiny that is rather improper to understand a complex Indian socio-cultural set-up. It is true that India has brought him so much pain because it is his ancestors' land where people are suffering due to their ignorance, superstition and uncivilized outlook. But then India as a nation is not static as he has wrongly viewed in *India: A Wounded Civilization*. He has however revised his opinion in the next travelogue *India: A Million Mutinies Now* in which he has tried to grasp the "pluralistic Indian society".

7.2. India as a Progressive Nation: An Evolutionary Assessment

7.2.1. *India as an Area of Darkness*

Naipaul in his early thirties has made unpleasant but mostly true comments on India in *An Area of Darkness*. He passes judgments about the systems of life and functioning of the administration. Naipaul says that India was a background to his childhood in a special way: "It was the country from which my grandfather came, a country never physically described and therefore never real, a country out in the void beyond the dot of Trinidad, and from it our journey had been final" (*AD* 27). He refers to his ancestral origin: "It was a country suspended in time; it could not be related to the country, discovered later. It remained a special, isolated area of ground which had produced my grandfather and others I knew who had been born in India and had come to Trinidad as indentured laborers, though that past too had fallen into the void into which India had fallen, for they carried no mark of indenture, no mark even of having been laborers" (27). He thought the journey of his grandfather had been final although his own trip to India was to see "how complete transference had been made from eastern Uttar Pradesh to Trinidad" (27). To Naipaul, "In its artefacts India existed whole in Trinidad. But our community, though seemingly self-contained, was imperfect. Sweepers we had quickly learned to do without. Others supplied the skills of carpenters, masons and cobblers. But we were also without weavers and dyers, workers in brass and makers of string beds" (29). Naipaul attacks the very Indian attitude of continuing with the ancient customs or a thing even if it has lost its relevance:

> Many of the things in my grandmother's house were therefore irreplaceable. They were cherished because

> they came from India but they continued to be used and no regret was attached to their disintegration. It was an Indian attitude as I was to recognize. Customs are to be maintained because they are felt to be ancient. This is continuity enough; it does not need to be supported by a cultivation of the past, and the old however hallowed, be it a Gupta image or a string bed, is to be used until it can be used no more. (29-30)

He explains that the "area of darkness" about India is featureless:

> To me as a child the India that had produced so many of the persons and things around me was featureless, and I thought of the time when the transference was made as a period of darkness, darkness which also extended to the land, as darkness surrounds a hut at evening, though for a little way around the hut there is still light. The light was the area of my experience, in time and place. And even now, though time has widened, though space has contracted and I have traveled lucidly over that area which was to me the area of darkness, something of darkness remains, in those attitudes, those ways of thinking and seeing, which are no longer mine. (30)

Naipaul is not a believer in Hinduism and the structure of its caste-system and uncleanliness: "Examining myself, I found only that sense of the difference of people, which I have tried to explain, a vague sense of caste, and a horror of the unclean" (32-35). He was against the irrational notion of caste in India:

> In India people were also to be tainted by their caste, especially when this was announced beforehand, approvingly or disapprovingly. But caste in India was not what it had been to me in Trinidad. In Trinidad caste had no meaning in our day-to-day life; the caste we occasionally played at was qualities; no more than an acknowledgment of qualities; the assurance it offered was such as might have been offered by a palmist or a reader of hand writing. In India it implored a brutal division of labor; and at its centre, as I had never

> realized, lay the degradation of the latrine-cleaner. In India caste was unpleasant; I never wished to know what a man's caste was. (33-34)

Naipaul was an unbeliever of Hindu religious rituals for which he refused to go through *Janaywa*, or thread ceremony of the newborn. He had a sense of ridicule to such irrational ceremony in Trinidad, which had no relevance in the life of a Brahmin there. He had the experience of the two opposite confronting worlds in Trinidad—the solid Indian world and the other worlds of Trinidad of other communities. However, the Indian world was gradually becoming non-existent. Naipaul therefore reiterates:

> Between my brother, twelve years younger than myself and me there is more than a generation of difference. He can have no memory of that private world which survived with such apparent society up to only twenty-five years ago, a world which had lengthened out, its energy of inertia steadily weakening, from the featureless area of darkness which was India. (35)

In Trinidad, Naipaul argues, the existence of the two worlds is even a marvel in the consciousness of a child. By coming to India he is now able to see the difference between the "Indian worlds of Trinidad" and the real India that he sees now. Though he rejects the Indian traditions of irrationality and superstition, he has also certain sense of love for some archaic Indian values. His Indian self is unable to accept the way people in Bombay "used candles and electric bulbs for the Diwali festival, and not the rustic clay lamps, of immemorial design" (36), which in Trinidad they still used. He understood that the Indians were an old people who continued to belong to the old world. Despite the fact that certain conventions in the Indian system were irrational and indefensible, they however gave deep impression on his self for which he became a bit emotional and sensitive: "I had been born an unbeliever. Yet the thought of the decay of the old customs and reverences saddened me" (36). The vastness and variety of India sometimes baffled Naipaul. In his youthful age of thirty, he was often puzzled how to conceptualize India as a country, a nation, a people, a culture. Remembering the past, he writes:

> The India, then, which was background to my childhood, was an area of the imagination. It was not the real country I presently began to read about and whose map I committed to memory. I became a nationalist; even a book like Beverley Nichols's *Verdict on India* could anger me. (41)

Naipaul admits that his lack of belief in the religion is the reason for which one whole aspect of India was not understood by him: "I was without belief or interest in belief; I was incapable of worship, of God or holy men; and so one whole side of India was closed to me" (41). His understanding of Gujarati business is intense, perceptive and critical. This community has no sense of anything like Indian identity. They are concerned with money and their work. Such a community has therefore no contribution to India because they live like an exclusive group, self-centered without any concern for the Indian problems:

> The Guajarati and Sindhi merchants were as foreign as Syrians. They lived enclosed lives of a narrowness which I considered asphyxiating. They were devoted to their work, the making of money; they seldom went out; their pallid women were secluded; and all day their houses screeched with morbid Indian film songs. They contributed nothing to the society, nothing even to the Indian community. (42)

There was much gap between these people and the other Indian community in Trinidad. Their journey to Trinidad was not final as they made frequent trips to India for buy and sell, marriage and recruitment. Naipaul's Indian journey is more a psychological exploration of his self—his illusions, notions and beliefs. He understands that India is a country of varieties. It is not governed by a single, plausible system. Being born in Trinidad and descending from Indian ancestry, he went to London for his studies. Now coming to India he questions his own self, his beliefs and his identity. He believes that London is not his centre, not his true identity. He therefore analyses his decision for coming to London:

> I came to London. It had become the centre of my world and I had worked hard to come to it. And I was lost. London was not the centre of my world. I had been misled; but there was nowhere else to go. It was a good place for getting lost in, a city no one even knew, a city explored from the neutral heart outwards until, after years it defined itself into a jumble of clearings separated by stretches of the unknown, through which the narrowest of paths had been cut. (42)

London has made his world narrow. He was confined to the bigness of this metropolitan city. It kept him away from his roots, ancestry and his natural identity. He therefore belonged to nowhere by staying in London. He was traumatized to explore his self, his identity:

> Here I became no more than an inhabitant of a big city, robbed of loyalties, time passing, taking away from what I was, thrown more and more into myself, fighting to keep my balance and to keep alive the thought of the clear world beyond the brick and asphalt and the chaos of railway lines. All mythical lands faded, and in the big city I was confined to a smaller world than I had ever known. I became my flat, my desk, my name. (44)

A sort of feeling for India as the mythical land of childhood was awakened in Naipaul as India was drawing nearer and nearer. Reaching India he lost his distinctiveness that he was enjoying in England. Now standing from his dual self, Naipaul observes the systems of society and attitudes of people in India. What struck Naipaul during his first India visit were the evils of poverty, uncleanliness and irrationality.

It was quite amazing for Naipaul to see the poverty of India in the lanes of Bombay. There was less concern how to improve the fortune of the people. Sympathy was more important than the action to improve the economic condition of the people. Beggars are sleeping on the pavements. The poor sweepers are sweeping the allotted area of pavement with "shrunken face". Poverty in India is not "an urge to anger or improving action, but poverty as an inexhaustible source of tears, an exercise of the purest sensibility" (44). During his visit to different parts of the country his observations of poverty in the rural areas were more startling:

> I had seen Indian villages: the narrow, broken lanes with green slime in the gutters, the choked back-to-back mud houses, the jumble of filth and food and animals and people, the baby in the dust, swollen-bellied black with flies, but wearing its good-luck amulet. I had seen the starved child defecating at the roadside while the mangy dog waited to eat the excrement. (45)

Naipaul's perceptive eyes were stuck at the scenes of degradation and dirt:

> In the dim, stinking corridors sat expressionless women, very old, very dirty, shriveled almost to futility; and already one had the feeling that people were negligible: these were the sweepers, the servants of the gay girls of the Bombay poor, doubtless lucky because employed: a frightening glimpse of India's ever receding degrees of degradation. (47)

Naipaul's sarcastic tone of disapproval is well marked in the above description of the miseries of the marginalized people in the postcolonial scenario. The division of labor in Indian society is also rejected by him for which he blames the sacred scripture *Gita* that persuades the individual to perform one's own duty rather than inclining towards other's work:

> To die in one's duty is life: to live in another's is death. This is the *Gita*, preaching degree fifteen hundred years before Shakespeare's *Ulysses* preaching it today. And the man who made the dingy bed in the hotel room will be affronted if he is asked to sweep the gritty floor. The clerk will not bring a glass of water even if you faint. The architecture student will consider it a degradation to make drawings, to be a mere draughtsman. And Ramnath, the stenographer so designated on the triangular block of wood that stands on his desk will refuse to type out what he has taken down in shorthand. (47-48)

Another important negative feature in the postcolonial Indian society was the colonial "mimicry". In their attitude, style and functions, the people of India had become "mimic men". These people were adopting a special type of mimicry that is different from other-postcolonial societies:

> The outer and inner worlds do not have the physical separateness which they had for us in Trinidad. They coexist; the society only pretends to be colonial; and for this reason its absurdities are at once apparent. Its mimicry is both less and more than a colonial mimicry. It is the special mimicry of an old country which has been without a native aristocracy for a thousand years and has learned to make room for outsiders, but only at the top. The mimicry changes, the inner world remains constant: this is the secret world of survival. And so it happens that to one whole area of India, a late seventeenth-century traveller like Ovington remains in many ways a reliable guide. Yesterday the mimicry was Mogul; tomorrow it might be Russian or American; today it is English. (56)

The insightful analysis of Indian mimicry by Naipaul is worth of understanding because he is very critical of the Indian people who mimic not the manners and attitudes of a real country, England, "but of the fairy-tale land of Anglo-India, of clubs and sahibs and syces and bearers" (57). Naipaul laments that "an entire society has fallen for a casual confidence trickster. Casual because the trickster has gone away, losing interest in his joke, but leaving the Anglo-Indians flocking to the churches of Calcutta on a Sunday morning to assert the alien faith, more or less abandoned in its country of its origin" (57). He thinks that the Indian English mimicry is like fantasy, an "undiminishing absurdity". V.S. Naipaul is therefore confused whether this is mimicry or schizophrenia:

> Mimicry might be too harsh for what appears so comprehensive and profound: buildings, railways, a system of administration, the intellectual discipline of the civil servant and the economist. Schizophrenia might better explain the scientist who before taking

> up his appointment: consults the astrologer for an auspicious day. But mimicry must be used because so much has been acquired that the schizophrenia is often concealed; because so much of what is seen remains simple mimicry, incongruous and absurd; and because no people, by their varied physical endowments, are as capable of mimicry as the Indians. (57)

Naipaul's keen observations on "beggary' and defecation are illuminating. He analyses the Indian attitude towards beggars and defecation in the public places as shameless. There are dissenting views on beggars: one argument is that automatic charity to the beggars is an act of reverence to God; there is also a contrasting opinion to such kind of charity: "If I had the power, I would stop every *sadavrata* where free meals are given. It has degraded the nation and it has encouraged laziness, idleness, hypocrisy and even crime. Such misplaced charity adds nothing to the wealth of the country, whether material or spiritual" (69). Naipaul comments: "It is the attitude of the foreigner who does not understand the function of the beggar in India and is judging India by the standards of Europe. He is too radical to succeed and of course in this matter of beggary he has failed" (69). Defecation in public places is quite natural in India. No law can prevent it. They defecate on the lower slopes of Shankaracharya Hill, bus station of Madras, banks of Mondovi River in Goa and in many other places:

> Indians defecate. They defecate, mostly, beside the railway tracks. But they also defecate on the beaches; they defecate on the hills; they defecate on the streets; they never look for cover. Muslims, with their tradition of purdah, can at times be secretive. But this is a religious act of self-denial, for it is said that the peasant, Muslim or Hindu, suffers from claustrophobia, if he has to use an enclosed latrine. (70)

The Indians do not see even if they look on. They have their own ways of defending their cleanliness. According to their religion they take bath every day. They have also devised their own rules to contain contamination:

> There is only one pure way to defecate; in love-making only the left hand is used; food is to be taken only with the right. It has all been regulated and purified. To observe the squatters is therefore distorting; it is to fail to see through to the truth. And the ladies in the Lucknow Club, after denying that Indians defecate in public, will remind you, their faces creased with distaste, of the habits of Europe—the right hand used in love-making, toilet paper and food the weekly bath in a tub of water contaminated by the body of the bather, the washing in a wash-basin that has been spat and gargled into-proving by such emotive illustrations not the dirtiness of Europe but the security of India. It is an Indian method of argument, an Indian way of seeing: it is so that the squatters and wayside filth begin to disappear. (70-71)

Despite such defense by the Indians, they have not been able to make their hamlets graceful because of the dung-heap for which the approach to many villages is not a refreshing experience: "Often one would like to shut one's eyes and stuff one's nose; such is the surrounding dirt and offending smell" (71). The civic sense of sanitation is therefore lacking in Indians. Their bad habits spoil the river banks which are turned into excellent breeding grounds for flies. It is the duty of every individual to cover one's waste. Hence those who go against it by spitting on the road and defecating in the public commit a sin against God and humanity. The Indians even defecate on the floors and in the urinals: "Fearing contamination, they squat rather than sit and every lavatory cubicle caries marks of their misses. No one notices" (72). Another Indian attitude that drew negative flak from Naipaul was to physical labor: "Labor is degradation; only a foreigner would see otherwise" (72). Mahatma Gandhi, the father of the nation observes: "Divorce of the intellect from body-labor has made of us the shortest-lived, most resource-less and most-exploited nation on earth" (73). Naipaul however thinks that Gandhi did not see like the Indians. He was like a visitor who wanted to bring reformation of these Indian lapses:

> He looked at India as no Indian was able to; his vision was direct, and this directness was, and is, revolutionary. He sees exactly what the visitor sees; he does not ignore the obvious. He sees the beggars and the shameless pundits and the filth up Banaras; he sees the atrocious sanitary habits of doctors, lawyers and journalists. He sees the Indian callousness, the Indian refusal to see. No Indian attitude escapes him, no Indian problem; he looks down to the roots at the static, decayed society. And the picture of India which comes out of his writings and exhortations over more than thirty years still holds: this is the measure of his failure. (73)

The people of India, Naipaul observes, do not have the qualities of clarity, criticism and discrimination for self-analysis. Gandhi, a curious combination of East and West, is able to understand the whole diseased, decadent Indian society. He has been able to link the sanitation problem to the divisive attitude of the people. Naipaul thus remarks: "Sanitation was linked to caste, caste to callousness, inefficiency and a hopelessly divided country, division to weakness, weakness to foreign rule. This is what Gandhi saw, and no one purely of India could have seen it. It needed the straight simple vision of the West" (74).

Gandhi's attitude to the ideal service to humanity is often correlated to the "selfless action" advocated by the *Gita*. But Naipaul considers this to be an Indian distortion. Gandhi is a revolutionary and his glorification of "service" is to put forward a practicable day-to-day ideal. In India caste division is responsible for poor functioning of all social structures. Work is not done to perform a duty properly. It has taken a form of ritualistic performance. Gandhi's spirit of service, the idea of excrement, bread-labor and the dignity of scavenging, "form a logical" whole; they answer the directness of his colonial vision" (74). Inefficiency and corruption have spoiled the Indian society. Naipaul believes that caste is responsible for this: "Service is not an Indian concept and this providing of services has long ceased to be a concept of caste. The function of the businessman is to make money" (75). Caste had been a convenient division of the classical India. It was functioning according to that society.

However in the present decadent society, it was irrelevant, obsolete and impractical: "Caste, sanctioned by the *Gita* with almost propagandist fervor, might be seen as part of the older Indian pragmatism, the 'life' of classical India. It has decayed and ossified with the society, and its corollary function, has become all: the sweeper's inefficiency and the merchant's short-sighted ruthlessness are inevitable" (78).

Naipaul is very harsh on this Indian attitude of exclusiveness and self-centered function. He condemns the Indian attitude of defending themselves by sheltering on the ideas of the *Gita:*

> Everyman is an island; each man to his function, his private contract with God. This is the realization of the Gita's selfless action. This is caste. In the beginning a no doubt useful division of labor in a rural society, it has now divorced function from social obligation, position from duties. It is inefficient and destructive; it has created a psychology which will frustrate all improving plans. It has led to the Indian function for speech making, for gestures and for symbolic action. (78)

The system of symbolic action in India is rather ridiculous. Seventy percent of the trees planted die soon after the symbolic action due to lack of care. The health minister would refuse to be vaccinated for religious reasons in the small-pox week; medical certificates can be bought by paying money. In coordination with the symbolic action, labels for things, places and people are also important. Naipaul's disapproval of such symbolic action is appropriate because it does not help in yielding any proper function of govt. machinery and welfare of the marginalized sections:

> An eastern concept of dignity and function, reposing on symbolic action: this is the dangerous, decayed pragmatism of caste symbolic dress, symbolic food, symbolic worship: India deals in symbols, inaction. Inaction arising out of proclaimed function, functions out of caste. Untouchability is not the most important effect of the system; a western conception of dignity alone has made it so. But at the heart of the system lies

> the degradation of the latrine cleaner, and that casual defecation in a verandah which Gandhi observed in 1901. (80)

Naipaul's remarks on untouchability, reservation policy and bravery awards are noteworthy because it critiques the Indian system of functioning, inefficiency and callousness:

> Reserving government jobs for untouchables helps nobody. It places responsibility in the hands of the unqualified; and the position of the untouchable civil servants, whose reputations always go before them, is intolerable. It is the system that has to be regenerated, the psychology of caste that has to be destroyed. (80)

Despite Gandhi's sincere efforts he was a great failure to enhance dignity of labor because the Indians did not practice the spirit of Gandhi in their life although they worshipped him like a God. His actions only remained symbolic. Gandhi remains, Naipaul thinks, a tragic paradox because of his nationalism, based on Hindu revivalism as he took India to archaism which deprived India of dynamism. It remained a static nation:

> The spinning-wheel did not dignify labor; it was only absorbed into the great Indian symbolism, its significance, rapidly fading. He remains a tragic paradox. Indian nationalism grew out of Hindu revivalism; this revivalism, which he so largely encouraged, made his final failure certain. He succeeded politically because he was reverenced; he failed because he was reverenced. (81)

Naipaul's tone has become more sarcastic when he attacks Gandhi for his failure to bring improvement on the system:

> It is so with Indians and Gandhi. He is the latest proof of their spirituality; he strengthens the private contract with God of all who revere him. Nothing remains of Gandhi in India but this: his name and the worship of his image; the seminars about non-violence, as though this was all he taught; prohibition, rich in symbolism and righteousness. (81)

Naipaul is not against the Gandhi vision. However, he is unhappy about the Indian attitude to understand Gandhi properly. They are complacent only by worshipping Gandhi as God rather than implementing his ideas and vision: "There is no inconsistency; the mahatma has been absorbed into formless spirituality and decayed pragmatism of India. The revolutionary became a God and his message was thereby lost. He failed to communicate to India his way of direct looking" (82). Gandhi's ideas have not saved India because people did not want to see like Gandhi. They were rather callous, self-complacent and indifferent. Naipaul is pained to record the miserable situation of the poor and deprived: "And in Uttar Pradesh town you might see the rich and very fat man in cool, clean white sitting in a cycle-rickshaw being pedalled by a poor and very thin man, prematurely aged, in rags. Beggars whine. Holy men give up all. Politicians are Grave and unsmiling" (75). This was the picture of India when Naipaul was traveling in 1962-63. The civil servants were conscious of their prestige rather than having any concern for the improvement of the system or conditions of the people on the margin. Corruption was pervasive in the system. The contractor made false bills which are passed with the understanding that the extra money will be shared from all the officials from top to bottom.

Even in Kashmir, Naipaul was preoccupied with the dirt of India. In a Srinagar-bound bus while he was traveling along with a Brahmin family, food was served according to the established norm. None other than "the dirty old servant' could touch with the "very fingers that a moment before had been rolling a crinkled cigarette and had then seized the dusty Dalda tins from off the dusty floor" (139-40). By using his right hand he distributed puris from one tin, "scooped out curried potatoes from another, and from a third secured dropping fingerfuls of chutney. He was of the right caste; nothing served by the fingers of his right hand could be unclean..." (140). Here the sarcastic tone of Naipaul is well marked. The vastness of India baffles the writer. He often compares with the rural landscape of small town of Indian Trinidad. He was sometimes not feeling homely in India. He felt like a visitor: "Its size, its temperatures, its crowds: I had prepared myself for these, but in its very extremes the country was alien. Looking for the familiar, I had again in spite of myself, become an islander: I was looking for the small and manageable" (140). From the day of his arrival he had learnt that racial similarities meant little. The people that he met in Delhi and Bombay and rural areas were all strangers, "narrower and grander" at once. These people were the natural inhabitants of a big country without any romantic notion about the size of the country. Naipaul does not find the linkage in his personal experience of Trinidad with India: "In all the striking detail of India there was nothing which I could link with my own experience of India in a small town of Trinidad" (141):

> The encounter with the tourist family in Kashmir had done more than dislodge a childhood memory; it awakened a suppressed consciousness. That food should be served in certain strict ways I at once understood. Equally I understood the mixture of strictness and dirt, the overdone casualness with which the puris and potatoes had been slapped into hands. It was partly a type of inverted asceticism by which a necessary pleasure is heightened...; it was partly the conviction, perhaps derived from a rural society poor in implements, perhaps derived from religion, that great elaboration was unnecessary, pretentious and absurd. It was above all a respect for the forms, for the way things had always been done. (141-42)

Naipaul sees that the medieval mindset of the Indians was, only for continuity. It did not develop any sense of history, which was a sense of loss. Such mentality did not have actually any sense of beauty for the beautiful Kashmir land and style of Mogul garden and other scenic beauties:

> The medieval mind, which saw only continuity, seemed so unassailable. It existed in a world which, with all its ups and downs remained harmoniously ordered and could be taken for granted. It had not developed a sense of history which is a sense of loss; it had developed no true sense of beauty, which is a gift of assessment. While it was enclosed, this made it secure. Exposed, its words

became a fairy land, exceedingly fragile. It was one step from the Kashmiri devotional songs to the commercial jingles of Radio Ceylon; it was one step from the roses of Kashmir to a potful of plastic daisies. (144)

His pilgrimage to Amarnath was an experience which combined both his joy and bitterness. He was happy because he saw the wonderful Himalayan. His joy had no linkage with the religious motif of the pilgrims although he wished to enjoy their mystic longing of peace of being religious. Naipaul was more concerned with sanitation than the spiritual aspects of his pilgrimage. India was the largest slum of the world. In this country, "cultural humility was sweet, but spiritual humility was sweeter" (162). His pilgrimage was not a thrilling experience because he thought that "the *Yatris* had no idea of sanitation. They polluted every river we came to; I wished they would follow Gandhi's advice about the need for a little spade" (162). The Himalayas were a special attraction for Naipaul:

> Yet a special joy had been with me throughout the pilgrimage and during all my time in Kashmir. It was the joy of being among mountains; it was the special joy of being among mountains; it was the special joy of being among the Himalayans. I felt linked to them; I liked speaking the name. India, the Himalayas: they went together. (167)

All these mountains were the "brightly colored religious pictures" in his grandmother's house in Trinidad. "They had become part of the India of my fantasy" (167):

> To be among them was fleetingly, and with a truer sense of their unattainability, to claim them again. To reject the legend of the thousand-headed sheshnag was easy. But the fact of the legend established the lake as mine. It was mine, but it was something I had lost, something on which I would soon have to turn my back again. Was it fanciful to think of these Himalayas, so well charted and perhaps once better known, as the Indian symbol of loss, mountains to which, on their burning plains, they looked back with yearning, and to which

> they could now return only in pilgrimages, legends and pictures? (160)

India's ruins have disturbed Naipaul deeply because Indians have no sense of history. Reading the history of India for the last one thousand years results in insult, humiliation and anger because India has been continuously destroyed by the attacks and foreign rulers. In 1962-63, Naipaul felt that the Indo-English encounter during the British Raj had harmed India to an irreparable loss: "The British had possessed the country so completely. Their withdrawal was so irrevocable" (187). Though he grew in British colony of Trinidad, a fantasy haunted him in his stay in India whenever he was reminded of their presence. Naipaul was rather at pains to note that "the Indo-British encounter was abortive; it ended in a double fantasy" (216). He clarifies: "Their new self-awareness makes it impossible for Indians to go back; their cherishing of Indianness makes it difficult for them to go ahead" (216). Though it appears that India has not been changed since Mogul time, it has actually been changed quite profoundly. The British encounter has diluted both the positive and negative indigenous values: "India's strength, her ability to endure, came from the negative principle, her unexamined sense of continuity. It is a principle which, once diluted, loses its virtue. In the concept of Indianness the sense of continuity was bound to be lost" (217). India has become a static country. It is not moving forward. That is because the creative urge failed:

> Instead of continuity we have the static. It is there in the "ancient culture" architecture; it is there in the much bewailed loss of drive, which is psychological more than political and economic. It is there in the political gossip of Bunty. It is there in the dead horses and immobile chariot of the Kurukshetra temple. Shiva has ceased to dance. (217)

The harmful effects of the British Raj were numerous. The British Empire in India remained incongruous. Though Trinidad was part of the British Empire, the people of West Indies knew very well that they were only "a dot on the map of the world, and it was therefore important to be British: that at least anchored us within a wider system. It was a system which we did not feel to be oppressive" (188). Since Trinidad was in the New World, the British were only one of the races known to them. However colonial India was quite different. Since the British were the dominant, all things relating to English were also dominant. The residues of the English that remained in India were rather painful to Naipaul: "But they revealed one type of self-deception as self-deception; and though this was lodged in that part of the mind where fantasy was permissible, the revelation was painful. It was an encounter with a humiliation. I had never before experienced, and perhaps more to me than to those Indians who hurried about streets with unlikely English names, in the shadow of imperial-grand houses, as others might have felt for me the colonial humiliation I did not feel in Trinidad" (158).

Naipaul's resentment against the mimicry of the Indians is obvious:

> It lived in the division of country towns into cantonments, civil lines, and bazaars. It lived in army officers' messes, in the silver so frequently given, so reverentially polished mannerisms and jargon. It lived in the collectorates, in the neat fading handwriting of these settlements which add up to a doomsday book of a continent: suggesting endless days in the sun on horseback, with many servants but few real comforts, and evenings of patient effort.... It lived in the clubs, the Sunday morning bingo, the yellow covered overseas edition of the *Daily Mirror* in the manicured hands of middle-class Indian ladies; it lived in the dance floors of city restaurants. It was an England more full-blooded than anyone coming from Trinidad might have thought possible. It was grander, more creative and more vulgar. (190)

Naipaul is not accepting the imposition of English culture on Indian systems because he feels that "the coming together of England and India is a violation" (190). He also feels that it is rather ridiculous when there is a comic mixture of costumes and the widespread use of an imperfectly understood language. In the building of Raj in India, there is the false vanity of Englishness. Naipaul resents that the architectural pattern built by the Raj neither belonged to India nor to England: "Their grounds were a little too spacious; their ceilings a little too high, their columns and arches and pediments a little too theoretical; they were neither of England nor India; they were a little to grand for their purpose, too grand for the puniness, poverty and defeat in which they were set. They were appropriate to a conception of endeavor rather than to endeavor. They insisted on being alien and were indeed more alien than the earlier British buildings.... It was embarrassing to be in these buildings; they still appeared to strive to impose attitudes on those within and those without" (190-91). Naipaul satirizes the Kipling administrators who are "perpetually sahib-ed and huzoor-ed, hedged around by fabulous state, is yet an exile, harassed, persecuted, misunderstood by his superiors and natives he strives to elevate; and on his behalf Kipling can rise to towering heights of mock-anger and can achieve a mock-aggressive self-pity; play within pity" (191). India inherits everything; nothing is abolished. The obsession for all that is English is so intense that the entire nation is inclined to these ridiculous English values. In Trinidad people accepted the English rule, English institutions and the English Language without questioning. However "England and Englishness, as displayed in India, were absent. And to me this remained the peculiar quality of the Raj: this affectation of being very English, this sense of a nation at play, acting out a fantasy. It was there in all the architecture of the Raj and especially in its faintly ridiculous monuments: the Victorian memorial in Calcutta, the India Gate in New Delhi. They were not monuments worthy of the power they celebrated (199). In India, the racial supremacy of the English people has ruined the country. They were not emotional with the problems of the country: "It is not properly an imperialist attitude. It points, not to the good or evil of British rule in India, but to its failure (201). The Indians have no sense of history because they squat among the ruins without any emotions. They cannot see their country directly. They rather depend on myths and legends. The Indians are not competent to interpret their own history. They look upon the western historians and scholars to know their past, their history, and their ruins:

> Indian interpretations of their history are almost as painful as the history itself; and it is especially painful to see the earlier squalor being repeated today, as it has been the creation of Pakistan and the reawakening within Indian of disputes about language, religion, caste and region. India, it seems, will never cease to require the arbitration of a conqueror. A people with a sense of history might have ordered matters differently. But this is precisely the saddening element in Indian history: this absence of growth and development. It is history whose only lesson is that life goes on. There is only a series of beginnings, no final creation. (202)

All creation in India is followed by "imminence of interruption and distraction" (205). Building is a very fundamental instinct in India: "It is building for the sake of building, creation for the sake of creation; and each creation is separate, a beginning and an end in itself" (205). To Naipaul, the ruins in India have a unity. They speak of the continuity and flow of Hindu India, ever shrinking. "In the North the ruins speak of waste and failure, and the very grandeur of Moghul building is oppressive" (205). In Europe, the monuments are symbolic of the country's spirit. They also express the refined sensibility of a nation. In contrast, the mosques and the great palaces speak of only personal plunder and a country's capacity to be plundered infinitely and endlessly. Naipaul is displeased with the racial dominance of the English rulers:

> An Imperial ideal, well on the way to a necessarily delayed realization, was founding on the imperialist myth, equally delayed of the empire-builder, on the English fantasy of Englishness, 'the cherished conviction', as one English official wrote in 1883, 'which was shared by every English man in India, from the highest to the lowest, by the planter's assistant in the lowly bungalow...to the Viceroy on his throne...that he belongs to a race whom God has destined to govern and subdue'. (210)

Even fifty years after independence, India remained a colonial country. The Chinese aggression exposed India's weakness:

"She continued to produce mainly politicians and speeches. Her 'industrialists' were mainly traders, importers of simple machinery; manufacturers under license. Her administration was still negative" (234). The emergency, declared during the war, spread rumors and panic. The passion of the aroused nation was responded with words, which had no meaning. India was not fully prepared for the unexpected war from China. The politicians did not prepare how to tackle the situations of poverty, disease and disintegration. India's poverty is visible everywhere—in the platforms, slums, streets and urban areas. The emotions of pity and compassion could not help to mitigate the critical situations. What was needed was to approach the difficulties with comprehensive planning to execute with all sincerity. Naipaul therefore laments:

> From the railway train and from the dusty roads India appeared to require only pity. It was an easy emotion, and perhaps the Indians were right: it was compassion like mine, so strenuously maintained, that denied humanity to many. It separated; it permitted the surprise and emotion I feel at these concerts, simple exhibitions of humanity. Anger, compassion, and contempt were aspects of the same emotion; they were without value because they could not endure. Achievements could begin only with acceptance. (249)

By the time Emergency was lifted, Naipaul's stay in India was almost over except his journey to Dubes, the village of his grandfather. In a year, he could not accept India: "I had learned my separateness from India, and was content to be a colonial, without a past, without ancestors" (252). Naipaul was not impressed by the magic of India: "It remained the land of my childhood, an area of darkness; like the Himalayan passes, it was closing up again, as fast as I withdrew from it, into a land of myth; it seemed to exist in just the timelessness which I had imagined as a child into which, for all that I walked on Indian earth, I know I could not penetrate" (252). The journey to Dubes distressed Naipaul more: "But food. Though they had overwhelmed me, my colonial prudence remained. It had prevented me emptying my pocket into Jussodra's sad, wrinkled hands" (256). He did neither take any food nor any water from Ramchandran's house. The journey therefore ended in futility: "So it ended, in futility and impatience, a gratuitous act of cruelty, self-reproach and flight" (263). Finally he concludes after twenty-four hours of his first Indian journey: "It was a journey that ought not to have been made; it had broken my life in two" (256). His reflections on Hindu philosophy of illusion take him further to go deeper into the meaning of India: its physical vastness and his duality of mind to belong to it or not:

> The world is illusion, the Hindus say. We talk of despair, but true despair lies too deep for formulation. It was only now, as my experience of India defined itself more properly off against my own homelessness that I saw how close in the past year I had been to the total Indian negation, how much it had become the basis of thought and feeling. And already, with this awareness, in a world where illusion could only be a concept and not something felt in the bones. It was slipping away from me. I feel it as something true which I could never adequately express and never seize again. (266)

Naipaul's diasporic situation has prompted him to see India with clarity and precision. Such a unique, fundamental encounter with India might not come to him again. Despite the fact that he has been ruthless in exposing the Indian deficiencies, he is however truthful and genuine. Some of his misconceptions might be due to his colonial self that he admits. Naipaul's India vision is however a landmark interpretation of India that is disturbing and explosive because it is a great effort of a young man who is seriously obsessed with India as a country, a people, a nation, a culture and a civilization. His efforts to understand India have always baffled him because his Western trained mind has analyzed it physically. Moreover, his high concerns for sanitation and hygiene, which India lacked as a postcolonial nation, were more a judgment based on his long stay in England where an advanced country gave more importance to it. It is true that Indians have not that sense when they defecate in public and pollute the environment. But then, India was a poor country, which was decolonized only fifty years before. It was a country plundered by the foreign invasions until the British ruled over it. The British Raj was a commercially oriented government, exploiting the Indian resources for England rather than utilizing the Indian resources for the welfare of the marginalized people who were living in poverty and misery continuously. His understanding, his dilemma, his confusion and above all his perceptions and judgments are not absolute. His statements are tentative, hypothetical subject to revision on a final analysis through continuous interpretation and evaluation.

Naipaul thus reconstructs the image of India through memories, interactions and personal decision. His colonial experience of Trinidad and London as well as his "distinct Indian ancestry" are always at the background to guide and influence his formations about India. India as an Area of Darkness haunts him to explore, and therefore he makes his own judgments about the function of the systems in India in the different spheres of life. The dominant factors that influenced his imagination are the important aspects, namely poverty, caste and cleanliness. Naipaul has been deeply perturbed by seeing the poverty of people, especially the "empty hands of the beggars", and the "beauty of poor prostitutes" has moved him to a considerable degree. The Indians endure poverty as a fact of life. Besides poverty, corruption is also a way of life for which there is no improvement. Naipaul laments: "In India everywhere the emphasis is on compassion and pity rather than on efficiency". The Indians are still under the influence of the "Britishness" in their use of "dress" and "drink". Naipaul is pained to note the "false glamours" of the Indian elites for their "Britishness and snobbery". He also observes that it is difficult to root out the Indian caste system from the society. Even J.S. Mill is very harsh on the Hindu idea of subordination which is 'degrading and pernicious'. The caste-system, initially a pragmatic means of classification has degraded due to inefficiency and corruption. The foreign rule further exploited the situation to their own advantage due to people's ignorance. The caste-system is against the values of humanity because it does not allow treating "man" as "man". He therefore writes in anguish: "To know Indians was to take a delight in people as people: every encounter was an adventure. I did not want India to sink; the mere thought was painful" (243). Naipaul refers to the inefficiency of the four sweepers in a Bombay Hotel because of the caste system. He is rather ashamed greatly to note the countryside Indians defecating in public. He has harsh words against the "misplaced idea of cleanliness" of the Indians.

Naipaul at 30 was perhaps not mature enough to understand the young Independent India. His construction of India in his early years of life in Trinidad was based on his observations of customs and traditions among the migrant Hindu and Muslim communities living there. The writer's training in the great Britain has framed his mental set-up to emphasize rationality, cleanliness, and reasoning and reject blind beliefs, myths, irrationalities and prejudices. Naipaul's reflections on food, cleanliness, behavior, rituals and irrational systems on the basis of caste, creed and religion show his concerns to question if India is truly a secular nation. Naipaul has therefore tried to make an authentic representation about its history and people, culture and socio-political practices, economic situations and so on. The Indian people still suffer from depravity even after independence which arouses pity and sympathy for them. Naipaul is unhappy to see that the British "babu culture" still persists. The Indian approach to "caste", "poverty" and "cleanliness" is strongly looked down upon by Naipaul. He feels that the caste system in the Hindu society and the continuation of the same by the British Raj is rather deplorable. Naipaul disapproves of the Indian attitude of "tolerance and compassion" at the cost of efficiency and order. He thinks that it is difficult to root out the British snobbery in dress and drink, the false glamour from Indian lifestyle. Naipaul in his subconsciousness loves the Indian Nation, his ancestral "home land". However he is keen to find out defects existing in its systems and people's attitudes. It is a great delight for him to know India—its people, history and culture. To him every encounter was on adventure and he did not want "India to sink; the mere thought was painful". He believes that the caste system in India has a degraded quality in not treating "man as man". This irrational division among the community has made the functioning of the Indian systems very much inefficient. The very Indian attitude to menial work is a great disappointment to Naipaul: "The man who makes the dingy bed in the hotel room will be affronted if he is asked to sweep the gritty floor. The clerk will not bring you a glass of water even if you faint. The architecture student will consider it a degradation to make drawings, to be a mere draughtsman" (47). Reacting strongly against the defecation system in the Indian rural set-up, Naipaul believes that it is a great shame on India as a Nation. It is uncivilized and barbaric. However, considering the poor condition of India as a postcolonial Nation in the 1960s, it was not possible on the part of the people and the government, to afford to construct Latrines with flush system for all the Indians. Naipaul mocks at this Indian attitude when they argue that the westerners are also unclean in many ways:

> The ladies at the Lucknow club will remind you...of the habits of Europe—the right hand used for love-making toilet paper and food, the weekly bath in a tub or water contaminated by the body of the bather, the washing in a wash basin that has been spat and gargled into—proving...not the dirtiness of Europe but the security of India. (71)

This argument indicates that "defecation in public" is a general trend in India. It signifies that India is "a static, decayed society" (73). Naipaul is not happy with the Indian people who are unable "to see" even if they "look on". Naipaul thinks that the nation's millions of people have always been "the sources of her greatest misfortune (Chatterjee 2000: 65). Naipaul argues that the caste system is responsible for all ills in the Indian system and lack of basic amenities for people. Naipaul's outright rejection of the concept of "*Maya*" and "*Karma*" is not in the proper perspective of understanding these two concepts. The Hindu idea of "*Karma*" is perhaps meant for motivating people to perform good actions for a great future and the Indian concept of "*Maya*" is meant for guiding people to work without being too much indulgent in greed and materialism. Naipaul's comments on the mimicry of this vast Nation are praiseworthy. Comparing with Trinidad, which is an insignificant dot in the world map, Naipaul is at pains to see that Indians imitate the

British manners and styles in all aspects of life. He is unable to reconcile to the fact that India should lose her identity. It is a country which is constantly ravaged, subjected to domination and ruins. In the process, its identity has been constantly challenged. He reflects on how the people of India do not cultivate a sense of history. The decay has made the country static. The political leaders, writers, economists, scientists and artists should have a vision to search for Indianness rather than this false "Englishness". The lack of a clear vision among the people has harmed India to an irreparable loss. He is therefore unable to see a clear India. It remains "an area of darkness" for him in his first visit. He would come to India again during Emergency to examine how the systems were functioning.

7.2.2. *India as a Wounded Civilization*

Naipaul's engagement with India again and again is due to his subconscious concern for this country. In the foreword to the book *India: A Wounded Civilization* he writes: "India is for me a difficult country. It's not my home and cannot be my home; and yet I cannot reject it or be indifferent to it; I cannot travel only for the sights. I am at once too close and too far" (IWC x). About Hundred years had passed by the time of his first journey to India in 1962 since his ancestors migrated to Trinidad. He has therefore washed himself clean of many Indian religious attitudes for which India seems to be "strange" to him. He further elaborates his stand on his inquiry about India:

> An inquiry about India—even an inquiry about the Emergency—has quickly to go beyond the political. It has to be an inquiry about the civilization itself, as it is. And though in India I am a stranger, the starting point of this inquiry...has been myself. Because in myself, like the split-second images of infancy which some of us carry, they survive, from the family rituals that lasted into my childhood, phantasmal memories of old India which for me outline a whole vanished world. (xi)

An analysis of India's history shows that it has an old civilization which has been constantly invaded. That is so because it has been ill "equipped to cope with the outside world;

no country was so easily raided and plundered, and learned so little from its disasters" (ix). Naipaul thinks that even in the late 20th century India is deeply "rooted in its own civilization" (IWC x):

> ...it takes time to understand that its independence has meant more than the going away of the British; that the India to which independence came was a land of far older defeat; that the purely Indian past died a long time ago. And already with the Emergency it is necessary to fight against the chilling sense of a new Indian dissolution. (x)

Naipaul visited India during Emergency rule of Indira Gandhi to observe the functioning of the Indian systems, and prospectus of this old civilization. He believed that further decay during Emergency might help in revitalizing this old civilization for strengthening the country to a better future. The stability of Gandhian India was an illusion; and India would not be stable again for a long time: "But in the present uncertainty and emptiness there is the possibility of a true new beginning, of the emergence in India of mind, after the long spiritual night" (161). In the past, India was constantly subjected to "intellectual depletion" due to frequent invasions: "In the history books, in the accounts of wars and conquests and plunder, the intellectual depletion passes unnoticed, the lesser intellectual life of a country whose contributions to civilization were made in the remote past" (8). In the periods of apparent revival, India hadn't only been making itself archaic again but intellectually smaller and vulnerable also. Naipaul comments on the contradictory nature of Indian nationalism based on political awakening and religion:

> But of independent India, with its five-year plans its industrialization, its practice of democracy, has invested in change. There always was a contradiction between the archaism of the national pride and promise of the new; the contradiction has at last cracked the civilization open. (8)

The archaism of India could neither move the country forward nor resolve its crises: "Her borrowed institutions have worked like borrowed institutions; but archaic India can provide no substitutes for press, parliament and courts. The crisis of India is not only political or economic. The larger crisis is of a wounded old civilization that has at last become aware of its inadequacies and is without the intellectual means to move ahead" (8). As back as in 1961, Narayan's remark about India, "India will go on", indicates that he believes in the continuity of India in spite of its multiple problems. Naipaul cannot reconcile with Narayan for such a view about India. He therefore writes:

> To get down to Narayan's world, to perceive the order and continuity he saw in the dereliction and smallness of India, to enter into his ironic acceptance and relish his comedy, was to ignore too much of what could be seen, to shed too much of myself: my sense of history, and even the simplest ideas of human possibility. I did not lose my admiration for Narayan; but I felt that his comedy and irony were not quite what they appeared to be, were part of a Hindu response to the world, a response I could no longer share. (11-12)

Referring to Narayan's novel of 1949 titled *Sampath* Naipaul understands that the individuals are indifferent to the problems of India. They do not think that their responsibility is to face the difficulties and make efforts for a better India. They think India can take care of herself: "...India is eternal and forever revives, there comes not a fear of further defeat and destruction but an indifference to it. India will somehow look after itself; the individual is freed of all responsibility" (15). In India, "responsibility" and "past" hung together. He refers to Indira Gandhi's speech published in *The Indian Express* in this context: "Mrs. Gandhi said no social welfare program could succeed unless the basic attitudes of mind change...'we must live in this age' Mrs. Gandhi said, adding that this did not mean that 'we must sweep away' all our past—while people must know of the past, they must move towards the future, she added" (16-17). His reading of Narayan's novel is also a reading of "a fable, a classic exposition of the Hindu equilibrium, surviving, the shock of an alien culture, an alien literary form, an alien language, and making harmless even those new concepts it appeared to welcome. Identity became an aspect of *karma,* self-love was bolstered by an ideal of non-violence" (17).

Though Naipaul is critical of Indian Philosophy, he is often puzzled to decide to which aspect he would embrace:

> But to those who embraced its philosophy of distress India offered an enduring security, its equilibrium, that vision of a world finely balanced that had come to the hero of *Mr. Sampath*, that arrangement made by the gods: only India, with its great past, its civilization, its philosophy and its almost holy poverty, offered this truth. So, to Indians, India could detach itself from the rest of the world. The world could be divided into India and non-India. And India, for as its surface terrors could be proclaimed, without disingenuousness as quality, as perfect. (23)

To the people of India, it provided great security and stability. The outside world is changing fast. India however does not change much, it is rather fixed and stable for which the foreign married girl of Delhi, whom Naipaul met, came to India whenever she felt void, isolated: "In the midst of world change India, even during this Emergency, was unchanging: to return to India was to return to a Knowledge of the world's order, everything fixed, sanctified, everyone secure" (26). The apparently stability of the Hindu world is destabilized the moment it comes in contact of the outside world, a non-Hindu idea of human possibility. This Hindu world is therefore fragile and subject to shattering at any moment. The ultimate Hindu retreat is a retreat to chaos. It is also a retreat from civilization and creativity, from rebirth and growth to magic and incantation, "retrogression to an almost African night, the enduring primitivism of a place like the Congo, where, even after the slave-trading Arabs and the Belgians, the past is yearned for as *le bon vieux temps de nos ancetres*. It is the death of a civilization, the final corruption of Hinduism" (33).

During the clean-up programme of Emergency the raids are like terrors. Since this was based on a political crisis, it did not frame any moral principle for the society. Even it did promise "a better regulated future". It only reinforced the high Hindu ideal of self-realization which may even take the form of worldly corruption. After a thousand years of defeat and withdrawal the Hindu society had broken down:

> The Emergency, whatever its immediate political promptings, only made formal a state of breakdown that had existed for some time; it needed more than a political resolution. In 1975, the constitution was suspended; but already in 1974, India had appeared to stall, with civil disobedience campaigns, strikes, and student disturbances. The political issues were real, but they obscured the bigger crisis. The corruption of which the opposition spoke and indiscipline of which the rulers spoke were both aspects of a moral chaos, and this could be traced back to the beginning, to independence. (35)

The Hindu society enabled by Gandhi during freedom struggle had started disintegrating with the rebirth and growth that came along with independence. In a harsh tone Naipaul therefore makes his own judgment of the post-independence Indian society:

> With independence and growth, chaos and loss of faith, India was awakening to its distress and the cruelties that had always lain below its apparent stability, its capacity simply for going on. Not everyone now was content simply to have his being. The old equilibrium had gone, and at the moment all was chaos. But out of this chaos, out of the crumbling of the old Hindu system, and the spirit of rejection, India was learning new ways of seeing and feeling. (38)

Referring to Tendulkar's play, Naipaul understands that his India has changed: "The world has opened out, and men have become more various and, individualistic; the will rages. Sensibility has been modified. India is less mysterious: "Tendulkar's discoveries are like those that might be made elsewhere" (39). Hinduism in its degradation has not helped much. It has rather brought a lot of negative aspects to the Indian society:

> Hinduism hasn't been good enough for the millions. It has exposed us to a thousand years of defeat and stagnation. It has given men no idea of a control with other men, no idea of the state. It has enslaved one quarter of the population and always left the whole fragmented and vulnerable. Its philosophy of withdrawal has diminished men intellectually and not equipped them to respond to challenges; it has stifled growth. So that again and again in India history has repeated itself: vulnerability, defeat, withdrawal. And there are not four hundred millions now, but something nearer seven hundred. (41)

Due to decay, the Indian civilization lost its vitality. During the Emergency, the intellectual deficiencies of archaic civilization are well-marked: "India stalled, unable to see its way ahead, to absorb and render creative the changes it has at last generated" (41). Naipaul keenly observes that the awakening of the marginal in the society has put the middle class people to rethink about their future. These marginalized people can no more be neglected: "Their illegal hutments in which they live are knocked down; but they rise again, a daily tide wrack on the margin of cities and beside the railway lines and the industrial highways" (43). Naipaul notes: "...it was this great uncertainty, this sense of elemental movement from below, and an almost superstitious dread of this land of impressive, unfinished ruins, that made professional man say in Delhi: "It's terrible to see your life's work turning to ashes." And his wife said "For the middle classes for people who live like us, it's all over. We have a sense of doom" (44).

Naipaul understands that the people in the lower rank are awakening in India. The big cities like Bombay are flooded with the rural people who go there in search of work and live in the slums. They live a very miserable life in the dirty slums. There are provisions of latrine. Every open space is a latrine in India. The division of labor in India is quite disturbing. Only the sweepers are to remove the excrement, people have wrong notions of cleanliness: "It was unclean to clean; it was unclean even to notice. It was the business of the sweepers to remove excrement, and until the sweepers came, people were content to live in the midst of their own excrement" (57).

Indians do not look for an objective Indian identity. An Indian identity is to belong to India, an established country with an established past. Naipaul's encounter with the journalist in Bombay reveals that an economist journalist who believes in the development and change believes that an

> Indian identity was not something developing or changing but something fixed, an idealization of his own background, the past he felt he had just lost. Identity was related to a set of beliefs and rituals, knowledge of the gods, a code, an entire civilization. The loss of the past meant the loss of that civilization, the loss of a fundamental idea of India, and the loss therefore to a nationalist-minded man, of a motive for action. (60-61)

This is however a part of the feeling of purposelessness of many Indians. It was also a middle class burden to have an idea of India after a long period of subjection. However in the slums and squatter settlements in Chawls, the real Indian Identity is quite obvious. These poor people who have migrated from the villages strive for their basic needs of life: food, shelter, water, a latrine. It was a great discovery of identity. These unacknowledged, unknown people actually represent India. Their needs are basic and India needs to address them rather than boasting on its glorious past. These emigrants from the villages are suffering due to suppression by the tyrant leaders, Sarpanches and Zamindars:

> All the way from Poona—except in certain defense areas—it was dotted with sodden little clusters of African-like huts: the encampments people in flight from the villages, people who had been squeezed out and had nowhere else to go, except here, near the highway, close to the towns, exchanging nullity: people fleeing not only from landlessness but also from tyranny, the rule in a thousand villages of men like the Patel and the Sarpanch. (77)

In the wake of Naxalite movement to save the poor and oppressed in the villages, many university students joined the battle to fight for justice knowing little about the problems of the country. It was just a rage, an excitement to sacrifice their lives, to stain their hands in violence and blood for the oppressed:

> India remains so little known to Indians. People just don't have the information. History and social inquiry, and the habits of analysis that go with these disciplines, are too far outside the Indian tradition. Naxalism was an intellectual tragedy, a tragedy of idealism, ignorance, and mimicry: middle-class India after the Gandhian upheaval, incapable of generating ideas and institutions of its own, needing constantly in the modern world to be inducted into the art, science, and ideas of other civilization, not always understanding the consequences, and this time borrowing something deadly. Somebody else's idea of revolution. (82)

Though Naxalite movement failed in India, it however alarmed everybody. The poor people are no more to be taken for granted. Millions of the people living in the margin both in cities and villages are on the move with a new claim on the land. Naipaul finds that the Indians have a defective vision because they are mostly guided by obsessions rather than observations and ideas. Referring to U.R. Anantmurti's book *Sanskar*, Naipaul comments: "Knowingly or unknowingly, Anantmurti has portrayed a barbaric civilization where the books, the laws, are buttressed by magic and where a too elaborate social organization is unquickened by intellect or creativity or ideas of moral responsibility" (97). The Acharya of *Sanskar*, imprisoned in his dead civilization, can only define himself within it. Like Gandhi he has no chance of coming into contact with an outside world. Gandhi had to work out his faith in alien societies:

> Gandhi, maturing in alien societies, defensively withdrawing into the self, sinking into his hard-won convictions and vows, becoming more obstinate with age, and always seemingly headed for lunacy, is constantly rescued and redefined by external events, the

> goading of other civilizations: the terror and strangeness of England, the need to pass the law examinations, the racial pressures of South Africa, British authoritarianism in India. (98)

Naipaul analyses that the Acharya's self-absorption at the time of crises is rather sterile, without any chance of bringing him any new idea whereas new ideas were peering to Gandhi at critical juncture. That is so because the Acharya remains an individual limited to his own perceptions. But India is to change, must come in contact with the outside world. In a changing society, according to Sudhir Kakar, the underdeveloped ego of the individual is a "dangerous luxury". The perceptions can be individual rather than a social function: "caste and clan and security and faith and shallow perception all go together; one cannot be altered or developed without the rest" (99). The individual therefore gets lost, gets "drowned in the immensity of the unknown world" (99).

The individual obsessions in India sometimes merge with the political movements of protest. Shiv Sena movement in Bombay and Dravidian movement in the South are brilliant examples. Jan Sangh is another such party. With the Emergency many such parties have been banned and the leaders imprisoned: "In India, where the problems are beyond comprehension, the goals have to be vague. The removal of poverty, the establishment of justice: these, however often stated now, are like abstractions. People's obsessions are more immediate" (103). Naipaul attacks the Indians for their intellectual confusion. Theoretically they go on professing how to eradicate poverty, but they have failed to do so because they have no sharp vision how to deal with it practically. Naipaul is therefore critical of the Indian concerns to eradicate poverty:

> In their attempt to go beyond the old sentimental abstractions about the poverty of India and to come to terms with the poor, Indians have to reach outside their civilization, and they are at the mercy then of every kind of imported idea. The intellectual confusion is greater now than in the days of the British, when the worlds seemed to stand still, the issues were simpler, and it was

> enough for India to assert its Indianness. The poor were background then. Now they press hard, and have to be taken into account. (105)

To cope with the problems of India, the leaders seek to exercise all the disciplines and skills borrowed from European civilization. Naipaul feels that " European methods of historical inquiry, arising out of one kind of civilization, with its own developing ideas of the human condition, cannot be applied to Indian civilization; they miss too much" (116). The idea of *dharma* in India accommodates bonded labour as it could accommodate widow-burning. The laws in India must serve *dharma*: "Yet *dharma*, as expressed in the Indian social system, is so shot through with injustice and cruelty, based on such a limited view of man" (119). Law therefore avoids any collision with *dharma*: "Yet it is this *dharma* the law must grapple with if the law is to have a 'dynamic role'. That is the difficulty: to cope with the new pressures, India has in some ways to undermine itself, to lose its old security" (121). The borrowed institutions are to function as an integral part of Indian institutions by way of synthesis. As a conquered people the Indians have been dependent on other civilizations:

> To survive in subjection, they have preserved their sanctuary of the instinctive, uncreative life, converting that into a religious ideal; at a more worldly level, they have depended on others for the ideas and institutions that make a country work. The Emergency—coming so soon after independence—dramatizes India's creative incapacity, its intellectual depletion, its defenselessness, the inadequacies of every Indian's idea of India. (121)

Naipaul does not appreciate Gandhi's approach to India and its problems though he acknowledges his great contribution: "'Archaic emotions': 'nostalgic memories'. When these were awakened by Gandhi, India became free. But the India created in this way had to stall. Gandhi took India out of one kind of *Kal Yug*, one kind of Black Age; his success inevitably pushed it back in another" (138-39). Gandhi's followers diluted everything he strived hard to emulate: Gandhi swept through India, but he has left it without an ideology. He awakened the holy land; his mahatmahood returned it to archaism. Naipaul argues that Bhave is a decadent Gandhian and does not know much about the Indian civilization: “Bhave, in the vanity of his spiritual perfection is more than a decadent Gandhian. His religion is a kind of barbarism; it would return men to the bush. It is the religion of poverty and dust” (149). Bhave’s ideals are not based on Gandhi’s vision: “Bhave, even if he understood Gandhi’s stress on the need for social reform, was incapable of understanding Hindu India; he was too much part of it. The perfect disciple, obeying without always knowing why, he invariably distorted his master’s message” (152). With his simplicity and distortions Bhave only offered Gandhianism as a kind of magic and he himself offered as a magician. He was unable to understand Gandhi’s complex vision: “It seems to be always there in India: magic, the past, the death of the intellect, spirituality annulling the civilization out of which it issues, India swallowing its own tail” (153). During the Emergency, India was however left alone “with the blankness of its decayed civilization” (154). The borrowed inherited democratic institutions were dismantled. There were no foreign rulers to establish a new order. These borrowed institutions that gave India freedom remained alien and “separated from the internal organization of the country, its beliefs and antique restrictions” (154). With independence, India grew with industrialization and five-year plans. However, India was unable to cope with the new problems: “The population grew; the landless fled from the tyranny of the villages; the towns choked; the restlessness created by the beginnings of economic development” (154). The triumph of democracy therefore brought the destruction of India. Politics and press could not save it. Press served the objectives of political anarchy: “India will at the end be face to face with its own emptiness, the inadequacy of an old civilization which is cherished because it is all men have but which no longer answers their needs” (155). India has come to this mess because it has no ideology. India and Gandhi as well have failed together: “Its people have no idea of the state, and none of the attitudes that go with such an idea no historical notion of the past no identity beyond the tenuous ecumenism of Hindu beliefs, and, in spite of the racial excesses of the British period, not even the beginnings of a racial sense" (154). Centuries of conquests have reduced the Indian civilization to such nullity. The idea of *dharma* in India is responsible for India's decline. Naipaul believes that "Indian poverty is more dehumanizing than any machine; and more than in any machine civilization, men in India are units, locked up in the straightest obedience by their idea of dharma" (157). Naipaul's severe indictment of India needs attention:

> So India ever absorbs the new into its old self, using new tools in old ways, purging itself of unnecessary mind, maintaining its equilibrium. The poverty of the land is reflected in the poverty of the mind; it would be calamitous if it were otherwise. The civilization of conquest was also the civilization of defeat; it enabled men, obeying an elastic dharma, to dwindle with their land. Gandhi awakened India; but the India he awakened was only the India of defeat, the holy land he needed after South Africa. (159)

Gandhi has awakened the emotions of people by which India could become free. However the Gandhian fantasies—his fantasies of spirituality, Ram raj, a return to the villages, simplicity and so on—cannot help India to deal with its multiple socio-economic crises and problems. Naipaul therefore thinks that India must not look to the past for its glory and spiritual revival. It must look to the past for enquiry and analysis: "The past can now be possessed only by inquiry and scholarship, by intellectual rather than spiritual discipline. The past has to be seen to be dead; or the past will kill" (161).

Naipaul therefore thinks that India must act according to its needs rather than bank upon past spirituality and Gandhianism. The India of 1975 was not the India of 1930 when Gandhi performed a symbolic act of picking up a handful of salt from the shore at Dandi. He firmly expresses his views: "The needs of 1975 were more worldly and difficult. India wasn't to be cleansed again; it was (as Mrs. Gandhi intuited) to be cleaned up and got going; it was to be seen to be offering worldly opportunities. The very fierceness of the Emergency answered the public mood, assuaged old frustrations (128). Naipaul's

India: A Wounded Civilization is his interpretation of India based on his rational analysis of Indian situations. Despite his explorations of truth about India, it cannot be argued that he was writing the only truth about India. It was only one of the interpretations about India. We will also examine how he analyses India in *India: A Million Mutinies Now*. The vastness of India and its diversity have often baffled the Western travelers to this country. Though Naipaul normally considers himself to be a westerner, he is however a doubly diasporic writer because his ancestors migrated to Trinidad from a village (Dubes) near Gorakhpur and he himself lived in England after completion of his studies there. Though his first Indian experience was bitter, he could not remain indifferent to India: "I cannot travel only for the sights. I am at once too close and too far" (18-19). His travel impressions during 1975-76 were recorded as socio-political/ethnographic analyses in the travelogue *India: A Wounded Civilization*. Naipaul resents the Indian attitude to begging when he writes that the Hindus consider it a "religious theatre, a demonstration of the workings of *Karma*, a reminder of one's duty to oneself and one's future lives" (58). His hatred of beggars is more conspicuous in his utterances: "...the beggars have become a nuisance and a disgrace. By becoming too numerous they have lost their place in the Hindu system and have no claim on any one" (58). Naipaul's judgment on Hinduism by seeing the ruins of Vijayanagar seems to be harsh: "Hinduism...had already reached a dead end, and in some ways had decayed, as popular Hinduism so easily decays, into barbarism" (16). Although there has been much development in the region of Vijayanagar, the peasantry does not understand the substantial changes that take place because of the intellectual depletion: "The crisis of India is not only political or economic. The larger crisis is of a wounded old civilization that has at last become aware of its inadequacies and is without the intellectual means to move ahead" (18). Naipaul's anguish is well-marked when he writes that for a thousand years India had always retreated before its conquerors and when it was about to revive it had always been moving itself archaic, intellectually smaller and vulnerable. Such a stand has been further elaborated by the writer focusing on a number of problems that have crumbled the foundation of Indian civilization. Poverty, slums, lack of facilities, illiteracy, exploitation, child labor, bonded labor, want of planning and leadership, overpopulation, corruption and lack of direction have shaken India. Naipaul feels that the Indians have no intellectual initiative to cope with such problems. The Indian intellectuals like Narayan, to Naipaul's disapproval, argue that "India will go on" in spite of all these problems.

Naipaul is not happy to note that Indians have a habit of ecstatic contemplation of the past and nostalgic reiteration of Gandhi. He also indicts the Indians for self-indulgence and self-pity rather than trying to solve the crises and grievances. The "mythology of the past", which has often a significant bearing on the "culture of the present", does not help much to lessen the problems: "The intellectual confusion is greater now than in the days of the British, when the world seemed to stand still, the issues were simpler and it was enough for India to assert its Indianness. The poor were background then. Now they press hard, and have to be taken into account" (118). Naipaul attacks the Indian concept of *Dharma* as a significantly cohesive force to the people, as it does not help remove bonded labor, widow-burning and other social atrocities. The law even does not interfere in the Indian concept of *Dharma*. He feels that the *dharma* in Indian Social System is replete with "injustice and cruelty based on such a limited view of man" (132). Being disturbed by this issue, he refers to Indira Gandhi's remarks published in *The Times of India* on 5th October 1975: "the Indian legal system should assist for liberation of human spirit and human institutions should strive for removing the obsolete customs" (132). It should function within the purview of the Indian ancient view that "society should uphold *dharma* so that *dharma* sustains society" (132). Naipaul therefore rejects the Indian idea of synthesis also:

> Indians say that their gift is for synthesis. It might be said, rather than for too long, as a conquered people, they have been intellectually parasitic on other civilizations. To survive in abjection they have preserved their sanctuary of the instinctive, uncreative life, converting

> that into a religious ideal; at a more worldly level. They have depended on others for the ideas and institutions that make a country work. (121)

Naipaul observes that the Indian political leaders have no progressive vision because of their obsession with such an archaic, outdated cultural tradition. He indicts the cultural primitivism of such leaders as Gandhi, Bhave, Indira, Jai Prakash Narayan, and Morarji Desai who have failed utterly to pull the Indian civilization out of the move of stagnation and decay. They could not regenerate the Indian strength and vitality. Gandhi was able to draw all India together in a new kind of politics during 1919-1930 because of his racial sense, which is not an Indian quality. This "racial sense" was qualified by such religious sense of Gandhi that he had exhibited in South Africa for which he viewed that "no man was an island and that the disunity of the high was bound up with the dignity of the low" (*IWC* 154). This attitude helped him remain away from the divisive politics of religion, caste and region. However such perspective changed later when he was elevated to a holy man in the emergence of his "Mahatmahood". This emergence did not serve his Indian cause. In the post-independence India, Naipaul thinks, religious ecstasy reduces Gandhianism to Mahatmahood as a result of which "racial sense", the individual sense of dignity is removed from the Indian scene: "...Gandhi awakened the holy land, his Mahatmahood returned it to archaism, he made his worshippers vain (159). His disciple, Vinoba Bhave, though regarded as a saint for his emphasis on the development of inner life, failed to bring any substantial creative change in the lives of the Indians. Naipaul criticizes him severely: "He is not particularly an intelligent man and, as perfect disciple of the Mahatma, not original; his political views came close to nonsense (107). Gandhi was unable to remove the inhuman social evils because his archaic ways were not visionary: "Bihar, where Bhave did much of his walking, remains—in matters of land and untouchability—among the most backward and crushed of the Indian states" (165). Naipaul's sincere indictment to Mr. Morarji Desai has been due to his pompous exhibitionist methods which are the "old Indian attitudes of defeat, the idea of withdrawal, a turning away from the world, a sinking back into the past" (141). Naipaul, thus, dismisses the Indian leaders who have merely spiritual fantasies without any coherent ideologies with a consistent vision:

> India is old, and India continues. But all the disciplines and skills that India now seeks to exercise are borrowed. Even the ideas Indians have of the achievement of their civilization are essentially the ideas given to them by European scholars in the nineteenth century. India by itself could not have rediscovered or assessed its past. Its past was too much with it, was still being lived out in the ritual, the laws, the magic—the complex instinctive life that muffles response and buries even the idea of inquiry. (129)

Naipaul interprets the concept of *Dharma* in the end of this travelogue. He views that the concept of *Dharma* must be understood in the perspective of *action* rather than *contemplation*. He refers to such writers as Balzac and Proust in this context. If Naipaul believes that *action* should be the basis of *Dharma*, then Indian concept of *Dharma* is also based on action, which is the key guiding principle of the *Gita*. Naipaul often indulges in European standards and "points of view" to judge India, to portray the Indian image. He sometimes fails to understand the Indian philosophy, culture and viewpoint. This does not however mean that *India: A Wounded Civilization* should be dismissed outright. What is significant about this travelogue is that it makes us understand our strengths and weaknesses, our achievements and failures. It also significantly argues that civilizations can thrive only on constant renewals and revitalization of the national energies and attitudes to avoid stagnation and decay.

During the second visit Naipaul was haunted by the duality of his consciousness: his childhood memories and his encounter with the 'strangeness of India'. Remembering the "old unchanging India", he is pained to observe the various invasions on it: the Muslim conquests, the British trade and the imposition of Emergency in 1975. Naipaul writes in grief about the invasions made by the Central Asian tribes:

> The invasions are in all the school books. But I don't think people understand that every invasion, every war, every campaign, was accommodated by slaughter, a slaughter always of the most talented people in the country. So these wars, apart from everything else, led to tremendous intellectual depletion of the country. ('A Million Mutinies' in *India Today International* August 18, 1997: 20)

Naipaul rejects the romantic notion of India regarding the Muslim attacks. He does not agree on the point that India always absorbed her conquerors. He feels that India has been esteemed low because of the invasion. Thus he argues that post-independent India must start afresh with "the memory of loss as the basis of nationhood" (Chatterjee 2000: 177). He therefore destabilizes the Indian notion of "wholeness" by questioning the socio-ethical issues. He supports his enquiries about India by referring to popular novels, newspaper headlines, journalistic writings, school buses and travel companions. His aim is to reconstruct the Indian consciousness about the past by deconstructing the socio-cultural and political history of India. Chatterjee's remarks are quite pertinent:

> His method is to catch prevalent culture and study some of its roots, such as the relevance of past history or the ionization of Gandhian philosophy. Most of his observations have the value of an outsider viewpoint, they are not meant to be deep philosophical reasonings—they are intended to cause a thoughtful ripple on modern Indian day-to-day existence. (2000: 177)

Naipaul's observations on a temple and Hindu kingdom of Vijaynagar in the South persuade him to comment on India's inability to face the challenges of the present world. The "archaic India" (*IWC* 18) has not yet been changed to understand the meaning of freedom of press and proper functioning of parliament and court. Naipaul is confused to understand why the Hindus go on chanting the mantras 50 million times while reinstalling the deity in the temple. He also feels that it 'is meaningless to remember the glories of the past of the Vijaynagar Kingdom. The need of the hour is to focus on the improvement of the people who are starving in the slums of India. Because of his too much obsession with European values and standards, Naipaul is perhaps unable to understand the meaning the starving people find in rituals of religion. During the thirty years of independence (1947-1976), though Indian politicians have not been able to tackle all the problems following the democratic model of governance, yet many changes are taking place in course of time. It is rather disheartening that the country is groaning under the pressure of corruption and nepotism, tyrannical governance of emergency. There are also some good efforts to develop the country. Naipaul's confusion is thus quite obvious:

> Since independence much money had been spent on the region. A dam has been built across the Tungabhadra River. There is an extensive irrigation scheme which incorporates the irrigation canals of the old kingdom.... A Vijaynagar steel plant is being planned; and a university is being built, to train men of the region for jobs in that steel plant and the subsidiary industries that are expected to come up, the emphasis is on training men of the region, local men. (*IWC* 17)

Naipaul's perception of India of 1976 has been mostly guided by the condition of Vijaynagar which seems to be myopic because India is not one; there are many "Indias" in different parts of the country. As a migrant with a European-centric mindset, Naipaul has not been able to understand the complexities of the Indian nation, "each having its own history and particular ways of negotiating with the present" (Chatterjee 2000: 179). Naipaul unknowingly diagnoses his own "myopic vision" when he says that "passions alone cannot give validity to ethics for ethical views also rise from the culture of the place in which they are held" (Chatterjee 179). Naipaul understands that the Indian nation is aware of her intellectual and creative depletion, but then people think that there is no escape from it. Naipaul is enraged and says that this is the antiquity of Indian attitude which has no relevance in the present context. Naipaul is therefore raged to note the stagnating attitude of the Indians to move forward for progress through a consistent ideology. He refers to the Indian villages in Bihar and Rajasthan. Bihar's poverty is due to the continuous ravages by famine, flood, earthquakes and political squabbles. Naipaul is disheartened to note the exploitation of child-labor and strong caste-discriminations. Referring to Rajasthan, Naipaul points out how the poor peasants and their children work as laborers in the estate of the prince of Bundi-Kotah region because they still retain a misplaced notion that his subjects still consider him to be their ruler. Naipaul is not happy with the situation because people have not yet changed their mindset due to the fact that they are under the pressure of food and survival.

7.2.3. *India as a Site for Million Mutinies*

After his visit to South American countries, Naipaul once again visited India during 1988-90. During this visit there had been a significant change in his perception on India because he found that the post-independent Indian nation was striving to life with enough vitality. In contrast his earlier visits made him realize that India was either "an area of darkness" or "a wounded civilization". Interacting with numerous people, he understood that India was overcoming its stagnation because of the overflow of energies by various groups and communities through million mutinies. India was now a country disturbed by a million mutinies. Acknowledging the pluralistic aspects of Indian nation, Naipaul realizes that the pattern of life that he encounters now is quite different from the monolithic identity of the Indian community of Trinidad. Such an identity has no relevance in the Indian context. Here, people stuck to smaller ideas of their own smaller groupings—their religion, class, caste and family. He confesses that he could not understand this earlier. By making a whirlwind tour to different regions of the country such as Kashmir, Madras, Bangalore, Calcutta, Uttar Pradesh, Delhi, Bengal, he interacts with the leaders of the Dalits and Shiv Sena in Bombay; he perceives the ongoing developmental programmes, communal problems in Madras, the state of the dying city of Calcutta, the history of Lucknow and the women's questions. The first-hand experience with the vastness of the Indian nation enables him to make empirical enquiries about the patterns of life in India. That is why he makes forceful positive remarks: "There was in India now what did not exist 200 years before: a central will, a central intellect, a national idea. The Indian union was greater than the sum of its parts.... They (the mutinies) were a part of the beginning of a new way for many millions, part of India's growth, part of the restoration" (*MMN* 518). This third Indian stand by Naipaul is a movement away from "depicting the confines of what Naipaul thinks to be a stagnation of culture" (Chatterjee 2000: 187). The various movements remained a source for reshaping the laws of the Indian state. These mutinies therefore strengthened the intellectual life, the wholeness of values and humanism in the country. Naipaul's first visit to India in 1962 was burdened with the anguish, abjectness, defeat and shame because his ancestors had to leave India as indentured servants for the sugar estates of Guyana and Trinidad. He confesses that some of his observations of 1962 were now reversible in 1989. The factual descriptions of William Howard Russell are also not acceptable to him now after his encounter in 1989 with the variety and vastness of India. He therefore revises his views and comments now: "In 27 years I had succeeded in making a kind of return journey, shedding my Indian nerves, abolishing the deadness that separated me from my ancestral past" (*MMN* 516). India had to travel through a series of traumatic darkness to revitalize itself. The Indian Dark ages can be attributed to the Muslim invasions, the repeated vandalizing of the North, the shifting empires, the wars and the 18th century anarchy. In 1962 he could not perceive India's revival:

> What I hadn't understood in 1962, or had taken too much for granted, was the extent to which the country had been remade; and even the extent to which India had been restored to itself, after its own equivalent of the Dark Ages.... The twentieth century restoration of India to itself had taken time; it could even seem like a kind of luck. It had taken much to create a Bengali reformer like Ram Mohun Roy (born in 1772); it had taken much more to create Gandhi (born in 1869). The

> British peace after the 1857 mutiny can be seen as a kind of luck. It was a kind of intellectual recruitment. India was set on the way of a new kind of intellectual life; it was given new ideas about its history and civilization. The freedom movement reflected all of this and turned out to be the truest kind of liberation. (517)

The first war of independence occurred in India in 1857. This mutiny was the beginning of a process which moved on and on even after India got her formal political freedom. The idea of freedom had gone to all learners during the 130 years from 1857. The last 90 years of the British Raj were phenomenal because the people of India increasingly protested against subjugation and domination. Even the first 40 years after independence made people conscious of their condition, status and identity. The idea of freedom was worked out at the top and transmitted to the bottom:

> The process quickened with the economic development that came after independence; what was hidden in 1962, or not easy to see, what perhaps was only in a state of becoming, has become clearer. The liberation of spirit that has come to India could not come as release alone. In India with its layer below layer of distress and cruelty, it had to come as disturbance. It had to come as rage and revolt. India was now a country of a million little mutinies. (517)

These mutinies were carried on by "twenty kinds of group excess, sectarian excess, religious excess, regional excess" (517). Naipaul feels that these are the beginnings of self-awareness and intellectual life that were negated by old anarchy and disorder. He could reach to such a conclusion through his encounter with a number of people from different sections of life through his traveling to different places of India beginning from Bombay to Kashmir via Delhi, Lucknow, Calcutta, Madras, Goa, Mysore and many other places. Although certain sections of people have a notion that India is changing from bad to worse, change is imminent. The people in the lower rank, the Dalits, the Harijans have became conscious of their own status and position in the society by way of getting some education and money to improve their conditions. It is true that soon after independence there were rampant corruption and criminalization of politics: "In seeking to rise India had undone itself" (4). There is no fixity, everything is in flux: "Policeman, thief, politician: the roles had become interchangeable. And with money—the money of which the crowded, ugly, skyscrapers towers of Bombay spoke—many long buried particularities had been released. These disruptive, lesser loyalties—of regions, caste, and clan—now played on the surface of Indian life" (4). The Dalit particularity is one of the sectarian movements visible in Bombay. But, more prominent was the Shiv Sena movement in the 1960s which through persistently pursued the cause of Maharashtrians and seized the power of Bombay Municipal corporation through election in 1988: "In the beginning of the movement hostility had been aimed mainly at poor migrants from South India; but other people had felt threatened as well. The movement was down as the Shiva Sena, the Army of Shiva, taking its name from Shivaji, the 17th century warrior leader of the Maharashtra people" (5).

Naipaul thinks that independence struggle is just on interim arrangement:

> Independence had come to India like a kind of revolution. Now there were many revolutions within that revolution. What was true of Bombay was true of other parts of India as well: of the state of Andhra, of Tamil Nadu, Assam, the Punjab. All over India scores of particularities that had been frozen by foreign rule, or by poverty or lack of opportunity or abjectness, had begun to flow again. (9)

The migrants from India to different parts of the world such as Fiji, South Africa, and Trinidad, Mauritius and so on develop a sense of Indian community identity without any consideration of caste, religion and regional identity. In the same manner, Naipaul had a sense of continental Indian identity when he came to India in 1962. On the one hand, he considered India to be the India of great civilization and the classical past. On the other hand, he was hammered by a neurosis that his poor ancestors had to leave India as indentured laborers. But on his arrival in India he found that a central Indian identity like the community identity in Trinidad was not a comfort at all: "In the torrent of India, with its hundreds of millions, where the threat was of chaos and the void, that continental idea was no comfort at all. People needed to hold on to smaller ideas of who and what they were; they found stability in the smaller groupings of region, clan, caste, family" (8). It was beyond his comprehension to understand these small groupings: "The poverty of Indian streets and the countryside was an affront and a threat, a scratching at my old neurosis. Two generations separated me from that kind of poverty: but I felt closer to it than most of the Indians I met" (8).

Naipaul's idea of India in 1962 was rather baffling. He could not understand how the Indian poverty was "a poetic concept, a prompting to piety and sweet melancholy, part of the country's uniqueness, its Gandhian non-materialism" (8). Naipaul, now in 1988-89, understands that the caste or group stability gives a more focused view in doing modest things rather than revolutionary things. During the 40 years since independence, many millions of people had immersed themselves in making immense national efforts to take the country forward. The result is quite visible now: "What looked sudden had been long prepared" (9). People are now very much confident: "One aspect of that confidence was the freeing of new particularities, new identities which were as unsettling to Indians, as the identities of caste and clan and region had been to me in 1962, when I had gone to India only as an Indian" (9). There are remarkable changes in the Indian way of life. Once regarded as untouchables, now they line up in the public roads with much confidence to honor the dead leader, Dr Ambedkar's statue, who championed their cause. Such type of pride is rather new in Indian standards of living: "It could be said to be something Gandhi and others had worked for; it could be said to be a vindication of the freedom movement. Yet it could also be felt as a threat to the stability many Indians had taken for granted; and a middle-class man might in a reflex of anxiety, feel that the country was going from bad to worse" (9).

In the first chapter "Bombay Theatre", Naipaul records his observations on the little mutinies that go on to bring about social transformation. Referring to the story of Papu, son of a migrant Indian to Burma during British Raj, Naipaul notes that he is better educated and well placed because of his stock market business. He also touches upon the industrialization of India that has changed the lifestyles in the society. He tells us the stories of Shiva Sena leader Mr. Patil, Raote, Malika, Anwar, Charu and some Dalits. The main thrust of these stories is how there is transformation in the personal lives of these people through struggle of generations. A change in the fortunes of the marginalized has a great impact on social, economic, political and cultural aspects of the people. Naipaul therefore observes that India is moving towards social revolution and that has been possible because people are conscious of their identity as human beings without disturbing much of their basic social structures. In the second chapter the secretary, Subramaniam, tells his personal story which also reflects the socio-political history of India and post-partition Hindu-Muslim conflicts and their effects on the lives of individuals. His story also tells us how India changes slowly and effectively and how people again rise like phoenix from their own ruins. Traveling through numerous hazards of life, Subramaniam, the secretary has a sense of loss as well as a sense of fulfillment:

> I am still left with the feeling that might have risen much higher, given a little more understanding and sympathy.... What keeps haunting me all the time is the feeling that I am doomed to rise no more than I have risen. Even in this job I have been like a ship's ladder. The sea rises, the ship rises, and the ladder rises with it. But the ladder cannot rise on its own. I cannot be independent of my employer and rise in life. (135)

However recalling the time when his father died, he feels that he has a sense of fulfillment. Inheriting no money from his father's death, he struggled hard to support his sister deserted by her husband and her children. Through his struggle he achieved a lot for this helpless lot. However, he has a dilemma which haunts him all along:

> I started off as a secretary, and am still a secretary, and shall probably end as a secretary. I have not yet risen

> beyond what my father and grandfather could rise to, at the beginning of the century. The only consolation is that, even as a secretary, I am not as badly off as most other secretaries are. And perhaps, even, I no longer believe I am just a secretary. (135)

With the help of new learning and the new tools of Europe, Hindu India got the idea of a country or a nation. Though it seemed that Hindu India might be on the verge of extinction due to new political ideas of Europe, but it did not happen: "Through all the twists and turns of history, through all the imperial venturing in this part of the world, which that Portuguese arrival in India portended and finally through the unlikely British presence in India a Hindu had grown again, more complete and unified than any India in the past" (143). Naipaul observes that like the Portuguese giving a great simplicity to Goa, "so British rule gave a direction to the later Indian history and made it easier to grasp" (143). The events were seen to be leading to the end of that rule: "To read of events in India before the counting of the British is like reading of many pieces of unfinished business; it is to read of a condition of flux of things partly done and then partly undone, matters more properly the subjects of annals rather than narrative history, which works best when it deals with great things being built up or pulled down" (144). Before independence Karnataka was divided into so many Kingdoms with so many boundaries and rulers. During post-independence period, Karnataka was a new creation, a linguistic state, answering the new pride, the new sense of self that the nationalist movement had fostered. Reflecting on the land of India's history and legends Naipaul becomes ecstatic and philosophical:

> The land was sacred, but it wasn't political history that made it so. Religious myths touched every part of the land outside colonial Goa. Story within story, fable within fable: that was what people saw and felt in their bones. These were the myths, about gods and the heroes of the epics, that gave antiquity and wonder to the earth people lived on. (144)

India's changes were well-marked in the field of science and technology. Bangalore was the centre of Indian space research program and one of the important centres of the Indian aircraft industry. Every kind of scientific institution was in Bangalore. The tree-lined roads of the garden city of the Maharajas were now full of the noise and smell and fumes of three-wheelers and cars. Like Dr. Srinivasan, chairman of the Indian Atomic Energy Commission, the other two scientists that Naipaul met in Bangalore, coincidentally had had also priestly grandfathers. Subramaniam tells Naipaul about the social revolution of Karnataka:

> A great social revolution took place in this state after independence. The social revolution was that the identity of the politically powerful classes changed in a few years. It was a bloodless revolution, but it was revolution, though people outside India don't know about it. Before independence, the administration in the state was in the hands of Brahmins. A few years after independence, power changed hands—and I mean the way power changed hands in other parts of the world. The people who now sit in the offices are of a different socials class. (161)

In post-independent India, change is the hallmark of Indian society. Pravas, a Bengali, expresses how there are changes in every generation:

> Because of his background, my father was philosophically oriented. Even within that his reading was different from my grandfather's. My grandfather would practice the hard-core Sanskrit, the original mantras as written in the Vedas or Puranas. It is the hallmark of ritualism that you don't necessarily understand the deeper meanings of everything you do, and my grandfather didn't necessarily understand what he chanted. Ritualism is perhaps, though not very crudely, a show-act. (167)

In a changing scenario, Pravas's father was not a performer, but a reader who interpreted the deeper meanings. Pravas finds that the Brahaminical values in his house continue with certain changes. The Puranic values were intermingled with nationalistic ideals, especially Gandhian truths based on simplicity. Pravas however changed some of these ideals in his own times:

> In my house the continuity of the Brahmanic value system remained, and then I also had my own change from an old world to a new world, from a hot room to a cold room. But this time the change was different. Nobody asked me, "why are you wearing long pants or "Did you eat food cooked by a Brahmin?" But like my father in his government job, I didn't have scaffolding. I had so to speak, to break down the door myself. (167)

He further argues that his interest in science is because of the mystery he feels about it and it is also one more level of transformation in the family history:

> I have made one more level of transformation that my father did from his father's time. I am more liberal in outlook than my father. I have probably become more questioning, because of what we may call "science". I am less knowledgeable about rituals. My father got a part of what his father had, and I have only a part of the rituals my father had. (167-68)

Change is therefore a continuous process. It does not stop. He understands that there will be further changes in the generation of his son. These changes will be big and significant:

> My son will go through a very large change in circumstances in many ways. In the family, in the school surroundings, in the job market, everywhere I grew up in a half-ritualistic background. My son will have no ritualistic background, but if my son loses the rituals even further, he could still be rooted locally, within his peer group. There will be many like him. Society is moving that way. (168)

Pravas views that too much obsession with the roots is a negative aspect because the society does not move on by that way. It is necessary for a society to keep in touch with the new trends. Indian society should therefore be progressive rather than being static, dead and fossilized:

> If you get too attached to your roots in the old sense, you might actually become uprooted fossilized. At least in form, at least in style, you must get into the new stream, get the new roots. More of India is doing that. Style becomes substance in one generation. Things one that starts to do because other people are doing it—like wearing long pants, in my father's case—become natural for the next generation. (168-69)

These views of Pravas remind Naipaul about the changes that the Indians in Trinidad experienced one or two generations before. The peasant India transported by his grandfather to Trinidad had begun to disintegrate when he was a child: first the language going, then the reverence for the rituals and the need for them only a group sense was left: it was merely a "Knowledge of family and clan, an idea of India in the background, an idea of India quite different (more historical, more political) from the India that had appeared to come with one's ancestors" (169). Naipaul extends the views of Pravas and argues that there has been a fundamental difference between the new generation Indians and the immigrants in Trinidad and elsewhere in South East Asia because Hindu theology has become difficult for these immigrants by being separated from the Indian earth. Naipaul analyses their position with clarity: ...the faith had been half possessed by many, abandoned by many. It had been part of a more general cultural loss, which had left many with no strong idea of who they were. That wouldn't happen in India, however much ritualism was left behind, and however much the externals changed (169).

Pravas is fully convinced that the primordial principles will remain though people will lose all the details about individual behavior. In group memory, the primordial streams such as "faith and its expression" will remain forever. India is awakening to a new life and new world which started for some people with either their grandfathers or fathers: "And people had traveled so far so fast that many active people had a success story to tell, their own sometimes, or that of someone in their family" (171). Naipaul knew one such story of a Tamil Brahmin girl, Kala, who joined a job of publicity for a big organization. However, recalling her mother's life of suffering Kala narrates:

> For a few years after her marriage she was virtually a chattel, working for the large joint family of her husband. Hard physical work—washing clothes and scrubbing vessels. She had no time to herself no freedom. She wasn't allowed to go and visit her people when she wanted to. She could make no decision as to what she would like to do with her own life. Somebody always decided for her. (178)

The in-laws of her mother, so-called philanthropists, were hypocrites with double standards. Though they were highly educated, they did not allow her mother to be a philanthropist because there was a lack of sensitivity in them; they were rather cruel. However, Naipaul thinks that Kala's perceptions were partially correct because Hindu family life was ritualized: "Just as there were rituals for every new stage in a person's life, so there were roles that people were required to fill as they progressed through their allotted years. Mothers-in-law were required to discipline the child brides of their sons, to train the unbroken and childish girls in their own duties as child-bearers and household workers, to teach them new habits of respect, to introduce them to the almost philosophical idea of the toil and tears of the real world: to introduce them, in this chain of tradition, to the kind of life and ideas they had been introduced to by their own mothers-in-law" (178-79). Such cruelty was quite common in Hindu family in India. Though the parents of the daughter knew about such cruelty to their daughter they would not protest: "Hindu parents were not supposed to question what was being done to their daughters after they had been married. It wasn't that they didn't know; they were not supposed to question. They would, nowadays" (179). Naipaul resents such cruelty in the Hindu families. He was reminded of the quarrels, politics, treachery and cruelty that he experienced in the joint family of his grandfather in Trinidad:

> Cruelty, yes: it was in the nature of Indian family life. The clan that gave protection and identity, and saved people from the void, was itself a little state, and it

> could be a hard place, full of politics, full of hatreds and changing alliances and moral denunciations. It was the kind of family life I had known for much of my childhood: an early introduction to the ways of the world, and to the nature of cruelty. It had given me as I suspected it had given Kala, a taste for the other kind of life, the solitary or less crowded life, where one had space around oneself. (178)

Naipaul comes to know from the state minister, Prakash on the attitude of the common men to power. Prakash explains how the people in power behave like feudal lords even in the democratic set-up. The ministers are the present-day maharajas and maharanis who misuse power to their own benefits, luxuries and advantages. Because of their submissive attitude even the common men have a fantasy of power even though they have a common tendency to hate the seat of power:

> Our people because of the long tradition of the rajas and maharajas and feudal lords, they always look with awe and fear on the seat of the power, and at the same time they nourish a dislike and hatred towards the seat of power. But there is a dichotomy. They like an accessible, simple, compassionate, benevolent man in the seat of power. But at the same time they have a mental picture of power of pomp, pageantry, authority and aristocracy. These things don't go together many times. (191)

Naipaul by way of interpreting his contacts and interactions with people from different social status and background focuses on the significant changes in people's attitudes and standings. In the context of the role of a Priest in 1989-90, Naipaul reflects:

> He went as a Brahmin, as he had always gone: bare-backed, with a dhoti and shawl, and bare-footed. But now he didn't go as an employee or palace servant. He went as a man in his own right. He went as a representative of a great and ancient religious foundation—though he just managed a marriage hall for them—and the gifts he took were not a retainer's gifts, but priestly offerings: a garland, two coconuts, and kumkum for the red holy marks on the forehead. (202)

In Trinidad, Naipaul notes the hatred of the South Indians towards the North Indians. There was strong revolt against the Brahmanical order and Hindi Language. However; there was a deeper irony in the anti-Brahmin movement in the South: "The anti-Brahmin movement was not a movement of all the non-Brahmin castes. It was a movement mainly of the middle castes. There was, as ever in India, a further lower level, a further level of disadvantage. For these people at the very bottom the DMK offered no protection" (225). The Periyar movement in Tamil Nadu and Kerala was rather provocative but progressive. To many people like Sadanand, Periyar "offered a vision of future bright with the fruits of science, and without the need for the idea of God" (220). Sadanand interprets Periyar's vision:

> In the world of the future, there will be no men without character and culture.... The depravity of the modern character is founded on culture, justice and discipline being used for maintaining caste and class differences among men...when these capitalist and individualist conditions are absent, the need for depraved character will not arise. (220)

The Periyar movement hated the Brahmins considering them more dangerous than a cobra and hence the killing of the former should be preferred to the latter. Mr. Palani, another follower of the Periyar movement, argues that the Tamil civilization is the oldest and purest. It had no caste system initially and the culture of the North affected this civilization when it came to them 2000 years ago. The Brahmanical tradition got a setback in the South during the 1950s when the anti-Brahmin movement resorted to "breaking idols, cutting of Brahmins' churkis and sacred threads rubbing off the religious marks on the foreheads" (253). Slowly the religious ceremonies were absorbed without the Brahmins. Thus the ritualistic nature of the Brahmin tradition was discouraged by anti-Brahmin movements in the South. Such little mutinies were felt in all walks of life in the Indian society. The Brahmo Samaj is another outfit in India which revolutionised thinking. It was a kind of purified or reformed Hinduism which aimed at synthesis of Hindu faith of the *Vedas* and the *Upanishads*: "It was a direct development of the ideas of Raja Ram Mohun Roy of Bengal (1772-1833), the first modern Indian reformer and educationist" (286). It focused on the abolition of the caste system and believed in the education of women and the ideals of democracy. Though it originated in Bengal, it spread all over India. It had a great impact on Indian social structures:

> What Raja Ram Mohun Roy began as a reform movement early in the 19th century, Devendranath Tagore made into a religion. It transformed the Bengali middle class. Rabindranath Tagore expanded that religion into a culture. And that culture became Nehru's politics. Because Rabindra Nath Tagore channeled it into a culture, and didn't restrict it to religion, it was soon absorbed by the wider middle class. Today the Brahmo Samaj is still technically there. But the life has gone out of the institution—and into the wider society. (288)

Another revolution started in Bengal in the field of science due to new learning. Though the Brahmanical tradition revolutionized the development of science in the South, in Bengal the new education made people more rational and conscious in the field of science and politics: In the South, science had grown over two or three generations out of the Brahmanical tradition of abstract learning. In Bengal, in the British built city of Calcutta, science had come with the New Learning; scientific achievement had come out of colonial competitiveness. With this new Learning the common people became conscious of the miserable life they are leading. Persons like Dipanjan, who involved in politics and also teaching the slum people, were concerned how to bring change in society because "society is so structured that the toiling people can never find their own voice, their own view of the world, their own identity" (327). This is a great development in the postcolonial Indian thinking because the people are moving in the proper direction. Another small rebellion that Naipaul elucidates through Ashok is the inter-community marriage by the young generation not through the traditional process of interviewing the girl by a group of family members but by way of personal interaction between the boy and the girl. It is a revolutionary way of marrying during these days because it results in breaking the family link with history and tradition without any vision for future. The younger generation in Bengal was also influenced by Marxism to transform the society. Debu, a high executive in a big company recalls his association with the Naxalite rebellion:

> Debu had taken part in the rebellion in its early stages. He had then fallen out ideologically with some elements of the leadership, and had to hide from both police and former associates. He could chart, precisely and convinced how the revolution of love and compassion had blurred into simple nihilism, with people talking of revolution and peasant power, but never actually taking on the state, or the powerful or the protected, concentrating instead on the weak and the exposed. But there was still in Debu some idea that a fresh and better start might be made. (332)

Debu is therefore still looking forward to a new true revolution. He is disheartened to see the increasing gap between the rich and the poor: "From beggars we have become borrowers. I am exercised by the gap between rich and poor, exercised by the lack of patriotism amongst the power-brokers, exercised by the number of industries going sick. And I am exercised by the fact that borrowers generally end up begging" (341). Naipaul in 1988-89 was disgusted with the amenities provided by the British built Calcutta which is a dying city now: "But I was overpowered this time by my own wretchedness, the taste of the water, corrupting both coffee and tea as it corrupted food, by the brown smoke of cars and buses, by the dug-up roads and broken footpaths, by the dirt, by the crowd; and could not accept the consolation offered by some people that in a country as poor as India the aesthetic side of things didn't matter" (346-47). Naipaul believes that such squalor at home and outside home is rather degrading. It gives people a low idea of their needs—air, water, space for stretching out. It might have also given people a low idea of their possibilities, as makers or doers. Calcutta as a city is dying slowly because it is unable to provide the civic amenities that can make life livable: "Perhaps cities died when they lost the amenities that cities provided, the visual excitement, the heightened sense of human possibility, and became simply places where there were too many people, and people suffered" (347). Naipaul thinks that the dogmatic policies of the government are responsible to destroy rather than creating anything new that can revitalize human life and needs. The old city of Calcutta started dying soon after the British left. The Anglo-Bengali culture—out of which modern India grew, is too old to cope with the present needs. It is therefore necessary to have a vision how to tackle the miseries and poverty of people by way of restructuring infrastructure and economy rather than merely contemplating on the "holy poverty" of India which were thought to be sacred in the eyes of Gandhi and Nehru. Naipaul believes that Calcutta had been ill prepared to the post-partition situation which was enormous. In 1946 the Hindu-Muslim massacre marked the beginning of the end of the city because the next year when India got her independence and Bengal was divided, a large Hindu refugee population overcrowded Calcutta which could provide no civic amenities to all of them.

At the time of partition, many middle class Muslims of Lucknow migrated to West Pakistan resulting in decline of Muslim culture—"the language, the manners, the music, the food". The dilemma of Muslims during this period was understandable. Some Muslims in Pakistan felt that they had no "identity-crisis", but they did not like the "money-culture", "the business aggressiveness of people who, when they had been in Lucknow, had been more easy-going" (370). Serious people like Rashid therefore were to return India where they found themselves in a new problematic communal situation:

> I (Rashid) would feel a change taking place in personal relationships. My Hindu friends started, lecturing. "What are Muslims doing with themselves?" They started becoming reformist about the Muslim faith and what they saw as our archaic practices "How long are you Muslims going to carry on like this? How long are you going to be so dependent on your mullahs?" The

> sad fact was that there was a lot of truth in what they said, I was hurt, but we had to take it. (371)

Rashid's experience is painful because he loves India as his native place. After partition, things had changed for which a true Indian Muslim experiences a sense of loss:

> What did it mean, being a Lucknow Muslim? It's like the Buddhist idea of "Not this, not this". I'm an Indian, but the temple is not for me. I'm Muslim, but in its details my faith cannot be the same faith as the one in Pakistan or Iran or Pakistan. I speak Urdu. I greet people in the Lucknow Muslim way. I say "My respects to you" instead of "Peace be up on you". I derive my sustenance from Lucknow. It gives me my sense of identity—the buildings, the monuments, the culture, the relationship. (385-86)

Naipaul wanted Rashid to elaborate his Pakistan experience and the reason of his coming back to India. Rashid's explanations were based on his first-hand perceptions about the attitudes of Pakistani Muslims. After 40 years of partition; he felt that the Pakistani Muslim was radically different from an Indian Muslim—worldlier, aggressive, corrupted, and money-minded. Elaborating on the attitude of his cousin, a trader Rashid expresses in anguish:

> He had a finger in every pie; he could bribe every officer; he knew that the main thing was to move and make money. He had been homeless twice, the first time in 1947, at independence, and then in 1971, in Chittagong in Bangladesh. He knew he could depend on nothing but money. Other values didn't matter. He was quite different from the person I remembered. (387)

Rashid tells Naipaul that the Pakistani Muslims had started their life afresh without being nostalgic about India, the people who still remembered them. They had been hardened in their approach to emotions and feelings. Rashid therefore felt relieved to leave Pakistan after his two months' stay in Pakistan:

> I felt relief to be back in India, after the claustrophobia of an Islamic society. I liked seeing women again on the

> streets. The dirt and filth of India didn't seem to matter. The people in Pakistan were relaxed enough about their religion. It was just the wretched laws, hanging like a cloud over one: the call to prayers, the moulvi coming to my friend's house and asking why he hadn't seen us at one mosque recently. The thought police. The Islam on wheels. (387)

As a real conscious Muslim, Rashid has not been able to reconcile to the partition of India. This partition has damaged his psyche. He feels that he is not a "complete man" like India itself. Like India, he himself feels fragmented because his "emotional life" is in jeopardy after partition. He therefore tells Naipaul:

> I felt relief to be back here. That sense of belonging, which I had in India I knew I couldn't find anywhere else. Yet I also know that I can never be a complete person now. I can't ignore partition. It's a part of me. I feel rudderless. If there had been no partition I might have been a married man with all the paraphernalia of a middle-class Muslim existence. But I've lived all my life so far as a bachelor and it's now too late for me to change. The creation and existence of Pakistan has damaged a part of my psyche. I simply cannot pretend it doesn't exist. I cannot pretend that life goes on, and I can have the normal full emotional life, as though what had been here before is still around me. (387)

Naipaul's understanding of Rashid's pain was in the area of his own experience. Indian history aroused a lot of emotions in him because he could not separate him from the misfortunes of India. India haunted his psyche at every encounter in India:

> What was pain for Rashid was also pain for me, I couldn't read with detachment of the history of this part of India. My emotions ran congruent for a while with those of Rashid; but we grieved for different things. Rashid grieved for the wholeness of the Lucknow world he had been born into, the world before partition. This world would have elements of old Muslim glory; the glory of the kings or nawabs of Oude and before them

> the glory of the Moghuls. There was no such glory in my past. My ancestors migrated to Trinidad, to work on the plantations there. (392)

Naipaul however had no contemplations of a recent past glory from which he had a break. Instead he developed a sense of an "idea of the kinship of Indians, the idea of the family of India" (399). He examines how a contemplation of Indian history through Russel's description takes him close to "cultural destitution and to wonder at the many accidents which brought us to the concepts—of law and freedom and wide human association—which give men self-awareness and strength, the accidents which have brought us to the point where we can in a way meet William Howard Russell, even in those, impressions made on my senses by the externals of things' not with equality—time cannot be bent in that way—but with something like lucidity" (398-99). Vishwa Nath, the editor of women's magazines such as *Sarita* and *Woman's Era* had his own idea of a mission to bring about social changes in India. He is critical of the great India civilization, Hindu religion and Indian social order. Though he was iconoclastic in his approach to religious ideas he had also high concern for preservation of the old social order: "The family is the hinge of civilization. My stress is that the family should be strengthened, not destroyed. Woman's Lib is responsible for quite a good deal of the disintegration of the family" (418). His views on religion are opposite to orthodoxy ideas: "I think religion is the greatest curse of mankind. It had killed more people, destroyed more property, than any other thing. Even today—Northern Ireland, the Middle East. Hindus, Muslims, Sikhs, all fighting each other in India. The oldest profession is not prostitution, it is the priesthood" (418). His ideas of Hindu religion are fairly perceptive:

> The Hindu religion is a conglomeration of faiths, 500 religions or faiths. We've had reformist movements from the very beginning. From the dawn of civilization we've had reformist movements against orthodoxy. What happens is that every reform movement degenerates into a sect—the Lingayats, the Arya Samajists everybody.

> Buddha rebelled. Mahavir, the founder of the Jaini rebelled. Guru Nanak the founder of the Sikhs rebelled. It's a long list. They rebelled and degenerated into and became as orthodox as the previous orthodox people. So I didn't put on those saffron robes and start going about to those conferences, or preaching in public. I published my magazines. (416)

Vishwa Nath therefore made efforts to give us a better Indian society in his own way of rebellion. By traveling and encountering various people and situations, Naipaul thinks that India has many mutinies, and through them she is awakening to a new rage, a new way of life shedding its stagnation and decay. It is fairly promising to note such pragmatic aspects in Indian way of life and culture:

> To awaken to history was to cease to live instinctively. It was to begin to see oneself and one's group the way outside world saw one; and it was to know a kind of rage. India was now full of this rage. There had been general awakening. But everyone awakened first to his own group or community; every group thought itself unique in its awakening; and every group sought to separate its rage from the rage of other groups. (420)

In the context of Hindu-Sikh conflict Naipaul thinks that there is some intellectual and emotional flaw in Sikh community for which there is no coordination between their attitude of adventure and tribal origin. Gutrej, an IAS tells Naipaul that people are not free. He thinks there are two ideas of India:

> It kept on nagging people that they were not free. It's all right to make two ends meet and have an animal existence, but there's more to life we have in India two absolutely opposed ideas about government and politics. The Hindu idea is that, government must have every right to do as it pleases. This is how the vacations of the constitution are tolerated by everybody. The Hindu idea is that whatever the government does is the law. It is more susceptible to dictatorship. The Sikh idea is that God is the only true sovereign, and that governments

> have a mandate to govern on the condition that they do justice. I was very happy that my people were resisting this subversion of the laws and constitution during the Emergency. (439)

Gutrej's understanding of history is partial. He refashioned history according to his own ideas and fundamental concepts; "people all over India, awakening to history and new knowledge of their place in the scheme of things, refashioned history according to their need" (444-45). Gutrej's took for granted "the constitution, the law, the centers of education, the civil service with its high idea of its role as guardian of the people's rights and improve of their condition, the investment over four decades in industrial and agricultural change" (445). Because of his association with the religious party of Sikhism, a fundamentalism based on religion, he rejected his discoveries as he applied this fundamentalism to human affairs.This reflects his narrowness:

> Like Papu the Jain stockbroker in Bombay, who lived on the edge of the great slum of Dharavi and was tormented by the idea of social upheaval, Gutrej had a vision of chaos about to come. Papu had turned to good works, in the penitential Jain fashion. Gutrej had turned to millenarian politics. It had happened with other religions when they turned fundamentalist; it threatened to bring the chaos Gutrej feared. (445)

Naipaul observes that establishment of a Sikh identity is a recurring need of the Sikh community. Religions is the basis of providing the emotional charge of this identity: "But that also meant that the Sikh cause had been entrusted to people who were not representative of the Sikh achievement, were a generation or so behind: Bhindran Wale had spent most of his life in a seminary in the country town of Mehta Chowk, not far from Amritsar" (445). The Hindu press of Punjab is controlled by the Arya Samajis who oppose the separate identity of the Sikhs. "At the beginning of this century the Aryan Samajis publicly converted some *Chamar*—Untouchable-Sikhs back to Hinduism at Jalandhar. And their hair was cut off, planted together into a rope, and the rope was sold at a public auction. The idea was to ridicule Sikhism and Sikhs" (472). In his final journey in India Naipaul perceives that it was a country of physical vastness and varieties in culture, religion and community. Though the same vastness was there in his 1962 journey, he could not comprehend the complexities of India as a nation, as a civilization. Because of his confidence, Naipaul now recalls that his earlier understanding was not based on fair judgment: "The physical country existed. I could travel to that, I had always wanted to. But on that first journey I was a fearful traveler" (491).

This chapter has focused on the 'Indian nation' from the perspective of a diasporic writer, doubly displaced from his ancestral homeland. In the contemporary world the "construction of nation" is to be understood by taking the voice of the diaspora into consideration. Corole Boyce Davies writes: "Migration creates the desire for home which in turn produces the rewriting of home. Homesickness or homelessness, the rejection of home or the longing for home become motivating factors in this rewriting. Home can only have meaning once one experiences level of displacement from it (1994: 113). Chatterjee remarks that migrant writers' journey to their ancestral homelands "holds the key to some answers about their own identity" (2000: 144). In the postcolonial scenario the meaning of "home", "tradition", "identity" and "past history" have been constantly reconstructed by the migrants through their multi-dimensional experience. Just as the colonial encounter was not only a political battle for dominance, but also a cultural battle, so the perspective of a post-national view on the nation serves to characterize an alternative vision. Both Said and Fanon argue that anticolonial nationalism should inevitably broaden its focus to include the views of an open-minded global community. Fanon thinks that such international solidarities are better placed to give both expansive and objective views on the culture of a nation. To Fanon, "National consciousness, which is not nationalism, is alone capable of giving us the only thing which will give us international dimension" (*WE* 2004: 179). Such a view is corroborated by Said when he says during postnationalism "there is the possibility of a more generous and pluralistic vision of the world" (1993: 277). A diasporic reading of the nation might avoid "the pitfalls of the fixities and the fetishes that form part of the single-minded notion of nation-building after the achievement of political independence from the colonial ruler" (Chatterjee 2000: 145). The idea of cultural dislocation that despotic communities are defined by can fall into what Spivak calls "the marginal specific or as the para-institutional" which in turn forms an ethnic land of their own, of value only as archaic rarities of a distant land. Diasporic thought can have independent validity when the plurality of its cross-cultural perspectives can be used to provide constructive ideas of socio-political progress. Chatterrjee has therefore rightly argued:

> Migration and decolonization have added further meaning to any ongoing discourse on nation. Estrangement and the sense of being far away from home can lead to the approaching of political and geographical issues with special emphasis on human interests and values. The notion of home and identity can be embedded in romantic, idealized viewpoints focusing more definitively on the 'people' who are affected by the political decision and therefore respecting the diverse viewpoints of those who inhabit the region. (2000: 147-48)

These remarks of Chatterjee are illuminating for understanding V.S. Naipaul's vision of the Indian nation in his Trilogy. A pragmatic stand on Indian caste system is that one might rigidly adhere to his own caste and should also be open to the idea of the plurality of the caste system because this goes along with the economic standing in the community. The diversity in socio-economic structures of India of the 1990s baffles Naipaul to construct ideological boundaries in his narrative in his third travelogue. Naipaul realizes that plurality had existed since antiquity, but had been suppressed by the colonial activity which had forced a faceless identity upon the nation. In *An Area of Darkness*, he has felt uneasy with his ethnic sameness in India. However in *A Million Mutinies*, Naipaul adopts a narrative distance by interpreting, analyzing and judging. Since the mutiny of 1857, India has gradually been remade. Freedom had been gained by the intellectual efforts of a handful of leaders but the knowledge of freedom was also spreading to the bottom too. For people who had known only ravages, the very idea of liberty was new, so the oppressed were asserting themselves. Naipaul's third travel book on India has enabled him to formulate a view of the everyday life of the Nation. Perhaps the changes, Naipaul has perceived, have been more a result of the ways of saying rather than in any revolutionary sense a change in the country itself. Aurobindo, Nehru and Gandhi were all at perils to categorize the Indian nation into definitions derived from religion and history. For them the struggle for liberation demanded unity as its first precondition. It was important to integrate India into a single culturally cohesive unit. They felt that it was their responsibility to bind by the numerous ethnic and religious diversities of India into an idea of the nation that had to be a monolithic one. These political activists and philosophers in fact sought to marginalize diversity, even as they could not overlook its existence. In a way they would not help sharing the British prejudice about the inefficiency of the illiterate Indian villager as being incapable of organizing himself since he was enslaved by either greed for the stagnating idea of history and tradition. Reservations about the ability of their countrymen led these thinkers to be wary of the creative potential of a pluralistic society, and seek ways of combining liberation with organization. They were able to establish their versions of unity by ingeniously combining the spiritual and the secular aspects of Indian life to infuse patriotism among the masses. The diasporic rewritings of India by Naipaul once again question the nation-centered ideologies of post-independence India. To his travelogues on India Naipaul brings a personal subjective narrative voice. The method of discovery used in the narrative also tries to bridge the gap between the India of Naipaul's inferences and the specific land he comes into contact with. On analyzing Naipaul's texts, it is quite evident that they bring in a perspective of the variety and plurality of Indian culture. Naipaul's "India vision" is based on a double perspective of outsider/insider divide. Chandra Chatterjee critiques Naipaul's vision of India:

> Tenderness and pleasure that come from the recognition of oneness with India are tempered by his impatience at the social inadequacies of destitutions based on caste and race. The Naipaulian sensibility attributes the Indian's acceptance of poverty to the embedded caste system. The migrant's short-sightedness intrudes upon his comments on Sanskrit texts and his limited understanding of the sociological realities of India. He is unable to accept Anglicisation as fact of Indian life. (202-03)

Naipaul's comments in the first two travelogues are often reductive because they do not take the vastness and variety of India into consideration. He however takes a third stand in his book *A Million Mutinies Now* in 1990 where he comes closer to "rigid humanity" (Aurobindo) and links it to the idea of social liberation. In his earlier books, he has discussed the issues from a colonial distance and has imposed codes of civility on a living Indian culture. However, *A Million Mutinies* focuses on the various vital aspects of Indian life by taking the interviews of people from the various communities, groups and individuals thereby bringing in a pluralistic perspective to his India vision.

The Islamic Journeys: Deconstructing History, Religion, Civilization

In the preceding two chapters, Naipaul's encounter with the West Indian societies and Indian situations has been elucidated. His Indian visits, which produced three important books, were undertaken from 1962 to 1989. The technique in the later travelogues is new because the characters are portrayed to explain their own experiences to Naipaul. In these books, his central concerns are related to people: how they live, think and visualize for a brighter future for their nations. After his second book on India *A Wounded Civilization* was written, Naipaul visited four Islamic countries such as Iran, Pakistan, Indonesia and Malaysia. He tried to understand the intricacies of Islamic culture and interpreted the split personalities of the intellectuals and the miserable conditions of these Muslim countries. Naipaul has focused on the complex situations of these converted people by traveling twice—once in 1979-80 and the other in 1997-98 in such travelogues as *Among the Believers* in 1981 and *Beyond Belief* in 1998. *Beyond Belief* is a sequel to the earlier book *Among the Believers: An Islamic Journey* (1981). This book was written after his second visit to the four Islamic countries. In this travelogue he makes serious reflections on the countries he visited. Naipaul writes about the book:

> It is less of a travel book; the writer is less present, less of an inquirer. He is in the background trusting to his instinct, a discoverer of people, a finder out of

> stories. These stories, opening out one from the other, make their own pattern and define each country and its promptings; and the four sections of the book make a whole. (*Beyond* 2)

Through Naipaul's interactions with numerous characters, anecdotes, narrations, there emerge deeper insights into the state of these countries. A clear vision of the Third World Islamic countries emerges when all the four sections are taken together.

8.1. The First Islamic Journey: Portrayal of a Disturbing Muslim World

Among the Believers is an interpretation of four non-Arab Islamic countries of "an unbelieving observer among believers". The idea of visiting the Islamic countries came to him when he was in U.S.A., and listened to the Iranian people speaking on the media during the Iranian revolution. Shah was overthrown in 1979 and the country was in turmoil for which people were leaving the country. Naipaul visited Iran and analysed the process of revolution referring to the forces of history operating in the country. This led him to visit other Islamic countries such as Pakistan, Malaysia and Indonesia to make an empirical study of Islam through the situations and characters that he encountered in these countries were different. Mustafa therefore rightly remarks that *Among the Believers* provides "a comprehensive and rigorous assessment of a major and historically rooted global phenomenon shaping twentieth-century politics: Islam" (1995: 153). He argues that the rise of Islamic fundamentalism is detrimental to the proper functioning of the First and Third World countries. Bhat thinks that *Among the Believers* is an "empirical study with philosophic and epistemological enquiries into the nature of Islamic civilization" (2000: 123). Naipaul's travelogues on Islamic nations are his searches for order and harmony to avoid the chaos that severely affects these societies for adopting sweeping changes.

Naipaul undertook the journey to the four Islamic countries "to see Islam in action". His objective is to understand Islam as a faith and its impact on day-to-day transactions in the Islamic world. In other words he has tried to explore how Islam as a faith has affected the people, society and other institutions including the functioning of the government and its policies. First, he visited Iran in 1979 when the Govt. of Shah had already been overthrown and Ayatollah Khomeini was installed as the chief of the state. A large number of executions were still taking place and the direction of the Iranian revolution was still unclear:

> In August 1979, six months after the overthrow of the Shah, the news from Iran was still of executions. The official Iran news agency kept count, and regularly gave a new grand total. The most recent executions had been of prostitutes and brothel-managers; the Islamic revolution had taken that wicked turn. The Ayatollah Khomeini was reported to have outlawed music. And Islamic rules about women were being enforced again. Mixed bathing had been banned. Revolutionary guards watched the beaches at the Caspian Sea resorts and separated the sexes. (*AB* 18)

Life in Iran has therefore seriously been affected due to fundamentalist ideas of Islamic revolutionaries. An Iranian doctor, a co-passenger in the plane tells Naipaul: "The revolution is terrible. They've destroyed the country. The army, everything. They've killed all the officers. Tehran was a nice city. Restaurants, cafes. Now there's nothing. That's why I sent my son away" (19). People like this physician consider America a sanctuary rather than merely a place of their education. The religion of the physician was Bahai. Bahais had their own frenzy which was derived from the Shia frenzy of Iran. Like the Shias' belief of Iran waiting for the Twelfth Imam, "the Bahais believed that in the nineteenth century a deputy or surrogate or the Twelfth Imam himself, had come and gone and only they, the Bahais, had recognized him" (21). Naipaul learnt that the Shia protest in the early part of the Islamic empire "was a political-racial protest among the subject peoples of that Arab empire; and the faith that had evolved with that protest had remained political, or liable, to political manipulation" (21). The Bahais suspected the authorities for their mourning for their own martyrs who died for the cause of the Shias. Like Khomeini's movement against Shah, the Bahai movement in the 19th century was subversive as it demanded for cutting off heads, burning books, demolishing places and murdering people. Even there was an attempt to kill the King in 1852. Naipaul writes: "Politically, though not in doctrine, the movement was like Khomeini's against the Shah. Politically, it didn't take; and the Bahais were left, or stranded, like many other Muslim sects, with the almost unapproachable intricacies of their faith: revelation within revelation, divergence within divergence" (21). Naipaul understands that the physician's comments on the persecutions were right. However, the Shias of Iran considered the Bahai claim about the Twelfth Imam the "most punishable kind of blasphemy" (21) for which there were sporadic cases of outburst of "revolutionary executions" against them. The physician had therefore made plans of his sanctuary in the United States. After the revolution, the first election which had been a referendum was in favor of an Islamic republic. The assembly of experts would work out for an Islamic constitution for which Khomeini advised people to elect priests:

> An Islamic constitution was something that had to be put together; and it had to be something of which the prophet, creating his seventh-century Arabian state, guided always by divine revelation, had very much ruled as his own man. That was where the priests came in. They might not have ideas about a constitution—a constitution was, after all, a concept from outside the Muslim world; but, with their knowledge of the Koran and the doings of the prophet, the priests would know what was un-Islamic. (23)

Visiting the different places of Teheran, Naipaul saw an allegorical painting of blood and revenge:

> In the foreground there was a flat landscape: flat, featureless sand bisected by a straight black road, marked down the middle by a broken white line. On the road a veiled woman, seen from the back, lay half-collapsed, using her last strength to lift up her child as if to heaven. The woman had a bloodied back; there was blood on the black road, out of that blood, higher up the road, giant red tulips had grown, breaking up the heavy crust of the black road with the white markings; and

> above the tulips, in the sky, was the face of Khomeini, the saviour, frowning. (27)

The meaning of such a painting is worth-noting. Khomeini saved and avenged. The artist has carefully portrayed that the blood of the martyrs had damaged the modern road for which it led nowhere. The wilderness and confusion during the aftermath of revolution had been well depicted by the artist. Khomeini had pushed Iran into whirlpool of disorder and chaos. The poster symbolized that personality was only allowed to the avenger. The wounded woman with whose pain the revolution started was veiled and faceless. Her pain was her pain. Naipaul also saw another election poster where a faceless women crowd held up photographs of candidates of a particular party: "In a newspaper the face of Ali, the Shia hero, the cousin and son-in-law of the prophet, was shown as a surrealist outline, transparent against a landscape. In one poster Khomeini himself had been faceless, his features replaced by a clenched fist" (28). These portraits bring out the idea that "facelessness had begun to seem like an Islamic motif" (28). The *Iran Week*, a post-revolutionary English language paper, was for the revolution. However, the paper was professing against the outcome of the revolution: "all the Islamic bans on alcohol, western television programmed, fashions, music, mixed bathing, women's sports, dancing" (28). Naipaul comments: "Individualism was to be surrendered to the savior and avenger. But when the revolution was over, individualism—in the great city the Shah had built—was to be cherished again. This seemed to be the message of the *Iran Week* (28). The editor-in-chief of the *Iran Week* suggested Naipaul to visit the holy city of QOM to understand Iran. Naipaul however observes that the *Iran Week* was hard to find in Tehran after his return from Islamic journey after six months. In Firdowsi Street, a Shia Muslim from Bombay remarked that "the Shah was a bastard" (31) who exploited the resources of Iran for his personal needs:

> When the Shah ruled, everything in Iran had been for him. He had drained the country of billions; he had allowed the country to be plundered by foreign companies; he had filled the country with foreign

> advisers and technicians. These foreigners got huge salaries and lived in the big houses; the Americans even had their own television service. The people of Iran felt they had lost their country. And the Shah never really cared for religion, the precious Shah faith. (32)

This man from Bombay enjoyed life in Iran for twenty good years under bad Shah. However he had all praise for the Rule of Ali: "What a nice thing is now...to see the rule of Ali! Getting women back into the veil, getting them off television. No alcohol" (22). Naipaul was however puzzled to note that this man who was leaving Iran for Bombay, remarked: "I don't know what's going to happen here how" (32). Mr. Jaffrey working in *Tehran Times*, a Shia from Lucknow sums up his views to Naipaul: "All Muslim people tend to put their faith in one man. In the 1960s the Shah was loved. Now they love Khomeini, I never thought the time would come when Khomeini would usurp the position of Shah (33). However Khomeini did not step down after the revolution. As a result, the country was being ruled by the fanatics who led the country to chaos and disorder. For Jeffrey, a follower of Khomeini, Islam was the answer to every political need. He explains that their religion stands for four things: "Brotherhood, honesty, the will to work, proper recompense for labor" (34). When Naipaul queried why he should relate these four things to religion, Jaffrey replies: "all my life I've wanted to see the true *jame to whidi*. I translate that as "society of believers". Naipaul is however unable to rationalize the argument of Jaffrey regarding the rule of Ali, "the dream of the society ruled purely by faith":

> But Mr. Jaffrey's faith was profounder than the faith of the man from Bombay: for him the rule of Ali was more than getting women back into the veil. Mr. Jaffrey's society of believers derived from an idea of the earliest days of Islam, when the prophet handed down the divine laws, led his people in war and prayer when every action, however worldly, served the true faith. (34)

That was the kind of society Mr. Jaffrey desired for Iran. With his Indian-British education Mr. Jaffrey thought that "such a society would be secured by institutions: by getting the mullahs back into the mosques, getting Khomeini to stand down, and putting politicians and administrators into the administration" (34). In his opinion mosque and state were to be divided. However, Jeffery was locked into the contradiction because of his faith, education and political instinct. Such a dream society for Iran was dashed by Khomeini. However, *Tehran Times* was to be closed down for their differences with Khomeini ideas. On his return after six months Naipaul notes: "Six months later, when I went back to Tehran, that office was desolate" (35). Another magazine titled *The Message of Peace*, published from the holy city of QOM, tried to spread the Islamic ideas. It was against the technology of the West. Though technology was evil, some of it had been so Islamized that the foreign origin was no more questioned. The second issue of the magazine published an article, namely "Islamic Urban Planning" which interested Naipaul:

> Islam was a complete way of life; it didn't separate the worldly from the spiritual. Hence it was necessary, in addition to avoiding materialist industrial excess, to plan for a theocentric society. In this society women also had to be sheltered. Problems! But the very existence of these problems proved the need for sensible Islamic planning. And a solution was possible. (36)

This magazine further illustrates that the residential areas along with mosque, nursing, clinic, hospital, school, maternity homes, bazaars, workplaces and offices, recreation clubs and games, and all other amenities should be built within the reach of the people so that prayers could be conducted without using the amplifiers. Since cars, radios and televisions were necessary, they were considered neutral, and possessing them was considered "part of a proper Islamic pride" (37). But these things were considered neutral; they were not associated with any particular faith or civilization. They were thought of as the stock of some great universal bazaar. Naipaul's resentment against the revolution is obvious in his sarcastic comments on the materialistic aspects that continue the Iranian revolution:

> Money alone bought these things. And money in Iran had become the true gift of God, the reward for virtue.

> Whether Tehran worked or not, seventy million dollars went everyday to the country's external accounts, to be drawn off as required: foreign currencies secured by foreign laws and institutions to keep the Islamic revolution going. (37)

By spending, a lot of money Iran was moving towards Islamization. The election results showed that people voted as per the instructions of Khomeini to elect the mullahs and ayatollahs to the constitution-framing Assembly of Experts. All sorts of suppressions were conducted as per Islamic ideas. All pre-revolution projects for modernization of Iran were cancelled. The American construction company was divested of constructing the six-lane project and it was given to an Iranian contractor. The minister made provocative speeches against Israelis, the Arabs and the Kurds. The minister for social welfare pleaded that a mosque "was not only a place of worship but also 'a base for launching anti-colonialist movements in a display of unity, thought and action'. Unity: it was the theme of a big Friday Sabbath feature in the *Tehran Times* 'Why has Islam the potential for revolution?'" (39). The motto of Islamisation is that individualism should be sacrificed for unity: "Unity, union, the backs bowed in prayer that were like drills, the faith of one the faith of all, the faith of all flowing into the faith of one and becoming divine, personality and helplessness abolished: union, surrender, facelessness, heaven" (39). Naipaul sees that unity is necessary, but in the name of unity the people of Iran are befooling themselves: "What, after the centuries of despotism, they really believed that the state was something apart, something that looked after itself and was ever restored. And even while with their faith they were still pulling it all down—hotel, city, state—they were waiting for it to start up again, to be as it was before" (40). Naipaul observes that Iran, despite the revolution, is still going back to be under despotism curtailing the freedom of press and suppressing people by medieval Islamic law. Having experienced a lot of contradictions of Iranian society in Tehran, Naipaul goes to the holy city of QOM to know more about the believers under the guidance of Behzad, his Iranian interpreter.

The rigidity and cruelty of Islamisation are reflected in whipping people who break the fast in the holy city of QOM. Behzad suggested Naipaul to eat something failing which he would not get anything to eat till the break of fast:

> It was Ramadan, the month when Muslims fasted from sunrise to sunset; and in QOM, the city of mullahs and ayatollahs, it wasn't going to be possible to eat or drink. In some parts of the country—with the general Islamic excitement—people had been whipped for breaking the fast. (5)

Behzad was without a religious faith though as a revolutionary he welcomed the overthrow of Shah. He however did not want the religious revolution that came to Iran. His communist father did not send him to a mosque to be trained in the Islamic faith:

> Islam was a complicated religion. It wasn't philosophical or speculative. It was a revealed religion, with a Prophet and a complete set of rules. To believe, it was necessary to know a lot about the Arabian origins of the religion; and take this knowledge to heart. (7)

In Iran, Islam was further complicated because of its divergence from its main belief. This divergence traces back to the issue of succession to the Prophet and rooted in political-racial dispute when the Prophet died in 632 AD: "Islam almost from the start, had been on imperialism as well as a religion with an early history remarkably like a speeded-up version of the history of Rome, developing from city state to peninsular overlord to empire, with corresponding stresses at every stage" (8). Shia Islam in Iran was based on ancient animosities and personal revenge even after thousand years. It was necessary to know a special list of heroes, villains and martyrs for which one was to be instructed. He did not learn about these complicated divergences from his father who spoke him about the general poverty as he was a communist.

By interpreting some of the revolutionary posters on the walls of Tehran, Behzad tries to make Naipaul understand the revolutionary ideas. By explaining one poster he tells him how the revolutionaries have been waiting for the Twelfth Imam:

"The Twelfth Imam was the last of the Iranian line of succession to the Prophet. That line had ended over eleven hundred years ago. But the Twelfth Imam hadn't died; he served somewhere, waiting to return to earth. And his people were waiting for him; the Iranian revolution was an offering to him" (10). It was difficult for Naipaul to comprehend the ecstasy of the Iranian believers. Though it seemed irrational to think of the survival of the Imam for the last eleven hundred years, but it has been a matter of faith with the Muslims. Naipaul could slightly understand this Muslim passion when he realized that legendary facts were more than factual. The Ayatollah Khomeini who was in exile during the revolution "turned out to be nothing less than the interpreter, for Iranians, of God's will. By his emergence he annulled, or made trivial all previous protests about 'fascism' of the Shah" (11). The duplicity and authoritarianism of Khomeini were quite conspicuous when he became the interpreter of God's will:

> I must tell you that during the previous dictatorial regime, strikes and sit-ins pleased God. But now, when the government is a Muslim and a national one, the enemy is busy in plotting against us. And therefore staging strikes and sit-ins is religiously forbidden because they are against the principles of Islam. (11)

This radio talk in 1979, when Naipaul was in Iran, evidently focused on the hypocritical attitude of Khomeini who exploited the religious belief of the people to his own advantage to rule over Iran. Naipaul from his Trinidad experience could not consider Islamic doctrines to be attractive. In spite of his travels, he could not know much about Islam: "The glories of this religion were in the remote past; it had generated nothing like a Renaissance. Muslim countries, where not colonized, were despotisms; and nearly all, before oil, were poor" (13). Islam as a religion has many sects: the Arabs and the Persians, being different sects, have different lines of succession to the Prophet. Historically they were rivals, and hence hated each other. That is why Naipaul comments on the reaction of the women with the *chador* on the television: "It was only in Iran that I understood the point, the woman with the *chador* had made about Saudi

Arabia. It was a sectarian point and might have been thought too involved for a television audience..." (15).

In QOM, Naipaul was disappointed when he talked to some students who were studying Islamic theology for about six years. He queries: "What did they study in all that time? This was not a place of research and new learning. They were men of faith. What was there in the subject that called for so much study?" (52). It was true that they were learning a bit Arabic and logic along with Islamic jurisprudence, Islamic sciences and Islamic philosophy and so on. But Naipaul had not expected this way of learning: "I hadn't expected this organization of learning or this hint of antique classical methods. I began to understand that the years of study were necessary. Faith still absolutely bounded the world here. And, as in medieval Europe, there was no end to theological scholarship" (52). The much awaited meeting with Khalkhalli, the hanging judge of Khomeini, was a bitter experience of Naipaul. The man was a clown, ill-mannered and rough. He was having a farming background and became an ayatollah by self-study. Naipaul comments on his ill manners: "Even before we had put our shoes on and got to the gate, he and the African couple were sitting down to dinner. It was big dinner; the clown ate seriously" (63). Behzad, the interpreter to Naipaul in Iran, was a revolutionary who had his own idea of oppression and freedom. Two days after the visit to QOM he told Naipaul that there was no true freedom in the West: "The workers were oppressed, exchanging their labor for the barest necessities. True freedom had existed only once in the world, in Russia, between 1917 and 1953" (67). When Naipaul countered by saying that during that regime in Russia a lot of people were killed, he was enraged and argued: "He had no religious faith. But he had grown up in Shia Iran, and his idea of justice for the pure and the suffering was inseparable from the idea of punishment for the wicked. His dream of the reign of Stalin was a version of the dream of the rule of Ali—the Prophet's true successor" (67). Commenting on the prayers of Muslims during Ramadan in the holy city of Mashood Behzad tells Naipaul: "You know what they pray for? They pray for money, a job, a son" (76). After reaching Tehran station it was learnt that "there had been riots over the weekend, between Muslims and the people of the left, and the left had suffered badly" (89). On his last evening in Tehran Naipaul meets Behzad for a few minutes. He observes how Behzad along with his communist friends was suffering under the despotic rule of Khomeini in Islamic Republic of Iran:

> He (Behzad) was dark with sun burn. He had been standing with the dispossessed communists across the road from the sand-bags and the machine-guns. He was sad but calm. He had found his battle. I asked after his mother, who had come to Tehran and was staying with him. But—old constraints still—he said little about her; and he said nothing about the girl. (90)

Naipaul therefore comments on the situations in the Islamic Republic of Iran where Muslim-communist conflicts were often common: "Such emotion, such bravery; and unavoidably in Iran, his cause was as simple as his enemy's and in the end really no more than a version of his enemy's. Both sides depended on revealed truth and a special reading of historical events; both required absolute faith. And both were fed by the same passion: justice, union, vengeance" (90). In the Islamic republic, the inhuman face of governance is well marked in the judgment of Khalkhalli, Khomeini's Islamic judge who had sentenced forty-five people to death for their violation of Islamic law:

> In no time, moving swiftly from place to place in the August heat, he had sentenced forty-five people to death. He had studied for thirty-five years and was never at loss for an Islamic judgment. When in one Kurdish town the family of a prisoner complained that three of the prisoner's teeth had been removed and his eyes gouged out, Khalkhalli ordered a similar punishment for the torture. Three of the men's teeth were torn out on the spot. The aggrieved family then relented, pardoned the offender, and let him keep his eyes. (91-92)

This was Islamic justice in Iran. This brutality under Khomeini was prevailing because of the faith in God. This kind of justice was administered because of the Will of God. This was sheer inhumanity: "It was Islamic justice, swift, personal, satisfying; it met the simple needs of the faithful" (92). But this side of the revolution was never reported in the media. People only read: "Down with fascist Shah". It was simply obsession of Khomeini to take revenge of his father's death by hanging the people in the Islamic republic:

> Only Iranians, and some foreign scholars, knew that when Khomeini was a child—while the Qajar kings still ruled in Iran—Khomeini's father had been killed by a government official; that the killer had been publicly hanged; that Khomeini had been taken by his mother to the hanging and told afterwards "Now be at peace. The wolf has attained the fruit of its evil deeds. (92)

The Islamic bigot Khomeini would argue that Islam was not a lesser religion. The government of the world should know that Islam cannot be defeated. Islam would defeat all the countries of the world, and the teachings of Koran would prevail. Khomeini twists his argument against the intellectuals by applying the logic and rhetoric taught at QOM:

> When democrats talk about freedom, they are inspired by the superpowers. They want to lead our youth to places of corruption.... If that is what they want, then yes, we are reactionaries. You who want prostitution and freedom in every matter are intellectuals. You consider corrupt morality as freedom, prostitution as freedom.... Those who want freedom want the freedom to have bars, brothels, casinos, opium. But we want our youth to carve out a new period in history. We do not want intellectuals. (92-93)

Khomeini did not want intellectuals because they could challenge his authority, his inhuman way of administering Islamic justice. He only wanted the *believers*, the faithful who would not protest; they would simply follow their ruler, the interpreter of God's Will. In Behzad's description, these believers are the *lumpen*. Before going to Pakistan, Naipaul made his final judgment of Khomeini and his manipulation of faith to rule the people of Iran:

> He required only faith. But he also knew the value of Iran's oil to countries that lived by machines, and he could send the phantoms and the tanks against the Kurds. Interpreter of God's Will, leader of the faithful, he expressed all the confusion of his people and made it appear like glory, like the familiar faith: the confusion of a people of high medieval culture awakening to oil and money, a sense of power and violation, and knowledge of a great new encircling civilization. That civilization could not be mastered. It was to be rejected; at the same time it was to be depended on. (93)

With this dilemma Naipaul proceeded to Pakistan to see another society of *believers*, the Muslim converts who practiced Islam in their day-to-day lives. Naipaul flew to Pakistan to know how Islam was in action there. With the advent of the Rule of Ali, Iran had been disintegrated. In the same way, Pakistan could be seen as "a fragmented country, economically stagnant, despotically ruled, with its gifted people close to hysteria. But Pakistan was also the country that had been founded more than thirty years before as a homeland for the Muslims of India, and for that reason was to be cherished as a pioneer of the Islamic revival" (97). The *Tehran Times* establishes a linkage between Iran and Pakistan as the countries of faith:

> The history of Pakistan and the Islamic Revolution in Iran is a reminder of the power of religion and the hollowness of secular cults. How the world works is the concern of society, and how society is to be governed is the affair of politicians, but the whole thing means is the main concern of Iran and Pakistan. Politics is combined with religion in Islam. Iran and Pakistan can join hands to prove to the world that Islam is not just a faith of the past, practicing ancient rituals. (97)

While making such comments the writer has ignored that both countries are lacking in science, the ability to run a twentieth-century state, and intellectual vigor. To him, honoring the faith was above everything. It was necessary for the writer to analyze the history of Pakistan: the uprooting and mass-migrations after the partition in 1947; the absence of the representative government; the land of faith turning into a land of plunder; the growth of regionalism; rule by the army in 1958; the bloody secession of far off Bangladesh in 1971. Naipaul therefore points out the flaws in the argument of the article:

> There was no hint in the article that the army ruled once again in Pakistan, that there was martial law once again; no hint that Mr. Bhutto, the country's only elected Prime Minister, deposed by the army in 1977, arrested on a murder charge, tried and sentenced to death, had been hanged after nineteen months in jail; no hint that this hanging, just four months old, had shocked, demoralized and further divided the country. All this history, all this secular failure and pain, had been conjured away by the logic of faith. (98)

Though both Iran and Pakistan are governed by Islamic faith, Pakistan is poorer than the oil-rich Iran. Despite its poverty it was less concerned for the poor than possessing an Islamic bomb:

> In Iran you felt, in spite of all that was said about the wickedness of the Shah, that the money had gone down far. Money, and the foreign goods and tools that it bought, gave an illusion of Islamic power. Seventy million unearned dollars a day kept the idle country on the boil, and fed the idea of the revolution. In Pakistan poverty had the same effect. The tensions of poverty and political distress merged with the tensions of the death. Thirty-two years after its founding as a religious state, an Indian Muslim homeland, Pakistan remained on the boil, and Islam was still an issue: failure led back again and again to the assertion of the faith. (100-01)

Reflecting upon the contemporary situations in Pakistan, Naipaul goes back to the history of the origin of Pakistan as an Islamic state. In 1930, Sir Mohammed Iqbal (1876-1938), a revered poet, in his speech to the All-India Muslim League argued that Islam, besides being an ethical ideal, was also a kind of polity. He further explained that the nature of Holy Prophet's religious experience described in the Koran should be considered.

Acceptance of Islamic religion results in acceptance of certain "legal concepts" which are revelatory with civic significance. The religious ideal of Islam, therefore, is organically related to the social order which it has created. The rejection of the one will eventually involve the rejection of the other. If the construction of a polity on national lines means a displacement of the Islamic principle of solidarity, it is simply unthinkable to a Muslim. The Muslims of India need a Muslim state because "India is perhaps the only country in the world where Islam, as a people-building force, has worked at its best" (102). Seven years later when such a state was carved out of undivided India, there was a communal holocaust in the border areas resulting in the death of millions of people and some millions becoming homeless. It was therefore proved that the plan of creating Pakistan was a terrible flaw. Reflecting on the post-partition history of Pakistan Naipaul understands that the armed forces flourished in the new Islamic state. These armed forces, as a well-organized group became masters, a country within country. The state failed because the people failed the faith. A quest was therefore for a purer faith:

> And in the quest of the Islamic absolute—the society of the believers, where every action was instinct with worship—men lost sight of the political origins of their state. They forgot the secular ambitions of Mr. Jinnah, the state's political founder, who (less philosophical than Iqbal) wanted only a state where Muslims wouldn't be swamped by non-Muslims. Even Iqbal was laid aside. Extraordinary claims began to be made for Pakistan: it was founded as the land of the pure; it was to be the first truly Islamic state since the days of the Prophet and his close companions. (103)

But the contemporary situation proves that Pakistan state is a failure. Naipaul's encounter with a civil servant during his journey shows that the civil servant has been completely disillusioned. He argues that the Muslim polity should have arisen naturally out of the faith. The feeling that Pakistan was God should have taken the country to the heights. However, the bad people of Pakistan didn't live up to the faith. The taxi driver in Karachi sea-beach was disgusted with the falsehood of Pakistani Muslims. He did not fast because he was angry with God: "Muslim people are bad. They lie too much. Too much lies from Muslim people. It is a sad story. I will not tell you about it" (110). Later on Naipaul understands his sad story when the driver's religious emotions are aroused near the mosques: "Like the pilgrims, my driver had moved from passion to calm. And his religious emotions had risen on a contrary curve, after the mosques, Mr. Jinnah's impressive white tomb, and the pilgrim centre. From being angry with God, and an indifferent Muslim, he had become at the end as passionate and secure a Muslim as any" (112-13). That is where his sad story lies:

> I believed that his father had risen fast in Mr. Bhutto's time, had risen to being the near neighbor of an Arabian king, but had lost everything with Mr. Bhutto's fall and had in some manner been put away: a peasant drama, the small change of Mr. Bhutto's tragedy, part of the thuggish public life of the Muslim Polity, where in practice the only morality (and also the eternal balm) was the possession of the faith. (113)

Since the faith in God alone cannot improve the economy, Pakistan was dragged into economic crisis because it could not meet the requirements of the poor, the marginalized sections who were to be exported to different countries such as Arabia, the Gulf states, Libya (Muslim country), Canada, United States, and many countries of Europe to earn their livelihood. These emigrant workers were to emulate some aspects of the alien civilizations whose virtues were not acceptable to them in their Islamic homeland. The idea of the Muslim state as God could not convert itself into political and economic organization. People suffered, and thus migrated for their survival. Pakistan therefore became a remittance economy. People's faith could not save them from their miseries:

> The dream of the Muslim homeland had had strange consequences. And strangest of all was this: the state which had appeared to some as God itself, a complete earthly record for the faithful, lived not so much by its agricultural exports or by the proceeds of its minor,

> secondary industries, as by the export of its people. The news paper advertisements called it "manpower-export". (114-15)

The migrants were to suffer a lot outside their Islamic homeland. They were at the mercy of civil liberties organization and very often "sought protection of the laws of the countries" where they landed down: "They or their representatives spoke correct words about the difference between poor countries and rich, south and North. They spoke of the crime of racial discrimination and the brotherhood of man. They appealed to the ideals of the alien civilizations whose virtue they denied at home" (115). However, people at home did not change their stand. They wished to establish that Islam, in full conformity with Holy Koran through reformation and adaptation with clarity of purpose, is a complete way of life. In the Muslim world Pakistan was considered the twentieth-century Islamic pioneer, "experimenting with Islamic law, with a Koranic alms-levy that would eventually sustain an Islamic welfare state, and with a banking system that would do away with interest" (117). In his search for knowing Islam in action Naipaul meets the Govt. Information officer Mr. Deien and his colleague Mr. Sherwani who suggest him to meet the pilgrims going to Mecca in the night of Ramadan. There is some difference in the celebration of Ramadan between Iran Shias and Pakistani Sunnis: "In Shia Iran Ramadan was a month of mourning, full of the calamities of the Shia heroes who had failed to be recognized as the Prophet's successors. For the Sunni Muslims of Pakistan, Ramadan was a happier month, the month of revelation and the foundation of the religion" (120). Visiting mosques in different areas, Naipaul saw that, "men were separate, engaged in private devotions" (121) in the better-off areas whereas in the poorer areas, there was a feeling of community: "Islam was each man's salvation, it was also the faith itself, the Prophet's story; it was also the community, stitched together by innumerable communal acts and occasions. Unity, faith, and discipline that was the theme of Islam" (121). Ahmad, a Govt. official who had warmth of relationship with him, told Naipaul: "The beauty of Islam lay in its mixture of law and compassion. To see Islam at its best, to understand the charity of which it was capable, I should go to some of the old shrines interior of Sind—he would arrange it" (127-28). Naipaul banked on Ahmad during his search for truth about Islam. Interviewing Mr. Mirza, considered to be one of the distinguished personalities of Pakistan, Naipaul understands that he had high political ambitions during the Islamization of institutions during martial rule: "But in Islam, you see, there is no separation. It's a complete way of life" (130). Mr. Salahuddin, the newspaper editor, dreams for the early Islamic state in Pakistan when Muslims would be guided by divine rules: "a fusion of history and theology, the indestructible alloy of faith" (131). That would result in Muslims living in purity. Khalid Ishaq, one of the leading lawyers of Karachi, a member of the Islamic Ideology council, and a member of a government commission inquiring corruption, was passionate for his faith: "Islam, I felt, was more than a private belief for him; to him, a Muslim from the subcontinent still insecure in Pakistan, Islam was his civilization and culture; it was fundamental to his idea of what he was; it was something, as a man and a lawyer, he had to serve and protect" (133).

To Ishaq, Muslims of Pakistan reject all that are Western. All westernized institutions are to be replaced by Islamic institutions—"institutions not of the west and not socialist, but institutions in keeping with people's emotional needs" (134). The Islamic enterprise is based on Koran as a guide of "a state mechanism that would function in the modern world and would be unlike anything else that had evolved" (134). He considered it a high intellectual enterprise for which Pakistan had neither talent nor resources. Naipaul however understood through interaction with Mr. Deen that "the great Islamic enterprise of Pakistan existed, but only as an ideal, at once an expression of the political insecurity in which Muslims lived in the Muslim homeland" (135). When Naipaul put Ahmad to Khalid Ishaq's views about emotional rejection of the West by Pakistani people, Ahmad explained: "The world is mixed up now. People are confused. There is no longer any symmetry in many people's lives" (138). As to question of faith Ahmad's doctor son in his twenties replies: "In the beginning men worshipped stones.

Then fire. Today we find those practices funny. Wouldn't men tomorrow find the practices of today funny?" (139). Ahmad's disapproval of Pakistan as a state was conspicuous: "They (Muslims) hated the foreigners and they hated the Hindus. So the country of Pakistan was built on hate and nothing else. The people here weren't ready for Pakistan, and people who don't deserve shouldn't demand" (140). Ahmad believed that "People were turning to Islam because everything else had failed. Even at the Universities the Islamic wave was swamping academic life" (141). Naipaul elicited a response from Ahmad putting the following queries: "Couldn't people now accept that they were Muslims in a Muslim country, and that Pakistan was what the faith had made of it? Did it make sense—after the centuries of Islamic history—to say that Islam hadn't been tried" (142). Ahmad however asserted that Islam had never been tried. Ahmad's dilemma is related to rethinking of creation of a Muslim state. It reflects the broken dreams of millions of Pakistanis. So, the people of Pakistan feel that they are still strangers in their Muslim homeland. Sometimes they feel dispossessed or threatened with dispossession. History in history textbooks in Pakistan is distorted to suit to false Muslim sentiments to arouse hatred towards Hindus and India. Before Mohammed, there was darkness, evil and slavery. With Mohammed, there is light. There is neither slavery nor exploitation. But this is far from truth. Still people suffer, there are slaves, poor people live with misery and degradation: "Faith begins to nullify or overlay the real world" (165). Military rule is continuing in Pakistan. The democratic activities are banned. Fundamentalism has stiffed the intellectual activities in the universities. Political parties have been banned. There is no development in industry and science. The economy is a remittance economy. There is large-scale immigration. But still the sixth class students in their social studies textbook read: "Conditions (caste system and other evils) in India are much the same to this day. But we are a democratic country. Here everyone is free to adopt the occupation of his choice. This is the secret of our progress" (165). In 1980, Naipaul's portrayal of plights of the people of the Islamic Nation of Pakistan is understandable. This is based on authentic observation.

In Pakistan the rule of law inherited from the British has been undone due to Islamic striving. As per Islamic rules, theft, drinking, illicit sex and rape are incurring severe punishments including "stoning to death", public whipping and so on. Naipaul is however surprised to know about them only after seven months of his stay:

> But if I hadn't so far been aware of these laws, it was because in the seven months they had been in force they hadn't been applied. One case had caused a scandal. A pir or holy man in provincial town had been charged with raping the thirteen-year-old daughter of one of his followers. The case against him couldn't get far in the sessions court because the new Islamic law under which he was tried required four eye-witnesses to the act. (191)

The requirement of four witnesses is irrational and impracticable. The reference to the Koran in such a case is not desirable at all: "It was easy to state the Koranic punishment; it was another matter to work out law. To work out law, with only the historical, geographical and cultural...particularities of the Koran as a guide, was to become entangled in textual-religious-sectarian disputes of this kind, and very quickly to get away from the idea of equity" (191-92). Quoting *Pakistan Times* Naipaul writes that the mullahs are responsible for such laws which are not workable by the government. These mullahs have "divided Islam into conflicting sects and made Islam a mockery. It is necessary to by-pass the mullahs, abolish the sects and refer to the holy book. Then only would there be light and enlightenment to remove darkness and confusion. An inclination towards fundamentalism implies a decay of the civilization that needs to be recreated. The intellectuals should assist that recreation. However, the claim of the fundamentalists that Islam is a complete way of life is also true of other religions like Hinduism, Buddhism or lesser tribal faiths in which in the early stage of their history there were "complete cultures, self-contained and more or less isolated, with institutions, manners and beliefs making a whole" (193). The Islamic fundamentalists wish to go back to such a whole "with the tool of faith alone—beliefs, religious practices and rituals" (193). However Naipaul argues that such a whole through faith without intellectual rationalization is meaningless as it can never make the society progressive, need-based, practical and useful:

> It is like a wish—with intellect suppressed or limited, the historical sense falsified—to work back from the abstract to the concrete, and to set up the tribal walls again. It is to seek to recreate something like a tribal or a city state that—except in theological fantasy—never was. The Koran was not the statute-book of a settled golden age; it is the mystical or oracular record of an extended upheaval, widening out from the prophet to his tribe to Arabia. Arabia was full of movement; Islam with all its Jewish and Christian elements was always mixed, eclectic, developing. (139)

It is therefore not desirable to reject the necessary things of the West in the name of Islam. What is important in the contemporary society is to look forward through intellectual freedom. The emotional rejection of the West—its science, machines, medicines and other technological tools—cannot help in uplifting the miseries of the common people. It will rather perpetuate their misfortunes. Attacking the attitude of the contemporary patron saint of Pakistan, Maulana Maudoodi, Naipaul believes that he was a man without any intellectual vision who "campaigned for Islamic laws without stating what these laws should be" (194). The same Maulana, who rejected the Western civilization and tried to keep his people from its enlightenment in his life, finally went to Boston for his own medical treatment: "...he had at the very end entrusted himself to the skill and science of the civilization he had tried to shield his followers from. He had sought...to reap where he had not wanted his people to sow" (194). Naipaul also sees people like Syed; the doctor's son has real concern for basics in his poetry. Despite his "fumbling response to the universal civilization", Naipaul "could see how Islamic fervor could become creative, revolutionary, and take men on to a humanism beyond religious doctrine: a true renaissance open to the new and enriched by it, as the Muslims in their early days of glory had been" (205). Naipaul therefore argues that fundamentalism, negativity, cannot prevent other good things to let in to make a progressive world:

> The fundamentalists, insecure, with their unhistorical view, feared alien contamination. But fundamentalism offered nothing. It pushed men to unappeasable faith; it offered a political desert. It violated the "basics"; it could never wall out the rest of the world. And I thought it was possible, looking not many steps ahead, to see how in Pakistan, by the very excesses of fundamentalism, Islam might be preparing its own transformation. (205-06)

The people of Pakistan should be more emphatic on the development of the country rather than emphasizing medieval Islamic adventures. While driving through the Kaghan valley Naipaul is moved to see the camp life of the different tribes who just live on with all the miseries in a desert valley: "I felt taken back to beginning: that life of animals and tents and the daily march. But what to me was the impulse of the moment was for them a way of life. I would move on, do other things; they would continue as I saw them And those girls, pretty as they were, with their lovely skins, were really far away, shut off in their own tribal fantasies, beauties now, well fed, conscious of their rising price but soon to be wives and workers" (217). Naipaul's descriptions about these poor tribal people are quite heart-touching:

> These women, wives, were workers; they were beasts of burden. Like the women of the Dakota Indians of Parkman saw on the Oregon trail in 1846. But these Afghans and all these mountain tribes lived in terrain which only they could master. No one could say of them, as Parkman could say of the Dakota Indians, that they were going to be wiped off the face of the earth. (216)

While on their return journey, Naipaul was thinking about the poor, neglected people on the roadside. The reaction of the driver to the attitude of the religiously bigot Maulanas of Pakistan is worth mentioning: "These maulanas...are using

Islam as a tool. We are all Muslims. We are not Muslims in their way. They want to destroy Pakistan. Our Islam is better. We are the only people who can save Islam and Pakistan" (230). Even Masood, the student-guide to Naipaul agrees with him. These Maulanas take the country backward. They only refer to Islam for everything without bothering for the development of the country taking the contemporary realities into account. Masood, who was one of the five best students of the University doing a Ph.D., is not finding a job due to corruption and lack of proper planning to move the country forward. Masood and his father, who had migrated from India in 1947 to a Muslim state, are completely disillusioned about the mess in the affairs of Pakistan: Listening to so many stories of people, Naipaul is really touched. He questioned himself what would happen to these unfortunate low class people in the Muslim state of Pakistan. He thought how these beliefs in Islam could save these workers, the herdsmen from their suffering:

> The Pakistan Govt. was unable to tackle the multiple social and economic problems for which there was severe crisis in the administration. Due to economic crisis, the press reported that there would be no salary rise, and there would not be any Govt. jobs for some time. Six ministries were wound up. Many officials were dismissed for corruption. The families of officials, who lost jobs, appealed to the Govt. to provide alternative jobs to save them from mental agony and starvation. Due to objections to issue no-objection certificates to the teachers, they could not go to Oman in south-east Arabia. So the Pakistan society was now on the brink of collapse, disorder and chaos. There was no discipline and stability among the people. The *Pakistan Times* therefore reported:
>
> It is now openly acknowledged that ours is a corrupt society, practicing every conceivable social evil imaginable. Children growing up in a domestic atmosphere where smuggling, black-marketing, hoarding, bribery and corruption...are indulged in quite blatantly, should not be expected to accept discipline in

> any form. When these children go to the educational institutions, they naturally try to project the home atmosphere there.... The solution was a greater firmness, "an iron hand in the schools (no politics to be allowed there) and in the courts. "Imprisonment, flogging" and even capital punishment will do the needful. (236-37)

A.H. Kardar, the former cricket captain of Pakistan, in an article in *The Muslim* wrote: "We look back in shame and anger at the utter lack of homework and preparedness of political leaders and administrators *vis-à-vis* economic issues...shame and anger as the ever-increasing shipload of imports of food grains..." (237). However, he was unable to give any concrete solutions. Pakistan, the Muslim state run by Muslim beliefs referring to Koran, was now facing serious economic crisis. The Govt. was unable to fight poverty, disease and starvation. Lack of intellectual strength and a concrete vision dragged the country to the brink of disaster. The Maulanas could only refer to God's Will, what the Prophet had said. They could not tell the Govt. how to frame the economic policy to produce more food grains and industrial requirement of the country. Lack of human resources in the field of Science and Technology would further deteriorate the condition of the country. Merely by rejecting Western things and education; the country might be facing more and more disasters. Pakistan must have to realize the hard realities of life and try to solve them depending on the contingency of the contemporary situations.

From Pakistan Naipaul moved to Malaysia to see "Islam in action". Religion came to the south-east Asia from the Indo-Pakistan subcontinent. The merchants and priests spread the Indian religions to these regions. Before Islam, Hinduism and Buddhism spread over there. These priests and merchants played great roles in taking Islam to Indonesia and Malaysia during the fourteenth or fifteenth century. When Islam went to south-east Asia as an Indian religion, there was no bloodshed, no slaughter, no loot and no devastation as in the case of Arab invasion of Sind. Naipaul traces the origin of Islam in this region:

> Islam went to south-east Asia as another religion of India. There was no Arab invasion, as in Sind, no systematic slaughter of the local warrior caste, no planting of Arab military colonies, no sharing out of loot, and no sending back of treasure and slaves to a Caliph in Iraq or Syria; no tribute, no taxes on unbelievers. There was no calamity, no overnight abrogation of settled world-order. (261)

Islam came here as an idea. In this region Islam was therefore a divinely sanctioned code which was mingled with older ideas. Thus it was an idea—"a Prophet, a divine revelation, heaven and hell" (261). The most passionate Islamic missionaries from the Indian subcontinent, especially from Pakistan, still come here to purify that mixed religion. These missionaries come with a special Muslim passion of the sub-continent to tell the other Muslims there that they are still "a threatened minority". They tell that they feel themselves on the margin of the true Muslim world: "The Persian distance from Arabia created the Shah faith and the Persian conviction that they are islamically purer than the Arabs. The Indian Muslim distance from Arabia is greater than the Persian; and that passion is as fierce or fiercer" (262). The subcontinent's passionate missionaries do not tell about the negativity that exists in Pakistan because they think the events related to the negativity are quite different from Islam: "They do not bring news of military rule, the remittance economy, the loss of law, the tragedy of the Bihari Muslims now wanted neither by Bangladesh nor by Pakistan. These events are separate from Islam, and these men bring news only of Islam and the enemies of Islam" (261). Naipaul is perhaps mocking at the vision of these missionaries to change the world after a four-day tent life of mass-prayers in the waterlogged desert of Punjab:

> Every Muslim is a missionary for Islam: that was the idea of the brotherhood assembled in the waterlogged desert of the Punjab. And after four days of tent life, of mass prayers, the simple men go out intoxicated by their vision of a world about to change. Some go to Malaysia; they have been going for years; and now their passion finds a response. (262)

Reflecting on the contemporary situation in Malaysia, Naipaul understands that the young generations of Malays, the Islamic revolutionaries, are the descendants of "simpler Malays, people of river and forest, half Muslims, half animist" (262). These young revolutionaries "have emerged after the colonial cycle, after independence, after money" (263). With the resources like tin, rubber, palm oil, oil, Malaysia has become rich and created "a whole educated generation of village people and drawn them into the civilization that once approached to be only on the outer edge of darkness but is now universal" (263). These young educated people understand that the present Malaysia has grown on the colonial foundations and is a British-Chinese creation. The British developed the mines and plantations, and brought in the diligent, rootless Chinese peasants and a lesser number of Indians, to do the work the Malays couldn't do. Later when the Chinese were advanced, they were prevented from the political power. The Malays therefore ruled the country:

> The country is officially Muslim, with Muslim Personal Laws; sexual relations between Muslims and non-Muslims are illegal and there is a kind of prying religious police; legal discriminations against non-Muslims are outrageous. But the Malays who rule are established, or of old royal families who crossed over into the new world some generations ago. (263)

The changes that money, development and education have brought have enraged the pastoral populace of Malay. However, these people have a new weapon in Islam which is their way of getting even with the world: "It serves their grief, their feeling of inadequacy, their social rage and racial hate" (264). This new Islam is an alternative kind of learning for the new men of the village. It is a passion without any constructive programme. The young generation hopes for a transformation in their country: "The materialistic world is to be pulled down first; the Islamic state will come later—as in Iran, as in Pakistan" (264). This "Malaysian disease" of new Islam's message spreads over to Indonesia. This new Islamic movement is considered to be nihilistic by its opponents. In order to know the new Muslim world of Malaysia, Naipaul met Anwar Ibrahim, the leader of ABIM, the most important and the most organized Muslim youth group and another organizer, Shafi, 32 years old, who lamented the modernization of Malaysia. Anwar was a visionary who had contact with the Muslim movements in Indonesia, Bangladesh, Pakistan and Iran. To him, " Islam was the energizer and purifier that was needed in Malaysia; true Islam awakened people, especially Malays, and at the same time it saved them from the corruption from the racialist politics of Malaysia, the shabbiness of the money culture and easy western imitation" (269). His grand view of Islam gave him security and confidence. As a man of travel with vision, he did not approve of the "'faddishness' of some Malaysian Muslim groups, their religious and political simplicities" (270). He was still in "the consccientization stage" about the economic side of things: "he genuinely believed that an Islamic economic system was something he might one day bring over from a place like Pakistan" (270). Since he was at the centre of all ABIM activities, he sent Shafi to accompany Naipaul to see Malaysia, its changes towards modernization and how Shafi reacted to such changes. Initial encounters with Shafi made Naipaul think about Shafi's resentment against the wastefulness of city life with its thrust on the changes towards modernization: "And I never became reconciled to the difference between the man who was talking to me—intelligent, self-possessed, scholarly-looking—and the slack village life he said he came out of and longed to go back" (270-71). Shafi's rejection of the world which had released his intelligence makes Naipaul reflective on this: "It would not have been easy for him to separate the past of himself that was purely traditional or instinctive from the part for which he alone was responsible. And his village has changed; and Malaysia had changed; and the world had changed" (271). The Malays, sons of soil, were given preferences for improvement of their economic development so that they might rise to the level of the Chinese. This method was however ineffectual which only created a favored class of Malay "front men". It was against this kind of racialism that Anwar Ibrahim and ABIM campaigned, setting up against it a vision of a purer Islamic way. The Muslim dominance in Malay is conspicuous:

> Only half the population was Muslim; but everyone had to make his obeisance to Islam. The pressures came from below: a movement of purification and cleansing but also a racial movement. It made for a general nervousness. It made people hide from the visitor for fear that they might be betrayed. It led oddly in this land of rain and steam of forest—to the atmosphere of ideological state. (273)

Naipaul's encounter with Shafi brought out so much knowledge about Malays. The Malay Muslim world is rotten by religious education, which prescribes strict rules and regulations. The backwardness of Malays is due to too much emphasis on Islamic law and more and more guidance by Mullahs. In a changing world, it is necessary to cope with the new ideas, scientific understanding and technological skills which can help the society to move in the path of progress. Shafi's argument is that the so-called progressive ideas lead people to moral lapses. They also drive them from humanitarian aspects of life and destabilize a society which has been based on human values of sanctity and peace. But then in his unconsciousness he also feels that there is necessity to have a road, good school and a bridge which put them in a quite advantageous situation. Even the Mullahs, who lack vision, skills and intellectuality due to their too much dependence on the outdated Islamic laws, are appreciative to the technical wonders that have changed the world so rapidly. Naipaul understands Shafi well—his confusions and inconsistency. Naipaul understands that Shafi's old world has been losing ground and moving towards a new world-order of progress and modernity. Naipaul therefore sums of Shafi's mental horizon: "And he was nagged by the inconsistency—as it had come out in our conversation—between his longing for the purity of village life and his recognition of the backwardness of Malays. Deep down he felt—he knew—that there was no inconsistency, no flaw; but he couldn't find the words to express that" (280). Shafi's village rule-books, approved by Islamic tradition and permitted by the Koran, were consulted for everything. This simple village-life was therefore a rigid life: "It had rules for every-thing; and everyone had to learn the rules" (290). Shafi's longing for the lost world of paradise is understandable in his conviction for Islamic vision. Naipaul therefore brings out a comparison between the Pakistani fundamentalists and Shafi's sense of loss, and brings out a difference in their shift of emphasis to Islamic faith:

> In Pakistan the fundamentalists believed that to follow the right rules was to bring about again the purity of the early Islamic way: the reorganization of the world followed automatically on the rediscovery of the true faith. Shafi's grief and passion, in multi-racial Malaysia, were more immediate; and I felt that for him the wish to reestablish the rules was also a wish to recreate the security of the childhood, the Malay village life he had lost. (281)

The brave girls in ABIM School were trained to have racial hatred towards the Chinese who were more competitive in their business acumen. The Malay Muslims were unable to compete with them. Unless someone was ethnic Malay even from Java or Indonesia, he could not be a Malaysian. The Chinese, despite staying in Malaysia for about 100 years, they were still considered immigrants. Naipaul thus remarks with disapproval: "To be Malay was to be Muslim—it was written in the laws of the new state. But the Malay was also to be denied the great rich British-Chinese city, where everything happened. Money had come to the tropical land of forest and river and villages: and money created now frenzies and frustrations" (293). Money, modernity and materialistic civilization have changed the world. They have invaded pastoralism by emphasizing industrialization. The paradox of this modernization is that it brings both good things and corrupt immoral practices. This is the dilemma, the contradiction in modernist mechanical civilization. In Malaysia the Hindu Tamils were a minority whose temples were always in attack. The Malay Muslims smashed their idols in the temple. There was a mutual hatred towards each other. The Tamil taxi-driver tells Naipaul that the Malay Muslims stab from the back. So, ethic conflict is a great problem in Malaysia. Naipaul understands that Malaysia has become a rich nation with tin, rubber, oil and palm-oil. However, the skills of people are not developed. They remained buyers of imported goods fixings the "country in a dependent relationship with the developed world, kept all men colonial" (308). Naipaul is therefore critical of Islamic faith that is not capable of lifting the country's technical strength: "It was possible to understand the withdrawal of someone like Shafi, the rage of the idol-smashers; and the wish, among the other Malays, to pretend that they were Arabs, living as purely as in the days of the Prophet" (308). It is already referred to the grief of Shafi for the lost village life. It is a kind of nostalgia. Despite his longing for past, Shafi had only been changed, not his village men:

> But that life—of community, old ways and peace—still existed for these men, in spite of the cars and the new kinds of job. It was Shafi who had changed. The Islam of these men was part of their contentment. Shafi's Islam—Islam the energizer and purifier of Malays, the destroyer of false ways and false longings—was revolutionary, serving no cause these men could understand. (326)

To Mohammed, a University teacher for many years, Islam was everything. He thinks that through Islam everything could be restructured:

> Malaysia—with its painful problems: the casualness of the Malays, the energy of the Chinese, the racial politics, the corruption of the new money, the technological dependence of the small, uneducated country—vanished, became an obstruction itself, a land of pure belief, of total submission to Allah. In that submission everything was solved. (333)

To Naipaul, Mohammed had no real intellectual vision. He had not any concrete ideas to his credit. He depended on other's ideas. He just criticized the Western ideas and systems—its vice and lust, alcohol and women, wild parties and tempting surroundings. His belief system was an "abstract system" called for the worship of Allah, no corruption, protection of women, "moral leanings" and so on. In his political system, he had only one thing to suggest: Malaysia should have a ruler like Khomeini of Iran, who was representative of God. Naipaul therefore rightly lashes at his bankruptcy of vision: "He had no idea of reform or any ameliorate process. He didn't deal in concrete. He wished only the world to be remade and repossessed as suddenly as.... It had been taken away from him. This was the promise of his Islam" (334). The University intellectual was therefore having no sense of history. He had no awareness for development of Malaysia. Even if, the Muslim world had been ravaged by bad news—gun battle in the mosque of Mecca, death of Mecca pilgrims in plane crash, imposition of Martial Law in Pakistan and torture of people and journalists there, seizure of American embassy in Iran and so on; but Mohammad and Abdullah were not to believe in bad news from the lands of faith.

Naipaul observes that Shafi did not bother to know about his country, its history: "At school, he was not interested in history. And now there wasn't time for learning or reading: there was his work for the movement. The rich past of his people remained closed to him: Hinduism, Buddhism, animist belief" (338). Shafi was therefore interested in his faith, to be an abstract man and to exist in limbo. As Malay, his only objective was to have faith, nothing else. To be a civilized man, one should know where he came from and where he was going to. And this was not a matter of history for him. It was rather a matter of correct religion and belief. He thought, "Everything flowed from the true faith. Out of his love for his Malay people, his wish to put the world right for them, he wished them to be as cleansed as he thought he was. That was the great task he had set himself" (338).

After his observation of "Islam in action" in Malaysia, Naipaul moved to Indonesia to see how the believers lived in their own world of faith, and how this attitude of the believers affected the functioning of the government and society there. In Indonesia, the army was ruling by this time and according to Shafi, the army was very much harsh to the Muslim movement in Indonesia. Although Indonesia, like Malaysia, was a Muslim country, there was a lot of difference in different aspects of life in the former:

> But the pre-Islamic past, that in Malaysia seemed to be only a matter of village customs, in Indonesia—or

> Java—showed as a great civilization. Islam, which had come only in the fifteenth century, was the formal faith. But the Hindu-Buddhist past that had lasted for 1400 years before that survived in many ways—half erased, slightly mysterious, but still awesome, like Borobudur itself. And it was this past which gave Indonesians—or Javanese—the feeling of their uniqueness. (347)

The recent Indonesian history might refer to the rule of Sunkarno who fought against the Dutch rulers with the help of Japanese army. However towards the end of his twenty years of presidency there was decline in his popularity for which the army deposed him by 1965, and took over the reign for about 15 years when Naipaul was there in Indonesia. Though the army rule brought stability and growth, there was much restlessness in the country: "The restless was expressed by the new Islam, the Islam that is more than ritual, that speak of injustices done to Allah's creatures and of the satanic ways of worldly governments: the Islam that makes people withdraw, the more violently to leap forward" (348). Naipaul wonders how the ruler managed in the recent past in Indonesia when the country had "so little to hold on to in the way of law or country" because the ruler was subject to so many assaults. Islam was the dominating faith of the people. However in the under current, there were the impulses of the older words, relics of the Hindu-Buddhist-animist past, but no longer part of a system. In Indonesia, the society has been transformed with the growth and industry, learning, peace and new technological civilization. Reflecting on Indonesia's recent history and contemporary situation, Naipaul questions himself how after the dizzying history of the last fifty years, the world had grown strange and people floated: "Whether they moved forward, into the new civilization, or back, like Suryadi's daughter, towards the purer Arab faith, they were now always entering somebody else's world, and getting further from themselves" (354).

While knowing about recent history of Indonesia from the famous poet Sitor who had been imprisoned by the army during 1965-1975 for his Sukarno connection, Naipaul came into contact with Adi Sassoon who told him to visit traditional

Islamic village schools, namely *pesantrens*. The business associate therefore planned the journeys to Yogyakarta to see a modern school and Surabaya to see a very old one: "These village *Pesantrens* preserved the harmony between community and school, village life and education. In this they were different from western-style schools which, set down in the Asian countryside, were psychologically disruptive" (369). Naipaul was told that Ivan Illich, the famous educationist had come to India to study the function of these village schools and wrote his "theory of deschooling" (369). Accompanied by Prasujo, a young college boy of 19, who had been to Arizona after getting a scholarship by the American Field Service, Naipaul went to Surabaya. Naipaul understands that Prasujo was a Javanese and a Muslim who lived with beautiful mysteries: "Scholarship, applied to his past, would have undermined what had become his faith, his staff" (371). Naipaul's confusion was removed by the English teacher Mr. Wahid who explained the name of this village school: "In Indonesian 'the world for the Chinese quarter of a town was *Perchinen*; *Per- China- en* "where the Chinese were so, *Pesantren was per- santrien*, 'the place where the wise men were', *santry* being a version of *shastry*, the Sanskrit word for a man learned in the Hindu *Shastras,* the scriptures" (371). These village schools were monasteries during Hindu-Buddhist days in Java. The community supported centers for spiritual guidance. However, when the old civilization cracked, the Sufi Muslims took over these places and continued as counseling centers for religious purposes. No formal education was instructed there. Anybody could seek the guidance of the leader or Kiyai on religious instructions or personal advice. That is why such schools were not "structured". By the end of the 19th century, these centers were converted into schools for religious instructions. Naipaul realizes that these schools are not of much use to the individuals, society and the country because nothing substantial and significant is thought here. He therefore comments:

> The Sufi centre turned schools: the discipline of monks and dervishes applied to the young: it wasn't traditional, and it wasn't education. It was a breaking

> away from the Indonesian past: it was Islamization; it was stupefaction, greater than any that could have come with a western-style curriculum. And yet it was attractive to the people concerned, because twisted up with it, was the old monkish celebration of the idea of poverty: an idea which, applied to a school in Java in 1979, came out as little more than the poor teaching the poor to be poor. (378)

Naipaul's perceptive analysis on the education system is noteworthy. He understands the conservative learning about Islamic faith could not take people anywhere. It was not possible to make any substantial economic development of the people and the country. The learning of religious faith had therefore no contemporary relevance. Even if some people like his companion Prasojo understood clearly, they still stuck to the traditional faith: "Prasojo was Muslim; he had friends among the new Muslims. But he was as yet far removed from the new Muslim wish to purify, to create abstract men of the faith, man who would be nothing more than the rules. Prasojo possessed his Javanese civilization too completely for that: it was his civilization that he had been talking about during the drive (383). An old archaic education system has no relevance in the contemporary context. It does not improve the intellectual vigor of the learned. Though some sort of village development is in the agenda, such village schools seem to be irrelevant. That is why an Australian visitor had written a letter to Tafiq in the context of his visit to Pabelan: "As I reflect on my visit to you all at Pabelan I am still confused.... What is it that you would like the students to do when they leave Pabelan? He has the skills to develop the village but can he do for those with little or no land? What kind of Islamic principles has he learned at Pabelan to help him in this situation?.... When does Islam tell you about Indonesia and what to do about poverty? (397)

Naipaul therefore reflects on this issue: "And that was the problem. What message did Islam have for the villages?" (398). Naipaul observes a Hindu connection to the concept of Muslim *Kown* in the village of Linus, a Catholic poet. In this village Naipaul sees the office of Muhammadiyah, a reformist, nationalist Indonesian Muslim movement, now said to be "conservative". Umar told Naipaul that *Kown*, meaning elder, performed the *Salamaton* ritual when he was called in by Muslim families on important occasions—a birth, a funeral, an anniversary or any Muslim religious ceremony. "This ritual was performed with consecration and distribution of food" Naipaul thinks: "From my Hindu childhood I recognized the ceremony as a Hindu survival and I thought of the Muslim *Kown* as a kind of successor to Hindu priest" (403). In Prambanam village, the idea of life was composite rather than being Muslim. It combines different things from different religions:

> The religion of the village was a composite religion; the idea of the good life was a composite idea. People lived with everything at once: the mosque; the church, Krishna, the rice goddess, a remnant of the Hindu caste, the Buddhist idea of nirvana, the Muslim idea of paradise. (406)

It is interesting to note that "the open-and-shut morality of Islam, always with its answers in the book or in the doings of the Prophet, gives way in the puppet theatre to something else. Hinduism and Buddhism shed their complexity. It is as if, at this far end of the world, the people of Java had taken what was the most human and liberating from the religions that had come their way to make their own" (409). Umar Khayam sees that the *wayang* and the epics (*Ramayana* and *Mahabharata*) as the core of Javanese religion and civilization. However the new Islam that was coming to the villages with borrowed ideas of wickedness of machines and the misuses of foreign aid. In the late 20th century, it rediscovered its political roots: "The Prophet had founded a state. He had given men the idea of equality and union. The dynastic quarrels that had come early to this state had entered the theology of the religion; so that this religion, which filled men's days with rituals and ceremonies of worship, which preached the after-life, at the same time gave men the sharpest sense of worldly injustice and made that part of religion" (411). Naipaul therefore points out the defects in the late twentieth century Islam. Though it appeared to raise political issues, it had the flaws of its origins—"the flaw that ran right through Islamic history; to the political issues it raised, it offered no political or practical solution. It offered only the faith. It offered only the faith. It offered only the Prophet, who would settle everything—but who had ceased to exist. This political Islam was rage, anarchy" (411-12).

In the late 20th century Indonesia, some people have lost their identities. They have become too rich or too important. To them, going back to village would be degeneration. They have lost the sense of security provided by the mutual help society of the village. At the same time they are not individuals in the western sense. They cannot stand on their own and individuals interact on an equal basis with others. This was how Darma-Sastro reacted to the attitude of this new class of people who were not like the nobles of past. These people were merely concerned with power and wealth alone:

> The people I'm talking about cannot function now as arbiters of right and wrong any more. Why? In their loss of identity they have lost all values except these associated with power. They are people continuing to look for their own security. (416)

His resentment was against the money-culture based on "oil-power". He viewed that there were some morally good people who had no power to enforce good. The middle class people, facing a threat to their identity, send their children for mental training: "They were children of the Jakarta middle class, people faced with the special Indonesian threat of the loss of personality. In Islam, the life of the mosque, with its rules and rituals, they found again, or reconstructed, something like the old feudal or rural community that for them no longer existed" (428). Naipaul analyses the views of the mental training course teacher, Imaduddin, an electrical engineer and a Muslim from Sumatra:

> Indonesia was a place to be cleansed. His faith was so great that he could separate his country from its history, traditions, art: its particularity. His faith was too simple for Indonesia, certainly for Java, too simple even for the *Kown* of Linus's village. And Indonesia—

> overpopulated, with so many people squeezed out, with only the army to hold the country together—was too fragile for his kind of protest. (435)

As a revolutionary teacher, Imaduddin thinks that he is preparing the next generation of leaders of Indonesia. He believes that the constitution has some Islamic value in it. He is preparing the new generation to replace all this. But Naipaul suspiciously questions: "*To replace* all this. But for what, and by what? Not by new institutions but only by men as pure and cleansed as himself" (437).

Most of the revolutionary leaders in Iran, Pakistan, and Malaysia and also in Indonesia blindly follow the Islamic rules and the Koran. They believed in cleansing the society for a pure faith through mass-slaughter. Killing was the instinct of Khomeini, as a Shia believer, killing was an instinct with Behzad, the communist son of a communist father. Even in Indonesia, the Islamic revolutionaries believed in violence and murder to overthrow all that was impure in their opinion: "It had happened before in Indonesia, this mass slaughter. In 1965 the communists had been wiped out. A million people had been killed.... And more should have been killed: there were two and a half million communists at the time. So a million and a half had escaped killing and many of them were still around. The Islamic faith was grounded in Allah. The owner of land and all men are his children. In the twentieth century this idea has been used more as a political faith rather than being religious. It was a great discovery in the opinion of the mental training teacher who is preparing the next generation of Islamic faith. Naipaul observes the situation of Indonesian Islamic resurgence, and therefore comments:

> After a generation of peace, the revolutionary current of 1965 flowed again. It was Islamic now, it was like what had gone before as though rage and the wish for revenge were always to be tapped in this overcrowded, once-feudal land, where many men were squeezed out, the old balance was broken, where every step forward took men further away from safety. Where the new

> world brought new gifts but made difficult demands, and all men, whether at the top or at the bottom, lived in fear of personality loss. (448)

Naipaul understands that too much belief in the Islamic religion leads the fundamentalists towards extremism, violence and mass-slaughter thereby endangering democracy, progress and enlightenment.

After completing the first Islamic journey, Naipaul feels that "the state still proclaimed its goal to be the true Islamic way" though it looked like terror and despotism. In Indonesia, Malaysia and Iran, Islam served or contained other causes. In Pakistan, the faith served itself though there were politicians and ambitious people among the fundamentalists. Pakistan is a special case of Islamic faith because people in Pakistan always felt threatened as a minority and therefore to them "Islam was more than personal salvation, more than a body of belief; it had become a country, culture, identity; it had to be served, at whatever cost to the individual or the state itself" (452). In Iran, Khomeini is "the regent of God, the representative on earth (or in Iran) of the Twelfth Imam (in hiding or in occultation for a thousand years)" (468). The Assembly of Experts had placed him above the president in their constitution. In Iran, Islamic revolution took place and established the rule of Islam. The Muslim world all over should realize that there is still an external world beyond faith. This world cannot be saved by faith alone. Therefore, people in the Islamic countries should compromise with the world outside shedding their extremist tag. Even the life of Islam had not been generated from within: "It had come from outside events and circumstances, the spread of the universal civilization. It was the late twentieth century that had made Islam revolutionary, given new meaning to old Islamic ideas of equality and union, shaken up static or retarded societies. It was the late twentieth country—and not the faith—that could supply the answers—in institutions, legislation, economic systems. And paradoxically, out of the Islamic revival, Islamic fundamentalism, that appeared to look backwards, there would remain in many Muslim countries, with all the emotional charge derived from the Prophet's faith, the idea of modern revolution" (494). Such a view of Naipaul very well establishes that he wants the "fundamentalist tag" of Islam to be uprooted. He scrutinizes the vision of Behzad, the communist in Iran who considers Russian revolution rather than Iranian revolution a turning point. People like Behzad may inverse the Islamic passion to work for "a society cleansed and purified, a society of believers" (491).

Naipaul's *Among the Believers* is a superb piece of travel writing in which he scrutinizes the four Islamic nations from his close observation, analysis, interpretation and inferences. Although it is a personal account his concerns are more vivid and passionate in the context of general human suffering, miseries and poverty in the Muslim world. Through his personal encounters with the "believers" of the Muslim world, he understands that Islamic faith without modernization has no place. Merely citing the past incidents of Prophet and deriving ideas from them to solve the contemporary situations are rather irrelevant, ineffective and invalid. It is now time the sanctity of Islam should be maintained by a curious blending of some of the contemporary ideas to Islam which are relevant to a contemporary society.

8.2. The Second Islamic Journey: Looking Beyond Islamic Fundamentalism

In the Prologue to *Beyond Belief* (1998), Naipaul writes: "This is a follow-up to a book I published seventeen years ago, *Among the Believers*, about a journey to the same four countries" (*Beyond* 1). Technically, the book follows the same method as in the case of *India: A Million Mutinies Now* (1990). Naipaul emphasizes the loss of identity of Muslim converts': "A convert's world-view alters. His holy places are in Arab lands; his sacred language is Arabic. His idea of history alters. He regrets his own; he becomes, whether he likes it or not, a part of the Arab story. The country has to turn away from everything that is his" (1). It is less a travel book and the four sections are integral and continuous to form a whole: "It is less of a travel book; the writer is less present, less of an inquirer. He is in the background, trusting to his instinct, a discoverer of people, a finder-out of stories. These stories, opening out one from the other, make their own pattern and define each country and its promptings; and the four sections of the book make a whole" (*Beyond* 2). This book contains four sections, namely Indonesia, Iran, Pakistan and Malaysian postscript. Through the descriptions of the countries, lovely scenes and lively narrations of interactions with a number of characters representing various types, a deeper insight about the state of a particular country emerges. If all the sections are considered together, a clear vision of the Islamic Third world countries emerges. Naipaul sees that emergence of Islam in these countries is significant. He also sees that Islam, and modern science and technology encounter with each other. Conversion, cultural identity, deconstruction of history, economic development and poverty dominate the descriptions and interactions.

Naipaul meets Imaduddin, a lecturer in electrical engineering after a gap of 15 years. Prof. Habib was a great scientist who was suspected during the 1970s for his views on combination of science and Islam. However, the situation by the end of the century was different for which he was considered a desirable leader. Imaduddin following Habib pursues scientific study along with his Islamic faith: "But this was precisely where Imaduddin's faith—as scientist and believer had coincided with Habibie's, where the careers of the two men had crossed, and Imaduddin had been taken up by his new patron to the sky of presidential favour" (9). Imaduddin believes that Islam could give them socialistic pattern of society. Naipaul therefore scrutinizes Imaduddin's Islamic faith: "I believe he (Imaduddin's) meant that all that was humane and attractive about socialism was also in Islam, and there was no need for him to take the secular way and risk his faith" (13). The decline in politics is a matter to be resented because "in politics the questioning of winning is the result" (13) rather than being honest and morally upright. Imaduddin has a clear vision for human resource development in his country rather than emphasizing technology: "Technology can be bought if you have the money. But you cannot buy human resources who are dedicated to doing things for their country" (17). Imaduddin is progressive in his vision although he feels that the next generations of students should also be devout Muslims along with pursuit of scientific study which will move the country in the path of progress of Industry and Technology: "When they become devout Muslims and good leaders of Indonesia, they will not think about revolution but about accelerated evolution.... We have to overcome our backwardness and become one of the new industrial countries by 2020" (22). Imaduddin attributes Industrial backwardness of Indonesia to the colonial administration by the Spanish, the British and the Dutch. He does not consider that Islamic faith has made the Muslims backward because science is inherent in Islamic teaching:

> Although Imaduddin refers to Islamic faith for everything, he also tries to establish the contemporary relevance of Islamic faith through deconstruction of Islamic religion and teaching. Naipaul's sense of history prompts him to scrutinize the dangers in the hereditary "religious feudalism" and "elitism" in the concept of Kiyai who owned *Pesantren* and passed down the ownership rights to his son. In this sense Islam is almost imperialism like European colonialism which simultaneously came to Indonesia to destroy the Hindu-Buddhist temples, traditions and cultures. Islam also seemed to feel like a colonized culture. The Forum for Democracy established in 1991 rejected the Islamic politics of Mr. Suharto and Professor Habibie. These appeal to the people to follow Islam by conscience, rather than by fear and tyranny spread by the rulers. Habibie and his friends create a fear among non-Muslims and non-practicing Muslims to show their identity. This is the first step to tyranny. Imaduddin remained a more cultural Muslim than Mr. Wahid who because of his liberal education became a more internationalist due to these Pesantren family pieties unlike Imaduddin who remained committed to the holy war. Imaduddin's worldview was that everybody was a born Muslim. That implies that outside the Muslim world everything was wrong till the Individual found his Muslim self. Naipaul therefore believes that

in the converted Muslim countries like Iran, Pakistan and Indonesia, "the fundamentalist rage is against the past, against history, and the impossible dream is of the true faith growing out of a spiritual vacancy" (59). Dewi, who had the background of a modern education through her uncle, believes that religious or cultural purity is a fundamentalist fantasy. To her except the tribal communities all others in Indonesia are mostly "culturally mixed in varying degrees, and every one lives in his own way with his complexity" (66). Her life is rich because all her different worlds converge. The converted people of Islam have no identity, no roots except the Arabs. This is purely the cruelty of Islamic imperialism:

> The cruelty of Islamic fundamentalism is that it allows only to one people—the Arabs, the original people of the Prophet—a past, and sacred places, pilgrimages and earth (eastern) reverences. These sacred Arab places have to be the sacred places of all the converted peoples. Converted peoples have to strip themselves of their past; of converted peoples nothing is required but the purest faith (if such a thing can be arrived at), Islam submission. It is the most uncompromising kind of imperialism. (72)

In Indonesia it is necessary to assimilate Science and Technology and Islamic faith to take the country forward. Materialism, which is now dominating, should be countered through the true development of religious ethics.

Naipaul brings out important insights on Iran by his interaction with various people. Iran was able to acquire wealth. It also brought about revolution through Khomeini and communists. There is a comparison between the histories of India and Iran: "India, as soon as it became a British Colony, began to be regenerated, began to receive the New learning of Europe, to get the institution that went with the learning.... Iran was to enter the twentieth century only with an idea of eastern kingship and the antiquated theological learning of places like QUM. Iran was to enter the twentieth century only with a capacity for pained nihilism" (250). In the different contexts different people, who have been marginalized during the tyrannical rule based on Islamic faith, have expressed their views which may be referred to finally formulate an insight on the functioning of the Government.

In Iran, women are to cover up their whole bodies with clothes (elegance overcoming the long gowns and the black headdress). Very few young women get the chance of freedom to work outside. However, Mehrdad, who is working in a publishing house considers herself to be lucky because "many young women didn't have that opportunity of leaving the house; it was not easy in revolutionary Iran for unmarried women to have a social life or even to move about" (146). From this it is quite clear how women are oppressed in Iran, governed by Islamic faith. Mr. Jaffrey, an Indian from Lucknow, went to Iran, the Shia state. However during Shah rule, there was tyranny, and "the great wealth when it came had led to corruption and sodomy and general wickedness" (154). He further thinks that "Iran under the Ayatollah should have been very close to Mr. Jaffrey's dream of the *jame to whi de*, the society of believers, the oneness of government and faith" (154). Mr. Pervez was disillusioned to see Iran under fundamentalist rule. He therefore reflected: "I never thought it would be like that in 1979. I thought that the regime of the Shah would go, and we would have a western-style democratic government as we had" (163-64). During the Khomeini regime, people's dreams and hopes were frustrated. He promised employment, saying he would take away employment from the Americans. In the Shah's time about one or two million people were unemployed or half-employed. Today there are ten millions unemployed.

The materialistic society of Iran has been reflected in the attitude of people preferring money to other aspects of culture like music and literature. On the voice of America it was heard that Iranian people were asking for new records to be played. In Tehran nobody cared about the war. Everybody was looking for money. Ali, a student in the United States of America supported the cause of revolution for getting liberty. However, in Iran despite there is a formal legal system, there is no much freedom especially for women. Paydar's mother's comments on the new education are noteworthy. Her mother says that the religious people are the most dangerous in the country. They are all against women: "You will never gain anything following these religious people. We have known them. We have seen them. These are the people who did not let me learn reading and writing" (194). The mentality of the religious people prevented women who were much interested in knowledge and books. There were religious regulations for women to wear chador and the full headdress. Music and cultural events were banned. There were also restrictions on the press. All the Universities were closed for some years. It was purely religious fanaticism. Paydar perceives murder of true culture in Iran: "I thought that ideologies are only a small part of our intellect which can help us in life. The main source lies in our cultural way of thinking. And natural behaviors of people like my mother. The revolution I worked for didn't understand me as an intellectual or my mother as a person" (197). The irrationality in some of the rules is obvious as Mehrad scrutinizes the rules of Islam vividly: "They are the rule makers. If you deny the rules you are denying the rule-makers. If you oppose the leader you are against the holy prophet. If you are against the holy Book, and the Holy book comes from God. Someone against God must be killed. But who does the killing? Only the rule-maker. Not God" (239). Even Parvez is more stringent in his attack on Islam who says: "The war (against Iraq) was fought in the name of Islam. It was a blessing in disguise. Without the war people wouldn't have got so fed up with Islam" (242). Revolt against the rigid rules is going on particularly by young people in respect of rigidity in the rule of sexuality on the Islamic lines: "There were rules and more rules. But young people, those who had known nothing but the religious state, were learning their own ways of disobedience. They had their bodies; their bodies were their own. There were stories of sexual revolution among the young; and there were other forms of disobedience" (246). Even feminist revolt is also going on because of too much oppressive measure against women: "Another kind of person, another kind of disobedience. In the high, well-lighted watch-post at the entrance to the commercial centre, a young girl stood blank and unabashed before the guard,...some unIslamic behavior; something against the rules, something perhaps about showing too much of her hair" (248). Reconstructing the histories of Iran and India, a comparative perspective is established. A hundred years after Jehangir, the Moghul glory in India was replaced by the British colonial rule during which India began "to be regenerated, began to receive the new learning of Europe, to get the institutions that went with that learning" (250). Although Iran never became a formal colony, "Its fate was in some ways worse.... Its great movements fell into decay.... And by the end of the 19th century its rulers were ready to hand over the country and its people, to foreign missionaries" (250).

When the land reforms started in the 1960s, the fertile land remained with the landowners whereas the "infertile or semi-fertile land was divided among the farmers, the people who always worked in the land" (257). Even if the landowners exploited the farmers, traditionally these farmers always looked to a landowner as their patron "who would lend them money, give them seed, and he would help when there was disaster" (257). However, after the land distribution the farmers lost their patron and the government did not replace with any alternative banking system. As a result the farmers "could not make their ends meet" (257) and migrated to the cities for work. In Iran, there has not been any integrated approach to solve the problems of the people by combining the ideals of Islamic faith and modern systems of governance. Only by faith and belief system, a country can never improve the conditions of the marginalized. Both the political leaders and religious leaders should sit together to chart out plans for well-measured economic, social, cultural educational and industrial development.

Delving deep into the history of Pakistan, Naipaul understands that Pakistan is not a settled country. The problem of Mohajirs and Pathans makes the situation more unsettled. The cause of partition can never be justified. It is actually a hurried decision. Because of this dangerous decision, there has been a lot of slaughter, bloodshed, rape and murder. The inhuman face of partition will remain to haunt the people of the subcontinent. The new state had been hurriedly created and had no true program. It couldn't be a homeland for the Muslims of the subcontinent; that was impossible. In fact, more Muslims were to be left behind in India than were to be in the new Muslim state. Without resorting to build the country on its own resources and thinking, Pakistan became a satellite of the Unites States: "Its various regimes were stored up right through the cold war. It didn't develop a modern economy; it didn't feel the need. Instead it began to export its people: it became in part a remittance economy" (267). The governance was less important than the triumph of faith. During pre-partition protest, "Islamic identity" was a very powerful evocative factor. However, it could not keep the two wings of the state together. In Pakistan there were two types of people who lived very well. They were people with names, and people with money. Everybody else lives like insects, worms. They have no power. Mostly people lived on the margin, without any power. People on the centre dominated. People also reacted against the law which was only meant for the poor; the rich people could violate them: "Justice is rubbish, Law is rubbish. Law is only for the poor, not for the rich" (23). The farmers were subjugated, they were treated like slaves. Shahbaz was astonished to see the miserable status of the farmers: "Shahbaz now saw that on their home ground the sons of these feudal didn't act like Oxford or Cambridge graduates. They treated their workers and peasants like serfs. The peasants would touch the feet of their landlord in submission and greeting; and the landlord would not ask the peasant to rise, Shahbaz, fresh from England, wanted to weep" (296). The nationalist question in Pakistan was one of important questions, the Marxist students discussed: "Punjab was the dominant province; people in other provinces felt left out" (*Beyond* 298). The complexity of Islamic culture is well marked in the diversity of various Muslim cultural identities. These refugees were pathans. So the pathans today are in a much stronger position than the Baluch in Baluchistan. The Pathans brought with them their fundamentalist trend. Madarasas (Karnic schools) are totally alien to the Baluch culture. This happened after the war. The longing for a separate Muslim state was a frustrating experience for some of the Muslims, the mohajir, strangers who came from India, are unwanted. So the dreamland of Pakistan has now become a curse to these mohajirs. Partition once a cause for joy, had become like a wound for some of these mohajirs. These foreigners (in the eyes of Pakistan) had a sense of loss and still longed for their identity in a Muslim state: "The people had their own history and language and feudal reverences. They had set up political barriers, some overt, some hidden, against the strangers from India, the mohajirs. And in Pakistan, the mohajirs had nowhere to go" (325).

Because of altering of history in Pakistan, after partition, there had been a decline in intellectual life. Moreover, freedom has not been given to people. Women were suppressed. They were prescribed specific rules of rigidity to follow. In the context of a small girl child who was playing joyfully, Naipaul makes a touching comment: "Purdah was soon going to fall on her; the rest of her life was going to be spent in that void where time was without meaning" (364). The feudal land-owners are shrewd enough to have alliances with religion and industry. Through marriage in the family of religious and industrial Functionaries, they move on: "This was how the feudal were moving: making alliances with industrialists and with religious dynasties like the pir's: religion and money and land locking together to rule" (362). The problem in the region of Sindh has been presented by Naipaul. The Muslim migrants, who had come to the feudal land of Sindh in large numbers from India after partition, found that that land belonged to them no more. It had become some other people's land. In Pakistan the functioning of the Govt. was miserable for which many people thought that the earlier British rule was better. Abdul's father feels that there is more injustice now. There are no street lights. However during British rule they had at least kerosene filled lanterns to move in the streets during the night. In 1971, Pakistan lost its entity and Bangladesh was formed for which Mustaq grieves for coming to Pakistan: "And then in 1971, Bangladesh seeded. That was an agony for Mustaq; the Pakistan of 1947, for which his family had given up India, had ceased to exist" (371). Scrutinizing the various systems—political, economic, cultural, religious—

Naipaul sees that high aspirations of Iqbal for Pakistan to be a people-building nation is rather proceeding towards violence, disorder, chaos. In the process, people remain, poor, ignorant and suffer to a great extent.

In the Malaysian post-script, there are vivid descriptions of Islamic missionaries spreading the success stories of Islamic faith. The Malays stuck to their traditions. When the Chinese people came, they dominated as business people and the Malays felt cheated. However, Islamic propaganda was used to awaken the youth movement. Awakening to their present reality the Malays, like Safi, felt that their country had almost been lost due to their dullness. Because of the fertile land, they could easily grow crops and produce much: "Things grew too easily in the warm, fertile land; the old life of river and forest was too rich and full. You could throw a seed", Safi said one day "and it would grow; you could put a bare hook in the water and catch a fish" (*Beyond* 386). These pastoral, tropical Malays were "timeless people" because they had no sense of time for which they were never bothered about commerce and prosperity. People like Philip felt that there was no separate identity in Malay. It was a mixing culture. Faith has given some identity to them. That is why Philip analyses his own life:

> I owe a lot to the faith. It gave me a certainty and belongingness, identity. It had all been confused. Who am I? Chinese, but not Chinese. In a Chinese cultural programme I would be lost. English, but not English. I have never been to England. The scriptures gave the original impetus to my love and passion for reading, which exists at this day. (395)

The Malay women consider marriage to give them security and identity. But all their expectations are frustrated after that. That happens to Nadezha who marries an ambitions *Kampung* boy like her mother. Despite the mother's warning "you are doing what I did" Nadezha however thinks that marriage is essential for her life: "She felt it was something she had to do as a woman; she thought that as a woman she could have a future only with a husband at her side. Later, when she was divorced her ideas changed" (400). When there was misunderstanding, the girl was to be divorced. But as she was pregnant, as per Muslim faith, she could not be divorced because the child was to be born legitimate. She was therefore to lead a miserable life for three years till her divorce. This was the status of a woman in Malaysia. It was not desirable on the part of a person to have doubts about religion and God. Rashid could not therefore question his father about that: "It was inconceivable, for instance, that he should ask his father whether God existed. His father was a bomah; he had mystical powers. To question him about religion, to express doubt, would be to show disrespect, and that was the last thing Rashid wanted to do" (412). Rashid's father, being a bomah and a Taoist-Buddhist, had a position in the society. He wanted his children to perform the rituals. However, Rashid could not do those although his mother and others in the family did them in the family altar after his father's death. This was the situation of cultural mixing in the Malay society. In Malay society, torment and malnutrition were also there. Syed Alwi's description of his father's childhood is evident to this. The society in Malaysia is a society where the native people are inefficient and incompetent for which the Chinese are dominant. However, they are not given the chance of administration. The village people of river and forest are not competent enough to take the country in the path of speedy economic development. Further, the culture is a mixed culture where the converts, though resort to their Islamic faith, are not too much against all these pre-Islamic culture such as Hindu-Buddhist faiths and religious beliefs.

Beyond Belief therefore deals with the complexity of governance of Islamic states where the leaders, while sticking to the Islamic faith to a large extent, are also influenced by the late twentieth century political and economic ideas. Simply, they cannot reject all these ideas altogether even if they follow the medieval religious beliefs. They must have to implement some of these important trends to take the country forward in consonance with the development of the other modern nations of the world. People in the lower rank who are deprived and marginalized understand that their conditions can only be improved when the political leaders and religious leaders sit together to integrate the policies of governance with human values rather than merely practicing/following, some of the irrelevant, obsolete Muslim beliefs and systems.

Beyond Belief deals with Naipaul's first-hand experiences and interactions during his visit to four non-Arab Muslim countries—Iran, Pakistan, Malaysia and Indonesia. He diagnoses the complex culture of these Islamic countries. However, he is very much satirical in tone. He generalizes the contradictions which he comes across in his interviews with the individuals. *Beyond Belief* is the sequel to his earlier travelogue *Among the Believers*. However, in this book he identifies the four countries as 'converted' though he does not give any convincing historical analysis regarding his claim. In this regard he seems to be universalizing his ideas and stands in the lines of European's claim of universal civilization. In these countries, Naipaul finds Islam as imperialism as it destroys all the past of 'converted' cultures in these countries. For Muslims, their faith is more important than anything else. However such a claim has not been elaborated in details. This seems to be a self-acclaimed truth for them. *Beyond Belief* may be predominantly informative and a factual text. In the "Prologue" he writes: "This is a book about people. It is not a book of opinions." He claims to present an undisturbed truth objectively. But his frequent encroachment in the narrative tends to be his commentary on Islam. Despite all his interviews and factual representations, he does not proceed forward before his personal comments and explanations. Though Naipaul takes long interviews with Imaduddin, he considers that Islam and science are contradictory and incompatible. When he comes across the tradition of learning the Koran by heart by the little boy, he doesn't show any interest to see that boy. In his capacity, Naipaul attempts to present a disturbing image of the Muslim world. Followers of Islam (esp. converted) are repeatedly referred to as violent, irrational, void and confused. In the era of globalization, such account of Muslim world, may widen the distance between Muslim and non-Muslim countries. Hiren Gohain makes a pertinent point about this book in his paper "The Post-Colonial Confusion and V.S. Naipaul": "This book confirms the colonial (Postcolonial) identity of Naipaul as he abandons all doubts and questions about the colonizers" (143). He further elucidates his resentment about the book: "The narrative (of *Beyond Belief*) presents deft portraits of a number of people caught in the great Post-colonial search for identity following the removal of colonial power from the immediate scene" (144). This book is an authentic critique of the Islamic belief system; it suggests a blending of faith as well as progressive ideas for the overall development of these converted Muslim nations rather than sticking to the obsolete Islamic Fundamentalism.

The South American Expedition: Exploring Racism, Culture, Civilization

A Turn in the South highlights the complex issues of the migrants and their marginalized status. This book is not just an account of his travel, but a serious interpretation of the civilization. Naipaul's concerns for the black marginalized people have been depicted vividly. The sweeping changes that were going on in the modern South American world have influenced these societies to a considerable degree. He focuses on the racial discrimination where the black people have been victims. They have become a marginalized lot. Naipaul writes about both black and white people who come from different backgrounds. South America is a land of voices; people speak with passion and hope for their future. Naipaul interviews both White people and Black people for interpretation of racial tension in South America. In his own childhood and adulthood Naipaul encounters this dichotomy of races that settle in the countries and coexist. In this land of slavery, the author tries to explore the truth about slavery and racism by visiting slave plantations, white expatriates and black settlements. Bhat scrutinizes Naipaul's encounter with the American South:

> However, in this book, he also distinguishes between the condition of black Americans, a powerless victimized minority and the self-governing black African or West Indians especially true of Trinidad and Tobago. The American South was associated with Trinidad and

> Tobago although the scenes in both differed. The final picture that emerges is a scattered one as several people speak through various voices. Naipaul's travelogue caters more to the metropolitan scathing criticism to the non-metropolitan people. (2000: 28)

Naipaul's travel to South America was aimed at focusing on the history of the Black people, the system of slavery and the adaptability of the Blacks to survive in a modern civilization. His serious interest in the "slavery question" makes him penetrate deeper into the lives of the people there. The racial issue, one of his important concerns, has been vividly probed into when he analyses the dichotomy between the White and the Black. In order to understand slavery, he visits slave plantations and compares the slavery in South America with the slavery in Trinidad and Tobago. It is interesting to note that Naipaul focuses on a scene of White and Black people living together. While he was visiting North Caroline, Hetty, Howard's mother notes

> Black people there, black people there. White people there, Black people, black people, White people, black people, white people. All this side black people, all this side white people. White people, white people, black people, white people (*TS* 10).

Naipaul was really hurt to see the Black people are suffering even after 100 years of the abolition of slavery. Comparing the position of the Black people there in Trinidad and Tobago, he notes that the Black people in Trinidad and Tobago are in majority in a postcolonial situation whereas the powerless South Americans are in minority in their own lands. That is why Naipaul expresses his agony: "A slave is a slave; a master need not think of humiliating or tormenting him. In the hundred years after the end of slavery, the Black man was tormented in the south in ways that I never knew about, until I began to travel in the region" (119). The negative impact of slavery on these people is more destructive: "But there could be no easy movement forward for the mass; they had lived through too much; the irrationality of slavery and the years after slavery had made many irrational and self-destructive" (119). Though

Naipaul is seriously disturbed by the sufferings of the Black minority in South America, the main theme of the book is related to the idea of home. Naipaul in the Prologue to the book acknowledges this:

> Jimmy was as struck by this as I was when Jimmy told me: that Howard had something neither Jimmy nor I had, a patch of the earth he thought of as home, absolutely his. And that where—many months after I had heard this story—I thought I should begin this book about the South: with the home that Howard had. (3)

Along with Jimmy and Howard Naipaul traveled to Howard's home where his mother lived:

> That little green wooden house, now closed up, just beside the high way, had been his mother's house. He had grown up there. His mother lived in another house now; another house—bigger and newer—was home. We saw it from the highway. It was a concrete block house set back from the road behind some other houses: no the old, tree—embowered house I had had in my imagination. (5)

Howard's mother Hetty had also lived in another more beautiful house for ten years. It was a farmhouse with a big green field and forest trees bounding the distance on every side. Naipaul notes that Howard's home had a richer and more complicated past:

> Home was not for Howard just his mother's house, the little green-house that was now closed up, or the new concrete-block house she had moved to. Home was what we had seen only a part: all about these country roads, within a few miles, were houses and fields connected with various members of Howard's family. It was a richer and more complicated past than I had imagined; and physically much more beautiful. The houses I was taken to were bigger than the houses many people in Trinidad or England might have lived in. But, still, in

the past there was that point where darkness fell, the historical darkness, ever here, which was home. (11)

Hetty, Howard's mother, had no regret for the past. She was more concerned with the present:

> What of the past, though? Had it been a reasonable sort of life? She said she had no regret for the past. Hadn't things got better for her? Hadn't things got better in the 1950s?
>
> She said, "I hardly think about my own past."
>
> And Howard Said, "I can hardly remember the past." (11)
>
> Even Hetty's sister's son said, "we've had too much of the past." (8)

The Southerners were more concerned with religion which they considered to be the centre of all their activities. It brings out a sense of community feeling, a union among them. Naipaul was too much touched by the idea of brotherhood and commitment in the Church gathering:

> There was hand-clapping from the choir, and swaying. One man stood up in the congregation—he was in a brown suit—and he clapped and sang. A woman in white with a white hat got up and sang. So I began to feel the pleasures of the religious meeting; the pleasures of brotherhood, union, formality, ritual, clothes, music, all combining to create a possibility of ecstasy.
>
> It was the formality—derived by theses black people from so many sources—that was the surprise; and the idea of community. (15)

Naipaul understands that church is the primal centre for these Blacks. Everything happens in the church: "Torture and tears, luck and grief: these were the motifs of this religion, this binding, this consoling union—union the unexpected, moving idea to me. And, as in Muslim countries, I understood the power, a preacher might have" (15). When Naipaul remarked that the idea of a Black community that he was given was quite startling, Howard said that the Black community might disappear in the next twenty to twenty-five years because of the mixing together of the Whites and Blacks in the region. Naipaul observes:

> Segregation had preserved the Black community. But now Blacks and Whites, especially of the younger generation, were doing more things together. This gave point to what Hetty (grieving for a son) had said the day before about black and white boys now "drinking together". And I wasn't sure whether Howard or Hetty wholly liked the new mixing and what it foreshadowed. I didn't think that Hetty could be as serene as she was, without her community. (16)

The Black people had a bad time in the past. Now when things were improving for them, there were new racial elements in the country: Mexicans and Cubans and the other foreigners. The Mexicans were soon going to be politically powerful in the country. The Asians were not just buying motels; they were going into other kinds of business as well. In a hospital not for away there were only two American doctors. So, the Black people's suffering continued. Howard therefore wanted to keep himself aloof from the past and from the "rage of Harlem" and live in New York:

> My rhythm is different. And they pick up on that Rhythm? It's like your energy level. How shall I put it? I'm not angry. Most people in Harlem are angry. And trying to explain more about himself, he said, "I'm different. I felt different at the high school. It's what you think and what you feel that makes you different. I always felt different. Which leads me to believe I was born in the wrong town like many people. (17)

However, Howard was a conservative because of his Southern Baptist background of Bowen. When Howard viewed that the Black community would disappear within twenty to twenty-five years, he meant that there would be less unity among them because of the changes that were taking place: "Change is like death. Good things come out of it. It's like the Civil War, when a whole way of life ended" (18). Naipaul observes that Howard was more abstract in his expressions. Though he said that he was not interested in the past or history, he was really linked to it in his attitudes and concerns. Naipaul therefore writes:

> So at the end it turned out that his early comment, about the continuity of his home town, had to do with history, as I had thought at the beginning. I had changed my mind because the word had then appeared to contain the idea of sameness and dullness: the same buildings, the ruins left standing in the fields, the dullness of the small town-life. He had meant that; but he had also meant the past living on. It was as though, talking to me, a stranger, he had had to find a way of talking about the unmentionable past. (18)

Naipaul's Southern journey started with a sense of unraveling the suppressed history of these people: their past torture, destruction of culture, resistance to retain the fundamentals and understand the hard realities of the Black civilization.

Before traveling to Atlanta from New York, Naipaul was suggested to visit Tuskegee in Alabama to have a look at the trades institute, now a University, that Booker T. Washington had founded more than a hundred years before for black people. A.I. Murray, who was living in Harlem, invited Naipaul to come to his apartment which would be part of his preparation for the southern journey. Murray, who was educated in Tuskegee, showed many photographs of the place to Naipaul who learnt from Murray that Washington was born a slave in 1856, five years before the civil war:

> And he would have grown up in the extraordinary period just after the civil war, when freed men asserted themselves here and there, and some of the gifted ones did well. He would have grown up with American ideas, the big ideas of the late nineteenth century. Booker Washington had to be seen as an American of the late nineteenth century, in his energy and in his understanding of the way capitalist America worked. He would have been at one with the very rich and powerful men he successfully appealed to. (21)

Naipaul with the help of A.I. Murray saw the neighborhood which was "a whole section of a great city in decay" (23). In Dallas in 1984, Naipaul had the idea of traveling in the American south. He observed that Trinidad, a former British colony (from 1797), and an agricultural slave colony (until 1833, when slavery was abolished in the British empire), would have had more in common with the old slave states of the southeast than with New England or the newer European-immigrant states of the North: "What I had heard as a child about the racial demeanor of the south had been too shocking. It had tainted the United States, and had made me close my mind to the South" (24). Racial question was crucial in the psyche of Naipaul behind his travel to the American south:

> My thoughts—in Dallas, and then in New York, when I was planning the journey—were about the race issue. I didn't know then that that issue would quickly work itself out during the journey, and that my subject would become that other South—of order and faith, and music and melancholy—which I didn't know about, but of which I had been given intimation in Dallas. (25)

Another important issue that was haunting Naipaul was "slavery" and the suffering of the marginalized black. He therefore correlates the Trinidadian Slavery system with the American South's slave trade:

> I began to think of writing about the south. My first travel book—undertaken at the suggestion of Eric Williams, the first black prime minister of Trinidad—had been about some of the former slave colonies of the Caribbean and South America. I was twenty-eight then. It seemed to me fitting that my last travel book—travel on a theme should be about the old slave states of the American Southeast. (25)

When Naipaul reached Atlanta, he was told that the talk about a black aristocracy in Atlanta was exaggerated. By American standards, the Blacks in America were not wealthy. A Black man might come at No. 201. The political power has no meaning without money: "Political power without the other sort of power is meaningless" (26). The black people were actually discriminated whenever there was a chance. The white dominance still continued. A black city councilor in Atlanta was attacked when he organized a march of "brotherhood" in protest against the displacement of Blacks from the country of Forsyth in 1912 in reference to the rape and death of a young white girl. The white-black conflict in Georgia was a long-standing one since the time of slavery. It was difficult to understand this complex issue. That is why a lawyer explains the issue to Naipaul in relation to Black identity:

> A lawyer I met said that to understand, it was necessary to remember that 120 years or so ago there had been slavery. For poor white people race was their identity. Someone well-off could walk away from that issue, could find another cause for self-esteem; but it wasn't that easy for the man with little money or education: without race he would lose his idea of who he was. (29)

The hatred of Whites towards Blacks was really painful. When Naipaul pointed out the stray case of Hetty's good relationship with her white master Bowen, the lawyer argued that some white people maintained relationship with the Blacks at the personal level. It did not go further: "Southern white people would do anything for black families, with whom they had a relationship, but that attitude stopped there; it wasn't extended to blacks in general" (29). The lawyer acknowledged that there was always a fear of racial violence when he was moving in the street: "But he also meant the larger fear of a world grown outside the more protective the bubble in which one lives, the more uncertain one's knowledge becomes of what lies out there" (29). The lawyer therefore genuinely wished that the Black middle class should grow and come to the centre in business, commerce and economic affairs. The economic power of the Blacks would result in the positive change of the black racial sentiment. The racial discrimination towards the Blacks was humiliating and frustrating:

> One day there was this story. IBM sent a black executive to Columbia, South Carolina: but there was no room for the black man in the country club, no party, invitations

> for his children. The next day there was this story: a black woman of thirty-one, a mother of two children aged five and two, took a revolver to work and shot herself in her office at Georgia power. She felt she was being discriminated by the company and passed over for promotion. She said in her suicide note that she wanted to give the managers and supervisors something to think about. (30)

Tom Teepan, the journalist commented that "white people in the United States don't have 'leaders'; only black people have leaders" (31). Naipaul thinks that Teepan was making this point because "the current scandals about black politicians in a number of states were being used to run down black people generally" (31). To Naipaul, this point about leaders was interesting because in many black or backward revolutionary countries the leader was everything, and the journalists unnecessarily poured much dignity on him. Since black politics in the United States was still racial or redemptive, they simply followed some people. These people were not leaders in true sense: "And I wondered whether it was possible in these circumstances for black people to stand apart from their leaders, any more than it was possible for people of the Caribbean or Africa to stand apart from the racial or tribal chiefs whom they had created" (31).

Identity is another great issue in the United States. There were the people who had planned out the system to keep everyone in his own place:

> In the United States, and especially in the South, religious faith was almost universal, and a religious vocation was as likely as any other. It was something a man could turn to for a number of reasons; and what I heard from the scholar was that some of the people he was in touch with (and he meant white people) had turned to the religious life in order to be confirmed in their identity: people from poor families who felt racially threatened by the new developments in the South, people who, in the booming new South, had gone into business and had then felt themselves drifting so far from the Southern

> world they had known that they had given up, to return to God and the life they felt more at ease in.

I heard this talk about religion and identity far from Atlanta, at an open air party on an estate in northwestern Georgia: hills, woods, long views, range beyond gentle range, blue upon blue (34).

The racial issue haunted everybody in the South. Even the sensitive intellectuals and writers were greatly disturbed by this. That is why Anne Siddons views that race as an issue can't be avoided: "I deal with race in some form in every book I've written. It's my great war, I guess, I write to find out where I am now, what I think, to make order and simplicity in my own world" (41). Naipaul reflects on his own views on slavery: "I talked of the oddity of slavery in the New world, of the two far removed races it had brought together African, European. Now there was a common language and even a common religion" (41). Naipaul's interactions with Anne Siddons unravel the multiple issues that existed in the Southern American region—racism, slavery socio-economic problems, woman's question, religion, culture, identity. It is pertinent to refer to Anne's comments in the context of woman being forced to depend on man:

> If we lived in the East—of the United States—we might have used our minds. In the West, we might have exercised a physical initiative and bravery. But we were here, and many of us were trapped here economically. And you can't aspire to what you can't imagine. And so, to survive, we had to look up with a man. My mother to this day would be happier if I had a teaching certificated and was married to a lawyer. (43)

Anne Siddons remarks on the futility of Civil War. After the Civil War women had lost their entire worlds. Their homes were burnt, their slave were scattered, and their men might have been killed. They perceived that this had happened through the sheer folly and childishness of their men: "That was a silly war. It was quixotic, romantic in the extreme. It was foolhardy. We fought a ridiculous war that any reflection would have told us we couldn't win" (43). Those women, who lost everything in the war, were now determined to ensure that their daughters and granddaughters should never handover their power to men: "And they determined then to control those men by guile and charm and feminine wiles, because those were the only weapons they had" (43). Acknowledging the fact that the South was very hard on women to keep them in discipline and order, she also expressed her anguish over her parents who did not allow her much freedom. However, she also appreciated them for their great love to her, and she was not like the "drunk women" in the street. It is noteworthy to understand the sensitive feelings of a Black politician like Michael Lomax who had the humiliating experience of being a black man:

> And yet for him with all that he had become, and all his future, there was still the burden of being black. He spoke of the burden in this way (and he might have spoken the words often before): "There's not a day, not a movement in my life when I don't have to think about the color of my skin. And being black is not just about what I see. It's about what I feel about myself. It's as much internal as external. (50-51)

Michael Lomax understands that Black people needed opportunity to rise. Economic opportunity was necessary. That could be achieved through political power. However without economic power political power had no meaning. This could only be provided through a system. Hence revolutionary rage was essential. Naipaul's understanding the southern people was also illuminated though his interactions with Arrington, the lawyer who viewed that "the civil rights movement was a great thing. But it freed up whites more than it did blacks" (66). Bob Wayher's views on white institutions regarding Blacks are also noteworthy: "I mean demise. Let me tell you why. In the teaching profession and the legal profession and any other profession you learn certain things from white institutions about Blacks. And they are ninety percent derogatory" (67). Naipaul's encounter with multiple voices in the South was a great learning experience. In the South, people resorted to religious faith at the time of great crisis. They surrendered before God for their needs and aspirations. The examples of Danny, the musician and the businessman, were rather inspiring to the people who wanted to give some order to their own chaotic lives:

> Religion was like something in the air, a store of emotion on which people could draw according to their need. The religious vocation would come to many. For some the vocation contained the ideas of service and community. For others, with a strange sense of self, who had gone out into the world with a will to win but had then withdrawn from various reasons, the vocation came as a wish to expound the word, to preach to make an offering to God and men of the life that had been lived. (69)

The various encounters in Atlanta helped Naipaul to come to terms with the various burring issues like racial tension and socio-economic concerns. However, Naipaul is yet to understand the Southern life comprehensively about the Negro issues, slavery, religion, culture, power structure, ethnicity and so on. He therefore moves to the historical place of Charleston to explore further the idea of Southern life. Naipaul comments: "It is only when you cross over from peninsular Charleston to what were once the slave plantations, the town's vast hinterland, that the slave past becomes more vivid—though there is now just forest for the most part" (78). With the help of Jack Leland, his guide, Naipaul could see the coastal South Carolina forest on a Sunday morning. The flatness and easiness and the extensiveness of the land made clear the need in the old days for abundant slave labor; and they also make painful the thought of the labor. Jack suggested Naipaul to see the old commissions of the Middleburg plantation house. On the lower floor there were two cells with bars on the windows: "These had been for slaves; not punishment cells, but 'holding' cells, where difficult new slaves would have been broken in or reconciled one at a time to plantation life" (81). Naipaul learns some aspects of plantation life which were not generally known. The planters were to face the problem of pacifying the new slaves. Old Mr. Gibbs, father-in-law of Leland, grew up in a family which believed the whites could be friends with Negroes, and had to respect them. However they could not take advantage of them. But the Negroes couldn't be elevated to being social equals.

The concept of "past", Naipaul believes, is a significant aspect in everybody's life. A sense of history is relevant to understand the present. The "idea of past" is also religion in Charleston. Here "past" was not merely referred to the old houses and the old families, the old names, the antiquarian side of principal or state history:

> It was also the past as a wound: the past of which the dead or alienated plantation spoke. Many of them still with physical memories of the old day, the house, the dependencies, the oak avenues. The past of which the more-black-than-white city now spoke, the past of slavery and the civil war. (99)

General Sherman had burned the State capital though he spared the Cathedral near the State House in Columbia. Naipaul was advised by Alex Sanders, chief judge of the South Carolina court of Appeals, to look at the Confederate Memorial. The judge told him that the inscription of the memorial was something that should be studied. It was poetic, and contained much of the South's idea of itself. Naipaul reflects on history on his way to see the monument on one side of which was engraved, "To South Carolina's dead of the confederate Army 1861-1865 and on the other side: Erected by the women of South Carolina, Unveiled May 13, 1879." He comments on seeing the engraving are noteworthy: "There was rhetoric in that reference to women; monuments of grief and revenge, or grief or piety, are most unsettling when they depict women bowed in grief" (99). The memorial makes Naipaul reflective on the "pain of defeat". The grand defeat that the memorial delineates makes one religious. With so much anguish and grief, he therefore comments:

> On one side: birth, faith, duty, suffering, and death. On the other side: the nameless, undefined cause, ennobled by these virtues. The words are grand, nevertheless. The pain of defeat is something that can be shared by everyone, since everyone at some stage in his life knows

> defeat of some sort and hopes in his heart to undo it, or at least to have his cause correctly seen. But the pain of the Confederate Memorial is very great; the defeat it speaks of is complete. Defeat like this leads to religion. It can be religion: the crucifixion, as eternal a grief for Christians as, for the Shias of Islam, the death of Ali and his sons. Grief and the conviction of a just cause; defeat going against every idea of morality, every idea of the good story, the right story, the way it should have been: the tears of the Confederate Memorial are close to religion, the helpless grief and rage (such as the Shias know) about an injustice that cannot be rehearsed too often. (100)

Naipaul however understands that the true past of the South had been lost. The world before the war and then the war itself were lost. Naipaul laments: "That grief was special and was like religion; it would last beyond the decline of the nineteenth-century empires, beyond the idea of empire itself" (101). The memorial about Spanish-American war was rather embarrassing to the cause of the earlier memorial. The grand words of the confederate Memorial could still be felt in the heart.

The suffering of the slaves was immense. All white boys had black slave boys to play with, and knock them down while playing. In the celebratory book *A Carolina Rice Plantation of the Fifties* published in New York in 1936 by William Morrow, there is reference to complete "economic security": "for this security, covertly, covering the whole period of their lives from boyhood to old age, a price was paid". "A price—that is the silent way in which, to preserve the idea of the classical world, slavery is referred to" (103). Another way of interpreting the slavery issue was more interesting:

> "For the South the slavery problem became the negro problem, and what in reality the Carolinian state strove against from 1831 to 1865 was a threatened 'solution' of the negro problem which would destroy them." The state required slaves; without slaves it couldn't get by: but the slaves threatened the state with extinction always. So the planter's special way of life in the rice

> lands of Carolina became "white civilization; that was the thing that had to be preserved". (103)

This is the irrational way in which the educated, sensitive people defended the shameful system of slavery. The dominance of North was generally not approved by people like Marion Saath who were engaging in political work. The so-called concept of "Americanization" was really "Northernization". To Saath, there was a great contribution of the South to the "idea of America". There was no need to define Southern values: "Southern culture is not simply a matter of the agrarian culture versus the industrial, or the ideals of honor against the crass values of commerce. Southern identity is important because it is southern. We are southern. That's enough" (105). Saath was really hurt by the superficial destruction of the South—the highways, the fast-food chains. Naipaul correlates the Shia connection to the past:

> The past as a dream of purity, the past as a cause for grief, the past as religion: it is the very prompting of the Shias of Islam to nobility and sacrifice, the dream of the good time of the Prophet and the first four Caliphs before greed and ambition destroyed the newly saved world. It was the very prompting of the Confederate Memorial in Columbia. And the very special Southern past and cause could be made pure only if it was removed from the squalor of the race issue. (106)

Judge Sanders comments on the life of the Southerners. As he gets older he realizes that the transgressions of the South were the transgressions of mankind. There are certain things that are superior. There is a cultural attitude in the South that embraces respect for family and God and in some ways for country. Among other things Sanders is rejecting racism altogether. Being a tolerant, he believes that common law is able to resolve so many issues, and gives people a larger identity:

> The common law is a majestic thing. It has a remarkable capacity to resolve disputes in a way which not only preserves civilization but enhances it. It is not unusual for me to find myself guided in a decision by a decision

> which a judge made a thousand years ago. I am aware I'm serving a larger civilization. And I know I'm serving it. (117)

In the British Empire slavery was only on a small scale. Soon after industrialization, the Empire could write off both the plantations and islands because it has now been a manufacturing and trading country. It abolished slavery in 1834 when slavery was very important in the United States. A slave is a slave who need not be tormented because the very state of slavery is rather disappointing and humiliating. The black man in the South was tormented. Naipaul was told that in the early days of motorcar in South Carolina Blacks had not been allowed to drive. In Tallassee he also heard that blacks were not allowed to try on clothes on stores. In Mississippi the blacks were not allowed to be educated beyond a certain level. In South Carolina, the blacks were not allowed to get education at all at a particular time. Violence and lawlessness were very much prevalent in the South:

> How did a black family react to news of lynching? What happened to the bodies? How were they buried? A man I met told me that when he was a child he was not allowed by his father to be a delivery boy. The father feared that a white woman might accuse the boy of being a Peeping Tom or attempting rape. (119)

Naipaul, comparing the West Indian Blacks with the Blacks of the United States, grieves for the ill-fated misfortunes of these deprived people. He understands that these men, despite so many possibilities, were kept in the darkness by the whites:

> In the Caribbean the black man, after a hundred years of colonial neglect, a hundred years of separation from slavery found himself in a majority on his own island with the power of electing his own leaders and his own government. The black American, at about the same time, found himself just liberated but in a minority in the world's most advanced country, and among the most denuded in that country. His possibilities as an American were far greater than these of a West Indian. But there could be no easy movement forward for the

> mass; they had lived through too much; the irrationality of slavery and the years after slavery had made many irrational and self-destructive. (119)

In the middle of his journey Naipaul began to wonder whether the truce that every black man looked for hadn't in fact been with the irrationality of the world around him. The Black people had a string. Religious heritage which Reverend Bernyce Clausell considered to come from slavery: "In slavery God was their deliverer. And they felt that someday God would work it out" (124). To these Blacks, churches were not merely the centers of worship; they were also community centers, and social centers. When there was segregation neither the Blacks nor the whites were happy: "Some people try to give impression that when we were segregated the whites were happy. But it's not true my son today has unlimited choices of career" (128). This was the resentment of Maurice Crockett who did not get her promotion despite her merit and qualification: "When, in 1964, I thought I was due for a promotion, they came and drove me around in the car and explained that I was qualified but they weren't ready for a colored person to do that kind of job yet. I went home and, I'll tell you, I cried. And it still hurts" (128). The discrimination and inhuman treatment to the Black people were beyond imagination. Their suffering perpetuated even after the liberation. Proper opportunities were not created for them. It was a great socio-economic issue when the Blacks were about to be released. The issue of racism was pervasive in the South. There were always dual laws, discriminations and indignities for the Blacks. Tuskegee was a Black Institute founded by Booker T. Washington, where the Blacks felt secured and safe. The campus of Tuskegee was a pretty one where the Blacks were not subjected to the type of life Black men were enduring in the rural areas during the time of Depression: "If I had been thrown out into the 'real world', it might, have been different. I might have become more aggressive—I can't tell what I may have done" (145). This is how a great musician, an old man, viewed about the Black Institute at Tuskegee that changed his life for better. This man further remarked how Tuskegee was a great oasis for the Blacks:

> It wasn't a conscious thing in my mind to seek safety. It was just the way my life developed. Though this environment did provide a lot of protection to the person against a lot of things that a person was subjected to in those days—I mean blacks. In the outside world we didn't have the same protection under the law that whites had. The moment you stepped off this campus you were subjected to all of the indignities. Everything was segregated. (145)

It was difficult to know when the irrational attitude of the whites would be going to end. The Blacks were however very much unhappy about it. The white people always claimed privileges and facilities because they thought they were above the blacks who were subordinate, and therefore should be discriminated. Inside the campus, the blacks were however secured and safe: "Indignity outside; within the campus, the erect pasture, the military correctness. Yet always—and how the irrationality would have twisted people—it was necessary to make signals to the people outside that you were not getting above yourself" (146). In course of time Tuskegee University achieved tremendous results for Black cause. The Blacks could be placed in the air-force for their talent. The Blacks were allowed to be admitted in the best hospitals meant for whites. But then the University was in decay; without funds the infrastructure was in ruins:

> The town—where once black students had worn their Tuskegee uniform as a kind of protection—was now safe: when black people had won the vote, the white people of Tuskegee had moved away. So, there had been a kind of victory here. But the town that had been taken over was small and poor, black-poor, with nothing of the life and money of the white University town of Auburrn, just twenty miles away. And Tuskegee Institute, now Tuskegee University, which could be said to have contributed to that local victory, was in decay. (148-49)

Despite its decay and without special funds, Tuskegee University was still needed for a "black experience". Black people preferred the Institute to study in an atmosphere of Black majority rather than in a minority place for Blacks:

> Tuskegee was still a going concern. It had a devoted committee: and it still had heart. Its financial predicament was the predicament of black schools generally: and it was better off than some. Its physical condition very far from that of Fisk University in Nashville, Tennessee, where in parts the campus looked ruined. There was a melancholy bronze statue there too, at Fisk, meant to set the seal on glory, but now seeming to watch over the ruins. The statue was of W.E.B. Du Bois, the rival and critic of Washington. (151)

Naipaul wanted to consider things from the point of view of the whites in Mississippi. In Alabama, he "found that Mississippi had a reputation for poverty and racial hardness" (155). Reaching there in Mississippi, Naipaul reflects on the situation of the "racially mixed society" there:

> But in a racially mixed society, especially one where race is a big issue, the different worlds have racial attributes or overtones. Distinctions and differences can have the force of taboos—things sensed rather than consciously worked out. In such a society participation is different from witness; they engage different sides of the person and it was with—old—relief that I put an end to my pleasure in the singing and dancing of the West Jackson Crusade, and returned to the silent healing of the air-conditioned room of the Ramada Renaissance in the north of the city. (158)

In Mississippi, violence was a dominant issue of the past. It was white violence during the childhood of Ellen, a white woman of sixty: "violence then; and there was violence now. The violence of her childhood had been white. The violence people spoke of now was black and was of cities" (162). The murder of Myrtle, the charming maid of her aunt always remained in her memory. She understood how a black woman's murder was just an insignificant event in Mississippi during her childhood:

> I think that if it had been a white woman killed like that they would have found out who did it. But I think that something, I'm thinking now. I don't think I thought that when I was eight years old. To me Myrtle was Myrtle. I didn't think of her being black. (163)

Ellen was greatly infringed by the thoughts of her father who told her that they could progress only when all of them work together. In this context Naipaul's comments are worth-noting: "That had been the great discovery of my travels so far in the south. In no other part of the world had I found people so driven by the idea of good behavior and the good religious life. And that was true for black and white (164). Referring to the present violence by Blacks in Mississippi, Louise, a woman of eighty recalled how in the past these people were so much oppressed that it had been a peaceful place: "They did not do the sort of thing they do now. We had very little trouble. They went their way; we went ours. We were used to having help" (168). Mary had been nostalgic while remembering the closeness between the whites and the Blacks during her grandfather's generation and her generation. Time had been changed to worse because the good relationship and cordiality between the two races no more existed:

> I don't think they did understand the race problem. I still don't think they do. I knew that people of, like my grandmother's generation—her generation and black people of the same generation had a closeness that doesn't exist anymore. In those days no one had money. You knew the depression and things. A lot of the jobs the black people had depended on the white people in the houses and yards and things. But the white people depended on the black people too. I think that at that time there was a better respect between the races. (182)

William, a businessman and also religious, deconstructing the crude attitude of the Northern Americans condemns their negative thinking:

> "People up North think they knew better than we about problems and people down here. They think they know

> how the black man thinks and the white man thinks. They have missed miserably on the black man." The North had disrupted the more economically active South in 1860; and they had done it again after World War II. (183)

Lewis, a local politician tells Naipaul that he has a great pride in his past even if it is filled with racism: "…I truly respect my past, be it segregated, be it filled with racism, be it whatever. Because I feel I have a place in the world, and I'm going to get it" (195). This sense of identity, laid by Lewis, is significant in the life of every individual. This Lewis, like many Southerners was however a religious man who believed that whatever he achieved was due to the grace of God. Through his encounter with a number of people around seventy, Naipaul was wondering how such people around seventy were able to live through many different worlds: "That the childhoods of solid citizens would have left memories of frontier life, primitive conditions, and closed communities; things hard now to recapture" (197).

Naipaul met the retired Supreme Court Judge Sugg in the hill town of Eupora, to the East of Delta. Judge Sugg, born in 1916 and retired in 1983, narrated his past since childhood when the Black River had no bridge, causing people suffer immensely. Recalling the immensities of hardships of the past life the Judge contrasts the modern life with all facilities like TV and instant entertainments. In the past everybody was poor and the town had only fourteen or fifteen hundred people. A white self-educated man, his father was a merchant. Mostly people were poor farmers. His family on both sides came to Mississippi between 1830 and 1840. In that hill town, there were no social distinctions like rich or poor, caste or class except between black and white. Since the people were very close because of a small populace, life was very much informal in the pioneer state. But, sometimes there were quick tempers leading to homicides and crimes of passion. However, people were co-operative to each other:

> They would just get angry, get into an argument. Some of them would be drunk. They would be, may be quarreling, and have a fight, and somebody would get

> killed. They were slow to arouse, but when you get somebody like that angry somebody would get hurt. Otherwise, helpful people lovely people. (200)

These Mississippi people were self-reliant and therefore hard-working agriculturists. That is so because "the idea of religion, threaded into the idea of the pioneer past" (200). Judge Sugg, with great satisfaction comments: "And I'm just thankful that I live in a country that has a heritage of people who are willing to look beyond the horizon and catch a vision of opening up new country for others to enjoy a better life" (201). That is so because the "pioneer spirit" was greatly guided by religious spirit, in the religious people of loving our neighbor. Religion had been so deeply intertwined with the practice of life in these pioneers. In the 1960s, Mississippi had the notoriety of being a place of violence because the Black population which consisted of 30 percent of total populace was treated with contempt and discrimination. They were not considered for similar privileges and rights as blacks: "I think this was a holdover from the days of slavery, when the blacks were servants and were looked upon as property, not people. And we white people have got to recognize the fact that God loves everybody" (202). Judge Sugg, through his "soul searching" realized that blacks were as much his neighbors as whites for which he took the mission of teaching to the poor Blacks. By that way, he was able to transform the lives of many black outcastes. This is essential in the society to bring about transformation through a change of heart. Reflecting upon the frontier life in respect of Judge Sugg's religious spirit Naipaul contemplates:

> The frontier, nature, faith, work, the contracts with other men—in Judge Sugg's world picture the ideas were as knitted together as they were in the world picture of William, the businessman. The Baptist faith made both men complete, each in his own way. But Judge Sugg had also been led by his faith and his past (the two things almost one) to an unlikely compassion—for black people, who had formed 30 percent of the population of his little home town. (201)

Naipaul's encounter with Campbell was also an experience of revealing the redneck society in Mississippi area. Campbell was the man "who represented the other side of the religious South, the authoritarian side" (204). He explained Naipaul that a redneck was "a lower blue-collar construction worker who definitely does not like blacks, he likes to drink beer. He's going to wear cowboy boots..." (206). These rednecks constituted sixty or sixty-five percent of the white population. They had the same old attitude as the black people. Originally the term referred to a person who lived by hard work, although it was changed in the 1950s, when the frontier or pioneer life was changing. Although Campbell praises the rednecks, he is also critical of both the blacks and rednecks:

> I admire them for their independence. But it's not right for the society now. No question about it. It was great a long time ago. But not now. You can't get business done in a modern city with that kind of mentality. We got to change that redneck society and that black society, or the wealth is going to be just in the few hands that it's been in. (210)

These rednecks were less materialists, free spirits. They were like tribal people "almost an Indian tribe, free spirits wandering freely over empty spaces" (211). The frontiersmen had a negative mentality, Eudor Welty believed because they had the motto: "Scare everybody, outwit everybody, bear everybody, kill everybody—that's the frontiersman's mentality" (214). Welty as a writer views about Mississippi region: "The great thing taught me here as a writer is a sense of continuity. In a place that hasn't changed much you get to know the generations. You can see the whole narrative of a town's history or a family's history" (214). For a final impression about the state of Mississippi Naipaul had a talk about the constitution of 1890 with the former Governor William Winter. History in Mississippi seemed to come in every thirty years: "Half the state Indian country in 1830; in 1860, the Civil War about to come; in 1890, after the Civil War and Reconstruction, a new constitution" (215). The Governor explained that the 1890 constitution was written with a motive to restore the 'white control' of the political processes of the state. It was a constitution which had provision for discouragement of black voting. Another negative provision was the anti-businesses one which prevented the state from rapid industrialization. The governor viewed that there was "an archaic tone to the whole document" (216). The Governor therefore argued:

> We need the psychological benefit now of a late-twentieth-country document. And the second thing, we need the restructuring of the manner in which we govern the state. We have to eliminate many of the processes designed to decentralize and fragment power. In 1890 there was distrust of any concentration of power in any one individual. With the result that's not a single law that's passed by the Mississippi legislature that is in strict accordance with the constitution of 1890. (216)

Because of the archaic nature of the constitution, it remained pastoral and the legislators were all ultra-conservatives who represented the "planter, agricultural interests". Many of them participated in the Civil War and mostly had strong racial bias: "They were committed to eliminating the black presence in the political process" (217). The constitution was a biased one which looked into the interest of the land-owners rather than the workers: "The constitution spoke to the economic interest of those who drafted it. For instance, it spoke of the maintenance of a levee system along the Mississippi River—which really has no place in a constitution" (217). It is a sort of Neo-colonial attitude of the constitution drafters. Because of this conservative, non-progressive attitude and selfish motives of the makers of the constitution, the state remained a backward one without any modern industries for a long time although there were amendments to the various provisions afterwards: "The Carolina and Georgia had tobacco-processing plants and textile plants. Alabama has a well-established industrial base going back to the nineteenth century. Mississippi never developed this kind of base (218). To the testimony to this, the 1984 map of the United States, kept on the desk of the Governor, reveals: "The map showed three concentrated areas of distressed counties: on the Mexican border; the Indian areas in the west; and, making almost one pink area, the Southern Black Belt of Alabama and almost all of Mississippi" (218).

Despite that, the frontier constitution was meant for representing truth about the state. The people have still grieved for the past that was more country-like, easy-going and unbusiness-like "when time was not money" (*TS* 218). The constitution of 1890 was able to give the security to the people about their "beauty of the past". Naipaul therefore makes some pertinent remarks about this state:

> It had been a frontier state, but always with this contradictory component of slavery. It was slavery that the old plantation land had around Natchez, on the river, spoke. The land, as flat and warm and soft as rice lands of South Carolina spoke of wealth and the need for black men, by the thousands. But Natchez also had its plantation houses, now days the object twice a year of "pilgrimages": the old sentimentality of the South, the divided mind, the beauty and sorrow of past containing the unmentionable ragged, black thing of slavery. (218-19)

Naipaul through traveling is searching for patterns of life in the Southern states. In the process, he encounters people from various professions and fields: common folk, politicians, judges, administrators, writers, businessmen, religious people, councilors and so on. Traveling provides a lot of romantic pleasures if one is not worried about its purpose. Though Naipaul had such an experience of pleasure while driving in Mississippi from the Delta to Jackson one stormy afternoon, his great pleasure was however diluted due to his botheration for writing, and meeting the next people and places for the purpose. Defining his own approach to traveling and inquiries on the themes and patterns, Naipaul comments reflectively:

> If you travel on a theme, the theme has to develop with the travel. At the beginning your interests can be broad and scattered. But then they must be more focused; the different stages of journey cannot simply be versions of one another. And, more than the other kind of

> travel, this traveling on a theme depended on luck. It depended on the people you met, the little illuminations you had. As with the next day's issue of a fast moving daily newspaper, the shape of the chapter in hand was continually being changed by accidents on the way. (222)

Naipaul recalls how the chance factor could enable him to encounter with Campbell who gave him a lyrical account of the rednecks of Rankin Country: "The outdoor life, relic of frontier self-sufficiency, mixed up with a dislike of black people, and oddly meshed with the love of country music, 'down-home music, crying music' and the cult of Elvin Presley" (222). Naipaul went to see the house of Presley at Tupelo where he began to get some new feeling about the Presley cult. Tupelo was the birthplace of Presley, "the man of the people, the saint of the people, made pretty and suitable, a shrine" (225). Later Naipaul was really surprised when he saw a poster in Charles Wilson's informal Presley collection in the centre for the study of Southern culture at Oxford, Mississippi:

> The most striking item was a poster that showed a tight-trousered full-bottomed Presley playing a guitar in the lower left-hand corner, with a staircase leading up to his mother and Graceland—the Presley house in Memphis—in the sky. Redneck fulfillment—socially pathetic at one level; at another, religious art of a kind, with Christian borrowings: the beatification of the central figure, with all his sexuality. Graceland like a version of the New Jerusalem in a medieval Doomsday painting. (225)

It was really astonishing to think of the impact of music on the people. Despite these people had political leaders, sportsmen, film stars as their heroes, they could not be close to them. Presley was however their singer who was one among them. Naipaul analyses the leadership cult in West Indies. The leader lived on behalf of his people and the people lived through them. It was not necessary for a leader to be modest and correct. To him ordinary ideas of morality and propriety did not apply. To the black people, a leader in the West Indies was to be grand and larger than life though in recent times, such an idea has been changed. Naipaul observes something like this black adulation in the Presley cult:

> It was strange—to me—that music should have carried so much of a people's emotional needs. And when, in Nashville, Tennessee, I went to performance of the "Grand Ole Oprey" the long-running country music radio program, I felt quite apart from what I was witnessing. It was like a tribal rite; it might all have been in a foreign language. (227)

In that performance of music some of the performers with Cowboy hats and over all working clothes gave a clue: "country music created a community, and was the expression of a community" (227). To Allen Reynolds, producer, country music is "real people's music, lyrically and melodically" (229). He further explained: "In country music the music itself was not important. What mattered were the words. But the words were few and simple, and the themes were so stylized" (229). The opinion of Reverend K.C. Ptoemy, the Presbyterian poster of Westminster Church, in one of the most prosperous parts of Nashville, is worth-mentioning:

> It's white soul music. It's comparable to the role that music played for slaves in the last century. It creates community among oppressed people. I like it. I listen to it because in the words I hear protest against the oppressive aspects of life as a poor white person experiences it. About the much-publicized religious faith of some of the singers, he said: "They're religious in a special way. Religion is to them a shared emotional experience rather than a shared doctrine." (232)

In this country music, the singer is both the star and victim. There is always a sense of loss for far-away things of the past. In that sense of loss, the entire community identify their own sense of loss: "Inseparable from this were the fundamentalist frontier religions, which had preserved for those people the idea of a complete, created world and a complete, divinely sanctioned code" (233). Naipaul therefore understands and learns: "Music and community, and tears and faith: I felt that

I had been taken, through country music, to an understanding of a whole distinctive culture, something I had never imagined existing in the United States" (233). Naipaul's enquiry into the identity of the Southerners is based on the distinctive culture and the Southern Baptist identity. The American Baptist is more open-minded unlike the religious rigidity of the Southern Baptist: "It has to do with sharing biblical literalism; it has to do with morality. For example to be a Southern Baptist is to be teetotaler. Morality, dancing, drinking—it encompasses the whole of life" (234). Reverend James Vandiver explained that the mid-south is at a pivotal point which is so near a place of American origins: "From a cultural and socio-economic point of view, the people in this area have common value systems and basically an agrarian economy. And basically people of that niche tend to be a bit more religious (235). James further told Naipaul that "the Church of Christ represented an abandoning of Protestantism and did not represent a return to Rome, but to the very beginning of the faith all the way back to Pentecost, the first Biblical dating of the Christian culture" (236). In his frank confession James told that the society in the South was rapidly changing "from agrarian to business and industry, from rural to urban from blue-collar to white-collar, from lower to middle and upper-class" (237). Henry was a man who was questioning the significance of the Christian faith and disillusioned. He was in a state of turmoil. Naipaul describes his state of mind: "An experience of Africa, the shock of a tribal Civil War, a new vision of missionary effort, leading to wider questioning: what had once been the complete, satisfying faith of a complete, clear, enclosed world no longer answered. And he was in a "whirlwind" (239). Ben who came from a church of Christ family had a great faith in the idea of service and brotherhood. But Melvin, who was in his early forties, and had drifted away from the church of Christ, did not believe in the idea of fellowship and viewed that the church would not exist in twenty-five years in its existing form. A rising professional man Melvin had grown to reject "the completeness of the culture of his childhood. Religion, the frontier faith had created this completeness; now it was a burden he could do without. In a new world, he wished religion to have its place, like everything else. Yes he knew that he was rejecting a part of his identity" (243). Melvin understood that the church of Christ was doing an excellent job by "meshing traditional values with Christian principles". However, Melvin felt that it was necessary to have the break with the South he had known. South had a certain identity, but because of its rigidity, creative people felt stifled for which they moved to places like California for business initiatives:

> Creative people have to get away from the South. It will be a very long time before that stifling will disappear. It will be my generation that will break the link. It's not something I say with any pride. Nor shame. No judgment. I say it purely as fact. (244)

Such an opinion of Melvin found confirmation with another distinguished man who told Naipaul that professional, successful people originally from small towns who had been Baptist or church of Christ were now Presbyterians. This Presbyterianism was socially acceptable because "it was more lenient, less demanding, less intrusive or encompassing" (244). Naipaul therefore reflects:

> The frontier had ceased to exist. And the religions it had bred were beginning slowly to die. In the old days when men, often of little education, had needed only to declare themselves ministers, people would have seen themselves reflected in the expounders of the word. This quality of the homespun would have made the religions appear creations of a community, personal and close and inviolable. Now a certain distance was needed. (244)

Naipaul's main concern in the South was to deconstruct history of the people, places and the states. Through this main concern he also focused on the politics, culture, identity, religion and civilization of these people. Looking at the present situations and crises, he goes back to the past and correlates the past way of life with the present. He also understands how the marginalized people like the Negroes and blacks had a kind of history which was humiliating to them for which they very often repulsed to look at the past life. As we know, history is also concerned with ruins and reconstructions, so also happens to all landscapes and cultures. That is therefore Naipaul views: "Every stage of history marked by small ruins, a landscape of small ruins—this had been my first impression of the South when I had come down at Easter with Howard, to see the place that to him was home, not very far from here" (277). Before completing his Southern travel, Naipaul moved to North Carolina. There was a great change in the fortune of poor North Carolina after 1960 because of the unusual industrial growth in the area as it provided thirty-thousand jobs to the people. Many modern technological and pharmaceutical names had been established in elegant style in the big industrial park of seventy-five hundred acres of land transforming the rural poverty and creating the impression that the agrarian South had been abolished here. This area was now known as the Research Triangle, bounded by the University campuses of Chapel Hill, Raleigh, and Durham. In this region of North Carolina, Tobacco was an old crop which was associated with the way of life. This tobacco culture was introduced to Naipaul by James Applewhite, a Duke University teacher of fifty-two at Durham. He was the grandson of a farmer, and also a poet. This tobacco crop needed hard, back-breaking labor and he was himself very close to this tobacco culture though he only smoked in the past for a little time. However, this crop that gave the region a distinctive cultural identity was a narcotic, dangerous crop although it had great commercial viability in the past. Applewhite liked tobacco as a culture, "for the formalities that went with the growing and curing and selling of the crop" (270). He was associated with tobacco as a "culture of his family history":

> Tobacco was associated with on older mode of living. Associated for me with my grandfather with a kind of ritualized cyclical time order, where the cycle of the seasons was marked by sowing the plant bed, preparing the land in the spring, setting out the plants in early summer, harvesting in midsummer. You'd be finishing up curing and grading in August. (272)

To Applewhite tobacco in its best incarnation was a sort of folk art practiced by people who were extremely good at it although they were illiterate. When the South was at a pretty disadvantageous position economically, it brought in cash money from the whole country and even from abroad. Tobacco had a final use as a social gesture although this crop was poisonous and therefore the South did not need to grow this crop any more: "I think of tobacco as an old Testament aspect of a past way of life, a kind of traditional conservative, fallen world, a world marked by original sin, of which tobacco was a kind of symbol (275).

In this part of American South modernization has always brought a sense of loss among people. Applewhite tells Naipaul now his mother-in-law was feeling lost due to electrification and other modern amenities just recently:

> Automobiles began to come into that area in the 1920s and electric light. Electrification tended to follow the roads. My wife's mother was reminiscing earlier this year, remembering when electrification got to the country. People did feel lost here. The sense of needing to form a life that had its own regularities, its own formalities—that was a reason that religion had the contour it had. That's why the formalities of tobacco-growing were so important. (275)

Religion and agriculture were so important to these people that any other change made them too much uncomfortable. They were conditioned to these factors. The rural agrarian economy was gradually being replaced by another modernized, industrial economy. But these communities were not much happy about this. Naipaul therefore comments: "Agricultural communities are conditioned, given a calendar, by the crops they grow, and the origin or first purpose of the crop becomes unimportant: rice in Java, tobacco in North Carolina, sugar cane in Trinidad in the old days" (272). Applewhite was sometimes baffled when he reflected upon the whole business of tobacco. To him this tobacco culture, which gave a way of life to the people of the region, was really a paradox of civilization because this tobacco is both poisonous and dangerous:

> It's mastery and a paradox. For me it has a certain resonance, the whole tobacco business, and it is close

> to the paradox of civilization itself. That this essentially poisonous substance formed the basis of a way of life that had so many attractive aspects—a formalized seasonal cycle to it, which left the land combed into its even furrows after the stalks had been cut in the autumn. Which had the spectacle of the tobacco market, with the golden piles of aromatic leaf being sold for what were really considerable sums of money? (275)

To Applewhite tobacco-farming was an aesthetic art, unique to North Carolina region. The tobacco produced here was a special kind with unique color and flavor. It could not be matched by the tobacco produced anywhere:

> ...one can argue that any successful agrarian economy has most of the aspects of tobacco-farming. What it doesn't have is the hand crafted, graded, aromatic sold-by-auction quality that tobacco has. The issue of quality, as determined by color, scent, and flavors, was central to tobacco. There's a region specificity to wine, and tobacco is in a sense analogous: there's a region specificity to tobacco as well. (276)

To Applewhite, the landscape of eastern North Carolina was, however a kind of landscape of the past: "There was this dichotomy in my own life between my father and my grandfather" (277). His grandfather had been born in that Civil War-era farmhouse. He was always associated, in Applewhite's mind, with agrarian economy. His father however ran a service station and believed in progress and sold electrical appliances for so many years. Though his father was always in a hurry, his grandfather was never hurried.

Reverend James Abrahamson, pastor of the Chapel Hill Bible Church, refuted the notion that the people of the region were indulging in "tobacco-politics, the small-farmer politics for getting continued support for tobacco farming. To him, the fundamentalist political impulse had always been there. Since the 1930s, the Universities moved to embrace the material and scientific aspects in life for a secular society. The eastern-North Carolina conservatism was therefore viewed "as being redneck and knee-jerk. Irresponsible—fanatical almost unenlightened, lacking what I call three 'I's—intelligence, information, and integrity" (284). However, the other side of this culture was that it was away from the materialism of the so-called secular society; "our culture may self-destruct before they have chance to articulate clearly the common sense they represent for a culture that is based on more than self and materialism" (284). Jim Abrahamson was himself a fundamentalist and believed that American society had been built on a religious base. However, he believed that the religious principles should be linked to the worldview of secularists who worked for the human society with some genuine concerns: "The religious right appears not to understand the worldview the left or the secular intelligentsia embrace. They tend to dismiss them as God-haters or infidels. And they have a difficulty about drown how to translate religious ideals into a political policy" (285). Naipaul is rather surprised to note the same concern for change and security in the left-behind corner of the United States. He considers that this was also the Islamic problem "since the Islamic state had never been defined by the founder—and it was the prompting to fundamentalism in many countries: how to know the truth and hold on to one's soul at a time of great change' (285).

However Barry McCarty, a professor of public speaking and debate since 1980 was more secure in his faith and in his politics. He combined politics and faith in his work-ethics. He was considered a New Right leader in the coming generation. McCarty, who lived in Elizabethan city two hundred miles away from Research Triangle, idolized Jesse Helms. He was therefore a Jesse-Crat that referred to "a conservative North Carolina Democrat who votes for Jesse Helms and people like Jesse Helms. They represent the conservative values of the old South-faith in God. It was a belief in limited government, a belief in free enterprise—Individual liberty and individual responsibility. In 1985, governor of North Carolina appointed him chairman of the State Social Services Commission for a four-year term. In that capacity he was trying to introduce the idea of workfare rather than welfare. The basic idea of workfare is that welfare recipients who are able to work are required to work in order to continue to be able to receive their benefits. It's part of the Southern work ethic. As a follower of Jesse Helm, he believes that the powers of the federal government should be strictly limited: "The more remote the government becomes, the less it should have to do with the life of the individuals" (288). His inclination to and passion for politics were influenced by the Bible which teaches that governments are necessary in order to establish order and justice in human society. In Chapter 13, Paul Apostle teaches that "governments have the authority of God" (288). Like God punishes the sinners, the government should also punish the lawbreakers. McCarty attacks the federal government for its taxation policy of exploitation in the name of charity:

> I question the very morality of the federal welfare system. If you were hungry, and I take you home and feed you, that is benevolence because I have chosen to show charity towards you. But when the federal government legally plunders me through taxation in order to give you, I consider that immoral. (290)

McCarty had tremendous faith in the Southern values and its people in rebuilding their state. People not only depended on farming, they also did other odd jobs like carpenters, mechanics and so on. These people believed in work and earned their livelihood through centuries. These people who worked hard were conservatives by choice not by ignorance: "what I'm saying is the conservatism and values that are held by choice and not through ignorance of what the modern world has to offer. They are timeless values, enduring values" (293). However he understood that the world constantly changes for which everybody should adapt. In spite of that, certain values however never change, they remains constant. He qualifies this argument by explaining that western civilization basically was Christian till the 17th century. However in the modern view "the world is just one damned thing after another. A horrible worldview ultimately a worldview human beings cannot live with. It cannot last. It will destroy itself" (295). He had all sympathies for the blacks who had the Southern work ethic and mostly were conservative; but he was puzzled to note that "they didn't vote conservative; they voted for black candidates" (296) in Elizabeth city. Naipaul's interaction with McCarty ended with the latter showing him the Confederate memorial which made Naipaul to reflect upon:

> The past transformed, lifted above the actual history, and given an almost religious symbolism; political faith and religious faith running into one, I had been told that the conservatives of North Carolina spoke in code. The code could sometimes be transparent: "Tobacco Is A Way of Life" being the small farmer's plea for government money. But in this flat land of small fields and small ruins there were also certain emotions that were too deep for words. (296)

In his final journey Naipaul accompanied Jim Applewhite to see the family farm in Wilson country, the heart of the Eastern-North Carolina tobacco country. Naipaul recalled how he accompanied Howard to see his mother's home at Bowen in the spring. Ten miles from the farmhouse of Applewhite they now went to the home of Applewhite's father at Stantonsburg at the end of summer. With Jim, Naipaul was considering another kind of past: "a past where the child had seen completeness, even in the stock-for tenants-of his grandfather's general store: mule collars, tobacco twine ten-penny nails..., bonnets, shoes for children" (301). In the beginning of his journey Naipaul was taken by Hetty, Howard's mother, to "the black cemetery, where her father was buried. She had shown me the farmhouse, now in ruin, with small trees and vines growing right up against it, where her father had lived as sharecropper" (301). She was however unwilling to go to the "gloom of her past" and the tobacco that she grew with her father and her husband made her cry. Applewhite reflecting upon his past unraveled to Naipaul that he had himself cut off from the past, "made a far journey. But that past was here still, a couple of hours way from Durham, or as much of the past as man of fifty-two might reasonably expect still to find. But a journey had been made; there had been a break" (302).

Applewhite told Naipaul that as a child he was always conscious of not belonging to his native world. Whenever he met Dee Grimes, his tenant in the farmhouse, he felt "a kind of kinship and a kind of separation" (303). He was the tobacco man who really belonged to that world: "Presumably, it began with that separation when I was a child, when I was set apart from those who were unself-consciously playing their part in this eastern-north Carolina world, which is a world of action, not of thinking" (303). Applewhite remembers occasions of visiting back during his early years of college and once again experiencing what he has now almost forgotten—"and that is a sensation of being so utterly at home in, and a part of a place, that one feels somehow coextensive with the place" (303). He further tells: "On the other hand, there is a sense of separateness in being in part of myself an observing stranger in my own native land. To the extent that at times I was fascinated by the idea of pre-existence of the soul" (303). Naipaul correlates how Jim's thoughts were his own thoughts in Trinidad when he himself was feeling that kind of sensation. It was also the same strange feeling of Howard, Hetty's son, in his own birth place: "I always felt different which leads me to believe I was born in the wrong town. Like many people" (304). Jim continued his reflections:

> My feeling of duality at that time was being physically in the world I identified with but which on the other hand completely left out a whole other side of my psyche or my soul. There was still a cultural transmission here—from something quite other—through the churches, the hymns, the words and the music, the poetry of the psalms in the king James Bible, and through books. (304)

He further tells Naipaul that there is a sense of self-subsistence about the South. Because of this sense of beleaguered self-sufficiency, it can be extremely pigheaded. It can cherish ignorance, the unreasonable and the unreasoning. Applewhite's intense contemplation of the physical world of his childhood drew Naipaul closer to him though his world was not at all like Naipaul's. Out of his separation Applewhite went beyond the religious faith of his ancestors and arrived at "a feeling of the sanctity of the smallest gestures" which was an imaginative poetic resolution, quite different from Barry McCarty's feeling as a politician. Despite differences such men had been created through their common sharing a common history, a special kind of past, the past as a wound. Appreciative of these Southern people's special history of defeat, a desperate kind of new world history, Naipaul feels happy to live among them, in the poorer land that reflected this history. *A Turn in the South,* deals with so many issues. The first thing we find here is a sense of loss. Life in South America seems to have lost a lot of the past forever due to Civil War. The whites lament the colonial period and the blacks lament their culture because of integration in the society. The sense of racism still exists even after the Civil Rights Movement. We find this in the attitudes of Blacks and Whites to the past. While the whites are full of nostalgia and regret, and they have a deep craze for the past, the blacks have hatred for the past as it gives them the sense of gloom. But at the same time Blacks too lament for the loss of the past, of the clannishness that existed among them. The Civil Rights have taken away this community spirit of the Blacks. In his visit to Tuskegee in Alabama for the University of Black people founded by Booker T. Washington, Naipaul finds a connection with Trinidad: colonial past, slave history and homelessness. Displacement also reminds him of his native land, Trinidad. In the very beginning of the book we find a kind of sense of homelessness, of exile, when Howard says, "I would go home to Mamma". A kind of bond he discovers through the book between Trinidad and South America is a bond of slavery, racial conflict and plantation society. In his observation of the third world countries he had been more disdainful and critical but here we find him more tolerant, empathetic, and tearful for them.

So far as the religious fundamentalism of Southern Christianity is concerned, Naipaul seems to advocate it as a compensation for the anguish and disturbed order of the past. His tone seems to be generous and reflective in contrast with his views on Indians and Islamic people in the travelogues, *AD*, *IWC* and *AB* where he condemns all forms of religion as irrational. *A Turn in the South* delineates Southern people's love of their culture, which was built upon the horrors of slavery. Naipaul's vivid descriptions and interpretations bring out the richness of this culture though he sets different Southerners sometimes in contrast in respect of their different views which are often puzzling. This travel book, which is a kind by itself, is a serious scrutiny into the nature of a civilization. Naipaul's inquiries to Southern resistances to modernization are quite illuminating and interesting. The descriptions and interactions are lively and enlightening; they focus on various aspects of life, manner, religion, politics, economy, culture and civilization. His inquiries into the racial tension are truth-based and authentic rather than being biased.

PART IV

Conclusion

10

Self, Culture and Universal Civilization

10.1. Notion of History and Civilization

Naipaul is concerned with the "suppressed histories" of peoples and nations. Through his fictions and travelogues, he has delineated the history of the vanquished. Dr. Horace Engdahl, the permanent secretary to the Swedish Academy therefore made the following remarks while delivering his speech in the Nobel Prize Award ceremony in 2001:

> Naipaul's literary domain has extended far beyond the West Indian Island of Trinidad, his first subject, and now encompasses India, Africa, America from south to north, the Islamic countries of Asia and, not least, England. Naipaul is Conrad's heir as the annalist of the destinies of empires in the moral sense: what they do to human beings. His authority as a narrator is grounded in his memory of what others have forgotten. (Ray xi)

Naipaul is original in his approach to the style and theme in his writings—whether it is fiction or travelogue. The comments of William Walsh are significant:

> Coleridge's words about Wordsworth are peculiarly appropriate to the nature of Naipaul's sensibility. He has the telescopic sight of the unattached observer, even an observer of genius, but one in whom the observation of others leads to analysis of self. (1973: 15)

Naipaul has tried to understand his self and background—his concern for his own history has led him to understand the civilization and culture of the world. Robert Hamner in the *Critical Perspectives on V.S. Naipaul* observes:

> For the fallacy of the primitive paradise, it seems to me, Mr. Naipaul wants to exchange that of the metropolitan paradise. The desire gives "*The Loss of El Dorado*" its bleak and caustic tone, yet also its persuasive sadness and the power of poetry. (158)

His further remarks are noteworthy:

> When there are words so rich in esthetic and humanistic value as Naipaul's are, it is unfortunate that many readers and critics are put off by such peripheral concerns at the author's political affiliations, or the quality of his compassion. (1979: xxix)

In Naipaul's final analysis, his predecessors, the sources of his material, and his political affiliations are not as important as the individual works, which stand on their own merits. Hamner glorifies Naipaul's efforts:

> ...By putting his finger on elusive problems, foibles, follies, and vices, recreating them within recognizable characters, he gives immediacy and comprehensible form to a reality which is otherwise too complex and expansive to grasp. This is no small achievement. (xxx)

Naipaul has not merged in the English tradition. He came from a multi-racial society of Trinidad which was an immigrant, slave, colonial society that had no concrete tradition. The English society did not belong to him. Although he read such great English and European writers as Dickens, Austen, Bronte sisters, Maupassant and Moliere who shaped his literary experience, they were unable to stir his imagination. He needed a tradition of his own which the English society could not provide to him. For every writer a literary tradition was needed so that he could be grounded in that tradition to flourish his literary career. But the English social tradition was completely different from that of Trinidad. These writers whom he read for becoming a part of the literary tradition however could not stir his imagination. He therefore felt the vacuum:

> The tradition that was not his was the particular social, political, philosophical structure of bourgeois society of England from the seventeenth century to the present day out of which the novel emerged and developed. Naipaul regrets this absence of a literary tradition as a handicap to a writer of fiction. (Kamra 14)

Naipaul thinks that every writer needs "a starting point for further observation.... Every writer is, in the long run, on his own; but it helps, in the most practical way to have a tradition" (Barracoon 26). However the society in which Naipaul grew up was a society without heroes. It was a colonial society with the "drive and restlessness of immigrants" where the forms of tradition and culture survived losing the essence of it. As a result the core of the tradition submerged and destroyed rendering it meaningless and insignificant. Naipaul therefore expresses in anguish: "To us, without a mythology, all literatures were foreign. Trinidad was small, remote and unimportant, and we know we could not hope to read in books of the life we saw about us" (1976: 24). Such anguish always haunted him in his writing career: "My material had not been sufficiently hallowed by a tradition; I was not fully convinced of its importance: and some embarrassment remained" (1976: 27).

In Naipaul's writings, the protagonist is a peripheral man. His struggle is against his marginalization, against anarchic, chaotic surrounding to achieve a fuller life. The suffering of the marginalized individual is so vast that it is not always possible on his part to reach the essence. However, his struggle is explicitly and implicitly a reflection of the efforts of attaining human dignity:

> He realizes that the core (essence) of life can never be touched as, like a mirage, it recedes before an ever-widening consciousness; to live intensely in the present... is the acceptance of the futility of such a search. The final release is the discovery that to live a full life, knowledge of the core is not necessary. (Kamra 14-15)

Naipaul understands that man is not secure in the universe. His protagonist is therefore an ordinary man. However, he searches for his identity, and strives for leaving a mark in society. In the process, he is trapped rather than being often successful. To Naipaul, so-called spiritual inclination is not real. It is the privilege of a few people who indulge in unreal rituals. He sees that life is more inclined to materialism based on the more visual conflicts, polarities and differences in the society. He therefore insists on the need of a tradition or a myth or a history as an external starting point for the self in order to become real: someone whose presence or absence is felt. If man is deprived of it, he will search for it or create it. A sense of reality is more than awareness of actuality. It is an eclectic perspective acquired through varied experiences. This is obvious in his novels as the protagonist's agonizing experience of the "sense of place" creates a sense of despair in the protagonist/narrator, and finally resulting in the objective artistic vision of the narrator.

The personal experience of the protagonist is unique; it cannot be objective. Naipaul thinks in terms of insecurity of man, and has immense doubts about human dignity and freedom in the chaos of modern life. In the existential writings of Sartre, Camus, Kierkegaard, and Heidegger, man is always trapped in a meaningless, chaotic and capricious universe and strives hard to maintain his dignity. Through his failings, he achieves his dignity. Individuality is supreme in such writings despite man's sufferings. John Press explains the fragmented and tortured modern consciousness in *A Map of Modern English Verse*:

> Two world wars, reintroduction of torture by governments generally reckoned to be civilized, the scientific planning of genocide the deliberate crushing of the individual by totalitarian states, the eviction of millions of families from their homes, the outbursts of irrational violence and of racial hatred in the great cities of the world, the possibility that *homo sapiens* may destroy himself—all the factors have lent urgency to the question "what is man?" It is the question which haunts modern English verse. (1977: 4)

Naipaul has been successful in transfusing the socio-political and literary problems into "a dialectic of his fictional technique"

(Kamra 17). To him, tradition, history and legend are of immense significance. They are however not of any mythic, archetypal and spiritual significance. They are not in any way related to an absolute cultural and religious life. On the other hand, his concept of tradition and history is more akin to Eliot's idea of tradition and history:

> Tradition is a matter of much wider significance. It cannot be inherited, and if you want it you must obtain it by great labor. It involves in the first place, the historical sense.... This historical sense, which is a sense of the timeless as well as of the temporal and of the timeless and of the time temporal together, is what makes a writer most acutely conscious of his place in time, of his own contemporaneity. (*SW* 49)

In the early fiction, Naipaul shows how "a sense of place" is an obstruction to the material prosperity of the protagonists such as attaining political power, wealth, holding higher positions in the society as well as owning a home. He portrays "a sense of place" as a historical reality in these novels. In the later novels, "a sense of place" is however imaginative, and it has been portrayed emotionally. In Naipaul's fiction, tradition is a major factor which dominates the individual in his struggle for dignity and self-glorification:

> Tradition, then, in all its aspects, as the trap of a static life, as the promise of the future, as the desired and the feared, as the controller of man's vision and action becomes internalized as 'mood' which being the expression of the total personality at any particular moment is incapable of analysis and hence of being captured. In his fiction it becomes a major objective correlative for the existential anguish of loss and impermanence, the effort to overcome it and the inability to do so except temporarily: it is the subjective and sensible apprehension of the metaphysical entrapment of the self. (Kamra 17-18)

Writing a work is a political act. The artist is to choose the political as well as sociological ideologies for representation in his work. Naipaul is concerned with the cultural, social and economic reality of the third world nations. He delineates the idea that man is in a state of helplessness in a hostile world. So far as tradition is concerned, the writer is to operate within an intellectual culture. The literature of the past influences a writer despite his desire for independence. Often, the writer is to incorporate the elements which he vigorously opposes in his life. However, tradition cannot influence sensitivity, style and sensibility of a writer. The writer can generate a new form to express his awareness of his material.

The traditional form of novel is not adequate to represent the multiple dimensions of a chaotic and capricious life. Naipaul therefore manipulates the narrative technique in his writings without sticking to any traditional theory of art. In the post World War II scenario, the post-modernists have shifted the focus from a study of man as the centre of universe to a study of the universe where man and society count equally important, and can be understood properly only when situated in the social as well as individual context. The existential context is significant to the postmodernist novelist. The postmodernist communicates a deeper nihilism than the existentialist writer because here man is aware of being dominated by an unstable universe as well as the materialism of machine-civilization.

Naipaul as a postmodernist is concerned with truth about contemporary life although he is more obsessed with historical sense. Through his art he represents truth by correlating history, truth, fiction and reality together as material and form of his novel. Naipaul often brings in contradictory visions in contact and conflict in his works. However, he gives a shape to all the conflicts and contradictions through his imagination and sensory experiences. Identity is not merely linked to one's parents alone; the individual is to be understood in the perspective of the totality of his historical heritage. Thus he has the anguish of a deeper existential loss when he emphasizes the lack of tradition in English literature. Such a view of "self" has been discussed by Camus in *The Myth of Sisyphus*:

> But in a universe that is suddenly deprived of illusion and of light man feels a stranger. His is an irremediable

> exile, because he is deprived of memories of a lost homeland as much as he lacks the hope of a promised land to come. This divorce between man and his life, the actor and his setting, truly constitute the feeling of absurdity. (Quoted in Heiney and Downs 1974: 295)

Camus expresses man's experience of absurdity. In Naipaul, the protagonist is a stranger. The protagonist is fully aware of it. Although it is a general perception that secure societies within a tradition can delimit aesthetic life of the self, it has been found in recent times that a man of sensibility, even if he is rootless, can more fruitfully pursue an authentic and creative life in the present political and economic situations. Naipaul thinks that sensibility is more a result of a viable tradition rather than purely related to heredity. It brings out one's sense of continuity with the past with its wider implication for the self. He thus identifies the problems of the writer with those of the man as "self". That is why he has attempted to illustrate a personal concrete metaphysics against the imagined frame of reference of Hindu India, the mythical land of his childhood and the land of his ancestors. He therefore undertakes a journey to this ancestral land, into his own past, the history of his ancestry. This existential journey into his self resulted in a most exciting and factual account. By undertaking such an important journey, Naipaul understands quite well how there exists a discrepancy between the imagined and the actual. He therefore refers to Charles Darwin's *Voyage of the Beagle* in *An Area of Darkness:*

> Only the other day I looked forward to this airy barrier as a definite point in our journey homewards; but now I find it, and all such resting places for the imagination, are like shadows, which a man moving onwards cannot catch. (Quoted in *AD* 27)

In his first journey which is full of difficult experiences for Naipaul, he could not comprehend the India of reality, and correlate it with the India of his imagination quite well. Because of his attitude he rejects the tradition of India, and therefore his understanding India remains partial. Although India is his ancestral land, he has neither been brought up here nor has he inherited its rich tradition. He has only known a few practices and rituals of Hindu India which were observed in Trinidad. Though he identifies some such practices nostalgically, there has always been a conflict of his "self" within—between his upbringing and unacknowledged inheritance. That is why he cannot reject India completely. His incomplete and partial understanding of India as a young man has puzzled him so much that he undertakes another journey with a mission to understand her past, her "wounded civilization" as he records it in his next book, *India: A Wounded Civilization* that outraged many Indians. Though Naipaul is apparently very harsh in criticizing the Indian attitude and her systems, he really loves this country. He does neither consider himself a complete outsider nor even an insider; but he is part of this ancient civilization. That is therefore he is seriously wounded, and therefore painfully portrays the wounded civilization of India: "India is for me a difficult country. It isn't my home and cannot be my home; and yet I cannot reject it or be indifferent to it; I cannot travel only for the sights. I'm at once too close and too far" (*IWC* x). In these two books, Naipaul has been apparently harsh to India and her people. These two books represent his deeper anguish and nostalgia for a great loss of his own "self". Kamra emphasizes her views through an interrogative statement: "Is it another paradoxical statement about existential loss becoming the grounds for identity and stability?" (24). Naipaul's involvement with India, her past, tradition and history, is fairly progressive. His psychic explorations of India remain a very important cause for his literary explorations. He cannot completely ignore the fact that India belonged to his ancestors and therefore his roots are grounded in this country, and thus partially defines his identity. He again visits India to understand it properly. This time his tone about India completely changes when he sees the "million mutinies" that are on footing that may lead to a great India in future. His understanding of India now becomes deeper, and quite significantly he tries to find some meaning in the indigenous systems and social manners which can only take India forward. The struggle within his "self" therefore enables him to produce such passionate books about India to describe its "area of darkness", its "wounded civilization" and "million mutinies".

Naipaul's sense of involvement to his "self" is obvious also in other travel writings—the result of his travel to other third world countries as well as to the American South. Naipaul's "idea of a nation" in the context of the "Caribbean islands" is significant. These slave islands, though politically independent, are still economically insecure. He believes that these islands are divisive and racial in nature for which they lack a larger vision of unity among them to take their country in the path of progress. The narrow attitude of racialism and disunity of the Caribbean has hurt Naipaul's sentiments to a great extent:

> I had seen how deep in nearly every West Indian, high and low, were the prejudices of race; how often these prejudices were rooted in self-contempt; ...Everyone spoke of nation and nationalism but no one was willing to surrender the privileges or even the separateness of his group. (*MP* 241)

The Middle Passage is also an attempt to define his self through his experiences of the Caribbean islands, the land of his birth.

Naipaul's obsession with the converted Muslim world is important because he has tried to know the meaning of "Islamic fundamentalism" in the context of the entire world-civilization. This is also related to his "self" because of his childhood experience of living along with the indentured, migrant Indian Muslims in Trinidad. The Muslims are the immediate neighbors of the Hindus. Though Naipaul cannot be branded as a Hindu, still his origin traces back to Hindu way of life—its traditions, rituals and cultural traits. Naipaul has therefore undertaken another kind of journey to his "self" and produced his analysis of the Islamic world by writing two books, namely *Among the Believers: An Islamic Journey* and *Beyond Belief*. In *Among the Believers*, his analysis of "Islamic Fundamentalism" in the four converted Muslim nations is an introspective interpretation of the "Muslim Self". Although the Muslim world has contributed significantly to the world culture and power, he has powerfully brought out both their strengths and weaknesses in these two travelogues. In the context of Islamic fundamentalism as a political experiment, he writes:

> No religion is more worldly than Islam. In spite of its political incapacity, no religion keeps men's eyes more fixed on the way the world is run.... I thought I could see how Islamic fervor could become more than a matter of prayers and postures could become creative, revolutionary, and take men on to a humanism beyond religious doctrine: a true renaissance, open to the new and enriched by it, as Muslims in their early days of glory had been. (*AB* 205)

Naipaul's anxiety to know about the origin of the Negroes of Trinidad has been partly responsible for his expedition to the American South. However, in the course of the journey, he has been inclined to the other aspects of the marginalized people—their aspirations, their miseries and their continuous displacement. This is a different kind of journey into his "self". *A Turn in the South* therefore explores the pattern of life of the marginalized blacks and whites—the communities on the periphery of mainstream of American culture of which they eagerly look for being a part. Among these people who see themselves as victims of a hostile past, Naipaul discovers a "sense of place", a sense of home—of being actively linked to their own land. In this travelogue, Naipaul describes the different situations in Mississippi, Tennessee, Alabama, Georgia, the two Carolinas and Atlanta. He has been greatly moved by the Biblical simplicity of the natives, their strong sense of material worth and personal dignity. Inclined to race issue he traveled the American South, but he had a different kind of interest while undertaking the journey: "I didn't know then that that issue would quickly work itself out during the journey, and that my subject would become that other South—of order and faith, and music and melancholy—which I didn't know about, but of which I had been given an intimation in Dallas" (*TS* 25).

Naipaul has a great concern for the reality of the people and society. His concern for the miseries of the underprivileged people of the colonial societies is expressed not only in his fictional texts and travelogues; it has also been reflected much in his journalistic writings. That is why when we read them; we find his clear understanding of the predicament of such societies. In *The Return of Eva Peron* Naipaul analyses the political and personal powers of Eva Peron, Mobutu and black power leader Michael de Freitas in relation to such colonial cultures as Jamaica, Argentina and Zaire. The local leaders lack a concrete vision of development of their societies. However they are affiliated to power groups in the West so that they can fulfill their ambitions whenever an opportunity arises. Naipaul is therefore critical of such societies:

> Much of the population is superfluous, and they know it. Unemployment is high but labor is perennially short. The physical squalor, the sense of a land being pillaged rather than built up, generates great tensions; ...but the situation is well suited to the hysteria and evasions of racial politics.... Malik, an operator acting always in the racial cause, found in Trinidad his perfect camouflage. (Eva Peron 59)

The writer critiques Eva's administration in the following:

> In the early Peronist days she was promoted as a saint, and she is now above Peronism and politics. She is her own cult; she offers protection to those who believe in her. Where there are no reliable institutions or codes or law, no secular assurances, people need faith and magic.... Desolation always seems close in the Argentine vastness: how did men come here how have they endured? (Eva Peron 162)

Naipaul relates to the Conradian world in his critical piece "Conrad's Darkness and Mine":

> Conrad's value to me is that he is someone who sixty or seventy years ago meditated on my world, a world I recognize today. I feel this about no other writer of the century. His achievement derives from the honesty which is part of his difficulty, that "scrupulous fidelity" to the truth of my own sensations".
>
> Nothing is rigged in Conrad. He doesn't remake countries. He chose as we now know, incidents from real life; and he meditated on them. (*LQ* 173)

His concern for India, Trinidad, Muslim World, Africa and South America is based on his notion that authentic books have not been written about these societies. He therefore writes: "And when that Indian need was satisfied, others became apparent: Africa, South America, the Muslim world. The aim has always been to fill out my world picture, and the purpose comes from my childhood: to make me more at ease with myself" (*LO*: Two Worlds 191). Naipaul has always been innovative in his writings. When he was asked why he was not going to Germany and China, he viewed that there was good writing about these countries and he had more concerns for the countries which were the areas of darkness: "Those were not the areas of darkness I felt about me as a child. So just there is a development in my work, a development in narrative skill and knowledge and sensibility so there is a kind of unity, a focus, though I might appear to be going in many directions" (*LO*: Two Worlds 192). To Naipaul, all literary forms are equally valuable. That is why both fiction and travelogue gave him new ways of looking at life and society. In *A Million Mutinies Now*, which he wrote twenty-six years after *An Area of Darkness*, he discovered a new form of writing:

> It came to me, for instance, when I set out to write my third book about India—twenty-six years after the first—that what was most important about a travel book were the people the writer traveled among. The people had to define themselves. A simple enough idea but it required a new kind of book; it called for a new way of traveling. And it was the very method I used later when I went, for the second time, into the Muslim world. (*LO*: Two Worlds 194)

Naipaul's skill rests on his exploration of new ideas as well as innovative prose style in all types of writings: novel, non-fictional travel writings and shorter fictions. In these texts, he is concerned with the issues of identities of the communities and nations. His serious obsession with the issues of rootlessness and racial discrimination in postmodern societies make his writings problematic. These issues are prevalent almost in all post-colonials, post-modern societies. Though Naipaul as a writer of novels and travelogues is well-known, he has also produced the shorter fictional texts which deal with the predicament of the postmodern societies. More specifically, *A Flag on the Island, Miguel Street* and *In a Free State* deal with the rootlessness of individuals. The consciousness of rootlessness has a damaging impact on their minds, making them vulnerable, for often their behaviors are absurd. They suffer from inferiority complex. *Miguel Street* refers to the multiracial and multi-cultural society of Trinidad composed of the Negroes, Asians, Chinese, English and Spanish, all of whom are expatriates. Colonialism has influenced significantly to their beliefs, attitudes, manners and habits. Though these people have attained political freedom, they have not yet been free intellectually and culturally. Unlike the stories in *Miguel Street,* the stories in *A Flag on the Island* do not form a "society street", because the characters belong to different times and locales. The characterization, thematic strands and narrative technique are also heterogeneous. The characters in these stories are full of vices such as hypocrisy, corruption, exploitation, selfishness, intolerance and superstition. However, the common phenomenon in these stories is confrontation. *In a Free State* explores the predicament of postcolonial societies which are politically free, but are still under cultural, psychological and social domination. Naipaul delineates that freedom is meaningless to an individual when he is living in an alien land being cut off from his roots. Kamal Mehta comments:

> All the three collections unfold the impact of colonialism on the minds of the people and the society as well. *Miguel Street* reveals the fact of the hampering of the physical, intellectual, emotional and social lives of the people. In the second collection, he makes his observation more general in the sense that he does not confine his stories to the Trinidadians and to the slum dwellers alone but expands the scope and thus tries to convey the same phenomenon symbolically. The author reveals in his third collection what happens to the citizens from such a country when they are out of their ancestral lands and enjoy complete independence. The third collection is a more general exploration of the same phenomenon

> with reference to people who are displaced, irrespective of their nationality. It reconstructs the disharmony between the people and the places they live upon in fictional terms. (Ray 293-94)

The shorter fiction of Naipaul, in the light of his later novels, can be regarded as precursors to the later serious fiction. A close reading of his fiction and non-fiction reveals that Naipaul is sincere in exploring the contemporary life and civilization. Despite different opinions on Naipaul's merits and talent as a writer, he is one of the most serious and progressive humanists, concerned with the universal civilization. That is why he writes:

> The new outlook fashioned by science implies a new outlook of man. They're going to realize that you have to respect man because he is man and that it's wrong to hand out charity. ("V.S. Naipaul in Paris," *The Guardian Weekly*, 125/4, July 26, 1981)

Naipaul also views:

> The "third World" notion is itself a cliché. I feel there's a great universal civilization at the moment which people would say is Western. But this has been fed by innumerable sources. It's a very eclectic civilization and it is so attractive, so liberating to people.... The mistake of Western vanity is to think that the universal civilization that exists now is a purer racial one. It's not the preserve of one race, one country but has been fed by many. ("The Master of the Novel," *Newsweek*, August 18, 1980)

His travelogues explore suppressed histories, cultures and political situations of different countries. Man is at the centre of his writings. Through them, he has tried to understand the predicament of man in a capricious universe. Such concern for man has lent all his writings a significant human face. Despite his severe criticism and harshness towards some of the aspects in the Third world countries like India, converted Muslim countries namely Iran, Pakistan, Indonesia and Malaysia, Caribbean islands and the slave land of the American South, his concern for truth is a powerful dimension in his travelogues. Sometimes it irritates some critics. Even Ezekiel has been too much harsh on Naipaul for his views on India in *An Area of Darkness* and *A Wounded Civilization*. Fukul Alam also disapproves of Naipaul's views on Islam in *Among the Believers* and *Beyond Belief*. He is however so happy that Naipaul was awarded Nobel Prize in literature in 2001. That is so because he considers Naipaul a supreme novelist with extraordinary style and powerful vision on man's predicament. He therefore comments:

> Nevertheless, I was happy to hear that Naipaul was awarded the Nobel Prize this year. If the Nobel Prize committee was wrong in appreciating the writer's "acuity" in his latest book on Islam, it is undoubtedly right in its assessment of his achievement as a novelist. The two novels that it singles out, *A House for Mr. Biswas* (1961) and *The Enigma of Arrival* (1987) are masterpieces of 20th century fiction, and for these works alone Naipaul deserved the Nobel Prize many years ago. And surely, the citation accompanying the award, distinguishing him "for having united perceptive narrative and incorruptible scrutiny in works that compel us to see the presence of suppressed lives, and is easily applicable to these two novels. (193)

Naipaul's achievement of "Nobel Prize" is however not a political one because he received the Prize purely on his personal merit. That is why Amit Chaudhuri thinks:

> The Nobel Prize for literature has always been a dubious accolade. It has been awarded, in the past, for political reasons rather than literary excellence; but one can't think of a good political reason for giving it to Naipaul. Perhaps this augurs well—for Naipaul's achievement has been to show us that the creation of a corpus of work, and the almost exclusive dedication to a writer's life and craft, have no less primacy in the life of the postcolonial writer than the nationalist or political impulses. The awarding of this year's Prize becomes an unlikely occasion on which to confirm what is an increasingly endangered and debated point of view: that a writer must be judged and assessed by his writing

> alone—and writing is Naipaul's great subject, as it is his great achievement. (189)

Chaudhuri is however puzzled about Naipaul's great achievement for his ironical presentation:

> It is paradoxical; of course, that this grand-sounding award should go to a man who has written so ironically about the makeshift and ambivalent, but perhaps nourishing, role that late literature played in the society he emerged from. In *Miguel Street*, the book he first wrote Young Elias takes tuition but keeps failing, or doing badly in, his school's Senior Cambridge exams: 'Is the English and litritcher that does beat me'. The narrator adds, "In Elia's mouth litritcher was the most beautiful word I heard. It sounded like something to eat, something rich like chocolate." (190)

Alam is not happy with Naipaul's travelogues like Nissim Ezekiel and Edward Said. Alam supports Edward Said's views on Naipaul's Islamic journeys: "How could a man of such intelligence and gifts as V.S. Naipaul write so stupid and boring a book." He therefore thinks that though Naipaul's travelogues on Indian and Islamic journeys show flashes of brilliance and reveal a master of narrative and shrewd delineator of people and setting" (192), these are rather the gifts of a writer of fiction: "In his travel writing and exposes of India and Islam Naipaul constantly overstates, over generalizes and quite misrepresents and even distorts what he comes across." Alam's toughness of disapproval as critic of Naipaul's travelogues, especially in the context of *Beyond Belief* has been well expressed in the following:

> Ezekiel's comments on Naipaul's rendition of India and what Said has observed about his depiction of Islam (and what Walcott has written about his reorientations of West Indies and Achebe of his portraits of Africa) appear to me to be tough-minded but accurate assessment of the writer. To put it somewhat differently, Naipaul's greatness does not reside in these books, although all of them have their moments of brilliance. Surely, works

> which seem to harbor deep-rooted prejudices against nations and religions and books which at times appear to be deficient in humanity should not be considered for the highest literary honor. This is why the following part of the Nobel citation about *Beyond Belief* strikes me as essentially wrong: "His travel books allow witnesses to testify at every turn, not least in his powerful descriptions of the eastern regions of the Islamic World.... The author's acuity finds expression in the acuity of his ear." Said, indeed, is right about Naipaul's lack of objectivity and antipathy to Islam and in pronouncing the Nobel Prize committee wrong! (192-93)

Such remarks on Naipaul are rather partial, and based on personal prejudices. An impartial, accurate study of travel writings reveals how Naipaul is not only a powerful writer of fiction; he is equally capable of writing about the human predicament, civilization and culture even in his travelogues. That has been discussed thoroughly in the chapters 6, 7, 8 and 9. He is a master of all the major forms of English prose—novels, travelogues, history, autobiography, and the occasional essay. In his autobiographical writings, he makes a journey into his own "self", and tries to correlate the contemporary reality to the living situations in his own life. That is why *The Enigma of Arrival* and *Finding the Centre* very well present Naipaul's "self" in "space and time as a phenomenon of 20th century, post-imperial history" (Alam in Panwar 195). Naipaul's vision is complicated in his autobiographical *The Enigma of Arrival*. He considers his presence in the English landscape an important event because England is reshaped by a contemporary diaspora. The Nobel committee therefore understands the exploration of England by Naipaul as "the placid course of the old ruling culture and the demise of European neighborhoods". Naipaul from the very beginning of his writing career has often baffled his critics. His immensity as a writer of contemporary relevance is to be understood in the proper perspective. It is not proper to outright dismiss Naipaul's travel writings without any useful meaning and significance. On the other hand our judgment should be free from personal, local, national and religious biases.

Then only, can we assess him quite truly and effectively. Though Alam's views cannot be fully supported, it is quite relevant to quote him before we discuss Naipaul's merits as an all-time great novelist:

> Naipaul, then, is a very great writer not in his travel writing and studies of other cultures and races but in his novels and his autobiographical writings. He has earned his Nobel Prize through these works for there is much to adhere in his fiction and self-explorations. But the Naipaul who presents himself as a conservative fastidious and truth-telling traveller is a less than agreeable and believable person. Why such an extraordinarily gifted writer could be so jaundiced in these works is, to me, the ultimate enigma posed by Naipaul, and it is something that continues to bother me even as I attempt to conclude my reflections on the Nobel Award he has so richly deserved. (195)

It is true that Naipaul has always been enigmatic—both in his life and writing career. He often baffles, but if he is judged with some bias, his true greatness as a writer and explorer of truth will be diminished. It cannot be refuted that in his novels he has been very brilliant. It is not proper to assess Naipaul's vision in the travel writings as "jaundiced". In the context of Naipaul's travelogues on India, we note that *An Area of Darkness* has views of a young man who himself considers to be an insider and outsider. His involvement with India makes him utter things quite painfully although he has not been able to comprehend India quite fully and properly because he has not understood the Indian perspective. However some of his observations are startlingly true. In *A Wounded Civilization*, the understanding is somehow greater and deeper. His anguish is rather motivated because of the "ruins" of the great Indian civilization and he himself considers of being humiliated by tracing his origin and roots to the Indian tradition and culture. India has always been in his psyche, and he therefore makes another visit to India to understand it better and deeper. The third travelogue *A Million Mutinies Now* is really a gripping narrative which represents Naipaul's vision of Indian situation.

Through a changed perception, he has been able to represent India through the voices of people from different walks of life. Through such encounters, he has understood India quite deeply. Similarly his visits of two Islamic countries, Caribbean island, American South and Africa have been quite fruitful by presenting the suppressed histories, political conditions, economic miseries, cultural and racial clashes and sociological situations. His representations of these nations are authentic, and therefore they are truthful explorations. Panwar, in her remarks on Naipaul's writing has been quite positive in her assessment:

> It may well be argued that with age the wisdom to anchor experience in perspective has acquired greater space in Naipaul's writing. His self-explorations and explorations of the world around, of nations, histories communities and cultures have evolved into a broad-based 'poetics of self-exile'. He continues to demonstrate the courage and ability to write whatever his intuitions, imagination and understanding drive him to; but he reflects larger comprehension and an easily discernible mellowness, especially in his works on India. (21-22)

It is quite true that Naipaul has dealt with history in his works. But, it is also equally true that it is difficult to extract any coherent view of history by way of interpreting these works. That is because Naipaul is such a difficult writer that summarizing his works is not that easy. However, his dominant authorial presence in his works enables us to extract Naipaul's views on "sense of historical awareness". In this context, Pratap Bhanu Mehta makes appropriate comments in his article "Naipaul and the Burdens of History":

> The centrality of the author in Naipaul's corpus might make it easier to extract Naipaul's views. After all Naipaul is a character in his own writing. But almost all attempts to recover Naipaul's views end up as attempts to do his psycho-biography, excavating the psychological complexes and anxieties at work in his writing. Naipaul's arguments just are Naipaul the character. To unravel his views is not to lay out an argument; it is to decipher

> a persona. That all of Naipaul's writing is extended autobiography in disguise has some truth to it. (44)

But it is not the entire truth about Naipaul, the persona which is shaped through his encounter with the world. That is why Mehta rightly argues: "The paradox of Naipaul's authorial presence is that censorious, overpowering and provocative as Naipaul's judgments, even in his fiction are, Naipaul's will himself seldom give reasons for those judgments" (2007: 44). Naipaul's concern is not merely with the physical aspects. He is more interested in the "moral-psychological" aspects. He explores how history produces ripples in the psyches of the various individuals and cultures. That is why he creates such characters that carry the imprints of their societies. Mehta in the context of *India: A Million Mutinies Now* also views in this direction: "*India: A Million Mutinies Now* is prescient precisely because it relates the characters of social movements like the Shiv Sena to the existential burdens Hindu society produces. A society that provides little by means of affirmation of any individual's self-worth is liable to produce an apocalyptic politics of self-esteem" (2007: 45). Naipaul's treatment of history is however not a burden of the past on the people. But then historical awareness of the people enables them to understand their own self and culture. To Naipaul, "historical sense" enables the individuals to be more "self-conscious" by which they will be able to understand the handicaps of their own culture and civilization. Such awareness will move the individuals towards "intellectual awareness". A historical amnesia, on the other hand is responsible for intellectual depletion. Unless the individuals have a real understanding of history, they will miss the very truth about their self, culture and nation. That is why in the travelogue *India: A Wounded Civilization* he views that Indians have not understood the "old" properly for which they do not understand the "wounds" of their civilization. On the other hand they are just glorifying their own past and culture. To Naipaul, the centuries of conquest did not help in enlivening India. On the other hand; he believes that such conquests have distorted "historical consciousness". He also thinks that the British conquest and European colonialism though helped

India to understand her inadequacies; they did not produce any intellectual movement that could help India overcome these inadequacies. In Naipaul's opinion, "suppressed histories" and forgotten historical complexes distort our consciousness when they are settled in our psyches. Embodiment of "self" in the historical perspective is very important. An individual in order to explore the possibilities in the world is to acknowledge the totality of our embodiment in history and society. In this process, the individual can attain its "fullest self". Naipaul does not approve of the religious identity that denies the individual to remain aloof from the outside world. He thinks faith and renunciation due to religion are detrimental to the entity of the "Self" for its overall flourishing in the world. Its denial of the world obstructs self-understanding and results in a lack of integrity. The individual should therefore be an embodiment of history in the perspective of the possibilities of the world. He must have to merge in the emerging universal civilization. Naipaul therefore writes in "Universal Civilization":

> A later realization—I suppose I have sensed it most of my life, but I have understood it philosophically only during the preparation of this talk—has been the beauty of the idea of pursuit of happiness. Familiar words, easy to take for granted; easy to misconstrue. This idea of the pursuit of happiness is at the heart of the attractiveness of the civilization to so many outside it or on its periphery. I find it marvelous to contemplate to what an extent, after two centuries, and after the terrible history of the earlier part of this century, the idea has come to a kind of fruition. It is an elastic idea; it fits all men. It implies a certain kind of awakened spirit. I don't imagine my father's parents would have even been able to understand the idea. So much is contained in it: the idea of the individual, responsibility, choice, the life of the intellect, the idea of vocation and perfectibility and achievement. It is an immense human idea. It cannot be reduced to a fixed system. It cannot generate fanaticism. But it is known to exist; and because of that, other more rigid systems in the end blow away. (*WW* 2003: 517)

This is the notion of Naipaul about the significance of the universal civilization. The pursuit of happiness is not related to anything beyond the "self" because such a thing is only a human ideal. He believes that man alienates himself from his own self, when he indulges in mortgaging himself to something other than the pursuit of happiness. Celebration of life is to open up all the possibilities by which life can give one a lot of happiness through these possibilities. Contrarily, denial to such a pursuit entails a life of condemnation which is inhuman in every aspect of it. However, Naipaul knows very well that attainment of happiness is not that easy because there are so many ulcers which haunt the universal civilization. That is why Mehta's comments are quite convincing in this context:

> Naipaul is not blasé that happiness can be easily possessed, for ulcers haunt the universal civilization. But not to have opened oneself up to that possibility is not to have lived. The relationship between and history remain somewhat obscure. There are hints, though only hints that have something to do with authenticity, creating conditions where one does not have to lie oneself. (Panwar 48)

Naipaul's treatment of history in the context of Hindu nationalism and Islamic religion is interesting because there is no symmetry in his attitude to these two contesting issues. Hindu nationalism is not a collective narcissism; it is however an attempt to recover a "suppressed history" which helps in removing historical amnesia and psychological burden of overcoming a non-existent supremacy of others imposed on the people of India. Despite the fact that such Hindu nationalism has incredibility of not being secular and dividing people on the basis of religion, it has the positive aspect of generating historical consciousness among the people. Of course, the political and social consequences are to some extent offensive. But Naipaul considers less important than the greater significance of making people aware of their history. In contrast Naipaul's attitude to Islam is different because he considers Islam responsible for erasing history, a kind of removing people from their selves. That is why in *Beyond Belief* he warns the convert Muslims in the four countries who have been trapped to turn away from their own "self" and "place" because of the uncritical way of sticking to their Islamic faith. He understands that the convert is a prisoner of defective vision of history. Such idea of history is not based on facts. The Islam practice of erasing the history is a kind of demeaning the "self", a kind of "self-eraser". In the context of Naipaul's views on Islamic faith erasing the "self", critics like Said have dismissed Naipaul's account as shallow, unformed and trite based on prejudices. They also argue that he has not understood the complex Muslim civilization properly. Critical puzzle is that sometimes the complexity of history poses some problems to an individual. Even Naipaul himself understands that truth does not always lie in facts. It is therefore important to take an "existential stand" whenever required. In his own life he has carried the burden of history: his ancestral roots in India, his Trinidadian nativity, his inclination to English culture and civilization and his own cosmopolitanism. In this context Mehta makes a remarkable point:

> This might explain a puzzle about Naipaul's own presentation of his self. Naipaul seems to carry with him all the layers of history he can decipher: his Indian roots, his Trinidadian inflections (now disowned in an act of bad faith), his anglophilia, and even his cosmopolitanism. It is writing of loss and anger, of unsettling confrontations, and confident certainties. (Panwar 2007: 49)

It is quite noticeable that Naipaul has a keen sense of sight towards the displaced and the unrealized that opens him up to other worlds. Contrarily it is also found that openness is belied by his sense of futility about most people he writes about. He often brings such seeming contradictions because he thinks without them it would be unreal as life is subject to all kinds of vulnerabilities. Quite appropriately, Mehta argues: "Naipaul can both be present in his work and can allow his characters to take over at the same time. It is as if Naipaul is saying: 'not to his judgment, his enlightenment, inheritances intrude would be an act of hypocrisy of the kind that purveyors of easy cultural sympathy always exhibit'. If the choice were between an attitude bordering on misanthropy on the one hand and the pieties of sympathetic understanding on the other, Naipaul would decidedly choose the former. Misanthropy is at least honest in a way almost nothing is" (Panwar 49).

Naipaul's concern for history is based on the fact that one must not escape his identity. But then, it is quite interesting to note that his works fail to bring out the pathos that the heroic integrity of a being enables him to see the world clearly and describe one's own place in it. His characters often have the limited perspective "like a frog living under a coconut shell" (*Beyond Belief*: *BB*). However, in his own case, Naipaul confesses that he has tried to escape from his native land because of the burden of his own history, his ancestry and roots. That is why; it is a great puzzle to understand Naipaul's contradictions, his convictions and his understanding the world in its perspective:

> It is difficult to see the kind of knowledge that Naipaul brings into the world as an ascent into a different order of being. It is rather that usual expectations associated with pathos of integrity are missing in Naipaul. An exhortation to honesty, a will to integrity, and a clear-eyed understanding of one's way in the world, is usually seen as the prelude to a more responsible politics. But in Naipaul the end point is almost always himself. History exists to give him the contradictions and pains he can work through. To demand that Naipaul have a clear politics would be unreasonable and unfair. But it is not entirely inappropriate to insist that history be not made into simply a template for the politics, in the wider sense of the term, of Naipaul's own story. After all, getting your own place clear in the world, involves letting it go sometimes, of letting it be, of eschewing fantasies of intellectual mastery, as if life and cultures could be easily possessed. In short, it is an integrity vitiated by what ought to accompany genuine integrity: some humility. (Mehta in Panwar 2007: 50-51)

Towards the end of his autobiographical novel *EOA* Naipaul the man and the narrator views that history establishes the identity of the individual: "Men need history; it helps them to have an idea of who they are. But history, like sanctity, can reside in the heart; it is enough that there is something there" (*EOA* 386). His warm feeling for the sanctity of the word is obvious when he becomes nostalgic about the passing away of the sacredness of the world:

> Our sacred world—the sanctities that had been handed down to us as children by our families, the sacred places of our childhood, sacred because we had seen them as children and had filled them with wonder, places doubly and trebly sacred to me because for always in England I had lived in them imaginatively over many books and had in my fantasy set in those places the very beginning of things, had constructed out of them a fantasy of home, though I was to learn that the ground was bloody, that there had been aboriginal people there once, who had been killed or made to die away—our sacred world had vanished. (*EOA* 386-87)

He views that generation-wise we move forward in the perspective of history and tradition. He therefore continues his point of view: "Every generation now was to take us further away from these sanctities. But we remade the world for ourselves; every generation does that, as we found when we came together for the death of this sister and felt the need to honor and remember" (*EOA* 387). From historical perspective Naipaul contemplates on his "self", a personal perspective which he links with history and tradition. His contemplation of death in his sleep is now a reality in the "death" of his younger sister, Sati. He therefore thinks that this tragic incident of personal life forced them to look into life afresh in its proper perspective: "It forced us to look on death. It forced me to face the death I had been contemplating at night, in my sleep; it fitted a real grief where melancholy had created a vacancy, as if to prepare me for the moment. It showed me life and man as the mystery, the true religion of men, the grief and the glory. And that was when faced with a real death and with this new wonder about man, I laid aside my drafts and hesitation and began to write very fast about Jack and his garden" (*EOA* 387). To Naipaul a traditional ritualism is not capable of creation and achievement. It is a closed world without any substantial meaning. He therefore creates his own world of sacredness through his writing "self", an existential stance that he undertakes. His writing of "self" is important for him and everything—his English education, colonialism, the West, his Worcestershire country garden—belong to his hallowed ground of writing: "Naipaul, at least in his own mind, seems to have found his home through writing, through the ability to imagine himself, and through writing to respond to his own fate. The binaries he creates between the West and the rest, in the end do not define a geographical space, they create, consecrate and reproduce a mode of being, an existential space that is not intellectually compromised, or willfully inert. It is no accident that the greatest tribute he pays to 'Universal Civilization' is that makes his writing possible" (Mehta in Panwar 51-52).

In the context of Trinidad's insignificance, Naipaul thinks that European colonialism has destroyed it and recreated it. It opened up the possibility of writing about it thereby making it a hallowed ground. Despite its negativity as a colonial power, European colonialism has some positive values whereas the Arab conquests are based on negativity because the Islamic faith is "a self-imposed tyranny" taking away all the positive aspects from life except faith. Naipaul's tryst with "history" is therefore enables him to see the world coldly although it also obstructs the vision casually: "But in Naipaul's engagement with Hindu nationalism with European colonialism and with Arab conquest, we find the same pre-occupation with the possibility of thinking in genuinely historical terms. Everything else is subordinate to that preoccupation, it is the tense, that enables Naipaul to see, at the same time as it shuts out much from him" (Mehta in Panwar 2007: 52). In this context, Mehta concludes his essay "Naipaul and the Burden of History" with the following remarks:

> Perhaps in the end, like Nietzsche, Naipaul's distortions are less a product of prejudice, but stem more from a fear of leveling, a fear of philistinism, and a fear of democracy. Flaubert had once written in a letter from Egypt, "poor wretches that we are, we have I think considerable taste because we are profoundly historical,

> we admit everything and adopt the point of view of everything we are judging. But have we as much inner strength as we have understanding of others? Is fierce originality compatible with so much breadth of mind?" Naipaul might himself pose this question: Does not empathetic understanding, involve a kind of self-alienation as well? To be able to adopt many viewpoints is for Naipaul not an achievement of understanding; it is dissolution of the self. We have to take history seriously, but only to the point that it does not compromise our self-possession and flatten our responses. That Naipaul cannot live up to the will to lead a life without illusions; that he cannot achieve clairvoyance that most ordinary and benighted characters he writes about cannot even dream of, is not a limitation of Naipaul's writing. Nor is it a particularly serious indictment to point out that an author does not live up to his own ideals. For that gap between ideals and reality is also an honest register of our history and our self. (Panwar 2007: 53)

Naipaul's ideas of "history" and "universal civilization" should be understood in the perspective of his life and achievements. In an interview with Dileep Padgaonkar in 1993, the journalist of *The Sunday Times of India* Naipaul clarifies his vision of the "universal civilization". His views were initially published on 18 July in 1993, in *The Sunday Times of India*. The interview is republished in Panwar's book with the title "An Area of Awakening: V.S. Naipaul in conversation with Dileep Padgaonkar" (Panwar 2007: 54-66). Like many Indians, Dileep Padgaonkar was enraged after reading *An Area of Darkness* and *A Wounded Civilization* in his early life. But when he understood the world better in his later years—different ideologies and world-views—, he was inclined towards Naipaul's deeper understanding about the world and universal civilization. He therefore writes:

> In later years, however when the attraction I had felt for ideologies or world views which claimed to explain everything about everything began to fade, Naipaul's books seemed to ring true. In the meanwhile, he, too,

> had changed. The opening sentence of his novel *A Bend in the River* (1979) read: "The world is what it is; men who are nothing, who allow themselves to become nothing, have no place in it." From this ominous note of dark despair to the celebration of a million mutinies in India ten years later Naipaul has indeed traveled quite a distance. (Panwar 55)

Naipaul's rootlessness has not detracted him from his mission of writing the world, understanding the world from his perspective of expatriate sensibility. He believes that the spread of education after the collapse of empire has enabled man to get away from concerns about roots and identities. Naipaul has been able to carry on in the postcolonial world despite his rootlessness and diasporic perspective because "nobody really lives in a single culture. Even Africa has been subjected to many, many influences. To talk about a 'pure African' culture makes little sense" (Panwar 2007: 56). Cultural identity in the contemporary situations cannot be treated in "isolated context". To understand "cultural identity", one must have to establish the linkages and contradictions that exist in a society. Culture is no more based on "either/or" notions. Very often culture is mixed and interactive. That is why Naipaul suggests that the alternatives—traditionalism versus Westernism—might be false. There is no either/or because the essence of literature, inquiry and philosophy is a constant examination of oneself and one's world and one's own culture. One hopes to leave the world with some more different ideas than those given to one when one enters the world.

Naipaul believes that the alternatives in India in the context of cultural identity could lead to brutal clashes, and destroy it further as in the past it had destroyed itself by wars. That had happened because there was absence of the "idea of a people, of a nation defending itself". Naipaul believes that "fundamentalism" even in Islam is a passing phase. He thinks that India is awakening to a new sense of history: "Today it seems to me that Indians are becoming alive to their history" (Panwar 57). Through this new historical awakening, people now understand that there has been a great vandalizing of

India. Earlier Indians were unable to understand because of the conquest and the nature of Hindu society. They had no notion of the Indian nation during the Pre-industrial society. However, things are changing faster: "What is happening in India is a mighty creative process. Indian intellectuals, who want to be secure in their liberal beliefs, may not understand what is going on, especially if these intellectuals happen to be in the United States. But every other Indian knows precisely what is happening: deep down he knows that a larger response is emerging even if at times this response appears in his eyes to be threatening" (Panwar 57-58). Naipaul feels that the Indian intellectuals should have to apply their minds, the emotional upsurge that is emerging in India. He also feels that the Hindu reaction is not motivated on the line of fundamentalism of the Islamic faith that is quite negative, "a protection against the world it desperately wishes to join" (Panwar 58). Aggressiveness in any culture and religion is not conducive to the universal civilization that Naipaul believes in: "We all live in a universal civilization some more than the others. We have our individual particularities. But we are all inhabited by a universal civilization. It is very hard to go back" (Panwar 59). To Naipaul, it is important to be critical in one's writings because by that way one becomes truthful: "It convinces that nothing matters more than to be truthful. Having your side, having to protect your side: that is so false. Such writing becomes redundant in five years. The other thing I have learnt is never to be taken in by passing events" (Panwar 60). Naipaul's truthful explorations in his writings are not confined to the East or West. He has written about the whole world, the entire human civilization. His concern is position of man in a chaotic, capricious world. He therefore comments: "I have written about American South too. My interest, however, began with who I am. I have explored the strands in my upbringing. India, Caribbean, slave society in the background (historically) England" (Panwar 61). Naipaul in his writings began with the immediate surrounding: Trinidad and its Hindu community, the racial movement, a racial movement handed by Eric Williams and the Muslim community in Trinidad, a community outside the Arab Islamic world. In the context of the Muslims in the non-Arab countries like Iran, Pakistan, Indonesia and Malaysia, Naipaul understands the tragic sense of injustice in these countries of the believers: "I think that the sense of injustice, the tragic sense of the world which you find in the countries I have mentioned will transmute itself into something very creative" (Panwar 61). Naipaul does not approve of Iqbal's vision of an Islamic nation, the creation of a society of believers. It is rather irrational and an outlook based on narrowness. Iqbal's vision is not profound, and is based on poor insight. To Naipaul, India is awakening to new ideas. This passion of the people is reflected in their new way of looking at things. Naipaul felt himself "wounded" to see the "Wounded Civilization" of India through a new awareness of historical sense. Every Indian should be aware of it. India is moving in that direction now. In the context of the African situation, Naipaul's feeling of authenticity is noteworthy:

> There are two issues about Black Africa I would like to go into. Why is there no Arab guilt about Black Africa? The Arabs were importing slaves all along. African eunuchs were employed to guard harems. Castration of black Africans was common practice in Sudan and Upper Egypt. And why is there no sense of guilt in Brazil where slaves were imported until 1888? It probably has to do with the intellectual traditions of these countries. A sense of guilt or shock is doubtless linked to analytical abilities.... (Panwar 65-66)

Naipaul's sense of history and concern for a universal civilization has motivated him to go on writing one book after the other. As an innovative writer he has been able to reshape the forms of fiction and non-fiction through his prose style. His style is interlinked to the theme and vision he has designed in his writings. Naipaul's narratives enable him to present his world-views that are not just stereotypes. Naipaul's novels are open-ended and multi-dimensional through which he explores/creates contextual situations relating to innumerable fundamental human issues. The protagonists are to face great situations for their existential stance. Through his novels, Naipaul wants to convert literature into "equipment for living

(Panichas 1974: 06). Sartre believes that "the written work can be an essential condition of action, that is, the moment of reflexive consciousness" (Sartre quoted in Garvin 1977: 12). Existential philosophy is at the core of all the fictional writings of Naipaul who considers that man can live an authentic life of his "self" without any belief in a "transcendent" power and authority. He can achieve an authentic life through imagination and commitment: "What all people want, some without being aware of it, is to be witness to their time, their lives, and above all to themselves" (Kem 1970: 100).

10.2. Narrative Techniques and Stylistic Devices

Naipaul's novels have definite styles according to the purpose of the novelist. They focus more on the unexplored, hidden issues rather than merely representing social or personal life. His novels release a meaning in the context which the novelist desires. That is why in an interview to *The Times of India* he expresses:

> I'm not concerned with style for its own sake. I try to destroy the rhythm of the prose if I find it. I'm concerned with letting each thing add to the other, trying to say exactly and clearly what I mean. It's not a problem of seeking a new form, but finding the reality of the situation. (24 August 1980)

Naipaul's fiction has a number of stylistic devices: dramatization, reflection, description, the centre of consciousness and the third person omniscient narration. Integrating all these devices of style in them, he creates an overwhelming mood to effect a major crisis. The mood is built up by selecting situations through multiple perspectives of the novel on various thematic dimension and polarities. It is created by dramatizing the episodes and incidents from the life of the protagonist through descriptions and reflections. The emotional atmosphere is created through the mood that holds together the elements of experience in time and space by the protagonist. The personal and the historical past mould the narrator's/protagonist's response to a present situation. Kamra remarks:

> In his fiction the existential polarities of tradition and personal meaning, the psychological polarities of the literal and literary, the unidimensional and the multidimensional man, the social polarity of small town and metropolitan life, the political polarity of the colonizer and the colonized (oppressor and oppressed) coalesce to create the experience of man trapped, fragmented and rootless struggling for release through a self-realizing order. It is the precise placing of images and phrases—their repetition in changing contexts—that builds up the rhythm and nuances of the novels. (30)

Garvin's views in this context are supportive to such an argument: "There is always an aura of mystery, of strangeness, awakened by the immanence of obsessive images and by incantatory language" (250-51). In Naipaul, style is not merely an arrangement of words. The important thing in his fiction is the unit of perception through which he creates memorable scenes and situations. That is why he writes: "I say things in visual images sometimes with sentimental torches. I put construction first. Every paragraph must have its color, its rhythm" (*The Guardian Weekly*, 125/4, July 26, 1981: 13). Naipaul is therefore able to create a complexity of situation through his style of descriptions, reflections and dramatization. This complexity of the situation is haunted by the existential despair of the protagonist reflected in his anguish because of living in a meaningless world. Since man is compelled to live in a void, which is beyond his control, the protagonist/narrator, has the possibility of reorientation of his life. The portrayal of despair in a moment of crisis in the life of the protagonist is a continuous process that comes to him in different circumstances. The critical moments of life in the protagonist of *The Mimic Men* can be illustrated in the following:

> ...all the activity of these years, existing as I have said in my own mind in parenthesis, represented a type of withdrawal, and was part of the injury inflicted on me by the too solid three-dimensional city in which I could never feel myself as anything but spectral, disintegrating,

> pointless, fluid. The city made by man but passed out of his control: break down the negative reaction, activity the positive: opposite but equal aspects of an accommodation to a sense of place which, like memory, when grown acute, becomes a source of pain. (*MM* 53)

Out of this despair and pain, there emerges a possibility of hope and community life. In most of the novels the protagonists have been thrust on such critical situations that lead them to experience the pains and dilemmas, and take an existential stand. Naipaul writes that the stories written by his father in *Gurudeva* "provided a starting point for further observation; they did not trigger off fantasy. Every writer is, in the long run, on his own; but it helps, in the most practical way, to have a tradition. The English language was mine; the tradition was not. Literature, then, was mainly fantasy" (Barracoon 27). Hel has made efforts to relate literature to life. His novels are multi-dimensional in structure. Through them, he transforms meaning and tradition into continuum as opening human potential from meaning and tradition as existential categories. By contextualizing meaning, Naipaul makes the protagonist aware of a widening, complex context. Through this, tradition is revitalized as an element of the contemporary situation:

> Meaning, as a source of power and community energizes the latent links between man and his environment so that man's 'meditation in the presence of otherness is also man's continuing search for a basic orientation in his situation'. The existential narrator, reflecting over the protagonist, seeks links (areas of concordance and discordance) between social and subjective meaning through empirical action which verifies the fact of a common humanity. (Kamra 33)

In Naipaul's novels, the protagonist, the narrator and the author himself are all rootless. Through their colonial experience, they strive to move towards a wider horizon to explore their potentiality as individual human beings. Through their search for excellence they have always been in a state of predicament and crisis. Satendra Nandan therefore comments on the protagonists of Naipaul thrown to critical situation:

> Virtually all of Naipaul's writings deal with the predicament of the "unanchored souls". In a dozen works, Naipaul's vision has never faltered, indeed it has widened, with a sense of urgency and immediacy, into a more universal fate moving into other cultures, other lands, other peoples. However, the underlying, unifying reality is always the same. That he has made the Caribbean experience an integral strand in the pattern of human condition in his signal achievement. (Narsimhaih 348)

The three—the narrator, the protagonist and the author—emerge from a common context, and meet in a situation quite understandable to all of them. However, the distinctive features of each protagonist in different books and their distinctive situations make each book a unique experience. To understand this simultaneous presentation of distinctiveness and wholeness the multiple contexts of his novels can be defined as the thematic relationship between three diverse personalities: between the protagonist and the narrator, between these two and Naipaul. Interpretation of Naipaul's novels reveals that each protagonist in each novel is placed in a definite situation that shapes the structure of that novel. The narrator treats the protagonist in such situations that the protagonist is evolved as a growing character. The physical and psychological reality in the novel is achieved through the chronological development of the story. The protagonist grows to face defeats and failures in life to understand that despite these failures, life has some meaning. He therefore faces the challenges with patience and calmness of mind. The protagonist is however an ordinary man struggling with the crisis of his life just like other common men in his society; he is not extraordinary. Though he seems to be heroic in the local context, all his fames and status are as temporary as his identity. The protagonist in Naipaul's novels therefore "affirms the homely sanctity of the commonplace, where there can be an acceptance of the imperfection of all things, human action chief among them" (Krieger 1966: 266). The narrator in Naipaul has control over other characters and situations. The self-conscious narrator has objectivity in his approach to life and situations in the universe. The reader always feels the presence of the narrator who fully dominates over the narrative, and always makes perceptive comments to emphasize his vision. The narrator pushes the protagonist from the margin to the centre so that he can play his role in politics and history on his pursuit of personal enhancement thereby enlarging the context of the particular situation. That is because Naipaul has great concern for the marginalized sections in the society. It has therefore rightly been commented:

> Until Naipaul wrote his novels the indentured laborer was featureless.... But it's Naipaul's writings which have given these dregs of humanity, a place in the educated consciousness of the world community. For the first time the face of the coolie acquires distinctive features which have the power to disturb a conscience. (Narasimhaiah 354-55)

Trapping the third world protagonist, Naipaul's narrator dramatizes his static situation for liberation to higher possibilities. Through his impartiality, the narrator reflects on his own sensibility and situation to crises with high degree of morality and freedom to make decisive choices:

> In his insistence on subjective empirical truth, he devalues the authoritarian power-oriented societies of the world. He is the perpetual anti-colonial and revolutionary. His hunger for "experience" makes him value his homelessness and rootlessness as assets in his enterprise to know the world to which he relates through the imagination and language. His mind ranges over the whole universe of discourse-myth, gesture, dream, silence, logic, symbolism and structuralism. The subjective and the objective are both possibilities of the narrator through irony, self-reflection and protection. (Kamra 37)

The protagonist is the "seer" of truth, and to him reality is a subjective term. He is portrayed as diametrically opposite to the narrator. Though both of them are intelligent and sensible, they are also entrapped to the static situations and thereby subscribe to the greater design of the novel. Through his satire and irony, the dominant narrative voice is rather a limited sensibility. This helps the author draw the attention of the readers to the situations of the novel with meticulous care. The dramatized world of materialism is contrived in the perspective of isolation where people are self-centered, and are less enthusiastic to objectivity. Naipaul therefore visualizes the world in terms of a barracoon: "But tranquility recedes. The barracoon is overcrowded; the escape routes are closed. The people are disaffected and have no sense of danger" (*Barracoon* 309). Naipaul's protagonist is thus subject to chaotic situations in the society for which he is on the move with a complex vision of his own life. The protagonist meditates continuously to overcome the crises. His fiction therefore moves forward by perpetual questioning of the "self" as well as the questioning of the situation. Robbe-Gillet's comments on art are appropriate to Naipaul's novelistic design: "Art is life.... Art cannot exist without this permanent condition of being put in question. But the movement of these evolutions and revolutions constitute its perpetual renaissance" (159). Naipaul's fiction is thus shaped by the purpose of the author. His aesthetic design ignites their minds by driving them to struggle for their survival and identity at any cost.

It is therefore a fiction of contemporary situations where alienation of man predominates as reality. It establishes a linkage between the actual and the artistic world of the author. Naipaul dramatizes the situations and confrontations between the Third world and First world from the 1950 onwards. He deliberately chooses neither the colonies of the immigrants who are imported as laborers to live in a country which is neither their home nor the civilization of the country is theirs. These people are thus subject to greater exploitation than the natives of a country who are exploited by the colonial administrators. The situations of these doubly displaced marginalized sections are more critical because they are stripped of their native culture and civilization. They have only the externality of their native culture. They are perpetually haunted by a sense of inferiority and backwardness, and hence are inclined to accept the Western values as absolute. Naipaul dramatizes this vision quite significantly through the narrator's multi-dimensional narrative design emphasizing the psychological and subjective aspects. The desire for moving to the Centre from the margin is the most important existential situation of the protagonist. Naipaul focuses on the cultural and historical aspects in his efforts to reinterpret the contemporary situation of these people. His rejection of all the institutions which practice subservience as a necessity illustrates his idea of equality. The notion of subservience by privileged society is reflected in these institutions, marriage and family life. Possessing a home is the symbol of a life with security and promise. Naipaul also believes that desire for home is sometimes detrimental for a full life because it takes the individual from the community, turning the individual to be more self-centered. Such a situation alienates him from the contemporary reality. Since security of home delimits the individual's horizon of life, he should therefore try to move out of home so that he may achieve a sense of self-realization through constructive action. *In a Free State* Naipaul's delineation of such a vision through the role of the narrator is significant because Naipaul believes that the individual can make his personal life more meaningful by taking interest in community life as he will be able to interact with the contemporary reality much better and deeper.

The most significant aspect in Naipaul's fictions is the continuous struggle of the protagonist to be free. This incessant search for freedom makes him aware of the sense of loss and his void of life. Naipaul combines the autobiographical and biographical mode so as to achieve the protagonist's predicament through paradoxical situations. Life is both paradoxical and ambiguous in nature. Concreteness is not the way life can move because life is always an abstract. His fictional structure therefore moves on through the interactions of various binary contexts producing tension between the opposites: past/ present, subjective/objective, historical/political, actual/ideal, place/time, concrete/abstract. In Naipaul's scheme, the narrator is a crucial figure, and his ambivalent relationship with the protagonist, brings out the balance between the opposites.

"Awareness of place" defines identity of individuals in his fiction. Because of affiliation to a place, the third-world individual is conscious of his racial, social and intellectual inferiority. However, he lacks an awareness of time, a historical sense. Through his anguish of inferiority racially, socially or intellectually, he tries to enhance his "place" by moving towards the modernity, but he is also disturbed on his way. Such instability leads him to strive for equality to reassert his identity as an individual. The protagonist's state of discontent with his place compels him to move away to escape. This causes his displacement. Naipaul expands his territory of the third world by including all people, displaced physically, mentally and emotionally. In Naipaul's fiction, the "sense of time" by the narrator and the "sense of place" of the protagonist balance with each other to carry on the design of the novelist. In Naipaul's novels, the narrator-protagonist-author triangle is complex because their interactions, oppositions and roles decide the directions in them. It is important to note how Naipaul, through his linguistic manipulation, is able to create new contexts to suit his design for portrayal of his vision. His use of third person narrator as well as the first person narrator depends on what type of role the narrator plays in the specific contexts of the specific situations. The use of first person narrative technique makes the situations existential because the narrator perceives the meaning about the contemporary world through interplay of his sensibility, situation and language:

> Structurally the novels emphasize the importance of the subjective, sensible life as the foundation of identity. They explore the possibilities inherent in man's imaginative and linguistic capacity to create a world out of the experience of absurdity. This narrative world is the culmination of the narrator's possibility for the time being. It leaves him emptied out, alienated and facing the void; he experiences the necessity for a fresh start. (Kamra 43-44)

Naipaul's vision could be understood clearly through the interaction of the narrator, protagonist and the author himself. When the narrator dominates over the protagonist, and goes on situating the latter into crises and struggles for his vanities and failures, he is not blind to objective realities of life and the world. He always presents himself as an extension to the narration of the narrator. His ironic presence lends the narrative deep philosophical dimensions. In his reflections Naipaul, the author blends past, future and present into one, a timeless entity. The narrator in his fiction is a distinctive voice, playing an important role to present the details of the life of the protagonist, rich with meaning. The narrator's dominance on protagonists makes him stand against all pressures to face the challenges to extend his own experiences through his agonies and anguish. Naipaul, the author is more important than Naipaul, the man. At best, the narrator and Naipaul, the man may have some common vision, which is sometimes subjective and existential. However, Naipaul, the author lends objectivity, balance and order to the overall vision of the fictional world by bringing a balance between the protagonist and the narrator.

10.3. The Book: A Contemporary Perspective

In his fiction and non-fiction, Naipaul has emphasized a "sense of history" and "identity" of the rootless margins across cultures and nationalities. "Postcolonialism" as a notion contests the canons of Western epistemology and advocates the alternative ways of seeing things from the perspective of the "other" knowledge systems. The thrust of emphasis is on the emancipation and empowerment of the marginalized sections in the society. Rejecting the existing, biased notion of the world order, it seeks to reconstruct the "suppressed histories and cultures", and therefore it aims at destabilizing the "power-equation" for uplifting the marginalized people, "the wretched of the earth". As has already been discussed, postcolonialism, by subverting the existing world-order threatens power and privilege of the high-ups repositioning the "margin" and the "centre". Naipaul deconstructs the "margin-centre" equation, and portrays the cultural predicament of the "marginalized" and the displaced individuals in a set-up where the migrant searches for his roots and identity in a bewildering universe. An interpretation of Naipaul's novels, short stories and travelogues has made us understand the issues related to marginality, cultural identity and sense of history. Postcolonial Reading involves an interdisciplinary approach because it draws on the insights and precision from different disciplines and areas of knowledge such as historical perspective of colonialism, political philosophy, culture, economics, and cultural anthropology, deconstruction, post-structuralism and postmodernism. Naipaul's works have therefore been interpreted drawing on different intellectual approaches.

As has already been mentioned, contemporary postcolonial theoretical approaches are not exclusive to other theoretical insights and precision. In contemporary research, postcolonial study therefore uses the insights and precision of a large number of post-structuralist theories. There are often controversies on Naipaul's commitment as a postcolonial writer. In this book, important postcolonial issues, namely "marginality", "cultural identity" and "deconstruction of history", have been taken up for discussion to explore Naipaul's "global vision" as a humanist with his concerns for the rootless marginalized. All the fourteen fictional texts, and seven travelogues have been interpreted for exploration of the "suppressed histories" of the people, their lack of historical sense, racial conflicts, cultural clashes and underdeveloped intellectuality of the independent citizens to take up the challenge for leading their countries in the path of socio-economic progress. Most of the existing books on Naipaul reveal that comprehensive interpretation of all fictional texts and travelogues have not been taken up in a single volume for study of colonial/postcolonial issues. However, a proper perspective of Naipaul's vision as a writer of the world can be understood better only when a rigorous project dealing with almost all the major works are undertaken for study. This book is an attempt to discuss his various works in proper perspective to each other. Naipaul has a great concern for a universal civilization based on "a globalized humanity" rather than on "narrow nationalism". "Consciousness of internationalism" intermingled with "broad nationalism" can turn the world into a place without borders, free from the evils of fundamentalism of "exclusive nationalism". He has always been conscious of evolution of a "Universal Civilization" based on enlightenment, understanding, and equality, with no discrimination of race, colour and caste. In his scheme of things, he has emphasized the destabilization of "margin-Centre" equation to a great extent. The evolution of a great Universal Civilization is possible if people realize their responsibility as "world-citizens" rather than indulge in fighting for false "issues of fundamentalism".

The present book is therefore relevant in the contemporary perspective because we still experience the different issues related to colonial situations of domination, inequality, subordination, hierarchy of power, marginalization, and identity crisis, lack of historical awareness, exploitation and poverty in the so-called postcolonial world. As has already been mentioned, "colonialism" is still continuing in the different contexts and situations—at home, in the society, in the office—wherever we find that there is "politics", the play of a "power-game". "Postcolonial theory" is not actually a theory in the sense of science that believes in a coherent set of principles which can bring out a verifiable result. On the other hand, it consists of a set of inter-related perspectives, juxtaposed and contradictory to one another. Postcolonialism as a perspective believes in dynamism rather than being static. It therefore enforces alternatives to the existing thinking in the field of metaphysics, power-politics and epistemology. The contemporary world is fast-changing, and the entire world is turned into a global village. As a result, most of the existing notions and assumptions soon become obsolete by losing relevance in the contemporary context. "Postcolonialism" therefore initiates a reorientation of values, perceptions and thoughts and carries them forward. It thus continuously displaces the ideas, thoughts, knowledge systems and perspectives. The idea of "displacement" is a complex issue because it is a continuous process wherein we are displaced constantly. "Rootlessness" or "displacement" is not negative because through change, there is freshness in thinking and development. In Post-structuralist thinking, the "notion of fixity" has been rejected. The deconstructionists and the feminists have made efforts for reconstruction of a new world-order by challenging the existing, stereotype notions and ideas which have not been founded on reason and sense. Similarly, "postcolonialism" as a notion has no belief in "fixity" and the dominant existing "epistemology" based on established ideas and notions. In that way, it has been able to force changes and development in the society not only materially, but also in all spheres of life. That is why Young makes a favorable evaluation of the postcolonial assumptions: "Above all postcolonialism seeks to intervene, to force alternative knowledge into the power structures of the West as well as the non-West. It seeks to change the way they behave, to produce a more just and equitable relation between the different peoples of the world" (2006: 7).

"Postcolonialism" as a concept is not moving in a single direction. It has not even a single source to generate its strength and power. It takes in and imbibes different insights and precision from different fields of knowledge and experience for which its operation is based on interdisciplinarity. In literary texts, a writer of the contemporary world cannot write good literary texts if he operates in an exclusive field. Inclusiveness can only bring in new insights and perspectives. V.S. Naipaul is a "world writer" who does not belong to one culture, one nation or one civilization; he is therefore a writer without borders. Even as a writer he does not think that novels, travelogues or short stories are all exclusive to each other in the form and technique. That is why his "global vision" is spread over to all his writings where he does not consider that "displacement" or "rootlessness" has been negative. He thinks that "marginality" must have to be discussed in the alternative perspective. He himself was a marginalized, rootless individual. Through his struggle he has been able to destabilize the "margin-Centre" dichotomy. Now as we know he has proved that "marginality" must have to be taken seriously because a marginalized individual can displace the Centralized figures and Knowledge Systems in a postcolonial world that gives him opportunities to displace the "Centre". In this perspective, Naipaul's life and works have been instrumental in displacing an entire world of knowledge, writings, notions and assumptions, beliefs and systems. That is why we consider that the present book, by interpreting Naipaul's entire corpus of writing, has been good enough to enable us to understand Naipaul's works better and deeper. However, this study has not been based on some fixed, rigid approaches of analysis and interpretation because such an approach will rather be narrow in exploring the complex ideas and vision of V.S. Naipaul. Young's views are relevant to quote:

> For much of postcolonial theory is not so much about the relations between ideas and practices: relations of harmony, relations of conflict, generative relations between different peoples and their cultures. Postcolonialism is about a changing world, a world that has been changed by struggle and which its practitioners intend to change further. (2006: 7)

This book has therefore contemporary relevance as it explores conditions of marginality, identity crisis and the suppressed histories of the peoples, nations and cultures. Naipaul's concern for marginality has motivated him to discuss the contemporary issues that have not received much attention. His experiences are unique because he has been doubly displaced—one displacement of his ancestors from India to Trinidad, and his own displacement from his native Trinidadian ethos. Living in England and looking back to his roots, he understands that the existing writings have not contained his situations—his predicament and frustrations as a writer as well as an individual. That is why he recorded his authentic experiences in the English language. Though he recorded them through this, he wrote in completely new modes that can be branded as "mixed mode" even though we sometimes categorize them as novels, travelogues, autobiographies, short stories, journalistic writings or non-fiction prose. He brought in some freshness to the structures and thought-patterns in literature. As a result, a study of his fictions/travelogues/other modes enables us to understand the contemporary world with some freshness of insight and outlook. Although the book is a postcolonial Reading of Naipaul's writings, it has not precisely or rigidly adhered to operations of postcolonial theories exclusively. An interpretation of texts in the light of postcolonialism has yielded many new areas of meaning hitherto escaped our notice.

Works Cited and Consulted

Abrams, M.H. *A Glossary of Literary Terms*. 6th ed. Bangalore: Prism Books, 1993. Print.

Acheson, James, ed. *The British Novel Since 1960*. New York: St. Martin's, 1966. Print.

Adami, Esterino. *Rushdie, Kureish, Syal: Essays in Diaspora*. New Delhi: Prestige, 2006. Print.

Ahmad, Aijaz. *In Theory: Classes, Nations, Literature*. 1992. New Delhi: OUP, 2008. Print.

———. "The Politics of Literary Postcoloniality". *Contemporary Postcolonial Theory: A Reader.* 1996. Ed. Padmini Mongia. New Delhi: Oxford University Press, 2002: 276-93. Print.

Ahmed, L. *Women and Gender in Islam: Historical Roots of a Modern Debate*. New Haven, CT: Yale University Press, 1992. Print.

Aikant, Satish C. "Determining the Post-colonial: Assumptions and Performance." *The Journal of Indian Writing in English* 27. 2 (1999): 56-64. Print.

Alam, Fukul. "The Enigma of V.S. Naipaul". *V.S. Naipaul: An Anthology of Recent Criticism*. Ed. Purabi Panwar. Delhi: Pencraft International, 2007: 190-95. Print.

Alavi, Hazma, et al. *Capitalism and Colonial Production*. London: Croom Helm, 1982. Print.

Aloysius, G. *Nationalism without a Nation*. New Delhi: OUP, 2008. Print.

Althusser, L. *Lenin and Philosophy and Other Essays*. Trans. B. Brewster. New York: Monthly Review Press, 1971. Print.

Ambedkar, B.R. *Thought on Pakistan*. Bombay: Thacker & Co., 1947. Print.

Amin, Samir. *Capitalism in the Age of Globalization:* The Management of Contemporary Society. London: Zed, 1997. Print.

Amur, G.S. *Indian Readings in Commonwealth Literature*. New Delhi: Sterling Publishers, 1985. Print.

Amur, G.S., and S.K. Desai, eds. *Colonial Consciousness in Commonwealth Literature*. Bombay: Somaya Publication, 1984. Print.

Ananthamurthy, U.R. *Samskara*. New Delhi: OUP, 1976. Print.

Andesron, B. *Imagined Communities: Reflection on the Origin and Spread of Nationalism*. 1983. London: Verso, 1991. Print.

Anzaldua, Gloria. *La Frontera / Border Lands*. San Francisco, CA: Aunt Lute Press, 1999. Print.

Appleby, Joyce, Lymn Haunt, and Margaret Jacob. *Telling the Truth about History*. New York: Norton, 1994. Print.

Apple White, James. "A Trip with V.S. Naipaul." *Raritan* 10.1 (1990): 48-54. Print.

Arnold, David. *Colonizing the Body*. New Delhi: OUP, 1993. Print.

Arnold, David, and David Hardeman, eds. *Subaltern Studies VIII: Essays in Honour of Ranajit Guha*. New Delhi: OUP, 2003. Print.

Arnold, David, and Ramchandra Guha, eds. *Nature, Culture, Imperialism: Essays of the Environment History of South Asia*. Delhi: Oxford University Press, 1995. Print.

Ashcroft, B., G. Griffiths, and H. Tiffin, eds. *The Post-colonial Studies Reader*. London: Routledge, 1995. Print.

———, eds. *The Empire Writes Back: Theory and Practice in Post-colonial Literatures.* New York: Routledge, 1989. Print.

Balibar, E., and Immanuel Wallerstein. *Race, Nation, Class: Ambiguous Identities.* London and New York: Verso, 1991. Print.

Bakhtin, M.M. *The Dialogic Imagination.* Ed. Michael Holquist. Trans. Caryl Emerson and Michael Holquist. Austin: University of Texas Press, 1981. Print.

Ballard, Roger, ed. *Desh Pradesh: The South Asian Presence in Britain.* Delhi: B.R. Publishing Corporation, 1994. Print.

Barker, F., P. Hulme and M. Iverson, eds. *Colonial Discourse/ Postcolonial Theory.* Manchester: Manchester University Press, 1994. Print.

Barua, Krishna. "'I Must not Unpack': The Rhetorics of Hiding in V.S. Naipaul's *Half a Life.*" *The Atlantic Critical Review* 3.2 (2004): 116-28. Print.

Bastolovich, Crystal and Neil Lazarus, eds. *Marxism, Modernity and Postcolonial Studies.* Cambridge: Cambridge University Press, 2002. Print.

Batra, Kanika. "Translating the Caribbean: V.S. Naipaul's Metaphorics of Mimicry". *V.S. Naipaul: An Anthology of Recent Criticism.* Ed. Purabi Panwar. Delhi: Pencraft International, 2007: 179-88. Print.

Baugh, Edward, ed. *Critics on Caribbean Literature: Reading in Literary Criticism.* London: George Allen and Unwin, 1978. Print.

Bauman, Emily. "Re-dressing Colonial Discourse: Postcolonial Theory and the Humanist Project." *Critical Quarterly* 40.3 (1998): 79-89. Print.

Beauvoir, Simone de. *The Second Sex.* Trans. and Ed. H.M. Parshley. London: Vintage, 1997. Print.

Beecroft, Simon. "Sir Vidia's Shadow: V.S. Naipaul, the Writer and *The Enigma of Arrival.*" *Journal of Commonwealth Literature* 35.1 (2000): 71-86. Print.

Bhabha, Homi K. *The Location of Culture.* London: Routledge, 1994. Print.

———. "The Other Question: The Stereotype and Colonial Discourse." *Screen* 24.6 (1983): 18-36. Print.

———. *Nation and Narration.* London and New York: Routledge, 1990. Print.

———. "Foreword Framing Fanon." *The Wretched of Earth.* Frantz Fanon. Trans. Richard Philcox. 1963. New York: Grove Press, 2004: vii-xli. Print.

Bhat, Yashoda. *V.S. Naipaul: An Introduction.* New Delhi: BR Publication, 2000. Print.

Birbalsingh, Frank. *From Pillar to Post: The Indo-Caribbean Diaspora.* Toronto: Tsar Publications, 1998. Print.

Blaut, James. *The Colonizer's Model of the World: Geographical Diffusionism and Eurocentric History.* New York: Guilford, 1993. Print.

Boehmer, Elleke. 1995, 2005. *Colonial and Postcolonial Literature.* New Delhi: OUP, 2008. Print.

———. *Empire, the National and the Postcolonial*, 1890-1920. Oxford: Oxford University Press, 2002. Print.

Bongie, Chris. *Islands and Exiles: The Creole Identities of Post/colonial Literature.* Stanford, Stanford University Press, 1998. Print.

Bornell, Victoria E., and Lymn Hunt, eds. *Beyond the Cultural Turn: New Directions in the Study of Society and Culture.* Berkeley: University of California Press, 1999. Print.

Boxhill, Anthony. *V.S. Naipaul's Fiction: In Quest of the Enemy.*, Fredericton, New Brunswick: York Press, 1983. Print.

———. "V.S. Naipaul's Starting Point". *The Journal of Commonwealth Literature.* 10.1 (1975): 1-9. Print.

Bradbury, Malcolm. *The Modern British Novel.* London: Secker and Warburg, 1994. Print.

Brathwaite, E.K. *Contradictory Omens: Cultural Diversity and Integration in the Caribbean.* Mona, Jamaica: Saracou Press, 1974. Print.

———. *Other Exiles*. London, OUP, 1975. Print.

Bratlinger, Patrich. *Rule of Darkness: British Literature and Imperialism, 1830-1914*. Ithaca: Cornell University Press, 1988. Print.

Breckenridge, Carol and Peter Van der Veer. *Orientalism and the Postcolonial Predicament: Perspective on South Asia*. Philadelphia: University of Pennsylvania Press, 1993. Print.

Brennan, Timothy. *At Home in the World: Cosmopolitanism Now*. Cambridge MA: Harvard University Press, 1997. Print.

———. *Salman Rushdie and the Third World*. London: Macmillan, 1989. Print.

———. ed. *West Indian Literature*. London: Macmillan, 1979. Print.

Bruce, F. Macdonald. "The Birth of Mr. Biswas". *Journal of Commonwealth Literature* 11.3 (1977): 50-54. Print.

———. "Symbolic Action in Three of V.S. Naipaul's Novels". *Journal of Commonwealth Literature* 9.3 (1975): 39-48. Print.

Buell, Frederick. *National Culture and the New Global System*. Baltimore & London: Johns Hopkins University, 1994. Print.

Burgess, Anthony. *The Artist as Novelist*. U.S.A.: The University of Alabama Press, 1979. Print.

———. *The Novel Now: A Student's Guide to Contemporary Fiction*. London: Faber, 1971. Print.

Burton, Antoinette, ed. *Gender, Sexuality and Colonial Modernities*. London: Routledge, 1999. Print.

Butler, Christopher. *Interpretation, Deconstruction and Ideology*. London: OUP, 1984. Print.

———. *Postmodernism: A Very Short Introduction*, 2002. New Delhi: Oxford University Press, 2006. Print.

Butler, Judith. *Gender Trouble*: New York and London: Routledge, 2007. Print.

Camus, Albert. "The Myth of Sisyphus". *Continental European Literature: Essentials of Contemporary Literature of the Western World*. 2nd edition. Woodbury, N.Y.: Barron's Educational Series, 1974: 295. Print.

Cantor, Norman F. *Twentieth-Century Culture*: Modernism to Deconstruction. New York: Peter Lang, 1988. Print.

Castle, Gregory, ed. *Postcolonial Discourses: An Anthology*. Oxford: Blackwell, 2001. Print.

Cesaire, Aime. 1950. *Discourse on Colonialism*. New York: Monthly Review Press, 1972. Print.

Chakrabarty, Bidyut, ed. *Communal Identity in India*. New Delhi: OUP, 2009. Print.

Chakrabarty, Dipesh. *Habitations of Modernity*. New Delhi: Permanent Black, 2002: Print.

———. *Provincializing Europe: Postcolonial Thought and Historical Difference*. Princeton, NJ: Princeton University Press, 2000. Print.

Chakrabarti, Santosh. "Alienation and Home: A Study of *A House for Mr. Biswas*". *V.S. Naipaul: Critical Essays*. Ed. Mohit K. Ray. Vol III. 2005: 45-52. Print.

Chakravorty, Swapan. Suzana Millevska and Tani E. Barlow. *Conversations with Gayatri Chakravorty Spivak*. London: Seagull Books, 2006. Print.

Chambers, Iain. *Migrancy, Culture, Identity*. London: Routledge, 1994. Print.

Chambers, I., and L. Curti, eds. *The Post-colonial Questions: Common Skies, Divided Horizons*. New York: Routledge, 1966. Print.

Chandra, D. Dorothy. "Identity Crisis: A Study of Derek Walcott and Nissim Ezekiel." *Critical Practice* 12. 1-2 (2005): 55-70. Print.

Chandra, Sudhir. *The Oppressive Present: Literature and Social Consciousness* in *Colonial India*. Delhi: OUP, 1992. Print.

Chaturvedi, Vinayak, ed. *Mapping Subaltern Studies and the Postcolonial*. London: Verso, 2000. Print.

Chatterjee, Chandra. *Surviving Colonialism: A Study of R.K. Narayan, Anita Desai, V.S. Naipaul*. New Delhi: Radha Publications, 2000. Print.

Chatterjee, P. *Nationalist Thought and the Colonial World—A Derivative Discourse*. Tokyo: Zed Books, 1986. Print.

———. *The Nation and its Fragments: Colonial and Postcolonial Histories*. Princeton: Princeton University Press, 1993. Print.

Chatterjee, Partha and Pradeep Jeganathan, eds. *Community, Gender and Violence*: New Delhi: Permanent Black, 2009. Print.

Chaudhuri, Amit. "Two Cheers for the Nobel Award." *V.S. Naipaul: An Anthology of Recent Criticism*. Ed. Purabi Panwar. Delhi: Pencraft International, 2007: 187-90. Print.

Chauhan, Vibha S. "Mythical and the Real: Protest and Marginalization. *Journal of the School of Language, Literature and Culture Studies* 4 (2005): 133-43. Print.

Childs, Peter and R.J. Patrich Williams. *An Introduction to Postcolonial Theory*. London: Prentice Hall, 1997. Print.

Christmas, Laura. Postcolonial Contraventions: *Cultural Readings of Race, Imperialism, and Transnationalism*, Manchester: Manchester University Press, 2003. Print.

Choubey, Asha. "A Critique of Naipaul's *Half a Life*: Searching for Identity in Limbo". http // 65. 107. 211. 208 / Caribbean / naipaul / Choubey 3. html, 2002.

Clifford, James. *The Predicament Of Culture*. Cambridge MA: Howard University Press, 1988. Print.

Clifford, James and George Marcus, eds. *Writing Culture*. Berkeley: University of California Press, 1986. Print.

Cohen, Jeffrey Jerome, ed. *The Postcolonial Middle Ages*. Houndmills U.K.: Macmillan, 2000. Print.

Connor, Steven. *Postmodernist Culture: An Introduction to Theories of the Contemporary*. Oxford and Cambridge: Basil Blackwell, 1989. Print.

Cooper, Frederick and Ann Laura Stales, eds. *Tensions of Empire: Colonial Cultures in a Bourgeois World*. Berkeley: University of California Press, 1997. Print.

Coulthard, G.R. *Caribbean Literature: An Anthology*. London: OUP, 1966. Print.

———. *Race and Colour in Caribbean Literature*. London: OUP, 1962. Print.

Crosby, Alfred. *Ecological Imperialism*. Cambridge: Cambridge University Press, 1993. Print.

Crow, Brian and Banfield, Chris. *An Introduction to Post-colonial Theory*. N.Y: University of Cambridge, 1996. Print.

Cudjoe, Selwyn, R. *Resistance and Caribbean Literature*. Athens, Ohio: Ohio University Press, 1980. Print.

———. *V.S. Naipaul: A Materialist Reading*. Amherst: University of Massachusetts, 1988. Print.

Das, Bijay Kumar. "Subaltern Studies as Postcolonial Criticism: A Note" *Critical Practice* 11.1 (2004): 48-56. Print.

———. "From Slavery to Freedom: A Study of V.S. Naipaul's *A House for Mr. Biswas*." *Aspects of Commonwealth Literature*. New Delhi: Creative Books, 1995: 93-103. Print.

Davies, Carole Boyce. *Black Women, Writing and Identity*. London: Routledge, 1994. Print.

Davis, A.Y. *Women Race and Class*. London: Women's Press, 1982. Print.

de Alva, J.J.K. "The Postcolonization of the (Latin) American Experience: A Reconsideration of 'Colonialism', 'Postcolonialism' and 'Mestizaje'. *After Colonialisms, Imperial Histories and Postcolonial Displacements*. Ed. G. Prakash. Princeton, NJ: Princeton University Press, 1995: 241-75. Print.

de Saussure, Ferdinand. *Course in General Linguistics*. Hazard Adams and Leroy Searle, eds. *Critical Theory Since 1965*. Gainesville, F.L.: University Press of Florida, 1986. Print.

Deane, Seamus, ed. *Nationalism, Colonialism and Literature*. Minneapolis: University of Minnesota Press, 1990. Print.

Delano, Laura. "The Postcolonial Paradox in V.S. Naipaul's *A Bend in the River*". *The Atlantic Critical Review* 3.4 (2004): 27-32. Print.

Derrich, A.C. "Naipaul's Technique as a Novelist". *The Journals of Commonwealth Literature,* 24.1 (1989): 155-62. Print.

Derrida, Jacques. *Writing and Difference*. Trans. Allan Bass (London): Routledge, 1978. Print.

———. "Structure, Sign and Play in the Discourse of the Human Sciences." *Contexts for Criticism*. Ed. D. Keesey. Mountain View, CA: Mayfield, 1994: 347-58. Print.

Dhawan, R.K., ed. *Commonwealth Fiction*. New Delhi: Classical Publishing Company, 1988. Print.

Dhawan, R.K. et al., eds. *Recent Commonwealth Literature*, 2 Vols. New Delhi: Prestige Books, 1989. Print.

Dhawan, R.K. and L.S.R. Krishna Sastry, eds. *Commonwealth Writing: A Study in Expatriate Experience*. New Delhi: Prestige, 1994. Print.

Dirks, Nicholas, ed. *Colonialism and Culture*. Ann Arbor: University of Michigan Press, 1992. Print.

Docherry, Thomas. *Postmodernism: A Reader*. Harvester: Hemel Hampstead, 1992. Print.

Donald, James and Rattansi Ali, eds. *Race, Culture and Difference*. Longman: Open University Press, 1992. Print.

Ducky, Rudy. "V.S. Naipaul and John Donne: The Morning After". *The Journal of Commonwealth Literature* 24.1 (1989): 155-62. Print.

Dulai, Surjit S. "The Ganges Flows through Africa: V.S. Naipaul's India and *A Bend in the River*." *Journal of South Asian Literature* 26.1-2 (1991): 303-21. Print.

Durix, Carole and Jean-Pierre. *The New Literatures in English*. Paris: Longman, 1993. Print.

Dutt, Shankar. "Indian Diaspora and The Constituency of Dissent." *Re-makings* 6.2 (2007): 11-20. Print.

Eagleton, Terry. *Exile and Émigrés*. London: Chatto and Windus, 1970. Print.

———. *Ideology: An Introduction*. London: Verso, 1991. Print.

———, ed. *Raymond Williams: Critical Perspectives*. Cambridge: Polity Press, 1989. Print.

Eagleton, Terry, Fredric Jameson, and Edward Said. *Nationalism, Colonialism and Literature*. Minneapolis: University of Minnesota Press, 1990. Print.

Eastley, Aason. "Joking with the Center: Naipaul's Ambiguous Treatment of Trinidadian English in *The Mystic Masseur*". *Journal of Contemporary Thought* (Special Numbers on Postcolonialism and the Discourse of Marginality) 4 (Summer 1999): 25-46. Print.

Eliot, T.S. "Tradition and Individual Talent" in *The Sacred Wood: Essays on Poetry and Criticism*. T.S. Eliot. Methuen, 1960: 47-59. Print.

Elliot, Michael. "Naipaulia." *New Republic*, 16 Nov. 1987: 13-14. Print.

Engdahl, Dr. Horace. "On Naipaul." *V.S. Naipaul: Critical Essays* Vol. III. Ed. Mohit K. Ray. New Delhi: Atlantic, 2005: xi-xii. Print.

———. "The Presentation Speech." *V.S. Naipaul: Critical Essays* Vol. III. Ed. Mohit K. Ray. New Delhi: Atlantic, 2005: xiii-xvi. Print.

Engels, D. and S. Marks, eds. *Contesting Colonial Hegemony: State and Society in Africa and India*. London: British Academic Press, 1994. Print.

Fanon, Frantz. *A Dying Colonialism*. Trans. H. Chevalier. New York: Grove Press, 1965. Print.

———. *Black Skin, White Masks*. (1952, 1967). Trans. Richard Philcox. New York: Grove Press, 2008. Print.

———. *The Wretched of the Earth*. (1961, 1963). Trans. Richard Philcox. New York: Grove Press, 2004. Print.

Fabian, Johannes. *Language and Colonial Power.* Berkeley: University of California Press, 1986. Print.

Feder, Lillan. *Naipaul's Truth*. New Delhi: Indialog Publications, 2001. Print.

Fieldhouse, D.K. *The Colonial Empires*. London: Macmillan, 1989. Print.

Foucault, Michel. *Madness and Civilization*. Trans. R. Howard. New York: Pantheon, 1965. Print.

———. *The Order of Things*. Trans. A. Sheridan. New York: Random House, 1970. Print.

———. *Discipline and Punish*. Trans. A. Sheridan. London: Allen Lane, 1977. Print.

———. "The Ethic of Care for the Self as a Practice of Freedom." *The Final Foucault*. Eds. James Bernauer and David Rasmussen. Cambridge: MIT Press, 1988: 13-14. Print.

———. *The History of Sexuality*. Trans. R. Huxley. New York: Vintage Books, 1990. Print.

French, Patrick. *The World is What it is*. London: Picador, 2008. Print.

Frow, John. *Marxism and Literary History.* Oxford: Blackwell, 1986. Print.

Gandhi, Lila. *Postcolonial Theory*. New Delhi: OUP, 2009. Print.

Gandhi, M.K. *Hind Swaraj*. Ed. A.J. Parel. Cambridge: CUP, 1947. Print.

Gandhi, Rajmohan. *Understanding the Muslim Mind*. New Delhi: Penguin, 2000. Print.

Garebian, Keith. "V.S. Naipaul's Negative Sense of Place." *The Journal of Commonwealth Literature* 10.1 (1975): 23-35. Print.

Garvin, Harry R. "Introductory Essay." *Makers of the Twentieth Century Novel*. Ed. Harry R. Garvin. Cranbury, New Jersey: Associated University Press, 1977. Print.

Gates, Henry Louis Jr., ed. *Black Literature and Literary Theory*. London: Methuen, 1984. Print.

Ghosh, Amitav. *Countdown*. Delhi: Ravi Dayal, 1999. Print.

Ghosh, Aurobindo. *Bande Matram*. 1907. Rpt. *Sri Aurobindo Birth Centenary Library*. Vol. 1, Pondicherry: Sri Aurobindo Ashram, 1972. Print.

Gikandi, Simon. *Writing in Limbo: Modernism and Caribbean Literature*. Ithaca and London: Cornell University Press, 1992. Print.

Gillner, Ernest. *Nations and Nationanalisms*. Oxford: Basil Blackwell, 1983. Print.

Gilkes, Michael. *The West Indian Novel*. Boston: Twayne, 1981. Print.

Gillis, John, ed. *Commemorations: The Politics of National Identity*. Princeton, NJ: Princeton University Press, 1994. Print.

Giri, B.P. and Prafulla C. Kar, eds. *Thinking Territory: Some Reflections*. Delhi: Pencraft International, 2009. Print.

Glover, David, and Cora Kaplan. *Genders*. London: Routledge, 2007. Print.

Gohain, Hiren. "The Postcolonial Confusion and V.S. Naipaul." *V.S. Naipaul: Critical Essays* Vol. III. Ed. Mohit K. Ray. New Delhi: Atlantic, 2005. Print.

Gokhale, B.G. *The Making of the Indian Nation*. Bombay: Asia Publication House, 2nd ed. 1960. Print.

Goonatilahe, Susantha. *Crippled Minds: An Exploration into Colonial Culture*. Bombay: Vikas, 1982. Print.

Gorra, Michael. *After Empire: Scott, Naipaul, Rushdie*. Chicago: University of Chicago Press, 1997. Print.

Gowda, H.H. *The Colonial and Neo-Colonial Encounters* in *Commonwealth Literature*. Mysore: Mysore University Press, 1973. Print.

Gramsci, A. *Selections from the Prison Notebooks*. Eds. Q. Hoare and G.N. Smith. London: Lawrence and Wishart, 1971. Print.

Greenblatt, Stephen J. *Learning to Curse: Essays in Modern Literature*. New York: Routledge, 1990. Print.

Greenblatt, Stephen and Giles Gunn, eds. *Redrawing the Boundaries*. New York: MLA, 1992. Print.

Griffiths, Gareth. *A Double Exile: African and West Indian Writing Between Two Cultures*. London: Marian Boyars, 1988. Print.

Grosby, Steven. *Nationalism: A Very Short Introduction*. Oxford: OUP, 2005. Print.

Grossberg, Lawrence et al., eds. *Cultural Studies*. New York: Routledge, 1992. Print.

Guha, R., ed. *Subaltern Studies*, Vol. I. New Delhi: Oxford University Press, 1982. Print.

Guha, R. and G. Spivak, eds. *Selected Subaltern Studies*. New Delhi: Oxford University Press, 1988. Print.

Guha, Ranajit, ed. *Subaltern Studies, I & II—Writings on South Asian History and Society*. Delhi: Oxford University Press, 1983. Print.

Gurr, Andrew. *Writers in Exile: The Creative Use of Home* in *Modern, Literature*. Sussex: The Harvester Press, 1981. Print.

Gaur, A.J. "Third-World Novel: Naipaul and After." *The Journal of Commonwealth Literature* 7.1 (1972): 6-13. Print.

Gussow, Mel. "Writer without Roots." *The New York Times Magazine* 26 Dec. 1976: 9. Print.

Gutmann, Amy, ed. *Multiculturalism: Examining the Politics of Recognition*. Princeton, NJ: Princeton University Press, 1994. Print.

Gutting, Gary. *Foucault: A Very Short Introduction*. Oxford: OUP, 2005. Print.

———. *The Cambridge Companion to Foucault*. Cambridge: Cambridge University Press, 1994. Print.

Haldar, Santwana. "V.S. Naipaul's *Half a Life*: The Colonial Context and Some Post Colonial Issues." *V.S. Naipaul: Critical Essays*, Vol. III. Ed. Mohit K. Ray. New Delhi: Atlantic Publishers, 2005: 226-49. Print.

Haley, Alex. *Roots*. London: Picador, 1976. Print.

Hall, Donald E. *Subjectivity*. London: Routledge, 2004. Print.

Hall, Stuart. "Cultural Identity and Diaspora." *Identity; Community, Culture, Difference*. Ed. Jonathan Rutherford. Lawrence and Wisher, 1990: 222-37. Print.

———. "Cultural Identity and Diaspora." *Contemporary Postcolonial Theory: A Reader*. 1996. Ed. Padmini Mongia. New Delhi: Oxford University Press,, 2002: 110-22. Print.

———. "On Postmodernism and Articulation" (Interview with Stuart Hall). *Critical Dialogues in Cultural Studies*. Eds. D. Morley and K.H. Chen. London: Routledge, 1996: 131-50. Print.

Hamner, Robert D. *V.S. Naipaul*. New York: Twayne, 1973. Print.

———, ed. *Critical Perspectives on V.S. Naipaul*. London: Heinemann, 1979. Print.

———. "V.S. Naipaul: A Selected Bibliography". *The Journal of Commonwealth Literature* 10.1 (1975): 36-44. Print.

Hardt, Michael and Antonio Negri. *Empire*. Cambridge, MA: Harvard University Press, 2000. Print.

Harrison, Nicholas. *Postcolonial Criticism: History, Theory and the Work of Fiction*. Oxford: Polity, 2003. Print.

Harry, R. Garvin. "Introductory Essay." *Makers of Twentieth Century Novel*. Ed. Harry R. Garvin. Cranbury, New Jersey: Associated University Press, 1977. Print.

Harrow, Kenneth W. "An African Reading of Naipaul's *A Bend in the River*." *Journal of South Asian Literature* 26.1-2 (1991): 322-36. Print.

Harvey, David. *The New Imperialism*. Oxford: OUP, 2003. Print.

Hassan, Dolly Zulakha. *V.S. Naipaul and the West Indies*. New York: Peter Lang, 1989. Print.

Hawkes, D. *Ideology*. London: Routledge, 1996. Print.

Hayman, Ronaldo. *The Novel Today*. New York: Orient Longman, 1976. Print.

Hayward, Helen. "Tradition, Innovation and the Representation of England in V.S. Naipaul's *The Enigma of Arrival.*" *Journal of Commonwealth Literature* 32.2 (1997): 51-65. Print.

Hazell, Stephen, ed. *The English Novel: Developments in Criticism Since Henry James*. London: Macmillan, 1978. Print.

Heiney, Donald and Lenthiel H. Downs. *Continental European Literature of the Western World*. 2nd ed. Woodbury, N.Y.: Barron's Educational Series, 1974. Print.

Hewitt, Douglas. *English Novel of the Early Modern Period*, 1890–1940. London: Longman, 1988. Print.

Hitchcock, Peter. *Dialogics of the Oppressed*. London: University of Minnesota Press, 1993. Print.

Hobsbawm, Eric. *On History*. 1988. London: ABACUS, 2008. Print.

———. *The Age of Empire*. New York: Vintage Books, 1989. Print.

———. *Nations and Nationalism Since 1780*. Cambridge: Cambridge University Press, 1990. Print.

Hogan, Patrick Colm. *Colonization and Cultural Identity: Crises of Tradition in the Anglophone Literature of India, Africa, and the Caribbean*. Albany: State University of New York Press, 2001. Print.

Howe, Irving. *Politics and the Novel*. Paris: Menton, 1967. Print.

Huggan, Graham. *The Post-Colonial Exotic: Marketing the Margins*. London: Routledge, 2001. Print.

Hughes, Peter. *V.S. Naipaul: Contemporary Writers*. London: Routledge, 1988. Print.

Hulme, P. *Colonial Encounters, Europe and the Native Caribbean 1492-1797*. London: Methuen, 1986. Print.

———. ed. *Post-Colonial Theory and Colonial Discourse*. Manchester: Manchester University Press, 1993. Print.

———. "Including America." *Ariel* 26.1 (1995): 117-23. Print.

Hutcheon, Linda. The *Politics of Postmodernism*. New York: Routledge, 1989. Print.

———. A Poetics of Postmodernism: History, Theory, Fiction. London: Routledge, 1988. Print.

Hutchinson, J. and A.D. Senath, eds. *Nationalism*. Oxford: Oxford University Press, 1994. Print.

Ilaiah, Kancha. *Post-Hindu India*. New Delhi: Sage Publications, 2009. Print.

Ingham, Patricia Clare and Michelle R. Warren, eds. *Postcolonial Moves: Medieval through Modern*. London: Palgrave, 2003. Print.

Innes, C.L. *Introduction to Postcolonial Literatures in English*. New Delhi: Cambridge University Press, 2008. Print.

———. *Race and Revolutionary Consciousness: A Documentary Interpretation of the 1970 Black Power Revolt in Trinidad*. Cambridge, Mass: Schenkman, 1971. Print.

Jain, Jasbir. *Problems of Post-colonial Literature and Other Essays*. Jaipur Printwell, 1991. Print.

———, ed. *Crossing Borders*. Jaipur: Rawat Publications, 2009. Print.

———, ed. *Writers of the Indian Diaspora*. Jaipur: Rawat Publications, 1998. Print.

Jain, Jasbir and Veena Singh, eds. *Contesting Postcolonialisms*. Jaipur: Rawat Publications, 2000. Print.

Jalal, Ayesha. *Democracy and Authoritarianism in South Asia: A Comparative and Historical Perspective*. New Delhi: Cambridge University Press, 1995. Print.

James, C.L.R. *Beyond Boundary*. Kasha: Duke University Press, 1993. Print.

———. *Spheres of Existence*. London: Allison and Busby, 1980. Print.

James, Louis, ed. *The Islands in Between: Essay on West Indian Literature*. London: Oxford University Press, 1968. Print.

Jameson, Fredric and Masao Miyoshe, eds. *The Culture of Globalization*. Durham, NC: Duke University Press, 1998. Print.

Jameson, Fredric. *The Political Unconscious: Narrative as a Socially Symbolic Act*. London: Methuen, 1981. Print.

———. "Third World Literature in the Era of Multinational Capitalism". *Social Text* 15 (1986): 65-78. Print.

Jan Mohammed, Abdul R. *Manichean Aesthetics: The Politics of Literature in Colonial Africa*. Amherst: University of Massachusetts Press, 1983. Print.

Janvis, Kelvin. *V.S. Naipaul: A Selective Bibliography with Annotations*. Metuchen: N.J. Scarecrow Press, 1989. Print.

John, La Guerre (ed.). *Calcutta to Caroni: The East Indians of Trinidad*. London: Longman, 1974. Print.

Jones, Stephanie. "The Politics and Poetics of Diaspora in V.S. Naipaul's *A Way in the World*." *Journal of Commonwealth Literature* 35.1 (2000): 87-97. Print.

Joshi, B. Chandra. *V.S. Naipaul: The Voice of Exile*. New Delhi: Sterling Publishers Private Ltd., 1994. Print.

Joshi, Navin Chandra, ed. *Democracy and Human Values: Essays in Honours of Shri V.M. Tarkunde*. New Delhi: Sterling Publishers, 1979. Print.

Kamra, Shashi. *The Novels of V.S. Naipaul: A Study in Theme and Form*. New Delhi: Prestige, 1990. Print.

Kabbani, R. *Europe's Myths of the Orient*. London: Pandora, 1986. Print.

Kakar, Sudhir. *The Inner World*. Oxford: OUP, *1978*. Print.

Kaul, R.K. "V.S. Naipaul and the Demythologizing of EL Dorado" *Commonwealth Fiction* 2 (1988): 119-27. Print.

Kelly, Richard. *V.S. Naipaul*. New York: Continuum, 1989. Print.

Kelvin, Jarvis. *V.S. Naipaul: A Selective Bibliography with Annotations, 1957–87*. Metuchen, New Jersey: Scarecrow, 1989. Print.

Kem, Edith. *Existential Thought and Fictional Technique*. London: Yale University Press, 1970. Print.

Kermode, Frank. *History and Value*. Oxford: Clarendon Press, 1988. Print.

———. "In the Garden of the Oppressor," *New York Times Book Review*, 22, Mar. 22 1987. Print.

Khan, A.J. "*V.S. Naipaul's Among the Believers*: An Indo-Islamic View." *Journal of Literary Studies* 22.1-2 (1998): 76-103. Print.

Kiernan, Victor. *The Lords of Human Kind: European Attitudes towards the Outside World in the Imperial Age*. Boston: Little, Brown & Co., 1969. Print.

———. *Marxism and Imperialism*. New York: St Martin's Press, 1974. Print.

King, Bruce. *V.S. Naipaul*. London: Macmillan, 1993. Print.

———. *Literatures of the World in English*. London: Routledge and Kegan Paul, 1974. Print.

———. *The New English Literatures—Cultural Nationalism in a Changing World*. London: Macmillan, 1980. Print.

———. *West Indian Literature*. London: Macmillan, 1979. Print.

King, Richard. *Orientalism and Religion: Postcolonial Theory, India and the Mystic East*. London: Routledge, 1999. Print.

Kirpal, Viney. *The Third World Novel of Expatriation*. New Delhi: Sterling, 1989. Print.

Klages, Mary. *Literary Theory: A Guide for the Perplexed*. London: Continuum International Publishing Group, 2008. Print.

Kortenaar, Neil ten. "Writers and Readers, The Written and The Read: V.S. Naipaul and *Guerrillas*". *Contemporary Literature* 31.3 (1990): 324-34. Print.

Krieger, Murray. *The Tragic Vision*. Chicago and London: The University of Chicago Press, 1966. Print.

Kumar, T. Vijay, Meenakshi Mukherjee, Harish Trivedi and C. Vijayarsee eds. *Focus India: Postcolonial Narratives of The Nation*. New Delhi: Pencraft International, 2007. Print.

Kundera, Milan. *The Art of the Novel*. 1988. Delhi: Rupa, 1995. Print.

Lamming, George. *Emigrant*. London: Alison and Busby, 1954. Print.

———. *In the Castle of My Skin*. 1953. London: Longman Drumbeat, 1979. Print.

———. *Natives of My Person*. 1972. London: Picador, 1974. Print.

———. *The Pleasures of Exile*. London: Michael Joseph, 1960. Print.

Langram, Phillip. "V.S. Naipaul: A Question of Detachment." *The Journal of Commonwealth Literature* 25.1 (1990): 132-41. Print.

Latimer, Dan. *Contemporary Critical Theory*. Harcourt Brace: Jovanovich Inc., 1989. 2nd Indian rpt. Delhi: Pearson Education, 2004. Print.

Lawrence, Daren R., ed. *Decolonizing Traditions: New Views of Twentieth-Century British Literary Canons*. Urbana and Chicago: University of Illinois Press, 1992. Print.

Lazarus, Neil. *Nationalism and Cultural Practice in the Postcolonial World*. Cambridge: Cambridge University Press, 1999. Print.

Lenin, V.I. *Imperialism, the Highest Stage of Capitalism.* Moscow: Foreign Languages Publishing House, 1947. Print.

Levine, Laurence. *Black Culture and Black Consciousness.* New York: Oxford University Press, 1977. Print.

Lewis, Maureen Warner. "Cultural Confrontation, Disintegration and Syncretism in *A House for Mr. Biswas.*" *Critical Perspectives on V.S. Naipaul.* Ed. Robert Hamner. London: Heinemann, 1977. Print.

Levy, Judith. *V.S. Naipaul: Displacement and Autobiography.* New York: Garland, 1995. Print.

Lichtheime, George. *Imperialism.* Harmondsworth: Penguin, 1974. Print.

Loclau, E. *Politics and Ideology in Marxist Theory.* London: New Left Books, 1977. Print

Lodge, David, ed. *Modern Criticism and Theory: A Reader.* 2nd ed. Delhi: Pearson Education, 2003, Second Indian Reprint, 2004. Print.

———. *After Bakhtin: Essay on Fiction and Criticism.* London: Routledge, 1990. Print.

Lodge, David and Miguel Wood, eds. *Modern Criticism and Theory: A Reader.* 1989. Print.

Loomba, Ania. *Colonialism/Postcolonialism.* 2nd ed. London: Routledge, 2007. Print.

Loomba, Ania, and Martin Orkin, eds. *Post-Colonial Shakespeare*, London: Routledge, 1998. Print.

Loomba, Ania, Suvir Kaul, Matti Bunzl, Antoinette Burton and Jed Esty, eds. *Postcolonial Studies and Beyond.* Ranikhet: Permanent Black, 2008. Print.

Lowenthal, David l. *West Indian Societies.* London: OUP, 1972. Print.

Lucy, Niall, ed. *Postmodern Literary Theory: An Anthology.* Oxford: Blackwell, 1999. Print.

Lyon, David. *Postmodernity.* 2nd ed. New Delhi, Mumbai, Chennai and Kolkata: Viva Books, 2002. Print.

Lyotard, Jean-François. *The Post-Modern Condition: A Report on Knowledge*. Manchester: University of Manchester Press, 1979. Print.

MacDonald, Scott B. *Trinidad and Tobago. Democracy and Development in the Caribbean*. New York: Praeger, 1986. Print.

Macherey, Pierre. *A Theory of Literary Production*. London: Routledge, 1978. Print.

Mackenzie, John. *Propaganda and Empire*. Manchester: Manchester University Press, 1984. Print.

Mahood, Molly. *The Colonial Encounter: A Reading of Six Novels*. London: Rex Collings, 1977: 165. Print.

Mair, Christian. "Naipaul's *Miguel Street* and Selvon's *Lonely Londoners*—Two Approaches to the Use of Caribbean Creole in Fiction." *The Journal of Commonwealth Literature* 24.1 (1989): 138-54. Print.

Malik, Yogendra. *East Indians in Trinidad: A Study in Minority Politics*. London: Oxford University Press, 1971. Print.

Mann, Harveen Sachdeva. "Variation on the Theme of Mimicry." *Modern Fiction Studies* 30.3 (1984): 472-73. Print.

Marx, K. *Surveys from Exile*. Ed. D. Fernbach. London: Pelican Books, 1973. Print.

Marx, K. and F. Engels. Collected *Works*. London: Lawrence and Wishart, 1976. Print.

Masih, I.K. "India Theirs and Mine: V.S. Naipaul's *An Area of Darkness*." *Commonwealth Fiction* 2 (1988): 156-66. Print.

Massie, Alan. *The Novel Today: A Critical Guide to the British Novel 1970-1989*. London: Longman, 1990. Print.

McClintock, A. *Imperial Leather: Race, Gender and Sexuality in the Colonial Context*. London: Routledge, 1995. Print.

———. "The Angel of Progress: Pitfalls of the Term 'Postcolonialism'." *Social Text* 31/32 (1992): 84-98. Print.

McLeod, A.L., ed. *Subjects of Worthy Fame: Essays on Commonwealth Literature*. New Delhi: Sterling, 1989. Print.

McWatt, Mark, ed. *West Indian Literature and its Social Context: Proceedings of the Fourth Annual Conference on West Indian Literature.* Cave Hill: University of the West Indies, 1985. Print.

Mehta, Kamal. "Naipaul as a Short Story Writer." *V.S. Naipaul: Critical Essays,* Vol. III. Ed. Mohit K. Ray. New Delhi: Atlantic, 2005: 279-94. Print.

Mehta, Pratap Bhanu. "Naipaul and the Burdens of History". *V.S. Naipaul: An Anthology of Recent Criticism.* Ed. Purabi Panwar. Delhi: Pencraft International, 2007. 43-53. Print.

Memmi, A. *The Colonizer and the Colonized.* Boston, MA: Beacon Press, 1967. Print.

Meyers, Jeffrey. *Fiction and the Colonial Experience.* Ipswich: The Boydell Press, 1973. Print.

Miles, R. *Racism.* London: Routledge, 1989. Print.

Miller Jr., James E., ed. *Myth and Method: Modern Theories of Fiction.* U.S.A.: University of Nebraska Press, 1960. Print.

Mishra, Binod. "Return and Reconciliation in V.S. Naipaul's Half a Life." *The Atlantic Critical Review* 3.2 (2004): 129-38. Print.

Mishra, Pankaj. "Introduction." *Literary Occasions* (V.S. Naipaul). Ed. Pankaj Mishra. Oxford: Picador, 2004: vii-xvi. Print.

Mommsen, Wolfgang, and Turgen Osteshammed. *Imperialism and After: Continuities and Discontinuities.* London: Allen and Unwin, 1986. Print.

Mongia, Padmini, ed. *Contemporary Postcolonial Theory: A Reader*. Oxford: OUP, 1996. Print.

Moore Gilbert, Bart. *Postcolonial Theory.* London: Verso, 1997. Print.

Morris, Robert K. *Paradoxes of Order: Some Perspectives on the Fiction of V.S. Naipaul*. Columbia: University of Missouri Press, 1975. Print.

Morton, Klass. *East Indians in Trinidad*. London: Columbia University Press, 1961. Print.

Mukherjee, Shreemati. "Subalternity as Event in History and Literature." *Journal of the School of Language, Literature and Culture Studies* Special Issues on "the marginal" (Spring 2006): 95-101. Print.

Murray, Stuart. "Introduction." *Not on any Map: Essays on Postcoloniality and Cultural Nationalism*. S. Murray. Exter: Univ. of Exter Press, 1997: 8. Print.

Mustafa, Fawzia. *V.S. Naipaul*. Cambridge: OUP, 1995. Print.

Nabar, Vrinda. *Caste as Woman*. New Delhi: Penguin Books, 1995. Print.

Naipaul, Seepersad. *The Adventures of Gurudeva*. New Delhi: Buffalo Books, 2001. Print.

Naipaul, Shiva. *Black and White*. London: ABACUS Book, 1990. Print.

Naipaul, V.S. *The Mystic Masseur*. 1957. London: Picador, 2002. Print.

———. *Miguel Street*. 1957. London: Picador, 2002. Print.

———. *The Night Watchman's Occurrence Book*. Suffrage, 1958; Mr. Stone, 1963; Flag, 1967. London: Picador, 2002. Print.

———. *A House for Mr. Biswas*. 1961. London: Picador, 2003. Print.

———. *The Mimic Men*. 1967. London: Picador, 2002. Print.

———. *In a Free State*. 1971. London: Picador, 2001. Print.

———. *Guerrillas*. 1975. London: Picador, 2002. Print.

———. *A Bend in the River*. 1979. London: Picador, 2002. Print.

———. *The Enigma of Arrival*. 1987. London: Picador, 2002. Print

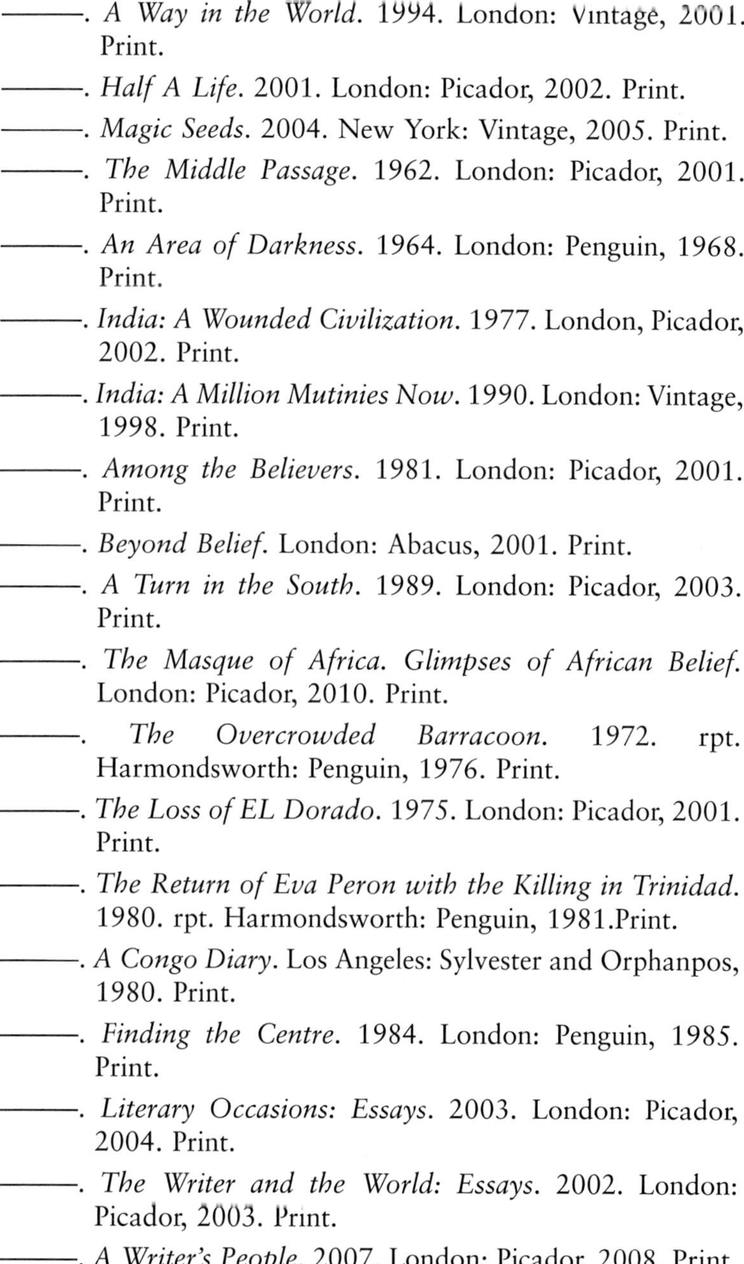

———. *A Way in the World*. 1994. London: Vintage, 2001. Print.

———. *Half A Life*. 2001. London: Picador, 2002. Print.

———. *Magic Seeds*. 2004. New York: Vintage, 2005. Print.

———. *The Middle Passage*. 1962. London: Picador, 2001. Print.

———. *An Area of Darkness*. 1964. London: Penguin, 1968. Print.

———. *India: A Wounded Civilization*. 1977. London, Picador, 2002. Print.

———. *India: A Million Mutinies Now*. 1990. London: Vintage, 1998. Print.

———. *Among the Believers*. 1981. London: Picador, 2001. Print.

———. *Beyond Belief*. London: Abacus, 2001. Print.

———. *A Turn in the South*. 1989. London: Picador, 2003. Print.

———. *The Masque of Africa. Glimpses of African Belief*. London: Picador, 2010. Print.

———. *The Overcrowded Barracoon*. 1972. rpt. Harmondsworth: Penguin, 1976. Print.

———. *The Loss of EL Dorado*. 1975. London: Picador, 2001. Print.

———. *The Return of Eva Peron with the Killing in Trinidad*. 1980. rpt. Harmondsworth: Penguin, 1981.Print.

———. *A Congo Diary*. Los Angeles: Sylvester and Orphanpos, 1980. Print.

———. *Finding the Centre*. 1984. London: Penguin, 1985. Print.

———. *Literary Occasions: Essays*. 2003. London: Picador, 2004. Print.

———. *The Writer and the World: Essays*. 2002. London: Picador, 2003. Print.

———. *A Writer's People*. 2007. London: Picador, 2008. Print.

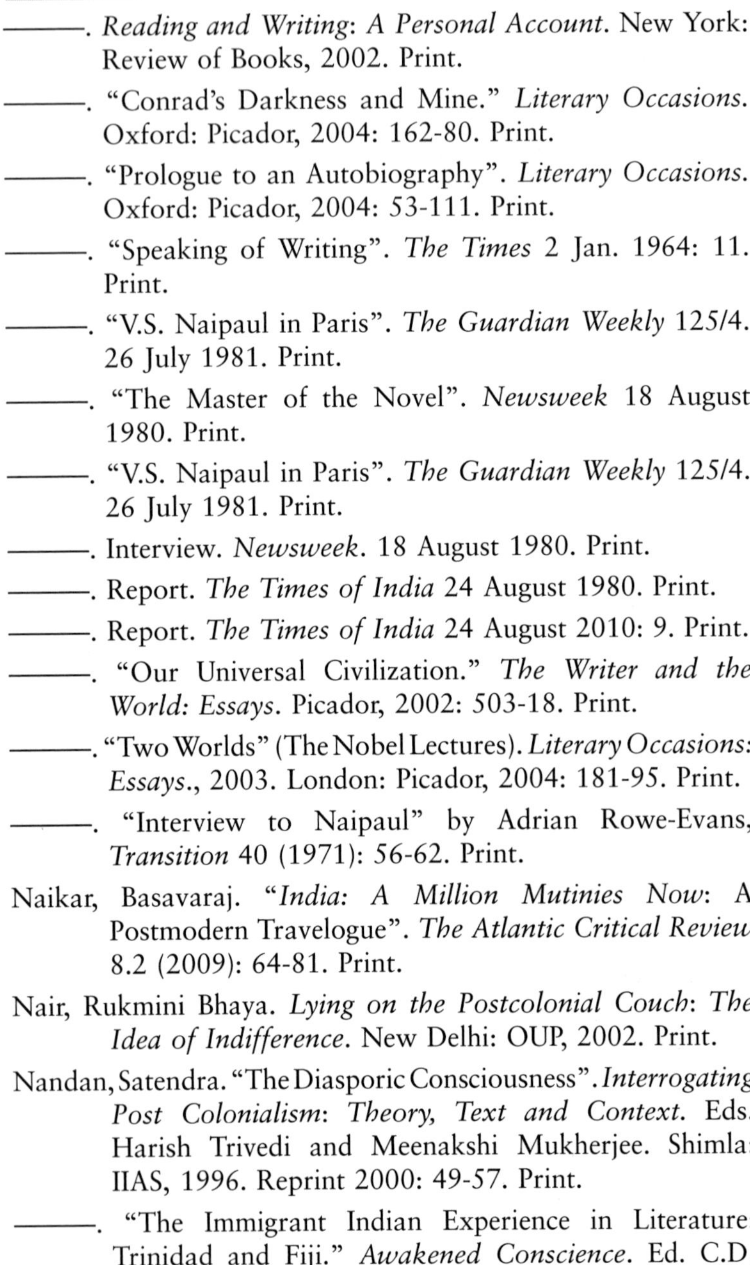

———. *Reading and Writing: A Personal Account*. New York: Review of Books, 2002. Print.

———. "Conrad's Darkness and Mine." *Literary Occasions*. Oxford: Picador, 2004: 162-80. Print.

———. "Prologue to an Autobiography". *Literary Occasions*. Oxford: Picador, 2004: 53-111. Print.

———. "Speaking of Writing". *The Times* 2 Jan. 1964: 11. Print.

———. "V.S. Naipaul in Paris". *The Guardian Weekly* 125/4. 26 July 1981. Print.

———. "The Master of the Novel". *Newsweek* 18 August 1980. Print.

———. "V.S. Naipaul in Paris". *The Guardian Weekly* 125/4. 26 July 1981. Print.

———. Interview. *Newsweek*. 18 August 1980. Print.

———. Report. *The Times of India* 24 August 1980. Print.

———. Report. *The Times of India* 24 August 2010: 9. Print.

———. "Our Universal Civilization." *The Writer and the World: Essays*. Picador, 2002: 503-18. Print.

———. "Two Worlds" (The Nobel Lectures). *Literary Occasions: Essays*., 2003. London: Picador, 2004: 181-95. Print.

———. "Interview to Naipaul" by Adrian Rowe-Evans, *Transition* 40 (1971): 56-62. Print.

Naikar, Basavaraj. "*India: A Million Mutinies Now*: A Postmodern Travelogue". *The Atlantic Critical Review* 8.2 (2009): 64-81. Print.

Nair, Rukmini Bhaya. *Lying on the Postcolonial Couch: The Idea of Indifference*. New Delhi: OUP, 2002. Print.

Nandan, Satendra. "The Diasporic Consciousness". *Interrogating Post Colonialism: Theory, Text and Context*. Eds. Harish Trivedi and Meenakshi Mukherjee. Shimla: IIAS, 1996. Reprint 2000: 49-57. Print.

———. "The Immigrant Indian Experience in Literature: Trinidad and Fiji." *Awakened Conscience*. Ed. C.D.

Narasimhaiah. New Delhi: Sterling, 1978: 344-56. Print.

Nandy, Ashis. *The Intimate Enemy: Loss and Recovery of Self Under Colonialism*. Delhi: OUP, 1983. Print.

———. *The Illegitimacy* of *Nationalism*. Delhi: OUP, 1996. Print.

Narasimhaiah, C.D., ed. *Awakened Conscience: Studies in Commonwealth Literature*. New Delhi: Sterling, 1978. Print.

———. "Musing on Award of the Nobel Prize for V.S. Naipaul." *The Literary Criterion* 35.4 (2001): 5-10. Print.

———, ed. *Commonwealth Literature: A Handbook of Select Reading List*. Delhi: OUP, 1976. Print.

———, ed. *Commonwealth Literature: Problems of Response*. Madras: Macmillan, 1981. Print.

Nasta, Susheila, ed. *Motherlands*. London: the Women's Press, 1991. Print.

Nazreth, Peter. "*The Mimic Men* as Study of Corruption". *Critical Perspective on V.S. Naipaul*. Ed. Robert Hamner. London: Heinemann, 1977. Print.

Nehru, J.L. *The Discovery of India*. Calcutta: The Signet Press, 1946.

Neill, Michael. "Guerrillas and Gangs: Frantz Fanon and V.S. Naipaul. *Ariel* 13.4 (1982): 22-62. Print.

Neill, S. *Colonialism and the Christian Missions*. New York: McGraw-Hill, 1966. Print.

Nelson, C. and L. Grossberg, eds. *Marxism and the Interpretation of Culture*. Basingstoke, Macmillan Education: 1988. Print.

Neogi, Tamil. "Naipaul's use of the Comic to Write Exilic Experience." *The Atlantic Critical Review* 3.4 (2004): 33-37. Print.

Nietzsche, Friedrich. *Twilight of the Idols and the Anti-Christ*. Trans. R.J. Hollingdale. 1960. Introduction. 1990. rpt. 2003. London: Penguin, 2003. Print.

Nightingale, Peggy. *Journey through Darkness: The Writing of V.S. Naipaul*. London: University of Queensland Press, 1987. Print.

Niven, Alastair, ed. *The Commonwealth Writer Overseas: Themes of Exile and Expatriation*. Brussels: Didier, 1976. Print.

Nixon, Rob. *Homelands, Harlem and Hollywood*. London: Routledge, 1994. Print.

———. *London Calling: V.S. Naipaul, Postcolonial Mandarin*. New York: OUP, 1992. Print.

Norris, Christopher. *Deconstruction: Theory and Practice*, 3rd Edition. London: Routledge, 2002. Print.

Nye, Malory. *Religion: The Basics*. London: Routledge, 2003 (1st Indian Reprint). Print.

O'Connor, Alan. *Raymond Williams: Writing, Culture, Politics*. Oxford: Blackwell, 1989. Print.

Osmania Journal of English Studies. V.S. Naipaul Special Number vol. 18, 1982. Print.

Padgaonkar, Dileep. "An Area of Awakening: V.S. Naipaul in Conversation with Dileep Padgaonkar." *V.S. Naipaul: An Anthology of Recent Criticism*. Ed. Purabi Panwar. Delhi: Pencraft International, 2007: 54-66. Print.

Panichas, George A., ed. *The Reverent Discipline*. Portland: Hawthorne Books, 1974. Print.

Panwar, Purabi, ed. *V.S. Naipaul: An Anthology of Recent Criticism*. Delhi: Pencraft International, 2007. Print.

———. "Introduction." *V.S. Naipaul: An Anthology of Recent Criticism*. Ed. Purabi Panwar. Delhi: Pencraft International, 2007. 13-25. Print.

Parekh, Bhikhu. *Rethinking Multiculturalism*. London: Macmillan, 2000. Print.

Parker, Michael, ed. *Postcolonial Literature: Contemporary Critical Essays*. Macmillan, 1995. Print.

Parrinder, Patrick. *The Failure of Theory*. The Harvester Press, 1987. Print.

———. "V.S. Naipaul and the Uses of Literacy." *Critical Quarterly* 21.2 (Summer 1979): 5-13. Print.

Parry, Benita. *Postcolonial Studies: A Materialist Critique.* London: Routledge, 2005 (Reprint). Print.

Patel, Vasant. *V.S. Naipaul's India.* New Delhi: Standard Publishers, 2005. Print.

Pathak, R.S. "Disorder Within, Disorder Without: Naipaul's Delineation of the Dilemma of The Fractured Indian Consciousness." *Commonwealth Fiction* 2 (1988): 128-57. Print.

Peterson, Kirsten Holst and Anna Rutherford, eds. *A Double Colonization: Colonial and Postcolonial Women's Writing.* Mundelstrup, Denmark: Kangaroo Press, 1986. Print.

Prakash, G., ed. *After Colonialism: Imperial Histories and Post-colonial Displacements.* Princeton: Princeton University Press, 1995. Print.

Pradhan, Prakash Chandra. *D.H. Lawrence's Novels*: A Stylistic Approach. New Delhi: Classical Publishing Company, 2002. Print.

———. *D.H. Lawrence's Novels*: A New Historical Approach. New Delhi: Atlantic, 2009. Print.

———. "Suppressed Histories, Racial Conflicts and Postcolonial Disorder in *A Bend in the River*". *Theory and Praxis: Indian and Western.* Eds. R.N. Rai, M.S. Pandey and Anita Singh. Newcastle upon Tyne: Cambridge Scholars Publishing, 2015: 80-103. Print.

———. "Race, Ethnicity, Sexual Violence and Neocolonialism in V.S. Naipaul's *Guerrillas*: A Postcolonial Reading." *V.S. Naipaul: An, Anthology of 21st Century Criticism.* Ed. Ajay Kumar Chaubey. New Delhi: Atlantic, 2015: 3-17. Print.

———. "V.S. Naipaul's *The Enigma of Arrival:* A Reference to Symbolic Death of Empire and Birth of Decolonization". *Orientation Matters: Studies in Transcultural Literature.*

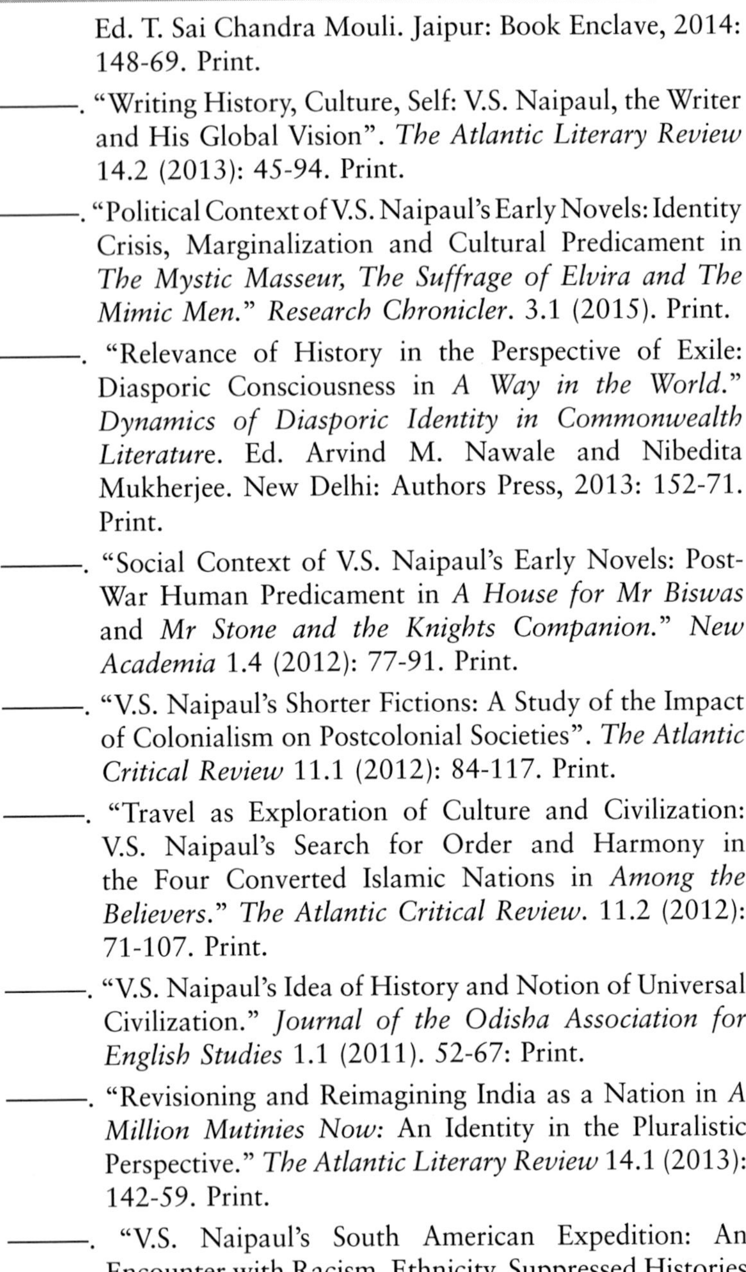

Ed. T. Sai Chandra Mouli. Jaipur: Book Enclave, 2014: 148-69. Print.

———. "Writing History, Culture, Self: V.S. Naipaul, the Writer and His Global Vision". *The Atlantic Literary Review* 14.2 (2013): 45-94. Print.

———. "Political Context of V.S. Naipaul's Early Novels: Identity Crisis, Marginalization and Cultural Predicament in *The Mystic Masseur, The Suffrage of Elvira and The Mimic Men.*" *Research Chronicler*. 3.1 (2015). Print.

———. "Relevance of History in the Perspective of Exile: Diasporic Consciousness in *A Way in the World.*" *Dynamics of Diasporic Identity in Commonwealth Literature*. Ed. Arvind M. Nawale and Nibedita Mukherjee. New Delhi: Authors Press, 2013: 152-71. Print.

———. "Social Context of V.S. Naipaul's Early Novels: Post-War Human Predicament in *A House for Mr Biswas* and *Mr Stone and the Knights Companion.*" *New Academia* 1.4 (2012): 77-91. Print.

———. "V.S. Naipaul's Shorter Fictions: A Study of the Impact of Colonialism on Postcolonial Societies". *The Atlantic Critical Review* 11.1 (2012): 84-117. Print.

———. "Travel as Exploration of Culture and Civilization: V.S. Naipaul's Search for Order and Harmony in the Four Converted Islamic Nations in *Among the Believers.*" *The Atlantic Critical Review*. 11.2 (2012): 71-107. Print.

———. "V.S. Naipaul's Idea of History and Notion of Universal Civilization." *Journal of the Odisha Association for English Studies* 1.1 (2011). 52-67: Print.

———. "Revisioning and Reimagining India as a Nation in *A Million Mutinies Now:* An Identity in the Pluralistic Perspective." *The Atlantic Literary Review* 14.1 (2013): 142-59. Print.

———. "V.S. Naipaul's South American Expedition: An Encounter with Racism, Ethnicity, Suppressed Histories

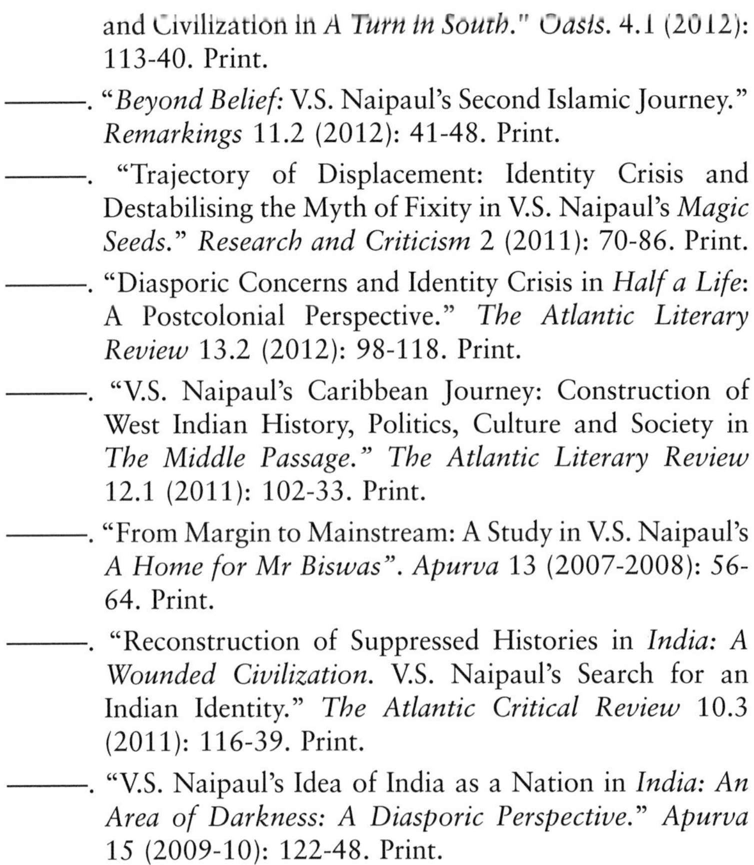

and Civilization in *A Turn in South*." *Oasis*. 4.1 (2012): 113-40. Print.

———. "*Beyond Belief:* V.S. Naipaul's Second Islamic Journey." *Remarkings* 11.2 (2012): 41-48. Print.

———. "Trajectory of Displacement: Identity Crisis and Destabilising the Myth of Fixity in V.S. Naipaul's *Magic Seeds*." *Research and Criticism* 2 (2011): 70-86. Print.

———. "Diasporic Concerns and Identity Crisis in *Half a Life*: A Postcolonial Perspective." *The Atlantic Literary Review* 13.2 (2012): 98-118. Print.

———. "V.S. Naipaul's Caribbean Journey: Construction of West Indian History, Politics, Culture and Society in *The Middle Passage*." *The Atlantic Literary Review* 12.1 (2011): 102-33. Print.

———. "From Margin to Mainstream: A Study in V.S. Naipaul's *A Home for Mr Biswas*". *Apurva* 13 (2007-2008): 56-64. Print.

———. "Reconstruction of Suppressed Histories in *India: A Wounded Civilization*. V.S. Naipaul's Search for an Indian Identity." *The Atlantic Critical Review* 10.3 (2011): 116-39. Print.

———. "V.S. Naipaul's Idea of India as a Nation in *India: An Area of Darkness: A Diasporic Perspective*." *Apurva* 15 (2009-10): 122-48. Print.

Prasad, Madhava. "The 'Other' Worldliness of Postcolonial Discourse': A Critique". *Critical Quarterly* 34.3 (1992): 74-89. Print.

Press, John, ed. *Commonwealth Literature*. London: Heinemann, 1965. Print.

———. *A Map of Modern English Verse*. London: Oxford University Press, 1977. Print.

Prince, Gerald. *Narratology: The Form and Functioning of Narrative*. New York: Mouton Publishers, 1982. Print.

Prince, Richard. *The Convict and the Colonial: A Story of Colonialism and Resistance in the Caribbean*. Boston: Beacon, 1998. Print.

Pritchett, V.S. *The Tale Bearers*. London. Chatto and Windus, 1980. Print.

———. "Climacteric." *New Statesman* 31 May 1963: 831-32. Print.

Puri, Shalini. *The Caribbean Postcolonial: Social Equality Post/ Nationalism, Cultural Hybridity*. New York: Palgrave, 2003. Print.

Rai, Sudha. *A Study in Expatriate Sensibility*. New Delhi: Heinemann, 1982. Print.

———. *Homeless by Choice*. Jaipur: Printwell, 1992. Print.

———. "Postcolonial Parables of Survival: V.S. Naipaul's *A Flag on the Island*." *V.S. Naipaul: An Anthology of Recent Criticism*. Ed. Purabi Panwar. Delhi: Pencraft International, 2007: 113-25. Print.

Rajan, P.K., et al., eds. *Commonwealth Literature: Themes and Techniques*. Delhi: Ajanta Books International, 1993. Print.

Rajeswaran, Sridar. "Re-defining Nation Spaces—A Movement from Chronos to Topos: Liberating 'marginalized or suppressed or forgotten histories'" *Critical Practice* 11.1 (2004): 1-47. Print.

Ramanathan, Vaidehi and Alastair Pennycook. "Talking Across Time: Postcolonial Challenges to Language, History and Difference". *Journal of Contemporary Thought* 25 (2007): 25-54. Print.

Ramchand, Kenneth. *The West Indian Novel and its Background*. London: Faber and Faber, 1970. Print.

———. *An Introduction to the Study of West Indian Literature*. London: Faber and Faber, 1976. Print.

Rao, Ranga. "Naipaul's Nobel Poise." *Indian Literature: Sahitya Akademi's Bi-Monthly Journal* XLVII.3 (2003): 199-210. Print.

Rath, Sura P. "Home(s) Abroad: Diasporic Identities in Third Spaces". *Journal of Contemporary Thought* 9 (1999): 7-24. Print.

Ray, Mohit K., ed. *V.S. Naipaul: Critical Essays*. Vol. III. New Delhi: Atlantic, 2005. Print.

Reinhard W. Sander. *The Trinidad Awakening: West Indian Literature of the Nineteen Thirties*. New York: Greenwood Press, 1988. Print.

Rice Philip and Patricia Waugh. *Modern Literary Theory: A Reader*. 1989. 4th ed. London: OUP, 2002. Print.

Rich, Paul B. *Race and Empire in British Politics*. Cambridge: Cambridge University Press, 1986. Print.

Rivkin, Julie and Michael Ryan, eds. *Literary Theory: An Anthology*. Oxford: Blackwell, 1998. Print.

Robbe-Grillet. *For a New Novel: Essays on Fiction*. Trans. Richard Howard. Freeport, N.Y.: Book for Library Press, 1970. Print.

Robins, Bruce. "Homelessness and Worldliness." *Diacritics* 13 (1983): 69-77. Print.

Robinson, Marilynn. *Mother Country*. New York: Faber, 1989. Print.

Rohlehr, Gordon. "Character and Rebellion in *A House for Mr. Biswas*." *Critical Perspective on V.S. Naipaul*. Ed. Robert D. Hamner. London: Heinemann, 1977. Print.

———. "The Ironic Approach: The Novels of V.S. Naipaul." *The Islands in Between: Essays in West Indian Literature*. Ed. Louis James. London: Oxford University Press, 1968. Print.

Ross, R., ed. *Racism and Colonialism*. The Hague: Mastinus Nighoff Publishers, 1982. Print.

Roy, Arundhati. *An Ordinary Person's Guide to Empire*. New Delhi: Penguin, 2006. Print.

———. *The Algebra of Infinite Justice*. New Delhi: Penguin, 2002. Print.

Rushdie, Salman. *Imaginary Homelands: Essay and Criticism 1981-1991*. London: Granta, 1991.

———. *Steps Across This Line*. London: Vintage Books, 2003. Print.

Rutherford, Jonathan, ed. *Identity: Community, Culture, Difference*. London: Lawrence & Wishart, 1990. Print.

Ryan, Selwyn D. *Race and Nationalism in Trinidad and Tobago: A Study of Decolonization in a Multiracial Society*. Toronto: University of Toronto Press, 1972. Print.

Said, Edward W. *Reflections on Exile*. London: Penguin, 2001 Print.

———. *Culture and Imperialism*. 1993. New York: Vintage, 1994. Print.

———. *Orientalism*. 1978. New Delhi: Penguin, 2001. Print.

———. *Reflection on Exile*. New Delhi: Penguin, 2001. Print.

———. *The World, the Text and the Critic*. Cambridge, MA: Harvard University Press, 1983. Print.

San, Juan E. Jr. *Beyond Postcolonial Theory*. New York: St. Martin's, 1998. Print.

Sandison, Alan. *The Wheel of Empire: A Study of the Imperial Idea*. London: Macmillan, 1976. Print.

Sartre, Jean Paul. "Preface". 1961. *The Wretched of the Earth*. Frantz Fanon. Trans. Richard Philcox. 1963. New York: Grove Press, 2004: xliii-lxii. Print.

Saul, John. *Decolonization and Empire*. Gurgaon: Three Essays Collective, 2007. Print.

Sertima, Ivan Van. *Caribbean Writers: Critical Essays*. London: New Beacon Books, 1968. Print.

Shapiro, Ian and Casino Hacker-Cardon, ed. *Democracy's Value*. Cambridge: Cambridge University Press, 1999. Print.

Sharma, Rajesh Kumar. "Holes in the Multicultural Canvas Hitting the Wall in Diaspora Studies." *Re-makings* 5.1 (2006). 79-84: Print.

Sharma, S.S. "The Theme of Selfhood in *A House for Mr. Biswas*." *Commonwealth Fiction* 2 (1988): 167-74. Print.

———. "Identity and Sensuality in *V.S. Naipaul's Half a Life*." *V.S. Naipaul: An Anthology of Recent Criticism*. Ed.

Purabi Panwar. Delhi: Pencraft International, 2007. 173-78. Print.

Sharma, T.R.S. "Naipaul's (Re)Figurations of Third World Cultures." *The Literary Criterion* 41. 3-4 (2006): 106-25. Print.

Sharma, Ursula. *Caste.* New Delhi: Viva Books, 2005. Print.

Sherry, Norman. *Conrad's Eastern World.* Cambridge: Cambridge University Press, 1971. Print.

———. *Joseph Conrad: A Commemoration.* London: Macmillan, 1976. Print.

Sheshadri, Vijay. "Naipaul from the Other Side." *Three penny Review* 22 (Summer 1985): 5-6. Print.

Shohat, Ella. "Notes on Postcolonial." *Contemporary Postcolonial Theory: A Reader.* 1996. Ed. Padmini Mongia. New Delhi: Oxford University Press, 2002: 322-34. Print.

———. "Notes on the Post-Colonial", *Social Text* 31/32 (1993): 99-113. Print.

Shohat, Ella and Robest Stam. *Unthinking Eurocentrism: Multiculturalism and the Media.* London: Routledge, 1994. Print.

Simpson, John. *The Oxford Book of Exile.* London: OUP, 1995. Print.

Sinfield, Alan. *Literature, Politics and Culture in Post-war Britain.* London: Continuum, 2005. Print.

Singh, M.I. *The Poetics of Alienation and Identity: V.S. Naipaul and George Lamming.* Delhi: Ajanta Books International, 1998a. Print.

———. *V.S. Naipaul.* Jaipur and New Delhi: Rawat Publications, 1998b. Print.

Singh, Manmohan. "Interrogating/Defending Postcolonialsm." *Re-markings* 5.1 (2006): 85-92. Print.

Singh, Pragnya M. "Adaptation in the Novels of V.S. Naipaul." *The Atlantic Literary Review* 10.2 (2009): 141-45. Print.

Singh, R.K. "New Indian English Writing: Post-Colonialism or Politics of Rejection." *Point of View* 11.1 (2004): 95-100. Print.

Singh, Shubha. *Overseas Indians: The Global Family*. Kolkata: Shipra Publication, 2005. Print.

Singh, Veena. "A Journey of Rejection: V.S. Naipaul's *The Mimic Men.*" *V.S. Naipaul: Critical Essays*. Ed. Mohit K. Ray. New Delhi: Atlantic, 2005: 156-66. Print.

Sinha, R.P. and R. Mishra. "Alienation as Creative Energy in V.S. Naipaul and Kiran Desai" *The Literary Vision* 3 (2008): 112-17. Print.

Sinha, Sunita, ed. *Post-colonial Imaginings*: Fissions and Fusions. New Delhi: Atlantic, 2009. Print.

Slemon, Stephen and Helen Tiffin, eds. *After Europe: Critical Theory and Post-Colonial Writing*. Sydney. Kangaroo Press, 1989. Print.

Smith, Mark J. *Culture: Reinventing the Social Sciences*. New Delhi: Viva Books, 2005. Print.

Smyer, Richard. "A New Look at V.S. Naipaul" *Contemporary Literature* 33.3 (1992): 573-81. Print.

Spenglar, Oswald. *The Decline of the West*. New York: Random House, 1962. Print.

Spivak, Gayatri Chakravorty. *A Critique of Postcolonial Reason: Toward a History of the Vanishing Present*. Cambridge: M.A: Harvard University Press, 1999. Print.

———. *In Other Worlds: Essays in Cultural Criticism*. London: Methuen, 1987. Print.

———. *The Post-Colonial Critic: Interviews, Strategies, Dialogues*. Ed. Sarah Harasym. London: Routledge, 1990. Print.

———. *Outside in the Teaching Machine*. London: Routledge, 1993. Print.

Spurr, D. *The Rhetoric of Empire: Colonial Discourse in Journalism, Travel Writing and Imperial Administration*.

Durham, NC and London: Duke University Press, 1993. Print.

Srinath, C.N. "Crisis of Identity: Assertion and Withdrawal in Naipaul and Arun Joshi." *The Literary Criterion* 14.1. (1979): 33-41. Print.

Srivastava, A.K., ed. *Alien Voice: Perspectives on Commonwealth Literature*. Lucknow: Print House, 1981. Print.

Steiner, George. *Extraterritorial.* Harmondsworth: Penguin, 1971. Print.

———. *Language and Silence: Essays 1958-1966*. London: Penguin, 1969. Print.

Stevenson, Randall. *British Novel since the Thirties: An Introduction*. London: B.T. Batsford Ltd., 1986. Print.

Suleri, Sara. *The Rhetoric of English India*. Chicago: Univ. of Chicago Press, 1992. Print.

Sundaram, P.S. "Naipaul on Narayan". *The Indian Journal of English Studies* XVII (1977): 129-37. Print.

Swinden, Patrick. *The English Novel of History and Society: 1940-80*. The Macmillan Press Ltd., 1984. Print.

Tabori, A. and Yahgeneh, N. *In the Shadow of Islam*. London: Zed Press, 1983. Print.

Tagore, R.N. *Nationalism*. 1917. rpt. Madras: Macmillan, 1976. 14. Print.

Tayab, Abdulkader. *Islam: A Short Introduction*. Oxford: One World Publication, 2006. Print.

Teverson, Andrew. *Salman Rushdie*. New Delhi: Viva Books, 2010. Print.

Thapar, Romila, ed. *India: Another Millennium?* New Delhi: Penguin, 2000. Print.

Tharoor, Shashi. *The Great Indian Novel*. New Delhi, Penguin, 1989. Print.

Theroux, Paul. *V.S. Naipaul: An Introduction to His Work*. London: Andre Deutsch, 1972. Print.

Thieme, John. *The Web of Tradition*: Uses of Allusion in V.S. Naipaul. Delhi: Hansib Printing Ltd.. 1987. Print.

———. "V.S. Naipaul's Third World: A Not So Free State." *The Journal of Commonwealth Literature* 10.1 (1975): 10-22. Print.

Thiong'o, Ngugi wa. *Decolonizing the Mind: The Politics of Language in African Writing*. London: James Currey, 1986. Print.

———. *Homecoming*. London: Heinemann, 1972. Print.

———. *Writers in Politics*. London: Heinemann, 1981. Print.

Thornton, A.P. *The Imperial Idea and its Enemies: A Study of British Power*. Basingstoke: Macmillan, 1985. Print.

Thorpe, Michael. *V.S. Naipaul*. Edinburgh: Longman, 1976. Print.

Tiffin, Chris and Lawson Allan, eds. *Describing Empire: Post-Colonialism and Textuality*. London: Routledge, 1994. Print.

Tinker, Hugh. *A New System of Slavery*. London: Oxford University Press, 1974. Print.

Tomlinson, John. *Cultural Imperialism*. London: Pinter, 1991. Print.

Trivedi, Deepkumar Jayprakash. "Identity Crisis in Indian Diaspora." *Re-makings* 7.2 (2008): 56-59. Print.

Trivedi, Harish and Meenakshi Mukherjee, eds. *Interrogating Post Colonialism: Theory, Text and Context*. Shimla: Indian Institute of Advanced Study, 1996. Print.

Trivedi, Harish. *Colonial Transactions*. Calcutta: Papyrus, 1993. Print.

Trollope, Anthony. *The West Indies and the Spanish Main*. London: Chapman and Hall, 1959. Print.

Trotter, David. "Colonial Subjects". *Critical Quarterly* 32.3 (1990): 3-20. Print.

Vaidyanathan, T.G. *Mr. Naipaul's Round Trip and Other Essays*. New Delhi: Penguin, 2003. Print.

Vaughan, M. *Curing their Ills: Colonial Power and African Illness*. Cambridge and Stanford, CA: Polity Press and Stanford University Press, 1991. Print.

——— "Madness and Colonialism, Colonialism as Madness." *Paideuma* 39 (1993): 45-55. Print.

Verdonk, Peter and Jean Jacques Weber, eds. *Twentieth Century Fiction: From Text to Context*. London: Routledge, 1995. Print.

Vincent, William. "Naipaul's *A Bend in the River:* Time, History, and Africa" *Journal of South Asian Literature* 26.1 (1991): 337-49. Print.

Viswanathan, Gauri. *Mask of Conquest: Literary Study and British Rule in India*. London: Faber and Faber, 1990. Print.

———, ed. *Power, Politics and Culture: Interviews with Edward. W. Said*. New York: Vintage Books, 2001. Print.

Volosinor, V. *Marxism and the Philosophy of Language*. New York: Seminar Press, 1973. Print.

Walcott, Derek. "The Garden Path" *New Republic* 13 April 1987: 27-31. Print.

Walder, Dennis. "How is it going, Mr. Naipaul? Identity, Memory and the Ethics of Post Colonial Literatures." *The Journal of Commonwealth Literature* 38.3 (2003): 5-18. Print.

———, ed. *Literature in the Modern World* 2nd ed. Oxford: OUP. 2008. Print.

Walker, W. John. "Unsettling the Song: V.S. Naipaul's *The Enigma of Arrival*." *Journal of Commonwealth Literature* 32.2 (1999): 67-84. Print.

Walsh, William. *A Manifold Voice: Studies in Commonwealth Literature*. London: Chatto and Windus, 1970. Print.

———, ed. *Readings in Commonwealth Literature*. Clarendon Press, 1973. Print.

———. *V.S. Naipaul*. London: Oliver and Boyd, 1973. Print.

———. *Commonwealth Literature*. London: OUP, 1973. Print.

Walvin, James. *Black Ivory: A History of British Slavery*. London: Harper Collins, 1992. Print.

Ward, J.R. *British West Indian Slavery, 1750-1834: The Process of Amelioration*. Oxford: The Clarendon Press, 1988. Print.

Watson, C.W. *Multiculturalism*. New Delhi: Viva Books, 2002. Print.

Weiss, Timothy. *On the Margins: The Art of Exile in V.S. Naipaul*. Amherst: University of Massachusetts Press, 1992. Print.

White, Hayden. *Tropics of Discourse*: *Essay in Cultural Criticism*. London: Johns Hopkins University Press, 1978. Print.

White, Jonathan. *Recasting the World Writing after Colonialism*. London: Johns Hopkins University Press, 1993. Print.

White, Landeg. *V.S. Naipaul*: *A Critical Introduction*. London: The Macmillan Press, 1975. Print.

Willett, Cynthia, ed. *Theorizing Multiculturalism*. Blackwell, 1998. Print.

Williams, Eric. *Capitalism and Slavery*. London: Andre Deutsch, 1964. Print.

———. *From Columbus to Castro: The History of the Caribbean*, *1492-1967*. New York: Harper and Row, 1970. Print.

Williams, R. *Marxism and Literature*. Oxford: OUP, 1977. Print.

———. *Culture and Society*, *1780-1950*. London: Chatto and Windus, 1958. Print.

William, P. and L. Chrisman, eds. *Colonial Discourse and Postcolonial Theory: A Reader*. New York: Columbia University Press, 1994. Print.

Wolf, Eric. *Europe and the People without History*. Berkeley: University of California Press, 1982. Print.

Wolfreys, Julian, Ruth Robins and Kenneth Womack. *Key Concepts in Literary Theory*. 2002. New Delhi: Atlantic, 2005. Print.

Wurgaft, Lewis. The *Imperial Imagination*. Middletown: Wesleyan Univ. Press, 1983. Print.

Young, Robert J.C. *Postcolonialism: A Very Short Introduction*. Oxford: OUP, 2003. Rpt. 2006. Print.

———. *White Mythologies: Writing History and the West*. London: Routledge, 1990. Print.

———. *Colonial Desire: Hybridity in Theory, Culture and Race*. London: Routledge, 1995. Print.

Index

C

D

G

H

I

M

N

S

T